THE MEASUREMENT OF MORAL JUDGMENT
VOLUME I

The Measurement of Moral Judgment

VOLUME I

Theoretical Foundations and Research Validation

Anne Colby and Lawrence Kohlberg

in collaboration with

Anat Abrahami, John Gibbs, Ann Higgins, Kelsey Kauffman, Marcus Lieberman, Mordecai Nisan, Joseph Reimer, Dawn Schrader, John Snarey, and Mark Tappan

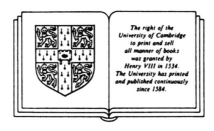

The right of the
University of Cambridge
to print and sell
all manner of books
was granted by
Henry VIII in 1534.
The University has printed
and published continuously
since 1584.

Cambridge University Press

Cambridge

New York   Port Chester

Melbourne   Sydney

CAMBRIDGE UNIVERSITY PRESS
Cambridge, New York, Melbourne, Madrid, Cape Town, Singapore,
São Paulo, Delhi, Dubai, Tokyo, Mexico City

Cambridge University Press
The Edinburgh Building, Cambridge CB2 8RU, UK

Published in the United States of America by Cambridge University Press, New York

www.cambridge.org
Information on this title: www.cambridge.org/9780521169103

First published 1987
Reprinted 1990
First paperback edition 2010

A catalogue record for this publication is available from the British Library

Library of Congress Cataloguing in Publication data

Colby Anne, 1946–
The measurement of moral judgment.
Bibliography: p.
Includes index.
Contents: v. 1. Theoretical foundations and research
validation – v. 2. Standard issue scoring manual.
1. Judgment (Ethics) 1. Kohlberg, Lawrence,
1927– . 11. Title.
BJ1408.5.C65 1987   155.2   86-28401

ISBN 978-0-521-24447-3 Hardback
ISBN 978-0-521-16910-3 Paperback

Contents

Preface

The Measurement of Moral Judgment presents the Standard Issue Moral Judgment Interview and Scoring System along with a statement of its theoretical assumptions and data on its reliability and validity. The measure provides a semistandardized method for identifying the developmental level of moral judgments used by a subject to resolve hypothetical moral dilemmas. We assume that moral judgment is a crucial component of human morality. However, it is not the only central component. For this reason, it is important to state at the outset that the measure presented in these volumes is not a measure of morality or moral maturity in general but rather a means of assessing the development of the structure or organization of an individual's moral judgments.

We intend these volumes to be of use not only to those who will use them to assign stage scores to moral judgment interviews, but also to anyone seeking a concretely grounded understanding of stages of moral development. An abstract knowledge of the moral stages, based on descriptions rather than case material, can lead to serious misconceptions. For example, Stage 4 is often mistakenly associated with a "law-and-order morality," Stage 3 with a concern for interpersonal relationships. In fact, as study of this stage scoring manual should make clear, some Stage 3 judgments are of the law-and-order type, and some Stage 4 judgments focus on the value of human relationships. In effect, then, Standard Issue Scoring is offered not only as a measurement and research tool, but also as an operational definition of the stages.

As described in the first chapter of this volume, our underlying conceptualizations of moral judgment stages were formulated over a 20-year period. They were worked out through a process of theoretical revision in response to empirical findings and close study of longitudinal case material. The stage indicators presented as "criterion judgments" in Volume II were generated empirically from individuals' responses to the moral judgment interview. The rules and procedures for moral judgment stage scoring were developed with the aim of creating a qualitative, structural, phenomenological method of analysis that simultaneously avoids subjectivity on the part of the rater and introduces much greater standardization than was characteristic of our earlier stage scoring schemes. This has resulted in a system that is quite complex and that may at first appear unwieldy. Much of the complexity represents an effort to make all aspects of the scoring process as explicit as possible. As the new rater comes to understand the rationale for the system's categories, rules, and procedures and becomes firmly grounded in a clinical or structural understanding of the stages, the procedural complexities become quite manageable, even automatic.

Becoming an expert at Standard Issue Scoring does require study and practice, however. In our experience, people learn the system with varying degrees of ease. For this reason, it is impossible to say just how much practice is required to develop facility with the system. However, a minimum of a month or two of concentrated study and practice is probably necessary even for those who learn the system with greatest ease. The annotated practice cases in chapter 7 are to be used along with Volume II to provide guided experience in using the Standard Issue Scoring System.

Volume I of *The Measurement of Moral Judgment* provides the necessary theoretical and empirical background for use of the reference manuals presented in Volume II. Chapter 1 lays out the theoretical and methodological assumptions underlying Standard Issue Scoring. It offers a history of moral judgment stage scoring, an account of the structural core of the stages, and a rationale for the conceptual framework of Standard Issue Scoring. Chapter 2 presents data on the instrument's reliability and a discussion of its validity. Chapters 3, 4, and 5 present longitudinal studies of moral judgment that have used Standard Issue Scoring. The data presented in these chapters support the validity of the construct and the measure in three very different cultures. Chapter 6 gives detailed instructions, procedures, and rules for Standard Issue Scoring. It should be studied very carefully before proceeding to use Volume II to score the practice cases in chapter 7.

The appendix to this volume presents a theoretical statement of moral types A and B; a method for coding the moral types is presented in an appendix to Volume II. This construct appears to be helpful in illuminating the relation of moral judgment to moral opinion and moral action. This coding procedure is entirely separate from Standard Issue Moral Judgment Scoring although it is also used to code responses to the Standard Moral Judgment Interview. Whether or not to use moral types coding as well as moral judgment stage scoring will depend on the aims of the research undertaken. It should be noted, however, that although the stage scoring system has been revised repeatedly and constitutes a finished product, the moral types construct and coding manual are still in preliminary form and may well undergo further revision. Of course, the question of whether the moral types construct and method hold up after further research does not bear on the validity of the moral judgment stages and Standard Issue Scoring.

Many people have contributed to the creation of this coding scheme over the 12 years of its development. Our primary collaborators are listed as authors of Volume II, but their contributions extend to all aspects of the moral judgment stages and this method for assessing the stages. These people who have invested so much of themselves over so many years are Betsy Speicher, Alexandra Hewer, John Gibbs, Dan Candee, and Clark Power. We would like to thank Bill Damon for his very helpful suggestions for rewriting several chapters in this volume; Jim Rest for providing support and encouragement even while challenging our thinking in many ways; Wolfgang Edelstein for detailed comments on earlier drafts; Bill Puka and Ann Higgins for help with numerous parts of the process; Jane Loevinger for providing a model of what could be done in her *Measuring Ego Development;* Carole Lee and many others who typed and retyped the numerous drafts; the graduate students who carefully worked through the practice cases; and the hundreds of boys and girls and men and women whose thoughtful responses to Kohlberg's hypothetical dilemmas have provided the raw material for the moral stage construct and Standard Issue Scoring. We are grateful to the National Institute of Child Health and Human Development for providing funding for the development of Standard Issue Scoring and to Susan Milmoe, Sophia Prybylski, and the other staff members of Cambridge University Press for taking on the cumbersome job of publishing this work. We would also like to acknowledge the support of the Danforth Foundation, and in particular the support of Vice-President Geraldine Bagby, which provided release time from teaching for Lawrence Kohlberg to work on this volume.

One

Theoretical Introduction to the Measurement of Moral Judgment

with Kelsey Kauffman

The Standard Issue Moral Judgment Interview and Scoring System is a theory-based assessment procedure that measures position on a developmental sequence postulated by Kohlberg's theory of moral judgment. It is therefore important to summarize at the outset the psychological and philosophical assumptions underlying the construct and the measure. (These assumptions are elaborated in more depth in Kohlberg [1984].) Accordingly, this chapter begins with a discussion of three concepts that represent the most general and basic assumptions underlying our approach to the definition and measurement of moral development: phenomenalism, structuralism, and constructivism. Next we present our position on the stage model of development and the controversies surrounding this model. We then discuss our conception of the moral domain and its relation to other domains in cognitive and social-cognitive development. The moral judgment levels and stages are introduced along with the concepts of sociomoral perspective and justice operations. In order to provide the background for understanding Standard Issue Scoring, we offer a history of moral judgment stage scoring and a description of the process through which Standard Issue Scoring was developed. We conclude the chapter with a detailed presentation of the conceptual framework of Standard Issue Scoring. Discussions of the measure's reliability, validity, and other psychometric properties and empirical studies using Standard Issue Scoring will be presented in later chapters of this volume. Volume II comprises the reference manual used in stage scoring moral judgment interviews.

Phenomenalism

A phenomenological approach to moral psychology assumes that moral judgments and rational argumentation are central to moral psychology. It assumes that such judgments must be seen as meaningful in their own terms, in some sense at face value, rather than treated as mere reflections or expressions of irrational feelings, unconscious motives, or external forces. That is, subjects' moral judgments are taken seriously and interpreted as referring to moral reality as they perceive it.

What this implies for the assessment of moral development is that the researcher must operate phenomenologically by looking at morality from the subject's viewpoint, understanding what the subject is saying in his or her own terms. That is, the researcher is seeking to understand what the *subject* means when making moral judgments rather than attributing meaning to the judgments from some outside system of interpretation not shared by the subject.

This phenomenological orientation is particularly important for the study of morality, because our judgments as to the moral nature of an action depend on imputing conscious motives to the actor. In order to judge whether an action such as physically harming another is moral or not, we must know something of the actor's moral judgment. For example, harming someone out of malice or for personal gain has a very different moral significance than harming someone to prevent him from causing much greater harm to someone else. To assess the moral quality of behavior requires one to confront complex issues of interpretation, for both motivation and judgment must be considered in such assessments before behavior can be said to be *moral* conduct or action. Thus, the study of moral development must consider the subject's own reasons and construction of moral meaning.

Therefore, we believe that in the study of moral behavior, it is essential to determine the actor's interpretation of the situation and the behavior since the moral quality of the behavior is itself determined by that interpretation. Furthermore, we make an additional assumption as to the importance of the subject's moral interpretations. We assume that the subject's thinking about moral questions and interpretation of moral right and wrong are important determinants of moral conduct. This is not to say that people always do what they think is right. The relation of moral judgment and conduct is complex and incompletely understood. No doubt the causality is bidirectional: Our overt behavior can influence our moral beliefs just as our moral beliefs can influence the course of our behavior. But our present point is that judgment is an integral component of action and that moral judgment must be assessed if moral conduct is to be understood. (This moral action issue is discussed at length in Kohlberg [1984, chap. 7].)

Structuralism

Following Piaget, we distinguish between the *content* of moral judgment and its *structure* or form. By structure we mean general organizing principles or patterns of thought rather than specific moral beliefs or opinions. That is, we assume that concepts are not learned or used independently of one another but rather are bound together by common structural features. Our focus is on the form of thinking rather than the content, because it is the form that exhibits developmental regularity and generalizability within and across individuals. Furthermore, as in the case of moral behaviors, the meaning of an individual's specific moral beliefs cannot be understood without understanding the more general moral world view or conceptual framework within which those beliefs are embedded and from which they arise. (The relation of content to structure is discussed at length in Kohlberg and Candee [in press].)

Our approach, then, focuses on the *relations* among ideas in the individual's thinking. We assume that there is a pattern of connections within the subject's meaning – a structure or set of relations and transformations. In this sense, the task of delineating the organization of moral thought is like that of the literary critic or humanist trying to analyze the pattern of ideas expressed in the work of Aristotle or Shakespeare. The developmental psychologist's interviews are like the humanist's texts. The test of accuracy of interpretation is that if it were claimed that certain ideas are related in certain ways in the text, this relationship should make sense in other places in the text, and in the text as a whole. That is, a thorough understanding of a literary work or a moral judgment interview allows one to see the underlying consistency of meaning despite apparent inconsistencies. In order to do this, the reader must discover the principle by which seemingly disparate ideas are related, the deeper organization or structure that gives rise to specific judgments. As William James (1909/1978) remarked in another context, ''Building up an author's meaning out of separate texts means nothing unless you have first grasped the center of his vision by an act of imagination.''

In order to achieve this kind of understanding, one must adopt the subject's point of view and grasp the sense the arguments make to that person. It is for this reason that the structuralist approach is related to phenomenalism in the study of moral judgment.

This interpretive aspect of assessing the form or structure of moral judgment can also be called hermeneutic. In the hermeneutic approach, stage scoring involves the identification and analysis of the organization of thought inherent in the individual's responses. That is, stage scoring becomes an act of interpreting a text around some philosophical categories of meaning shared by subject and investigator. In order to clarify this concept, we will quote from J. Habermas's (1984) article, ''Interpretive Social Science vs. Hermeneutics'':

In the interests of connecting the problem of interpretation with the topic of the social sciences and morality, let me first explain what I mean by hermeneutics. Any meaningful expression – be it an utterance, verbal or nonverbal, or an artifact, such as a tool, an institution, or a scripture – can be bifocally identified, both as an observable event and as an understandable objectification of meaning. We well might describe, explain, or predict a noise that is equivalent to the phonetic utterance of a sentence without having any idea of what this utterance means. To grasp (and state) its meaning, one must participate in some (actual or imagined) communicative actions, in the process of which one must use that very phrase in such a way that it is intelligible for speakers, hearers, and bystanding members of the same speech community. . . .

If one compares the third-person attitude of those who say (or think) how things are (the attitude of scientists, among others) with the performative attitude of those who try to understand what is said (interpreters, among others), the methodological consequences of a hermeneutic dimension in research come to the fore. Let me indicate the important implications of hermeneutic procedures.

First, interpreters sacrifice the superiority of observers' privileged positions, since they are involved in the negotiation about validity claims. . . .

Second, in adopting a performative attitude, the interpreters not only give up a position of superiority to their subject matter, but they also face the issue of the context-dependency of their interpretation. They cannot be sure, in advance, that they and the hearer start from the same background assumptions and practices. . . .

In short, every science that admits meaningful expressions as part of its object domain has to cope with the methodological consequences of the participatory role of an interpreter, who does not ''give'' meaning to things observed but instead explicates the ''given'' meaning of expressions that can be understood only from within processes of communication. These consequences threaten the very conditions for the objectivity of theoretical knowledge.

Some who face the problem of interpretation are prepared to drop the conventional postulate of value neutrality, abstain also from assimilating the social sciences to the model of pure nomological science, and yet advocate the desirability *and* possibility of approaches which promise to generate some sort of objective and theoretical knowledge. This position needs justification. . . .

Let me first mention an argument that when fully developed would show that the interpreters' participatory involvement at the same time deprives them of the privileges of an observer's, or third-person, position and yet provides them with the means for maintaining a position of negotiated impartiality from within. The paradigm case for hermeneutics is the interpretation of a traditional text. The interpreters appear at first to understand the sentences of the author; then they have the disturbing experience that they do not adequately understand the text, that is, not to the extent that they can respond to the author. The interpreters take this to be a sign that they are embedding the text in another context than the author did, that they are starting with other questions. This disturbance in communication marks the initial situation. They seek, then, to understand why the author – in the tacit belief that certain states of affairs obtained, that certain values and norms were valid, that certain experiences could be attributed to certain subjects – made certain assertions in the text, observed or violated certain conventions, and described certain intentions, dispositions, feelings, and the like. Only to the extent that the interpreters grasp the reasons that allow the author's utterance to appear rational do they understand what the author could have meant.

Thus, the interpreters understand the meaning of the text only to the extent that they see why the author felt entitled to put forward (as true) certain assertions, to recognize (as right) certain values and norms, and to express (as sincere) certain experiences.

(Copyright © 1983 Columbia University Press. By permission.)

Although our approach to assessing moral development can be seen as interpretive or hermeneutic, it should not be seen as a form of the extreme hermeneuticism that denies the validity of the scientific method. Our approach attempts to combine aspects of the interpretive or hermeneutic method with means for minimizing subjectivity in the interpretive process (see Kohlberg, 1984, chaps. 4 and 5).

As we have said, the measurement of moral judgment involves the analysis of observable patterns of thought revealed in the subject's responses to the moral judgment interview. The scorer abstracts stage structure from observation. The rules of inference are made explicit in the scoring manual, thereby permitting independent interpreters or raters to agree in their interpretations of the material.

Constructivism

A third basic assumption of cognitive developmental theory is that by thinking about and acting on the world, human beings construct meaning for themselves. As they interact with the world, they actively construct and reconstruct reality. As Piaget (1965/1971) writes:

The human subject in general . . . uses norms of every kind, cognitive, ethical, etc. . . . He is engaged in the world and attributes to everything a ''meaning'' from vital, social or personal, as well as epistemological, points of view. . . . What needs to be strongly emphasized is that it is the subject himself in his interpersonal relationships and in his own spontaneity who is the origin of these ''meanings,'' not the philosopher or the psychologist. (p. 225)

In the constructivist view, functioning is creative in that the individual is always inventing or constructing anew responses to each situation encountered.

However, although each response is a creation of the moment, its form is constrained or determined by the person's current developmental level. Furthermore, the individual's current developmental stage has arisen from his or her developmental history such that the present mode of construction is an outgrowth of the prior mode. Each new stage of development represents a qualitative reorganization of the individual's pattern of thought, with each new reorganization integrating within a broader perspective the insights achieved at prior stages. Thus, as they develop, patterns of thought become more complex, differentiated, and adaptive. Because each stage presupposes the understanding gained at previous stages, development occurs in a predictable sequence of stages. It is assumed that individuals will pass through each stage in order, without skipping any stage in the sequence.

This assumption is supported by longitudinal research and by attempts to teach higher level reasoning (Turiel, 1966; Walker, 1982a). These studies indicate that subjects cannot simply internalize higher stage reasoning but instead are only able to move forward to the logical next step of cognitive reorganization. For example, Walker (1982a) assessed subjects' stages of moral development, then presented them with reasoning either one (+1) or two (+2) stages above their present stage. He found that some subjects in both the +1 and +2 conditions showed some developmental advance from pretest to posttest. However, subjects in both conditions showed +1 change if they changed at all. That is, subjects who were presented with reasoning two stages above their own moved not to the modeled stage but to the next stage above their own, which was not modeled.

This inability to internalize higher stage thinking in a rote way or to produce high-level responses without having achieved that level of development has important implications for the measurement of moral judgment. In effect, it disarms any attempt by subjects to misrepresent their moral reasoning as ''better'' than it is for the sake of social desirability. The use of phenomenological self-reports of moral reasoning as data naturally raises the question of a social desirability bias. We argue that this is not a problem for our system. In fact, we assume that individuals responding to the moral judgment interview *will* present what they consider to be their most morally desirable or defensible position. This assumed ''social desirability effect'' does not compromise the validity of the measure, because the coding criteria are structural and developmental in the sense described earlier and because the Standard Moral Judgment Interview attempts to measure the most advanced level of reasoning of which the individual is capable. In this regard, we draw on the distinction between competence and performance. We assume that competence and performance in moral judgment may differ to some degree depending on the problem being addressed, the context, and other factors. That is, people do not always use their highest stage of moral reasoning. We have attempted to minimize the gap between the competence and performance by using hypothetical dilemmas, by using probing questions that attempt to elicit the upper limits of the subject's thinking, and by our scoring rules according to which only the most mature expressed version of a particular moral idea is scored.[1]

---

1 See chapter 3 for a discussion of this scoring rule and an explanation of why it does not result in an artificially high degree of internal consistency of stage scores within an interview.

The Stage Model[2]

In this section, we will present the stage model that is assumed by Kohlberg's moral judgment stages and by Standard Issue Scoring. In order to clarify the nature of this model, we will contrast it with the Eriksonian model of functional stages (Erikson, 1963), which traces the maturing person through his or her experiences of new sociocultural spheres and roles. In this section we will attempt to clarify the meaning and significance of our assumptions without examining them empirically. Empirical support for our claims about the stage model will be presented in chapters 3, 4, and 5 of this volume.

In his discussions of this issue, Kohlberg (1973) has termed Piaget's theory *structural* because it starts by abstracting a structure or form of thinking from the *function* the thinking is serving or the content on which the thinking focuses. For Piaget, the same function, moral judgment, is served by successive structures of judgment, each of which displaces or reintegrates prior structures for serving this function. Kohlberg has termed the Erikson model functional because it defines stages not by new structures for old functions but by new functions of the self, person, or ego, or new foci of concern and choice for the person.

In Erikson's model, the individual moves on to face the next stage or task regardless of whether prior tasks have been resolved successfully. Rather than being subsumed in the next stage, as in structural development, earlier functions or choices remain as background to the later functional stages. Later stages of functional ego development are more adequate than prior stages in their ability to order personal experience in a way that is stable, positive, and purposive. In contrast, the later structural stages are more *cognitively* adequate in that they provide more internally consistent, universally applicable, and inclusive solutions to the same problems. The functional conception assumes that there are age-typical changes in personality, linked to focal tasks, and that successful resolution of these tasks leads to characteristic attitudinal outcomes. That is, Erikson's stages can be thought of as a sequence of sociocultural tasks, related to personality trait change, rather than as structural-developmental stages as defined by Piaget.

In the traditional cognitive-developmental literature, the following four general criteria have been used to identify Piagetian (1960) cognitive stages (these criteria also define the stage concept as used by Kohlberg):

1. Stages imply a qualitative difference in structures (modes of thinking) that still serve the same basic function (for example, intelligence) at various points in development.
2. These different structures form an invariant sequence, order, or succession in individual development. Cultural factors may speed up, slow down, or stop development, but they do not change its sequence.
3. Each of these different and sequential modes of thought forms a "structural whole." A given stage response on a task does not represent simply a specific response determined by knowledge and familiarity with that task or tasks similar to it; rather, it represents an underlying thought organization. The implication is that various aspects of stage structures should appear as a consistent cluster of responses in development.

---

2 Parts of this section are adapted from Kohlberg and Armon (1983).

4. Stages are hierarchial integrations. As noted, stages form an order of increasingly differentiated and integrated *structures* for fulfilling a common function. Accordingly, higher stages displace (or, rather, integrate) the structures found at lower stages.

In the next three sections, we will present our interpretation of the meaning of these criteria for Kohlberg's theory of moral development.

Transformational versus Additive Model

Even among researchers working in the area of moral judgment within the cognitive-developmental framework, some of the formal properties attributed to stages by Piaget and Kohlberg are controversial. One area of controversy concerns the issue of the transformational versus the additive model. Some have interpreted "hierarchial integration" to mean that lower stages are no longer accessible once the individual has developed beyond those stages. Others (e.g., Rest, 1979) have rejected this "transformational" model for an additive or "layer-cake" model in which higher stages are added to the repertoire with no loss of availability of the lower stages. Of course, these two different views of the hierarchial nature of stage development imply different views of the "structural whole assumption" (the third criterion of stages) as well. Clearly, a transformational model of development tends to be linked conceptually with the assumption of very great internal consistency of reasoning (the stage as strongly holistic), whereas the layer-cake or additive model is consistent with greater heterogeneity of stage use.

In order to understand our position on this issue, it is important to recognize that moral judgment in the broad sense includes within it a number of distinct modes or processes including comprehension of judgments made by others, preference for or evaluation of statements made by others, and spontaneous production of moral judgments in response to questions about what is right or wrong and why. In our view, the development of moral judgment as a whole (including comprehension and preference as well as spontaneous production) is too broad in scope to be described by a single model. In fact, it is quite clear that a transformational model entailing a great degree of structured wholeness is not appropriate to describe comprehension and preference of moral judgments. There is certainly little reason to expect that subjects will comprehend statements at only one stage. Rather, they have been shown (Rest, 1973; Walker, deVries, & Bichard, 1984) to comprehend all stages below their own spontaneous production stage as well as sometimes comprehending a stage or two above their own. Thus, we would not characterize the development of moral judgment comprehension as conforming to a transformational model. Evaluation of or preference for judgments made by others may also fail to conform to a transformational model. This is because, due to hierarchial integration, lower stage judgments often retain their validity when seen from a higher stage perspective. The higher stage subject may attribute a somewhat different meaning to the statement than would someone reasoning at the lower stage, but that does not prevent the higher stage subject from endorsing as valid many ideas that have first become available at lower stages. We hold, then, that a transformation model is appropriate for describing the development of spontaneous production of moral judgments, but not of comprehension and preference. (For further discussion, see chap. 3.)

A discussion of our position on the appropriateness of the transformational model for the development of spontaneous production in moral judgment requires reference to the distinction between competence and performance. As noted earlier, we do not assume that people always use their highest stage of moral reasoning. However, the Standard Moral Judgment Interview does attempt to tap the most advanced reasoning of which the subject is capable. Insofar as we are successful in eliciting the respondent's highest level, we expect that the thinking exhibited will be quite internally consistent, and with the exception of some very slight *decalage,* will form a structured whole across widely varying content. That is, the stage properties presented earlier characterize competence though not necessarily performance in moral judgment.

This contrasts with Selman's (1980) account of the development of social perspective taking and interpersonal understanding, which should be considered an additive rather than transformational model. In Selman's scheme, responses can vary across a number of levels even if the highest competence is being assessed, because for solving some kinds of problems a lower level may be all that is required and thus the most appropriate response. Because of the prescriptive nature of morality, lower level responses can never be said to be more *morally* appropriate than higher level responses, though one might want to argue that under some circumstances they could be more psychologically appropriate. Thus, although we do distinguish between competence and performance in moral judgment, we hold that lower levels are used only in situations with a significant downward press. Hickey and Scharf (1980), for example, have found that convicts living in what may be called the low-level ''moral atmosphere'' of a traditional prison exhibit significantly less mature moral reasoning on hypothetical prison dilemmas than on the Heinz dilemma and others that are further removed from the prison setting. At this point, the performance variables that determine fluctuation of stage use have only begun to be delineated, and this represents a particularly important direction for future research.

Generality versus Specificity of Structures

Theoretical controversy also surrounds the question of defining the unit over which the structured whole extends. The issue is the generality or specificity of developmental structures. At one extreme is a global interpretation of structure: the position that the structure of an individual's thinking forms a single coherent system across all domains (Loevinger, 1976; Kegan, 1982). The differences between thinking in different domains result from the application of a single cognitive structure to different contents.

At the other extreme, still within a structural-developmental framework, is the view that even within a domain such as moral judgment, different concepts exhibit different developmental sequences of cognitive structures. This approach is exemplified by Damon's (1977) contention that judgments about distributive justice, authority, and social rules are best represented by ''partial structures'' that do not extend beyond the specific area of morality in question.

We have taken an intermediate position, namely, that cognitive and social-cognitive development can be divided into a number of internally coherent domains including logicomathematical development, social perspective taking, moral development, social-conventional development, and others. Within each of these domains, general structures or patterns of thought can be identified, and these structures organize and underlie the more specific concepts within the domain. In the moral domain, we have called these underlying patterns of thought levels of sociomoral perspective and justice operations. These will be discussed in a later section of this chapter.

In addition to asserting that there are cognitive structures that organize thinking within the moral domain, we have also argued that there are parallels and interdependencies among structures in different domains. We will take up this question of the relations among domains in a later section.

Universal Invariant Sequence

Perhaps the most controversial of all of the stage properties is the contention that stage sequences are not only invariant across individuals within a particular culture or subculture but are also culturally universal. Some theorists (Simpson, 1974; Schweder, 1982) have argued that there are likely to be different structures and developmental sequences resulting from different social contexts, for example, in widely different cultures. On the other hand, Kohlberg has argued that the most general core structures of moral judgment are universal, although many other very important aspects of moral judgment do vary from one culture to the next. In later chapters we present longitudinal data from Turkey and Israel that trace the development of all five stages. Other supporting data have been reported by Parikh (1980), Lei and Cheng (1982), Grimley (1973), and Edwards (1975, 1981, 1982). Edwards (1981) provides a review of cross-cultural research on moral judgment in which she concludes that there is strong evidence for the cross-cultural universality of the stages and their sequence at least for the first four stages. The fifth stage is somewhat more problematic since it is less commonly found in simple than in complex societies. She tentatively explains this latter finding in terms of correspondences between moral judgment (psychological) structures and legal-political (societal) structures. For a more extensive discussion of the cultural relativity issue, see Kohlberg (1984, chap. 4) and Snarey (1985).

The universality claim has also been questioned with regard to gender. That is, even within the American middle-class culture, Gilligan (1982) and others have argued that male and female experience is different enough to generate different developmental structures and sequences. So far there is no evidence that there are two tracks of development, one for women and one for men. Those sex differences that do exist appear to be differences in mode or style rather than structure. Furthermore, there is abundant evidence that girls' and women's responses to Kohlberg's hypothetical dilemmas are readily scorable by the Standard Issue Scoring System and that, when education and occupation are controlled, there are no sex differences in stage (Gibbs, Arnold, & Burkhardt, 1983; Rest, 1983; Walker, 1983; Snarey, Kohlberg, & Reimer, chap. 5, this volume). Furthermore, longitudinal studies of moral judgment (Snarey et al., chap. 5, this volume; and Erickson, 1980) have demonstrated that males and females show the same sequence of stage development and equivalent regularity of sequence. We will return to this issue in chapter 2, "Reliability and Validity of Standard Issue Scoring."

The Moral Domain

A critical point in the study of moral judgment is the recognition that moral judgment refers to a mode of *prescriptive* valuing of the obligatory or right. Other modes of judgment may pertain to prescriptive evaluations of logic and truth, to descriptions of naturally occurring phenomena, to pragmatic calculations of consequences, or to aesthetic judgments. It is quite possible, of course, to engage in psychological and philosophical study of one of these other modes of judgment. The development of judgments of logicomathematical and physical knowledge is Piaget's primary field of study. The development of descriptive judgments of social behavior and institutions is represented in, for example, studies of levels of social cognition or role taking (Selman, 1976) and social-cognitive epistemology (Broughton, 1978b). It is only when social cognition is extended into prescriptive judgments as to what is right or good that we can identify a moral judgment. When someone is asked, ''What is a constitutional government?'' or ''What is a husband–wife relationship?'' a level of social cognition can be inferred from the answer. It is when the person is asked, ''Should you always obey the laws of a constitutional government?'' or ''Should you break a husband–wife relationship by divorce?'' that the answer is likely to include not only a social-cognitive judgment, but, beyond that, a judgment of prescriptive valuing.

Moral judgments, then, have certain properties that make them *moral* judgments. They are, first, judgments of value, not of fact. This distinguishes them from cognitive reasoning and judgment studied by Piaget. Second, they are social judgments, judgments involving people. Third, they are prescriptive or normative judgments, judgments of ought, of rights and responsibilities, rather than value judgments of liking and preference.

The prescriptive nature of moral judgments implies that they direct, command, or oblige us to take some action. Moral prescriptions are not merely commands to *perform* particular actions, however. They are imperatives deriving from some rule or principle of action that the speaker takes as binding on his own actions. These rules or principles may be very instruction specific and idiosyncratic to the person speaking, but they are still rules or principles with specific features built into them. For example, to say a promise-keeping act is right or obligatory may have to be phrased for a given action as: ''Let any person who has promised to do something, where the promise was not obtained by force or fraud, do what he has promised to do unless it conflicts with helping a person in overwhelming need'' (Hare, 1963, p. 107). According to Hare, then, a moral judgment is an implicit commitment to action by the speaker and by others who share his principle, a commitment specifiable as a rule or principle.

The notion of a rule or principle in turn requires logically that moral judgments are *universalizable prescriptions.* Kant (1785/1948) argued that mature moral principles are morally universalizable in the sense of the categorical imperative, ''Let the maxim of thy conduct be the universal will.'' In this sense principles are universalizable if they are framed to be justifiable to, and applied by, *all* moral agents. Hare, however, does not demand universalizability in this strong normative sense. Rather, he holds universalizability as a logical or metaethical statement about the meaning of words, as the necessary requirement of moral words. This is a condition that can be met even by cultural or ethical relativists' moral judgments.

In this delineation of the moral domain, it is important to clarify our position on the distinction between moral judgments and social-conventional judgments (judgments about such issues as manners, dress, protocol, and so on). Because Kohlberg has used the terms *preconventional, conventional,* and *postconventional* to describe the developmental levels of moral judgment (as discussed later in this chapter), readers have sometimes incorrectly assumed that this implies a belief that the moral domain is undifferentiated from the domain of social convention at the preconventional and conventional levels. We fully recognize that young children have been shown to distinguish between the two domains (Turiel, 1983), at least in unambiguous cases. Our use of the term conventional to describe the second developmental level implies not a failure to distinguish the two domains but rather a focus on socially shared moral norms and roles as the basis for making *morally* prescriptive judgments of rights, responsibilities, and so on.

Justice

Kohlberg (1981a, chaps. 2, 5) has written reinvoking the Socratic claim that ''virtue is not many but one and its name is justice.'' In reiterating the claim for the primacy of justice, he drew on Rawls's (1971) *A Theory of Justice,* in which justice is seen as the first virtue of a society. Although Kohlberg characterizes his stage scheme as the development of justice reasoning, this should not be interpreted to imply that the system can handle only judgments that are *explicitly* rights or justice oriented (Kohlberg, 1984, chap. 4). Kohlberg (1984) has described four moral orientations reflected in responses to his hypothetical dilemmas, only one of which focuses *explicitly* on justice. These orientations, discussed further in chapter 6, are the following: (1) general and normative order or impartial following of rules and normative roles; (2) utilitarian maximizing of the welfare of each person; (3) perfectionistic seeking of harmony or integrity of the self and the social group; and (4) fairness, balancing of perspectives, maintaining equity, and social contract.

The emphasis on justice is most explicit and direct in the fairness orientation, but implicitly underlies all of the orientations. Justice within the normative order orientation is impartial, just, or consistent maintenance of general rules. The utilitarian orientation considers justice as the operation of quantitatively maximizing social welfare consequences. In the perfectionist orientation, the central element is treating the self, the other, and the self's relations to others as ends, not as means. Implicit in this orientation is fairness or avoidance of exploitation of others and the need to benefit them.

This question of the scope of moral thinking included within the stages described in this volume has been controversial. Gilligan (1982) has argued that because of the focus on justice as the central defining feature of the moral domain, the system fails to account for an important area of morality that she calls caring and responsibility. Although it is true that the dilemmas in the Standard Moral Judgment Interview pose conflicts of rights, the actual judgments made by respondents may focus on concern and love for another person, on personal commitments, on the need for sympathy and understanding, on responsibility to humanity and one's fellow human beings as well as rights, rules, and duties. As long as these concepts are used prescriptively, as defining what is morally right or good, they fall within the scope of the moral domain as we construe it. In this sense, the scope of the domain we assess is considerably broader than is conveyed by the term *justice reasoning.* We will return to this issue in our discussion of the content classification scheme used in Standard Issue Scoring.

Metaethical Thinking

In order to understand the nature of the moral domain over which Kohlberg's stage theory extends, one must distinguish between normative ethics and metaethics (Kohlberg, 1984, chap.4). Normative ethical questions ask what is right, wrong, good, morally obligatory, and the like, and why. Normative judgments assert that a choice, action, or policy is morally right or wrong and may take the form of a principle such as, "It is always wrong (other things being equal) to harm someone or cause unhappiness." Metaethical thinking does not address either particular or general questions about what is good or right. It addresses instead logical, epistemological, or semantic questions like the following: What is the *meaning* of the expressions *morally right* or *good*? How can ethical judgments be established or justified? What is morality? Is morality relative to the individual or is it universal?

Although subjects' normative ethical and metaethical thinking are closely interrelated, Kohlberg's stage sequence and the Standard Issue Scoring System deal only with normative judgments, not with metaethics. Occasionally, a subject's expressed position on metaethical issues can be used to illuminate the stage significance of an ambiguous normative judgment, but the metaethical position itself is not stage scored.

From a Piagetian perspective, normative judgments can be considered to be operational reasoning, whereas metaethical thinking represents second-order or reflective reasoning. We follow Gibbs (1979) in arguing that a strong Piagetian stage model is appropriate to operational but not to reflective judgment. Two theorists that deal more directly with metaethics are Perry (1970) and Fowler (1981). Neither of these theories, which deal respectively with intellectual and moral epistemology and with religious faith, conforms to a strictly Piagetian model of development.

Relations among Cognitive, Social-Cognitive, and Moral Domains

Let us take up again the question of generality versus specificity of structure and the hypothesis of parallel and interdependent structures in different domains. We have argued elsewhere (Colby, 1975) for a fairly global and integrative view of structure, i.e., that cognitive structures or operations develop in parallel in the domains of logicomathematical thinking, social perspective taking, and moral judgment, and that justice structures are operations of social interaction parallel to the operations of logicomathematical thought. Justice operations of reciprocity and equality parallel operations of reciprocity and equality in the logicomathematical domain (Kohlberg, 1984, chap. 4).

Specifically, we have argued that Piagetian concrete operations are necessary but not sufficient for Stage 2 in Selman's (1980) social-perspective-taking scheme, which, in turn, is necessary but not sufficient for Stage 2 moral judgment. Early formal operations are said to be necessary for Stage 3 role taking and moral judgment, and consolidated formal operations are posited as the prerequisite for Stage 4 role taking and moral judgment.

One way of interpreting the meaning of these claims is to see them as conceptual or definitional issues for which empirical evidence is irrelevant. That is, Kohlberg has argued that logical and role-taking operations are built into the definitions of the moral stages. In this interpretation, the higher moral stages by definition require a high level of logical and social-cognitive sophistication, but advanced logical thinking and social cognition can be expressed within the moral domain without constituting thinking that is *morally* advanced. It is clearly true that, in a general sense, one must be capable of intellectually and social-cognitively sophisticated responses within the moral domain if one is to exhibit an advanced stage in Kohlberg's scheme. This is evident from reading examples of higher stage reasoning in Volume II of this book. It is also clear that one can exhibit intellectual and social-cognitive sophistication about a moral problem without meeting the criteria for advanced moral thinking. The question of whether the intellectual sophistication required within the moral domain is best described in terms of the specifically suggested parallel operations of logicomathematical and moral judgment must be answered by scrutinizing the justice operations said to define the moral stages and considering their relation to logicomathematical structures of thought. The justice operations will be presented in a later section of this chapter.

This interpretation of the hypothesis that Piagetian cognitive stage, and especially Selman's (1980) social-perspective-taking level, is necessary but not sufficient for moral stage is especially useful for the researcher and scorer of moral judgment interviews to keep in mind since it makes clearer what is being scored as moral stage. This is, in the first place, *the sociomoral perspective of prescriptive reasoning* of a stage and in the second place, the justice operations of the stage (these will be defined later in this chapter). Even if there are parallel operations across stages of logic, social perspective taking, and moral judgment, scoring for moral stage does not, from our point of view, involve scoring the application to moral dilemmas or problems of a level of cognitive reasoning (e.g., formal operations) or a level of social perspective taking (e.g., a third-person mutual perspective). Rather, it involves scoring a developing domain with its own unique structures, the domain of prescriptive moral reasoning. We hold that conceptually distinct developmental domains can and should be delineated and that each is characterized by its own qualitatively different sequence, even if there are isomorphisms and interdependencies among domains. The specific structures of thought within a domain are determined in part by the nature of the function they serve, and each domain can be said to represent a different function.

There is, in addition to the preceding interpretation, a more radical interpretation of the claim that logical cognition is necessary but not sufficient for role taking, which is in turn necessary but not sufficient for moral judgment. In this view, it is claimed that the operations in question will necessarily be exhibited first in response to logicomathematical or physical problems, next in response to social problems, and last in response to moral problems. Empirical research on the relations among domains focuses, of course, on this interpretation of the "necessary but not sufficient hypothesis." In fact, a substantial amount of evidence has been accumulated in support of this position. For the most part, the evidence has come from studies in which scores on tests from two or three domains are compared either correlationally or through contingency table analyses in which a zero cell is expected (Selman, 1971; Selman and Damon, 1975; Kuhn et al., 1977; Kohlberg et al., in press). That is, if concrete operations are necessary but not sufficient for Stage 2 moral judgment, one would expect to find subjects in the preoperational X MJ Stage 1 cell, in the concrete operational X Stage 1 cell, in the concrete operational X Stage 2 cell, but *not* in the preoperational X Stage 2 cell. This has, in fact, been found. However, this research has been criticized as inconclusive since the same pattern of data could result from a correlation of each developmental sequence with age and a somewhat slower rate of development in moral judgment, even if development in the domains progressed independently. Further methodological problems arise in connection with choosing appropriately "equivalent" measures in very different domains.

A stronger design for evaluating the necessary but not sufficient hypothesis is provided by the use of an intervention designed to increase the subjects' role-taking or moral stage. In such a study, subjects are chosen who have and who do not have the hypothesized logical prerequisite of a particular moral stage, for example, but do not exhibit the parallel moral stage. These subjects then undergo a series of training sessions designed to increase their moral stage. The prediction, if the hypothesis is correct, is that only the subjects with the necessary logical prerequisite will advance to the next moral stage. Arbuthnot et al. (1983), Faust and Arbuthnot (1978), and Walker and Richards (1979) have used this design to study the relation of the logical, perspective-taking, and moral stages and obtained the predicted results.

Probably the strongest single study supporting the hypothesis that there is a necessary but not sufficient relationship between (a) logical operations and Selman's (1980) social perspective taking and (b) social-perspective-taking level and prescriptive moral stage is that of Walker (1980). Walker summarizes his study as follows:

Kohlberg has proposed that both cognitive and perspective-taking development are necessary though not sufficient conditions for moral development. This study examined that proposition by attempting to stimulate moral development to stage 3 as a function of attainment of hypothesized prerequisites in cognitive and perspective-taking development. After assessing stage of development in each domain of reasoning, fourth-through seventh-grade children were exposed to moral stage 3 reasoning in a brief role-playing situation. This treatment was followed by a moral reasoning posttest and a follow-up. Results indicated that transitions to moral stage 3 were found only for those children who had attained the hypothesized prerequisites of "beginning formal operations" and "perspective-taking stage 3," thus confirming Kohlberg's proposition and implying the relevance of these prerequisites for the efficacy of moral education programs. (p. 131)

Nevertheless, the developmental model that posits interdependent relations among domains has been criticized by Turiel and others. Turiel argues for the importance of making clear distinctions between domains of social thought and between different types of cognitive function. He hypothesizes that "there are domains of social knowledge which are not dependent upon non-social cognitive structures and which are constructed through the individual's interactions with the social environment" and that "thought is organized . . . within domains and not across domains." He argues that

since conceptual knowledge is constructed through an interactive process, the nature of conceptual constructions, though not determined by the environment, would be influenced by it. Therefore, individual-environment interactions with fundamentally different types of objects and events should result in the formation of distinct concepts. In sum, if thought is organized within domains and if developmental change entails reorganization of thought, it then follows that there would be separate developmental sequences for each domain. (Turiel, 1979)

Turiel and his colleagues have presented convincing data that support his argument that the domains of social conventional judgment and moral judgment are differentiated by young children. However, to show that two domains are psychologically distinct is not to show that they are independent. That is, the fact that children from the beginning can tell moral concerns apart from conventional concerns does not imply that these two sets of concerns do not inform and influence one another. Conventional and moral concerns, in fact, are so closely intertwined that one frequently becomes the other in the course of development, as when certain issues of sexual propriety are transformed from moral into conventional issues in individuals' thinking. We would hold, then, that it is more accurate to think of morality and social convention as distinct but closely interrelated rather than completely independent conceptual systems.

Rest (1979) has argued that the question of the relations among developmental sequences in the various domains should not even be taken seriously. His reasons derive from his rejection of the strong Piagetian stage model. Rest agrees with our claim that qualitatively different forms of moral judgment can be identified and that development involves the increasing use of more advanced or sophisticated reasoning, and the decreasing use of less sophisticated reasoning. He disagrees, however, with our claim that development proceeds through a stepwise sequence of internally consistent stages. He holds instead that individuals simultaneously use reasoning of many types and that an adequate description of an individual's moral judgment must include a quantitative account of the proportion of each type rather than a global designation for the person. Rest argues that the question of correspondence between stages on different developmental dimensions assumes that it makes sense to stage type the subject on both measures, an assumption he considers invalid.

The problem with such statements is that they represent development as a point rather than as a range within which the subject operates, depending on the test characteristics, response mode, content domain, or level of attainment. Mapping out one developmental variable on another can be done point for point only if it is understood that the points have little generality to other situations, test instruments, response modes, or scoring conventions (which makes point for point comparisons rather trivial). (p. 74)

From our perspective, this critique of research on the relations among stage sequences in different domains is unwarranted at least in regard to those domains that we claim do fit the Piagetian stage model. Of course, the competence–performance distinction is again relevant here and the "necessary but not sufficient" relationship refers to highest level of competence in each domain in question. We will return to Rest's critique of the stage model in chapter 3 and will present data in support of our position along with an interpretation of Rest's discrepant findings.

The Moral Judgment Levels and Stages

The basic developmental concept underlying the stage sequence presented here is level of sociomoral perspective – the characteristic point of view from which the individual formulates moral judgments. In discussing level of sociomoral perspective, let us again say that we believe the perspective taking underlying the moral stages is intrinsically moral in nature rather than a logical or social-cognitive structure applied to the moral domain. In this interpretation we agree

15

with Turiel (1979) and Damon (1983) in their contentions that there are many types of perspective taking, each of which develops separately, although not necessarily independently, as a result of experience in a particular domain. In this view, spatial, social, and moral perspective taking are fundamentally different processes rather than applications of a single general structure to different content areas. That is, the form of spatial perspective taking is intrinsically spatial, not moral or social, and the form of moral perspective taking is intrinsically moral, not spatial or social.

The levels of moral perspective, briefly described in Table 1.1, provide a general organization of moral judgment and serve to inform and unite other more specific moral concepts such as the nature of the morally right or good, the nature of moral reciprocity or moral rules, of rights, of obligation or duty, of fairness, of welfare consequences, and of moral values such as obedience to authority, preservation of human life, and maintenance of contracts and affectional relations (moral norms and elements, to be defined later). Within each of these specific moral concepts (norms and elements), the form of developmental change is to some extent specific to the nature of the particular concept in question. However, the general moral perspective can be seen to underlie its more specific manifestations.

The six moral stages are grouped into three levels: *preconventional level* (Stages 1 and 2), *conventional level* (Stages 3 and 4), and *principled* or *postconventional level* (Stages 5 and 6).

To understand the stages, it is helpful to begin with the three moral levels. The preconventional level is the level of most children under age 9, some adolescents, and many adolescent and adult criminal offenders. The conventional level is the level of most adolescents and adults in American society and in most other societies. The postconventional level is reached by a minority of adults and usually only after the age of 20–25. As noted earlier, the term *conventional* does not mean that individuals at this level are unable to distinguish between morality and social convention but rather that morality consists of socially shared systems of moral rules, roles, and norms. Individuals at the preconventional level have not yet come to really understand and uphold socially shared moral norms and expectations. Those at the postconventional level understand and generally accept society's rules, but acceptance of society's rules is based on formulating and accepting the general moral principles that underlie these rules. These principles in some cases come into conflict with society's rules, in which case the postconventional individual judges by principle rather than by convention.

One way of understanding the three levels is to think of them as three different types of relationships between the self and society's moral rules and expectations. From this point of view, Level 1 (preconventional) is a perspective from which rules and social expectations are something external to the self; in the Level 2 perspective the self is identified with or has internalized the rules and expectations of others, especially those of authorities; and the Level 3 (postconventional) perspective differentiates the self from the rules and expectations of others and defines moral values in terms of self-chosen principles.

Within each of the three moral levels, there are two stages. The second stage is a more advanced and organized form of the general perspective of each level. Corresponding to the three levels of moral judgment, Kohlberg has postulated three levels of sociomoral perspective as follows:

[margin notes:] Cannot assume all pts. have moral principles, or "typical" moral principles.

And at any given moment, we can be thinking in any of the levels, using that levels framework to determine our course of action, etc.

Shared viewpoint of group

Moral judgment	Sociomoral perspective
1. Preconventional	Concrete individual perspective
2. Conventional	Member-of-society perspective
3. Postconventional or principled	Prior-to-society perspective

Let us illustrate the meaning of sociomoral perspective in terms of the unity it provides for the various ideas and concerns of the moral level. The conventional level, for example, is different from the preconventional in that it uses the following reasons: (1) concern about social approval; (2) concern about loyalty to persons, groups, and authority; and (3) concern about the welfare of others and society. We need to ask what underlies these characteristics of reasoning and holds them together. What fundamentally defines and unifies the characteristics of the conventional level is its sociomoral perspective, a shared viewpoint of the participants in a relationship or a group. This perspective subordinates the needs of the single individual to the viewpoint and needs of the group or the shared relationship. To illustrate the conventional level perspective, consider 17-year-old Joe's response to the following question:

Why shouldn't you steal from a store?

It's a matter of law. It's one of our rules that we're trying to help protect everyone, protect property, not just to protect a store. It's something that's needed in our society. If we didn't have these laws, people would steal, they wouldn't have to work for a living and our whole society would get out of kilter.

Joe is concerned about keeping the law, and his reason for being concerned is the good of society as a whole. Clearly, he is speaking as a member of society. "It's one of *our* rules that *we're* trying to help protect everyone . . . It's something that's needed in *our* society." This concern about the good of society arises from his taking the point of view of "us members of society," which goes beyond the point of view of Joe as a concrete, individual self.

Let us contrast this conventional member-of-society perspective with the preconventional concrete individual perspective. The latter point of view is that of the individual actor in the situation thinking about his or her interests and those of other individuals he or she may care about. Seven years earlier, at age 10, Joe responded from a concrete individual perspective in answer to the same question:

Why shouldn't you steal from a store?

It's not good to steal from the store. It's against the law. Someone could see you and call the police.

Being "against the law," then, means something very different at the two levels. At Level 2, the law is made by and for "everyone," as Joe indicates at age 17. At Level 1 it is just something enforced by the police and, accordingly, the reason for obeying the law is to avoid punishment. This reason derives from

17

Table 1.1. *Six stages of moral judgment*

Level and stage	Content of stage		Sociomoral perspective of stage
	What is right	Reasons for doing right	
Level 1: Preconventional: Stage 1. Heteronomous morality	To avoid breaking rules backed by punishment, obedience for its own sake, and avoiding physical damage to persons and property.	Avoidance of punishment and the superior power of authorities.	Egocentric point of view. Doesn't consider the interests of others or recognize that they differ from the actor's, doesn't relate two points of view. Actions are considered physically rather than in terms of psychological interests of others. Confusion of authority's perspective with one's own.
Stage 2. Individualism, instrumental purpose, and exchange	Following rules only when it is to someone's immediate interest; acting to meet one's own interests and needs and letting others do the same. Right is also what's fair, what's an equal exchange, a deal, an agreement.	To serve one's own needs or interests in a world where you have to recognize that other people have their interests, too.	Concrete individualistic perspective. Aware that everybody has his own interests to pursue and these conflict, so that right is relative (in the concrete individualistic sense).
Level 2: Conventional: Stage 3. Mutual interpersonal expectations, relationships, and interpersonal conformity	Living up to what is expected by people close to you or what people generally expect of people in your role as son, brother, friend, etc. "Being good" is important and means having good motives, showing concern about others. It also means keeping mutual relationships, such as trust, loyalty, respect, and gratitude.	The need to be a good person in your own eyes and those of others. Your caring for others. Belief in the Golden Rule. Desire to maintain rules and authority which support stereotypical good behavior.	Perspective of the individual in relationships with other individuals. Aware of shared feelings, agreements, and expectations which take primacy over individual interests. Relates points of view through the concrete Golden Rule, putting yourself in the other guy's shoes. Does not yet consider generalized system perspective.
Stage 4. Social system and conscience	Fulfilling the actual duties to which you have agreed. Laws are to be upheld except in extreme cases where they conflict with other fixed social duties. Right is also contributing to society, the group, or institution.	To keep the institution going as a whole, to avoid the breakdown in the system "if everyone did it," or the imperative of conscience to meet one's defined obligations.	Differentiates societal point of view from interpersonal agreement or motives. Takes the point of view of the system that defines roles and rules. Considers individual relations in terms of place in the system.

Stages		Social perspective of stage
Level 3: Postconventional or principled: Stage 5. Social contract or utility and individual rights	Being aware that people hold a variety of values and opinions, that most values and rules are relative to your group. These relative rules should usually be upheld, however, in the interest of impartiality and because they are the social contract. Some nonrelative values and rights like life and liberty, however, must be upheld in any society and regardless of majority opinion. A sense of obligation to law because of one's social contract to make and abide by laws for the welfare of all and for the protection of all people's rights. A feeling of contractual commitment, freely entered upon, to family, friendship, trust and work obligations. Concern that laws and duties be based on rational calculation of overall utility, "the greatest good for the greatest number."	Prior-to-society perspective. Perspective of a rational individual aware of values and rights prior to social attachments and contracts. Integrates perspectives by formal mechanisms of agreement, contract, objective impartiality, and due process. Considers moral and legal points of view; recognizes that they sometimes conflict and finds it difficult to integrate them.
Stage 6. Universal ethical principles	Following self-chosen ethical principles. Particular laws or social agreements are usually valid because they rest on such principles. When laws violate these principles, one acts in accordance with the principle. Principles are universal principles of justice: the equality of human rights and respect for the dignity of human beings as individual persons. The belief as a rational person in the validity of universal moral principles, and a sense of personal commitment to them.	Perspective of a moral point of view from which social arrangements derive. Perspective is that of any rational individual recognizing the nature of morality or the fact that persons are ends in themselves and must be treated as such.

Source: Reprinted from Kohlberg (1976).

the limits of a Level 1 perspective, the perspective of an individual considering his or her own interests and those of other isolated individuals.

Let us now consider the perspective of the principled or postconventional level. It is like the preconventional perspective in that it returns to the standpoint of the individual rather than taking the point of view of "us members of society." The individual point of view taken at the postconventional level, however, can be universal; it is that of any rational moral individual. Aware of the member-of-society perspective, the postconventional perspective questions and redefines it in terms of an individual moral point of view, so that social obligations are defined in ways that can be justified to any moral individual. An individual's commitment to basic morality or moral principles is seen as preceding, or being necessary for, taking society's perspective or accepting society's laws and values. Society's laws and values, in turn, should be ones to which all reasonable persons could commit themselves – whatever their place in society and regardless of the society to which they belong. The postconventional perspective, then, is prior-to-society; it is the perspective of an individual who has made the moral commitments or holds the standards on which a good or just society must be based. This is a perspective by which (1) a particular society or set of social practices may be judged and (2) a person may make a rational commitment to a society.

An example is Joe, our longitudinal subject, interviewed at age 24:

Why shouldn't someone steal from a store?
It's violating another person's rights, in this case to property.

Does the law enter in?
Well, the law in most cases is based on what is morally right so it's not a separate subject, it's a consideration.

What does morality or morally right mean to you?
Recognizing the rights of other individuals, first to life and then to do as he pleases as long as it doesn't interfere with somebody else's rights.

The wrongness of stealing is that it violates the moral rights of individuals, which are prior to law and society. Property rights follow from more universal human rights (such as freedoms that do not interfere with like freedoms of others). The demands of law and society derive from universal moral rights, rather than vice versa.

It should be noted that reference to the words *rights* or *morally right* or *conscience* does not necessarily distinguish conventional from postconventional morality. Orienting to the morally right thing, or following conscience as against following the law, need not indicate the postconventional perspective of the rational moral individual. The terms *morality* and *conscience* may be used to refer to group rules and values that conflict with civil laws or with the rules of the majority group. To a Jehovah's Witness, who has gone to jail for reasons of conscience, *conscience* may mean God's law as interpreted by the religious group rather than from the standpoint of any individual oriented to universal moral principles or values. To be considered postconventional, such ideas or terms must be used in a way that make it clear that they have a foundation for a rational or moral individual who has not yet made a commitment to any group or society or its morality. Trust, for example, is a basic value at both the conventional and postconventional levels. At the conventional level trustworthiness is something one expects of others in the society. Joe expresses this as follows at age 17:

Why should a promise be kept, anyway?

Friendship is based on trust. If you can't trust a person, there's little grounds to deal with him. You should try to be as reliable as possible because people remember you by this, you're more respected if you can be depended upon.

At this conventional level, Joe views trust from the perspective of a truster, as well as from the viewpoint of someone who could break a trust. He sees that individuals need to be trustworthy, not only to secure respect and to maintain social relationships with others, but also because, as members of society, they expect trust of others in general.

At the postconventional level, individuals take a further step. They do not automatically assume that they are in a society in which they need the friendship and respect of other individuals. Instead they consider why any society or social relationship presupposes trust, and why they, if they are to contract into society, must be trustworthy. At age 24, Joe is postconventional in his explanation of why a promise should be kept:

I think human relationships in general are based on trust, on believing in other individuals. If you have no way of believing in someone else, you can't deal with anyone else and it becomes every man for himself. Everything you do in a day's time is related to somebody else and if you can't deal on a fair basis, you have chaos.

We have defined a postconventional moral perspective in terms of the individual's reasons *why* something is right or wrong. We need to illustrate this perspective as it enters into making an actual decision or defining *what is right*. Postconventional thinking is aware of the moral point of view that each individual in a moral conflict ought to adopt. Rather than defining expectations and obligations from the standpoint of societal roles, as someone at the conventional level would, postconventional thinking holds that persons in these roles should orient to a "moral point of view." Although the postconventional moral viewpoint also recognizes legal-social obligations, recognition of moral obligations may take priority when the moral and legal viewpoints conflict.

At age 24 Joe reflects the postconventional moral point of view as a decision-making perspective in response to Heinz's dilemma about stealing a drug to save his wife:

It is the husband's duty to save his wife. The fact that her life is in danger transcends every other standard you might use to judge his action. Life is more important than property.

Suppose it were a friend, not his wife?

I don't think that would be much different from a moral point of view. It's still a human being in danger.

Suppose it were a stranger?

To be consistent, yes, from a moral standpoint.

What is this moral standpoint?

I think every individual has a right to live and if there is a way of saving an individual, he should be saved.

Should the judge punish the husband?

Usually the moral and the legal standpoints coincide. Here they conflict. The judge should weigh the moral standpoint more heavily but preserve the legal law in punishing Heinz lightly.

Sociomoral Perspectives of the Stages

This section will briefly describe sociomoral perspective differences involved in moral judgment Stages 1 through 5. Stage 6 will be briefly discussed in the section on justice operations since its sociomoral perspective is not clearly distinct from Stage 5. In this discussion of the first five stages, we will attempt to show how the second stage in the preconventional and conventional levels completes the development of the perspective entered at the first stage of that level. After providing an overview of the stages, we will turn to a more detailed account of the "justice structures" that characterize each stage.

We will start with the easiest pair of stages to explain in this way – Stages 3 and 4, comprising the conventional level. In the preceding section we quoted the "isolated individual" perspective of Stages 1 and 2 and contrasted it with Joe's full-fledged member-of-society perspective at age 17, a perspective that is Stage 4. Joe's statements about the importance of trust in dealing with others clearly reflect the perspective of someone taking the point of view of the social system. The social perspective at Stage 3 is less aware of society's point of view, or of the good of society as a whole. As an example of Stage 3, let us consider Andy's response to a dilemma about whether to tell your father about a brother's disobedience after the brother has confided in you.

He should think of his brother, but it's more important to be a good son. Your father had done so much for you. I'd have a conscience if I didn't tell, more than to my brother, because my father couldn't trust me. My brother would understand; our father has done so much for him too.

Andy's perspective is not based on a social system. It is rather one in which he has two relationships: one with his brother and one with his father. His father as authority and helper comes first. Andy expects his brother to share this perspective, but as someone also centered on their father. There is no reference to the organization of the family in general. Being a good son is said to be more important, not because it is a more important role in the eyes of, or in terms of, society as a whole or even in terms of the family as a system. The Stage 3 member-of-the-group perspective is that of the average good person, not that of society or an institution as a whole. The Stage 3 perspective sees things from the point of view of shared relationships between two or more individuals – relations of caring, trust, respect, and so on – rather than from the viewpoint of institutional wholes. In summary, whereas the Stage 4 member-of-society perspective is a "system" perspective, the Stage 3 perspective is that of a participant in a shared relationship or shared group.

Let us turn to the preconventional level. Whereas Stage 1 involves only the concrete individual's point of view, Stage 2 is aware of a number of other individuals, each having other points of view. At Stage 2 in serving my interests, I anticipate the other guy's reaction, negative or positive, and he anticipates mine. Unless we make a deal, each will put his own point of view first. If we make a deal, each of us will do something for the other.

An example of the shift from Stage 1 to Stage 2 is shown by the following change in another subject's response between ages 10 and 13 to a question about whether an older brother should tell his father about his younger brother's misdeed, revealed in confidence. At 10, the subject gives a Stage 1 answer:

In one way it was right to tell because his father might beat him up. In another way it's wrong because his brother will beat him up if he tells.

At age 13, he has moved to Stage 2:

The brother should not tell or he'll get his brother in trouble. If he wants his brother to keep quiet for him sometime, he'd better not squeal now.

In the second response, there is an extension of concern to the brother's welfare as it affects the subject's own interests through anticipated exchange. There is a much clearer picture of the brother's point of view and its relationship to his own.

Turning to the postconventional level, the Stage 5 orientation distinguishes between a moral and a legal point of view, and defines a moral perspective that is linked with the perspective of contractual-legal rights. Bill, at Stage 5, says with regard to why it is important to obey the law:

I think it relates in the sense that laws are generally passed to protect rights that have been recognized in some social sense, have become prevailing norms and recognition of the norm usually follows — they follow in a sense, but they also — law has been used to establish rights, too, to define them, to codify them, to provide sanctions and constraints against the imposition or the taking away of those rights. Rights are a recognition of those things which an individual has a claim on, in terms of time or whatever else, by virtue of being a human being.

Although Bill recognizes the importance and validity of the legal system, he sees its legitimacy as deriving from its function in establishing, codifying, and protecting fundamental human rights. Those rights stand as prior to or more basic than the laws that protect them and are due to each person "by virtue of being a human being." That is, the moral perspective is a prior-to-society view of basic human rights and welfare, and social systems are seen as derivative from this prior, ethical perspective.

Justice Operations

Among moral philosophers (Frankena, 1973; Boyd, 1977) it is customary to distinguish three types of ethical judgment: (a) deontic judgments of rightness and obligation, (b) aretaic judgments of the moral worth or virtue of particular persons or actions, and (c) judgments about the goodness of lifestyle or of ideals of the good life. The central focus of our moral judgment stages is deontic judgments, e.g., answers to the question: "Is Heinz right to steal the drug?" or "Does Heinz have a duty to steal the drug if he doesn't love his wife?" Closely related to deontic judgments of obligation are judgments of rights. Duties and rights are typically correlative at higher stages: If Heinz's wife has a right to life, Heinz has a duty to steal or procure the drug to preserve this right. In a structural sense, our moral stages center on deontic reasoning about justice.

In discussing the moral domain Gilligan (1982) not only has postulated sex differences in moral judgment but has made an ideal-typical distinction between a "care and response orientation" and a "justice orientation" and claims that our moral stages only capture development of the justice orientation. This complex issue is discussed in detail in Kohlberg (1984). In this context it may be noted that many or most moral concerns of care are concerns about enhancing the welfare of other persons or not hurting them and about preserving and embracing relationships with others. We consider these concerns as falling within the domain of justice as the orientations of social utilitarian concern for the welfare of others or the perfectionistic orientation of promoting harmonious social relations, Plato's conception of justice. We do, however, find our most structurally distinctive feature of moral stages in the fairness orientation, where balancing operations of reciprocity, prescriptive role taking, equality, and equity are most explicit and are most parallel to Piagetian logicomathematical thought operations. Kohlberg (1982) explicates how these operations, most explicit in the fairness orientation, are also implicit in the other three orientations to justice.

In stressing an account of moral stages in terms of justice, we should also note that our moral dilemmas not only probe deontic questions of rightness, duties, and rights, but are themselves dilemmas of justice. They do not attempt to capture moral situations raising issues of supererogation, of moral goodness beyond duty, or of special responsibilities to friends and family in situations that do not centrally raise issues of justice.

The moral dilemmas in the Standard Issue Moral Judgment Interview addresses three problems of justice that have been identified in Aristotle's *Nichomachean Ethics* (1962). The first problem is one of *distributive justice*, that is, the way in which society or a third party distributes "honor, wealth, and other desirable assets of the community." This is done in terms of such operations as equality, desert, or merit (i.e., reciprocity defined in terms of proportionality) and, finally, equity in light of need or extenuating circumstances. The second type of justice problem is *commutative justice*, which focuses on voluntary agreement, contract, and equal exchange. A third and closely related type of justice problem is *corrective justice*, "which supplies corrective principle in private transactions" that have been unequal or unfair and require restitution or compensation. In addition, corrective justice deals with crimes or torts violating the rights of an involuntary participant and in this sense requires restitution or retribution.

There is a fourth type of justice problem that is not independent of the three just mentioned. It is the problem of *procedural justice*, which must be addressed in issues of distributive, commutative, and corrective justice. This problem of procedural justice, a concern more clearly distinguishable in high-stage moral judgments, often represents the considerations that moral philosophers treat as validity checks on moral reasoning. These checks are derived from a concern for balancing perspectives or making one's judgments reversible (e.g., employing the Golden Rule) and from a concern for making one's judgments universalizable (e.g., employing Kant's categorical imperative). The reversibility check asks, ''Would you judge this action as fair if you were in the other person's shoes?'' The universalizability check asks, ''Would you judge this action right if everyone were to do it?'' Procedural justice, which involves a special set of considerations at lower stages, becomes a solution to substantive justice problems of distribution and correction at Stage 6, where universalizability and reversibility constitute self-conscious validity checks on one's reasoning.

In order to fill out in more detail what we see as the form or organization of reasoning at the six stages, we will present for each the stage-typical conception of each form of justice. Having already presented the sociomoral perspective of each stage, we will include here a discussion of how the sociomoral perspective informs and underlies the justice operations at each stage.

Stage 1: Heteronomous Morality

The perspective at Stage 1 is that of naive *moral realism*. That is, there is a literal reification of the moral significance of an action such that its goodness or badness is seen as a real, inherent, and unchanging quality of the act just as color and mass are seen as inherent qualities of objects. This realism is reflected in an assumption that moral judgments are self-evident, requiring little or no justification beyond assigning labels or citing rules. For example, telling on your brother is wrong because that is tattling and breaking into the druggist's store is wrong because ''you're not supposed to steal.'' Punishment is seen as important in that it is identified with a bad action rather than because the actor is attempting pragmatically to avoid negative consequences. Likewise, there is an absence of mediating concepts such as deservingness or intentionality through which the particular circumstances of the case alter its moral significance. Thus, moral rules and labels are applied in a literal, absolute manner and both distributive and retributive justice are characterized by strict equality rather than equity. Characteristics of persons that determine their authority, power, or moral worth tend to be physicalistic or categorical. For example, ''The father is the boss because he's bigger;'' ''You should steal to save a woman's life if she's Betsy Ross, who made the flag.'' The perspective of moral realism represents a failure to differentiate multiple perspectives on the dilemmas. This means that authority and subordinate, self and other, and other individuals in conflict or disagreement are assumed to share a single perception of the situation and of the morally appropriate response to it. Morality at Stage 1 is heteronomous in the Piagetian sense. That is, what makes something right or wrong is defined by the authority rather than by cooperation among equals. In formal terms, Stage 1 reasoning is characterized by the uncoordinated use of equality and reciprocity.

Distributive justice is guided by strict equality, and special considerations of need or deservingness are not taken into account. In cases where an authority is involved, distributive justice is guided by heteronomous obedience to or respect for authority. This is illustrated by the following response to Dilemma I:

Should Joe refuse to give his father the money?

If his father told him to give the money up, I'd give it to him, because he's older than you and he's your father.

25

Does he have the right?

No.

Then why should he give it?

Because he's older than him.

Corrective justice tends to be retributive and based on strict reciprocity. For example, "The doctor should be given the death penalty [if he performs the mercy killing] – he killed the woman so they should kill him." Again, moderating circumstances such as intentionality are not incorporated. Also characteristic of Stage 1 is the notion of immanent justice – that punishment necessarily follows as an automatic consequence of transgression. For example:

Why is it important to keep a promise?

If you don't then you're a liar. You're not supposed to lie because you'll get pimples on your tongue.

Commutative justice, as already illustrated, is a matter of following externally defined rules: "You should keep a promise because if you don't, you're a liar." Avoidance of the punishment that would inevitably follow transgression is another reason to follow the rules that govern promise keeping (as is also the case with other rules).

Stage 2: Individualistic, Instrumental Morality

Stage 2 is characterized by a concrete individualistic perspective. There is an awareness that each person has interests to pursue and that these may conflict. A moral relativity develops out of the understanding that different persons can have different yet equally valid justifications for their claims to justice. That is, there is a recognition of more than one perspective on a situation and respect for the moral legitimacy of pursuing one's own interests. The morally right is relative to the particular situation and to the actor's perspective on the situation. Since each person's primary aim is to pursue his or her own interests, the perspective at Stage 2 is pragmatic: to maximize satisfaction of one's needs and desires while minimizing negative consequences to the self. The assumption that the other is also operating from this premise leads to an emphasis on instrumental exchange as a mechanism through which individuals can coordinate their actions for mutual benefit. Thus, the moral realism of Stage 1 is no longer in evidence. An important limitation of Stage 2 is that it fails to provide a means for deciding among conflicting claims, ordering or setting priorities on conflicting needs and interests.

Distributive justice involves coordinating considerations of equality and reciprocity, so that judgments take into account the claims of various persons and the demands of the specific situation. There is reference to individual needs or intentions as the basis for equity rather than strict equality or literal reciprocity in distributive justice. However, equity at Stage 2 is based on concrete, pragmatic considerations rather than on an appreciation of mediating concepts such as deservingness. That is, the Stage 2 conception of equity is based on the reasonable pursuit of individual needs and interests, not equity as referring to shared social norms as at Stage 3. The coordination of reciprocity with equality in distributive justice at Stage 2 is illustrated by the following response to Dilemma I:

Should Joe refuse to give his father the money?
He shouldn't give him the money, because he saved it and should use it however he wants. If his father wants to go fishing he should make his own money.

In this judgment, the reciprocal relation between working for money and being able to spend it is seen as applying equally to both father and son.

Corrective justice also involves reference to individual needs or intentions as the basis for equity. For example, "The doctor should not be given the death penalty for mercy killing the woman, because she wanted to die, and he was just trying to put her out of her pain." This represents a beginning recognition that one person can see another's point of view and modify his or her own action in response. Another example is the following: "The judge shouldn't punish the doctor, because the judge would think that if it was him who was sick he would want the doctor to kill him too."

Commutative justice is based on instrumental exchange that serves to coordinate in a simple way the needs and interests of individuals. For example, it is seen as important to keep promises so that others will keep their promises to you, or do nice things for you, or to keep them from getting angry with you.

Stage 3: Interpersonally Normative Morality

At Stage 3 the separate perspectives of individuals are coordinated into a third-person perspective, that of mutually trusting relationships among people, which is embodied in a set of shared moral norms according to which people are expected to live. These moral norms and expectations transcend or are generalized across particular persons and situations. Stage 3 norms can be distinguished from Stage 1 rules in that norms represent an integration of perspectives that have been recognized as separate, a coming to general social agreement on what constitutes a good role occupant, whereas the orientation to rules at Stage 1 represents a failure to differentiate individual perspectives. The primacy of shared norms at Stage 3 entails an emphasis on being a good, altruistic, or prosocial role occupant and on good or bad motives as indicative of general personal morality. This recognition of the importance of motives also distinguishes Stage 3 norms from Stage 1 rules. As a result of the socially shared perspective, the individual at Stage 3 is particularly concerned with maintaining interpersonal trust and social approval.

The justice operations of Stage 3 are most clearly represented in Golden Rule role taking: Do unto others as you would have others do unto you. This involves a second-order operation whereby a Stage 2 reciprocal exchange is subjected to evaluation by reference to a superordinate or shared norm against which its fairness can be judged. That is, reciprocal exchanges are not necessarily fair but must be negated or affirmed in relation to standards of morally good conduct that stand outside the reciprocal exchange.

Distributive justice at Stage 3 involves equity as at Stage 2. But at Stage 3, strict equality and literal reciprocity are modified by reference to shared norms or to motives that indicate a good or bad person or deservingness rather than by reference to individual needs or interests as at Stage 2. An example is provided by the following response to Dilemma III: "That must be a pretty terrible druggist. A druggist is like a doctor; he's supposed to save people's lives." The reciprocity of "he made the drug so he can do what he wants with it" is negated by reference to socially shared norms of a good druggist.

Corrective justice at Stage 3 also emphasizes the relevance of motives and whether the transgressor is living up to a shared conception of a good person. If so, punishment is not warranted:

Should the judge sentence Heinz?

The judge should see why he did it and see his past record, let him go free and give a warning.

Why?

He did it from the fondness of his heart . . . What most humans would do.

Commutative justice also involves the modification of reciprocity by reference to shared norms and deservingness. For example, a young child might freely agree to trade his dollar for an adult's 25-cent candy bar. At Stage 3 the fairness of this exchange would be denied on the grounds that the adult knows better and should not take advantage of the child's ignorance. That is, the adult should live up to a socially shared conception of his benevolent, protective role in relation to the child.

A similar idea is represented by the following response to Dilemma I:

Joe shouldn't give his father the money because even though, as his parent, his father can demand the money, he shouldn't do it because that would be selfish and childish.

Stage 4: Social System Morality

At Stage 4 the individual takes the perspective of a generalized member of society. This perspective is based on a conception of the social system as a consistent set of codes and procedures that apply impartially to all members. The pursuit of individual interests is considered legitimate only when it is consistent with maintenance of the sociomoral system as a whole. The informally shared norms of Stage 3 are systematized at Stage 4 in order to maintain impartiality and consistency. A social structure that includes formal institutions and social roles serves to mediate conflicting claims and promote the common good. That is, there is an awareness that there can be conflicts even between good role occupants. This makes it necessary to maintain a system of rules for resolving such conflicts. The perspective taken is generally that of a societal, legal, or religious system that has been codified into institutionalized laws and practices. Alternatively, the perspective may be that of some higher moral or religious law that is embodied in the individual's conscience and that may conflict with institutionalized law. In this case, internal conscience or moral law is equated with some system of divine or natural law. Moral judgments at Stage 4 are made in reference to institutions or systems – either legal or social institutions or moral and religious institutions and systems of belief.

Distributive justice is based on a concern for impartiality, respect for social institutions such as systems of authority and private property, and considerations of social merit or contribution to society. Generally, maintaining respect for property rights as a return for investment of effort is considered to be central to social organization. On the other hand, property rights may also be seen as contingent on demonstration of social responsibility. This is exemplified by the following response to Dilemma III:

Did the druggist have the right to charge that much?

No, for him to make that much profit is ignoring his responsibility to people.

Corrective justice at Stage 4 centers on the notions of impartiality in application of the law and corrective action as protecting society through deterrence, by removing threats to society, or by providing a means for the offender to "pay a debt to society." The importance of upholding impartiality or consistency reflects a concern about procedural justice that emerges as a central consideration at Stage 4. This is illustrated by the following response to Dilemma III:

What would be the best reason for the judge to give him a sentence?

Exceptions to the law cannot be given. This would lead to totally subjective decisions on the part of the law enforcers.

Commutative justice is based on a recognition of the importance of contractual agreements to maintaining a smoothly functioning society or on the value of upholding one's moral character, integrity, or honor. For example:

Is it important to keep a promise to someone you don't know well?

Yes. Perhaps even more so than keeping a promise to someone you know well. A man is often judged by his actions in such situations, and to be described as being a man of honor or a man of integrity is very fulfilling indeed.

Stage 5: Human Rights and Social Welfare Morality

The Stage 5 prior-to-society perspective is that of a rational moral agent aware of universalizable values and rights that anyone would choose to build into a moral society. The validity of actual laws and social systems can be evaluated in terms of the degree to which they preserve and protect these fundamental human rights and values. The social system is seen ideally as a contract freely entered into by each individual in order to preserve the rights and promote the welfare of all members. This is a "society-creating" rather than a "society-maintaining" perspective. Society is conceived as based on social cooperation and agreement. Within the Stage 5 perspective, the primary focus may be either on rights or on social welfare. The former orientation emphasizes that some rights must be considered inviolable by the society. These rights cannot be abridged even through freely chosen contracts. Each person has an obligation to make moral choices that uphold these rights even in cases where they conflict with society's laws or codes. There is a concern for protection of the rights of the minority that cannot be derived from the social system perspective of Stage 4. The social welfare orientation reflects a rule utilitarian philosophy in which social institutions, rules, or laws are evaluated by reference to their long-term consequences for the welfare of each person or group in the society.

Distributive justice at Stage 5 is structured around respect for fundamental human rights and a rational hierarchy of rights and values or around a process of social cooperation and agreement. The latter is exemplified in the following response to Dilemma III:

Last time we talked you mentioned something about a priori rights . . .

It revolves around what I was saying just now about rights that kind of go with being a human being, but really those rights have been defined by us as people, by agreements that we have reached through some kind of social process and so I may be kind of backing off from the concept.

Corrective justice also focuses on human rights and social welfare, and retributive notions of punishment are given up. Procedural justice, including a concern for due process, is closely related to corrective justice at Stage 5. It is assumed that the practice of consistently applying due process will (in a reasonably just legal system) lead to more equity than will the practice of making each individual decision on an ad hoc basis. Corrective justice may also be oriented toward effecting social change through the judge's discretion in interpreting the law. For example, "I can see the point of the judge trying to act as a reforming force in law by handing down a sentence which is so light as to effectively say the law itself is wrongly applied here."

Commutative justice focuses on contract as a necessary form of social agreement, the foundation of human relationships. That is, making and being able to depend on agreements is the basis for social relationships and a source of moral obligation: "Society is interrelationships with other individuals. You would have no basis for that relationship if there were no trust or acting in good faith, so to speak." As is true of distributive and corrective justice, commutative justice at Stage 5 may also focus on respect for the rights of the parties to an agreement. The importance of upholding contracts is seen as deriving from the fact that persons warrant respect in their own right as individuals having intrinsic worth and dignity. Breaking an agreement is seen as a violation of the other's intrinsic dignity or value.

The justice structures of Stage 6 are defined tentatively as follows:

Stage 6: Morality of Universalizable, Reversible, and Prescriptive General Ethical Principles

The sociomoral perspective of Stage 6 is that of "the moral point of view," a point of view that ideally all human beings should take toward one another as free and equal autonomous persons. This means equal consideration of the claims or points of view of each person affected by the moral decision to be made. This prescriptive role taking is governed by procedures designed to ensure fairness, impartiality, or reversibility in role taking. Procedures of this sort are formalized in various ways. One formalization is Rawls's (1971) original position of choosing justice principles under a "veil of ignorance" in which the chooser does not know which person in a situation or society one is to be and must choose a principle or policy with which one could best live in any position, including especially the position of the persons who would be most disadvantaged in the society. A second formalization is that of "moral musical chairs,'' a second-order application of the Golden Rule (Kohlberg, 1981a, chap. 5). Not only is Heinz to take the point of view of the dying person, of the druggist, and of himself, but in doing so each person (druggist, dying person) is expected to take the point of view of the other in putting forward his or her claim and so modifying it. A third formalization is expressed through an emphasis on actual dialogue as in what Habermas (1984) calls an ideal communication situation, a dialogue among free and equal persons considering and modifying their claims in light of one another, the equivalent of internal dialogue as described by Kohlberg. A fourth utilitarian formalization by Harsanyi (1982) is considering preferences under the condition of having an equal probability of being any of those involved in a situation or a society. It is manifested in response to a dilemma by considering the point of view of each involved and balancing these points of view. It is also manifested in explicit statements of the intrinsic worth, dignity, or equality of every human being, that is, in expressing the attitude of respect or care for persons as ends in themselves, not solely as means to achieving other values, no matter how lofty or desirable, such as the good of society or human survival and development. It is manifested in using the criterion of universalizability; i.e., would I want anyone in my (or Heinz's) position to choose the way I do? It is manifested, fourth, in using one or more general principles to make a decision. General principles are distinct from either rules or rights, first, in being positive *pre*scriptions rather than negative *pro*scriptions (do not kill, do not steal or cheat) and second in that they apply to all situations. Respect for human dignity may imply sometimes breaking the rules or violating societally recognized rights (e.g., stealing the drug, giving a lethal dose of morphine at the request of a dying woman in pain). General principles at Stage 6 may be one or several. Single principles include the principle of justice or respect for human personality or dignity and the principle of utility or benevolence; i.e., act so as to maximize the welfare of all individuals concerned, the attitude of universal human care or agape. Multiple principles of justice include the principle of the maximization of quality of life for each, of maximum liberty compatible with the like liberty of others, of equity or fairness in distribution of goods and respect. These principles may be expressed either in terms of the language of human rights (and reciprocal duties) or in the language of care and responsibility for human ''brothers and sisters.''

Operations and Principles

At Stage 6 the operations we have been discussing form a coordinated whole that constitutes a self-conscious structure for moral decision making. At Stage 5 law and moral norms are grounded on the operations of equality, equity, and the like. At Stage 6 these operations become self-conscious principles. Given this self-consciousness of moral agency and decision making, the operations of prescriptive role taking (i.e., balancing perspectives) and universalizability become operative principles as well as being validity checks on the reasons given for upholding moral laws or norms. Stage 6 is based not so much on a new social perspective beyond Stage 5's notion of a prior-to-society perspective as on a *deliberate* use of the justice operations as principles to ensure that perspective when reasoning about moral dilemmas. These characteristics of Stage 6 reasoning require that Stage 6 raise dialogue to a principle, a principle of procedure or ''moral musical chairs.'' Thus, whereas Stage 5 is grounded on the notion of contract or agreement, Stage 6 is oriented to the *process* by which agreements or contracts are reached as well as to ensuring the fairness of the procedures that underlie such agreement. Underlying the social contract and agreement of Stage 5, designed to protect human rights, is the notion of the importance of maintaining human trust and community. At Stage 6 the notion of trust and community becomes the precondition for dialogue, human rights, and so on. (We should note that Stage 5 has difficulty balancing the notion of fixed contract with the underlying notions of trust and community, a problem that Stage 6 resolves through the operation of dialogue, a derivative of moral musical chairs.)

Distributive Justice. At Stage 6 distributive justice is determined by the principle of equity or fairness in addition to the principle of equality. At this stage equity does not include reference to special rewards for talent, merit, or achievement. These are largely seen as resulting from differences in genetic endowment or in educational and social opportunities, which are morally arbitrary, or to unequal distributions by society. However, Stage 6 equity does include the recognition of differential need, i.e., the obligation to consider the position of the least advantaged. Where distribution of scarce basic goods must be unequal (e.g., issues of who should live in lifeboat-type dilemmas), a lottery approach is preferred to favoring the strong or more socially useful.

Corrective Justice. Although punishment through either incarceration or restitution is seen as necessary to protect the rights or welfare of potential or actual victims of crime through isolation or deterrence, it is not retributive – it is not based upon inflicting suffering or death as "repayment" for demerit or immorality. The offender is still seen as a human being with human dignity to be respected as far as this is compatible with justice principles. For example, Heinz's stealing the drug, or Dr. Jefferson's performing euthanasia are seen to require no punishment but rather to require the consideration of issues of procedural justice.

Commutative Justice. Exchanges between persons are partly regulated by contracts or promises. Promises are seen as the foundation of contracts. Promises presuppose and affirm a moral relationship between promisor and promisee. A violation of a promise is both a violation of trust and of a relationship of mutual respect between the promisor and promisee as autonomous persons of worth and dignity. It is the violation of a right awarded to the promisee by the promisor in making the promise. Promises may be modified or violated only insofar as they maintain a moral relation of mutual respect or reversible role taking; e.g., one may break an appointment to serve the urgent need of a third party, a violation of promise which the promisee as a moral person would necessarily understand through ideal role-taking or moral musical chairs. Violation of promises is seen not so much as a violation of the self's integrity (Stage 4) as an issue of the integrity of the other and of the relationship.

Current Status of Stage 6

The exact nature and definition of Stage 6 are uncertain at this point. First, none of the longitudinal subjects in the studies reported in this volume clearly indicate a focus of reasoning distinct from Stage 5 after attaining Stage 5 itself. Second, identification of Stage 6 with a particular normative theory like those of Kant and Rawls and identification of Stage 5 with rule utilitarian theories like that of Hare (1981) seems arbitrary or biased. Hare's utilitarian theory of justice is as formally concerned with universalizability and reversibility as is Rawls's (1971) deontological theory. There is, however, an intuitive immediacy to a recognition of rights and justice as based on respect for human personality, autonomy, and dignity that tends to be associated with the formal perspective of Stage 6. Fundamentally, these are twofold. Although Stage 5 orients to universal human rights and value hierarchies, it does not elaborate one or perhaps two fundamental principles that are (a) general to all moral situations and (b) universalizable to all moral agents. Principles, as distinct from rules, resolve conflicts between rules, generate particular rules, and define a mode of viewing concrete moral situations.

Kohlberg (1984, chap. 7) reports a case we take to be illustrative of Stage 6. The interviewee is a 32-year-old woman with graduate training in philosophy whom we call Joan. Joan starts by framing the Heinz dilemma as one of potential communication and dialogue, the reversible role taking stressed by Habermas.

Now the first question is, what do you see as the problem in this situation?

The problem for Heinz seems to be that his wife is dying and that he's caught in between obeying the societal law of not stealing and committing a crime that would result in saving his wife's life. I would like to think that there's a conflict for the druggist as well, in that the druggist has to make a profit, and assuming it's a capitalistic society, doing all those things that are a part of that. But at the same time, I would like to think that there is a conflict for him too; of the fact that his desire to make money and fulfill his own desires are done at the expense of another person. There might also be a conflict for the woman as well in that she would prefer to live – but at the same time her desire to live is what is putting Heinz in the dilemma.

And why do you think it's important to take into consideration the conflicts facing the other two characters in the situation?

Well, because I think anytime there are conflicts in a situation . . . As soon as more than one person knows about a situation, O.K., then there's shared conflicts and the conflicts of each person sort of play off one another. And I think that the conflicts can be resolved to some extent by kind of pooling – so that as soon as more than one person becomes aware of the conflict then there are automatically problems to be resolved by each, things to be considered by each; and each person then has the power to affect what happens in the conflict. If I were Heinz, you know, would keep trying to talk with the druggist . . . I have a hard time thinking of any decision as being static, and it seems to me that dialogue is very important and a continuing dialogue in this kind of situation. But if it came to a point where nothing else could be done, I think that in consultation with his wife, if he and his wife decided that that would be an acceptable alternative for Heinz, then yes he should. Because I think that ultimately it comes down to a conflict of duties . . . I hate to put it this way, but I really tend to think of things in a Kantian sense – I don't think that Heinz should do anything that he wouldn't be willing to say that everyone should do. And breaking into a store and stealing is not an action that can be prescribed for humanity, for our societal group as a whole. On the other hand, Heinz, I think as, just by virtue of being a member of the human race, has an obligation, a duty to protect other people – I guess that's a way to put it. And when it gets down to a conflict between those two, I think that the protection of human life is more important.

Is it important for people to do everything they can to save another's life?

No. I have this natural responsibility I'm talking about – to preserve your dignity, integrity, as an autonomous human being. And now when I think, Do I have a responsibility to save your life? I think that depends a lot. If I'm walking down the street, yes, I would do anything I could to save somebody else's life. I mean if I saw somebody walking in front of a car, I would jerk that person out of the way of the car. That would be the way I would react automatically. But, in other situations it depends. If you are terminally ill and you have decided that you would prefer rational suicide, or would prefer to not go through any more chemotherapy, any number of those things, I don't feel that I have the right to intrude on that position of yours, to say that you must take this chemotherapy, it's going to extend your life for a week longer, or a month longer or something. I don't see myself doing that, no.

Let me ask you this question: in looking at the original situation of Heinz and the drug and deciding whether to steal or not, is there any one consideration that stands out in your mind above all others, in making a decision of this sort?

I would say that there are two things. The first thing is that no person has the right to make a decision that affects the dignity and integrity of another person without there being cooperative discussion among the people involved. Number one. The second thing is that, you know, in this very strange situation where it would come down to being, you know, the single person's decision, and I have trouble conceiving that as ever happening, then it comes down to preserving the dignity and integrity . . . and for the reason of life usually is involved in that, of another person. So I guess I'm saying that, well . . . I'm not saying that preserving life is *the* essential or ultimate thing. I think that preserving a person's dignity and integrity are the important things.

If Heinz doesn't love his wife, should he steal the drug for her?

I don't think that he should steal it out of a sense of love. I think that Heinz should steal the drug, if it comes down to that far-reaching point, out of a sense of responsibility to preserve life, not out of love. I think responsibility, as I'm using it here, means a recognition of dignity, on the part of every living being, but I could narrow it down, if you like, to persons. And responsibility is really something that's entailed in that recognition. If I respect you as a creature with dignity and your own unique, special being, in recognizing that I won't intrude on you, I won't purposefully harm you – there's this whole series of negatives that go along with being responsible and there's also some positives. And that's to recognize you as being unique, important, and integral, in some sense, and to do what I can to preserve all that.

Suppose the person dying is not his wife but a stranger. Should Heinz steal the drug for a stranger?

Assuming going through the whole situation again – you know, of talking and . . . sure, yes.

Is it a duty or obligation for Heinz?

When I think of my being obliged to do something I think of another person as having a special claim, a claim that goes beyond the sort of minimal claims we all have on one another. To me that's obligation. And responsibility is what I naturally feel for every person. It's not imposed on me from the outside, it's part of my nature as a human being.

Is there really some correct solution to moral problems like Heinz's or when people disagree is everybody's opinion equally right?

Well of course, there is some right answer. And the right answer comes out of the sense of recognition of other people in the ways that I described and out of a recognition of one's responsibility, well, to do a couple of things: to preserve all of the integrity, dignity, and to, in a general sense, act as you would like to see other people acting. I don't know really how to explain that I expect that when I do things, particularly things that I do not really want to do very much, you know, but what I really feel is the right thing to do, usually what sort of sets me over the edge and makes the motivation enough for me to do it has to do with, well, how would I like to see people in general act in this case. What do I think is right in general, and that's what I do.

We may summarize this interview around several points. First, Joan believes in actual dialogue or communication and a correlated reversible role taking or moral musical chairs in coming to a solution. Second, she follows Kant in thinking that a decision must be universalizable. Third, she has a single general principle for resolving moral dilemmas, namely, responsibility to other human beings as autonomous moral beings possessing dignity and integrity. This single general principle is clearly distinguished from a general rule to preserve life since she spontaneously says that it need not dictate keeping a person alive under conditions such as our euthanasia dilemma (Dilemma IV). Fourth, this principle defines both rights and caring responsibilities and integrates the two. Fifth, Joan is nonrelativist but not an absolutist; for instance, she does not define the preservation of human life as an absolute in all situations. Rather she has a sense of the features of a moral point of view that she thinks everybody should take to resolve moral dilemmas.

We include this discussion and example of Stage 6 for theoretical completeness even though our scoring manual does not attempt to define a sixth stage nor do we claim to have validated its existence as a culturally universal sequential "natural" structure. Gibbs (1979) has claimed that Stage 5 is not a "natural," "operational," or "standard Piagetian" stage but is rather a purely theoretical or reflective "meta-level." In Kohlberg (1984, chap. 5) we attempt to respond to Gibbs's critique of Stage 5 but would allow for Gibbs's interpretation of Stage 6. Stage 6 may perhaps be viewed as part of a broader level of "ethical and religious philosophy" supporting moral action (Kohlberg, 1984, chap. 12).[3]

History of Stage Scoring

The stage definitions just presented are the culmination of more than 25 years of work by Kohlberg and his colleagues, and they differ substantially from earlier definitions of the six stages.

Since Kohlberg began studying the development of moral judgment in 1958,

---

3 The authors of this chapter would be interested in potentially Stage 6 interviews that readers of this volume might intuitively classify as such.

there has been a continuing evolution in the proposed definitions of moral judgment stages and in the accompanying assessment methodology (stage scoring procedures). Unexpected empirical findings and case material discrepant from Kohlberg's assumptions have led to theoretical and methodological reorganization. These empirically guided reformulations have resulted in refinement and redefinition of exactly what is being described or measured, of the moral judgment stage descriptions, and of the procedures used to assign stage scores to interviews. The aim of this section is to describe the evolution of our approach to assessing moral judgment stage. This should help to clarify the nature of Standard Issue Scoring and the rationale behind it.

The method we have used in responding to early theory–data discrepancies is not strictly hypotheticodeductive. In other discussions we have called this method *bootstrapping* (Colby, 1978; Kohlberg, 1981b; see also Loevinger, 1976). By bootstrapping we mean the notion of an evolving research program in which data feed back into theory and method to improve the account of development we offer. This process is not unique to our efforts. In fact, it could be argued that it is the model used in all scientific endeavors.

In justifying the legitimacy of this model, we shall refer to a critique of Kohlberg's theory by Nicolayev and Phillips (1979). (See Puka [1979] and Lapsley and Serlin [1983] for replies to Nicolayev and Phillips.) These authors have attempted to evaluate Kohlberg's theory in relation to criteria set forth by Lakatos (1976). Lakatos sees a theory not as a closed conceptual structure but as an evolving research program. As Nicolayev and Phillips point out, Lakatos distinguishes between a theory's "hard-core" assumptions (those elements of theory that cannot be changed without abandoning the theory) and its "protective belt" (those aspects of the theory that are subject to change in light of experience). A progressive research program includes "a partially articulated set of suggestions or hints on how to change, develop the 'refutable variants' of the research program, how to modify, sophisticate, the 'refutable' protective belt." The resulting modification of the protective belt must anticipate new facts or be "content increasing" rather than simply be a means to explain away discrepant findings.

Though we agree with Nicolayev and Phillips in identifying the stage concept as part of the hard core,[4] we are led to conclusions very different from theirs. Our point here is not to argue that the data support our claims about the stage model (as we will argue in chap. 3) but rather to defend the theoretical revision process as progressive rather than "a readjustment of scoring procedures to give the results required by the theoretical assumptions" (Nicolayev & Phillips, p. 241). As will become apparent in this section, the procedure for revising the stage descriptions, constructing the current scoring manual, and scoring the longitudinal data presented in chapters 3, 4, and 5 did not in any sense guarantee the results obtained. The theoretical and methodological evolution did not consist in generating new scoring rules that would force internal consistency or postulation of new stages to explain sequence regression. In-

---

4 One need not accept Phillips and Nicolayev's statement that "the assumption that moral development occurs in fixed stages . . . could not be given up, for then nothing of the program would remain." As Lapsley and Serlin (1983) point out, the stage concept should be considered part of the hard core, but the specific stage model adopted is subject to revision, i.e., is part of the protective belt or "positive heuristic." This can be seen clearly in the work of Rest (1979), who posits a quite different version of the stage model while remaining within the cognitive-developmental framework.

stead, the evolution entailed a sweeping revision of the entire stage sequence, a radical redefinition of the basic structures in moral judgment development, and the presentation of moral types A and B, where B type conventional stage thinking was originally considered principled (see appendix to Volume I).

The evolution of moral judgment stage scoring (like the development it describes) has been a gradual and organic process, with new themes or variations on old themes emerging almost every year. In order to highlight the central trends in the process, we will focus on only three points and will treat the transitions from one to the next as more clear-cut than they were in reality. The three reference points will be the systems of Sentence and Story Rating (Kohlberg, 1958), Structural Issue Scoring (Kohlberg, 1971a), and Standard Issue Scoring (this volume).

The two interrelated issues that have been most central to the evolution of Kohlberg's model are the differentiation of content and structure and the definition of the unit of analysis. We can view this history as a progressive differentiation of content from structure. Each major scoring change has involved an important redefinition of the content–structure distinction, and each differentiation has led to (or has been accompanied by) a redefinition of the unit of analysis.

Sentence and Story Rating

In 1958, Kohlberg developed his moral judgment interview, a clinically probed, semistructured interview about hypothetical moral dilemmas. His first coding schemes were methods for assessing what he called developmental ideal types.

In addition to Piaget's ideas, this method rested on Weber's (1949) conception of the ideal type in studying values. An example of such an ideal type is Weber's construct of the Protestant ethic. The Protestant ethic represents a complex of values, a sort of composite photograph of historical individuals. The "photograph" however, does not represent a single individual or the average or mean value of a group of individuals. It is rather a caricature designed to highlight the meaningful coherence uniting the elements of values involved, i.e., their understandable or logical connection with one another. Weber uses the Benjamin Franklin of *Poor Richard's Almanack* as expressing traits of the Protestant ethic, though Benjamin Franklin as a historical individual was a complex personality poorly captured by Weber's type. The ideal type (the Protestant ethic), however, not only captures a value gestalt better than a more literal picture, but it makes it easier to give a causal-genetic account of phenomena subsumed under it. Thus Weber's fundamental hypothesis was that the rise of modern capitalism rested on a religious precondition as providing a nonhedonistic motivation for the accumulation of capital.

The 1958 ideal-typical approach, then, assumed a coherent moral type that was associated with prototypical value contents rather than looking directly for the organization of thought represented in each subject's response to the interview. The stages were defined as "composite photographs" of response to the dilemmas. Any one choice or statement of value would not be adequate to classify an individual as to stage, but the overall fit of the individual's choices and modes of defining value to the composite picture or ideal type determined that person's stage. Particular responses, then, were "signs" of a stage, signs with a greater or lesser probability of being indicators of that stage.

The identification of an individual's moral stage from an interview protocol followed two methods: sentence scoring and story rating. Sentence scoring used a manual listing prototypical sentences for each moral dilemma. Every statement of a subject was scored by stage; these statement scores were then converted into percentages, generating a profile of stage usage for each subject.

The second method was story rating. Here the subject's total response to a story was assigned a stage in terms of that stage's overall definition. Stage mixtures were handled by intuitively weighting a dominant and a minor stage of response.

In effect, the early scoring systems (Kohlberg, 1958), Global Story Rating and Sentence Scoring, were based on what was essentially a content analysis. That is, both systems focused on what content concerns a subject brought to bear in resolving a dilemma and treated these concerns as signs or indicators of the developmental stage with which they were presumably associated. For example, responses to Dilemma III (the Heinz dilemma) that focused on Heinz's fear of punishment were considered to be indicative of Stage 1; those emphasizing Heinz's love for his wife were Stage 3; and respect for the law was identified with Stage 4.

These scoring methods were used to analyze longitudinal moral judgment data that Kohlberg had collected over a 10-year period (Kramer, 1968). The results of this analysis were quite discrepant from Kohlberg's theoretical assumptions. First, Kramer found very little internal coherence in stage scores within a single interview. Perhaps this is not surprising given a probabilistic sign approach to measurement. On the other hand, the method was, at the very least, a poor way to evaluate empirically the Piagetian assumption of the stage as a structured whole. Furthermore, the analyses yielded a substantial amount of deviance from the predicted sequence of subjects' movement through the stages. In an early report of these results, Kohlberg and Kramer (1969), although reporting some measurement problems leading to anomalies, stressed a genuine failure of the stage sequence hypothesis in the college years leading to so-called sophomore retrogression in development. In 1973, Kohlberg reinterpreted the anomalies as resulting not from retrogression but from incorrect conceptualization of stages as they appear in development after high school. He reported some clinical analyses of cases suggesting that college retrogressors were exhibiting a Stage "$4\frac{1}{2}$" (having moved out of conventional morality but not yet into principled moral judgment) and proposed revised conceptual definitions of the fourth and fifth stages. In fact, such revisions accounted for only a few of the anomalies reported by Kohlberg and Kramer. This implied that there were general problems in the reliability and validity of the stage criteria and scoring method. It was the recognition of these problems that led to the redefinition of stages and the development of Structural Issue Scoring.

Structural Issue Scoring

The redefinition of structure and content that accompanied the transition from the 1958 scoring systems to Structural Issue Scoring can best be described through specific examples. As we have pointed out, in Kohlberg's early work Stage 4 moral judgment was identified with a focus on law, authority, and so on – that is, Stage 4 was unified by a "law-and-order" orientation. However, in subsequent work with longitudinal data, it was found that statements considered indicative of Stage 4 were often made by subjects who seemed on the basis of most of their other judgments to be using another stage, e.g., Stage 3.

In addition, longitudinal subjects who made law-and-order judgments at Time A were found to satisfy the criteria for Stage 3 moral judgment at Time B. At this point, a closer study of law-and-order responses revealed that they could be reliably differentiated by level of sophistication. Law-and-order thinking was then construed as content that could be present at more than one stage. Using case material, it was possible to identify a more general characteristic (social system perspective) of Stage 4 law-and-order and Stage 4 non-law-and-order thinking that differentiated them from less sophisticated conceptions of the same content. The same kind of in-depth case analysis was used to differentiate "true Stage 2" judgments from Stage 2-like judgments made in a context of ethical relativity from a postconventional rather than preconventional perspective (Stage $4\frac{1}{2}$). As a result of this conceptual analysis of interview material, a single unifying construct was identified that could be shown to unify or generate all of the various ideas and concerns at each moral judgment level and stage. This construct, the sociomoral perspective, has been discussed here as the basis of Standard Issue Scoring as well as the earlier Structural Issue Scoring System.

In line with the conceptual redefinition of the stages, the transition from the 1958 scoring systems to Structural Issue Scoring entailed a shifting of methodological focus from specific content concerns (law, affiliation, life) to the broader sociomoral perspective in which they are embedded. The shift arose from the redefinition of the structure and content of each moral stage, with a reliance now on level of sociomoral perspective as defining moral structure (see Kohlberg, 1976).

Reformulating the core structures of the moral stages implied a need to redefine the scoring unit of analysis. In the 1958 systems, there was no clear recognition of the fact that each content concern could be used at any stage (but would be used or defined differently in terms of the stage's sociomoral perspective). The significance of affiliation between husband and wife (or respect for the law) for a person at one stage may be very different from its meaning for someone at another, even though both persons consider it a crucial consideration in resolving the dilemma. For this reason, responses to a hypothetical dilemma should not be taken as a whole and assigned a stage score based on the kinds of concerns on which the individual focuses. Instead, one must go a step further and ask what developmental level or stage the person construes those concerns. The concerns that were identified with particular stages in the 1958 scoring systems became the *unit of content* for stage analysis in the 1971 Structural Issue Scoring System, with a stage assigned to material *within* each content unit on the basis of the respondent's level of sociomoral perspective. Thus, Structural Issue Scoring represents an attempt to resolve the basic content–structure confusion of the earlier systems by redefining as content that which had been considered structure. In Structural Issue Scoring, the interpretation was guided by a reference manual that described, at a fairly abstract level, the way each of nine moral issues is construed at each of the six stages. It was assumed that the rater was thoroughly familiar with Kohlberg's theory, including the concept of level of sociomoral perspective.

Structural Issue Scoring proved to be a substantial advance over earlier systems. The new stage definitions focusing on level of sociomoral perspective not only yielded more orderly data, they also made possible a more convincing rationale for the internal logic of the moral judgment stage sequence.

There were a number of problems with this approach, however. The need to determine level of perspective in stage scoring an interview implied that the scoring unit must be large and that scoring criteria must be very general and abstract. This meant that scoring decisions were subjective and often unreliable. Moreover, the reliance of this scoring system on very general features of stage structure meant that findings of invariant longitudinal sequence and stage consistency across issues could be attributed to consistency in or a universal sequence of the general features rather than providing evidence for consistency or sequentiality of the detailed conceptual differentiations included in more specific moral stage definitions.

Standard Issue Scoring

Standard Issue Scoring was intended to overcome the limitations of Structural Issue Scoring – to achieve greater objectivity and reliability in scoring by specifying clear and concrete stage criteria and to define the developmental sequences of the specific "moral concepts" within each stage as well as the sequence of the global or general stage structures. The redefinition of the scoring unit was the key to achieving these aims.

This change from an intuitive scoring method to a standardized scoring technique maintains the hermeneutic or phenomenological orientation but reflects a change from a view of interpretation as an art to a view of interpretation as a science, i.e., as a research activity employing an objective and reliable method of observation. This method, however, still rests on the communicative stance of an interpreter, not on the positivistic stance of someone trying to classify and predict behavior as distinct from meaning.

The procedure for construction of the Standard Issue Scoring System was designed to avoid the problem of circularity (theoretical verification as a self-fulfilling prophecy). With this in mind, seven cases were selected from Kohlberg's longitudinal sample. These *construction cases,* chosen at random from among those tested at all six times, were assigned global stage scores based on intensive discussion and analysis using concepts from Structural Issue Scoring. The responses to each dilemma were then classified into clearly defined scoring units, or *interview judgments.* Each of these interview judgments formed the basis for a *criterion judgment* to be entered in the scoring manual. The stage score of each criterion judgment was assigned on the basis of the global score of the interview from which it was derived and a conceptual analysis of the idea it embodied. The criterion judgments generated by these seven construction cases were later used to score the remaining interviews in the longitudinal study through a process of matching interview material to criterion judgments in the manual. Those cases not in the construction sample comprised a blind sample that was not used at all until the scoring manual had been completed.

A particularly noteworthy aspect of Standard Issue Scoring is the omission of Stage 6 from the system. Stage 6 was omitted partly because none of the interviews in the longitudinal sample seemed intuitively to be Stage 6 and partly because the standard dilemmas are not ideal for differentiating between Stages 5 and 6. The question of whether Stage 6 should be included as a natural psychological stage in the moral development sequence will remain unresolved until research (using more appropriate moral dilemmas and interviewing techniques) is conducted with a special sample of people likely to have developed beyond Stage 5.

The Moral Judgment Interview

The Standard Issue Moral Judgment Interview consists of three parallel forms. Each form comprises three hypothetical moral dilemmas, and each dilemma is followed by 9–12 standardized probe questions designed to elicit justifications, elaborations, and clarifications of the subject's moral judgments. For each dilemma, these questions focus on the two moral issues that were chosen to represent the central value conflict in that dilemma. For example, the familiar Heinz dilemma (Dilemma III: Should Heinz steal a drug to save his dying wife if the only druggist able to provide the drug insists on a high price that Heinz cannot afford to pay?) is represented in Standard Scoring as a conflict between the value of preserving life and the value of upholding the law. Life and law are the two standard issues in this dilemma, and the probing questions are designed to elicit information on the subjects' conceptions of these two issues. Of course, the dilemma also can be seen to involve other value conflicts, for example, between the husband's love for his wife (affiliation) and the druggist's property rights (property). In order to standardize the set of issues scored for each interview, the central issues for each dilemma were predefined. This preidentification of standard issues allows not only the sampling of moral judgments about the same six issues (per interview) for each subject, but also the construction of three parallel forms of the moral judgment interview. Thus, the first dilemma in interview Forms A and B focuses on the same two issues, life and law. The second dilemma of the two forms concerns the conflict between morality/conscience (whether to be lenient toward someone who has broken the law out of conscience) and punishment (whether to punish someone who has broken the law). The third dilemma involves a conflict between authority (e.g., obeying one's parent) and contract (abiding by or holding someone to an agreement). Form C involves the same six issues but in somewhat different pairs than in Forms A and B (see chap. 6 for further discussion of the Moral Judgment Interview).

The Process of Standard Issue Scoring

The Unit of Analysis

The first step in Standard Issue Scoring involves the classification of the subject's responses to a dilemma into the two standard issue categories. This is a fairly simple procedure. In the Heinz dilemma, for example, all responses arguing *for* stealing the drug are classified as upholding the life issue; all those arguing *against* stealing the drug are classified as upholding the law issue. In the follow-up dilemma (Dilemma III': Should Heinz be punished if he does steal the drug?), all responses arguing for leniency are classified as morality/conscience; all those arguing for punishment are classified as punishment.

The first step in scoring responses to a dilemma, then, is to separate material into the two issue categories. Since the issue units are large and often contain a great deal of material, Standard Issue Scoring involves two further subdivisions (by element and by norm; see Table 1.2) before stage scoring begins. This results in a fairly small unit of analysis. The Standard Scoring unit, the interview judgment (IJ), and corresponding criterion judgment (CJ) in the man-

Table 1.2. *Categories of moral content*

Modal elements

Upholding normative order:

1. Obeying/consulting persons or deity. Should obey, get consent (should consult, persuade).
2. Blaming/approving. Should be blamed for, disapproved (should be approved).
3. Retributing/exonerating. Should retribute against (should exonerate).
4. Having a right/having no right.
5. Having a duty/having no duty.

Value elements

Egoistic consequences:

6. Good reputation/bad reputation.
7. Seeking reward/avoiding punishment.

Utilitarian consequences:

8. Good individual consequences/bad individual consequences.
9. Good group consequences/bad group consequences.

Ideal or harmony-serving consequences:

10. Upholding character.
11. Upholding self-respect.
12. Serving social ideal or harmony.
13. Serving human dignity and autonomy.

Fairness:

14. Balancing perspectives or role taking.
15. Reciprocity or positive desert.
16. Maintaining equity and procedural fairness.
17. Maintaining social contract or freely agreeing.

Norms

1. Life	4. Affiliation	(9. Civil rights)
a) Preservation	(5. Erotic love and sex)	(10. Religion)
b) Quality-quantity	6. Authority	11. Conscience
2. Property	7. Law	12. Punishment
3. Truth	8. Contract	

ual are defined by the intersection of dilemma × issue × norm × element. Classification of responses by issue involves determining which choice in the dilemma is being supported or which of the two conflicting issues is being upheld. Classification by norm is a further subdivision of the interview material by its value content. The norm represents the moral value or object of concern used by the individual to justify his or her choice in the dilemma. For example, one might argue that Heinz should steal the drug to save his wife's life (life issue) because of the importance of their loving relationship (affiliation norm). The elements represent the different ways in which the significance of a norm may be construed. They are the reasons for endowing the norms with value. To continue the example, Heinz's love for his wife (affiliation norm) might be considered an important reason to save her (life issue) because that is a husband's proper role (duty element), because of his gratitude toward her (reciprocity element), or for a number of other reasons. Each of these is treated by Standard Issue Scoring as a discrete moral idea, and each represents a separate unit of material. The procedural complications of subdivision by norm and element were found to be necessary in order to define a unit that was narrow enough to be homogeneous, to capture what seems to be a single, discrete moral concept or idea, yet broad enough to represent the idea's full conceptual or structural significance for the subject. That is, the system provides a way for the scorer to categorize interview material in a nonarbitrary way into manageable, conceptually coherent units (interview judgments) that can then be stage scored by matching them to very specific and concrete criteria in the scoring manual (criterion judgments).

This system of content classification provides for meaningful definition of the scoring unit that, in addition to being essential to those preparing the scoring manual, is also necessary for each scorer in the process of analyzing an interview. In effect, material in the interview transcript is classified according to three types of content category before it is classified by stage or structure.

In addition to resolving the unit problem, this approach is useful in preventing some of the content–structure confusions that have been problems for earlier moral judgment scoring systems. For example, Stage 3 reasoning often focuses on love or the affiliative relationship as a reason for Heinz to steal the drug in Dilemma III. That is, the content of affiliation is likely to occur in the context of a Stage 3 (interpersonal concordance) structure. Earlier scoring systems, which failed to clearly differentiate content and structure, tended to misscore as Stage 3 reasoning that was in fact structurally more advanced but that focused on affiliative content. (For example, "Heinz should steal the drug for his wife because of his deep commitment to her and to the marriage and the responsibility that results from that commitment.") By first categorizing according to content and then addressing the questions of structure or stage, Standard Scoring procedures involve explicit differentiation of form and content, and, in effect, remind the rater that identification of a particular content has not answered the stage scoring question.

Scoring for more detailed, concrete, and narrowly defined concepts rather than for the stage structures in their most general form has also made it possible to gather evidence for sequentiality and consistency in all aspects of the more detailed stage descriptions. That is, the smaller scoring unit has allowed us to describe the developmental distinctions among parallel moral ideas across the stages. For example, in Dilemma III', which poses the question of whether Heinz should be punished for following his conscience in stealing the drug, the idea of deterrence as an argument for punishment is used at seven points in the sequence, beginning at transitional Stage ½ and proceeding through Stages 2, ⅔, 3, ¾, 4, and ⅘. The criterion judgments specify exactly what the conception of deterrence is at each point and explain the differences among the seven interpretations.

In order to clarify further the unit of analysis as the intersection of issue × norm × element, let us consider some examples of criterion judgments. All of these examples are taken from the Heinz dilemma (Dilemma III in Form A) and are examples of Stage 3 reasoning. The first criterion judgment uses the *issue* of life, the *norm* of property, and the *element* of blaming/approving and appears in Volume II, Manual A, as follows:

CJ #:	10
DILEMMA:	III
ISSUE:	Life
NORM:	Property
ELEMENT:	Blaming/approving

Criterion Judgment   Heinz should steal the drug because the druggist is selfish, cold-hearted, or greedy.

Let us compare this criterion judgment with three others that differ only by issue, norm, or element. As with our first example, the following criterion judgment also uses the norm of property and the element of blaming/approving at Stage 3, but here the issue being supported is law:

CJ#:	12
DILEMMA:	III
ISSUE:	Law
NORM:	Property
ELEMENT:	Blaming/approving

Criterion Judgment   Heinz should not steal the drug because the owner worked hard for what he has and you shouldn't take advantage.

Although this criterion judgment is representative of the same norm, element, and stage of thinking as the first, it supports an action diametrically opposed to that supported by the first criterion judgment and is thus classified under the opposing issue.

A third criterion judgment differs from the first only in terms of the norm that is used. Thus, unlike the second criterion judgment, this one also supports the issue of life (steal the drug). And, like the first two, it uses the element of blaming/approving. But unlike the first two examples, the *norm* used in this third example is affiliation, not property.

CJ#:	12
DILEMMA:	III
ISSUE:	Life
NORM:	Affiliation
ELEMENT:	Blaming/approving

Criterion Judgment   Heinz should steal the drug out of love or concern for his wife.

Our first and third examples differ only by norm, but they may be seen to represent quite different ideas.

Finally, let us consider a fourth criterion judgment that differs from the first only in the *element* used. Again, the issue is life and the norm is property, but here the *element* is retributing, not blaming/approving.

CJ#:	11
DILEMMA:	III
ISSUE:	Life
NORM:	Property
ELEMENT:	Retributing

Criterion Judgment   Heinz should steal the drug because the druggist is selfish, heartless, or inhumane and deserves to be stolen from.

In the first criterion judgment there is a condemnation of the druggist but there is no note of retribution, whereas in the fourth criterion judgment the druggist's blameworthiness is seen as warranting retribution. Again, the criterion judgment expresses a different moral judgment or idea from the others. Thus, issue, norm, and element are all essential components of the scoring unit. It is their intersection at a particular stage that represents a discrete moral judgment.

The Explicated Criterion Judgment

A structural or theoretical explication has been provided for each criterion judgment in the manual. Each explication includes a statement of the underlying stage structure reflected in the criterion judgment (Stage Structure), detailed criteria for defining a match to the criterion judgment (Critical Indicators), explanations of distinctions among criterion judgments a scorer is likely to confuse, and several examples of interview material that can be considered to match the criterion judgment. (See Table 1.3 for illustration of the explicated criterion judgment.)

This criterion judgment format was an important advance over earlier scoring systems. The subjectivity of scoring decisions is minimized by the concrete and explicit specification of exactly what constitutes a match between interview material and a criterion judgment in the scoring manual.

Standard Issue Scoring Rules

As we have said, Standard Issue Scoring involves first classifying the responses to each dilemma into two broad categories – the standard moral issues for that dilemma. Within each issue a stage score is entered for each match between a criterion judgment in the manual and a moral judgment in the interview. Usually, somewhere between one and five such matches are assigned for the issue. Although in practice these matches tend to cluster at a single stage or at two adjacent stages, there is no restriction in the scoring rules that requires such consistency. The rules allow scores to be assigned at all five stages if matches are found at those stages.

In calculating an overall score for a three-dilemma interview form, one assigns a summary score for each of the six issues. As many as three stages may be represented in the issue summary score. The six issue scores are then combined to yield a global interview score and a continuous weighted average score for the interview.

The Issues

As we have noted earlier, the conflict between moral issues is central to every dilemma in the Standard Moral Judgment Interview. Each of the standard di-

Table 1.3. *Explicated criterion judgment*

DILEMMA:	III
ISSUE:	Life
NORM:	Life
ELEMENT:	Good (bad) individual consequences (8)
STAGE:	2

Criterion judgment [Heinz should steal the drug] because his wife needs it or will die without it.

Note: Match score this criterion judgment only if Life is the subject's chosen issue: E.g., when a subject says that stealing the drug might be best for Heinz's wife but it is still wrong and should not be done, do not match to this point.

Stage structure Breaking rules is justified if doing so is instrumentally necessary because of Heinz's wife's needs. The connection between her desire to live and the rightness of stealing is direct and unmediated. That is, the woman's need to live is used as a sufficient reason and is not stated in terms of empathy or concern of a moral person considering her desire.

Critical indicators Required for a match are all three aspects of a reference to: (a) the woman's needs or negative physical consequences (without the drug she'll die) which (b) is used to support life as the chosen issue, and (c) appears in the absence of any higher stage idea of the value of life (life norm CJs).

Match examples 1. *Should the husband have done that?*
Yes. It's right. *Why?* If he doesn't steal she will die. (0-66)

2. *Why doesn't that make it morally wrong?*
His wife is dying. She needs the drug, so he should steal it.

Guess example *Should the husband have done that?*
It's better that he steals. But after he steals, he must tell the man. Because at that moment, there is a need.

lemmas is constructed so that two issues and their associated courses of action are in conflict; e.g., life versus law in the Heinz dilemma. The subject must choose between these two. That decision represents an action choice: for example, to steal a drug to save a life or not to steal the drug, thereby upholding the law. Thus the issue choice tells us what the interviewee thinks should be *done*.

The standard probe questions that follow each dilemma are designed to elicit reasoning on both issues in the dilemma as well as on the relationship between the two issues. The subject's action choice on a dilemma may be taken as representing a choice of one value or issue over the other. Thus, a subject who thinks Heinz should steal the drug is valuing life over law, and that subject's responses will stress either reasons valuing the wife's life (or life in general) or reasoning leading to a hierarchy of one issue over the other, i.e., of life over law.

In Standard Issue Scoring, the first step is to divide interview content according to the issue being supported. Thus, in Dilemma I (which concerns Joe and his father), reasoning that supports Joe's giving his father the money is categorized under the authority issue whereas arguments against his giving him the money are categorized under the contract issue.

The issues and norms represent the same nine values. They are identical except in the role they play in the scoring process, that is, in the level of content classification in which they are used. We have given the two functions different names to underline their differences in function and level in the classification process.

The set of nine issues and norms is empirically based. They represent those concerns raised spontaneously by subjects in response to the hypothetical dilemmas. The decision as to which two issues are the focus of each dilemma was somewhat arbitrary, because more than two issues can be involved in a single dilemma, for example, affiliation and property in addition to life and law in the Heinz dilemma.

Three criteria guided the selection of the two standard issues for each dilemma: (1) In order to sharpen the issue conflict within each dilemma, the issue was selected on which the strongest arguments could be made in favor of taking a particular action (e.g., law as the issue opposing theft of the drug). (2) Where salience of issue appeared to vary by stage, the two issues most salient at the higher stages (Stages 4 and 5) were selected. For example, individuals at Stages 4 and 5 typically view the Heinz dilemma as presenting a conflict between life and law. Individuals reasoning at Stages 2 and 3, on the other hand, may structure that dilemma as a conflict between family love (in favor of stealing) and property rights (opposed to stealing). (3) The system was constructed so as to represent the same issues in all three of the interview forms. Each of the three interview forms, A, B, and C, includes three dilemmas. With one exception, each set of three dilemmas samples the same six issues: life, law, conscience, punishment, authority, and contract. The single exception is that the authority issue is not represented on Form C.

The Norms

We use the term *norm* to represent that moral value or object of concern that is brought to bear by the subject in justifying the choice of which action to support in the dilemma. In other words, the issues reflect what the subject thinks should be done; the norms begin to clarify *why* the subject thinks it should be done. As noted earlier, the difference between them is functional. Unlike the issues, the norms are introduced by the respondent, rather than being predetermined by the interviewer.

Some examples should help clarify the functional difference between issues and norms. The following are three criterion judgments taken from the Standard Issue Scoring Manual A for Dilemma III (the Heinz dilemma) at Stage 4. In all three cases, support is given to stealing the drug in order to save the woman's life; that is, life is the chosen issue. The element used in each case is "serving social ideal or harmony."

In the first example, the worth of human life itself is the value supporting the decision to steal the drug; i.e., the life *norm* is supporting the life *issue*.

CJ#:	24
DILEMMA:	III
ISSUE:	Life
NORM:	Life
ELEMENT:	Serving social ideal or harmony
STAGE:	4

Criterion Judgment   People should do everything they can to save another's life because people must have some sense of responsibility for others for the sake of society or humanity.

In the second example, thinking about the life issue focuses not on the life norm but instead on an appeal to a ''higher'' moral law, that is, on the norm of conscience. The issue, element, and stage are the same as in the preceding example.

CJ#:	29
DILEMMA:	III
ISSUE:	Life
NORM:	Conscience
ELEMENT:	Serving social ideal or harmony
STAGE:	4

Criterion Judgment   Heinz should steal the drug because the commandment or obligation to save a human life is actually the highest expression of law.

A third example, one still supporting the life issue, and using the element ''serving social ideal and harmony,'' focuses on the property norm. The concern is with property ownership.

CJ#:	26
DILEMMA:	III
ISSUE:	Life
NORM:	Property
ELEMENT:	Serving social ideal or harmony
STAGE:	4

Criterion Judgment   The druggist has no right to charge that much because in his exploitation he has failed to show any responsibility to his fellow man.

Although all three criterion judgments favor the same action (stealing the drug) and thus the same issue (life), using the same element, at the same stage, the reasons given for stealing the drug are quite different. Those differences are the differences in the norms used.

Although in theory, any of the nine norms could be used in discussing a particular issue, in practice only three or four norms are used for each issue (e.g., the life, affiliation, conscience, and property norms for the life issue in the Heinz dilemma). This reflects the fact that relevant values, even when used as norms, are to a large extent determined by the nature of the moral dilemma in question. It is in this sense that we say the issues represent clusters of norms or values. A particular subject may use any or all of these several norms in discussing an issue. Whether a particular norm is used by a subject is a function of both the salience of that norm to the subject and the kind of questioning done by the interviewer.

Rationale for the System of Issues and Norms

We have said that the issues and norms are empirically based, that they represent the categories used spontaneously by the respondents themselves in the dilemmas. But the issues and norms are also grounded in philosophical considerations. They are *moral* norms in that they (1) regulate human claims and conflicts, (2) define basic human rights, (3) are culturally universal, (4) are subject to sanctions, and (5) are nonreducible. Not all norms or values in a society are moral norms or values; for example, norms of fashion and etiquette are social conventions, rather than moral norms. To clarify the distinction, let us consider each of these criteria in turn.

1. The issues and norms are values that regulate human claims and conflicts. One of the functions of morality and moral judgment is the resolution of conflicts between individuals, their interests, rights, and claims. For instance, law norms and norms for the preservation of life and health regulate conflicts. As we elaborate later, social roles and institutions are built around each of the norms. Thus, the legal system and its roles (e.g., that of a judge) serve to resolve social conflicts as do the life and health system and its roles (e.g., those of doctor, pharmacist).

2. The issues and norms define basic human rights. Among the most fundamental human rights or freedoms are the rights to life, the protection of law, freedom of conscience (moral-religious beliefs) and affiliation (friendship, marriage, parenting), the right not to be subject to arbitrary authority or punishment, the right to a voice in the government or political authority system, the right to property, and the freedom to make contractual agreements. Morality involves a concern for injustice and human rights.

3. The issues and norms are universal. All humans have needs and rights relating to life, property, affiliation, law, and so on. These values have been found to be central in every culture studied. They are universal values regulating universal human conflicts.

4. Issues and norms are subject to social sanctions. According to Durkheim and other sociologists, a central criterion of a moral norm or value is that it defines an act that is subject to social sanction. Thus, one way in which moral norms or values differ from nonmoral norms or values is that violation of moral norms can be punishable or criminal offenses, i.e., can be deviations forbidden by law and requiring punitive sanctions as opposed to the restitutive sanctions of civil law. Although violation of moral norms may also lead to moral self-blame and guilt, the fact of social punishment is an indication of the status of the norms as moral.

5. The issues and norms are nonreducible. They are in some sense "intrinsic" values. Although the issues and norms can be used as instrumental to each other, they are not reducible to one another, and each can be seen as valuable in its own right. Life, truth, conscience, and the other norms all can be seen to have intrinsic value. Thus if the question, "Why should a life be saved?" is answered, "To avoid grief to loved ones," then "life" may be seen as "serving" some other value. But when the same question, "Why should a life be saved?" is answered, "Because it is intrinsically valuable," then life is seen as a value in and of itself, not dependent for its worth on any other norm.

In addition to being moral values, issues and norms are objects of social institutions. Societies have created institutions whose purpose is to protect these central values. These "moral" institutions are complexes of rules and roles that define rights and obligations and that center on some overall purposes or values. For example, law as an institution is not only a set of legal rules, but also a system of roles (judge, police officer, lawyer, criminal, legislator) defining specific rights and duties. It is an institution with an overall value or purpose – civil order and justice.

Although a strict one-to-one relationship does not exist between the issues and norms and the social institutions of any particular society, the set of issues and norms is related to the set of social institutions. For each issue and norm there are institutions designed to protect it.

Not all social institutions are moral institutions just as not all values are moral values. For example, the institutions of engineering and technology and their value object, production, are not considered moral institutions, that is, institutions intended by society to protect the most basic of rights. We would not want to say that there are fixed positive rights to technological development, or at least not in the sense that we speak of a right to life or freedom of conscience.

We have already discussed functional differences between issues and norms. Although the issues and norms represent the same nine values, their functions differ conceptually as well as operationally. We noted that the issues and norms are nonreducible, that they represent values in their own right. The issues, however, can be seen as instrumental to other values. If we ask, "Why is law valuable?" and the answer is "Because it preserves life," then law (the issue) is valuable because it is instrumental to life (the norm). Thus, the norm is the more basic value justifying the choice of issue.

A related difference between values as issues and values as norms is that issues may be seen as more external, and norms more internal to the subject. Issues, whether they be valued social objects, institutions, or events, are outside the subject. Thus, when we conceptualize values in terms of moral institutions, we are really speaking of values as issues, rather than of values as norms. This "externality" of the moral issues is underscored in moral judgment interviewing by the fact that the issues are predetermined for the subject by the moral dilemma itself. That is, the moral issues in an interview are chosen by the experimenter who presents the dilemma. The choice of which norm is brought to bear on the issue in any given response, however, is to a large extent a function of the respondent's own values and beliefs. It is the subject who introduces the norms to the dilemma.

Almost any moral dilemma involving interpersonal relations and social justice will tap the nine issues and norms we have discussed. Other researchers with special interests have devised dilemmas using sex (Gilligan et al., 1970), civil rights (Lockwood, 1975), and religion (Oser, 1980) as issues and norms. We have not included these three additional issues and norms in our list because they are not used in the scoring system presented here. Interested readers may consult the references cited for pertinent structural issue rating guides.

The Elements

In Standard Issue Scoring, the scoring unit is designed to capture a single, complete moral judgment. The issues and norms are moral values, that is, objects of moral concern. A complete moral judgment goes beyond that, giving a reason, principle, or concern for which the norm serves as object. These ultimate reasons or principles are designated *elements*.

In essence, selection of the issue in a dilemma represents a choice of action that is in need of justification. The norm represents a partial justification, but is itself in need of further justification. The elements represent the final justification. Thus a full moral judgment is a concern about a norm in terms of an element, in the service of an issue.

Each of the three components – issue, norm, element – is in need of the others. They must be considered as a unit. Their intersection represents a single, complete moral judgment and is the unit of analysis for stage scoring, that is, the criterion judgment. It is important to realize that identifying the issue × norm × element unit does not itself yield the moral stage of a judgment. The same issue × norm × element unit can be found at several stages.

In defining the elements, the authors drew on philosophical categories in ethics that define types of normative moral philosophies. (These categories are set out in some detail in most ethics texts, e.g., William Frankena, *Ethics* [1973], to which the reader may wish to refer.) The first division within the elements is between deontological reasons, principles, or philosophies and teleological reasons, principles, or philosophies. In essence, deontological ethics center on concerns for duty and rightness per se. Teleological ethics center on concerns for the consequences and purposes of moral actions.

Within deontology, we identify two orientations: the normative order orientation and the fairness orientation. In the normative order orientation, there is a focus on duty or rightness as deriving from ''rulefulness'' or ''lawfulness.'' As the name indicates, there is a concern for maintaining the normative order, that is, maintaining regularity of a system whether of conscience or of social order. Kantian ethics are an example in which duty is the primary or first consideration in morality (deontology). Within deontology, Kantian ethics are oriented to ideal normative order. Duty is the maintenance of lawfulness, consistency, or regularity at all costs. For example, Kant held that it is wrong to lie even to a murderer bent on seeking a victim because such lying contradicts the universality of the norm of truth.

There is a somewhat different orientation toward duty and rightness that comes from seeing them as deriving from principles of justice or fairness, as is clearly done by Rawls (1971). Following Rawls and Kohlberg's (1981a, chap. 5) extension of Rawls, one would not, for instance, say that it is wrong or unfair to the potential murderer to lie to protect the intended victim. Yet the concern about fairness or unfairness is still deontological; it is not reducible to a concern about utilitarian positive and negative consequences of the act. In defining an ultimate and rational ethic, this orientation takes justice to be the first virtue of society and of moral action. Justice, in turn, is a set of considerations and agreements rational persons would make if they tried to imagine law and moral decisions from the perspective of someone who did not know who they would be in a society or situation (the ''original position''). These justice decisions would give primacy first to the element of liberty, then to that of equity-equality, both elements within the justice orientation.

Teleological ethics center on the purposes, aims, or consequences of action, as distinct from the deontological emphasis on lawfulness and justice. Returning to the example from Kant, the sense that it is right to lie to a murderer to protect someone also, or alternatively, implies concern for the welfare consequences and purposes of action. Teleological ethics can be divided into two orientations: utilitarianism and perfectionism. Utilitarianism, as propounded by Bentham and Mill, tries to reduce the moral value of actions to their predictable consequences for the welfare or pleasure–pain of individuals or groups of individuals. Actions are morally right if they maximize the welfare or happiness consequences of all the individuals affected; i.e., morality is evaluated in terms of the greatest good or happiness for the greatest number. The utilitarian orientation can be subdivided into egoistic utilitarianism, in which concern is for consequences to oneself, and social utilitarianism, in which concern is for consequences to the group.

Perfectionistic ethics see the moral value of actions as coming from their expression or realization of a moral self and the perfection of that self and the social group. Perfectionism does not reduce moral value to harm or benefit to individuals or groups. The concern is rather with movement toward harmony both within and among persons. The classical Greek ethics of both Aristotle and Plato were perfectionistic. The moral value of action derives from its contribution to the harmony of the acting self or to the harmony of society.

This general categorization into orientations is further subdivided to yield the elements. This is because, for the purposes of analyzing interview material, how one defines fairness, utility, or perfection is important. Fairness as equality is quite a different concept from fairness as reward for merit. These distinctions are important in moral philosophy, as they are in moral judgment assessment. The 17 elements, grouped by orientation, are listed in Table 1.2.

The elements represent conceptual distinctions within the orientations that make sense logically and philosophically and that make a difference empirically. Further divisions could have been made. For example, Element 7 (seeking reward/avoiding punishment) could have been divided into two elements, but the distinction between seeking reward and avoiding punishment is not particularly important for scoring moral stage. Alternatively, one might argue for combining Element 15 (reciprocity or positive desert) with Element 3 (retributing), which could also be called "negative reciprocity." But there is a considerable philosophical and psychological difference between looking at positive reciprocity or deservingness as fair and looking at negative reciprocity or retribution as fair. An individual might well use positive reciprocity as a basic principle while denying the validity of retribution or negative reciprocity. The philosophical difference between the two is borne out by the data. All of the elements identified here are actually used in the moral judgment scoring process, and together, they cover all the moral judgments we have encountered.

Modal Elements and Value Elements

As indicated in Table 1.2, the normative order elements are labeled modal elements; all the other elements are labeled value elements. A fully elaborated moral judgment uses both a modal element and a value element in addition to an issue and norm. If a value element is present, then a modal element also is, though usually implicitly. The reverse is not necessarily true, however. Especially at lower stages, a moral judgment often involves only a modal element. If both are present, the material is classified by value element, ignoring the modal element. If only the modal element is present, it serves as the basis for classification.

Modal Elements

A moral judgment is like a sentence, with the norm corresponding to the subject and the value element corresponding to the predicate. Thus, the value element is the property or quality whereby the norm has value. The modal element in moral judgment is analogous to the modal in grammar (words such as *should, could, would, must, can* that express the mood of a verb). The modal elements are, in a sense, the key moral words – *should, must, deserves, has a right, approves,* and so on. They express the mood or modality of moral language. A moral judgment, like a sentence, can be expressed in different modalities; e.g., as an expression of duty, of rights, or of blame. It is a judgment's reference to rights, duty, or the like that make it a *moral* judgment; for example, "Heinz should (has a duty to) steal the drug"; or "You can't blame Heinz for stealing the drug"; or "The druggist deserves to have the drug stolen." Judgments or statements of value can be stated using nonmoral modalities: "Most people *would* steal the drug"; or "Heinz *could* steal the drug and get away with it." Without using one of the five moral modals, a statement would not be prescriptive and thus would not be considered a *moral* judgment.

The distinctions among modal elements become fully clarified only at the higher stages. An individual reasoning at Stage 1, for example, does not recognize the difference between having a right and having a duty or between having a right and *being* right. Thus, one is not seen as having a right to do anything that is not right, rendering incomprehensible to someone reasoning at Stage 1 the familiar statement, "I disagree with what you say, but will defend to the death your right to say it." At the higher stages, the distinctions among the modal elements are important, and judgments using different modal elements are clearly distinguishable from one another. Thus, at Stage 5 the judgment that Heinz has a *right* to steal the drug is seen as different from the judgment that he has a *duty* to steal it. In fact, the ability to differentiate among the modal elements is an essential characteristic of higher stage reasoning. It is the salience of this philosophical difference to the person reasoning at the higher stages that leads us to distinguish among the modal elements in the scoring process.

As we have mentioned, a modal element can be used with a value element or it can be used alone. When used in conjunction with a value element, the modal element serves to place the judgment within the moral realm and to express the "mood" of that judgment. Used in this way, modal elements do not represent reasons or values in themselves. They are "empty" in the sense that they do not bring a value per se to bear on the moral norm at hand. That is why moral judgments are not classified by modal element when a value element is used as well.

Often, however, modal elements are used by the subject as terminal values or justifications. In fact, approximately one quarter of the criterion judgments in Standard Issue Scoring take that form. We may view such judgments as somehow incomplete. They may tell us, for example, that a good husband has a duty to steal to save his wife's life or that his wife has a right to life. But they do not tell us *why* that duty or right exists. That is what a value element would do. It is important to realize, however, that subjects using modal elements in this way do not themselves see such judgments as being incomplete. They see their responses as answering the question *why* and thus feel that they are providing sufficient justification. That is why the use of a modal element without a value element still provides a scorable unit. It must be remembered that the unit is a single moral judgment or idea in the respondent's thinking. *We* might regard a simple statement of duty as incomplete and wish to go beyond it to some underlying principle or concern. That the interviewee does not in itself provides useful information. It tells us that the respondent is speaking from the normative order orientation in which maintaining a norm is an end in itself.

One final point about the modal elements. We have classified them as deontological. However, the modal elements are not in themselves deontological. It is only when they are used as ends (i.e., without a value element) that they are deontological. When duty itself is seen by a subject to be a final justification, then the judgment is deontological – a judgment concerned with rules and norm following, not one concerned with welfare consequences. That is, a judgment is not deontological simply because it makes reference to duty. It is deontological when duty *is* the reason; e.g., "You have a duty, and that's *why* you should do it."

Value Elements

The modal elements, when used alone, affirm the importance of a norm via a particular modality without further justification. The value elements, on the other hand, are used as final justifications that go beyond norm and modality. They represent the ultimate ends, values, or reasons held by the subject. At least at the higher stages, value elements are synonymous with principles. When seen as principles, it is clear why value elements are the terminal or ultimate values. Why is happiness valuable? At least for the utilitarian, the value of happiness is self-evident and is not reducible to any other value or principle. When a respondent uses a value element as a principle underlying a norm and issue, the researcher may, of course, continue to press for further justification. But such a tack would, in a sense, be a case of asking *why* too many times. The respondent, on realizing that the first element he or she has used has not been accepted as terminal by the interviewer (otherwise, why ask for further justification?), might eventually shift ground to a different value element. But the respondent would not go beyond elements to something more fundamental. That is why, both empirically and logically, the value elements are seen as the terminal values.

To clarify the difference between a judgment using only a modal element and one using both an implicit modal element and a value element, let us consider two examples. Both of the following criterion judgments use the same issue (life), norm (affiliation), and modal element (having a duty) at the same stage (Stage 3), but only the second uses a value element as well.

CJ#:	13
DILEMMA:	III
ISSUE:	Life
NORM:	Affiliation
MODAL ELEMENT:	Having a duty
STAGE:	3

Criterion Judgment Heinz should [has a duty to] steal the drug even if he doesn't love his wife because . . . he is still her husband.

The second criterion judgment, like the first, uses the modal element ''having a duty'' but also uses the value element ''reciprocity or positive desert'' to justify that duty.

CJ#:	15
DILEMMA:	III
ISSUE:	Life
NORM:	Affiliation
MODAL ELEMENT:	Having a duty
VALUE ELEMENT:	Reciprocity or positive desert
STAGE:	3

Criterion Judgment   Heinz should [has a duty to] steal the drug even if he doesn't love his wife because . . . she has shared her life with him and the least he can do is save her.

In both cases the husband is seen as having a duty to save his wife. But it is only in the second example that we are fully apprised of a reason for that duty – in this case positive reciprocity between husband and wife.

At the preconventional or conventional level, a person may or may not spontaneously use a value element in addition to a modal element. Even when pressed to give a reason (e.g., ''*Why* does a husband have a duty to his wife?''), the respondent may be unable to produce a further justification. By the postconventional level, however, there should always be a value element in addition to the modal element. At the postconventional level, a person would see immediately that it is not sufficient simply to say ''a husband has a duty'' and leave it at that. The subject would be able to go beyond that, to give an ultimate reason or principle underlying that obligation, for at the postconventional level, duties, rights, and obligations are grounded in principles. As is true with the modal elements, individuals reasoning at the higher stages are capable of clearly differentiating the value elements.

A reasonable question to ask at this point is why the rater needs to classify material by issue, norm, *and* element. Why are elements important in addition to the issues and norms? Alternatively, given that we can classify by element, why do we bother with the issues and norms? To help answer these questions, let us draw some further distinctions between the elements and the issues and norms.

Issues and norms refer to shared values that are outside the self. As such, issues and norms are more sociological, whereas elements are more philosophical and psychological. As we have seen, issues and norms correspond closely to rules and institutions in society. Elements, on the other hand, may be considered general internal dispositions that give value and definition to those norms or institutions. For example, justice and human welfare are decision-guiding principles that may be applied to different institutions or norms. They are used to define and give value to an institution (e.g., law as an institution that protects justice) and to resolve conflicts between norms or institutions.

But justice and welfare as moral elements or principles are not institutions in themselves. The Department of Justice, for example, represents a normative institution of law. Its name reflects a societal concern that the institution be guided by principles of justice. But we would not want to say that the Department of Justice *is* the justice principle. Thus, although a principle or element gives value to an institution or norm, it is not itself a social norm or role.

The elements can also be seen as reasons or motivations behind action. Thus, we speak of someone acting out of a *sense* of justice or injustice. In that way, justice is not merely a principle, but an attitude or motive or reason for doing something. We are not speaking here of motives as drives or needs but rather as concerns. Thus, one may have a fundamental concern for good reputation, for human dignity, or for equity, in which case good reputation, human dignity, and equity can be seen as reasons for action. The norms define kinds of moral action (e.g., lawbreaking, lifesaving); the elements provide the ethical reasons for those actions.

It follows that the norms are more situation specific than the elements. Few people, for example, would consider it useful or appropriate to use the property norm as a basis for resolving the mercy-killing dilemma (Dilemma IV). Elements such as "serving human dignity" or "maintaining equity," on the other hand, can be appropriately applied to any moral dilemma. As principles, the elements are something that individuals "carry around" within themselves. For this reason, we often find individuals characterzied by the use of a particular orientation although not necessarily the same element within that orientation.

Although the elements are less situation specific than the issues and norms, they are more stage related. We may orient toward one issue or norm as opposed to another in a particular situation, but the issues and norms per se are relevant considerations at every stage. Everybody recognizes life, law, property, truth, affiliation, authority, contract, conscience, and punishment, and takes them into account in some way or another. In choosing life over law in a particular dilemma, one is not rejecting the value of law. When law conflicts with life under different circumstances, the same individual may choose law. Thus, all norms are valued. It is a question of which is the more important value under the particular circumstances presented.

The same is not true with elements. An individual may reason on the basis of a number of different elements, but fail to consider or actually deny the validity of other elements. This selectivity helps to define the subject's own personal philosophy. The selectivity is also stage related. We have already seen why the modal elements are not used as terminal values in postconventional thinking. Nor would the element "seeking reward/avoiding punishment" be seen as a valid reason or principle for moral action in Stage 5 reasoning. At the other end of the spectrum, an individual reasoning at Stage 1 would not use Element 14 (balancing perspectives) because she would not yet be capable of the necessary role taking. Nor would Stage 1 reasoning permit use of Element 17 (maintaining social contract or freely agreeing). An individual using Stage 1 moral reasoning can have a concern for keeping a promise (contract norm), but would not use the social contract element to justify keeping that promise, because use of that element requires at least a social system perspective, if not a prior-to-society perspective, something not yet accessible at the preconventional level.

For many of the same reasons, categorization of material by element is less arbitrary than is categorization by norm. The norms overlap to a certain extent, so some leeway exists in assigning material to one norm as opposed to another. The Heinz dilemma, for example, involves laws that uphold property rights.

Reasoning about upholding the law and about maintaining respect for property are often indistinguishable here. Similarly, ideas about property and contract overlap in Dilemma I. Because of this overlap, it was possible to streamline the scoring process by limiting the number of norms for each issue on a given dilemma. This was not possible with the elements, however. As we have seen, the elements are more logically distinguishable and mutually exclusive. Thus, there is no restriction on the number of elements used in scoring any of the dilemmas.

To help appreciate how the issues, norms, and elements differ, let us look at the case in which they most closely resemble one another. Maintaining social contract or freely agreeing is an element. The system also includes a contract *issue* and contract *norm*. When used together, how do we differentiate the idea of contract at these three levels?

Contract and authority are the two issues in Dilemma I, which asks if a boy, Joe, should hold his father to a promise to let him keep money he has earned. If the interviewee feels that Joe ought to keep the money he has earned, then the chosen issue is contract. That choice merely defines an action, namely, Joe should keep the money. If the subject then focuses on the importance of keeping the contract or promise as the *reason* for keeping the money, then the *norm* is contract.

Thus far, the individual is supporting an action (keep the money – contract issue) by reference to the contract norm. But the question still remains, Why value the contract norm? There are a number of reasons why one might do so. For example:

CJ#:	32
DILEMMA:	I
ISSUE:	Contract
NORM:	Contract
ELEMENT:	Upholding self-respect
STAGE:	4

Criterion Judgment It is important to keep a promise for the sake of personal honor, integrity, or self-respect.

In this case, the contract norm is being upheld out of concern for self-respect (Element 11). Or we might have:

CJ#:	30
DILEMMA:	I
ISSUE:	Contract
NORM:	Contract
ELEMENT:	Good group consequences
STAGE:	4

Criterion Judgment It is important to keep a promise for the sake of the orderly or smooth functioning of society or so that society can survive or be productive.

Here the contract norm is being upheld out of a concern for good group consequences (Element 9).

Or the contract norm may be valued because of a concern for contract itself, as we see in both the following examples:

CJ#:   33
DILEMMA: I
ISSUE: Contract
NORM: Contract
ELEMENT: Maintaining contract or freely agreeing
STAGE: 4

Criterion Judgment   It is important to keep a promise, or the father does not have a right to demand the money, because a promise is a pact, contract, commitment, sacred covenant, formal agreement, or final word.

And:

CJ#:   42
DILEMMA: I
ISSUE: Contract
NORM: Contract
ELEMENT: Maintaining contract or freely agreeing
STAGE: 5

Criterion Judgment   Joe should refuse to give his father the money, or it is important to keep a promise, because promises are a necessary form of social agreement if people are to live together in society.

In these latter two cases, maintaining a contract and keeping one's word are seen as values or principles in themselves. Social order is founded in agreement or social contract and thus contract is the source of moral obligation.

Issue defines choice or action. Norm defines the general value guiding that choice. Element defines the underlying principle and provides the moral motive or concern behind whatever action is prescribed.

We have seen that we need the elements because the norms tell us only *what* an individual is valuing (e.g., life, law) without telling us why it is valuable. But it is reasonable to ask why we must concern ourselves with the norms and issues if we know the elements. The reason is that we are concerned with actual moral judgments. We are not trying to measure an individual's abstract philosophical positions, but rather what is going to make a difference when that individual is faced with an actual moral choice. An individual could read Mill, Kant, or Rawls and state what sounds like principles. But unless such "principles" can be used to resolve moral conflicts, they amount to empty phrases. A person may say, "I am a utilitarian, I believe in the greatest good for the greatest number." But that does not help us much in determining that person's stage of moral reasoning. What we care about is how moral judgments are made when that utilitarianism is actually applied to values in conflict.

Morality is a matter of choice and decision. It is not just a matter of using abstract concepts like justice. It concerns the use of such concepts to guide moral choice. It is through the issues and norms that we define the choice. For example, someone can believe that human dignity is important in morality, but that person will not be able to resolve the Heinz dilemma unless he or she is able to decide whether upholding the law or saving the life is more consistent with human dignity. This is why the moral judgment interview asks subjects to resolve moral dilemmas rather than to state their moral philosophy in the abstract. It is also the purpose of classifying judgments by issue, norm, and element.

We can appreciate the importance of the juxtaposition of norm and element when we see that the same element, when applied to different norms, can have quite different implications – in fact, may result in opposite action choices. Good group consequences (Element 9), when used as a reason for preserving life, for example, is quite different from good group consequences as a perceived basis for supporting law. Both positions can be maintained at the same stage, yet express very different ideas. Thus, at Stage 4 we have the following two criterion judgments on the Heinz dilemma using the element good group consequences. The first involves the life norm:

CJ#:	23
DILEMMA:	III
ISSUE:	Life
NORM:	Life
ELEMENT:	Good group consequences
STAGE:	4

Criterion Judgment   Heinz should steal the drug because his wife can contribute to society.

In the second, good group consequences is applied to the law issue and norm:

CJ#:	25
DILEMMA:	III
ISSUE:	Law
NORM:	Law
ELEMENT:	Good group consequences
STAGE:	4

Criterion Judgment   It is important to obey the law because laws serve to protect productive and orderly functioning of society.

Although the same element – good group consequences – is used in both judgments, it is used to express very different ideas. The two criterion judgments, in fact, support opposite stances or action choices on the dilemma.

Our purpose in classifying the interview material has been to isolate each separate, complete moral judgment or idea advanced by the respondent. Using the issue × norm × element unit, we are able to do that reliably in a way that makes sense to the scorer without distorting the subject's meaning. This unit, when found in the interview itself, is the *interview judgment*. Its idealized counterpart in the manual is the *criterion judgment*.

When the scorer has identified a unit of content – issue × norm × element – stage assessment can begin. We must emphasize, however, that the issue × norm × element will be different when used at different stages. For example, both of the following criterion judgments represent the life issue, life norm, and serving human dignity and autonomy elements. The first is representative of Stage 3, the second of Stage 5:

CJ#:	9
DILEMMA:	III
ISSUE:	Life
NORM:	Life
ELEMENT:	Serving human dignity and autonomy
STAGE:	3

Criterion Judgment Heinz should steal the drug even if he doesn't love his wife or even for a stranger because we are all human beings and should be willing to help others.

CJ#:	36
DILEMMA:	III
ISSUE:	Life
NORM:	Life
ELEMENT:	Serving human dignity and autonomy
STAGE:	5

Criterion Judgment Heinz should steal the drug because the right to life supersedes or transcends the right to property.

Similarly, the following two criterion judgments both use the law issue, law norm, and seeking reward (avoiding punishment) element. The first is representative of Stage 1 reasoning, the second Stage 2/3. Again, they may be seen to have quite different meanings.

CJ#:	3
DILEMMA:	III
ISSUE:	Law
NORM:	Law
ELEMENT:	Seeking reward (avoiding punishment)
STAGE:	1

Criterion Judgment Heinz or one should not steal, because if he does he will be caught, locked up, or put in jail.

CJ#:	10
DILEMMA:	III
ISSUE:	Law
NORM:	Law
ELEMENT:	Seeking reward (avoiding punishment)
STAGE:	2/3

Criterion Judgment Heinz or one should not steal if he doesn't love his wife or for a stranger because he shouldn't risk that much for someone not as close to him or who means less to him.

Conclusion

In this chapter we have presented the theoretical assumptions that underlie our approach to assessing moral judgment. Let us conclude by reviewing the connections between our general assumptions and specific aspects of the Standard Issue instrument and procedures.

First and most important is the question of what the instrument is intended to measure. As discussed earlier in this chapter, the Standard Issue Moral Judgment Interview is designed to elicit a subject's (1) own construction of moral reasoning, (2) moral frame of reference or assumptions about right and wrong, and (3) the way these beliefs and assumptions are used to make and justify moral decisions. We have described this as a phenomenological approach in that it involves viewing the moral world from the subject's perspective. The interviewer, through the use of hypothetical dilemmas and intensive probing, attempts to elicit the most mature reasoning of which the respondent is capable. The questions asked are explicitly prescriptive so as to draw out normative judgments about what one *should* do rather than descriptive or predictive judgments about what one *would* do. The Standard Scoring System is a method for interpreting or identifying the organization or structure exhibited in the individual's moral judgments. The rater uses a hermeneutic approach in that he or she interprets what the subject *means* by the various statements and judgments made in response to the interviewer's questions. Through a number of procedures such as standardization of content, matching to the critical indicators and stage structures of the criterion judgments, the use of explicit rules for computing total scores, and so on, the subjectivity of the interpretive process is minimized. In line with our phenomenalist orientation to assessing moral judgment, the categories of analysis, the issues, norms, and elements, are taken from philosophy and sociology. That is, the individual's moral judgments are taken seriously as moral positions to be analyzed on their own terms rather than reduced to psychological epiphenomena reflecting unconscious processes. These categories of analysis serve to define the scoring unit in a conceptually meaningful, nonarbitrary manner and allow the rater to differentiate moral judgment content from structure. It is assumed that the organization of thought exhibited in responses to the moral judgment interview will conform to five patterns, described by the five stages of moral judgment. The core features of these stages are the levels of sociomoral perspective and justice operations as applied to the universal problems of distributive, corrective, and commutative justice.

Two

Reliability and Validity of Standard Issue Scoring

Reliability Data

Reliability data of several types have been compiled for the Standard Issue Moral Judgment Interview and Scoring System. As the following results indicate, the instrument has proven to be highly reliable.

Test–retest Reliability

Test–retest moral judgment interviews were conducted with 43 subjects using Form A, 31 subjects using Form B, and 10 subjects using both A and B. The same forms were used at Times 1 and 2 with conditions of testing held constant and intervals between Time 1 and Time 2 ranging from 3 to 6 weeks. Subjects were chosen from among volunteers in several Boston-area elementary and high schools, colleges, and graduate schools. The college and graduate school students were paid for their time. Subjects ranged in age from 8 to 28 years; approximately half were male and half female. Interviews were scored blind by two raters using Standard Issue Scoring.

Test–retest reliability figures are summarized in Table 2.1. As shown there, correlations between Time 1 and Time 2 for Forms A and B are both in the high .90s. Since the correlations could be very high without much absolute agreement between scores at Time 1 and Time 2, we have also presented percent agreement figures. For almost all subjects, the scores on Times 1 and 2 were within one-third stage of each other (one step – from 1 to 1[2] or 1[2] to 2[1] or 2[1] to 2, and so on). If we look at global scores based on a nine-point scale (the five stages and the four transition points between stages), we find between 70% and 80% complete agreement. We also calculated percent agreement using a more differentiated system of global scores with 13 categories. This system includes two transition points between each stage, distinguishing, for example, between an interview that is primarily Stage 2 with some Stage 3 and an interview that is primarily Stage 3 with some Stage 2. The agreement levels for this system were in the 60s for the separate forms, 70% for the two forms combined.

Overall, then, it appears that on the two interviews conducted 3–6 weeks apart, almost all subjects receive scores within one-third stage of each other. About three quarters receive identical scores on the two interviews when a nine-point scale is used, and between one half and two thirds receive identical scores

Table 2.1. *Test–retest reliability*

	Form A	Form B	Forms A and B
Percent agreement			
Within one-third stage	93	94	100
Using pure and mixed stage scores[a]			
(Ns = 43, 31, and 10)	70 (Rater 1)	75 (Rater 2)	80 (Rater 2)
	77 (Rater 2)		
Using major/minor stage differentiations[b]	59 (Rater 1)	62 (Rater 2)	70 (Rater 2)
	70 (Rater 2)		
Correlation $T_1 - T_2$	.96 (Rater 1)	.97 (Rater 2)	—
	.99 (Rater 2)		

[a] Nine categories: 1, 1/2, 2, 2/3, 3, 3/4, 4, 4/5, 5.
[b] Thirteen categories: 1, 1/2, 2/1, 2, 2/3, 3/2, 3, 3/4, 4/3, 4, 4/5, 5/4, 5.

with the more finely differentiated 13-point scale. When scores do change from Time 1 to Time 2, the change is as likely to be negative as positive, so it cannot be attributed to practice effect. There were no age or sex differences in test–retest stability.

Interrater Reliability

The test–retest interviews were also used for assessing interrater reliability. Twenty Form A interviews were scored independently by five raters. Ten Form B interviews were scored by four raters. In addition, 20 Form C longitudinal interviews were scored independently by two raters.

Percent agreement figures for interrater reliability on Form A ranged from 88% to 100% for agreement within a third of a stage, from 75% to 88% for complete agreement based on the nine-point scale, and from 53% to 63% for complete agreement using the most finely differentiated 13-point scale. The correlation for Raters 1 and 2 on the Form A test–retest interviews was .98. Interrater figures for Forms B and C are about the same as those for Form A (see Table 2.2).

Raters who scored these reliability data varied in degree of experience using the manual. Of the five Form A raters, two were familiar with Structural Issue Scoring as well as Standard Issue Scoring and, in fact, were authors of Standard Issue Forms A and B. The third rater was also highly experienced but was not an author of the manual. The other two less experienced raters had learned to score within the prior 6–8 months using the manual. They consulted with more experienced raters as they learned to use the manual to score a separate set of practice cases, but this consultation was no more extensive than would be provided at a brief training workshop. Interrater reliability figures between the two ''new scorers'' and between each of them and an experienced scorer were at least as high as reliability among the experienced scorers. The same was true for Form B interrater reliability, which involved two experienced and two new scorers. Thus it seems warranted to conclude that the Standard Issue Scoring Manual can be reliably mastered by relatively inexperienced users.

This conclusion is further supported by interrater reliability achieved be-

Table 2.2. *Interrater reliability*

| | Agreement (%) | | |
	Agreement within 1/3 stage	Complete agreement (9 categories)	Complete agreement (13 categories)
Form A:			
Rater pair 1	100	88	53
Rater pair 2	100	88	63
Rater pair 3	100	75	63
Rater pair 4	88	88	63
Rater pair 5	88	88	63
Form B:			
Rater pair 6	100	78	78
Rater pair 7	100	88	63
Form C:			
Rater pair 8	91	76	52

Note: Correlation: Raters 1 and 2, Form A test–retest interviews = .98; Form B = .96; Form C = .92.

tween an experienced rater and a group of research assistants from another university who had participated in a 4-day seminar on Standard Issue Scoring. On 10 of the interviews from a study being conducted at the University of California at Berkeley, percent agreement between the experienced rater and the new raters was comparable to reliability figures achieved among experienced raters. All pairs of scores were within one-third stage of each other; 83% agreed perfectly when a nine-point scale was used.

In general, then, the figures for interrater reliability look roughly comparable to the test–retest figures: Almost all interviews were scored within one-third stage of each other by any two raters, and on about one half to two thirds of the interviews the two raters assigned identical scores even when using the 13-point scale.

Alternate Form Reliability

Alternate form data between Forms A and B are based on those 10 test–retest subjects who received both Forms A and B and on 193 longitudinal interviews that included both forms. A single rater independently scored both forms of the 20 test–retest sample interviews. Percent agreement between Forms A and B for this sample was comparable to test–retest and interrater reliability: 100% of the interviews were given scores within one-third stage of each other for the two forms, 75% received identical scores for A and B using the nine-category system, and 67% received identical scores for the two forms using the 13-category system. The correlation between moral maturity scores for Forms A and B in this sample was .95.

The level of agreement across forms for the longitudinal data is not as high (see Table 2.3). This is to be expected since Form A was scored by Rater 1 and Form B by Rater 2. That is, the reliability figures confound form and rater

Table 2.3. *Alternate form reliability*

Longitudinal sample (N = 193):
Correlation Form A × Form B = .84
  (Rater 1 for Form A, Rater 2 for Form B)
85% agreement within 1/2 stage
  (other % agreement figures not available)

Test–retest sample (Rater 2 for both forms):
Correlation Form A × Form B = .95
% agreement (9 categories) = 75%
% agreement (13 categories) = 67%
% within 1/3 stage = 100%

differences. The correlation between Forms A and B for the longitudinal sample is .84.

Alternate form reliability figures between Form C and Forms A and B also represent conservative reliability estimates since they too confound form and rater effects. The correlation is .82 for Forms A and C, .84 for Forms B and C. That is, Form C is as highly correlated with each of the other two forms as they are with each other. Percent agreement figures are also comparable across all two-form comparisons.

Since essentially unrelated developmental variables may be correlated if a wide age range is included, we have also computed alternate form correlations with age partialed out. The partial correlations are .78 for Forms A and B, .76 for Forms A and C, and .78 for Forms B and C. Correlations between alternate forms were also computed within each age group. As shown in Table 2.4, the correlations are low, .37–.56 (probably due to restricted range), before age 16, but at age 16 and above they are primarily in the .60s and .70s. In view of the relatively small sample sizes, the fairly restricted moral maturity score range even at the later ages, and the fact that each form was scored by a different rather, these correlations among the alternate forms can be considered psychometrically adequate.

Equivalence of Forms A, B, and C [1]

It has been demonstrated that there are high correlations among the three forms using the continuous weighted average score (WAS) and a high correspondence between the qualitative global stage scores. However, there are small absolute differences between the forms. These differences affect the results of intervention studies with a pre- and posttesting design where one form is used as the pretest and the other as a posttest.

Table 2.5 reports the stage usage and moral maturity scores on each of the three forms at various ages. It can be seen that each form gives slightly different estimates of moral maturity than the others, and has slightly different pulls for certain stages, for example, for Stage 1 and for Stage 5.

1 In order to assess the ability of scores based on two dilemmas to predict scores based on a full three dilemma form of the interview, we calculated the correlation between WAS derived from the first four issues and WAS derived from all six issues for each of the forms, A, B, and C. The correlations ranged from .83 to .98. The percentage of modal stage agreement between scores from the first four issues and all six issues for the three forms ranged from 58% to 85%.

Table 2.4. *Alternate form correlations within age groups*

	Age (years)						
	10	13–14	16–18	20–22	24–25	28–30	32–33
Form A × Form B:							
r	.37	.39	.73	.65	.78	.78	.68
N	19	35	43	29	22	35	22
Form A × Form C:							
r	.37	.40	.67	.59	.83	.70	.47
N	19	35	42	31	21	26	11
Form B × Form C:							
r	.56	.46	.62	.67	.77	.55	.61
N	21	35	43	30	21	26	11

Because of the slight difference in "pull" between the forms, it is appropriate to provide a conversion formula or scale score that would equalize the three forms. Such a conversion formula adds a constant to the score on each form and a weighting factor for each form based on its correlations with the scores for the forms combined. This formula allows estimation of an absolute change value, given the use of one form for pretest and another for posttest.

Regression analyses were performed to create scale scores based on the overall moral maturity score and using the score on each form as a single predictor variable.

For the sample of 199 interviews with all three forms used, Table 2.6 shows the coefficients and the proportion of variance accounted for by each form in predicting the overall score.

Regression was also performed on each age group, but the number of subjects ranged only from 20 to 40 and the results were highly unstable. In pretest–posttest designs, it is recommended that every individual be randomly assigned to one interview form for the pretest and receive a different form as a posttest. Raw scores should be converted to scale scores using the linear transformations (Table 2.6) before analysis and interpretation of the data.

Internal Consistency

Cronbach's α was computed for each of the three interview forms using issue scores as items. The results were as follows: Form A, .92; Form B, .96; and Form C, .94. These figures indicate that the measure meets the psychometric criterion of internal consistency of a test. That is, they provide strong evidence that the moral judgment interview is measuring a single construct. Recall in this regard that each of the three dilemmas within each form was scored independently.

Conclusions: Reliability of Standard Issue Scoring

A review of the correlational reliability data for Standard Issue Scoring indicates that the instrument is well within the limits of acceptable reliability. A

Table 2.5. *Stage distributions of scores within age groups for Forms A, B, and C (% of subjects at each stage)*

Age (years) and form	Stage								Mean MMS
	1	1/2	2	2/3	3	3/4	4	4/5	
10:									
A	5.3	26.3	42.1	15.8	10.5	.0	.0	.0	204
B	.0	52.4	33.3	9.5	4.8	.0	.0	.0	184
C	4.8	57.1	19.0	19.0	.0	.0	.0	.0	181
13–14:									
A	.0	11.1	8.3	58.3	16.7	2.8	.0	.0	249
B	2.8	5.6	33.3	36.1	11.1	8.3	.0	.0	235
C	.0	11.1	16.7	55.6	13.9	2.8	.0	.0	246
16–18:									
A	.0	2.3	4.5	22.7	31.8	36.4	.0	.0	299
B	.0	4.5	9.1	27.3	16.4	20.5	.0	.0	280
C	2.3	9.1	22.7	36.4	27.3	.0	.0	.0	288
20–22:									
A	.0	.0	.0	6.5	25.8	54.8	9.7	3.2	335
B	.0	.0	3.3	12.2	40.0	26.7	13.3	3.3	319
C	.0	.0	.0	18.2	27.3	45.5	9.1	.0	325
24–26:									
A	.0	.0	.0	4.3	17.4	43.5	21.7	13.0	365
B	.0	.0	4.2	4.2	25.0	37.5	16.7	8.3	354
C	.0	.0	.0	4.5	22.7	50.0	18.2	4.5	350
28–30:									
A	.0	.0	.0	.0	21.6	48.6	16.2	13.5	362
B	2.8	.0	.0	.0	13.9	52.8	16.7	13.9	366
C	.0	.0	.0	.0	33.3	59.3	7.4	.0	338
32–33:									
A	.0	.0	0	.0	4.5	68.2	18.2	9.1	366
B	.0	.0	.0	4.3	8.7	43.5	26.1	13.0	363
C	.0	.0	.0	.0	9.1	81.8	9.1	.0	351
36:									
A	.0	.0	.0	.0	.0	77.8	11.1	11.1	375
B	.0	.0	.0	.0	12.5	37.5	50.0	.0	369
C	.0	.0	.0	.0	.0	.0	100.0	.0	400

Note: Rows indicate percentage of scores assigned at each stage on a given interview form at a given age.

comparison with related measures may be helpful here. Loevinger and Wessler (1970) report interrater reliability correlations for their Sentence Completion Test of ego development in the mid .80s (using total protocol scores) as compared to our .98. Rest (1979) reports test–retest reliability of .68–.92 and internal consistency reliability of .77 and .79 for the Defining Issues Test of moral development. Recall that test–retest reliability for Standard Scoring ranged from .96 to .99 and that internal consistency ranged from .92 to .96.

Table 2.6. *Regression coefficients and R^2 for each interview form*

Form	Constant	Coefficient (SE)	R^2
A	18.618	.913(.024)	.880
B	55.400	.833(.020)	.895
C	29.152	.909(.024)	.876

The qualitative analyses emphasized in many studies of moral development require more than high correlational reliability, however. Percent of absolute agreement between global scores is also important. In this regard, the Standard Issue System again compares favorably with Loevinger's Sentence Completion Test. Interrater agreement on total protocol Sentence Completion scores using a 10-point scale is reported to range from 50% to 80% (median 61%). This is substantially lower than the 75%–88% for the 9-point Standard Scoring scale and is, in fact, lower than even the 53%–78% agreement on our 13-point scale. Loevinger and Wessler find that most protocols receive scores within a half-stage step of one another (88%–100%, median 94%), whereas we find most protocols to be scored within one-third stage of each other (88%–100%). Rest (1979) does not report percent agreement figures since his instrument does not yield stage typology scores.

In addition to test–retest, interrater, and alternate form reliability, we have also calculated the standard error of measurement for the moral judgment measure. With the standard error of measurement defined as $\sigma_{meas} = \sigma\sqrt{(1-r_{xx})}$ (Nunnally, 1978), we have entered the standard deviation of the total longitudinal sample (69.87) as σ and .95 as r_{xx}, the reliability estimate of the measure. The standard error of measurement of the instrument based on these figures is 15.62 "moral maturity points."

Validity of Standard Issue Scoring

As we have argued elsewhere (Colby, 1978; Kohlberg, 1981b), the appropriate validity concept for a developmental measure such as the Standard Issue System is construct validity, not prediction to an external criterion. For a measure of moral judgment stage, the two most critical empirical criteria of construct validity correspond to the two most central theoretical assumptions of the stage construct. They are invariance of stage sequence and structural "wholeness" or internal consistency (generality of stage usage across moral issues or dilemmas). As noted in the descriptions of longitudinal moral judgment data presented in later chapters of this volume, the results confirm both invariant sequence and internal consistency. Among other things, we interpret construct validity to mean the fit of the data obtained by means of the test to primary components of its theoretical definition. The primary theoretical definition of structural moral development is that of an organization passing through an invariant developmental sequence. In other words, positive results of the longitudinal analyses reported in chapters 3, 4, and 5 support not only the theoretical assumptions but also the validity of the measure. Negative results, of course, could have been due to an incorrect theory, an invalid test, or both. Furthermore, validity and reliability of a test are closely related notions since both refer to the generalizability of performance on a test, or a set of test items, to performance in other situations including the performance on other forms of the test or at other times of testing. In the case of structural stage, construct validity demands high generalizability or test–retest and alternate form reliability. If a stage is a structural whole, the individual should be consistent over various stimuli and occasions of testing. Our reliability data fit this demand rather well.

In regard to the instrument's validity, one might also wonder whether Standard Issue Scores on responses to hypothetical dilemmas predict to moral judgment in real life. One should not expect, however, to find an exact correspondence between developmental stage of hypothetical and real moral judgments. As Damon (1977) has shown, the relation between moral judgments made by children in real and hypothetical versions of the same distributive justice situation is mediated by a number of factors including the individual's developmental level on the hypothetical judgments. Moreover, the most salient features of real-life dilemmas are not always unambiguously moral. Many of the issues dealt with in attempts to resolve such dilemmas may be practical or factual rather than moral. To the extent that such situations do elicit moral reasoning, the scores on individuals' responses to hypothetical dilemmas should be predictive of, although not identical to, the scores on the real-life moral judgments. Of course, evaluation of this aspect of construct validity is limited by the absence of techniques for scoring real-life moral judgments.

One study that has reported data on the relation between Standard Issue Scoring and scores on real-life situation is Gilligan and Belenky's (1980) longitudinal study of women deciding whether to have an abortion. Gilligan and Belenky (1980) reported that rank order correlations on the relation between scores on the hypothetical abortion dilemma and on the standard dilemmas at Time 1 and Time 2 were .83 and .92, respectively. They present percent agreement figures but not correlations between scores on the real hypothetical abortion dilemmas: 59% were scored at the same stage, and all but one of the remainder were scored within one-half stage of one another. Gilligan and Belenky do not, however, interpret the discrepancies between actual and hypothetical abortion dilemma scores as measurement error. Rather, they argue that the discrepancies are important psychological phenomena that have significant implications for the future development and mental health of these women facing unwanted pregnancies. Like Selman and Jaquette (1977), they find that when individuals are unable to bring to bear their cognitive capacities (as measured in the hypothetical interview) in thinking about the real-life situation, they are more likely to exhibit emotional disturbance both at the time of the initial interview and in longitudinal follow-up 1 year later. Gilligan and Belenky also report that changes in moral judgment scores on the standard dilemmas in the year following the abortion were strong predictors or psychological adjustment at the time of the follow-up interview.

Discussion of Reliability and Validity

Taken together, the data presented in this volume (chaps. 2, 3, 4, and 5, indicate that Standard Issue Scoring has succeeded in addressing the central methodological concerns raised in critiques such as the widely cited paper by Kurtines and Greif (1974). The criticisms of Kohlberg's method presented by Kurtines and Greif fall into three general categories: (1) nonstandardization of the interview and coding scheme; (2) questionable reliability of the coding schemes, especially important given their complexity and "subjectivity"; and (3) questionable validity of the coding schemes, particularly a failure to present clear evidence of invariant stage sequence.

As its name indicates, the Standard Issue Moral Judgment Interview and Scoring System represents an attempt to standardize the assessment of moral judgment stage. The nine hypothetical dilemmas constitute three parallel interview forms and the probing questions are specified. Although the system remains complex, it can be mastered by individuals who are relatively inexperienced as indicated by the interrater reliability figures presented here. Test–retest and alternate form reliability are also high, as is internal consistency of scores assigned an interview. This should both assure reliable scoring within each study that uses the measure and provide enough standardization to allow comparison of results across studies by different investigators. This increase in reliability and objectivity in scoring was achieved by the creation of a small but conceptually, rather than arbitrarily, defined unit of analysis, by the elaboration of clear rules for classification of material and for defining a match between manual and interview judgments, and by the construction of specific and detailed stage criteria, the critical indicators, which specify exactly what is required in the interview in order for a stage score to be assigned. On the other side of the reliability–validity balance, structural explications of each manual item were provided in order to minimize loss of validity due to excessively literal interpretation of the manual.

With regard to validity, we have argued that prediction to an external criterion such as action taken in a moral conflict situation is not an appropriate indicator of the instrument's validity. The appropriate question is whether the interview and scoring system provides a valid assessment of moral judgment stage, not of moral character as a whole. If validity is understood in this way, the longitudinal data presented in this volume can be considered to provide substantial support for the validity of Standard Issue Scoring. That is, when Standard Issue Scoring is used to score longitudinal interviews not used to construct the measure, it yields scores that agree very closely with the theoretical predictions of invariant sequence and internal consistency.

Three longitudinal studies of moral judgment have been included in this volume. Two others that have used Standard Issue Scoring and several that have used earlier scoring systems have been published by other investigators. The two that used Standard Issue Scoring are Erickson's (1980) study of girls and young women and Gilligan and Murphy's (1979) study of male and female college students. Both studies were conducted in the United States with middle-class samples.

Unfortunately, design problems make it difficult to interpret these researchers' results. Both samples participated between Times 1 and 2 in courses intended to promote moral development. Particularly problematic is that these courses included direct study and discussion of Kohlberg's theory. Furthermore, these studies used different forms of the moral judgment interview at different testing times rather than maintaining a consistent set of dilemmas across all waves of data collection. Since scores on different dilemmas may differ somewhat, the unsystematic variation in dilemmas used may introduce error into the data. A further limitation of these studies is that Erickson's subjects at each testing time and Gilligan and Murphy's at Times 1 and 2 filled out a written version of the moral judgment interview rather than participating in individually administered taped interviews. Since responses to written interviews are less well elaborated than responses to oral interviews, misscoring of the former is more likely to occur.

Possibly as a result of these methodological problems, both Erickson and Gilligan and Murphy report somewhat more frequent sequence reversals than were found in our study. Over three 3–8-year intervals, the Gilligan and Murphy data show 12%–15% downward stage movement as compared to 3% in our American male data. Over a 4-year interval (between Time 1 and Time 5), the Erickson data show 9% downward stage movement. Calculated over all 1-year testing intervals, Erickson finds 13% downward stage movement. It should be noted that in spite of indicating somewhat more frequent stage reversal, all of these figures fall within the limits of measurement error as represented by our test–retest data.

The difference between Erickson's 1-year and 4-year interval data is consistent with earlier findings (Kuhn, 1976; White, Bushnell, & Regnemer, 1978) that the longer the time interval between subsequent testings, the more likely a subject is to have advanced rather than regressed. These results have been interpreted as evidence that short-term fluctuations in moral judgment occur in the context of long-term progression. Whether it is most appropriate to treat the short-term fluctuations as measurement error or as actual stage change is impossible to determine with certainty. Of course, the present study does not allow us to compare short-term fluctuation with long-term progression within the same individuals since all interviews were conducted 3–4 years apart. However, we have seen that downward changes from Time 1 to Time 2 in our test–retest sample are substantially more frequent than from time n to time $n + 1$ in our longitudinal sample.

We interpret the differences between Time 1 and Time 2 in the test–retest sample as measurement error rather than as true developmental fluctuation, primarily because the percent agreement and correlation coefficients are essentially the same for test–retest, interrater, and alternate form reliability. That is, there seems to be slippage or error of about one-third stage in the system. When this confidence interval is superimposed on negligible developmental progress, as in the case of testings 1 year apart, the result will be relatively more frequent occurrence of lower scores at time $n + 1$ than at time n. When the measurement error is superimposed on developmental progress, as in the case of testings 3 years apart, the occurrence of a score one-third stage below the individual's "true stage" would result in either no change from time n to time $n + 1$ or a smaller positive change than would otherwise appear. If most individuals move forward at least one-third stage in 4 years, this interval will not yield many cases of apparent regression.

To sum up, there have been five reported longitudinal studies of moral judgment using Standard Issue Scoring (chaps. 3, 4, and 5, this volume; Gilligan & Murphy, 1979; and Erickson, 1980). In two of these studies there were methodological problems that might be expected to increase measurement error. The stage sequence data are in fact somewhat less orderly in these two studies than in the others. However, the frequency of sequence anomalies even in these studies is quite low, substantially lower than the frequency of downward stage change in our test–retest data. In the two cross-cultural studies the sequence data are essentially identical to those reported in our American male study. Of the five studies, only two (Snarey [1982] and Colby and Kohlberg [1983]) present internal consistency data. The results of these studies regarding internal consistency of moral judgment are very clear. In a factor analysis only one general factor emerged, and very few subjects showed reasoning at more than two adjacent stages.

In light of criticisms of Kohlberg's theory by Holstein (1976), Gilligan (1977), and others, one might wonder whether subjects in the studies that report more orderly stage sequence data are more predominantly male and subjects in the studies with less orderly data are more predominantly female. The fact that Erickson's subjects were all females and Nisan and Kohlberg's (chap. 4, this volume) subjects as well as those in our American study (chap. 3, this volume) were all male may seem to support this interpretation. However, the subjects in Gilligan and Murphy's and Snarey's studies were approximately half male and half female. The issue of sex differences in orderliness of stage sequence may be addressed by calculating separately the percentage of reversals among males and females in the Gilligan and Murphy and Snarey studies. In fact, there do not appear to be significant sex differences in either of these studies in either developmental stage or in orderliness of stage sequence.

Overall, these five studies using Standard Issue Scoring are consistent in yielding more orderly sequence data than have been reported by investigators using earlier scoring systems. We have already referred to Kramer's analysis of Kohlberg's data and we shall discuss it further in chapter 3.

Holstein (1976) has reported 3-year longitudinal data on Kohlberg's moral judgment interview with 52 13-year-old boys and girls and their parents. Using Structural Issue Scoring on interviews that were primarily written, she found that a substantial number of subjects skipped stages or reverted from a higher to a lower stage between Time 1 and Time 2. Holstein found both age and sex differences in the frequency of stage skipping. Whereas 21% of the adolescents skipped at least one stage between Time 1 and Time 2, only 7% of the adults did so. Stage skipping in males tended to be from Stage 1 or 2 to Stage 4, in females from Stage 3 to Stage 5. Holstein also reported a substantial amount of regression from Time 1 to Time 2 along with a dramatic difference in frequency of regression for lower-stage (1–3) subjects and for higher-stage (4–6) subjects. Virtually none of the lower-stage subjects regressed, whereas many (20%–33%) of the higher stage subjects did revert to a lower stage at Time 2. Without rescoring Holstein's interviews, it is impossible to determine whether the differences between her results and ours are due to scoring differences, sampling differences, or some other feature that differs across the two studies. Holstein interprets the high rate of regression among higher stage subjects as an indication that Kohlberg's Stages 4 through 6 do not represent an invariant developmental sequence but rather are alternative and equally mature forms of moral judgment. An alternative interpretation is that the higher stages were inadequately defined in scoring systems prior to Standard Issue Scoring. Perhaps the strongest evidence for the validity of this interpretation is that Kramer's (1968) analysis of Kohlberg's longitudinal data showed patterns of regression and stage skipping that were almost identical to those Holstein found. On rescoring using Standard Issue Scoring, virtually all of the anomalies in Kohlberg's data disappeared. That is, in the study reported in chapter 3, Stages 4 and 5 do appear to be developmentally ordered. The relation between Stages 5 and 6 cannot be addressed, or course, since Stage 6 has been dropped from the system. Among the other longitudinal studies that used Standard Issue Scoring, only two traced the stage sequence up to Stage 5. The results with regard to sequence in these two studies are inconclusive. Although Snarey (1982) finds virtually no downward stage change at either low-stage or high-stage levels, Gilligan and Murphy (1979) do report a tendency for subjects to regress from Stage 5 to transitional level 4/5. This difference may be an artifact resulting from the fact that the latter subjects had studied Kohlberg's theory but the former subjects had not. On the other hand, it might indicate some remaining unresolved inadequacy in the differentiation of Stage 5 from transitional level 4/5.

White et al. (1978) present longitudinal data collected on the island of Eleuthera in the Bahamas. Their data include a 3–7-year longitudinal sample and a series of 2–7-year longitudinal samples. Like Holstein, they used Structural Issue Scoring. Although the findings indicate a general pattern of upward stage change over time, some respondents in all subsamples did regress. Since the authors report analyses of variance rather than frequency of regression, we cannot directly compare their results with those from the other studies discussed here. White et al. point out that in their data, the longer the time interval between subsequent testings, the more likely a subject was to have advanced rather than regressed. They argue that their findings suggest that moral judgment stages develop sequentially, but short-term fluctuations either up or down often may take place in the context of long-term progression. This is the same pattern that Erickson (1980) found using Standard Issue Scoring. We have argued earlier here that the pattern is probably an indication of measurement error superimposed on steady developmental progression.

Another instance of this pattern has been reported by Kuhn (1976) in a 1-year longitudinal study of 50 5–8-year-old children. Kuhn used simplified versions of the dilemmas from Standard Form A and used global story scoring to analyze the responses. The children were interviewed three times – at Time 1, 6 months after Time 1, and 1 year after Time 1. Kuhn found that at 6-month intervals the data showed considerable downward as well as upward stage movement. In fact, between Times 1 and 2, and between Times 2 and 3, subjects were not significantly more likely to move upward than downward. The pattern of change from Time 1 to Time 3 was drastically different, however. Although there was a substantial amount of upward stage change, only 1 subject out of 50 (2%) showed any downward movement (using our nine-point scale). There were no occasions of stage skipping. It is worth noting that at this age level, an interval of 1 year is sufficient to show steady progression, whereas at older ages 1-year intervals show the kind of short-term fluctuation that Kuhn found in her 6-month intervals. This is no doubt due to age differences in rate of development.

Also noteworthy is that the sequence in Kuhn's 1-year data is as orderly as it is in our data despite the fact that she used an earlier scoring system. This further illustrates the point made earlier that in Standard Issue Scoring the higher stages were more radically redefined than were the lower stages.

Turning to our own longitudinal data, we see a dramatic improvement over Kohlberg and Kramer's earlier analysis in the fit between theory and data in relation to both structured wholeness and invariant sequence (see chap. 3). In considering the significance of that improvement, we must raise the question of circularity. Is the improvement simply the result of post hoc manipulations that ensure our obtaining the desired results (i.e., it could not have been otherwise)? We think not. Standard Issue Scoring rules do not force consistency of stage scores assigned an interview. According to the rules, scores could have been scattered across three or four stages for an individual subject, yet they were not. Our design could not prevent the halo effect of scorer bias toward consistency within dilemmas but did prevent such an effect across dilemmas by requiring that each of the nine dilemmas for each subject be scored independently of one another. Furthermore, the interviews from which sequence and internal consistency data were derived were not used at all in reformulating the stages or creating the scoring manual. If there were no clear sequence in moral judgment development, it should not have been possible to derive a system from seven "construction cases" that would yield such clear sequence for the blind cases. The fact that the raters were required to use specific, objective criteria in assigning scores makes the sequence and internal consistency findings even more convincing. The records kept on each subject document exactly the sense in which the subject was judged to have developed (or remained the same) from one time to the next, as well as the sense in which that subject's responses can be considered structurally consistent from one dilemma to the next at the same testing time.

In conclusion, then, we have presented here data that document both the reliability and validity of the Standard Issue Moral Judgment Interview and Scoring System. In order to establish even more completely the validity of the system, there is a need for further research on discriminant and construct validity. In order to illuminate more fully the broader psychological significance of scores on this measure, further research is needed relating responses to the standard dilemmas to reasoning about spontaneously framed moral dilemmas and to moral conduct. The availability of Standard Issue Scoring should help to facilitate a systematic approach to these areas of investigation.

Three

A Longitudinal Study of Moral Judgment in U.S. Males

with John Gibbs and Marcus Lieberman

This chapter presents the results of a 20-year longitudinal study of moral development. The study represents an attempt to document the basic assumptions of Kohlberg's cognitive developmental account of moral judgment. According to this account, moral judgment is said to develop through a sequence of six stages.[1] In line with a Piagetian notion of stages, the cognitive developmental approach to moral judgment focuses on the qualitative form of the child's moral reasoning and on developmental changes in that reasoning. Kohlberg has attempted to describe general organizational or structural features of moral judgment that can be shown to develop in a regular sequence of stages. The concept of structure implies that a consistent logic or form of reasoning can be abstracted from the content of an individual's response to a variety of situations. It implies that moral development may be defined in terms of the qualitative reorganization of the individual's pattern of thought rather than the learning of new content. Each new reorganization integrates within a broader perspective the insights that were achieved at lower stages. The developing child becomes better able to understand and integrate diverse points of view on a moral conflict situation and to take more of the relevant situational factors into account. In this sense, each stage presupposes the understanding gained at previous stages. As a result, each stage provides a more adequate way of making and justifying moral judgments. The order in which the stages develop is said to be the same in each individual, not because the stages are innate, but because of the underlying logic of the sequence. (See Table 1.1 for a summary of the stages.)

Kohlberg has hypothesized that the developmental levels that he has described are stages in a strict Piagetian sense. To test this hypothesis, longitudinal data are required following subjects over a relatively long span of time. First, the stage concept implies that under normal environmental conditions the direction of change will always be upward. Second, it implies that there will be no stage skipping. The individual must pass through each stage in order to reach the next stage in the sequence. Third, the stage concept implies that an individual's thinking will be at a single dominant stage across varying content,

A longer version of this chapter was published in 1983 as "A Longitudinal Study of Moral Judgment," *Monographs of the Society for Research in Child Development, 48,* 1–124.

1 Although Kohlberg's theory describes six stages of moral development, we will deal in this chapter only with Stages 1 through 5. Stage 6 is not represented in Standard Issue Scoring, the method of stage scoring used in this study. Therefore, it does not enter into our results or the discussion of their significance.

though use of the adjacent stage may also be expected. Previous research has supported the general notion of an age developmental order of qualitative responses and a hierarchy of preference and comprehension in these levels. Such an order has been shown by cross-sectional age studies in a variety of cultures (see Edwards, 1981). It has also been shown by a number of training studies that support the assumption that change after exposure to moral judgments at other stages is always to the next stage up. For example, Blatt and Kohlberg (1975), Colby et al. (1977), and Lockwood (1977) found that exposure to group moral discussions in which a range of stages was presented in general led to movement to the next stage up. Rest (1973) found that there was a Guttman scale hierarchy in comprehension of the stages; that is, individuals comprehended all stages lower than their own dominant stage, they comprehended the next stage up if they exhibited on the pretest some (15%) usage of that stage, but they did not comprehend stages more than one above their own dominant stage.

In addition to data supporting the general idea of a developmental hierarchy in Kohlberg's levels, a large number of studies reviewed by Blasi (1980) have generally found significant associations between moral judgment level and moral conduct. Reviews of the extant published literature on research in the development of moral judgment based on the Kohlberg levels generally support the cognitive-developmental assumptions about the antecedents and correlates of moral judgment development (see Rest, 1983).

The data we have just cited as supporting the developmental level hypothesis have usually compared group means. The results of these studies have not directly supported the strong stage claim, as critics like Kurtines and Greif (1974) have pointed out. In part, the ambiguity in some of these findings has been due to the limited reliability of Kohlberg's (1958) method of interviewing and scoring moral stage. The longitudinal data published by Holstein (1976), Kuhn (1976), and White, Bushnell, and Regnemer (1978) have shown some anomalies in stage sequence. It has not been clear whether these anomalies represent a failure of fit of the strict stage model to moral judgment development or whether they have represented confusions in the conceptual definitions of the stages or problems in the reliability or validity of the measure. In an early report of his own longitudinal data over 10 years, Kohlberg (Kohlberg & Kramer, 1969), while reporting some measurement problems leading to anomalies, stressed a genuine failure of the stage sequence hypothesis in the college years leading to so-called sophomore retrogression in development. In 1973, Kohlberg reinterpreted the anomalies as resulting not from retrogression but from incorrect conceptualization of stages as they appear in development after high school. He reported some clinical analyses of cases suggesting that college retrogressors were exhibiting a Stage "$4\frac{1}{2}$" (having moved out of conventional morality but not yet into principled moral judgment) and proposed revised conceptual definitions of the fourth and fifth stages. In fact, such revision accounted for only a few of the anomalies reported by Kohlberg and Kramer. This implied that there were general problems in the reliability and validity of the stage criteria and scoring method.

The present chapter attempts to address the validity of the stage model as applied to longitudinal data and the associated problems of stage definition and measurement this task has involved. It reports a reanalysis of 1956–68 longitudinal data along with analysis of the subsequent data collected from the same subjects from 1968 through 1976. The current analysis involved the application of a new scoring method, Standard Issue Scoring, based on a substantially revised account of the stages.

Methods

Design

The design of the original cross-sectional study, which was later followed up longitudinally, was determined by a number of theoretical concerns. Three variables were included in the design: age, socioeconomic status, and sociometric status. Socioeconomic status was expected to be positively associated with moral judgment development in part because it was assumed to be an indicator of sense of participation in the society as a whole. Kohlberg, drawing on G. H. Mead (1934), considered this sense of participation to be an important determinant of moral development. Sociometric status was intended to be an indicator of peer group participation, which Piaget (1932/1965) argued was crucial to moral development. The age variable was intended to establish the age developmental characteristics of types of response to the moral dilemmas. These originally cross-sectional subjects, stratified by three levels of age and two levels of social class and sociometric status, were followed longitudinally at regular 3–4-year intervals for 20 years.

At each testing time subjects were interviewed on the nine hypothetical moral dilemmas making up the three forms of Kohlberg's moral judgment interview: Forms A, B, and C. At some testings subjects also responded to additional instruments not reported in this volume, including interviews concerning attitudes toward social and occupational roles and attitudes toward sex, the Thematic Apperception Test, Loevinger's Sentence Completion Test, Piagetian cognitive measures, and Selman's role-taking interview.[2]

Subjects

The basic sample consisted originally of 84 boys filling the following $2 \times 2 \times 3$ factorial design (see Table 3.1).[3] The population had the following characteristics:

1. *Age.* Subjects were 10, 13, and 16 years old at Time 1.
2. *Class.* To facilitate filling the design, two suburban Chicago school systems were selected, one predominantly upper middle class, the other predominantly lower middle and working class. Fourth-, seventh-, and tenth-grade classes formed the basis for selection. A dichotomous judgment of a boy's socioeconomic status was based on his parents' occupation and education, as reported in the school folder. In spite of efforts to obtain discrete groups, it was necessary to take children along a fairly broad continuum with a rather arbitrary, though conventional, dividing point. The parents of boys in the lower- and lower-middle-class group included unskilled, semiskilled, and skilled laborers

---

2 All of the data from Kohlberg's longitudinal study are archived at the Henry A. Murray Research Center of Radcliffe College where they are available to interested researchers for further analysis.

3 Girls were not included in Kohlberg's original sample because adding gender as a fourth variable would have required doubling the sample. Given the laboriousness of the interviewing and scoring procedures, such a large sample was not feasible. In retrospect, however, the omission of girls is regrettable.

Table 3.1. *Design of study*

	Lower SES		Higher SES		
	Integrates	Isolates	Integrates	Isolates	Totals
10 years	6(6)	4(6)	6(6)	5(6)	21
13 years	4(6)	3(6)	5(6)	5(6)	17
16 years	6(6)	2(6)	3(6)	4(6)	15
Totals	16	9	14	14	
		25		28	
			53		

Note: Figures not in parentheses indicate number of cross-sectional subjects who were followed up longitudinally. Figures in parentheses indicate number of subjects in the original cross-sectional sample. As noted in text, five additional working-class subjects, age 19 at Time 3, were added in 1964, at Time 3.

and white-collar workers without a college education. The parents of boys in the upper-middle-class group included small businessmen, accountants, and salespeople with a college education, semiprofessionals, executives, and professionals.

3. *Sociometric status.* When entering a given classroom the investigator described the procedures to be followed, including a "revealed differences" discussion among three boys. The boys were then asked to write the names of three other boys with whom they would like to have the discussion. The sociometric test was informally discussed with the teacher and compared with notes in the school folder before a final selection was made, in order to somewhat reduce determinants of school and athletic achievement and temporary fluctuations of popularity. The teachers were asked to comment on the boys' social connectedness, not on their moral characters or reputations.

As in the case of socioeconomic status, there were not enough subjects available to obtain only extreme groups, so that the dichotomy tends to divide a continuum. Boys who were never chosen or who where chosen once or twice but never by someone they had themselves chosen were designated sociometric isolates. Boys with at least two reciprocal choices or who were chosen at least three times, at least once reciprocally, were designated as integrates.

4. *Intelligence.* IQ scores were taken from school records at Time 1 and were based on various group tests routinely administered in the various schools (e.g., the Otis and the Thurstone PMA). An attempt was made to equalize intelligence for the social class and sociometric groups. Those whose IQs were above 120 or below 100 were excluded from the study. Although complete equalization was not achieved, the IQ differences were small and nonsignificant. Mean IQ for middle-class boys was 109.7; for lower-class boys was 105.9. Mean IQ for integrates was 111.2, for isolates 104.4.

5. *Religion and ethnic.* The ethnic and religious composition of our sample is presented in Table 3.2.

Longitudinal Follow-up and Sample Attrition

The study included six testing times – the original interview and five follow-up interviews. Because not every subject could be reached at each time, the

Table 3.2. *Religious composition of cross-sectional sample*

Group	N
Working-class group	
Catholic	14
Protestant	22
Upper-middle-class group	
Catholic	3
Jewish	2
Protestant	31

number of interviews per subject ranged from one to six. Only those subjects with at least two interviews were included in our current analysis. This condition was met by 58 of the subjects. As shown in Table 3.3 the most typical number of interviews completed for a single subject was four. All but three subjects were interviewed at least three times. Age, sociometric status, and socioeconomic status of origin of these 58 longitudinal subjects are presented in Table 3.1.

There was no attempt to locate for later longitudinal follow-up those boys who were unavailable for follow-up at time 2. As shown in Table 3.1, the initial dropout from the cross-sectional sample was not evenly divided by age and social class. Whereas 12 working-class boys dropped out, only 8 upper-middle-class boys did so. Ten of the Time 1 16-year-olds dropped out, whereas only 3 of the 10-year-olds did so. To compensate for the attrition of working-class subjects, in 1964 (testing Time 3) we added 5 working-class 19-year-olds to the sample. Because IQ and sociometric status data are missing for these subjects (subjects 91–96), they are not included in our analyses of social class, education, IQ, and sociometric status in relation to moral judgment. However, because they were each interviewed three or four times, they were included in our analyses of longitudinal sequence and internal consistency of moral judg-

Table 3.3. *Frequency of longitudinal follow-up*

Number of interviews completed and scored	N
2	3
3	8
4	25
5	12
6	10
Total	58

Note: Because interviews from seven of these subjects were used to construct the scoring manual, the blind sample used for data analysis included only 51 subjects.

Table 3.4. *Time 1 moral maturity scores for dropouts from sample*

	Age at time 1 (years)		
	10	13	16
Mean MMS at Time 1 of subjects:			
Dropping out after Time 2	203(2)	—	—
Dropping out after Time 3	—	—	—
Dropping out after Time 4	176(4)	240(2)	260(5)
Dropping out after Time 5	191(5)	227(2)	249(5)
Mean MMS at Time 1 of dropouts	190(11)	234(4)	255(10)
Mean MMS at Time 1 of total sample	189(21)	236(17)	262(14)

ment. Thus the final longitudinal sample was skewed somewhat toward the younger cohort but was balanced in terms of socioeconomic status. The cohort bias should not affect the basic findings of the study, however, because orderliness of longitudinal sequence and internal consistency of responses to the interview were not related to age cohort.

To determine whether the subset of subjects who dropped out after Time 3 were higher or lower in their moral judgment than the sample as a whole, we compared Time 1 weighted average score (WAS) of the whole sample, subdivided by age group, with Time 1 moral maturity scores of the dropouts, again subdivided by age group. As shown in Table 3.4, the dropout means were almost identical to the total sample means, and there was no tendency for subjects who dropped out earlier in the study to show lower scores at Time 1 than those who dropped out later. Thus, mean increase in moral maturity scores over time cannot be attributed to lower stage subjects dropping out of the longitudinal sample.

Moral Judgment Interviews and Scoring

Subjects were interviewed first in 1955–56 and at 3–4-year intervals thereafter. The last set of interviews (including 35 subjects) was completed in 1976–77. Although the probe questions differed slightly from one testing time to another, the same nine dilemmas were used each time. These dilemmas were later used in constructing the Standard Issue Interviews and represent in effect the use of all three Standard Forms (A, B, and C) at each testing time for each subject. All interviews were conducted individually and were tape recorded and transcribed.

Interviews were scored according to Standard Issue Scoring Manual Forms, A, B, and C. Because the number of interviews to be scored was very large, a different rater scored each of the three forms. All three raters were highly experienced and reliability among them fell within the limits discussed in the reliability section of this volume. None of the interviewers participated in coding the interviews. Scoring of all interviews was done blind. That is, raters coded the responses to each dilemma at each time without knowing the subject's age, identity, responses to (or scores on) other dilemmas at the same testing time, or responses to (or scores on) any of the dilemmas at other testing times.

Results

Invariant Stage Sequence

According to our theoretical assumptions, the developmental sequence should be identical in every individual studied. Except under extreme circumstances, there should be no deviations from perfect sequentiality. That is, there should be no stage skipping and no downward stage movement. Let us first consider downward stage movement. Theoretically, our data should never yield a lower score at time $n + 1$ than at time n. Since we have not constructed an error-free measure, however, some discrepant scores must be expected to result from measurement error. A reasonable estimate of the number of such deviations attributable to measurement error can be derived from analysis of test–retest reliability data. That is, we can assume that virtually none of our subjects will have changed in stage of moral judgment within the short test–retest interval. Any differences between scores at Times 1 and 2 can be attributed to measurement error. Therefore, the analysis of longitudinal sequence involved a comparison of the frequency of sequence reversals (downward stage movement) in the longitudinal data with the frequency of negative Time 1–Time 2 changes in our test–retest data. (Of course, this comparison depends on a psychometrically adequate level of test–retest reliability.) If sequence reversals exceed test–retest instability, we cannot consider our data to support the invariant sequence assumption. Table 3.5 presents global stage scores for the three interview Forms A and B and C separately and combined. The sequence reversals are noted with a *c*. In Form A these sequence reversals (downward changes) occurred in only 7% of the adjacent times using even our most differentiated 13-point scale of global interview scores. The reversals were 6% in Form B, 6% in Form C, and 5% in Forms A, B, and C combined. A comparison with downward stage change in test–retest data for Forms A and B is presented in Table 3.6. Since in every case the test–retest reversals are well over twice as great as the longitudinal reversals, it seems reasonable to attribute the violations of longitudinal sequence to measurement error.

A second type of sequence analysis involves comparing the proportion of positive to negative stage change rather than focusing on negative change alone. Such a comparison is important because the invariant sequence assumption implies both that individuals will move upward through the developmental sequence and that they will not move downward. Data showing infrequent downward movement would be interpreted very differently if upward movement was equally infrequent. Although it is somewhat difficult to know what would constitute an adequate preponderance of upward stage change, Rest (1979) reports a ratio of 9.4:1 for positive to negative change on longitudinal data from the Defining Issues Test (DIT). If we define change as one step of movement along our nine-point scale, the ratio of positive to negative change in our study is 14.75:1.

In addition to predicting that at no time will a subject move downward in the developmental sequence, cognitive-developmental theory holds that each stage is a prerequisite for those that follow it. That is, the concept of invariant stage sequence implies that no stage will be omitted as development proceeds. Since within a 4-year interval a subject might enter and leave a stage, we could not necessarily expect our data to corroborate this aspect of sequentiality. Fortunately, however, the interval seems to have been short enough in relation to

Table 3.5. *Moral judgment stage scores*

Subject and testing time	Standard global score			Standard global score (A, B, and C combined)	Kramer scores	Structural issue scores
	Form A	Form B	Form C			
1-1	1[b]	2	2	1/2	—	—
1-2	1/2	2	2/3	2	—	—
1-3	2/3	2[b]	2/3	2/3	—	—
1-4	2/3	3	2/3	3	—	—
1-6	3/4	3/4	—	3/4	—	—
2-1[a]	1/2	1/2	1/2	1/2	2/4	1/2
2-2	3	3	3/4	3	—	3
2-3	3/4	3/4	3/4	3/4	3/4	3/4
2-4	3[c]	2/3[c]	3/4	3[c]	2/3	4/5
2-5	4/5	4/5	4/5	4/5	—	5
2-6	4/5	4/5	—	4/5	—	—
3-1	1/2	2	1/2	2	1/2	2
3-2	2/3	2/3	2/3	2/3	—	2/3
3-3	3/4	3	3/4	3/4	3/4	3
3-4	3/4	3/4	3[c]	3/4	—	3/4
3-5	3/4	3/4	—	3/4	—	4
3-6	3/4	4	3/4	3/4	—	—
4-1	2/3	2	2	2	2/3	2
4-2	3	2/3	2/3	2/3	—	2
4-3	3/4	2/3	3/4	3	3/4	3/4
4-4	3/4	2/3[b]	3[c]	3	3/4	3/4
4-5	3/4	3/4	3/4	3/4	—	3/4
5-1	2	1/2	1/2	1/2	1/2	1
5-2	2/3	2	1/2	2/3	—	2
5-3	2/3	1/2[c]	1[c]	1/2[c]	—	2
5-4	3	2	2/3	2/3	—	2/3
5-5	2/3[c]	2	3	2/3	—	2/3
6-1	—	1/2	1/2	1/2	—	1/2
6-2	—	2/3[b]	2/3	2/3	—	2
6-3	—	3	3	3	—	2/3
6-4	—	3	2/3[c]	2/3[c]	—	2/3
6-5	—	2/3[b,c]	2/3	2/3	—	3/4
8-1	2	1/2	1	1/2	—	1/2
8-2	2	1[c]	2	2	—	1/2
8-4	3/4	3	3	3	—	3
9-1[a]	1/2	1/2	1/2	1/2	1/2	1/2
9-2	2/3	2/3	1/2	2/3	1/2	2
9-3	2/3	3	3	3	3/4	3
9-4	3	3	3/4	3	—	3/4
9-5	3/4	3/4	3/4	3/4	—	3/4
9-6	4	3/4[b]	—	4	—	—
11-1	1/2	2	1/2	1/2	—	—
11-2	2/3	2[b]	2/3	2/3	—	—
12-1	2	1/2	1/2	1/2	1/2	1/2
12-2	3	2	3	2/3	—	2
12-3	3/4	3/4	3	3/4	4	3
12-4	3/4	3[c]	3/4	3/4	3/4	3

Table 3.5. (*cont.*)

Subject and testing time	Standard global score			Standard global score (A, B, and C combined)	Kramer scores	Structural issue scores
	Form A	Form B	Form C			
13-1	1/2	2	1/2	2	—	—
13-2	2	2	2	2	—	—
13-3	3	3	3	3	—	—
14-1	2/3	2	2/3	2/3	—	1/2
14-2	2/3/4	2/3	3	2/3	—	2/3
14-4	4	4	4	4	—	4
14-5	—	4/5	—	4/5	—	4
15-1	2/3	2/3	2/3	2/3	—	—
15-2	2/3	3	2/3	2/3	—	—
16-1	2/3	2/3	2	2/3	—	1/2
16-2	3/4	3	2	2/3	—	2/3
16-3	3/4	3/4	3	3/4	—	3/4
16-4	4	4	3/4	4	—	4
16-6	4	4	—	4	—	—
17-1[a]	—	2	1/2	1/2	2/3	1/2
17-2	2/3	2/3	2/3	2/3	2/3	2/3
17-3	3/4	3	3/4	3	3/4	3
17-4	3/4	3	3/4	3/4	—	4
17-5	4	4	3/4	4	—	4
17-6	4/5	4/5	—	4/5	—	—
18-1	3	3	2/3	3	—	2
18-2	2/3[c]	3	2/3	2/3[c]	—	3
18-4	3/4	3/4	3/4	3/4	—	4
18-5	3/4	3/4[b]	4	3/4	—	4/5
18-6	4	4	—	4	—	—
19-1	2	1/2	2/3	2/3	—	2
19-2	2/3	3/4	3	3	—	2/3
19-3	—	—	3/4	3/4	—	—
19-4	3	3/4	3/4	3/4	—	2/3
19-5	3/4	3/4	—	3/4	—	2/3
19-6	3/4	4	—	4	—	—
21-1	2	1/2	1/2	1/2	—	2
21-2	2/3	2	2	2/3	—	—
21-3	3	2/3	2/3	2/3	—	2/3
21-4	2/3[c]	3	3	3	—	2/3
22-1	2	1/2	2	2	1/2	2
22-2	1/2[c]	2/3	1/2[c]	2/3	—	3
22-3	3/4	3/4	3/4	3/4	2/4	3
22-4	3/4	4	3/4	3/4	—	4
22-5	3/4	—	3/4	3/4	—	—
22-6	4	4/5	—	4	—	—
23-1[a]	2	1/2	1/2	1/2	—	1/2
23-2	2/3	3/4	—	3/4	—	—
23-3	3/4	3/4	3/4	3/4	—	4
23-4	3/4	4/5	3/4	3/4	—	—
23-5	4/5	5	4	4/5	—	4/5
23-6	4/5	—	—	4/5	—	—

Table 3.5. (*cont.*)

Subject and testing time	Standard global score			Standard global score (A, B, and C combined)	Kramer scores	Structural issue scores
	Form A	Form B	Form C			
24-1	3	1/2	1/2	1/2	1/3	1/2
24-2	3	2/3	2/3	2/3	—	2/3
24-3	3/4	3	2/3	3	2/3	3
24-4	3/4	3/4	3/4	3/4	2/4	3/4
25-1	2/3	1/2	2/3	2/3	—	2/3
25-2	3/4	3	2/3	3	—	2/3
25-5	3/4	3/4	3/4	3/4	—	4/5
25-6	3/4	4	—	4	—	—
26-1	2	2	2/3	2	2/4	2
26-2	3	2/3[b]	3/4	3	3/4	3
26-4	3	3	3[c]	3	—	3
26-5	3	3/4[b]	3/4	3	—	3
26-6	3/4	3/4	—	3/4	—	—
27-1	2/3	1/3	2/3	2/3	3/4	3
27-2	3/4	3	3	3	3/4	3
27-4	3/4	3	3/4	3/4	—	3
27-5	3/4	3/4	3/4	3/4	—	3
29-1	2/3	2/3	2/3	2/3	3/4	—
29-2	3	3	3	3	2/4	—
29-4	3/4	3	3	3/4	—	—
29-5	4	3/4	3/4	3/4	—	—
31-1	1/2/3	2	2/3	2/3	—	—
31-2	3	2/3	3/4	3	—	—
31-5	3/4	3/4	3/4	3/4	—	—
32-1	1/2	2	2/3	2	—	—
32-2	2/3	2	2/3	2/3	—	—
32-5	3	3/4	3	3	—	—
32-6	3/4	3/4	—	3/4	—	—
36-1	2/3	1/2	1/2	1/2	1/2	—
36-2	1/2/3[c]	2	1/2	1/2	1/2	—
36-5	3/4	3	3/4	3/4	—	—
36-6	3/4	3/4	—	3/4	—	—
37-1	3	2/3	3	3	3/4	3
37-2	3/4	3/4	3	3/4	3/5	3/4
37-3	3/4[b]	3/4	3	3/4	3/4	3/4
37-4	4	4[b]	3/4	4	3/4	3/4
37-5	4/5	4/5	—	4/5	—	5
37-6	—	4/5	—	4/5	—	—
38-1	2/3	2	2/3	2/3	2/4	—
38-2	3/4	3/4	3	3	3/4	—
38-5	3/4	4	3/4	3/4	—	—
38-6	3/4	3/4[b]	—	3/4	—	—
39-1	2/3	2/3	2/3	2/3	3/4	2/3
39-2	3/4	3	3/4	3/4	4/5	3/4
39-3	3/4	3	3/4	3/4	2/3	4
39-4	4	3/4	3/4	3/4	4/5	4/5

Table 3.5. (cont.)

Subject and testing time	Standard global score			Standard global score (A, B, and C combined)	Kramer scores	Structural issue scores
	Form A	Form B	Form C			
41-1	2/3	2	2	2	2/4	2
41-2	2/3	2/3	3	3	3/4	3
41-3	3	3	3/4	3	3/5	3/4
41-4	3	3	3/4	3	3/4	3/4
41-5	3	3	3/4	3	—	4
41-6	3/4	4	—	4	—	—
42-1[a]	2/3	2/3	3	2/3	2/4	2/3
42-2	3	3	3/4	3/4	3/4	3/4
42-3	—	—	4	4	3/5	—
42-4	4/5	4	4	4	3/4	4/5
42-5	4/5	4/5	4	4/5	—	4/5
42-6	4/5	4/5	—	4/5	—	—
43-1	3[b]	2/3	2/3	2/3	3	—
43-2	3/4	3/4	3	3/4	3/5	—
43-3	3/4	3/4	3	3/4	3/4	—
43-4	3/4	3/4	3/4	3/4	3/5	—
44-2	2/4	3	3	3/4	4/5	—
44-3	4/5	3/4	4	4	4/5	—
44-4	4[c]	4	3/4[c]	4	4/5	—
44-5	—	—	—	4/5	—	—
44-6	4/5	4/5	—	4/5	—	—
45-1	2/3	2	2	2/3	2/4	2/3
45-2	3	2/3	2/3	2/3	3/4	2/3
45-4	4	3/4	3/4	3/4	3/4	4
45-5	4	4	4	4	—	4/5
45-6	4	4	—	4	—	—
47-1	2/3	3/4	2/3	2/3	2/3	—
47-2	2/3	3/4	3	3	2/4	2/3
47-3	3	—	2/3[c]	3	3/4	2/3
47-4	3	3/4	3	3/4	3/4	2/3
47-5	3/4	3/4	3	3/4	—	2/3
47-6	3/4	2/4[c]	—	4	—	—
48-1	2/3	—	2/3	—	—	—
48-2	3/4	2/3	3	3	—	2/3
48-4	3/4	3	4	3/4	—	3/4
48-5	3/4	3/4	3/4[c]	3/4	—	—
48-6	3/4	4	—	4	—	—
49-1	3/4	3	3/4	3	—	—
49-4	3/4	3/4	3/4	3/4	—	—
49-5	3/4	3[c]	3/4	3/4	—	—
49-6	3/4	3/4	—	3/4	—	—
50-1	3	2/3	2	2/3	—	—
50-4	3/4	3	3	3	—	—
50-5	3/4	4	3/4	4	—	—
50-6	3/4	4	—	4	—	—
51-1	2	2	—	2	—	—
51-4	3/4	3/4	3	3/4	—	—

Table 3.5. (cont.)

Subject and testing time	Standard global score			Standard global score (A, B, and C combined)	Kramer scores	Structural issue scores
	Form A	Form B	Form C			
51-5	3/4	4	3/4	3/4	—	—
51-6	3/4	3/4[c]	—	3/4	—	—
53-1	3	1/2/3[b]	2	2/3	—	—
53-2	3/4	2/3/4[b]	2/3	3/4	—	—
53-4	3[c]	3/4	3/4	3/4	—	—
54-1	2/3	2/3	2	2/3	—	—
54-5	3/4	3/4	3/4	3/4	—	—
56-1	2	—	—	2	—	—
56-4	3	—	—	3	—	—
56-6	3/4	—	—	3/4	—	—
59-1	2/3	1/2	2/3	2/3	—	—
59-2	3	2/3	3	2/3	—	—
59-4	3	3	3	3	—	—
59-5	3/4	2/3[c]	3/4	3	—	—
62-1	2/3	3	3	3	—	—
62-2	3/4	4	3/4	3/4	—	—
62-4	3[c]	3[b,c]	3/4	3[c]	—	—
62-6	3/4	4	—	4	—	—
64-1	3	2/3	3	3	—	—
64-4	3	3/4	3	3/4	—	—
64-5	3/4	3/4	3/4	3/4	—	—
65-1[a]	3	3	3	3	4/5	—
65-2	4	2	2/3[c]	2/3/4[c]	2/4	—
65-4	3/4[c]	3/4	3/4	3/4	—	—
65-5	3/4	3/4	4	3/4	—	—
65-6	3/4	4	—	4	—	—
67-1[a]	3	2/3	2/3	2/3	3/4	—
67-2	3	3	3/4	3	3/5	—
67-3	—	—	—	—	4/5	—
67-4	3/4	3/4	3/4	3/4	—	—
67-5	4/5	3/4	3/4	4	—	—
67-6	4/5	3/4	—	4/5	—	—
68-1	3	3	2	2/3	—	—
68-2	3/4	3	3	3/4	—	—
68-4	3/4	3/4	3	3/4	—	—
68-5	4	3/4[b]	3/4	3/4	—	—
68-6	4	3[c]	—	3/4	—	—
70-1	2/3	2/3	2/3	2/3	—	—
70-2	3/4	3/4	3/4	3/4	—	—
70-4	3/4	3/4	3[c]	3/4	—	—
70-5	4	3/4	3/4	3/4	—	—
70-6	3/4[c]	4	4	4	—	—
71-1	3	3	2/3	2/3	—	—
71-2	3/4	3	3	3	—	—
71-4	3/4	3/4	3	3/4	—	—
71-5	3/4	3[c]	3	3/4	—	—

Table 3.5. (*cont.*)

Subject and testing time	Standard global score			Standard global score (A, B, and C combined)	Kramer scores	Structural issue scores
	Form A	Form B	Form C			
81-1	3	1/2	2/3	2/3	—	—
81-2	3	2/3	3	3	—	—
81-5	3/4	3/4	3/4	3/4	—	—
91-3	3	3/4	3	3/4	—	—
91-4	2/3[c]	3[c]	3	3[c]	—	—
91-5	3/4	3	3/4	3	—	—
91-6	4	4	—	4	—	—
92-3	2/3	3	3/4	3	—	—
92-4	3/4	3/4	3/4	3/4	—	—
92-5	3[c]	3/4[b]	3/4	3/4	—	—
93-3	3/4	3	3	3	—	—
93-4	3/4	3	3	3	—	—
93-5	3/4	3/4	3	3/4	—	—
93-6	3/4	4	—	4	—	—
95-3	3	2/3	3	3	—	—
95-4	3/4	—	3	3/4	—	—
95-5	3/4	3	3/4	3[c]	—	—
95-6	—	3	—	3	—	—
96-3	3/4	3	2/3	3	—	—
96-4	3[c]	3	3	3	—	—
96-5	3/4	3/4	3/4	3/4	—	—
96-6	3/4	3[c]	—	3[c]	—	—

Note: Slight discrepancies between this table and the version published in 1983 (*Monographs of the Society for Research in Child Development*) are due to typographical errors in the earlier version.
[a]"Construction case" used to develop scoring criteria.
[b]Guess score.
[c]Sequence inversion.

Table 3.6. *Comparison of downward stage change: longitudinal and test–retest*

Longitudinal	Form A (Rater 1)	Form B (Rater 2)	Form C	Forms A, B, and C combined
Pure and mixed stage scores (9-point scale)				
$Tn \rightarrow Tn + 1$	5%	6%	4%	3%
Test–retest T1 $\rightarrow$ T2	19%	23%	No data	No data
Major/minor and pure stage scores (13-point scale)				
$Tn \rightarrow Tn + 1$	7%	6%	6%	5%
Test–retest T1 $\rightarrow$ T2	19%	33%	No data	No data

Note: Only the longitudinal interviews that were scored blind are included in this analysis.

our subjects' rate of development to capture each stage in the sequence for each subject. In fact, Table 3.5 shows that in no case on any form did a subject reach a stage in the sequence without having gone through each preceding stage. For the most part, changes across the 4-year intervals were less than a full stage. In Forms A and B only 3% changed more than a full stage in 4 years. In Form C only 2% changed more than a full stage in 4 years. Scores combined across all three forms show only half a percent changing more than a full stage.

Internal Consistency

According to our theoretical assumptions, the logic of each stage forms a "structured whole." In line with this assumption, one would expect to find a high degree of internal consistency in stage scores assigned, at least within those units that are conceptually and psychologically coherent. The data support this assumption as clearly as they do that of invariant sequence.

One indication of degree of internal consistency in moral judgment is provided by distributions for each subject of proportion of reasoning scored at each of the five stages. Our analysis of these distributions showed that most interviews received all of their scores either at a single stage or at two adjacent stages. The mean percentage of reasoning at the individual's modal stage was 68% for Form A, 72% for Form B, 69% for Form C, and 67% for Forms A, B, and C combined. The mean percentage of reasoning at the subject's two most frequently used stages (always adjacent) was 98% for Form A, 97% for Form B, 99% for Form C, and 99% for Forms A, B, and C combined. (Remember that there are three dilemmas per form and each dilemma was scored without knowledge of responses to the other dilemmas, so these figures cannot be an artifact of scorer bias.) The high correlations among alternate forms and high Cronbach's α figures reported in the chapter 2 provide further support for the consistency of subjects' stage of reasoning across differing content.

Some interviews, however, received scores at three stages. In order to determine the number of interviews that did exhibit reasoning at three stages, it was necessary to establish a boundary below which the entry would be treated as error and above which it would be treated as real. For example, if an interview received 80% of its scores at Stage 1, 19% at Stage 2, and 1% at Stage 3, we would probably want to treat the 1% at Stage 3 as error and consider the interview to exhibit only two stages of moral judgment. We established the error boundary at 10% with entries of 10% and below treated as error, entries above 10% treated as real. Our choice of the 10% figure can be justified as follows. The 10% boundary derives from the relation between the number of criterion judgment (CJ) matches assigned to an interview at a stage and the percentage of reasoning at that stage in the interview's distribution of stage scores. Through a comparison of distribution of stage use for each interview with a record of each individual CJ match score assigned, we determined that using a cutoff point of 10% would assure that in every case where the interview received one full criterion judgment match at a stage, the percentage use of that stage would fall above the cutoff and thus be treated as real. That is, any stage represented in the distribution at a level of 10% or below reflected less than one full criterion judgment match at that stage across the entire interview. For example, the existence of 8% Stage 2 in a distribution of scores for an interview might reflect the assignment of a transitional CJ score at Stage 2/3 in a predominantly Stage 3/4 interview. Proportions of reasoning greater than 10% often reflected less than a full CJ on the score sheet, but proportions less than 10% never reflected a full CJ or more. Therefore our error boundary is conservative. Using the assessment of one full CJ as an indication of stage presence would have allowed us to treat many more entries as error. That is, our 10% boundary errs in the direction of treating as real some entries that are in fact error rather than in treating as error entries that are real. Even so, we find that only 9% of our longitudinal interviews show a third stage of reasoning greater than 10%. Using a less conservative cutoff, we find that only 1% of our interviews show a third stage of reasoning greater than 20%.

It is safe to say, then, that very few interviews show any use of three stages of moral judgment. Where three stages do appear, they are always adjacent stages. It is unclear, however, whether the instances where a third stage is used should be interpreted as cases of measurement error not caught by our conservative error boundary or as real but unusual cases of stage heterogeneity in the subject's thinking. In at least two cases, to be discussed in more detail later, we interpret the lack of consistency as a real phenomenon. These two cases – Subject 2, Time 4, and Subject 65, Time 2 – were the two that Kohlberg (1973) identified as representing a relativistic, transitional type of thinking that he called "Stage $4\frac{1}{2}$." Note that both of these cases represent sequence anomalies in our analysis as well as the absence of "structured wholeness."

Factor Analyses

Theoretical expectations lead us to believe that moral judgment development is a single general domain cutting across verbal dilemmas and issues. To examine this hypothesis, we factor analyzed the correlations among stage scores on each of the issues across the dilemmas.

Correlation matrices for the whole population and for the 16–17-year age group are given in Tables 3.7 and 3.8. The correlations are all positive and moderately high, consistent with our expectations. Table 3.8 indicates that the correlations among moral issues are not due simply to their common correlation with age since the correlations remain positive and moderately high even within a single age group. The 16–18-year age group was used for this analysis because it is the group in which the number of subjects is largest.

Table 3.9 shows the results of the principal components analysis. The first row of each age group shows the highest and second highest eigenvalue and corresponding percentage of variance accounted for. The succeeding eigenvalues were much smaller (21) and therefore were not reported. The next three rows give the highest and second highest eigenvalues for each of the three forms. With all subjects pooled, the second eigenvalue is less than 1 and therefore, by convention, is disregarded. Within the different age groups the second eigenvalue barely exceeds 1 and adds very little to the percentage of variance contributed by the first factor.

Table 3.10 gives the unrotated first factor loading, for the entire sample on all 18 issues and for each separate form. The loadings of each issue varied from one dilemma to another, so that no single issue is the best representative of a general moral judgment level.

In spite of the marginal contribution of succeeding factors in the age group with the largest number of subjects, we extracted all factors with eigenvalues greater than 1. The unrotated loadings for that age group (16–18 years) are given in Table 3.11. After the first general factor, the loadings on the specific

Table 3.7. *Correlations among 18 moral issues for total sample* (Ns *in parentheses*)

	Life (A1)	Law (A2)	Morality and con-science (A3)	Punish-ment (A4)	Contract (A5)
Law (A2)	.74 (204)				
Morality and conscience (A3)	.73 (165)	.67 (149)			
Punishment (A4)	.69 (156)	.76 (154)	.68 (115)		
Contract (A5)	.70 (219)	.66 (200)	.61 (166)	.65 (156)	
Authority (A6)	.67 (290)	.63 (193)	.61 (159)	.59 (154)	.66 (212)

	Life (B1)	Law (B2)	Morality and con-science (B3)	Punish-ment (B4)	Contract (B5)	Authority (B6)
Law (A2)	.74 (174)	.66 (167)	.74 (161)	.69 (170)	.67 (165)	.76 (139)
Morality and conscience (A3)	.74 (144)	.70 (138)	.73 (135)	.66 (140)	.52 (136)	.70 (113)
Punishment (A4)	.69 (136)	.65 (128)	.68 (121)	.69 (135)	.61 (131)	.77 (103)
Contract (A5)	.68 (187)	.69 (179)	.71 (171)	.64 (180)	.62 (182)	.67 (149)
Authority (A6)	.64 (178)	.65 (175)	.64 (170)	.64 (171)	.59 (175)	.66 (144)

	Life (quality) (C1)	Life (quan-tity) (C2)	Morality and con-science (C3)	Punish-ment (C4)	Contract (C5)	Law (C6)
Law (A2)	.65 (115)	.70 (77)	.71 (152)	.74 (132)	.70 (161)	.68 (159)
Morality and conscience (A3)	.57 (97)	.55 (68)	.60 (119)	.67 (100)	.60 (127)	.62 (125)
Punishment (A4)	.64 (87)	.75 (58)	.67 (113)	.79 (104)	.66 (121)	.66 (117)
Contract (A5)	.62 (131)	.60 (93)	.55 (165)	.61 (144)	.62 (177)	.62 (174)
Authority (A6)	.57 (129)	.66 (86)	.57 (160)	.57 (141)	.53 (172)	.60 (167)

Table 3.7. (*cont.*)

	Life (A1)	Law (A2)	Morality and conscience (A3)	Punishment (A4)	Contract (A5)	Authority (A6)
Life (B1)	.69 (188)	.74 (174)	.74 (144)	.69 (136)	.68 (187)	.64 (178)
Law (B2)	.60 (179)	.66 (167)	.70 (138)	.65 (128)	.69 (179)	.65 (175)
Morality and conscience (B3)	.71 (176)	.74 (161)	.73 (135)	.68 (121)	.71 (171)	.64 (170)
Punishment (B4)	.61 (178)	.69 (170)	.66 (140)	.69 (135)	.64 (180)	.63 (171)
Contract (B5)	.50 (180)	.67 (165)	.52 (136)	.61 (131)	.62 (182)	.59 (175)
Authority (B6)	.66 (148)	.76 (139)	.70 (113)	.77 (103)	.67 (149)	.66 (144)

	Life (B1)	Law (B2)	Morality and conscience (B3)	Punishment (B4)	Contract (B5)
Law (B2)	.86 (161)				
Morality and conscience (B3)	.88 (163)	.83 (152)			
Punishment (B4)	.81 (159)	.83 (161)	.79 (148)		
Contract (B5)	.71 (164)	.66 (157)	.66 (156)	.66 (158)	
Authority (B6)	.74 (143)	.78 (131)	.74 (135)	.72 (128)	.83 (133)

	Life (quality) (C1)	Life (quantity) (C2)	Morality and conscience (C3)	Punishment (C4)	Contract (C5)	Law (C6)
Life (B1)	.66 (116)	.66 (83)	.68 (149)	.70 (133)	.63 (155)	.70 (153)
Law (B2)	.62 (110)	.56 (76)	.67 (142)	.67 (127)	.62 (152)	.62 (144)
Morality and conscience (B3)	.68 (116)	.64 (78)	.66 (145)	.75 (130)	.64 (152)	.67 (150)
Punishment (B4)	.72 (111)	.69 (74)	.64 (138)	.74 (125)	.61 (142)	.66 (140)
Contract (B5)	.56 (118)	.49 (86)	.60 (149)	.64 (132)	.52 (161)	.58 (159)
Authority (B6)	.62 (102)	.55 (74)	.73 (119)	.77 (108)	.63 (127)	.64 (130)

Table 3.7. (*cont.*)

	Life (A1)	Law (A2)	Morality and con-science (A3)	Punish-ment (A4)	Contract (A5)	Authority (A6)
Life (quality) (C1)	.65 (130)	.65 (115)	.57 (97)	.64 (87)	.62 (131)	.57 (129)
Life (quantity) (C2)	.62 (91)	.70 (77)	.55 (68)	.75 (58)	.60 (93)	.66 (86)
Morality and conscience (C3)	.62 (168)	.71 (152)	.60 (119)	.67 (113)	.55 (165)	.57 (160)
Punishment (C4)	.67 (147)	.74 (132)	.67 (100)	.79 (104)	.61 (144)	.57 (141)
Contract (C5)	.59 (177)	.70 (161)	.60 (127)	.66 (121)	.62 (177)	.53 (172)
Law (C6)	.62 (175)	.68 (159)	.62 (125)	.66 (117)	.62 (174)	.60 (167)

	Life (B1)	Law (B2)	Morality and con-science (B3)	Punish-ment (B4)	Contract (B5)	Authority (B6)
Life (quality) (C1)	.66 (116)	.62 (110)	.68 (116)	.72 (111)	.56 (118)	.62 (102)
Life (quantity) (C2)	.66 (83)	.56 (76)	.64 (78)	.69 (75)	.49 (86)	.55 (74)
Morality and conscience (C3)	.68 (149)	.67 (142)	.66 (145)	.64 (138)	.60 (149)	.73 (119)
Punishment (C4)	.70 (133)	.67 (127)	.75 (130)	.74 (125)	.64 (132)	.77 (108)
Contract (C5)	.63 (155)	.62 (152)	.64 (152)	.61 (142)	.52 (161)	.63 (127)
Law (C6)	.70 (153)	.62 (144)	.67 (150)	.66 (140)	.58 (159)	.64 (130)

	Life (quality) (C1)	Life (quan-tity) (C2)	Morality and con-science (C3)	Punish-ment (C4)	Contract (C5)
Life (quantity) (C2)	.83 (75)				
Morality and conscience (C3)	.65 (120)	.57 (86)			
Punishment (C4)	.70 (101)	.64 (71)	.89 (146)		
Contract (C5)	.58 (129)	.59 (89)	.62 (167)	.69 (146)	
Law (C6)	.63 (127)	.66 (91)	.68 (164)	.75 (146)	.82 (182)

94

Note: All correlations are significant at $p < .001$.

Table 3.8. *Correlations among 18 moral issues for 16–17-year-old age group* (Ns *in parentheses*)

	Life (A1)	Law (A2)	Morality and conscience (A3)	Punishment (A4)	Contract (A5)
Law (A2)	.58 (37)				
Morality and conscience (A3)	.41[a] (26)	.22[c] (23)			
Punishment (A4)	.77 (29)	.68 (27)	.11[c] (19)		
Contract (A5)	.49 (42)	.30[a] (37)	.11[c] (26)	.52[b] (29)	
Authority (A6)	.47 (37)	.29[c] (33)	.25[c] (24)	.21[c] (28)	.41[b] (38)

	Life (B1)	Law (B2)	Morality and conscience (B3)	Punishment (B4)	Contract (B5)	Authority (B6)
Life (A1)	.49[b] (37)	.45[b] (34)	.64 (30)	.38[a] (30)	.28[a] (36)	.44[a] (28)
Law (A2)	.57 (33)	.47[b] (30)	.50[b] (27)	.70 (29)	.46[b] (32)	.71 (25)
Morality and conscience (A3)	.13[c] (24)	.46[a] (25)	.27[c] (19)	.22[c] (20)	.05[c] (24)	.51[a] (19)
Punishment (A4)	.64 (29)	.35[a] (24)	.57[b] (21)	.61 (23)	.37[a] (27)	.49[a] (19)
Contract (A5)	.42[a] (37)	.53[b] (34)	.48 (29)	.44[b] (30)	.37[a] (37)	.33[a] (29)
Authority (A6)	.26[c] (33)	.46[b] (32)	.59 (28)	.36[a] (28)	.10[c] (35)	.22[c] (26)

	Life (quality) (C1)	Life (quantity) (C2)	Morality and conscience (C3)	Punishment (C4)	Contract (C5)	Law (C6)
Life (A1)	.24[c] (28)	.18[c] (19)	.45[b] (33)	.60 (28)	.27[c] (37)	.29[a] (36)
Law (A2)	.41[a] (25)	.46[a] (17)	.59 (28)	.57[b] (25)	.54[b] (33)	.50[b] (32)
Morality and conscience (A3)	.29[c] (21)	−.07[c] (14)	.19[c] (21)	.33[c] (16)	.07[c] (24)	.19[c] (23)
Punishment (A4)	.07[c] (19)	.35[c] (13)	.41[a] (22)	.71 (22)	.61 (26)	.50[b] (24)
Contract (A5)	.21[c] (29)	.31[c] (20)	.17[c] (32)	.37[a] (27)	.47[b] (38)	.49[b] (37)

Table 3.8. (*cont.*)

	Life (quality) (C1)	Life (quantity) (C2)	Morality and conscience (C3)	Punishment (C4)	Contract (C5)	Law (C6)
Authority (A6)	.27[c] (27)	.17[c] (19)	.20[c] (29)	.42[a] (25)	.09[c] (34)	.29[c] (33)

	Life (A1)	Law (A2)	Morality and conscience (A3)	Punishment (A4)	Contract (A5)	Authority (A6)
Life (B1)	.49[b] (37)	.57 (33)	.13[c] (24)	.64 (29)	.42[a] (37)	.26[c] (33)
Law (B2)	.45[b] (34)	.47[b] (30)	.46[a] (25)	.35[a] (24)	.53[b] (34)	.46[b] (32)
Morality and conscience (B3)	.64 (30)	.50[b] (27)	.27[c] (19)	.57[b] (21)	.48[b] (29)	.59 (28)
Punishment (B4)	.38[a] (30)	.70 (29)	.22[c] (20)	.61[b] (23)	.44[b] (30)	.36[a] (28)
Contract (B5)	.28[a] (36)	.46[b] (32)	.05[c] (24)	.37[a] (27)	.37[a] (37)	.10[c] (35)
Authority (B6)	.44[a] (28)	.71 (25)	.51[b] (19)	.49[a] (19)	.33[a] (29)	.22[c] (26)

	Life (B1)	Law (B2)	Morality and conscience (B3)	Punishment (B4)	Contract (B5)
Law (B2)	.67 (32)				
Morality and conscience (B3)	.74 (28)	.56[a] (26)			
Punishment (B4)	.78 (27)	.63 (26)	.77 (21)		
Contract (B5)	.45[b] (34)	.38 (31)	.14 (28)	.69 (27)	
Authority (B6)	.41[a] (26)	.24[c] (25)	.39[c] (19)	.50[a] (20)	.55[b] (25)

	Life (quality) (C1)	Life (quantity) (C2)	Morality and conscience (C3)	Punishment (C4)	Contract (C5)	Law (C6)
Life (B1)	.29[c] (25)	.57[b] (19)	.31[a] (30)	.54[b] (27)	.43[b] (34)	.52[b] (33)
Law (B2)	.23[c] (26)	.35[c] (18)	.34[a] (28)	.36[a] (24)	.26[c] (33)	.55[b] (31)

Table 3.8. (*cont.*)

	Life (quality) (C1)	Life (quantity) (C2)	Morality and conscience (C3)	Punishment (C4)	Contract (C5)	Law (C6)
Morality and conscience (B3)	.55[b]	.57[a]	.38[a]	.50[b]	.21[c]	.46[b]
	(21)	(14)	(25)	(23)	(27)	(27)
Punishment (B4)	.49[a]	.68[b]	.43[a]	.68	.48[b]	.62
	(22)	(16)	(26)	(21)	(27)	(26)
Contract (B5)	.18[c]	.24[c]	.18[c]	.23[c]	.21[c]	.38[a]
	(26)	(20)	(28)	(25)	(35)	(33)
Authority (B6)	.03[c]	−.05[c]	.40[a]	.55[b]	.38[a]	.37[a]
	(23)	(16)	(22)	(19)	(27)	(27)

	Life (A1)	Law (A2)	Morality and conscience (A3)	Punishment (A4)	Contract (A5)	Authority (A6)
Life (quality) (C1)	.24[c]	.41[a]	.29[c]	.07[c]	.21[c]	.27[c]
	(28)	(25)	(21)	(19)	(29)	(27)
Life (quantity) (C2)	.18[c]	.46[a]	−.06[c]	.35[c]	.31[c]	.17[c]
	(19)	(17)	(14)	(13)	(20)	(19)
Morality and conscience (C3)	.45[b]	.59	.19[c]	.41[a]	.17[c]	.20[c]
	(33)	(28)	(21)	(22)	(32)	(29)
Punishment (C4)	.60	.57	.33[c]	.71	.37[a]	.42[c]
	(28)	(25)	(16)	(22)	(27)	(25)
Contract (C5)	.27[c]	.54[b]	.07[c]	.61	.47[b]	.09[c]
	(37)	(33)	(24)	(26)	(38)	(34)
Law (C6)	.29[a]	.50[b]	.19[c]	.50[b]	.49	.29[c]
	(36)	(32)	(23)	(24)	(37)	(33)

	Life (B1)	Law (B2)	Morality and conscience (B3)	Punishment (B4)	Contract (B5)	Authority (B6)
Life (quality) (C1)	.29[c]	.23[c]	.55[b]	.49[a]	.18[c]	.10[c]
	(25)	(26)	(21)	(22)	(26)	(23)
Life (quantity) (C2)	.57[b]	.35[c]	.57[a]	.68[b]	.24[c]	−.05[c]
	(19)	(18)	(14)	(16)	(20)	(16)
Morality and conscience (C3)	.31[a]	.34[a]	.38[a]	.43[a]	.18[c]	.40[a]
	(30)	(28)	(25)	(26)	(28)	(22)
Punishment (C4)	.54[b]	.36[a]	.50[b]	.68	.23[c]	.55[b]
	(27)	(24)	(23)	(21)	(25)	(19)
Contract (C5)	.43[b]	.26[c]	.21[c]	.48[b]	.21[c]	.38[a]
	(34)	(33)	(27)	(27)	(35)	(27)
Law (C6)	.52[b]	.56[b]	.46[b]	.62	.38[a]	.37[a]
	(33)	(31)	(27)	(26)	(33)	(27)

Table 3.8. (*cont.*)

	Life (quality) (C1)	Life (quantity) (C2)	Morality and conscience (C3)	Punishment (C4)	Contract (C5)	Law (C6)
Life (quantity) (C2)	.75 (17)					
Morality and conscience (C3)	.43[a] (25)	.47[a] (17)				
Punishment (C4)	.01[c] (19)	.34[c] (12)	.87 (26)			
Contract (C5)	.28[c] (28)	.67[b] (18)	.49[b] (31)	.59[b] (27)		
Law (C6)	.22[c] (29)	.60[b] (19)	.58 (30)	.69 (27)	.77 (37)	

Note: All correlations not marked by [a], [b], [c] are significant at $p < .001$.
[a] $p < .05$.
[b] $p < .01$.
[c] Not significant.

Table 3.9. *Eigenvalues and associated percentage of variance for 18 issues and for each form in the total sample and three age groups*

Groups and issues	First eigenvalue	Variance (%)	Second eigenvalue	Variance (%)
All subjects (N = 190):				
18 issues	12.35	68.6	.84	4.7
6 issues A	4.35	72.5	.47	7.8
6 issues B	4.83	80.6	.49	8.3
6 issues C	4.43	73.8	.63	10.4
16–18 years (N = 40):				
18 issues	8.27	46.0	1.87	10.4
6 issues A	3.06	50.9	1.30	17.1
6 issues B	3.69	61.4	1.05	17.5
6 issues C	3.63	60.6	1.29	21.5
20–22 years (N = 29):				
18 issues	7.91	43.9	2.05	11.4
6 issues A	2.57	42.8	1.16	19.4
6 issues B	3.90	65.0	.99	16.5
6 issues C	3.26	54.3	1.12	18.6
28–30 years (N = 30):				
18 issues	8.62	47.9	2.46	13.7
6 issues A	3.50	58.4	.86	14.4
6 issues B	4.30	71.7	.74	12.3
6 issues C	2.68	44.6	1.64	27.4

Table 3.10. *First factor loadings* (N = *190*)

	18 × 18	6 × 6
Form A (alone):		
Life	.80	.87
Law	.86	.86
Morality and conscience	.79	.80
Punishment	.84	.82
Contract	.78	.79
Authority	.75	.76
Form B (alone):		
Life	.89	.92
Law	.84	.91
Morality and conscience	.88	.90
Punishment	.85	.87
Contract	.75	.79
Authority	.86	.86
Form C (alone):		
Life	.79	.81
Law	.77	.78
Morality and conscience	.80	.83
Punishment	.87	.90
Contract	.78	.79
Authority	.81	.86

Table 3.11. *Unrotated loadings for five factors in the 16–18 age group*

	1	2	3	4	5
Life	.68	.34	.24	.19	−.14
Law	.79	.09	−.10	−.04	.26
Morality and conscience	.33	.29	.29	.24	.29
Punishment	.76	.24	−.17	−.09	−.27
Contract	.58	.05	.11	−.16	−.28
Authority	.46	.08	.41	.20	−.16
Life	.77	−.08	.12	−.26	−.15
Law	.65	.01	.30	−.11	−.09
Morality and conscience	.77	−.12	.46	.12	−.16
Punishment	.88	−.15	.08	−.28	.12
Contract	.51	.10	−.03	−.59	.28
Authority	.61	.54	−.07	−.12	.38
Life	.46	−.60	.30	.20	.38
Law	.64	−.75	−.12	.01	−.03
Morality and conscience	.66	−.03	−.32	.48	.22
Punishment	.80	.29	−.31	.33	−.12
Contract	.65	−.18	−.53	.01	−.10
Authority	.74	−.12	−.29	−.01	−.11
Eigenvalues	8.27	1.87	1.65	1.34	1.19
Variance (%)	46.00	10.40	9.20	7.20	6.60

factors are greatly diminished and reveal no consistent patterns that could be interpreted. Similar factor matrices resulted from the other age groupings.

In attempting to determine the existence and nature of a multifactorial solution, the factors were rotated using both orthogonal and oblique methods. Here, too, no clear interpretation is evident on inspection across the five factors. In summary, then, for several age groups and for the sample as a whole, no more than one interpretable factor emerged even when the multiple factors were subjected to orthogonal and oblique rotations. In all cases, the eigenvalue and corresponding proportion of variance accounted for by the first factor far exceeded those of succeeding factors. Therefore we conclude that moral judgment, as measured by the Interview Forms A, B, and C and scored using the Standard Form Scoring Manual, is a single, general domain.

Relation of Moral Judgment Stage to Age

As one would expect of a developmental variable, our data show a clear relationship between age and moral judgment stage. The correlation between age and WAS was .78. As shown in Table 3.12, mean weighted average score increases monotonically from 189 (Stage 2) at age 10 to 375 (Stage 4[3]) at age 36. As shown in Figure 3.1, the frequency of usage of Stages 1 and 2 decreases from age 10 on, Stage 3 increases up to age 16–18 and then decreases, and Stage 4 begins at zero and rises monotonically to 62% at age 36. Stage 5 also increases monotonically after its entry at age 20–22 but never rises above 10% of the reasoning in the sample as a whole.

Table 3.12 presents the data in terms of global as well as weighted average scores. As that table indicates, the proportion of subjects at Stage 1/2 in the sample decreases from a high of nearly 48% at age 10 to 2% (one subject) at age 16–18. No subject is below Stage 2 after that. Subjects at Stage 2 decrease from about one third of the 10-year-olds to 11% of the late adolescents (age 16–18). No one beyond age 18 was scored as Stage 2. Very few subjects at age 20 or beyond were scored at Stage 2/3. Most of our 2/3 subjects were in the 13–14-year age group. The proportion of Stage 3 subjects increases up to age 18, then decreases to zero at our oldest age (36). The transition to Stage 4 does not seem to begin before late adolescence – we found only one Stage 3/4 subject before the 16–18-year age group. The proportion of 3/4 subjects in the sample increases through the early 20s and then levels off to a little less than half the sample. Consolidated Stage 4 did not occur in our sample before age 20, and the proportion of Stage 4s continued to increase through the oldest age in the study (age 36). The transition to Stage 5 occurs even later, with no Stage 4/5 subjects occurring before the mid-20s. The proportion of subjects reaching Stage 4/5 remains low (11%–16%) throughout the age range in which it appears, from the mid-20s through the mid-30s.

Looked at from the point of view of age norms in our sample, the interviews of most 10-year-olds were scored at Stage 1/2 or 2, a few were scored at 2/3. Most early adolescents (13–14) were 2/3, though some were Stage 2 or 3. Almost half of the late adolescents were scored as Stage 3, about one fourth had begun the transition to Stage 4, and a little less than one fifth were still in transition from Stage 2 to Stage 3. Youths in their early 20s were most likely to be in transition between Stages 3 and 4 or to be still solidly at Stage 3. About one fifth of these subjects had completed the transition to Stage 4. Most subjects from the mid-20s through the mid-30s were scored as Stage 3/4 mixtures

Table 3.12. *Percentage of subjects of each age group at each stage*

	Age (years)							
Global stage	10	13–14	16–18	20–22	24–26	28–30	32–33	36
1/2	47.6	8.1	2.2	0	0	0	0	0
2	33.3	16.2	11.1	0	0	0	0	0
2/3	14.3	56.8	17.8	9.4	8.0	0	0	0
3	4.8	16.2	44.4	31.3	12.0	16.2	8.7	0
3/4	0	2.7	24.4	40.6	48.0	51.4	47.8	44.4
4	0	0	0	18.8	16.0	18.9	30.4	44.4
4/5	0	0	0	0	16.0	13.5	13.0	11.1
Mean WAS	189	246	290	327	357	361	369	375
S.D. WAS	31.4	37.7	43.7	36.1	49.1	42.3	41.5	25.6
N	21	37	46	33	25	38	23	9

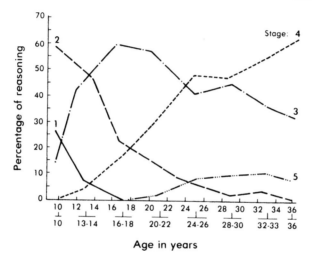

FIGURE 3.1.—Mean percentage of moral reasoning at each stage for each age group.

(or transitionals) with decreasing numbers at Stage 3 and increasing numbers at consolidated Stage 4. Subjects scored as postconventional (4/5 or 5) represent about one sixth to one eighth of the sample from the mid-20s on.

Curves of mean stage usage for a group do not necessarily represent curves of growth for any of the individuals in the group. Accordingly, we present figures of changes in stage usage over time from four representative individuals (Figures 3.2–3.5). These subjects were randomly chosen from among those who were tested at all six times, and they can be considered typical of our data. Subject 3, for example, never shows reasoning at more than two adjacent stages.[4] His reasoning at age 10 is scored at Stages 1 and 2. At age 13, his moral judgment remained dominantly Stage 2, but the Stage 1 has dropped out and has been replaced by substantial use of Stage 3. At age 14 the Stage 3 has become dominant and Stage 4 has entered as a second stage. This pattern re-

---

4 Note that we treat reasoning that represents less than 10% of the subject's total as error. For example, the 4% of Stage 3 at age 10 reflects less than one full CJ across all dilemmas scored and thus should not be considered to be true use of Stage 3 reasoning.

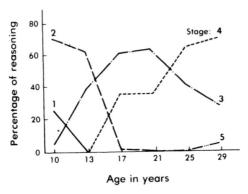

FIGURE 3.2.—Percentage of moral reasoning at each stage for each age: subject 3 (10 years old at time 1).

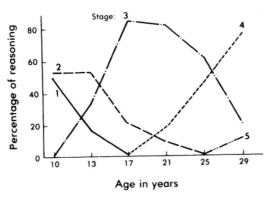

FIGURE 3.3.—Percentage of moral reasoning at each stage for each age: subject 9 (10 years old at time 1).

mains stable between ages 17 and 21, but as he reaches young adulthood Stage 4 begins to predominate over Stage 3. Between ages 21 and 25 this trend continues, with the proportion of Stage 4 usage increasing and the proportion of Stage 3 decreasing. Perhaps most noteworthy is the orderliness and regularity of the developmental curves, with earlier stages dropping out as later stages enter such that the subject seems to be always in transition from one stage to the next. Also noteworthy is the fact that development continues throughout the age range sampled, never reaching a final plateau. The figure for Subject 9 shows a similar pattern, except that some use of Stage 1 seems to linger even after the entry of Stage 3 at age 13. (This may be due to the fact that scoring errors confusing Stages 1 and 3 are common when responses are ambiguous or poorly probed.) The rate of development for Subject 9 is slower than that for Subject 3, with Stage 2 still in evidence at age 17 and Stage 4 barely above the error boundary at age 21. Development between ages 25 and 29 is particularly striking in this subject, however, and at age 20 he is scored globally as consolidated Stage 4, whereas Subject 3 remains globally at Stage 4(3) at that age. Subjects 37 and 42 also show the regular pattern of movement through the stages. These figures are of particular interest in that they show substantial

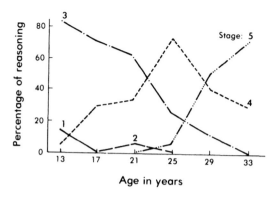

FIGURE 3.4.—Percentage of moral reasoning at each stage for each age: subject 37 (13 years old at time 1).

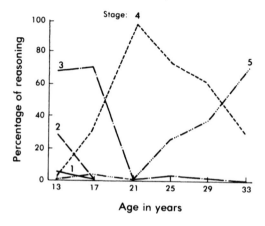

FIGURE 3.5.—Percentage of moral reasoning at each stage for each age: subject 42 (13 years old at time 1).

development occurring into young adulthood – between ages 29 and 33. Stage change with age in all four subjects seems to alternate between periods of fairly rapid development and periods of slower development or consolidation. The curves for Subject 3, for example, are especially steep between ages 13 and 17, plateau to some degree between 17 and 21, and become steep again, indicating a second growth period between ages 21 and 25. Furthermore, in all four cases a fairly saltatory model of development appears justified. That is, the absence at each time of three-stage mixture not only supports the assumption that reasoning at a given time forms a structured whole, it also bears on the process of development. The point here is that for the most part Stage 1 has dropped out by the time use of Stage 3 has begun, Stage 2 had dropped out by the time use of Stage 4 has begun, and so on. The holistic character of the developmental change is evident across the entire age range in our study.

Cohort Effect

Our sample can be considered to be composed of subjects from three cohorts: those who were 10 years old at Time 1, those who were 13 at Time 1, and

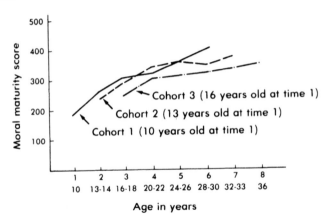

FIGURE 3.6.—Mean weighted average scores at each age for each cohort.

those who were 16 at Time 1. When data from these three groups are analyzed separately, we find that they all show the same moral judgment patterns. That is, subjects from all three groups demonstrate "structured wholeness" and invariant stage sequence in their moral judgment. As is shown in Figure 3.6, the mean weighted average scores for the three groups differed somewhat, particularly in that the means for the Time 1 16-year-olds were lower at each testing time than were the means for the Time 1 10-year-olds. The difference is not significant, however, and is most likely due to sampling procedures. The 10- and 13-year-olds were chosen from an elementary school; the 16-year-olds were chosen from a high school in the same community. Although each cohort was composed of half working-class and half middle-class subjects, there was a tendency for the high school subsample to come from somewhat lower socio-economic origins within the broader working-class and middle-class categories than was true for the younger subjects. That is, the high school tended to draw the lower end of both the working-class ("lower" rather than "upper lower" class) and the middle-class (lower middle and middle rather than upper middle class) categories. This may have resulted in the consistent though nonsignificant tendency for the Time 1 16-year-olds to score a little lower than the others at each testing time. Based on the information available to us, there is little reason to believe that the slight group mean differences represent a historical cohort effect. Neither do we interpret the data as indicating a practice effect on the moral judgment interview since in our test–retest analysis we found no such practice effect.

Stability of Individual Differences

Our data bear on the question of whether there are stable individual differences in rate of moral judgment development. The issue here is whether scores at one age predict to scores at a later age. As Table 3.13 shows, the correlations between weighted average scores at age 10 and scores at ages 13, 17, and 21 are positive and significant but not very high. The age 10 scores do not predict adulthood scores at all. In contrast, moral judgment scores at age 13 are much more highly correlated with later scores, even with scores at age 32–33. Though the *highest* correlation between scores at age 10 and those from a later testing

Table 3.13. *Correlations among weighted average scores at different ages* (Ns *in parentheses*)

Age (years)	Age (years)						
	10	13–14	16–18	20–22	24–26	28–30	32–33
13–14	.395[a]						
	(21)						
16–18	.456[a]	.699[a]					
	(15)	(30)					
20–22	.473[a]	.464[a]	.683[a]				
	(18)	(24)	(31)				
24–26	.198	.696[a]	.732[a]	.710[a]			
	(13)	(23)	(21)	(19)			
28–30	−.249	.668[a]	.685[a]	.481[a]	.905[a]		
	(10)	(23)	(36)	(23)	(16)		
32–33		.571[a]	.448[a]	.764[a]	.862[a]	.809[a]	
		(10)	(23)	(12)	(7)	(21)	
36			.164	−.119		.083	.880[a]
			(10)	(6)		(10)	(8)

[a] $p < .05$.

was .47, the *lowest* correlation between scores at age 13 and later ones was .46 and the correlations ranged up to .70. Scores at age 16 do not seem to predict later scores any better than do the scores at age 13, but at age 20 the scores again seem to increase in stability to some degree.[5] (By stability we mean maintenance of relative rank order rather than a decrease in developmental change within individuals.) It seems, then, that there are two periods during which stabilization in this sense occurs. The first occurs between ages 10 and 13, that is, as the subjects enter adolescence. The second period of stabilization occurs between the ages of about 17 and 21, that is, as the subjects enter early adulthood. This does not necessarily imply that these are periods of particularly rapid development in moral judgment. In fact, the mean increase for the group as a whole was not much greater between ages 10 and 13 than between ages 13–14 and 16–18, nor was it greater between ages 16–18 and 20–22 than between 13–14 and 16–18. As was shown in Table 3.12, the increase in mean WAS with age is gradual and quite even across the age range studied. Rather, these periods of stabilization reflect a tendency for subjects to shift their positions in relation to each others' moral judgment scores as they enter adolescence and again as they enter adulthood.

The Relationship of Moral Judgment to Other Variables

Given the existence of fairly stable individual differences in moral judgment stage, the question arises as to what determines these differences. Our study provides data on a number of variables that might be expected to be related to moral judgment stage. These variables include socioeconomic status of origin,

5 Recall that the test–retest correlations were in the high 90s. This indicates that the unexplained variance in predicting from earlier to later ages cannot be attributed to measurement error.

Table 3.14. *Correlations between moral judgment and social class, sociometric status, IQ, and education*

	Age (years)							
	10 (N = 21)	13–14 (N = 36)	16–18 (N = 46)	20–22 (N = 34)	24–26 (N = 24)	28–30 (N = 38)	32–33 (N = 23)	36 (N = 10)
$r_{WAS, SES}$	.60[a]	.41[a]	.41[a]	.56[a]	.36[a]	.22[a]	.41[a]	.59[a]
$r_{SMS, SES}$	.36	.12	.17	.04	−.17	.22	.18	−.35
$r_{IQ, WAS}$	.19	.25	.17	.27	.37[a]	.51[a]	.60[a]	.37
$r_{education, WAS}$	—	—	—	—	.69[a]	.54[a]	.59[a]	.77[a]

[a] $p < .05$.

sociometric status (as measured at Time 1), IQ (group test scores taken from school records at Time 1), and educational level attained.

Socioeconomic Status. As Table 3.14 indicates, correlations between parents' SES and subjects' moral judgment scores were moderate at every age. They ranged from .22 to .60, and all but two were above .40. There was no tendency for the relationship to either strengthen or attenuate with age, and the fluctuations of correlations across age showed no clear pattern.

Perhaps more enlightening is a comparison of working-class and middle-class subsamples on mean percentage of each stage used at each age. As shown in Figure 3.7, the distributions are quite different for the two subsamples. Both Stages 3 and 4 exceed the 10% error cutoff level at earlier ages in the middle-class group. Stage 3 is present at age 10 for middle-class subjects but not until age 13 for working-class subjects. Stage 4 appears at age 16 in the middle-class group but not until age 20 in the lower SES group. Furthermore, Stage 2 remains above the 10% cutoff somewhat longer for lower SES subjects. Whereas Stage 5 use exceeds 10% at age 28 in the upper SES group, it never exceeds the error cutoff in the lower SES group.[6]

Sociometric Status. Correlations between weighted average score and sociometric status were substantially lower than correlations between moral judgment scores and SES. Except at age 10 they did not achieve significance. Again no clear pattern emerged in fluctuation of SMS/WAS correlations across time (see Table 3.14).

A comparison of stage × age figures (Figure 3.8A, B) for sociometric integrates and isolates reveals that Stage 3 exceeds the 10% cutoff at age 10 in the integrated group but does not do so among the isolates until age 13. In addition, the isolates at age 10 show substantially more Stage 1 use than do 10-year-old sociometric integrates. Stage 1 drops below 10% at age 13 for integrates but not until age 16 for isolates. As the correlations show, differences in sociometric groups beyond age 13 are minimal. Overall, then, the data show that at the time that sociometric status was evaluated, integrates tended to show more

6 The Stage 5 present in the low SES group is due to one subject (Case 2) reaching Stage 4/5 at age 24. Since he was age 10 at Time 1 and age 28 at Time 6, he was not interviewed at age 32 or 36. That is, the decrease in mean percentage of Stage 5 does not reflect a decrease in Stage 5 use in any one subject, but rather the absence of the one Stage 4/5 subject at the last two ages.

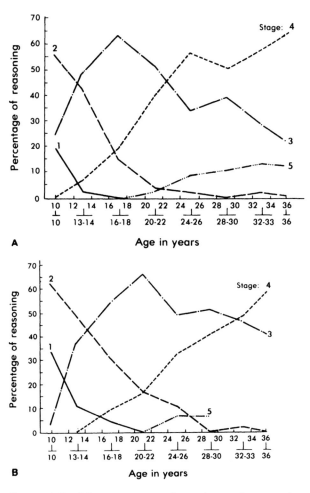

FIGURE 3.7.—Mean percentage of moral reasoning at each stage for each age group. A, High-SES subject. B, Low-SES subject.

Stage 3 and less Stage 1 than sociometric isolates. However, the difference between groups is not maintained over time.

A multiple regression analysis indicates that age accounts for 60% of the variance in weighted average scores. Adding SES raises the proportion of variance accounted for to 67%, and adding sociometric status adds very little, raising the proportion of variance accounted for to 68%. Because SES was not reassigned for adult subjects who may have changed in social class and because sociometric status was assessed only at Time 1, these figures on the relative importance of age, SES, and SMS should be interpreted cautiously.

Intelligence. Correlations between weighted average score and IQ were nonsignificant and ranged from .17 to .27 in childhood and adolescence for our sample but become substantially higher at age 24 and above (.37–.60) (see Table 3.14). Except at age 36 (an analysis that included only 10 subjects), the correlations increase steadily from age 24 on and are significant at the three age levels between 24 and 33. This occurs in spite of the fact that IQ was assessed only at Time 1. It appears, then, that whereas rate of moral development in

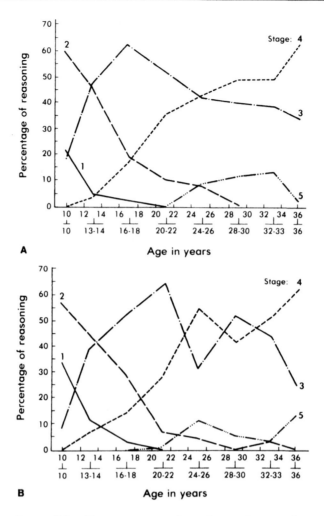

FIGURE 3.8.—Mean percentage of moral reasoning at each stage for each age group. A, Sociometric integrates. B, Sociometric isolates.

childhood and adolescence is only slightly related to IQ, the final level achieved in adulthood is more closely related to intellectual capacity, perhaps partly via differential educational experiences that are related to intelligence.

Educational Level Attained. Correlations between adult weighted average score and educational level attained ranged from .54 to .69 ($p < .05$), with no clear relationship between strength of correlation and age (see Table 3.14). (Only ages 23, 27, and 31 are reported because formal education for many subjects was not completed before age 23 and the N at age 36 is small.) Note that these correlations are somewhat higher than the correlations between moral judgment and either social class or IQ.

Partial correlations substantiate the interpretation that moral judgment stage is related to educational experience itself rather than to educational level as a reflection of IQ and SES differences. The correlation between WAS and sub-

Table 3.15. *Relation between education and moral judgment divided by social class*

| Stage | Education (%) | | | |
	Finished high school only	Some college	Four years college and/or B.A.	Graduate school, M.A. and/or Ph.D.
Working class				
4/5	—	—	—	33 (N=1)
4	—	17 (N=1)	33 (N=1)	33 (N=1)
3/4	75 (N=3)	83 (N=5)	67 (N=2)	33 (N=1)
3	25 (N=1)			
Middle class				
4/5	—	—	14 (N=1)	50 (N=5)
4	—	33 (N=1)	57 (N=4)	50 (N=5)
3/4	50 (N=2)	67 (N=2)	29 (N=2)	—
3	50 (N=2)	—	—	—

Note: Data taken from age groups 28–36.

ject's education with IQ partialed out is .36 ($p < .05$), at age 28, the only age at which the N was large enough to make a partial correlation feasible. The correlation between WAS and subject's education with parents' SES partialed out is slightly higher, $r = .45$ ($p < .05$) at age 28. The correlation between WAS and education with both IQ and SES partialed out was somewhat lower but still significant, $r = .26$, $p < .05$. It appears, then, that educational experience per se is related to moral judgment maturity beyond the association of education to SES and IQ.

Table 3.15 presents the moral judgment × education data in a way that is perhaps more revealing than a correlational analysis. The table indicates that no subjects from either working-class or middle-class origins achieved consolidated Stage 4 moral judgment without attending at least some college and no subject from either social class achieved Stage 4/5 without having completed college. (Recall in this regard that no one reached Stage 4 before age 20 and no one reached Stage 4/5 before age 24.) Whereas more middle-class than working-class subjects reached Stages 4 and 4/5, both of these moral judgment levels were attainable by subjects of working-class origins who had attended college. (No statistical analysis was performed on these data because expected values in the tables' cells were less than 5.)

Discussion

The results of this study provide strong support, at least within the limits of the sample, for the central claims and assumptions of Kohlberg's theory of moral development and for the validity of the Standard Issue Moral Judgment Interview and Scoring System as a measure of Kohlberg's stages. As discussed in chapters 1 and 2, Standard Issue Scoring yields more orderly data than did earlier scoring systems. This is no doubt due both to the psychometric advantages of the current system and to the radical redefinition of the stages that preceded and accompanied development of Standard Issue Scoring.

Age Norms

An important aspect of the change in moral judgment scoring criteria is that the current system stresses more heavily the need for the rater to look beyond the subject's superficial verbal responses to the conceptual significance of those responses for the individual. This is achieved methodologically through intensive probing of statements made in the interviews (e.g., What do you mean by that? Why is that important?) and by requiring each interview–manual match to undergo a structural evaluation based on the stage structure paragraph provided with each criterion judgment. One result of this shift is that people are less likely to be "given credit" for clichés and language that resemble those of higher stages if they do not exhibit the appropriate conceptual underpinning. This means that stage criteria are in general more stringent than in earlier scoring systems. The result is a fairly radical change in age norms.

Figure 3.9 presents percentage of stage usage for the middle-class longitudinal subjects aged 10 through 24 using Sentence Rating scores (Figure 3.9A) and Standard Issue scores (Figure 3.9B).[7] The distributions are clearly very different. One noteworthy difference is that the Sentence Rating scores show spread across a wider range of stages for each age. This no doubt reflects a tendency for the early scoring system to treat content differences as developmentally significant both within and across subjects.

Along with the greater variance in the Sentence Rating scores, we see a tendency for Sentence Rating scores to be higher than those using the Standard Issue System. In the early analysis, Stage 4 is in evidence at age 10 and is relatively heavily used at ages 13 and 16. In our analysis there is no use of Stage 4 at age 10, less than 10% at age 13, and less than 20% use of Stage 4 even at age 16. The difference in use of Stage 5 is even more dramatic. Sentence Rating assigns some Stage 5 scores to subjects as young as age 13 and shows Stage 5 as the group's most frequently used stage at age 16. We show no use of Stage 5 until age 24.

As subjects move from age 16 to age 20, Stages 4 and 5 reverse in the early analysis. That is, at age 16 Stage 5 predominates over Stage 4 whereas at age 20 Stage 4 predominates over Stage 5. This reversal indicates the presence of sequence anomalies in the early data such that a number of subjects scored at Stage 5 at age 16 were scored as Stage 4 at age 20. The Standard Issue data show no such reversal. Between ages 16 and 20 Stage 4 use increases steadily and Stage 3 use decreases. There is no evidence of Stage 5 until age 24 and

---

7 Only the middle-class subsample is used because a comparable figure for the total sample based on Sentence Rating scores was not available.

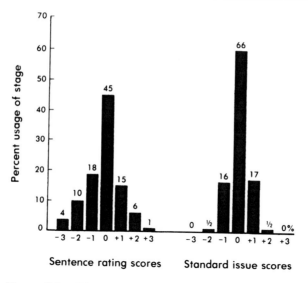

FIGURE 3.9.—Distribution of stage usage. Sentence rating for high-SES subjects. Standard scoring for high-SES subjects.

Stage 5 use does not decrease once it has occurred. This results in a very different picture of stage use in late adolescence and early adulthood than had been assumed previously. According to Standard Issue Scoring, moral judgment at age 20 is essentially completely conventional, whereas using the 1958 system subjects show substantial representations of Stages 4, 5, 3, and 2.

In summary, both within and across subjects, Standard Issue scores show greater homogeneity than scores reported in earlier analyses of these data. The range of moral judgment stages used by middle-class American boys at a given age seems to be fairly limited. From our current perspective it is clear that Sentence Rating profiles were reflecting a range of content emphases or orientations rather than a range of qualitatively different structures. Superficial differences that in the earlier system were treated as structurally significant are no longer represented by different stage scores.

One important issue raised by the difference in the two analyses is the question of adulthood stages. In light of the emergence of Stages 5 and 6 in adolescence, Kohlberg and Kramer (1969) concluded that "there was no new way of thinking about the moral situations that was found in adulthood and not found in adolescence" (p. 105).[8] Our interpretation of this finding is that the early scoring systems could not discriminate properly among superficially similar moral judgments at Stages 3, 4, and 5. This meant that when "true Stage 5" began to emerge in early adulthood, it was not recognized as a qualitatively new form of reasoning. We can now discriminate principled reasoning from superficially similar conventional reasoning, and we no longer see Stage 5 being used in junior high or high school. This means that there *is* a new stage in adulthood and that many of our subjects continued to develop in their 20s and 30s, rather than reaching a ceiling in mid-adolescence. This result is intuitively appealing since 30-year-olds often do seem to be more sophisticated in their moral judgment than 16-year-olds. However, it does raise the question of whether

8 Kohlberg and Kramer analyzed interviews of some longitudinal subjects as old as age 24 as well as the moral judgment interviews of their fathers.

Stage 5 is a "naturally developing" stage in the strict Piagetian sense (see Gibbs, 1979).

Along with the age shift in onset of Stage 5, we also see a reduction in the prevalence of principled moral judgment once it begins to appear. In our analysis, Stage 5 scores do not rise above 15% even at age 36, whereas Kramer (1968) shows almost 30% Stage 5 use at age 16. According to Standard Issue Scoring, the percentage of individuals who reach at least the 4/5 transition in adulthood is only 16%. Kramer reports that about 30% of the subjects in his analysis have at some point shown substantial usage of Stage 5.

In evaluating studies that used Structural Issue Scoring, it is important to note that there is closer agreement between Standard and Structural Issue Scoring than between Standard Issue Scoring and Story or Sentence Rating. In this longitudinal sample, the correlation between global scores derived from Standard and Structural Issue Scoring Systems is .84 ($n = 115$).

Individual Differences

Our results support the assumption that relative maturity of moral judgment is a fairly enduring characteristic of individuals throughout their development and becomes even more stable in adulthood. That is, if an adolescent is advanced in his moral judgment relative to his age peers, he is likely to be advanced in adulthood as well. However, the correlations are not so high as to preclude some changes in relative position for many subjects. Bloom (1964) has suggested that shifts in stability of individual differences in intelligence are useful in defining open periods for educational intervention. There are a number of problems in taking this idea literally in the domain of intelligence (Kohlberg, 1968) and in moral judgment. However, the fairly dramatic increase in correlation with adult scores that occurs between the ages of 10 ($r = .20$) and 13 ($r = .70$) suggests that the period before 13 years may be particularly fruitful for educational stimulation or intervention. This implication of the findings is discussed at length elsewhere (Kohlberg, 1970).

Social Role and Status Variables and Moral Development

The variable of sociometric status was included in the original design in order to illuminate Piaget's (1965) argument that peer group participation is an important determinant of moral judgment maturity. Our data provide some very limited support for this hypothesis in that our sociometric integrates used more Stage 3 and less Stage 1 than the sociometric isolates. Of course, there is no way of knowing whether these results are due to Stage 3 children being more popular or whether more active peer group involvement and social interaction facilitate the transitions out of Stage 1 and into Stage 3. Both are theoretically possible, and both may have occurred. In any case, the effect of sociometric status in childhood, at least as measured here, does not seem to extend beyond the transition to Stage 3.

Differences in socioeconomic status, on the other hand, seem to be associated with moral judgment differences across the entire stage range. Whereas peer group participation may be especially important for the onset of Stage 3, social class seems to be related to the development of Stages 4 and 5 as well as 3. Many more middle-class than working-class subjects reached both consolidated Stage 4 and the postconventional 4/5 level, although Stages 4 and 4/5 do seem to be accessible to college-educated subjects with working-class origins. In previous writing, Kohlberg (1969) had interpreted social class differences in rate and terminus of development as reflecting differential participation in and identification with the society and its secondary institutions. It is argued that this differential participation creates differential role-taking opportunities for middle-class and working-class children which allow those from the middle class to experience, for example, being integral participants in the society and thus to develop the social system perspective that characterizes Stage 4. Since the design controlled for IQ, the relation between moral judgment and SES cannot be accounted for by IQ differences between working-class and middle-class subjects.

Educational attainment is, however, confounded with social class. Formal education is itself a very important experience that is more often available to middle-class individuals and may mediate at least to some degree the relation between moral maturity and social class. Whereas only 37% of our working-class sample completed college, 71% of our middle-class sample did so. However, when the variables of social class and educational attainment are separated, as in Table 3.15, it appears that social class is related to moral judgment stage even with educational level held constant. Although the small Ns preclude any definite conclusions, the table indicates that, except for the "high school only" group, the scores are higher for middle-class than working-class subjects within each of the three education levels – some college, completed college, and graduate school. This suggests that the differential experiences of middle-class and working-class children include but go beyond differential opportunities for formal education.

Formal Education and Moral Development

The finding of a moderate relationship ($r = .54$) between moral judgment stage and education is not surprising given the cognitive-developmental nature of the moral judgment stages. As noted earlier, we found that none of our subjects reached Stage 4 without having attended some college, and none reached the 4/5 level without having completed college. This does not imply that college study is always necessary for development of consolidated Stage 4 or movement to Stage 5. In an era or a culture with less emphasis on formal education or less accessibility to college, one might find many self-educated people at Stage 4 or 5. However, the relationship does suggest that development to the higher stages is facilitated by educational experience. Using Rest's Defining Issues Test (DIT), G. Rest (1977) found a comparable moderate correlation ($r = .45$) between education and moral judgment in adults.[9]

IQ and Moral Development

The cognitive basis of Kohlberg's stages is also reflected in moderate correlations between IQ and moral judgment. Although the positive correlations point to the cognitive component in moral development, the modest size of the cor-

---

9 Rest's Defining Issues Test involves the presentation of hypothetical moral dilemmas along with a set of stage-keyed ideas, issues, or considerations relevant to resolution of each dilemma. The subject is asked to rate and rank the importance of these considerations in this thinking about the dilemma. Scores are based on the relative importance for the subject of considerations at the six moral judgment stages.

relations (.37–.59 for our sample) indicates that moral judgment is not reducible to intelligence. As in the case of educational experience, correlations between IQ and moral judgment as measured by the DIT are comparable to those between IQ and moral judgment in our sample. Rest (1979) reports that most studies have found IQ × DIT correlations in the .20–.50 range. (Recall that ours range from .37 to .59 between ages 19 and 36.)

College Relativism and "Regression" in the Longitudinal Sample

Readers familiar with the work that was generated in response to Kramer's (1968) finding of sequence anomalies may wonder what happened to "Stage 4 1/2." This phenomenon – an apparent regression from Stage 5 to Stage 2 or 3 in late adolescence – was first interpreted (Kohlberg & Kramer, 1969) as a "functional regression in the service of the ego." Kohlberg (1973) later reinterpreted the phenomenon as a structural progression characterizing the transition from conventional to principled moral judgment for some subjects.

In fact, only one of the anomalous cases in the original analysis can be attributed to the phenomenon Kohlberg called Stage 4 1/2. As Table 3.5 indicates, Standard scores for Case 2 went from a 3/4 score at the end of high school to college-period scores of Stage 3 on Form A, Stage 2/3 on Form B, and Stage 3/4 on Form C. This scatter and regression in moral judgment scores coincided with nonscorable metaethical views of ethical relativism and ethical egoism. On follow-up 4 years later, Case 2 had moved to a postconventional score of 4/5, as Table 3.5 indicates. Case 2 was one of the cases discussed in Kohlberg's (1973) account of college transitional relativism.

A second case discussed as "Stage 4 1/2" in Kohlberg (1973) was Case 65. Table 3.5 indicates that Case 65 was scored as Stage 3 (Standard Issue Scoring) at the end of high school. In college his scores were Stage 4 on Form A, Stage 2 on Form B, and Stage 2/3 on Form C. Like Case 2, Case 65 gave evidence of moral cynicism and relativism in spontaneous college interview material. Unlike those of Case 2, however, Case 65's scattered college scores, including Stage 2 judgments, did not represent a transition from conventional to principaled or postconventional reasoning. Before his college moral "crisis," Case 65 had reasoned primarily at Stage 3. After this crisis, his reasoning was successively Stage 3/4 and Stage 4.

Our current interpretation of the phenomenon of "college-age relativism" is that it does not necessarily represent a transitional period between Stages 4 and 5. Instead, moral relativism appears to be a metaethical position that can be taken at a number of different developmental stages. Whereas the level of sophistication of the relativistic metaethic may differ developmentally, the effect of this stance on normative judgments appears to be very much the same whether the subject is moving from Stage 4 to Stage 5 or shifting within the conventional level. The increased stage scatter in these interviews can be interpreted as reflecting a breakdown of faith in the currently held moral frame of reference with no substitution of a more adequate system. Subjects in this position sometimes refuse to make moral judgments. When they do make moral judgments they seem to rely on whatever has some lingering validity for them even if these intuitions from Stages 2, 3, and 4 fail to represent a coherent whole.

The Stage Model

Let us turn now to the more usual pattern of moral judgment development. Our data seem to provide strong support for the strict Piagetian stage model of development. With regard to the criterion of "structured wholeness" or internal consistency, we found that the great majority of our interviews were scored at only one moral judgment stage or at most two adjacent stages. Only 9% showed evidence of a third stage. On the average, across nine independently scored dilemmas, two thirds of all scores were assigned at the subject's modal stage and almost all the remaining scores (32%) were assigned to a single stage adjacent to the modal stage. The structured wholeness assumption was also supported by the high degree of alternate form and test–retest reliability, the high Cronbach's α, and the results of factor analyses of issue and dilemma scores.

The factor analyses indicate that there was a single factor of general moral level across the domain of dilemmas and issues. The absence of issue or dilemma factors along with the absence of scatter across more than two adjacent stages indicates that we have succeeded in defining a coherent moral domain united by a single underlying organizational structure. This position contrasts with that taken by Damon (1977), who argues that, at least in young children, the moral domain is broken down into a number of issues or dimensions each with its own unique structure. The two moral issues on which Damon has focused are authority and distributive justice. Although Damon's research does not use Kohlberg's hypothetical dilemmas, it is clear that Kohlberg's dilemmas do involve both authority and distributive justice. If Damon's interpretation of the moral issues as independently organized were true at the age level addressed by our study, the factor analysis should have indicated multiple factors rather than a single general factor of moral stage that cuts across the content of the dilemmas.

This high degree of structural coherence within each interview leads to a relatively saltatory picture of development if we compare interviews across time for any single individual. Developmental change in any given 3-year period seems to involve predominantly an increase in the next higher stage of reasoning along with a simultaneous decrease in the lower stage. This means that the subject is most often in transition between two adjacent stages, has given up using all earlier stages, and uses no reasoning more than one stage above his modal stage. This contrasts with a model in which the distribution of a subject's reasoning extends across all five stages and in which development involves the gradual increase in use of the higher stages along with decrease (but not decrease to zero) in use of lower stages. Kohlberg's early results based on the Sentence Rating method may have appeared to support this latter model but we now interpret those results as artifactual (i.e., due to inappropriate definition of the scoring unit and a confusion between moral judgment content and structure).

Our results also support the Piagetian stage models' assumption of invariant developmental sequence. With a few exceptions that can be attributed to scoring error, each of our subjects proceeded through the stages in the prescribed order, neither skipping stages nor regressing to an earlier level once a later stage had been attained.

This stage model of development has recently been criticized – in the cognitive domain by Flavell (1971) and, most directly, in the moral judgment domain by Rest (1979). As discussed in chapter 1, Rest argues for a "complex" (rather than "simple") stage model in which individuals use several stages simultaneously and development consists of increased usage of the higher stages and decreased usage of the lower stages. He interprets our finding of internal consistency as a methodological artifact and points to his own results with the DIT as consistent with a more complex model of development.

One interpretation of the discrepancy between Rest's results and ours derives from the fact that the DIT is measuring comprehension and preference of moral judgments made by others while the Standard Issue System is measuring an individual's spontaneous production of moral judgments in response to very open ended questions. We suggest that the development of moral judgment as a whole (including comprehension and preference as well as spontaneous production) may be too broad in scope for what Rest calls the "simple stage model." Development of moral judgment comprehension and preference may not follow a stagelike pattern even though spontaneous production appears to do so when assessment conditions pull for the subject's competence.

This would mean that the developing individual has one basic framework for resolving moral dilemmas and justifying those resolutions. This framework has some coherence for the individual and undergoes developmental transformation, hierarchically integrates the insights from lower levels, and so on. On the other hand, other aspects of moral development such as the comprehension of judgments made by others may not be stagelike in this sense. In fact, given Kohlberg's assumptions, there is little reason to expect that subjects will comprehend statements at only one stage (or at two adjacent stages). Rather, they can be expected to comprehend all stages below their own as well as possibly a stage or two above their own. Thus we would not characterize the development of moral judgment comprehension as following a stagelike sequence. Preference for moral judgments made by others is somewhat more problematic, however. According to a simple stage model, how would one explain the endorsement of judgments that represent stages below one's own level of spontaneous production? One possible explanation derives from the Piagetian assumption of hierarchical integration. That is, although the stage as a whole may undergo transformation as the individual develops, many of the insights achieved at the lower stages remain valid from the higher stage perspective though they are now embedded in a more complex and sophisticated position. For example, the Stage 3 judgment that "you ought to keep a promise because the person you promised trusts you" would be endorsed or agreed to by individuals who reason predominantly at Stages 4 and 5 as well as Stage 3. The difference is that at the higher stages one's conception of trust and reasons for its importance have developed beyond what is available at Stage 3.

Another consideration with regard to Rest's preference data is methodological. When subjects endorse an item on the DIT, it is not clear how they understand the item. The Standard Issue Moral Judgment Interview involves probing for elaboration and clarification and pooling all responses to the dilemma that refer to a single idea (as defined by norm and element). This system will naturally lead to greater internal consistency than assigning a score for each unelaborated statement the subject judges to have some validity. We do not interpret our finding as an artifact. It is true, as Rest points out, that according to Standard Issue Scoring rules an interview cannot receive more than one stage (or stage transition) score for a single norm–element intersection. However, scores at all five stages may be assigned to a single issue, dilemma, or interview if interview–manual matches at those stages occur. In fact, such variance does not occur in our data even though the nine dilemmas were scored independently and by three different raters. We agree with Rest that moral judgment comprehension and preference are important aspects of moral development that are separable from spontaneous moral judgment production and that a full developmental account of an individual's moral judgment requires scores on all those aspects (that is, the information from the various sources is not redundant). However, we feel that a careful look at our methods and data should convince the reader of the validity of the Piagetian stage model for describing the development of spontaneous moral judgment at least within the limits of our instrument and sample.

In general, then, we interpret the results of this study as consistent with cognitive-developmental theory, in particular as consistent with a stage model of development. The results in relation to moral judgment compare favorably with longitudinal studies of the stage model in purely cognitive development (Kohn, 1969). Our subjects did seem to use a coherent structural orientation in thinking about a variety of moral dilemmas. Their thinking developed in a regular way up the stage sequence, neither skipping stages nor reverting to use of a prior stage. Our results also serve to validate the moral judgment stages as operationally defined in Standard Issue Scoring and to indicate that the Standard Issue System is a reliable and valid measure of moral judgment.

Four

A Longitudinal Study of Moral Judgment in Turkish Males

with Mordecai Nisan

Basic assumptions of cognitive-developmental approaches lead to the proposition that both stages and sequence in the development of moral reasoning are universal, or culturally invariant. According to cognitive-developmental theorists (Piaget, 1932/1965; Kohlberg, 1969), moral judgment represents underlying thought organization rather than specific responses; its development results from a process of interaction between organismic structuring tendencies and universal features of social experience, rather than from "transmission" through genetics or direct shaping; and the direction of development is toward greater equilibration in the organism–environment interaction and reciprocity between the self and other. These features of the development of moral judgment are said to lead to a culturally invariant sequence of stages, or hierarchical organizations, each more differentiated and integrated, and thus more equilibrated, than its predecessor (Kohlberg, 1971c). Although the specific content or moral judgment may vary among cultures, the basic structures are said to be universal. Kohlberg's description of the stages (Kohlberg, 1976) is an attempt to expose such structures.

The hierarchical organization attributed to the stages implies that the individual should proceed through them in an invariant order. Evidence for this claim is provided by cross-sectional (Kohlberg, 1963; Rest, Davison, & Robbins, 1978), longitudinal (Kohlberg, 1973; Kuhn, 1976; Rest et al., 1978), and experimental (Turiel, 1966; Rest, Turiel, & Kohlberg, 1969) studies with U.S. subjects. Cross-sectional studies in Kenya (Edwards, 1975), Honduras (Gorsuch & Barnes, 1973), the Bahamas (White, 1975), India (Parikh, 1980), and New Zealand (Moir, 1974) provide support for the universality claim. However, universality is properly tested by longitudinal studies of individuals in different cultures. In one such short-term longitudinal study, White, Bushnell, and Regnemer (1978) assessed the level of moral judgment in Bahamian pupils over 2 or 3 consecutive years. Their results support the hypothesis that moral judgment advances with age (at least through the first three stages). However, their analysis is limited to group means. They do not examine whether all observed individuals do indeed develop in the sequence delineated by the theory. Turiel, Edwards, and Kohlberg (1978) did examine this point. Theirs was

This chapter was originally published as M. Nisan and L. Kohlberg, 1982, "Universality and Cross-Cultural Variation in Moral Development: A Longitudinal and Cross-Sectional Study in Turkey" *Child Development, 53,* 865–76. The original citation reflects the author's relative contributions to the paper.

a longitudinal and cross-sectional analysis of moral judgment among village and city subjects in Turkey. The sequential advance of each individual anticipated by Kohlberg's theory was indeed found in this sample. The results also indicated that the rate of development was slower among village than among city subjects.

The first aim of the present study is to examine further the universality claim by broadening and elaborating the study of Turiel et al. Included are data collected in 1976, providing data over a longer time period. The study now includes subjects who were interviewed four times, into their 20s. More subjects were also added to the cross-sectional study in the oldest age group. The invariant sequence hypothesis can thus be examined more adequately and for more mature subjects. The broadening of age range is of special interest in light of results from the United States that show that moral development continues into the third decade of life. We would like to see whether this holds true for the Turkish subjects, and also whether there is a ceiling in moral development not passed by our oldest village subjects, as is the case in at least one traditional society (Edwards, 1975).

Furthermore, all the material used in this study (i.e., both earlier and recent interviews) was scored according to Standard Issue Scoring. The increased objectivity of this scoring method over earlier systems is especially valuable in a cross-cultural study, where interpretations of the material are more prone to personal bias.

Methods[1]

Subjects

Data were collected from male subjects in three locations in Turkey: a rural village (population 1,580 in 1960); a seaport provincial capital (population 520,000); and the national capital (population over 1 million). Subjects from the village were boys attending the local school, young workers, and young men who had recently returned from serving in the Turkish army. These subjects represent a fairly traditional society according to the criteria used by Lerner (1958) in dealing with Turkish society. Subjects from the cities were elementary school, high school, and college students or young workers. All city subjects analyzed in the present study were middle-class (judged by parental occupation).

Interviewing took place in 1964, 1966, 1970, and 1976. In 1964, 23 village subjects, aged 10–17 years, were tested. In 1966, 15 of these subjects were retested and 10 village subjects were added to the sample. In 1970, 6 of the village subjects were retested and 15 college students ages 18–25 were interviewed. In 1976, 9 of the village subjects and 5 of the city subjects were retested. Thus some of the subjects were interviewed only once, whereas others were interviewed two, three, or four times. All the subjects are included in the cross-sectional study; only those interviewed two or more times are included in the longitudinal study. The number of subjects in the longitudinal and cross-sectional studies, by age and social group, is presented in Tables 4.1 and 4.2. A complete picture of the longitudinal sample is given in Table 4.4.

1 Parts of this section are taken from Turiel et al. (1978). See that source for more details.

Table 4.1. *Number of subjects in the longitudinal study by year and age at testing*

Year of testing	Age at testing				
	10–12	13–15	16–18	19–23	24–28
1964	7	5	3	—	—
1966	7	9	6	2	—
1970	—	—	3	3	—
1976	—	—	—	9	5

Table 4.2. *Number of subjects in the cross-sectional study by age and social group*

Social group	Age (in years)				
	10–12	13–15	16–18	19–28	Total
Village	17	14	16	16	63
City	11	9	6	20	46

Note: Longitudinal subjects are represented more than once.

Moral Judgment Interview and Scoring

Each subject was given an individual oral interview, including (each year) the same six hypothetical moral dilemmas and a standard set of probing questions. These dilemmas were revised versions of Kohlberg's standard stories adapted to make them more suitable for the Turkish setting. An example of one such dilemma is presented in Table 4.3. In 1964 and 1966, the interviews were administered through an interpreter. In 1970 and 1976, the interviews were given by the same Turkish-speaking graduate student attending a university in the United States, who had been trained in the technique of moral judgment interviewing.

For the purpose of this study, all the interviews were organized by dilemmas, randomized by subjects and year, and then scored using the Standard Issue Scoring Manual which entails matching interview judgments to stage-oriented moral judgment criteria organized by moral issue (two issues per dilemma). Scoring was done by dilemma, not by protocol. Thus, one dilemma was scored for all subjects, then a second dilemma, etc. Scorers were blind to the identity, age, and social group of respondents. For each subject, percent usage of each of five stages of moral judgment was then computed as a function of all scored judgments. The subject then received a stage score, which could be a single stage (if only one stage had more than 20% of his judgments) or a mixed stage, indicating his dominant stage and secondary stage (when more than 20% of his judgments fell in this stage).[2]

2 Thus, in principle one could obtain a score indicating a mixture of more than two stages, and these could be far apart, e.g., 1(3)(5). This never happened in the present sample, where all subjects were either in one stage or in a mixture of two adjacent stages. Note that the coding and analysis of these data were completed prior to a change in algorithm which now requires 25% usage of a stage in order for that stage to be represented in the global score.

Table 4.3. *An example of a dilemma used in the study*

Dilemma III. Equivalent to Kohlberg's (1958) ''Heinz and the Drug''

A man and wife have just migrated from the high mountains. They started to farm, but there was no rain and no crops grew. No one had enough food. The wife became sick from having little food and could only sleep. Finally, she was close to dying from having no food. The husband could not get any work and the wife could not move to another town. There was only one grocery store in the village, and the storekeeper charged a very high price for the food because there was no other store and people had no place else to go to buy food. The husband asked the storekeeper for some food for his wife, and said he would pay for it later. The storekeeper said, ''No, I won't give you any food unless you pay first.'' The husband went to all the people in the village to ask for food, but no one had food to spare. So he got desperate and broke into the store to steal food for his wife.

1. *Should the husband have done that? Why?*
2. *Is it a husband's duty to steal the food for his wife if he can get it no other way?*
3. *Did the storekeeper have the right to charge that much?*
3a. *(If the subject thought he should steal the food:)*
   Why is it all right to steal if it is to save a life?
4. *If the husband does not feel very close or affectionate to his wife, should he still steal the food?*
4a. *(If the subject thought the husband should not steal the food:)*
   Would you steal the food to save your wife's life?
5. *Suppose it wasn't his wife who was starving but it was his best friend. His friend didn't have any money and there was no one in his family willing to steal the food. Should he steal the food for his friend in that case? Why?*
5a. *If you were dying of starvation but were strong enough to steal, would you steal the food to save your own life?*
6. *(Everyone:)*
   The husband broke into the store and stole the food and gave it to his wife. He was caught and brought before the judge. Should the judge send him to jail for stealing or should he let him go free?

Thirty protocols, randomly selected, were scored by another trained scorer. For 23 protocols (77%) there was complete agreement for the stage score, whereas for 7 protocols there was a discrepancy of a half stage (e.g. 2[3] and 3[2]). In no case was there a larger discrepancy. The correlation between the weighted average score (WAS) given by the two scorers was .83. Internal consistency was calculated over the scores received by the individual on the six dilemmas. The obtained Cronbach α figure was .72.

Results

Stage of Moral Judgment

Table 4.4 presents the global scores and WAS of subjects in the longitudinal study at each testing point. Each row presents one subject. The table allows us to follow the development of an individual's moral judgment at two, three, or four points in time, where the range of ages represented is 10–28 years. The table shows a clear sequence of advance in moral judgment: Out of 35 changes,

Table 4.4. *Global score and weighted average score (WAS) for longitudinal subjects*

Subject	10–11 Years		12–13 Years		14–15 Years		16–17 Years		18–19 Years		20–21 Years		22–23 Years		24–25 Years		26–28 Years	
	Stage	WAS	Stage	WAS	Stage	WAS	Stage	WAS	Stage	WAS	Stage	WAS	Stage	WAS	Stage	WAS	Stage	WAS
1	1	118	1(3)	186	—	—	—	—	—	—	—	—	2(3)	218	—	—	—	—
2	2(1)	150	2(3)	224	—	—	2(3)	239	—	—	—	—	3	281	—	—	—	—
3	1(2)	133	2	178	—	—	3(1)	229	—	—	—	—	3	296	—	—	—	—
4	—	—	1(2)	158	2(1)	177	—	—	3(2)	263	—	—	—	—	—	—	—	—
5	—	—	2(1)	192	2(3)	198	—	—	3(2)	247	—	—	—	—	3	294	—	—
6	—	—	—	—	2(3)	207	2(3)	208	—	—	—	—	—	—	—	—	—	—
7	—	—	—	—	—	—	3(2)	216	2(3)	243	—	—	3	311	—	—	3(2)	283
8	—	—	—	—	—	—	2	192	2	196	—	—	—	—	—	—	4(3)	365
9	1(2)	124	2	200	—	—	—	—	—	—	—	—	—	—	—	—	3	261
10	1(2)	146	2	209	—	—	—	—	—	—	—	—	—	—	—	—	—	—
11	—	—	1(2)	160	2	203	—	—	—	—	—	—	—	—	—	—	—	—
12	—	—	2(1)	176	2(3)	247	—	—	—	—	—	—	—	—	—	—	—	—
13	—	—	2(1)	188	1(2)	150	—	—	—	—	—	—	—	—	—	—	—	—
14	—	—	2	216	2(3)	207	—	—	—	—	—	—	—	—	—	—	—	—
15	—	—	—	—	—	—	2	217	2(1)	198	—	—	—	—	—	—	—	—
16	1(2)	153	—	—	—	—	—	—	—	—	4(3)	340	—	—	—	—	—	—
17	1(2)	172	—	—	—	—	—	—	—	—	4(3)	347	—	—	—	—	—	—
18	2	183	—	—	—	—	—	—	—	—	2(3)	231	—	—	—	—	—	—
19	2	191	—	—	—	—	—	—	—	—	4(3)	353	—	—	—	—	—	—
20	—	—	3(2)	259	—	—	—	—	—	—	—	—	4(5)	434	—	—	—	—
21	—	—	3(2)	277	—	—	—	—	—	—	—	—	3(4)	367	—	—	—	—
22	—	—	—	—	—	—	2(3)	230	—	—	—	—	—	—	—	—	2(3)	241
23	—	—	—	—	—	—	—	—	—	—	3(2)	218	3	296	—	—	—	—

Table 4.5. *Number of subjects in various stages by age and social group*

Age and social group	Stage 1	1/2	2	2/3	3	3/4	4	4/5	Total
10–12 years									
Village	1	12	3	1	—	—	—	—	17
City	—	4	2	4	1	—	—	—	11
13–15 years									
Village	—	5	3	6	—	—	—	—	14
City	—	1	—	8	—	—	—	—	9
16–18 years									
Village	—	2	2	12	—	—	—	—	16
City	—	—	—	4	1	1	—	—	6
19+ years									
Village	—	—	—	5	9	2	—	—	16
City	—	—	—	4	7	8	—	1	20

only 4, or 11.4%, go against our prediction, a distribution whose chance probability is only .001 (by sign test; Siegel, 1956). In no case do we find the skipping of a stage.

Table 4.5 presents the distribution of subjects in the cross-sectional study according to stage, by age and social group. Table 4.6 presents means and standard deviations of WAS according to age and social group. The WAS data were subjected to analysis of variance by age (four groups) and social group. The analysis showed a strong effect of age $F(3,101) = 48.1$, and of social group, $F(1,101) = 26.7$, both significant at .001 level, and no significant interaction. Further analysis (post hoc t tests) revealed that all age-group differences in each social group were significant at the .05 level.

An examination of Tables 4.5 and 4.6 suggests the following points: (1) In both village and city groups, the findings of the cross-sectional study are consistent with those of the longitudinal study. The results show a sequential advance with age through the stages of moral judgment. The correlation between WAS and age is .71 ($N = 109$). In no case do we find a regression in WAS mean of a group with advancing age. (2) The data show that the development of moral judgment continues after the age of 18 in both village and city subjects. This result is similar to findings in the United States, which show that moral development continues at least into the third decade of life (Kohlberg, 1973). This result is of special interest for the village population in light of the following points. (3) We find that the rate of moral judgment development is slower in the village than in the city and that this is also true for our oldest subjects. The differences between village and city subjects are statistically significant for each of the four age groups (significance is at the .01 level by post hoc t test in all four cases). (4) We find no subject older than 15 in the city or 18 in the village within a pure preconventional stage (i.e., Stages 1 and 2), although even in the oldest age group sampled we do find subjects in a mixed Stage 2–3. (5) Among the village subjects there is an indication of stabilization at Stage 3. Only 2 out of 16 (12.5%) in the oldest age group show any sign of

Table 4.6. *Means and standard deviation for WAS by age and group*

Social group	Age (in years)			
	10–12	13–15	16–18	19+
Village				
M	167.05	202.6	228.7	279.3
SD	31.19	31.4	27.7	39.9
City				
M	206.7	243.3	274.8	312.6
SD	51.4	32.9	34.3	41.0
t value	2.549[a]	2.979[a]	3.266[a]	2.457[a]

[a]$p < .01$.

Stage 4 development, as compared to 9 out of 20 (45%) city subjects of this age. The impression that village subjects stabilized at Stage 3 is strengthened by the tendency noted in point 6. (6) Table 4.4 shows that, in general, subjects tend to show a mixed rather than a pure stage. However, this tendency is weaker after the age of 18, especially for our village subjects. Up to the age of 18, only 13 out of 73 (17.8%) are in a pure stage (where a pure stage indicates that only one stage gets more than 20% of the scored responses of the subject), while after this age we find 9 out of 16 (56.3%) village subjects and 7 out of 20 (35%) city subjects showing pure Stage 3 responses. The difference between percentage of subjects of pure stage in the 10–18-year-old group and in the older age group is statistically significant, $\chi^2 = 7.18$, $p < .01$. The consistency in the moral reasoning of the older subjects, especially those from the village, suggests a tendency to stabilize, at least temporarily, at this stage of reasoning. Is it then the case that the village people tend to remain in Stage 3, as do Edwards's (1975) Kenyan subjects? No decisive answer is possible here without further follow-up of the village subjects.

Discussion

Universality in Development of Moral Judgment

The first aim of this study was to examine whether the claim of universal structures in moral reasoning, which grew mainly out of research in the United States, would find support in a different culture. Our Turkish village subjects represent a traditional culture quite distinct from the Western urban culture that characterized the subjects of the American longitudinal study reported in chapter 3. Two aspects of the claim of universality are that moral responses of individuals in any culture fit the structures suggested by Kohlberg (i.e., are classifiable in one of his stages) and that the stage sequence is constant across cultures. A longitudinal study is essential in examining this second element.

The present study has found support for both aspects of the claim, support that should be seen as only a single step in a necessarily much larger body of research in different cultures. The longitudinal study presents a consistent picture of sequential advance in the stages of moral development up to Stage 4, as well as in the quantitative WAS. This picture was supported in the cross-sectional study both in the village and in the city. It should be mentioned, however, that the sequence observed in this study is limited to the first four stages in Kohlberg's scheme – with the exception of one city-born youth.

Turning to the fitting of Kohlberg's stages to the Turkish data, it seems quite remarkable that the scorers had no difficulty and achieved satisfactory agreement analyzing the Turkish responses according to Kohlberg's stages, using a manual that requires a matching of responses. There were differences between Turkish and American responses, as well as between city and village. However, these differences did not interfere with the identification of basic structures that framed the responses. The scorers generally felt the match between actual responses and criterion judgments in the manual to be satisfactory and not forced.

One may argue that this apparent ease in scoring the Turkish data results from an inevitable overlaying of preconceptions on the data, leading to biased interpretation of the responses. This argument is somewhat weakened both by the relatively high reliability between judges and by the observed sequence in development. However, a more important – although far from conclusive – test of this argument would be the judgment of a sensitive and open person who is aware of the possibility of bias (Piaget, 1929). The scorer in this study was aware of the possibility of bias and sought for cross-cultural variance in addition to searching for universality. Our analysis rests, not on one standard and mechanical response, but on a multitude of judgments generated by several moral dilemmas, each possessing a number of questions. This seems to add to the credibility of the scoring. Yet there is no doubt that more research with maximal openness to the possibility of bias is needed (Price-Williams, 1975).

A related issue concerns the representativeness of our data. Do the dilemmas presented to the subjects constitute true moral issues in their lives? Do their responses to these dilemmas represent genuine thinking in these domains rather than "playing the researcher's game"? The best we can do in regard to these basic problems of cross-cultural research is to examine the dilemmas and the responses from this viewpoint, using relevant ethnographic material (Cole et al., 1971). Our impression is that the dilemmas are representative. The least we can say is that the Turkish responses were given with an appropriate sense of reality and involvement. Again, more research and further examination of these issues are clearly needed.

The universality claim may have another ramification to which this study does not relate. A strong claim of universality would imply that the structures described by Kohlberg exhaust more or less the whole domain of morality in every culture. Even if one assumes a degree of success in representing the moral domain of one's own culture, such an assumption does not seem as simple for other cultures. It is possible that in other cultures, principles are held that are distinct from ours, and moral reasoning is used that does not fit the structures described by Kohlberg. This is likely in regard to higher stages of moral development. Gibbs (1977) has suggested that only the first four stages described by Kohlberg meet the criteria for a naturalistic developmental sequence, whereas the higher stages, which are almost absent in our interviews, appear to be formalized extensions of earlier stages. Such extensions seem to be culture dependent and may take forms that are hard for "outsiders" to identify. Examination of this argument would require – in addition to an agreed-upon definition of the moral domain – the study of a broader sample of moral dilemmas, composed though cooperation with expert and sensitive informants from other cultures.

The Rate of Development and Cultural Variation

The universality claim allows for the possibility of differences in the rate and end point of development. Such differences are indeed revealed in this study. The rate of development is slower among village than among city subjects. The findings do indicate that after the age of 16, all village subjects develop beyond the preconventional level and show Stage 3 judgment (or a mixture of Stages 2 and 3). At the same time, they show scarcely any sign of development beyond Stage 3. Clearly, the data cannot show whether village subjects will adopt Stage 4 judgment in the future. However, the high frequency of a pure Stage 3 and the almost complete lack of Stage 4 among the oldest subjects indicate that Stage 3 may be the stage in which the judgment of village subjects is stabilized, later development being mainly in a further decline of Stage 2 judgments. This coincides with the finding of Stage 3 as the final point of development in the traditional culture studied by Edwards (1975) and supports her suggestion that Stage 3 is a necessary and sufficient level of functioning in societies having a social order based on face-to-face relationships and a high level of normative consensus. These conditions may not necessitate differentiation and integration beyond Stage 3. Thus we have here an equivalent – in the moral domain – of what Berry (1971) has called ecological functionalism.

Five

The Development of Moral Reasoning among Kibbutz Adolescents: A Longitudinal Study

with John Snarey and Joseph Reimer

This chapter presents the results of a longitudinal study of moral reasoning among Israeli adolescents. The research objectives were to evaluate Lawrence Kohlberg's theory of moral development from the cross-cultural perspective of an Israeli kibbutz and to gain an understanding of the cultural uniqueness of kibbutz social-moral reasoning from the perspective of Kohlberg's theory.

The data presented, based on a sample of 92 kibbutz-born and Middle Eastern aliyah adolescents (those whose families have immigrated to Israel from the Arab countries), are able to address these objectives since this is the largest and longest cross-cultural longitudinal study of moral reasoning to date, in contrast to most cross-cultural studies of moral development, which have been cross-sectional. These studies have previously been reviewed by Edwards (1981, 1982) and Snarey (1982, 1985). The sample also includes males and females in contrast to Kohlberg's original longitudinal study in the United States (Kohlberg, 1958, 1981a; Colby et al., 1983) and Nisan and Kohlberg's longitudinal study in Turkey, both of which included only males (Turiel, Edwards, & Kohlberg, 1978; Nisan & Kohlberg, 1982). Finally, the present study also attempts to replicate many of the same analyses that were performed in the United States and in Turkey, the two previous longitudinal studies that have used the standardized scoring system (Colby et al., 1983). This will enable us to make specific comparisons among the samples and to begin to clarify the cross-cultural validity of Kohlberg's model and method.

Hypotheses

This study considers six specific research questions. The first four apply conventional psychological indicators of reliability and validity to Kohlberg's theory. To what degree does the development of moral reasoning in a kibbutz population, as measured by Kohlberg's instrument, follow the same patterns as shown by other populations who have been studied? The final two research questions apply anthropological methods to Kohlberg's theory. In what ways does the moral reasoning of kibbutzniks differ from that of people from other cultures studied using comparable methods?

This chapter was originally published as J. Snarey, J. Reimer, and L. Kohlberg, 1984, "The Sociomoral Development of Kibbutz Adolescents: A Longitudinal, Cross-Cultural Study." *Developmental Psychology, 21*, 3–17.

Developmental Questions

1. Stage Sequence. The invariant-sequence assumption of Kohlberg's moral development theory should be supported by the combined results of the blind-scored longitudinal data. Stage change should be upward and sequential, and stage regressions should not be found beyond the level explainable by scoring error (Kurtines & Greif, 1974; Broughton, 1978a; Kohlberg, 1984).

2. Structural Wholeness. Structural wholeness is a critical empirical criterion of construct validity. The internal consistency of the stages was previously established for subjects in the United States, using the standardized scoring manual (Kohlberg, 1981a; Colby et al., 1983). A replication of their analyses on the kibbutz longitudinal data should yield similar findings.

3. Age Norms and Stages. Moral judgment can be expected to be positively correlated with age, as developmental theory suggests and previous research has found. The age norms among kibbutz subjects will also be compared with the findings from previous research.

4. Sex Differences. Kohlberg's theory predicts that although there will be no difference cross culturally in the sequence of stages in the moral development of males and females, there may be differences in the rate of development due to an inequality of sex roles in particular societies. From an anthropological perspective, however, the general equality of sex roles in the kibbutz socialization process also suggests that sex differences in the rate of moral development should not be expected among kibbutz subjects. The issue of sex differences in moral judgment is a topic of current debate (Gilligan, 1977, 1982), of course. Yet, because kibbutz ideology stresses equality of sex roles, at least as an ideal, we would anticipate that there would not be sex differences in the development of moral reasoning among kibbutzniks.

Cultural Questions

5. Culturally Defined Moral Issues. There may be culturally based differences in choices that subjects make regarding the issue or content within a dilemma they will consider the most important. Each of Kohlberg's dilemmas requires the subject to make a content choice between two moral issues, for example, to steal or not to steal a drug. From an ethnographic perspective, one might expect Middle Eastern aliyah youth to more commonly favor particular kinds of action (such as upholding the law and authority) that reflect the content of moral reasoning stressed in their culture and families, whereas kibbutz-born subjects might be expected to more commonly select other choices (e.g., upholding conscience, life, contract). This difference between two groups, if it exists, would also be expected to decrease as aliyah students spend more time on the kibbutz.

6. Culturally Defined Moral Structure. Another aspect of the cultural uniqueness question, aside from content differences, is the possibility that the scoring manual simply misses or misunderstands particular structures of moral reasoning because of cultural differences between the subject and theoretician (Simpson, 1974; Bloom, 1977). We assessed the cultural uniqueness of stage formulations by examining interview material that the scorers indicated was difficult to score. This material was analyzed for patterns that relate to kibbutz norms and values.

Methods

Samples

Kibbutzim are intentionally created collective communities in Israel characterized by communal childrearing, collective economic production, and direct participatory democracy. The kibbutz under study, which we will call Ramat Yedidim, was founded in 1949 in the northern Galilean hills by a group of young Jewish men and women who had grown up in the Young Guard (Hashomer Hatzair) youth movement.

Kibbutz Ramat Yedidim's educational system, in general, is typical of the approach of other kibbutzim within the National Kibbutz Federation (Kibbutz Artzi), the federation most loyal to the traditional approach to structuring a kibbutz living environment. Small age-graded peer groups (kvutzot) live together in their own houses from infancy until age 18, when they enter the army. Each of these cohorts is given a name that serves some of the same identification functions as a family surname in the United States, although they also have family surnames. Each cohort of children has one or more full-time teachers who guides their formal education and also a houseparent or caretaker (metapelet) who is responsible for directing and socializing the children in the communal living and work activities of the children's house. Since, to a limited degree, their peers are experienced as their family and their educators as parental figures, there is an unusual unity to their educational, work, and social experiences. Kibbutz Ramat Yedidim has, however, modified an element of the traditional kibbutz movement's approach to educating adolescents in that it fully integrates city-born youth into the kibbutz educational system. Most of these youth are so-called Middle Eastern Jews, and they come from economically disadvantaged backgrounds. A group of these 12–13-year-olds is brought to the kibbutz, through the services of the Youth Aliyah organization, and after a year is fully integrated with a parallel cohort of kibbutz-born youth. This new cohort of kibbutz- and city-born youth is educated and lives together until early adulthood (Kohlberg and Bar-Yam, 1971; Reimer, 1977; Snarey, 1982).

The 92 adolescents in this study are divided into four subsamples, each of which corresponds to a kibbutz cohort. Each subsample of kibbutz-educated students includes both kibbutz-born and city-born adolescents. The subjects in all four subsamples were residing at Kibbutz Ramat Yedidim, with two exceptions: Subsample I was supplemented with kibbutz-born subjects from Kibbutz F and with two groups of city-born and city-educated youth; Subsample II was supplemented with a group of city-born kibbutz-educated youth from Kibbutz M (Table 5.1).

Research Instrument

Kohlberg's moral judgment interview, Form A, was used to collect the longitudinal data on moral development. The three dilemmas in Form A are III, the classic Heinz dilemma, involving a conflict between the issues of life and law;

Table 5.1. *Sample description*

Cohort number	Cohort name	Place of birth	Place of residence	Background data at first interview				
				Age	Grade	Males	Females	N
I A	Cyclamen Youth Aliyah	City	Kibbutz RY	15–17	10	10	0	10
I B	Federation Kibbutz Sabras	Kibbutz F	Kibbutz F	15–17	10	9	0	9
I C	Middle-class academic students	City	City	15–17	10	9	0	9
I D	Lower-class vocational students	City	City	15–17	10	10	0	10
II A	Sparrow Kibbutz Sabras	Kibbutz RY	Kibbutz RY	13–14	8	4	3	7
II B	Sparrow Youth Aliyah	City	Kibbutz RY	13–14	8	4	4	8
II C	Gazelle Youth Aliyah	City	Kibbutz M	13–14	8	6	5	11
III A	Crane Kibbutz Sabras	Kibbutz RY	Kibbutz RY	12–13	7	6	2	8
III B	Crane Youth Aliyah	City	Kibbutz RY	12–13	7	8	3	11
IV A	Turtledove Kibbutz Sabras	Kibbutz RY	Kibbutz RY	13–15	8	2	3	5
IV B	Turtledove Youth Aliyah	City	Kibbutz RY	13–15	8	1	3	4
Total						69	23	92

III', the Officer Brown dilemma, involving a judge's conflict between conscience and punishment; and Dilemma I, the Joe dilemma, involving a father–son conflict between contract and authority. Each dilemma is followed by 9–12 standardized probe questions designed to clarify the reasons why a subject has made a particular moral judgment.

The dilemmas and probe questions were translated into Hebrew and were also modified slightly; for example, U.S. dollars became Israeli pounds, Heinz became Moshe, and so forth.

Data Collection Procedure

The subjects were interviewed individually in Hebrew. Each interview was conducted privately, tape-recorded, and later transcribed. Moral judgment interviews were collected from the entire cohort shortly after a group of Youth Aliyah students arrived at Kibbutz Ramat Yedidim or shortly after the Youth Aliyah group was integrated with the parallel group of kibbutz-born subjects. All subjects in a particular subsample were then reinterviewed 1 or 2 years later and again 5 years later. For some kibbutz cohorts a city-residing comparison group was also interviewed. The interview schedule, according to both sample subgroups and frequency of interview, is presented in Table 5.2. The frequency of the longitudinal follow-up interviews may be summarized as follows: 32 subjects were interviewed three times each for a total of 96 interviews, 32

Table 5.2. *Interview schedule*

Cohort number	Cohort name	Time 1		Time 2		Time 3		Time 4		Time 5		Total interviews per cohort
		N	Ages	N	Ages	N	Ages	N	Ages	N	Ages	
I A	Cyclamen Youth Aliyah	10	(15–17)	6	(17–19)					6	(24–26)	22
I B	Federation Kibbutz Sabras	9	(15–17)							4	(24–26)	13
I C	Middle-class academic students	9	(15–17)									9
I D	Working-class vocational students	10	(15–17)									10
II A	Sparrow Kibbutz Sabras			7	(13–14)			7	(15–17)	7	(20–22)	21
II B	Sparrow Youth Aliyah			8	(13–14)			8	(15–17)	8	(20–22)	24
II C	Gazelle Youth Aliyah			11	(13–14)			11	(15–17)			22
III A	Crane Kibbutz Sabras					8	(12–13)			8	(18–19)	16
III B	Crane Youth Aliyah					11	(12–13)	11	(13–14)	11	(18–19)	33
IV A	Turtledove Kibbutz Sabras							5	(13–15)	5	(18–20)	10
IV B	Turtledove Youth Aliyah							4	(13–15)	4	(18–20)	8
Total interviews per year		38		32		19		46		53		188

subjects were interviewed twice for a total of 64 interviews, and 28 subjects were interviewed only once. Thus, altogether, there was a total of 188 interviews from the 92 subjects.

Scoring and Analysis

Moral development interviews were scored using the new *Standard Issue Scoring Manual* (Colby et al., 1983). This standardized scoring method yielded two indexes of moral development: a global stage score and a moral maturity score.

To assign each of the 188 interviews in this study a global stage score and a moral maturity score, they were divided and distributed randomly to three expert scorers, one of whom was a coauthor of the scoring manual. All interviews were scored blind from English transcripts, i.e., *without* knowing the subject's name, age, sex, cohort membership, time of testing, or scores assigned to other interviews. To assess *interrater reliability,* 20 interviews were selected randomly and scored independently by all three scorers. Comparing the level of agreement between the global stage scores, we found that in 65%–70% of the cases an interview received the exact same score from any two scorers. In 95% of the cases the interview received the same score or within one half of a stage score from all three scorers. The mean reliability between all three scorers was estimated to be .89 for the categorical global stage scores and .91 for the continuous weighted average score. To assess the *translation reliability,* seven interviews were also randomly selected for independent scoring in Hebrew by a bilingual scorer. The interrater correlation was .84 for the global stage scores and .93 for continuous scores. Translating the interviews, therefore, did not significantly alter the scoring reliability.

Findings and Analysis

Developmental Findings

The findings from the four samples will be combined in order to evaluate the degree to which they support the first three hypotheses regarding the basic theoretical assumptions of Kohlberg's developmental model and the reliability of the new scoring method. The results will also be compared with findings from two previous longitudinal moral development studies (chaps. 3 and 4) that have used the standardized scoring manual.

Developmental Sequence and Regressions.   According to Kohlberg, developmental sequence or stage change should be consecutive and upward, i.e., without regressions or omissions. Table 5.3 summarizes the types of stage changes that occurred in the interval from time n to time $n + 1$ among the 64 longitudinal subjects. Table 5.4 presents the actual interview scores for each of the 64 longitudinal subjects in the study.

As an examination of Tables 5.3 and 5.4 indicates, small amounts of regression occurred in 6 out of 96 longitudinal steps (6.3%) using the customary 9-point scale and regressions occurred in 7 out of 96 cases using the most differentiated 13-point scale. To evaluate this finding, previously reported test–retest reliability data can be used as an estimate of the number of such deviations that can be attributed to measurement error. Colby et al. (1983) have reported test–retest error for the Form A interview to be 19%. Colby and colleagues also report that the longitudinal regressions in the United States were 5% for the Form A interview using the 9-point scale and 7% using the 13-point scale and thus conclude that since the test–retest reversals are well over twice as great as the longitudinal reversals, it seemed reasonable to attribute the violations of longitudinal sequence to measurement error (1983). One might add, of course, that some of the nonreversals might also be due to measurement error, but it still seems reasonable to conclude that the assumptions regarding developmental sequence and regressions are supported by the kibbutz findings since the percentage of violations of the longitudinal sequence in this kibbutz longitudinal study was nearly identical to the finding in the U.S. longitudinal study reported in chapter 3. This conclusion is also supported by the fact that in no case did a longitudinal subject completely skip a stage. Each subject reached his or her highest stage at the last interview time by going through each of the preceding intermediate stages between the first and last interview stage scores.

Structural Wholeness.   Kohlberg has suggested that in addition to invariant sequence, the most critical empirical criterion of construct validity is structural wholeness or internal consistency. This refers to the generality of stage usage across moral issues and dilemmas within the interview.

One indication that a stage forms a structured whole would be the degree to

Table 5.3. *Summary of longitudinal stage sequence*

Type of stage change	Frequency	Percentage
Stage progression		
2 to 2/3	1	
2 to 3	1	
2/3 to 3	13	
2/3 to 3/4	12	
2/3 to 4	1	
3 to 3/4	23	
3 to 4	8	
3/4 to 4	1	
3/4 to 4/5	3	65.6
No stage change		
2/3 to 2/3	5	
3 to 3	10	
3/4 to 3/4	12	28.1
Stage regression		
3 to 2/3	3	
3/4 to 3	3	6.3
Total	96	100.0

which any particular individual reasoned at the same stage at any one interview time. Each subject's percent stage usage is presented elsewhere (Snarey, 1982). The 188 interview profiles indicate that in 156 (83%) of the cases all reasoning was at one major stage or in transition between two adjacent stages and 32 (17%) of the cases included reasoning at three adjacent stages. In no case was a subject reasoning at two nonadjacent stages. To analyze such interviews with three stages represented, Colby and Kohlberg have previously established a conservative error boundary of 10% with entries of .10 and below treated as error and entries above .10 treated as real (Colby et al., 1983). Applying this formula, 16 (8.5%) of the 188 interviews exhibit reasoning at three stages. This is comparable to the U.S. longitudinal study in which 9% of the interviews exhibited reasoning at three adjacent stages, though the stage range is narrower in the current study.

Another procedure for evaluating the structural wholeness claim is to examine the correlations among the stage scores for each of the six issues that make up the global or overall interview score. A correlation matrix for the entire sample is presented in Table. 5.5. Consistent with Kohlberg's assumptions, the correlations were all positive, significant, and moderately high (.745–.422). If the structural wholeness hypothesis is correct, one would also expect to find one major factor, not several factors, accounting for the major portion of the variability. Factor analysis and principal components analysis were thus conducted for three age groupings (12–15, 16–19, 20–26) on all six moral issues. The results indicated that the first factor accounts for 79%–100% of the variance, with eigenvalues of 3.49, 2.88, and 2.74. The second factor's eigenvalue is always less than 1 for each age group and for the sample as a whole. Nevertheless, to consider the possibility of a multifactorial solution, the factors were

Table 5.4. *Longitudinal sequence by subjects*

Subject ID[a] and testing time	Moral development scores		Stage usage (%)				
	Global stage	Maturity scale	1	2	3	4	5
IA. Cyclamen cohort: Youth Aliyah subjects at Kibbutz Ramat Yedidim							
01-1	3/4	352			48	52	
01-2	3/4	350			50	50	
01-5[a]	4/5	429			6	59	35
03-1	3/4	338			62	38	
03-2	3/4	332			68	32	
03-5	3/4	350			50	50	
05-1	2/3	266		33	67		
05-2	3/4	316		17	50	33	
05-5	4/5	437				63	37
07-1	2/3	246		50	50		
07-2	3	302			100		
07-5	3/4	355			45	55	
09-1	3	310		10	70	20	
09-2	3	300		12	76	12	
09-5	3/4	338			62	38	
10-1	3	300		10	80	10	
10-2	2/3[b]	280		33	54	13	
10-5	3/4	326			73	27	
IB. Federation cohort: kibbutz-born subjects at other kibbutzim							
11-1	3	290		9	91		
11-5	4	377			23	77	
13-1	3	320			80	20	
13-5	4	415			8	69	23
14-1	3/4	350		10	30	60	
14-5	3/4	367			33	67	
16-1	3	314			86	14	
16-5	3/4	373			27	73	
IIA. Sparrow cohort: kibbutz-born subjects at Kibbutz Ramat Yedidim							
39-2	2/3	256		39	61		
39-4	3	315			83	17	
39-5	3/4	343			43	57	
40-2	3	322			77	23	
40-4	3/4	350			50	50	
40-5	4	396			19	65	16
41-2	3	320			80	20	
41-4	3/4	341			59	41	
41-5	3/4	332			68	32	
42-2	3/4	335			64	36	
42-4	3/4	341			59	41	
42-5	3/4	350			50	50	
43-2	3/4	327			72	28	
43-4	3[b]	318			82	18	
43-5	4	400			23	54	23

Table 5.4. (*cont.*)

Subject ID[a] and testing time	Moral development scores		Stage usage (%)				
	Global stage	Maturity scale	1	2	3	4	5

IIA. Sparrow cohort: kibbutz-born subjects at Kibbutz Ramat Yedidim (cont.)

Subject ID[a] and testing time	Global stage	Maturity scale	1	2	3	4	5
44-2	3/4	325		4	67	29	
44-4	3/4	340			60	40	
44-5	3/4	350			50	50	
45-2	3	300			100		
45-4	3/4	327			73	27	
45-5	3/4	334			65	35	

IIB. Sparrow cohort: Youth Aliyah subjects at Kibbutz Ramat Yedidim

Subject ID[a] and testing time	Global stage	Maturity scale	1	2	3	4	5
46-2	3	283		17	83		
46-4	3/4	336			64	36	
46-5	3/4	350			60	30	10
47-2	2	200		100			
47-4	2/3	245		59	27	14	
47-5	3	300		15	70	15	
48-2	2/3	253		67	33		
48-4	3	310			89	11	
48-5	3/4	357			42	58	
49-2	2/3	263		37	63		
49-4	3	315			83	17	
49-5	4	423				77	23
50-2	2	190	18	73	9		
50-4	3	316			81	19	
50-5	3	316			79	21	
51-2	2/3	272		28	72		
51-4	3	300			100		
51-5	3/4	323			77	23	
52-2	2/3	283		27	62	11	
52-4	3	296		13	77	10	
52-5	3/4	346			58	42	
53-2	2/3	250		50	50		
53-4	3	300			100		
53-5	3/4	362			38	62	

IIC. Gazelle cohort: Youth Aliyah subjects at Kibbutz M

Subject ID[a] and testing time	Global stage	Maturity scale	1	2	3	4	5
54-2	2/3	255		44	56		
54-4	3	300			100		
55-2	3	300			100		
55-4	3	300			100		
56-2	3	311			89	11	
56-4	3	300			100		
57-2	3/4	340			59	41	
57-4	3[b]	300			100		
58-2	2/3	250		50	50		
58-4	3	282		18	82		

Table 5.4. (*cont.*)

Subject ID[a] and testing time	Moral development scores		Stage usage (%)				
	Global stage	Maturity scale	1	2	3	4	5

IIC. Gazelle cohort: Youth Aliyah subjects at Kibbutz M (cont.)

Subject ID[a] and testing time	Global stage	Maturity scale	1	2	3	4	5
59-2	3	307			86	14	
59-4	3/4	338			61	39	
60-2	2/3	250		50	50		
60-4	3	300			100		
61-2	3	300			100		
61-4	3	300			100		
62-2	3	300			100		
62-4	3	310			89	11	
63-2	3	300			100		
63-4	3	318			82	18	
64-2	3	300			100		
64-4	3	311			89	11	

IIIA. Crane cohort: kibbutz-born subjects at Kibbutz Ramat Yedidim

Subject ID[a] and testing time	Global stage	Maturity scale	1	2	3	4	5
65-3	3	286		14	86		
65-5	3/4	335			65	35	
66-3	3	306		13	69	18	
66-5	3/4	347			60	40	
67-3	2/3	276		35	54	11	
67-5	3/4	326			73	27	
68-3	2/3	263		37	63		
68-5	3/4	325			75	25	
69-3	3	300			100		
69-5	4	380			20	80	
70-3	3	285		15	85		
70-5	4	382			18	82	
71-3	2/3	230		69	31		
71-5	3/4	350			50	50	
72-3	3	300			100		
72-5	3/4	366			33	67	

IIIB. Crane cohort: Youth Aliyah subjects at Kibbutz Ramat Yedidim

Subject ID[a] and testing time	Global stage	Maturity scale	1	2	3	4	5
73-3	2/3	244	4	50	46		
73-4	2/3	254		45	55		
73-5	3/4	332			68	32	
74-3	2/3	250		50	50		
74-4	2/3	278		39	44	17	
74-5	3/4	336			64	36	
76-3	2/3	277		27	73		
76-4	2/3	266		33	67		
76-5	3/4	319		19	42	39	
77-3	2/3	263		36	64		
77-4	3	280		19	81		
77-5	4	386			13	87	
78-3	2/3	267		44	44	12	

Table 5.4. (*cont.*)

Subject ID[a] and testing time	Moral development scores		Stage usage (%)				
	Global stage	Maturity scale	1	2	3	4	5
IIIB. Crane cohort: Youth Aliyah subjects at Kibbutz Ramat Yedidim (cont.)							
78-4	3	283		17	83		
78-5	3/4	331			69	31	
79-3	3/4	356			44	56	
79-4	3[b]	300			100		
79-5	3/4	379			32	68	
80-3	2/3	253		46	54		
80-4	2/3	270		29	71		
80-5	4	392		7	93		
81-3	3	281		19	81		
81-4	2/3[b]	269		31	69		
81-5	3/4	333			67	33	
85-3	2/3	256		44	56		
85-4	2/3	272		27	73		
85-5	3/4	370			30	70	
87-3	3	293		11	86	3	
87-4	2/3[b]	264		43	50	7	
87-5	3/4	380			30	60	10
88-3	3	311			88	12	
88-4	3	271		21	79		
88-5	3/4	340			60	40	
IVA. Turtledove cohort: kibbutz-born subjects at Kibbutz Ramat Yedidim							
89-4	3	306			96	4	
89-5	3/4	373			27	73	
90-4	3	318			82	18	
90-5	4	404			8	79	13
91-4	3/4	346			54	46	
91-5	3/4	371			36	57	7
92-4	3/4	350			50	50	
92-5	4/5	436				64	36
93-4	3	286		14	86		
93-5	3/4	350			50	50	
IVB. Turtledove cohort: Youth Aliyah subjects at Kibbutz Ramat Yedidim							
95-4	2/3	263		37	63		
95-5	3/4	350			50	50	
96-4	3	293		10	90		
96-5	3/4	357			43	57	
97-4	3	234		22	78		
97-5	3/4	359			41	39	
99-4	3	304		8	81	11	
99-5	3	311			89	11	

[a]The gaps in the subject ID numbers refer to cross-sectional subjects who have not been included in this longitudinal report.
[b]Indicates a score reversal.

139

Table 5.5. *Correlations among six moral issues in Form A interview for total sample*

Moral issues	2	3	4	5	6
1. Life	.72	.65	.48	.50	.42
2. Law	—	.75	.70	.52	.46
3. Conscience		—	.63	.47	.53
4. Punishment			—	.47	.48
5. Contract				—	.49
6. Authority					—

Note: The probability level for all correlations was < .001.

rotated. Again, using a varimax (orthogonal) rotated factor matrix, no underlying consistent pattern is interpretable across the factors. Thus, in summary, the eigenvalue and proportion of variance were predominantly accounted for by only one general factor, and rotation of multiple factors did not yield any consistent pattern across the factors. The structural wholeness hypothesis, therefore, cannot be rejected; the findings suggest that there is a general dimension of moral reasoning that is not issue specific. These findings are also clearer than those from the U.S. study in which the second eigenvalue was greater than 1 (1.05–2.05) for similar age groups.

Age Norms and Moral Stage. Moral development would be expected to show a clear relationship with age. The actual relationship between age and moral stage can be summarized by observing the mean and range of stages for each age. Stage 2/3 was the lowest commonly assigned stage; 61% of the subjects at age 12 were assigned this stage. No kibbutz subject aged 18 or over scored at stage 2/3. Stage 3 was the modal stage for ages 13–14 and 15–17. No one in the 13–17 age group scored higher than Stage 3/4. Stage 3/4 was assigned to 62 (33%) of the interviews and was the modal stage for the 18–26 age groups. Stage 4 was assigned to 10 (5%) of the interviews; it did not appear until the 18–19 age group, at which time 14.3% of this cohort was assigned Stage 4. Stage 4/5 also appears for the first time in the 18–19 age group, but it does not become common until the 24–26 age group. Stages 4/5 and 5 thus appear to be confirmed on the kibbutz as stages of adulthood and not of adolescence.

In sum, the mean weighted average score gradually and consistently increased from 278 at age 12 to 377 at ages 24–26. A regression analysis indicated that age accounts for 40% of the variance in moral maturity scores.

As Table 5.6 indicates, the Israeli sample's age norms compare favorably with the findings from the two previous longitudinal studies that have used the standardized scoring system. Colby and co-workers (chap. 3, this volume) found that the scores on the Form A interview in their American sample ranged from Stage 1 to Stage 4/5 between ages 10 and 26, and Nisan and Kohlberg (chap. 4) also found that in their Turkish sample the scores ranged from Stages 1 to 4/5 between ages 10 and 28. The Israeli scores are somewhat similar in that they ranged from Stage 2 to Stage 4/5 between ages 12 and 26, but there were

Table 5.6. *Percentage of subjects in each age group at each stage by cultural setting*

Ages	Country	N	\multicolumn{9}{c}{Global moral stages}								
			1	1/2	2	2/3	3	3/4	4	4/5	Mean
12	Israel	18				61.1	33.3	5.6			278
10	U.S.	21	5.3	26.3	42.1	15.8	10.5				204
10–12	Turkey	28	3.5	57.1	17.9	17.9	3.5				183
13–14	Israel	40			2.5	32.5	55.0	10.0			288
13–14	U.S.	37		11.1	8.3	58.3	16.7	2.8			249
13–15	Turkey	23		26.1	13.0	60.2					219
15–17	Israel	70			1.4	17.1	57.1	24.3			303
16–18	U.S.	46		2.3	4.5	22.7	31.8	36.4			299
16–18	Turkey	22		9.1	9.1	72.7	4.5	4.5			241
18–23	Israel	50					14.0	68.0	16.0	2.0	348
20–22	U.S.	33				6.5	25.8	54.8	9.7	3.2	335
19–28	Turkey	36				25.0	44.4	27.8	0.0	2.8	298
24–26	Israel	10						50.0	30.0	20.0	377
24–26	U.S.	25				4.3	17.4	43.5	21.7	13.0	365
28–30	U.S.	38					21.6	48.6	16.2	13.5	362
32–33	U.S.	23					4.5	68.2	18.2	9.1	366
36	U.S.	9						77.8	11.1	11.1	374

Note: The three samples are equivalent in that each includes an approximately equal number of lower- and middle-class subjects.

no scores at Stages 1 or 1/2. The kibbutz sample's mean scores at *all* ages were consistently higher than the mean stage scores in samples from the United States and Turkey. Stage 2/3, for instance, disappeared on the kibbutz by age 16, whereas it continued to be present until age 24 in the United States and until age 26 in Turkey. On the other hand, Stage 4/5 was first exhibited in the kibbutz sample at age 18, but in the United States sample Stage 4/5 was first present at age 24; and the one subject in the Turkish sample who scored at stage 4/5 was age 23.

Another dimension of the relationship between age and stage is the stability of individual differences, i.e., the relationship between a subject's score at one age and the same subject's score at a later age. The correlations among weighted average score for the different ages were thus examined. The correlations between moral maturity scores at one age and scores at a later age were positive but not always high or significant. The highest correlation within our sample was between scores at ages 15–17 and scores at the adjoining 18–19 age range (.75, $p < .05$), but scores at ages 13–14 were the best general predictors of scores in later adolescence and early adulthood (.48 with scores at ages 15–17, .49 with scores at ages 18–19, and .56 with scores at ages 20–23). Kohlberg and Colby's longitudinal study in the United States also found that scores at ages 13–14 were better predictors of later stages, presumably because this age represents a period of stabilization after entering adolescence. The correlations reported by Colby and Kohlberg between scores at age 13–14 with later ages were generally higher than was found in the present study (.70 with scores at ages 16–18, .46 with ages 20–22, .70 at ages 24–26, and .67 at ages 28–30).

Sex Differences. One assumption of Kohlberg's theory is that the sequence of stages found in the all-male samples of the U.S. longitudinal study will apply cross-culturally to female samples as well. Furthermore, although there may be differences in the rate of development of males and females, these are not inherent gender differences, but are due to the unequal social and political status of men and women in particular societies. Gilligan has challenged this idea (1977, 1982), and the kibbutz data provide an opportunity to test this assumption as kibbutz society strives to provide general equality to its female and male members. Table 5.7 presents a cross tabulation of sex by global stages for all cohorts that included both male and female subjects (i.e., Samples, 2, 3, and 4). There is no significant relationship between sex and stage scores ($\chi^2 = 4.65$, $df = 3$, $p =$ NS).

The relationship between sex and specific moral stages can be further examined by considering the percentage of reasoning at each stage for males and females. This information is presented in Table 5.8. Sex and stage usage are cross-tabulated for each stage. The strength of the association between sex and percentage using a particular stage is always weak (V ranged from .16 to .25), and the sexes do not differ significantly in the degree to which they use any of the stages.

Possible sex differences in stage of moral judgment were also considered separately for kibbutz-born males and females and for Middle Eastern Youth Aliyah males and females because of the variation in their cultural backgrounds in terms of the distribution of sex roles. The relationship between stage and sex for the kibbutz-born youth at their first and last interview times was examined as was the relationship between stage and sex for the Youth Aliyah subjects at their first and last interview times. The analyses for the kibbutz-born youth did not reveal any significant sex difference at their first interview ($\chi^2 = 4.45$, $df = 2$, $p =$ NS) or at their last interview (Fisher's Exact Test, $p =$ NS). The aliyah youth also showed no significant differences at either their first interview time ($\chi^2 = 3.62$, $df = 2$, $p =$ NS) or at their last interview time ($\chi^2 = 3.05$, $df = 2$, $p =$ NS).

In sum, there were no significant sex differences in the sequence or rate of development of moral judgment for the age groups under study, even when controlling for cultural background, stage usage, and interview time.

Cultural Findings

The findings reported in the previous section supported the developmental assumptions underlying Kohlberg's theory and strengthen arguments for the cross-cultural universality of his model as well as his method of studying moral judgment. They have not spoken, however, to the cross-cultural particularity of moral reasoning among kibbutzniks. This section will focus on the cultural content of moral reasoning and the ways in which the cultural characteristics of kibbutz moral reasoning may be different.

Culturally Defined Moral Issues. For each of the moral dilemmas included in each interview, the subject is first asked to make a choice between two alter-

Table 5.7. *Cross-tabulation of sex by global stage scores*

Sex		Global stage scores				
		2, 2/3	3	3/4	4, 4/5	N
Males	n	21	25	25	7	78
	%	26.9	32.0	32.0	8.9	
Females	n	9	25	20	2	56
	%	16.0	44.6	35.7	3.5	

Note: $\chi^2 = 4.65$, $df = 3$, $p = \text{NS}$, $V = .19$.

Table 5.8. *Cross-tabulation of sex with percentage of stage usage at each stage*

Stage and sex		Stage usage				
		0%	4–24%	25–49%	50–74%	75–100%
Stage one						
Males	n	76	2	0	0	0
	%	97.4	2.5			
Females	n	54	2	0	0	0
	%	96.4	3.5			
Stage two						
Males	n	47	11	15	4	1
	%	60.2	14.1	19.2	5.1	1.2
Females	n	40	7	5	4	0
	%	71.4	12.5	8.9	7.1	
Stage three						
Males	n	2	6	11	34	25
	%	2.5	7.6	14.1	43.5	32.0
Females	n	1	2	8	19	26
	%	1.7	3.5	14.2	33.9	46.4
Stage four						
Males	n	31	15	17	9	6
	%	39.7	19.2	21.7	11.5	7.6
Females	n	21	14	8	13	0
	%	37.5	25.0	14.2	23.2	
Stage five						
Males	n	74	4	0	0	0
	%	94.8	5.1			
Females	n	52	3	1	0	0
	%	92.8	5.3	1.7		

Note: $N = 134$ (males, 78; females, 56). Percentages refer to rows. All χ^2 p values were not significant.

native moral actions that could be taken in the dilemma. These alternative actions are referred to as issue choices since each affirms the value of one of the two issues that are in conflict in that dilemma. The Heinz dilemma, for instance, requires a choice between life and law. The Officer Brown dilemma represents a conflict between morality and conscience and punishment, and the Joe dilemma presents a conflict between contract and authority.

The possibility that these issues are related to the cultural differences was considered. For instance, one might expect kibbutz subjects to more commonly choose the life, conscience, or contract issues since these values are given stress in kibbutz ideology. The Middle Eastern aliyah youth, whose families are more tradition bound, might be expected to more commonly choose the law, punishment, and authority issues. This possible cultural difference in issue choice was examined for both cultural groups at different ages in order to compare their issue choices when the Middle Eastern aliyah youth first came to the kibbutz and again 5–7 years later after being kibbutz educated.

With regard to the issue choices for the Heinz dilemma, the kibbutz-born and aliyah youth do not differ at ages 12–15, at ages 15–17, or at their final interview at ages 18–26. On average kibbutz-born (96%) and Middle Eastern youth (94%) nearly always choose the life issue and advocate that the drug be stolen to save the woman's life. For the Officer Brown dilemma, again the groups do not differ at any of the age intervals; on average the conscience issue is the slight favorite for both groups (55% and 63%). Looking at the father–son dilemma, however, the Middle Eastern aliyah youth are less likely to choose the contract issue than are the kibbutz-born subjects. At ages 12–15 the trend is not significant at the .05 level, but the trend becomes stronger and reaches significance among the 15–17-year-olds ($\chi^2 = 3.98$, $df = 1$, $p < .05$, Phi = .40). The Middle Eastern youth, both on the kibbutz and in the city, often choose the authority issue (i.e., give the father the money) in spite of the unfairness of the father's request. The kibbutz-born youth consistently choose the contract issue (i.e., the father must keep his promise). In hindsight, this particular dilemma seems the most likely to capture the different cultural origins of the groups. Kibbutz children tend to find the fact that the father has broken his promise and asked for his son's money to be amazing within the context of the kibbutz childrearing and economic system. Middle Eastern youth, on the other hand, could be expected to find it more reasonable to give in to the father's request within the context of the Middle Eastern patriarchal family system, which emphasizes parental respect and authority. By the time of the final interview, after 5–9 years of kibbutz residence, the difference between kibbutz-born and aliyah youth has completely disappeared and both nearly always choose the contract issue (i.e., they think Joe should not give his father the money).

Since all of the subjects in the age range for which differences in issue choices were found were also reasoning at the conventional stages, it appears that their choices were guided by the different conventions of their subcultures. This is further suggested by observing the frequency with which the Israeli subjects drew on specific culturally defined values and norms from the social institutions to which they belonged in order to justify or support their moral judgments. That is, references to kibbutz democratic and family norms, Israeli legal and military protocols, Jewish religious and ethnic values parallel the aforementioned issue choice patterns. The number of cultural references made by the 12–14-year-old subjects in both the kibbutz-born and Youth Aliyah cohorts was quite low ($M = 6\%$), and these subjects also had the highest use of preconventional reasoning. Among the older subjects, however, the number of references to social institutions rose dramatically, with an average of 50% of the 15–17-year-old and 40% of the 18–26-year-old subjects supporting their moral reasoning by referring to specific social institutions.

In sum, no significant differences between kibbutz-born and non-kibbutz-born youth were found on the Heinz dilemma or on the Officer Brown dilemma, but a culturally predictable difference was found on the father–son dilemma among the 15–17-year-olds. These findings contrast somewhat with the results of Colby and Kohlberg's United States study (chap. 3, this volume) since in their sample 67% of the subjects argued that Heinz should steal the drug compared to 95% of the kibbutz subjects; 45% of their American sample argued for leniency in the Officer Brown dilemma compared to 55% of the kibbutz-born youth; and 61% of their sample argued that the father must keep his promise compared to 93% in the kibbutz-born sample. In each case, the kibbutz subjects are more likely to choose the response most often chosen at the principle stage; the differences remain essentially the same when age and stage of development are controlled. The kibbutz findings are also in contrast with the results of Nisan and Kohlberg's Turkish study (chap. 4, this volume), which found the opposite pattern: In their sample Turkish village subjects were significantly more likely than Turkish city subjects to choose the law issue in the Heinz dilemma and the punishment issue in the Officer Brown dilemma, but there were no significant differences on the father–son dilemma. Nisan and Kohlberg's discussion, however, similarly accounts for these differences in terms of subcultural differences between the two groups. The next section will consider cultural differences among kibbutzniks as they relate to the higher stages of moral development.

Culturally Defined Postconventional Morality. Another aspect of the cultural uniqueness question can be assessed by examining the interview material the scorers considered to be difficult to evaluate in terms of stage structure. Occasionally the reason a subject gives for prescribing a particular moral action cannot be matched with a structural example in the scoring manual. Under these circumstances the scorer assigns a "guess" score to the judgment and it is included, but weighted less, in the scoring algorithm. Such difficult material, especially within cross-cultural interviews, may indicate aspects of moral reasoning that the stage model and scoring manual miss or misunderstand because they were created from interviews collected in the United States (Cole et al., 1971; Price-Williams, 1975).

Systematic examination of the guess-scored material at the conventional stages reveals that the items are usually unclear because of the briefness or incompleteness of that particular judgment by the subject. The higher stage judgments that are difficult to score, however, are not only usually complete judgments but also appear to be culturally patterned around the cooperative and collective working-class values of the kibbutz (Snarey & Blasi, 1980; Snarey, 1982). Young adult kibbutzniks bring much more of a collective communal emphasis to solving the dilemmas than do middle-class North Americans, and they express a much greater investment in the preservation and maintenance of social solidarity. Thus, although all of Kohlberg's five stages are present among kibbutz members, not all elements of kibbutz postconventional reasoning are present in the criterion judgments of the scoring manual. In particular, some judgments that were guess-scored as Stage 4 or 4/5 could be understood as full

145

postconventional Stage 5 judgments if one took a kibbutz perspective rather than a middle-class American perspective to the data. The following two examples illustrate this thesis.

**EXCERPT ONE
(KIBBUTZ FEMALE):**

It is against the law for Moshe to steal the drug. Does that make it morally wrong?

It will be illegal or against the formal law, but not against the law which is the moral law. Again, if we were in a utopian society, my hierarchy of values, and the hierarchy of others through consensus, would be realized.

What are those values?

Socialism. But [laughter] don't ask me to explain it.

What is wrong with a nonsocialistic society that makes it unjust?

In a utopia there will be all the things I believe in. There would not be murder, robbery, and everyone will be equal. In this society, the greatest value, the value of life, is perfectly held. Disvaluing life is forbidden. It is like our dream, our ideal. In one way it is ridiculous since this utopia will never be achieved, of course. You can even observe children in the kindergarten; they can be very nasty and cruel to each other.

Should people still do everything they can to obey the law in an imperfect world?

Yes, unless it will endanger or hurt another important value. . . . But generally speaking, people should obey the law. The law was created in order to protect . . . from killing, robbery, and other unjust uses of power. . . . I believe everyone has the right to self-growth and the right to reach happiness.

"Unjust uses of power" interfere with this?

People are not born equal genetically and it is not fair that one who is stronger physically should reach his happiness by whatever means at the expense of one who is weaker because the right to happiness is a basic human right of everyone, equal to all. A society that is based on power negates the right and possibility of those who are weaker to get their happiness.

**EXCERPT TWO
(KIBBUTZ MALE):**

Should Moshe steal the drug? Why or why not?

Yes. . . . I think that the community should be responsible for controlling this kind of situation. The medicine should be made available to all in need; the druggist should not have the right to decide on his own . . . the whole community or society should have the control of the drug.

Is it important for people to do everything they can to save another's life? Why or why not?

If I want to create a better community, a nice and beautiful one, an ideal world, the only way we can do it is by cooperation between people. . . . We need this cooperation among ourselves in order to achieve this better world. . . . The happiness . . . principle underlies this cooperation – the greatest happiness for the greatest number of people in the society.

Should people try to do everything they can to obey the law?

In principle, yes. It is impossible to have any kind of state, country, society without laws. [Otherwise], it will be complete anarchy and those who have the power will dominate the weaker.

Why is that wrong?

I am not strong . . . [laughter]. But really, you can see in the totalitarian countries today in contrast to, for example, the kibbutz. You damage the principle of democracy and, most importantly, you destroy the principle of equality. Which is why I live on a kibbutz.

In scoring these excerpts as *guess* Stage 4 or 4/5, the scorer made two judgments: (1) There was not a clear match to a criterion judgment in the scoring manual by which to evaluate these judgments, and (2) clinically, these statements seem to be at least Stage 4, but they do not seem to be fully postconventional Stage 5 judgments. Since the subjects do appear to be arguing for the maintenance of the social system, it seems reasonable, in the absence of material in the scoring manual, that these excerpts were so scored. Yet, we would argue that there is a clear sense in which the collective equality and happiness perspective common to these interviews is more mature than Kohlberg's definition of Stage 4 and should be included as a type of Stage 5 reasoning. One notes that the kibbutz functions for the subjects as an imperfect embodiment of a more utopian ideal. Furthermore, in commonly asserting that the community or kibbutz should control the drug, they are making a solid Stage 5 judgment to the extent that they view community membership as based on a commitment to collective equality and the aim of cooperative happiness. Allusions in some interviews to the social system becoming dysfunctional are also not necessarily conventional judgments if the reason they are protecting the social system is because they see it as ideally embodying universal moral principles. The clear recognition by the subjects that the kibbutz does not fully meet these ideals also supports our assumption of the autonomous use of moral principles that are prior to a social perspective, even if these principles are more collectively articulated than is typical of middle-class Americans. Poland's Lech Walesa would perhaps recognize this, but the scoring manual clearly does not.

A more culturally sensitive scoring of the preceding excerpts would have assigned a score of Stage 5 to these interviews. Such a culturally sensitive scoring would not, however, have drastically increased the number of Stage 5 interviews in the sample. Whereas the current stage distribution included three young adults who scored at Stage 4/5, the foregoing considerations would have increased the number to five interviews scored as fully Stage 5.

Summary and Conclusions

The moral development of 92 adolescents in Israel was studied with the aim of evaluating the cross-cultural validity of Kohlberg's theory of the development of moral judgment. The research questions focused both on the degree to which the moral development of kibbutzniks follows the patterns reported for samples in other cultures and on possible culturally defined variations in moral development between kibbutz and other populations.

Universality of Moral Judgment Stages

The longitudinal findings indicated that stage change was consecutive, gradual, and upward. The number of stage regressions was not higher than one would

147

expect due to scoring error and in no case did a subject skip a stage. Colby and Kohlberg's analyses regarding structural wholeness and internal consistency were also replicated. The 188 kibbutz interview profiles indicated that in 83% of the cases all reasoning was at one major stage or at two adjacent stages. The correlations among the stage scores for each of the six moral issues within each interview were all positive, significant, and moderately high. Finally, in a factor analysis the variance was predominantly accounted for by only one general factor.

Age showed a clear relationship with stage and accounted for 40% of the variance in weighted average scores. The age norms compare favorably with the findings from the U.S. and Turkish longitudinal studies. The Israeli sample, even at the lowest age of 12, shows no usage of Stage 1 or 1/2 and little usage of Stage 2. Furthermore, the kibbutz mean stage scores at all ages are consistently higher than the mean stage scores in the United States and Turkey. This distribution of the kibbutz stage scores is also impressive when one considers that previous research has found that children in rural communities generally progress more slowly than city children (Turiel, 1969, p. 125; Edwards, 1975). Yet in all studies to date, Stages 4/5 and 5 have been relatively rare: 8 subjects in the United States (Colby et al., 1983), 18 kibbutz founders in Israel (Snarey, 1982), 1 subject in Turkey (Nisan & Kohlberg, 1982), and 3 kibbutz youth in the present study.

Regarding the stability of individual differences, Colby and Kohlberg have found that scores at ages 13–14 are the best predictors of later stages. The finding from the United States was replicated in Israel, although the correlations between scores at ages 13–14 with later scores were generally lower in this present study than had been the case in the United States.

There were no significant differences in development between males and females in stage scores. Controlling for cultural background, interview time, and age also revealed no significant sex differences.

Cultural Variation in Moral Judgment

Regarding the content of moral reasoning, there were no significant differences in moral issue choice between kibbutz and nonkibbutz subjects in moral issue choice on the Heinz dilemma or the Officer Brown dilemma but there was a culturally comprehensible difference on the father–son dilemma among the 15–17-year-olds. The kibbutz-born youth nearly always made the contract choice and argued that the father should keep his promise, whereas the Middle Eastern youth often chose the authority issue and argued that the son should give his father the money. The 15–17-year-old subjects were more likely to draw on culturally defined values and norms from the social institutions to which they belonged in order to justify their moral judgments. In essence, the youngest age cohorts, whose members were primarily at the preconventional stages, seldom reflected cultural conventions in their reasoning; the middle 15–17 age cohorts, whose members were primarily at the conventional stages, were significantly more likely to make moral choices that reflected the conventions of their society; finally, for the oldest cohorts, whose members had begun to make greater use of the less convention bound Stages 4 and 4/5, there was again a drop in the use of or conformity to conventions.

Culturally defined structural variations in kibbutz postconventional reasoning were suggested by an analysis of interview material that the scorers had labeled as difficult to score. The kibbutzniks' communal emphasis, greater investment in the preservation of social solidarity, and greater emphasis on collective happiness seem to have been missed or misunderstood when evaluated solely by the existing criterion judgments of the scoring manual. Five interviews that were rated as Stage 4 or 4/5 by the standard scoring procedure were evaluated as Stage 5 under a culturally sensitive second scoring. This suggests that in cross-cultural research, one may need to revise the scoring manual in two ways. First, one may have to add culturally indigenous examples of higher stage judgments to those currently included in the scoring manual to avoid bias when considering the content of reasoning by subjects from a cultural background other than the one of the original subjects on which the manual was based. Since it is not possible for one scoring manual to contain the universe of cultural variation, this first point also underscores the importance of the researcher's being thoroughly immersed in the culture of the population under study. Second, and more interestingly, there appear to be additional postconventional moral principles other than those currently represented in the scoring manual. There is thus a need for more cross-cultural research on populations such as kibbutzniks to develop in the future a more pluralistic understanding of the development of principled moral judgment around the globe.

In conclusion, Kohlberg's model and method have fared well: The kibbutz findings are remarkably consistent with a structural understanding of the development of moral reasoning. The data, however, also revealed some degree of cultural uniqueness in the moral judgments of kibbutzniks. These findings should be seen, of course, as only one part of a broader investigation of the validity of Kohlberg's theory within diverse cultural settings.

Six

Instructions for Moral Judgment Interviewing and Scoring

with Kelsey Kauffman

Procedure for Conducting a Moral Judgment Interview

We will begin this "how to" chapter with some guidelines for conducting a Moral Judgment Interview. The critical importance of high-quality interviews for assessing moral judgment stage should become clear in the next section, which deals with the procedures for stage scoring an interview.

The Standard Issue Moral Judgment Interview is a directed conversation between interviewer and respondent concerning the resolution of three moral dilemmas. Since the interview will ultimately be used to score the respondent's stage of moral reasoning, all techniques that encourage fully elaborated, stage-scorable reasoning are desirable. The design of the interview itself and the following suggestions for interviewing techniques will help you obtain scorable data.

Design of Interview

The Interview consists of three parallel forms: Forms A, B, and C. Each form includes three dilemmas or "stories." Each of the stories poses a conflict between two moral issues. For example, the Heinz story (Dilemma III) poses a conflict between the issues of life and law. Arguments that favor stealing the drug support life, arguments that oppose stealing support law. The goal of interviewing is to obtain stage-scorable reasoning on each issue. In order to increase the chances that a subject will give scorable material on each issue, we have posed a number of issue-related questions. For example, in the Heinz story, Questions 1–7 are either general questions (can be answered with regard to either issue) or pertain to the life issue directly (e.g., should people do everything they can to save another person's life, and why or why not)? Questions 8 and 9 focus on the law issue.

Several questions have special designations. Starred questions are designed to be scored for moral stage but may be eliminated if time pressures require a researcher to shorten the interview. Questions such as Number 10 (Dilemma III) are designed to reveal the subject's moral type as well as moral stage. Studies using moral type information should be sure to include this question. Other questions (e.g., 7–12, Dilemma III') are designed to illuminate the subject's theory of ethics, or metaethics. These questions should not be scored for stage and need be administered only if material on metaethical thinking is desired. A single interview session consists of the three stories in any one form.

Mode of Presentation

Interviews can be conducted in either of three ways: (1) oral interviews (tape-recorded and transcribed); (2) oral interviews with responses written by interviewer; and (3) written interviews. Oral interviews that are tape-recorded and transcribed are ideal. This method allows for both probing of ambiguous responses and a full record of the subject's reasoning. However, the method is very expensive. An alternative that preserves the interviewer's opportunity to probe the subject's reasoning is the second method, in which the subject's responses are hand-recorded. When using this method, the interviewer should begin writing before the subject finishes speaking, since responses may be distorted by remembering incorrectly. In writing down the subject's responses, the interviewer should be sure not to paraphrase them. Slight variations in language may suggest concepts used at different moral stages. The goal of recording is to preserve the subject's train of thought using the subject's own words. Obvious repetitions and false starts may be eliminated. We suggest that beginning interviewers using the handwritten method tape-record their first few interviews to check the accuracy of their transcription.

An alternative is to tape-record the interviews and to score directly from the tapes rather than from typed transcripts. This approach makes the scoring somewhat more laborious and time-consuming, but is much less expensive than having the interviews transcribed. Scorers using this method should be sure to move backward and forward on the tape repeatedly as this is necessary to organize interview material and to reach confident decisions regarding issue, norm, element, and stage as described later in this chapter.

Interviews that are filled out directly by the subject (written interviews) are not as desirable but may be the only feasible method of collecting data from large numbers of subjects. If possible, the investigator should quickly review each interview as it is returned and ask subjects who have provided only short responses to explain their reasoning in more detail. Written interviews may be obtained by the same Standard Moral Judgment Interview as is used for the oral interview. The written form of presentation is not appropriate for subjects younger than about 16 or for subjects without good verbal and writing skills. Pilot testing with subjects comparable to the research sample is strongly recommended. Instructions for presentation of the written interview are included in the next section.

Administration

Oral Interviews. In administering the oral interview, begin by reading the moral dilemma aloud and making sure the subject is clear on the facts of the case. Younger subjects may be asked to repeat the facts. Ask each interview question in turn, following the ideas described in the section, "Interviewing Techniques." It may be helpful to give the subject a copy of the interview form with which to read along. The following introductions are suggested. Researchers may vary the wording to suit their situation:

I am going to read several stories to you that involve questions of right and wrong. I would like you to answer some questions about each of these stories. In answering the questions, it is very important that you tell me not only *what* you think should be done or *what* you think is right but also *why* you think it is right.

Oral interviews take about 45 minutes for three stories. The stories are generally not meaningful to children under the age of 10. Techniques for testing younger children can be found in *The Growth of Interpersonal Understanding* by Robert Selman (1980) and in *The Social World of the Child* by William Damon (1977).

Written Interview.   Distribute interview forms to subjects and read the following instructions. Wording may be varied to suit particular situations:

The Moral Judgment Interview consists of several stories that we believe present some challenging issues. Some of you might choose one solution to these stories, others of you may choose another. We are primarily interested in the explanations or reasons you give for your decisions. Try to justify and explain your statements as fully as possible. Very short answers are of no help to us so be sure to elaborate fully. Keep in mind that we are more interested in your answers to the ''why'' questions than to the ''what'' questions. Even if you give a long description of what you think is right or what you think should be done, it is of no help if you do not explain *why* you think it is right or *why* you think it should be done.

The approximate writing time for each story is 20 minutes, though subjects should always be given as much time as they need to write out complete answers to all questions.

Interviewing Techniques

The Moral Judgment Interview includes standard probing questions. For many subjects, the interviewer will not have to do any more than ask the standard probe or follow-up questions. However, in cases where the subject is inarticulate, is giving opinions rather than reasons, or where a particularly significant moral concept needs clarification, additional probe questions may be necessary. The following are some suggestions for eliciting scorable responses in an oral interview.

1. Explain or paraphrase questions if the subject is unsure of what is being asked.   Be careful not to suggest any particular answer to the question when paraphrasing. If the subject asks for facts not in the dilemma, suggest ones that seem reasonable (e.g., ''Let's assume that the drug will work'') or ask the subject to explain why the particular factual information requested is critical to her or his moral decision.

2. Use ''why'' questions to encourage subjects to express reasons and justifications.   Almost any reasoning can be relevant to answering a moral question if the subject explains why that reasoning justifies a moral decision or answers a probe question. Although all standard probes include a ''why'' question, it is often necessary for the interviewer to ask for further explanation. Common forms of ''why'' questions are, ''Why does that mean that Heinz should steal the drug [break the law, be let free, and so on]?'' ''Why is that the right thing to do?'' ''Why is that important?'' The following are examples:

EXAMPLE   *Should Heinz steal the drug?*

Yes. If he doesn't steal his wife will die.

153

Why is it important that his wife not die?

Because he is poor, he can't marry after his wife dies. The children will be desolate and his family will fall apart.

Comment: The initial response here is ambiguous and probably would be scored as a Guess Stage 2 if it had not been probed further. When the subject was asked why saving the wife's life is important, a Stage 3 response based on the family's welfare was given.

EXAMPLE *What is the most important thing a good son should recognize in his relations to his father? Why that?*

Try to keep their relationship as good as possible. They should trust each other. *Why?* Because if the kid doesn't like his father he's not going to do stuff his father wants him to and if his father trusts him, he'll let him do more stuff he wants to do.

Comment: The initial response here is not scorable because it is hard to tell what he means by *trust*. Although the content of the initial response is often associated with Stage 3 reasoning (the importance of mutual trust in father–son relationships), the subject's elaboration reveals a less mature (Stage 2/3) conception of relationships and trust between people.

3. Other useful probes are, "What do you mean?" "Could you explain that further?" "What do you mean by trust, justice, friendship, and so on?"

EXAMPLE *Which would be worse, stealing like Karl or cheating like Bob? Why?*

Cheating like Bob, because when you steal something, you're taking something, but when you're lying, you're hurting someone else.

What do you mean by hurting someone else?

The old man might have needed the money later on but couldn't get it.

Comment: Here the subject's notion of "hurting someone else" needed to be clarified in order to be scored. He could have meant the physical loss of money, as at Stage 2, or hurt feelings over the violation of a personal trust, as at Stage 3. Probing revealed that the subject's reasoning on this question was, in fact, Stage 2.

EXAMPLE *Should the judge send Heinz to jail for stealing the drug?*

No, because it would oppose what I view as justice.

What do you mean by justice?

To the best of my ability to operate in society not infringing on the rights of others. But the impossible part of it is that certain rights of John Doe are going to be infringed upon because of my right to do something. You have to look at what is more important. In this case the woman's right to life was far more important than the druggist's right to his property. Justice would not be served by punishing someone who protected the right to life of another human being.

Comment: The concept of justice means something different at each stage. Only by specifically asking can we know what a subject means by any concept or issue.

4. Ask probing questions when the subject tells only what should be done. Even if the description of what should be done is long and detailed, the answer should not be considered complete unless the subject tells *why* it should be done.

EXAMPLE *Should Heinz steal the drug? Why?*

No, he should go to other possible friends or ultimately authorities who might be able to help. If this fails, then he should steal it. I think he should eventually try to pay for it, though.

Comment: The subject has only answered the question, "What should Heinz do?" He has not told us why. To elicit stage-scorable moral reasoning, the interviewer should now ask, "Why should Heinz steal the drug if going to friends and authorities fails?"

EXAMPLE *The doctor kills the woman and is brought to court. He is found guilty of murder. The usual sentence is life imprisonment. What should the judge do? Why?*

He should get a life sentence but be eligible for parole. The judge should be lenient. *Why?* Because he knew the doctor was acting in good faith when he killed the lady.

Comment: Again the initial response only answered the question, "What should the judge do?" To elicit scorable moral reasoning, the interviewer had to ask *why*. This example is illustrative of one problem with group-administered interviews. Almost invariably, subjects respond only to the *what* in some of the questions.

5. Ask probe questions when the subject merely recounts the facts of the dilemma.

EXAMPLE *Should Heinz steal the drug? Why?*

He should steal it because he can't get it any other way. He has tried to borrow the money or pay later. His wife would die if he didn't get it.

Comment: The interviewer should have asked, "But why is it so important to save her?" This tendency to recount the facts of the dilemma as a justification or reason can be indicative of a particular stage of moral judgment, but it is not necessarily. Unless the subject is encouraged to go beyond this kind of response, it tells us little about his moral stage.

EXAMPLE *Which would be worse, stealing like Karl or cheating like Bob? Why?*

Cheating like Bob because he lied to him about why he needed the money. He said he needed it for an operation when really he just needed it because he was in trouble. Karl just robbed a store.

Comment: The interviewer should ask, "But why is cheating the old man worse? Could you explain a little further what you mean?"

6. Distinguish ''would'' from ''should'' responses. If the subject answers a "should" question ("What should the judge do?") with a "would" response (e.g., "He would probably punish Heinz" or "I would let Heinz go if I were the judge"), let him finish since this may indicate something about his moral

155

judgment level. After he has finished, ask him again to answer the "should" question. (But is that what he *should* do? Do you think that's the *right* think to do?). If the subject continues to answer in terms of "would," let it drop and go on to the next question.

EXAMPLE

Should Heinz steal the drug? Why?

I don't know. I don't think it is right for him to steal the drug, but if I was in his position, I would. *Why?* Because I feel if it was somebody that I was close to, I would feel if it was somebody close to me dying, that it would be my loss and I would be acting just off my feelings and I would go ahead and do it. But if I was to think about it, *I still wouldn't think it was right.*

How about if the person was not close to you?

It depends, it depends on the circumstances. I might still go out and steal it. If I knew somebody, a stranger, who was dying, I still might go out and do it, but *I still wouldn't think it was right.*

Comment:

The interviewer here made a very common mistake. The subject's response ("if I was in his position, I would") does tell us something about his moral judgment level and role-taking ability. However, he clearly does not equate what he would do in the situation with the "right" thing to do. He twice states, "I still wouldn't think it was right." Because the interviewer did not ask, we do not know why he thinks it wouldn't be right, a distinction that could be crucial in the assignment of a stage score.

7. Don't restate the subject's response in your own words or "put words in his mouth." Interviewers with training in nondirective counseling seem to have an almost irresistible tendency to "reflect" the subject's responses back to him by saying, "So you think he should . . ."; "Do you mean he should . . ."; "Are you saying . . . ?" You may inadvertently bias an interview by suggesting rewordings of the response to the subject.

EXAMPLE

Which is worse, letting someone die or stealing? Why?

Letting someone die. *Why?* Because stealing is simply a defiance of the law and laws are made by men. By dying – there is more to it, it is not man-made, it is a spiritual thing as well as physical and it does more. There is more to someone dying than someone stealing from you. If you steal something, you break a law. If a person dies, other people's feelings are bothered, and there are feelings like spiritual love and stuff.

Are you saying that you think life is sacred?

Yes.

Comment:

Here the interviewer is suggesting a concept to the subject that he has not expressed spontaneously. This biases the interview.

8. Don't suggest alternatives to the subject when he or she is stuck and can think of nothing to say.

EXAMPLE

What should the judge do?

Send him to jail. *Why?* I don't know.

156

Is it because it's against the law or so he won't do it again or what?
Both I guess.

Comment:

Here the interviewer has suggested reasons to the subject that she might not have come up with spontaneously. This is very biasing and should never be done. Instead, the interviewer should have said, ''Think carefully – Why do you think it's important for the judge to send Heinz to jail?''

9. Don't push too hard when the subject can't think of any answer or any reason for an answer. Suggest gently that he relax and think about it for a minute but don't badger him when it's getting nowhere. Of course, one could go on asking ''Why?'' and ''What do you mean?'' forever, so it is equally important to know when to stop pushing for more. Stop if the subject seems really unable to answer the question. Stop when he begins to repeat the same answer he has already given.

10. Higher stage probes. Perhaps the most difficult stages to distinguish in scoring are Stages 4 and 5. We have found that certain interview probes help the discrimination to be made. For example, when the subject asserts the greater importance of a certain value but does not explain why it is most important, it is important to ask for clarification. Additional probes may determine whether the subject sees one value as ''prior to'' or ''derivative of'' another value, which can be an important clue in distinguishing Stage 5 from Stage 4.

EXAMPLE

Should Heinz steal the drug?
Yes. A human life is more important than money or the druggist's property.

Why is human life more important?
Because property or money means nothing without life. Laws are made to protect life, not the other way around.

Comment:

In this case the subject clearly demonstrates the structure of Stage 5 ''a priori rights.''

Subjects often fail to show the relationship of one value to the major competing value. At Stage 5 the subject appreciates not only the preeminence of values such as human rights but also sees how those values should be integrated into, or protected by, the law.

EXAMPLE

Should Heinz steal the drug?
Yes. If he did not it would cost a human life. If a life can be saved, I believe that one should go to any extent necessary to save it. Life is the most important ''possession'' that any of us have.

I understand, but in this case Heinz must break a law in order to save a life. How can you justify breaking a law to save a life?

Comment:

This type of question is usually not asked at the beginning of the interview. Give the subject a chance to relate the issues to each other. But, if the subject persists in assigning greater value to one issue without explaining its relationship to the other, place the conflict squarely before the subject. Other examples of such questions are, ''How can one justify following the law here if it will cost a life?'' or ''How can one justify letting Valjean go free when he has broken a law?''

A third common ambiguity between Stages 4 and 5 is the subject's apparent hesitation to generalize a moral judgment.

EXAMPLE

Should Heinz steal the drug?

Yes. In many value systems human life is of far greater value than the druggist's property rights.

Is this your value system or do you think this should be true for everyone?

Comment:

The suggested probe here may help determine whether the subject sees the relationship between life and law as one that is determined by the nature of the values themselves (Stage 5) or whether it is seen simply as one's own personal hierarchy (Stage 4/5).

As we have indicated, it is permissible to confront higher stage subjects to clarify the structure of their reasoning. However, the interviewer should always see his or her role as posing alternatives rather than suggesting solutions.

Instructions for Standard Issue Scoring

We have dealt in chapter 1 with the theoretical assumptions that underlie Standard Issue Scoring and the rationale for scoring procedures adopted. This chapter will take a more practical approach by presenting a detailed account of how actually to score a moral judgment interview.

Standard Issue Moral Judgment Scoring involves (a) breaking down interview material into discrete interview judgments; (b) matching these interview judgments with their conceptual counterparts, the criterion judgments, in the scoring manual according to strict rules; and (c) assigning stage scores at the issue and global levels on the basis of the interview judgment – criterion judgment matches.

A number of steps are involved within each of these three broad tasks. Table 6.1 presents the step-by-step scoring process. The 17 steps involved in scoring are discussed in detail in the pages to follow. Where relevant, rules are laid out and examples of various procedures are given. To help illustrate each step as well as to provide continuity from one step to another, a sample interview is analyzed at the end of the discussion of each procedure. The step-by-step scoring procedures are followed by a set of Skills Sections that present examples of some of the more difficult steps.

We do not intend that experienced raters refer to this lengthy discussion of rules and procedures each time they score. Rather, we hope that raters will study the material carefully and then use it principally for reference when difficulties arise at a particular step. The same is true, of course, for the Skills Sections. However, Table 6.1, which summarizes the 17 steps, should be used as a checklist of procedures each time an interview is scored. For this reason, this table is included in Volume II as well.

In the process of learning to score, it will be necessary to refer to several sections of this chapter, specifically, Appendix A – the moral dilemmas and probing questions with questions classified by type (dilemma-related, issue-centered, and general-issue questions); Appendix B – a transcript of one di-

Table 6.1. *Overview of scoring procedures*

Section I: Breaking down interview material into interview judgments

1. Orientation to the dilemma as a whole
2. Identification of chosen issue
   Determine which of the two standard issues is the subject's chosen issue, i.e., which course of action on the dilemma is recommended.
3. Classification by issue
   Classify all responses to the dilemma questions according to which of the two standard issues they represent.
4. Tentative stage orientation by issue
   Make an initial and tentative evaluation of the stage of reasoning reflected in the responses classified under the first issue to be scored (the chosen issue).
5. Classification into interview judgments
5a. Classification by norm
   Separate the material classified under the chosen issue into subcategories according to the norm reflected by the response.
5b. Classification by element
   Separate the material classified under the first norm to be scored into units that reflect a single element.
6. Scorability criteria
   An interview judgment (IJ), to be considered scorable, must provide a reason that is considered valid by the subject and must be prescriptive in nature.

Section II: Matching interview judgments with criterion judgments (CJs)

7. Locating a potential IJ–CJ match (Phase 1 of match evaluation)
   Guess the stage of the first IJ to be evaluated, and identify a CJ that seems to correspond to the IJ.
8. Surface evaluation of proposed match
   Evaluate the correspondence between IJ and CJ according to the CJ critical indicator (Phase 2).
9. Structural evaluation of proposed match
   Evaluate the correspondence between the IJ and CJ stage structure (Phase 3).
10. Accepting or rejecting the proposed match
    The following criteria must be met if a match score is to be assigned:
    a) The IJ must provide a reason that is attributed at least some validity by the subject and is at least implicitly prescriptive.
    b) The IJ must exhibit all the required critical indicators of the CJ.
    c) The IJ must be consistent with the specific stage structure of the CJ.
    d) The IJ must not provide a clearer match for the critical indicators and stage structure of any other CJ.
11. Entering a match score on the score sheet
    If the IJ–CJ match is accepted (as a clear or marginal match), it is noted on the score sheet.
12. Scoring the remaining IJs on the issue
    a) After scoring the first IJ of the issue, attempt to match any other IJs on the same issue that use the same norm.
    b) Then score the remaining IJs on the issue that use other norms. A score for each successful IJ–CJ match is entered on the score sheet.
    c) Material for which no clear or marginal match can be found should be bracketed for possible use in guess scoring.
    d) Check for inclusions.
13. Guess scoring
    If no match scores have been assigned but moral judgment material is available, enter a guess score for the issue. If no match or guess scores have been assigned, enter a note of ''no material'' for the issue.

159

Table 6.1. (*cont.*)

lemma from a sample interview that is referred to throughout this chapter; and Appendix C – the standard scoring sheet. The reader will also want to use the Form A section of Volume II while reading through the step-by-step instructions.

Knowledge of material presented in chapter 1 of this volume is assumed. Before beginning this chapter, the reader may want to review those sections of chapter 1 that deal with dilemmas, issues, norms, elements, and interview and criterion judgments.

Step-by-Step Scoring: Section I (Steps 1–6)
Breaking Down Interview Material into Interview Judgments

A Standard Issue Moral Judgment Interview includes three dilemmas, each of which taps two different standard issues and a number of norms and elements. The first procedure in scoring each of the three dilemmas is to break down this large quantity and range of material into manageable scoring units within each dilemma. We have defined our scoring unit, the interview judgment (IJ), as consisting of all interview material on an issue of a particular dilemma that represents the same norm and element at the same stage.

The scorer begins by reading through all the material on the first dilemma of the interview to gain a general sense of what the subject said (Step 1). Next the scorer determines the "chosen issue" (i.e., the action choice favored by the subject in that dilemma, Step 2). All the material on the dilemma is then classified by issue (Step 3). Beginning with the chosen issue, a preliminary estimate of stage is made (Step 4), and material on that issue is loosely classified by norm and element (Steps 5a and 5b). Finally an evaluation of the "scorability" of the individual IJ scoring units is made (Step 6). At that point, the scorer will be ready to evaluate potential CJ matches for the IJs, procedures to be taken up in Step-by-step Scoring: Section II (Steps 7–14).

Step 1: Orientation to the Dilemma as a Whole

The three standard dilemmas of an interview are scored one at a time. Thus, if interview Form A is being used, Dilemma III is scored first in its entirety before Dilemmas III' and I are each scored.

You should begin the scoring process by reading through all the responses to the first dilemma, including the responses to all the probe questions of that dilemma. This first reading will provide a general sense of the subject's approach to the dilemma, the points covered, and the relative emphasis on the two issues of the dilemma.

SAMPLE INTERVIEW

We will use one subject's responses to Dilemma III, the first dilemma of Form A, as our sample interview. You should begin by reading through all the responses to the dilemma.

Step 2: Identification of Chosen Issue

Each dilemma in the Moral Judgment Interview represents a conflict between two moral issues. The subject is asked to make a choice as to which issue should take priority (i.e., which action choice should be pursued) in the hypothetical situation. The chosen issue is determined by the subject's choice in regard to the original conflict posed by the dilemma.

Thus, the first task in reading the material on a dilemma is to determine the subject's chosen issue (i.e., which side of the argument the subject basically supports). To determine the chosen issue on a dilemma, you should read over all the subject's responses, asking what basic choice the subject makes. In Dilemma III, for example, the choice is whether Heinz should steal the drug to save his wife's life, or whether he should not steal but should instead uphold the law. If the action choice is "yes, steal," then the chosen issue is life; if it is "no, don't steal," then the chosen issue is law.

One of the two issues of a dilemma must be designated as the chosen issue for the dilemma even if the choice is ambiguous. There is no option of designating no chosen issue on the dilemma even if the choice is ambiguous. This is because a dichotomous choice yields greater agreement among raters than does the addition of a third, "undecided," category.

The probe questions that follow each dilemma are designed to elicit reasoning on both of the standard issues. Not surprisingly, most subjects say more about the issue they favor (i.e., the chosen issue) and attribute greater validity to arguments supporting that issue than they do for the issue they oppose (the "nonchosen" issue). The interviewer must often push the subject to provide arguments on the nonchosen issue. As a result, subjects may sometimes use arguments in support of the nonchosen issue that represent slightly less mature thinking than that of which they are capable. For these reasons, scores for the subject's chosen issue on each dilemma are weighted more heavily in the calculation of global interview stage scores than are scores on the nonchosen issue. Designation of chosen issue can thus have a substantial effect on the global stage score.

Identification of chosen issue is often straightforward as in the case of the sample interview. But the situation is not always as clear-cut. Generally it is preferable to determine chosen issue at the outset of scoring a dilemma. However, when it is especially difficult to decide which is the chosen issue, this step may be postponed until Step 14. In determining chosen issue, the following rules apply:

Rules for Designating Chosen Issue

1. If the subject makes a clear action choice in response to the first question of the dilemma (e.g. "Should Heinz steal the drug?") and holds consistently to that choice throughout the interview, then that choice represents the chosen issue.

When subsequent probe questions introduce new situational factors (e.g., "Suppose Heinz doesn't love his wife?"), the responses to these questions are not relevant in determining the chosen issue. Thus if a subject clearly states that Heinz should steal for his wife but later qualifies that by saying that he should not steal if he doesn't love his wife, the chosen issue is still life.

2. If the subject spontaneously reverses his or her choice without any input from the interviewer other than a repetition of the original question ("should he?" or "why?") or a factual clarification of the dilemma itself, and if the subject holds consistently to the second choice, then the chosen issue corresponds to that second choice.

3. If the subject reverses his or her choice after probing by the interviewer beyond simple repetition of the original question or factual clarification of the dilemma, then the chosen issue corresponds to the subject's original (i.e., first) choice.

4. If the subject reverses his or her decision with or without input from the interviewer but then does not hold consistently to the second choice, the original choice determines the chosen issue.

5. If the subject answers the original probe question with arguments for both sides of the dilemma, the chosen issue should reflect the subject's emphasis. For example, if the subject is basically in favor of a particular choice but qualifies this judgment by arguments against that choice or for the other choice, then that basic choice rather than the qualifications determines the chosen issue. This occurs frequently on Dilemmas III' and IV'.

6. Determination of chosen issue for Dilemmas III' (Form A) and Dilemma IV' (Form B) focuses on the decision of the judge (whether or not to *punish* the individual) rather than on the decision of the police officer or doctor (whether or not to *report* the individual). Thus, morality and conscience is the chosen issue if the subject feels that the judge should not punish the individual or should impose only token punishment. Alternatively, punishment is the chosen issue if the subject advocates more than a token punishment or if arguments in favor of punishment are stressed even if some leniency is also advocated.

7. In Dilemma VIII (Form C), the chosen issue is determined by the question of whether to *report* Valjean, rather than by the question of whether to *punish* him if he is reported. (Note that this is the opposite of Dilemmas III' and IV' discussed in Rule 6 above.)

SAMPLE INTERVIEW

Determination of chosen issue is unambiguous in the sample interview (Appendix B). The subject says that Heinz should steal the drug for his wife. Although he later expresses doubt as to whether Heinz should steal for a stranger, he does not waver from his initial judgment that Heinz should steal for his wife. Thus life is the chosen issue; law is the nonchosen issue.

Step 3: Classification by Issue
The next step in scoring is to divide all the interview material on the dilemma according to the two standard issues of that dilemma. The issue classification of a particular statement is defined by the dilemma choice for which the statement argues or by the value it upholds. Issues are scored independently both within dilemmas and across dilemmas. Therefore, it is important that material classified under one issue not be used in scoring the other issue on that dilemma or the same or another issue on another dilemma. (The only exception to this rule is the case in which very little material exists for a particular issue. In this

case, material from the opposing issue may be used to interpret that material in order to assign a guess score to the problematic issue. See Step 13.)

The response to a single question may, of course, include more than one idea. These distinguishable ideas (interview judgments) presented in response to a single question need not be classified under the same issue. It is only necessary that the same interview material not be classed under (and thus used in scoring) both issues.

One important factor to consider in classifying material by issue is the probe question to which it is a response. There are three types of probe questions used in the interviews: (1) dilemma-related questions (e.g., "Should Heinz steal the drug?"); (2) issue-centered questions (e.g., "It's against the law for Heinz to steal. Does that make it morally wrong?"); and (3) general-issue questions (e.g., "Should people try to do everything they can to obey the law?"). Responses to the three types of questions are handled somewhat differently in terms of issue classification. *Dilemma-related* questions ask the subject to make a judgment in relation to the particular dilemma. *Issue-centered* questions elicit the subject's reasoning about the significance of an issue (e.g., law) in a particular dilemma (e.g., the Heinz dilemma). *General-issue* questions concern the value of the issues (e.g., life or law) in general rather than a particular dilemma.

Rules for Issue Classification

1. Interview material should be classified under only one issue and should be used for scoring that issue alone. It should not be used in scoring the opposing issue on that dilemma or the same or another issue on another dilemma. However, the response to a single question may include arguments on both issues in which case these arguments should be separated and classified each under the appropriate issue.

2. Assignment by issue on dilemma-related questions corresponds to the choice that the subject is making or defending in the particular response being classified (e.g., arguments in favor of stealing the drug in Dilemma III are classified under the life issue; arguments opposed are classified under the law issue).

Other than the actual choice being supported in a response to a dilemma-related question (e.g., steal, don't steal), the content of the response is irrelevant in issue classification. For example, if in response to the question, "Should Heinz steal the drug?" the subject says, "Yes, because the laws weren't designed to value property over life," the subject is presenting a particular conception of law as a way of justifying theft of the drug. Because arguments supporting that position are made in response to a dilemma-related question and are justifying the choice defined as life, the response is classified under the life issue, not the law issue. (The subject's conception of law is not lost here, of course, as it becomes the focus of the next content classification, that by norm. The issue here would be life, but the norm would be law. See Step 5a.)

3. Issue classification is not affected by which issue is the chosen issue for the dilemma as a whole. Thus, if the subject says that Heinz should steal to save his wife's life but should not steal to save a stranger's life, then arguments that support stealing to save the wife are classified under the life issue (which would also be the chosen issue in this case), whereas arguments against stealing for the stranger are classified under the law issue.

4. Responses to issue-centered questions are sometimes classified under the issue focused on by the question and sometimes under the issue of the choice being supported in the response. Issue-centered questions (and general-issue questions) are asked in order to ensure that material is generated about both issues on the dilemma. Thus, an attempt should be made first to classify responses to issue-centered questions under the issue evoked by the question. However, if the subject uses the facts of the dilemma to reject the validity of the issue addressed by the question, then the response is classified under the issue upheld by the subject. For instance, the following response would be classified under the life issue even though the issue focused on is law. "It is against the law for Heinz to steal. Does that make it morally wrong?" "It doesn't matter what the law says, Heinz really loved his wife so he should have stolen for her."

5. A response to a general-issue question that does not refer to the original dilemma is classified under the issue raised by the question even if it denies the value of the issue being probed. Thus, responses to the question "Is it important for people to do everything they can to save another's life?" are usually classified under the life issue, and responses to the question "Should people try to do everything they can to obey the law?" are usually classified under the law issue. If, in response to a question about the importance of upholding the law, the subject denigrates the value of maintaining the law, the response is still classified under the law issue. If CJ matches can be found for the responses under both issues, enter a score only for the issue of the question. Remember, never score the same material twice.

6. When in doubt about the issue classification of some material either because it is dilemma related and the choice is ambiguous or because it is a response to an issue-centered or a general-issue question and unclear as to issue, check both issues and score the material under the CJ that seems to be the closest match. Again, keep in mind that the same material should not be scored twice.

7. Sometimes a CJ from one issue seems to provide a match for interview material that, according to the rules presented here, clearly belongs to the second issue. If no other interview material is available for scoring the first issue, then the CJ may be used in assigning a guess score for that issue, but may not be used for match scoring.

In addition to these general rules, two specific rules apply to Dilemmas III′ and IV′.

8. Dilemma IV′ includes questions on capital punishment. Arguments against capital punishment or arguments for leniency are classified under the morality and conscience issue. Arguments for capital punishment are classified under the punishment issue. Responses that deny the value of capital punishment by arguing for the value of another type of punishment (rather than by arguing against capital punishment itself) are also classified under the punishment issue.

9. Questions 7–12 of Dilemma III′ and Questions 8–13 of Dilemma IV′ are designed to elicit metaethical reasoning. Responses to these questions are never match scored on either issue. When a response to one of these questions seems to match a criterion judgment on one of the standard issues, it may be used as material for a guess score in the issue if no match scores have been found. Otherwise, material in response to these questions is not stage scored.

Issue classification is fairly straightforward in the sample interview. Questions 1, 2, and 3 are dilemma related. In Questions 1 and 2 the subject supports Heinz's stealing the drug to save his wife (whether he loves her or not), and thus the issue is life (Rule 2).

In Questions 3, he opposes stealing the drug for a stranger and thus the issue is law (Rules 2 and 3).

Question 5 is a general-issue question regarding life. In it, the subject does not refer back to the original dilemma and the classification is life (Rule 5).

Question 6 is issue centered. It poses the conflict of the dilemma abstractly. This can make issue classification more difficult than is the case with either general-issue or dilemma-specific questions. In response to Question 6 the subject argues for upholding life. Therefore the classification is life (Rule 4).

Question 7 is another general-issue question, this time focusing on law. The respondent does not refer back to the dilemma and thus the issue is law (Rule 5).

Question 8 is a dilemma-related question. The respondent again supports stealing the drug and the classification is life (Rule 4).

Thus, material in Questions 1, 2, 5, 6, and 8 is classified as life and the responses to Questions 3 and 7 are classified as law.

Step 4: Tentative Stage Orientation by Issue

Responses to the first dilemma in the interview have now been classified according to issue. The chosen issue has been designated, and it is with that issue that scoring begins. Material within the chosen issue must still be broken down by norm and element into discrete IJs. Before doing that, it is helpful to gain an overall sense of what stage or stages the material on that issue represents.

You should reread all the responses classified under the issue you are scoring and think about what they mean and what level of sociomoral perspective they seem to reflect. Be careful, however, not to place too much confidence in this initial assessment. It can aid in the search for appropriate CJ matches for the IJs, but it is not essential to that search. In fact, too great a reliance on this initial guess could lead to inadequate consideration of CJs at other stages. In any case, if intuitively interpreting the stage significance of the material proves difficult at this point, simply proceed to the next step.

Since the chosen issue for our sample interview on Dilemma III is life, we begin scoring with that issue. Turn to the Table of Life Issue Criterion Judgments, Dilemma III, Form A in Volume II.

Reading all the statements from the sample interview on the life issue (i.e., responses to Questions 1, 2, 5, 6, and 8), you should ask yourself which, if any, of the reasons for stealing the drug found in the Table of Life Issue Criterion Judgments seems to capture the thrust of the subject's argument.

Stage 1 with its confusion of the value of life with external factors (e.g., property, position) can be ruled out as can Stage 5 with its emphasis on a hierarchy of rights. Stages 2, 3, and 4 are all reasonable alternatives to consider. However, the material seems to lack the Stage 2 concern with instrumental needs and exchange and perhaps falls short of a Stage 4 social system perspective. The Stage 3 emphasis on motives and relationships for their own sake may best capture the meaning of the subject's responses. But that is only a guess, a preliminary impression.

Steps 5a and 5b: Classification into Interview Judgments

The interview judgment is the basic scoring unit into which the interview material is divided. A single IJ embraces all interview responses within a single dilemma that represent the same issue × norm × element.

Formally speaking, classification of issue material into IJs involves two additional steps: (a) classification by norm, and (b) classification by element. In practice, the scorer need not divide the material on the issue being scored into discrete IJs before looking for appropriate CJs in the manual. A review of the CJs in the manual usually helps to clarify which norms and elements, that is, which IJs, are represented in the issue material.

For the moment, however, let us consider the formal two-step approach of classifying material by norm and element. (See Tables 6.2 and 6.3 for norms and elements.)

Step 5a: Classification by Norm

Classification by norm is essentially classification by the value content of the moral judgment. Thus the norm represents the moral value or object of concern that is being brought to bear by the subject in justifying a choice in the dilemma.

As discussed in chapter 1, each issue encompasses between one and four norms. An individual will evidence in moral judgments on an issue a concern with at least one of those norms. Material relating to a particular norm may extend through many questions on an issue, may be found sporadically throughout responses to the dilemma, or may make up only a part of the answer to one question.

The best way to learn how to differentiate interview material on the basis of norm is to look at criterion judgments within the same issue and stage that differ from each other by norm (e.g., CJs 9, 19, and 12 and CJs 25, 26, 27, and 28 in Form A).

SAMPLE INTERVIEW

On the life issue five norms are listed as possible choices: life, law, property, affiliation, and conscience. In our sample interview, a single norm seems to stand out on the life issue, the norm of affiliation. (Question 1) "He is desperate for one he loves." (Question 2) ". . . he's married to this woman. And I'm sure one time he loved her. Love keeps coming to my mind." (Question 8) ". . . he's stealing to help someone he loves." In addition, most of the life issue material on the issue-specific questions 5 and 6 seems to be focused on the norm of life itself. (Question 5) [It is important for people to do everything they can to save another's life] "because people are human beings." (Question 6) "It's instinct to reach out and help another human."

On the law issue, five norms are listed as possible choices: life, property, affiliation, law, and conscience. In response to Question 7 the subject focuses on the law norm. (". . . [you] have to have laws [to] say what is right and wrong. We have people who are crazy and unstable, so we have to have the law.") Norm classification of the remaining law issue material, found in the response to Question 3, is also fairly straightforward. The argument presented here is that whether you should steal to save someone depends on how close you are to that person and in the case of the stranger you are not as close as you are with someone you love. This argument is basically the same idea that was used to argue for stealing to save a loved wife. But in the case of the

Table 6.2. *The moral norms*

1. Life
   a) Preservation
   b) Quality/quantity
2. Property
3. Truth
4. Affiliation
(5. Erotic love and sex)
6. Authority
7. Law
8. Contract
(9. Civil rights)
(10. Religion)
11. Conscience
12. Punishment

Table 6.3. *The moral elements*

Modal elements

Upholding normative order
1. Obeying/consulting persons or deity. Should obey, get consent (should consult, persuade).
2. Blaming/approving. Should be blamed for, disapproved (should be approved).
3. Retributing/exonerating. Should retribute against (should exonerate).
4. Having a right/having no right.
5. Having a duty/having no duty.

Value elements

Egoistic consequences
6. Good reputation/bad reputation.
7. Seeking reward/avoiding punishment.

Utilitarian consequences
8. Good individual consequences/bad individual consequences.
9. Good group consequences/bad group consequences.

Ideal or harmony-serving consequences.
10. Upholding character.
11. Upholding self-respect.
12. Serving social ideal or harmony.
13. Serving human dignity and autonomy.

Fairness
14. Balancing perspectives or role taking.
15. Reciprocity or positive desert.
16. Maintaining equity and procedural fairness.
17. Maintaining social contract or freely agreeing.

stranger the idea is being used to justify *not* stealing. Thus it is classified by the same norm, affiliation, but under a different issue (law rather than life).

Step 5b: Classification by Element

The 17 elements represent the different ways in which the significance of a norm may be construed. An element is the reason given for endowing the norm with value.

As with the norms, the best way to learn how to differentiate the elements from one another is to look for CJs with the same issue, stage, and norm that therefore differ only by element. (These are easily found as they are grouped together in each issue's Table of Criterion Judgments, e.g., CJs 12, 13, 14, 15 and CJs 23, 24, 25, on the life issue, or CJs 24, 25, 26, and 27 on the law issue, Form A.)

For those who compiled the scoring manual this final division of interview material by element into CJs was critical, but it is a step that need not unduly delay the scorer.

In practice, subdivision by element into interview judgments is often accomplished by comparing the relevant interview material with the CJs listed in the issue's Table of Criterion Judgments. This process is explained more fully in Step 7 (discussed later).

SAMPLE
INTERVIEW

In looking over the sample interview material of the life issue, bear in mind that we have identified two norms in this subject's responses: affiliation and life. Let us consider first the affiliation norm material in Questions 1, 2, and 8. One idea expressed here is that Heinz's action is not blameworthy because his motives were good, he had no choice, he was desperate, and so on. In looking through the Table of Life Issue CJs, it should become clear that this kind of argument reflects the blaming (approving) element. (See, for example, CJs 8 and 12.) Another idea expressed within the affiliation norm material is that "he's married to this woman . . . one time he loved her." In focusing on the marital relationship per se, the subject is using the having a duty element. (See, for example, CJ#13.) Turning to the life norm material we see basically one idea – that she should be saved because she is a human being, and it's right or natural to help another human being. This direct focus on the value of human life or human beings reflects the serving human dignity element.

Turning to the law issue, the element good group consequences seems to stand out for the material under Question 7 (already classified under the law norm). The appropriate element classification for the rest of the material seems less obvious and must be determined by comparison of the interview material with the criterion judgments in the manual. In thinking about the element designation of the response to Question 3, let us look at the CJs on the law issue with the affiliation norm to see what elements are used with this issue and norm. CJ#13, affiliation norm and blaming (approving) element, looks like a good possibility for a potential match.

In separating material into interview judgments, it is important to remember that within a single issue and norm, the material can sometimes represent two or more elements. If this occurs, each issue × norm × element combination constitutes a separate interview judgment. Further discussion of identifying interview judgments is provided in the skills section for Step 5.

Step 6: Scorability Criteria

An interview judgment, to be considered scorable, (1) must provide a reason that (2) is considered valid by the subject and (3) is prescriptive in nature. These three "scorability" criteria lie at the very heart of moral judgment scoring as they define what does and what does not constitute a moral judgment within this system. For that reason, evaluation based on these criteria can take place at any point in the scoring process. At the very least, careful scrutiny is appropriate here and as part of Step 10 (discussed later).

We will state the three scorability criteria and then go on to explain them in some detail. Examples of how to apply these criteria in practice are provided in the Skills Section. The scorability criteria are as follows:

1. An interview judgment must offer a reason or justification for the action being defended or value being upheld.
2. An interview judgment must be accepted as valid by the subject.
3. An interview judgment must be at least implicitly prescriptive if it is to be used for match scoring.

1. An IJ must offer a reason or justification for the action or value being defended. In scoring moral judgments, we are not cataloging the individual's moral opinions or values. We are concerned instead with the way that person thinks and with what he or she thinks is right; the material cannot be used for scoring unless an explanation is offered for why the action should be taken or why a particular position is morally preferable or right.

In order to qualify as a statement that offers a reason, a response must assert some general, basic, or terminal value as an argument for a recommended action or as justification for a less terminal value. In terms of the scoring system presented here, this means that a potentially scorable statement must refer to either a moral norm and modal element or a value element. (See chapter 1 for a discussion of modal and value elements.)

A reason in this context is a statement that relates one value to another. In the criterion judgments, this relation is usually reflected in the use of the word *because;* for example, "Heinz should steal because his wife means a lot to him." This statement reflects a concern for a general positive value that can be distinguished from the action or value that it is upholding.

If, however, in response to the question of whether Heinz should be punished for stealing the drug, the subject replies flatly, "He should pay the druggist for the drug," then the response cannot be said to embody a reason for what should be done – that is, why Heinz should pay the druggist. One might argue here that the response implies restitution or reciprocity as a value. It does not, however, use reciprocity as a value element; it simply states *what* should be done without explaining why it should be done. In other words, the response involves merely the assertion of a value, not the assertion of a relationship *between* two values. Thus, a statement that can be said to offer a reason is defined as one that refers to a relation between a recommended value or action and another value that serves to justify or support the action or the first value. This means that any potentially scorable statement must refer to a norm or an element that is not simply implied by the recommended action or value.

The example we cited, "He should pay the druggist for the drug," clearly does not fit the criterion of providing a reason. A statement that at first glance seems to be equally impoverished is, "[Heinz should be punished because]

Heinz should be made to pay for what he has done.'' However, this example can be said to offer an implicit reason for punishment and thus may be usable for guess scoring (see Step 13). This response differs from the preceding one (which could not be used even for guess scoring) in that it includes an implicit reference to retribution (or expiation). This assertion of retribution/expiation as a value is separable from the action being recommended (punish Heinz). The subject is saying, in effect, that Heinz should be punished because he deserves it, i.e., that there is a value of negative reciprocity or retribution providing a reason for punishment. Retributing is one of the modal elements. The problem of distinguishing among match material, guess material, and ''no material'' using the criterion of having a reason is taken up in the Skills Section.

As we have seen, not every identifiable value constitutes a moral concern. To qualify as a moral concern (norm or element), the value must be used as a reason. It is also true that not every reason reflects an underlying value. Some statements that seem to offer a reason are classified as unscorable because the reason offered is ''empty'' of value content from the standpoint of Standard Issue Scoring. Consider the statement, ''Heinz should be punished because stealing is wrong.'' Such a statement does not include any information about the value that underlies it, i.e., the norm or element on which it is based. Although the statement seems to offer a reason or a justification for an action that is separable from the reason, it does not refer to any of the elements. ''Stealing is wrong'' could reflect a concern for the importance of property rights, respect for the law, possible negative consequences to the thief, and so on. The subject has not asserted a general positive value or a terminal value as a justification for punishing and thus has not, in the relevant sense, told us why Heinz should be punished.

This rule must be modified in regard to Stages 1 and 1/2. Stage 1 is in part defined by the inability of the individual to take intention into account and by a tendency to simply label some actions as wrong with no real understanding of why they are wrong. Thus in scoring for Stages 1 and 1/2, the interview response must be considered in the context of the subject's inability to elaborate when probed. The statement ''Heinz should be punished because stealing is wrong'' is a case in point. If the subject makes such a statement in the context of a well-probed interview with no evidence of an ability to go beyond it to say why stealing is wrong, then that statement is scored at Stage 1. But if the same statement were made and not probed to elicit further justification, it would not be scored because it does not present a reason for why stealing is wrong.

2. An IJ must be accepted as valid by the subject.   Judgments that are explicitly disavowed or rejected as invalid by the subject are not scored. Moral judgment stage scores should reflect the kind of reasoning the subject subscribes to or considers valid, not reasoning he or she understands and can generate but rejects as invalid; for example, ''Maybe he would feel he had to steal the drug even if he didn't love his wife because he's still her husband. But I wouldn't think like that. I think that's crazy.'' This requirement excludes from scoring statements that describe what the subject takes to be the socially accepted position on an issue if he or she does not subscribe to that position (e.g., ''I guess most people would argue that Heinz should be punished to deter others, but I think they are wrong''). All material to be match or guess scored must offer a moral reason or justification that has some validity for the subject. Judgments that fail this criterion are those that are clearly disavowed or rejected by the person making them. However, judgments that are considered by the subject to have some validity but that are overridden by other, more important considerations are scored. When validity for the subject is questionable, the material can be used for guess scoring.

3. An IJ must be at least implicitly prescriptive if it is to be used for match scoring. Interviewees are asked what they think should be done in a moral dilemma or conflict, not what they think would be done or even what they themselves would do in the situation. Thus, to be used for match scoring an IJ must involve some element of *should* or *ought;* that is, it must be prescriptive. Statements such as "I would steal the drug because my wife means a lot to me" or "Most people would not steal the drug because they would be afraid of going to jail" fail the criterion of prescriptivity and are not usable for match scoring. Prescriptivity, however, is not a requirement for guess scoring.

Some caution should be used in applying the criterion of prescriptivity to Stage 1 and Stage 2 protocols. Individuals reasoning at these stages do not distinguish clearly between would and should. For them the questions "What should Heinz do?" and "What would Heinz do?" may have the same meaning. Much the same problem was encountered with the requirement that a reason be given. As in that case, if the interview has been well probed and the individual does not seem to differentiate would and should, then the rater should attempt a lower stage match for the material. If the subject has demonstrated a clear understanding of prescriptivity in other parts of the interview, then the nonprescriptive material should not be used for match scoring. When individuals at the conventional or postconventional stages clearly designate a position as nonprescriptive, they are often in effect rejecting the position as morally invalid (Scorability Criterion 2). In other words, in saying that a reason is not meant to be prescriptive, the subject also may be saying that it is not a morally valid argument (e.g., "Maybe he wouldn't steal the drug for his wife if he didn't love her because he would be afraid of going to jail, but he should steal it. Whether he loves her or not shouldn't make any difference, but it probably would").

SAMPLE INTERVIEW	Most of the material in the sample interview satisfies the scorability criteria.

Providing a Reason: The subject begins his response to Questions 1, 2, 3, and 5 with "because" and provides a reason why the proposed action should or should not take place. The responses to Questions 6 and 7 also provide reasons for the positions taken. An example of a statement that does not provide a reason for upholding a value is the statement in question, "Stealing is wrong but sometimes you don't have any other choice, and that's what you have to do. And ask God to forgive you." No reason is given here for why "stealing is wrong" and therefore it does not provide scorable material for the law issue. If instead he had said, "Stealing is wrong according to God's law [or because God has said it is], but sometimes you don't have any other choice," then you would have a reason and a potentially scorable IJ.

Validity: The subject attributes validity to the arguments made. In response to Question 3 he states that Heinz should not steal the drug for a stranger, "Because she is a stranger and other than feeling sorry for her as a human being, but not like a closeness that you have for one you love." Here he is raising an argument in favor of stealing for a stranger, "feeling sorry for her . . . ," which he overrides due to other considerations. But he does not reject the reason of "feeling sorry for her as a human being" as invalid. In fact, he uses that as a major theme elsewhere in the interview. Similarly, he declines to apply his reasons for obeying the law (Question 7) to the Heinz case itself (Question 8), but he also does not deny the validity of his general arguments for obeying the law. If, in Question 1, he had said "Stealing is wrong according to God's law, but sometimes you don't have any other choice, and that's what you have to do," that would also be an example of overriding an argument, not invalidating it.

Prescriptivity:

There are two statements made in the interview where prescriptivity is questionable. The interviewee concludes his response to Question 3 by saying, "I would have to have a strong feeling for someone before I could do it . . ." This statement would not be used for match scoring since the protocol is clearly not Stage 1 and the subject does seem to comprehend prescriptivity. It might be usable in guess scoring. Another ambiguous statement is found in Question 6, where he says, "It's instinct to reach out and help another human." This might be a mere statement of perceived fact. Or it may be a statement of how he thinks humans ought to behave. In the context of the interview, the statement does seem implicitly prescriptive. It appears to be an assertion that helping is a universal "natural law" imperative for human beings, rather than an individual subjective wish unique to the particular person.

Step-by-step Scoring: Section II (Steps 7–14)
Matching Interview Judgments with Criterion Judgments

Evaluating the proposed match between an IJ from the interview being scored and a CJ in the manual is probably the most difficult task in Standard Issue Scoring. It is also the point at which most unreliability arises.

Once you have divided the interview material into IJs, you must make a tentative stage assessment and locate a potential match for the IJ with a CJ in the Table of Criterion Judgments for the issue being scored. You must then determine whether the correspondence between the IJ and the CJ is substantial enough to warrant its being scored as a match. That is, you must decide if the IJ is really an example of the kind of thinking demonstrated in the CJ.

In making this decision, the scorer must strike a balance between focusing on the deeper structural significance and the more concrete and objective features of the material to be scored. Operationally, this means that the scorer must be able to interpret the essential meaning of an interview response without distorting or misinterpreting the data by reading into it some meaning that is not really there. For this reason, in order for a IJ–CJ comparison to be considered a match, (1) the IJ must exhibit the surface features of the CJ in question, and (2) the IJ must be consistent with the stage structure of that CJ.

Our requirement that the IJ exhibit the surface features is designed to prevent an excessively loose interpretation in which the scorer attributes to the subject ideas that the subject may not in fact have been expressing. Our requirement that the IJ also be consistent with the underlying moral judgment structure of the stage represented by the CJ is an attempt to minimize the invalidity of scores based on a literal matching of surface features of the IJ and the CJ.

A scoring system based on a very literal, "strict interpretation" approach might yield greater reliability, but responses could be misscored from the structural point of view. The increase in reliability would be outweighted by a decrease in validity. The adoption of a very structural orientation or "loose interpretation" approach might increase the validity or incidence of correct classification for very experienced scorers, but would involve greater unreliability in general as well as less valid scoring among less experienced scorers.

Because the careful evaluation of each proposed IJ–CJ match is so crucial and is also the point at which most unreliability arises, we have divided the evaluative process into three phases, corresponding to Steps 7, 8, and 9.

Phase 1 (Step 7): Locating a potential IJ–CJ match. Using a general conception of the five stages, the scorer makes a tentative estimate of the stage of the IJ and locates a CJ that seems to be a potential match for the IJ.

Phase 2 (Step 8): Surface evaluation of proposed match. The scorer evaluates the proposed IJ–CJ match in terms of the critical indicators of the CJ. The scorer decides whether the critical indicators are clearly present, ambiguously present, or absent. Each CJ is defined in terms of one or more critical indicators that are required in an IJ for a match to be given.

Phase 3 (Step 9): Structural evaluation of proposed match. The scorer evaluates whether the structural significance of the IJ is consistent with the structural features of the proposed CJ match.

Once the surface and structural evaluations have been made, the IJ must be accepted or rejected as a match according to rules presented in Step 10. If the match is accepted, it is entered on the score sheet (Step 11). All of the remaining IJs on the first issue are then scored following the same procedures used for the first IJ (Step 12). If no clear or marginal IJ–CJ matches have been found for the issue, then a guess score must be assigned to the issue as a whole (Step 13). After the chosen issue has been completely scored, then the nonchosen issue of the first dilemma is scored, followed by the chosen and nonchosen issues of the second and third dilemmas (Step 14). At that point, stage scores for each issue and for the interview as a whole can be computed. A global stage score and a weighted average score (WAS) are assigned – procedures to be taken up in Step-by-step Scoring: Section III (Steps 15–17).

Step 7: Locating a Potential IJ–CJ Match

The first part of the scoring process, "breaking down interview material into IJs," involved classifying responses to an entire dilemma. In the next set of procedures, IJs are considered one at a time, and one issue at a time. All the IJs on the chosen issue are scored individually before all the IJs on the nonchosen issue are scored.

The search for an appropriate match begins by choosing material from the issue being scored that seems clearest as to norm and stage and that meets the scorability criteria of providing a reason accepted as valid by the subject and being prescriptive in nature. Remember that material on any one norm within an issue may be contained in a response to a single question or may be spread out over a number of responses to the dilemma.

Reading over the interview material to be scored, you should think about what the subject seems to be saying and make a general orienting guess as to the probable stage of the material. Making this very tentative initial guess will help to bring into focus the ideas being expressed and will also serve as a guide in the search for a CJ to match the material being assessed. However, it is important to keep in mind that both this initial stage orientation and the initial assumptions about which norm the material represents are tentative and merely serve as aids in the search for an appropriate CJ. It is important that CJs at different stages be considered as well as norm or element classifications different from the initial guess.

With the interview material in mind, you should read the stage overviews in the appropriate Table of Issue Criterion Judgments in Volume II, beginning with the section of the stage of your initial assessment. Each of these stage overviews not only introduces the basic orientation of that stage toward the issue at hand, but also introduces the CJs included under that stage. (Note, however, that the transitional CJs are not included in this review. Be sure that the transitional CJs are not overlooked.) You should then look for a promising CJ match among the CJs of the stage that seems most appropriate, as well as among CJs of adjacent stages and stage transitions. You may find more than one possible match. If so, you should note all of the possibilities since each one should be considered. (Remember that material using the same norm can represent more than one IJ if several elements are used.)

The initial search for a possible CJ match is not difficult, but it must be thorough. You should not settle on the first CJ that sounds remotely similar to the interview material before you. Beginning scorers in particular should be careful not to restrict their choices to CJs at the stage of their initial stage guess, since that initial guess may well be wrong.

After selecting the CJ that most closely resembles the IJ being scored, evaluation of the match begins.

SAMPLE INTERVIEW

Beginning with life, the chosen issue, let us consider first the often repeated idea that Heinz is desperate for one he loves, he didn't have a choice, he has no other way, he's stealing to help someone he loves, and so on. We have determined that this material reflects the affiliation norm and the blaming (approving) element. In looking over the Table of Life Issue Criterion Judgments, the two CJs that look like a potential match for this IJ are CJ#8, Stage 2/3 and CJ#12, Stage 3.

Step 8: Evaluating the IJ–CJ Match – Surface Evaluation

After choosing from the Table of CJs the CJ that most closely resembles the IJ in question, the scorer should turn to the fully explicated Criterion Judgment and begin the surface evaluation of the IJ–CJ match.

The surface evaluation seeks to answer the question "Does the IJ match the CJ according to certain required specifications?" These required specifications have been labeled critical indicators. Each CJ has at least one critical indicator. The scorer must decide whether the IJ has the same features referred to in the CJ critical indicators.

Critical Indicators. If you turn to any of the explicated CJs in the manual, you will find the paragraph labeled Critical Indicators. You should read through a number of such paragraphs to become familiar with the types of requirements imposed. As you will see, different CJs require different numbers and combinations of critical indicators for a match. For example, CJ#1 of the life issue,

Form A, requires that one of its two critical indicators be met; CJ#2 requires that both of its critical indicators be met, and so on.

Examples. The examples provided for each CJ of clear and marginal matches and sometimes of nonmatch material from actual interview protocols are invaluable aids in evaluating what does and does not constitute a match. These examples can be profitably used not only to help evaluate individual IJs, but also as a means of understanding the scoring procedures themselves.

In deciding whether interview material should be considered to match a CJ, the scorer should use a strict interpretation of the critical indicators. This does not mean that the interview material must use the exact words of the CJ. However, the essence of each required critical indicator must be present in the interview. The scorer should not supply a mediation between the IJ and CJ that involves "filling in" the essence of a critical indicator implied but not stated by the subject. Furthermore, in assessing an IJ–CJ correspondence, close attention should be paid to the question to which the interview material is a response to avoid giving credit for words or phrases that simply repeat the probe question (unless, of course, there is some appropriate elaboration in the response).

On the other hand, you should also avoid rejecting stage-scorable material just because the ideas in it are not articulately or precisely presented. We all make false starts when we speak, beginning an idea, going on to others, combing back later to the same idea. People do not speak in criterion judgments. The scorer must often construct meaning out of garbled words and mangled sentences. This reconstruction process is called *transposition,* and it can be used at any stage of the evaluation process, although it is perhaps most frequently used at Phase 2 (where literal comparisons from the data to the manual are most important).

Transposition involves restating the relevant interview material in a way that is more coherent than the subject's own expression of his or her thoughts. Transposition is especially useful when the responses included within an IJ are scattered throughout an interview. In such cases, the fragments must be pulled together to provide a complete account of the subject's thinking on the norm-element in question. Another appropriate use of transposition is to extricate the relevant IJ material from a long interview passage that includes material on several norms and/or elements. It is also helpful in making sense of an interview response that is unclear as to meaning or one that is expressed rather incoherently or idiosyncratically.

Transposition entails making rearrangements, distillations, or other grammatical alterations, but no substantive modifications of the response. The idea is to establish a more concise or focused representation of the response. In the process, you must be careful neither to read extraneous ideas into the subject's judgments nor to exclude relevant material from the restated version.

Step 8: Surface Evaluation

Outcome of Surface Evaluation. The evaluation of an IJ in relation to the critical indicators of a CJ may have one of three results:

Clear Pass: At least the minimum number of required critical indicators is clearly present in the interview response. (Although the IJ need not use the exact words of the critical indicators, the equivalence of the ideas referred to must be clear and unambiguous.)

Marginal Pass: The subject expresses ideas that are essentially the same as those required by the critical indicators, but the correspondence between them involves some ambiguity.

Fail: At least one of the required critical indicators of the CJ is absent in the IJ. If one or more critical indicators is clearly present in the IJ, but another required critical indicator is not at least marginally present, then the IJ fails.

Thus the surface evaluation involves distinguishing among ideas that clearly express the critical indicators (clear match), those that ambiguously express the critical indicators or differ from them in superficial ways (marginal match), and those that may resemble the critical indicators but that differ significantly from them (fail). Again, the examples section provided for each explicated CJ should help the scorer to understand in a concrete way what it means for an IJ to exhibit the critical indicators. It is especially instructive to contrast clear match, marginal match, and fail examples to see what degree of explicitness or clarity we have required for a match.

If, after careful evaluation you are still uncertain whether an IJ can be said to exhibit the critical indicators, note this uncertainty and proceed with the next step, structural evaluation (Step 9).

SAMPLE
INTERVIEW

To begin with, let us consider whether our first IJ matches the critical indicators of CJ#8. (See Volume II, Form A, for the complete CJ#8.) In this case the IJ must exhibit both of the CJ's critical indicators. Clearly these conditions are met by the IJ from our sample case. The subject does indicate that Heinz can't be blamed because of his circumstances (". . . sometimes you don't have any other choice . . .") and also refers explicitly to Heinz's desperation (". . . he is desperate for one he loves"). Thus the IJ–CJ correspondence receives a clear pass. Let us go on to consider, however, the correspondence of the IJ with CJ#12 since, as noted in the Stage Structure, Distinctions, and Inclusions paragraph of CJ#8, the Stage 2/3 CJ#8 is included within the Stage 3 CJ#12. That is, if the interview material matches both, only the score for CJ#12 is entered on the score sheet. Refer to Volume II, Form A, for the complete CJ#12. Required for a match is reference to either (a) a normative motive of love or concern, or (b) the close relationship. Clearly, critical indicator (a) is present in responses to Questions 1, 2, and 8. This IJ–CJ correspondence also receives a pass for the surface evaluation.

Step 9: Structural Evaluation of Proposed Match
Having evaluated the surface features of the match, the scorer must determine whether the structural level of the IJ material is consistent with the stage structure said to underlie the CJ. The purpose of this phase is to allow the scorer to veto a proposed match either when the IJ matches the CJ critical indicators but does not seem to be structurally representative of the stage of the CJ, or when the IJ is clearly more representative of another CJ of the same or different stage. In making this judgment be sure to limit your consideration to the discrete IJ in question rather than taking the whole issue beyond that IJ into account.

Scorers must be particularly careful in evaluating structural consistency of a match when the match has been given only a marginal pass at Phase 2. A subject's failure to clearly express the ideas embodied in the critical indicators of a CJ may be due to the fact that the subject is using reasoning representative of a different stage, rather than to a failure to elaborate the ideas fully or express them clearly. In such cases, the scorer must look especially carefully at the stage structure descriptions and the IJ for evidence that the response might be inconsistent with the structure of the proposed CJ stage.

Each explicated CJ in the manual provides two aids in making the structural evaluation: the Stage Structure and the Distinctions and Inclusions paragraphs. The latter section points out cases in which a lower stage idea can be said to be included within a higher stage idea. Due to the hierarchical nature of the moral judgment stages, ideas are often expressed within a higher stage context, which when taken literally or out of context would be scored at a lower stage. The function of the Phase 3 structural assessment is to weed out or "veto" those literal matches for which the stage of the criterion judgment is not a true reflection of the structural significance of the interview material.

The scorer should veto a proposed match if clear inconsistencies exist between the CJ stage structure and the IJ being scored. The scorer also may veto the match if there is clear evidence of a positive match between the IJ and a stage other than that of the CJ at hand. However, Phase 3 vetoes based on structural evidence for another stage should be used cautiously and only by experienced scorers. Novice scorers should focus instead on evaluating the IJ's consistency with the proposed CJ stage structure rather than on proposing positive correspondence of the IJ with the structure of a different stage.

The IJ must not only be consistent with the CJ stage structure, it must also fail to provide a better match to another CJ. To make this decision, the Distinctions and Inclusions paragraph(s) of each explicated CJ should be examined.

In the Distinctions paragraph, the CJ in question is distinguished from parallel or similar CJ ideas at the same and different moral stages. The Distinctions notes are designed to further clarify stage structure and to prevent misscoring an IJ as a match to a particular CJ when in fact it would be a better match to a similar-sounding – although conceptually distinct – CJ found elsewhere (either a CJ at a different stage or a CJ at the same stage but with a different norm and/or element). Operationally, the scorer proceeds by reading each distinction while keeping in mind the IJ to be scored. If one of the CJs referred to in the distinctions sounds as if it might provide at least as good a match as the CJ under consideration, the scorer should turn to the explicated version of the new CJ. An evaluation must then be made of the relative appropriateness of the two candidates by comparing the outcomes of the surface and structural evaluations for each.

Included with the distinctions are notes on possible inclusions of some CJs within other CJs. Within a single dilemma and issue, a set of hierarchical inclusions has been defined so that a particular CJ may be considered to include within it other CJs and/or to be included itself within other CJs. A given CJ may include lower stage CJs that express parallel but developmentally less advanced concepts. Alternatively, a given CJ may be included within higher stage CJs that express parallel but developmentally more advanced concepts.

In order for one CJ to be defined as included within another, the idea expressed by the higher stage CJ must logically entail acceptance of the simpler or more partial idea expressed by the lower stage CJ. These inclusion relationships most often but not always involve CJs with the same norm and element but different stages.

Whenever interview material matches two CJs of the same norm and element but different stages, the lower stage CJ is considered to be included within the higher stage CJ. Only the score of the highest match on that norm and element is included when assigning a score for the issue. This same inclusion relationship sometimes holds for CJs with different elements but the same norm. Look carefully at the inclusion notes of the explicated CJ to determine when one CJ is included within another.

Once a structural evaluation has been made of the proposed IJ–CJ match using the Stage Structure and the Distinctions and Inclusions sections of the explicated CJ, the structural evaluation of the proposed match must be assigned either a pass or a fail.

Outcome of Structural Evaluation

Pass: In order to pass the structural evaluation, all of the following must be true: (a) The IJ does not contradict or violate the stage structure described in the CJ Stage Structure paragraph; and (b) nothing in the IJ suggests that the structure of a stage other than that of the proposed CJ would provide a closer match to the IJ; and (c) no other CJ, especially those mentioned in the CJ Distinctions and Inclusions, provides a better match for the IJ.

Fail: A fail on the structural evaluation is assigned if one or more of the following is true: (a) The structural significance of the IJ seems to be inconsistent with the stage structure of the proposed CJ stage; or (b) something in the IJ suggests that it is structurally either more or less advanced than the proposed CJ; or (c) a different CJ provides a better match for the IJ.

In order to give the scorer a thorough understanding of the underlying stage structures, the manual provides greater elaboration of the structural significance of each CJ than will be expressed by any one subject. In addition, many CJ stage structure descriptions provide an in-depth analysis of structure that may be quite far removed from the way in which such ideas are normally expressed. Therefore, the scorer should give the IJ material the benefit of the doubt unless something in the subject's conceptualization actually seems to contradict or suggest a substantive inconsistency with some aspect of the CJ's stage structure.

SAMPLE INTERVIEW

Having decided that the IJ in question provides at least a surface match for both CJs #8 and #12, let us now consider the IJ's consistency with the Stage Structure paragraphs of these two CJs. The Stage Structure paragraph of CJ#8 indicates that the IJ–CJ correspondence is to be given a match only if the idea expressed is truly ambiguous as to whether it reflects a Stage 3 recognition that Heinz had no antisocial motive or a Stage 2 notion that Heinz's stealing was instrumentally reasonable. In fact, the material seems to exhibit a fairly clear recognition that Heinz was acting out of good motives. Let us, therefore, turn to the stage structure of CJ#12. The responses to Questions 1, 2, and 8 do seem to be consistent with the requirement that "the justification for stealing be based on an evaluation of life made in terms of the relationships of love, concern, closeness, attachment, etc." Since the IJ correspondence with CJ#12 passes both the surface evaluation and the structural evaluation and CJ#12 includes CJ#8, we will drop CJ#8 from further consideration.

Step 10: Accepting or Rejecting the Proposed Match
A match score is a fully weighted stage score assigned on the basis of a correspondence between an interview judgment and a criterion judgment. The following criteria must be met if a match score is to be assigned:

1. The IJ must provide a reason that is attributed at least some validity by the subject and is at least implicitly prescriptive.
2. The IJ must exhibit all the required critical indicators of the CJ.
3. The IJ must be consistent with the specific stage structure of the CJ.
4. The IJ must not provide a clearer match for the critical indicators and stage structure of any other CJ.

If the IJ meets all of the preceding criteria clearly and explicitly, it is considered to be a match to the CJ. Whether a clear pass or a marginal pass has been given using the critical indicators, it is in any case scored as a match. Otherwise, the proposed IJ–CJ match fails.

Table 6.4 presents the possible outcomes for a proposed match based on the surface and structural evaluations, assuming that the scorability criteria have been met.

As Table 6.4 indicates, a match versus nonmatch decision is straightforward once the outcomes of the critical indicator and structural evaluations have been determined.

If the proposed IJ–CJ match fails, then you should return to the Table of Criterion Judgments for the issue to find another CJ that may provide a match for the IJ at hand. Evaluate this next CJ as you did the first attempted match using Steps 8 and 9. Continue this process until a match meeting all the criteria has been found for that IJ or until you have determined that no match exists. If no clear or marginal match exists for the IJ, you should bracket it as possible guess material to return to in case no match scores are assigned to any material on that issue and guess scoring becomes necessary. Then proceed with the next IJ.

We have provided several examples in the Skills Section of how to decide on a match along with the rationale for the scoring decisions made at each phase.

SAMPLE INTERVIEW

The sample interview that has been examined at each step of the scoring process has posed few problems in evaluating the IJ–CJ match (it was selected in part for its simplicity).

The scoring outcome for the IJ–CJ correspondence considered here is a match since a pass was given both for Phase 2 (critical indicators) and for Phase 3 (stage structure).

Step 11: Entering a Match Score on the Score Sheet

If the IJ–CJ match is accepted, it should be noted on the score sheet.

A single score sheet is used for all three of the dilemmas for a particular interview form (see Appendix C). Begin in the upper left-hand corner by filling in the dates of the interview and of the scoring, the interviewee's code number, and the name of the scorer. In the upper right-hand corner, circle either Form A or Form B depending on which interview you are scoring.

The section for the first dilemma (Dilemma III in the case of Form A, Dilemma IV in the case of Form B) is found on the upper third of the scoring sheet. It is divided into two sections, Life Issue (or Life Quality in the case of Form B) on the left, and Law Issue (or Law/Life Preservation for Form B) on the right.

There are three columns under each issue, labeled Q#, CJ#/Norm & Element, and Stage (Notes). Under the first, Q#, you list the interview question

Table 6.4. *Possible outcomes for a proposed IJ–CJ match based on surface and structural evaluation (assuming that the scorability criteria have been met)*

Description of correspondence	Phase 2 critical indicators	Phase 3 stage structure	Scoring outcome
IJ is structurally consistent with stage of CJ as well as showing clear evidence of critical surface features (critical indicators).	Pass	Pass	Match
There is some evidence that critical indicators are present but evidence is ambiguous. IJ is structurally consistent with CJ.	Marginal pass	Pass	Match
There is some at least ambiguous evidence of surface features (critical indicators) but IJ is not consistent with underlying structure of CJ.	Marginal pass	Fail (veto)	Nonmatch (match or guess for another stage)
IJ exhibits surface features of CJ but is not structurally consistent with the proposed stage.	Pass	Fail (veto)	Nonmatch (match or guess for another stage)
IJ is structurally consistent with the proposed stage but does not exhibit the critical surface features.	Fail	Pass	Nonmatch (guess or match to another CJ at same stage)
IJ is not consistent with the structure of the proposed stage and, moreover, does not exhibit the critical surface features.	Fail	Fail	Nonmatch (match or guess for another stage)

number(s) from which the material for the particular IJ–CJ match was drawn. Under the second column, CJ#/Norm & Element, you fill in the number of the CJ that matches the IJ being scored. Listing the norm and element of the CJ is optional since this information is included in the CJ number. In the third column, Stage (Notes), you should list the stage of each CJ and make any relevant notes about the match. In particular, you should note here if the match is a marginal match, or if two scorers have disagreed as to the appropriate CJ, or if the CJ scored has included material at a lower CJ.

Immediately below these columns are spaces for the issue score. We will discuss the assignment of issue scores later, in Step 15. As you will see on the form, the section for the second dilemma occupies the middle third of the scoring sheet, and that for the third dilemma is found on the bottom third.

Finally, at the very bottom of the page you will find spaces for calculating the overall stage scores (global stage score for the interview as well as the weighted average score). These will be taken up in Steps 16 and 17.

Thus, once you have successfully made an IJ–CJ match (clear or marginal), you should enter the interview question numbers corresponding to the interview material you have just scored, the CJ number, and the stage of the CJ on the scoring sheet under the appropriate issue.

Step 12: Scoring the Remainder of the IJs on the Issue

After scoring the first IJ of the issue, you should attempt to match any other IJs on the same issue that use the same norm. Then go on to score the remaining IJs on the issue, norm by norm. A score for each successful IJ–CJ match should be entered on the score sheet. Material for which no clear or marginal match can be found should be bracketed for possible use in guess scoring.

Once scores have been entered on the score sheet for all the IJs on the issue, the inclusion notes for each of the CJs listed should be checked to see if any of the CJs are included within any of the other CJs listed. Any CJ found to be included in another matched CJ should be bracketed as it will not be used in assigning a stage score for the issue.

SAMPLE
INTERVIEW

In Step 7 we identified two other IJs on the life issue. Rather than proceed through Steps 8–11 for these IJs, we will simply note here the conclusions reached in those steps. The IJ that was identified as affiliation norm, duty element (response to Question 2) was scored as a match to Stage 3 CJ#13. The life norm/human dignity element IJ (responses to Questions 2, 5, and 6) was scored as a match to Stage 3 CJ#9. Before going on, look over the interview materials and the CJs to be sure you understand why these match scores were assigned.

Step 13: Guess Scoring

Sometimes an interview will not yield even a single match (clear or marginal) for the issue being scored. In such cases, if any moral judgment material is available on the issue in question, the scorer must assign a guess score to the issue, however ambiguous the material on the issue might be.

There are two categories of reasons why material sufficient for match scoring may not exist for an issue. The first category concerns how the interview was done; an oral interview may be poorly probed, a written interview may be poorly elaborated, a subject may prove to be very reticent or resistant in the interview, or the nonchosen issue may be neglected in an otherwise well-probed interview. The second category acknowledges the limits of the scoring manuals. The subject's ideas, though structurally scorable and fully elaborated, may be original or idiosyncratic, or the particular expression of a stage used by a subject may not be represented in the CJs of the scoring manuals. The CJs were generated empirically and are not exhaustive of all possible CJs at each stage.

We have introduced the concept of a guess score in order to (a) increase the likelihood of each subject's receiving a score for each of the six standard issues, thus maximizing standardization in sampling across the domain of moral judgment; (b) make possible the scoring of novel responses not represented in the manuals; (c) minimize the introduction of experimental bias; the use of guess scores should minimize any tendency to eliminate as unscorable data that violate the scorer's expectations; and (d) compensate for the fact that raters often disagree as to the point at which material should no longer be considered stage scorable.

Because the guess category uses material that is often very ambiguous and relies on scorers' general stage conceptions rather than well-defined scoring criteria, issues on which a guess score is given are not weighted as heavily in relation to other, more clearly scorable issues in computing total interview scores. (See Steps 15–17.)

Guess scores can be assigned either on the basis of individual IJ–CJ correspondence applying less stringent standards than those used in match scoring or on the basis of an overall assessment of the interview material pertaining to the issue; or these two approaches may be combined. Whatever approach is used, the unit of analysis in guessing is the issue as a whole. Thus, only one guess score is entered for the whole issue. That score reflects the scorer's best estimate of the stage or stages represented by all the material on that issue.

In order to be considered for guess scoring, material must meet two of the three of the scorability criteria:

1. A reason must be offered in support of the value of the issue or in support of the action choice corresponding to the issue, or the scorer must be able to construct a reason for the action choice or value from the subject's responses to the dilemma without adding any substantive material (either by minor syntactic reorganization or by using relevant material embedded within a response to the opposing issue).

2. The reason given in support of the issue (action choice or value) must be seen by the subject as having some validity, although its importance may be overridden by some other consideration deemed more important or more valid by the subject. That is, the reason being guess scored must not be rejected by the subject as an invalid argument. When doubt exists about the validity of a reason in the subject's eyes, the reason can be used for guess scoring but it cannot be used for match scoring.

3. Material used for guess scoring need not fulfill the third scorability criterion, prescriptivity.

You should begin the process of assigning a guess score by rereading all the material on the issue and looking for interview judgments considered valid by the subject that have failed as matches to any CJs. In many cases in which a guess score is required, only a single statement will be available on the issue. An IJ with potential for guess scoring may approximate – but not quite match – the critical indicators of a CJ and be consistent with, or at least not violate, the stage structure of the CJ. You should not assume that because an IJ comes close to matching a CJ a guess score should be assigned for the stage of that CJ. The IJ may have failed to match the critical indicators of the CJ because it is in fact more representative of a different stage. You should instead consider the correspondence of the IJ to the general structure of the other stages as well as to the specific stage structure of the CJ being considered. Regardless of the apparent similarity an IJ may have with a particular CJ, the guess score should reflect your best estimate of stage structure.

If you are still unable to make an acceptable guess for any material on the issue, you can turn to the other issue for help. The opposing issue on the dilemma can be used to help interpret the meaning of the material on the issue you are scoring. Failing that, you can attempt to extract reasoning on the issue being scored that may be embedded in the reasoning on the opposing issue,

Finally, a CJ corresponding to an IJ on the issue being guess scored may be sought among CJs of a different issue. We will briefly look at these three options in turn:

1. *Using other issue material as context:* Material from the opposing issue may be used as context or background from which to interpret the meaning of material on the issue for which you are attempting to assign a guess score. Material from the opposing issue used to interpret the material from the guess issue should, if possible, not be relied on to provide a score for the other issue. For example, if in scoring the life issue you use material from the law issue to help interpret the life issue material, then try not to use that same law material to score the law issue. This precaution is again to allow issues to be scored using separate material, thus providing some independence of measurement.

2. *Extracting arguments from the opposing issue:* Sometimes an interview does not yield any responses that can be classified in their entirety under a particular issue. This usually occurs on the nonchosen issue. In many of these cases, material usable for a guess score may be extracted from the arguments for the opposing issue. The guess material is usually presented as a consideration that is overridden by arguments for the opposing issue. However, in constructing the subject's position on a neglected issue in this way, you must keep in mind the second scorability criterion, namely, acceptance of the reason as valid by the subject. If the reasoning is merely overridden by other considerations, it can be used for a guess score; if it is disavowed as invalid, it cannot be used.

3. *Illuminating an IJ with a CJ of another issue:* If a response does not resemble a CJ from its "own" issue, occasionally it will seem to resemble a CJ from another issue, in which case that IJ–CJ correspondence may be used for a guess score. Sometimes an IJ on one issue will be an almost perfect match for a CJ on another issue. However, an IJ–CJ correspondence involving two different issues is always considered to be a guess, no matter how perfect the fit. (In such cases, check to be sure you have classified the IJ under the appropriate issue.) If you do turn to CJs of a different issue to provide a guess for an issue, be sure to consider all the possible CJs from the other issue just as you would when attempting to match score within an issue.

If material on an issue seems clearly scorable from a structural point of view but does not seem to correspond to a CJ from any of the six issues, then you should enter a score on the basis of an overall structural estimate. Your guess score here should reflect your best possible estimate of the stage of reasoning on the issue as a whole, although inevitably in making this assessment you will rely most heavily on the material that seems clearest as to stage structure.

You can, of course, combine looking for IJ–CJ guess correspondence with attempting an overall stage assessment. This approach is most useful with interviews on which you may have a great deal of material available on an issue, but no match scores at all. (This is usually the result of unskilled interviewing.) In such a situation, you may want to assign individual guess scores to each IJ unit and then make an overall assessment of stage.

If all these efforts fail and the only material available for an issue is quite ambiguous with regard to stage, you should still make a best estimate of the stage significance of the material. These estimates can be based on CJ stage structures in the manual or on the rater's general knowledge of the stages.

Whatever approach is used in making a guess score, only a single guess score is assigned to the issue. This score should be entered in the score sheet under the issue in question on the line marked Issue Score. The score should be preceded by a *G*, e.g., G4 or G3/4.

No material: If any moral judgment material is available on the issue, then a match or guess score must be assigned. Occasionally, however, not even a guess score can be assigned.

An issue is judged to include no moral judgment material and is designated "no material" (rather than being assigned a stage score) when either (a) no responses can be classified as relevant to the issue, or (b) no issue-relevant responses are available that pass the two scorability criteria of providing a reason accepted as valid by the subject. Issue-relevant material is considered to be present if one can construct from the subject's responses to the dilemma an answer to the question "Why or how is the issue in question to be valued?" or "What reason can be given for the dilemma choice corresponding to that issue?" If the scorer cannot construct from the interview material an answer to either of these questions, then no material is available for the issue. If issue material is available but does not constitute a reason for the recommended value or action, or is rejected by the subject as invalid, then no moral judgment material is available.

In either case, a notation of "no material" should be made on the score sheet for that issue.

Rules for Guess Scoring

1. A guess score is assigned only if no IJ–CJ matches have been found for the issue.
2. The material used for guess scoring must meet the scorability criteria of providing a reason accepted as valid by the subject. However, it need not be prescriptive.
3. The best estimate of stage is the main guide in attempting to guess score an IJ.
4. In the absence of an IJ–CJ guess using only interview material and CJs within an issue then:
   a) Material from the opposing issue may be used as context or background with which to interpret the meaning of material on the issue being guess scored; or failing that,
   b) Material usable for guess scoring can be extracted from the arguments of the opposing issue; or failing that,
   c) A CJ corresponding to an IJ on the issue being scored may be sought among CJs of another issue.
5. If an IJ–CJ guess can be found, an overall estimate of stage structure should be based on whatever material is available on the issue.
6. A single guess score for the issue should be entered on the score sheet, with a *G* preceding the score.
7. If absolutely no material is available on an issue or if the available material fails to provide a reason considered valid by the subject, then a notation of "no material" is made on the score sheet.

SAMPLE
INTERVIEW

Match scores were assigned for the life issue of the sample interview. Therefore, guess scoring is unnecessary on this issue.

Step 14: Scoring the Remainder of the Interview

After the chosen issue of the first dilemma has been completely scored, proceed to score the nonchosen issue of the first dilemma and then the chosen and nonchosen issues of the second and third dilemmas. If there were problems in assigning a chosen issue on any dilemma in the beginning phases, complete this process at the end. On the basis of the preponderance of match scores for the two issues of a dilemma, assign as the chosen issue the issue with the most CJ matches. You will recall that if there are guesses on both issues, no chosen issue is assigned.

Step-by-step Scoring: Section III (Steps 15–17)
Assigning Stage Scores at the Issue and Global Levels

Once all the IJs for an interview have been scored (and, where no clear or marginal IJ–CJ matches have been found for an issue, a guess score has been assigned to that issue), stage scores are then calculated for the interview. The rater begins by calculating the stage score for each issue (Step 15). Using the issue scores, a global score can then be calculated for the interview as a whole (Step 16) as can a weighted average score for the interview (Step 17).

Step 15: Calculating Issue Scores

Stage scores for each issue are calculated after all the material on a dilemma has been scored and all the IJ–CJ matches have been noted on the score sheet. All IJ–CJ matches on an issue are considered equally in calculating the score on that issue. No distinction is made between clear and marginal matches.

When there is only one IJ–CJ match on an issue or where all of the IJ–CJ matches for that issue represent the same stage or stage transition, then no further calculation need be made: The issue score is the stage of the single IJ–CJ match or identically scored IJ–CJ matches. When there are two or more matches for an issue and they represent different stages or stage transitions, then the issue score is calculated as follows:

1. Add up all the times each stage is represented by a IJ–CJ match for the issue (e.g., the number of Stage 2 or Stage 3 or Stage 4 matches, etc.). When a match is for a stage transition, each stage is counted one half; e.g., if a match is for transition Stage 2/3, Stage 2 receives $\frac{1}{2}$ point and Stage 3 receives $\frac{1}{2}$ point. Thus, if there were four matches on a particular issue and these represented Stages 2, 2/3, 3, and 3/4, Stage 2 would be assigned $1\frac{1}{2}$ points, Stage 3 would receive 2 points (1 whole and 2 half-points), and Stage 4 half a point.
2. If only one stage is represented by 25% or more of the scores, then that stage score is the issue score.
3. If two or more stages each are represented by 25% or more of the IJ–CJ matches on the issue, but one stage is represented most often, then that stage is the "major" stage and the stage(s) represented less often (but at least 25% of the total) is (are) the minor stage(s). The minor stages are noted in parentheses after the major stage, e.g., 2(3) or 3(2)(4).
4. If two or more stages are represented by 25% or more of the CJs on an issue and their frequency is the same, then a transition score is assigned to the issue, e.g., 2/3, 3/4, or 2/3/4.

185

Guess scores are assigned when no suitable IJ–CJ match can be found for an issue. Therefore, the guess score *is* the issue score.

When a score has been calculated for an issue it should be noted on the score sheet. Scores for chosen issues should be circled unless they are guess scores. Guess scores are not circled even on the chosen issue.

Step 16: Calculating Global Stage Scores

Once stage scores have been calculated for each of the six issues, then the global stage score for the interview is computed.

Issue scores are not all treated equally in computing the global score. Scores for chosen issues are given greater weight than those for nonchosen issues, and guess scores (whether for chosen or nonchosen issues) are given least weight of all (see Steps 2 and 13 for reasons why nonchosen issues and guess scores are given less weight). The weights assigned are as follows:

3 points for chosen issue
2 points for nonchosen issue
1 point for guess score (whether on a chosen or nonchosen issue)

The rules for calculation are as follow:

1. For chosen issues: If the issue score is a "pure" stage score (i.e., Stage 2, Stage 3), assign 3 points to that stage. If it is a transitional score (e.g., 2/3), assign $1\frac{1}{2}$ points to both stages. If the stage score includes a major and a minor stage (e.g., 3[2]), assign 2 of the 3 points to the major stage and 1 point to the minor stage. In the case of a major stage and two minor stages (e.g., 3[2][4]), assign two points to the major stage and one half point to each of the minor stages.
2. For nonchosen issues: If the issue score is a pure stage score, assign 2 points to that stage. If it is a transitional stage score, assign 1 point to both stages. If it includes a major and minor score, assign $1\frac{1}{3}$ points to the major stage and $\frac{2}{3}$ point to the minor stage. If the issue score includes three stages, assign $\frac{2}{3}$ point to each.
3. For guess scores: If a guess score on an issue is a pure stage score, assign 1 point to that stage. If it involves two stages (whether transitional or major/minor) assign $\frac{1}{2}$ point to each stage (see Table 6.5).

Weighted points are assigned to all stages represented in the issue scores of an interview according to the previously defined rules. Then the percent of weighted points assigned to each stage is calculated (i.e., the number of weighted points per issue is divided by the total number of weighted points for the interview) and the global stage score is assigned.

In assigning global stage scores, only pure stage and mixed stage scores are used. No distinction is made between major and minor stages. If only one stage is represented in the issue totals, or if only one stage reaches 25% of the total number of weighted points assigned, then that stage is the global stage for the interview. If two or more stages are represented each by 25% or more of the points assigned, a mixed score is given that includes all stages at or above the 25% level.

For example, the issue scores for an interview were:

Table 6.5. *Weights for chosen and nonchosen issues and guess scores, according to whether the issue score is a pure stage score, a transitional stage score, or a major/minor score*

	Pure	Transitional	Major/Minor
Chosen issue	3 points	$1\frac{1}{2}$ points each issue	2 points major 1 point minor
Nonchosen issue	2 points	1 point each issue	$1\frac{1}{3}$ points major $\frac{2}{3}$ points minor
Guess score	1 point	$\frac{1}{2}$ point each issue	$\frac{1}{2}$ point each issue

Life (chosen)   Law

③   2(3)

M&C (chosen)   Punishment

②(1)   G2/3

Contract   Authority (chosen)

G3   ②/3

This interview involves the use of three stages, Stages 1, 2, and 3. Stage 1 is assigned only 1 point because it occurs only once, as the minor stage of a chosen issue score, morality and conscience. The major stage of this issue, Stage 2 receives 2 points. Stage 2 also receives $1\frac{1}{3}$ points for the law issue (i.e., $\frac{2}{3}$ of the 2 points given to a nonchosen match-based score), $\frac{1}{2}$ point for the punishment issue (half of the 1 point given for a guess score), and $1\frac{1}{2}$ points for the authority issue (half of the 3 points for this chosen issue). The total number of weighted points for Stage 2 is $5\frac{1}{3}$. Stage 3 receives 3 points for life (a chosen issue), $\frac{2}{3}$ of a point for law, $\frac{1}{2}$ point for punishment, 1 point for contract, and $1\frac{1}{2}$ points for authority for a total of $6\frac{2}{3}$ points.

Stage	Weighted points
1	1
2	$5\frac{1}{3}$
3	$6\frac{2}{3}$
Total	13

The total number of weighted points assigned for the interview is 13. Stage 1 represents 8% ($\frac{1}{13}$) of the weighted issue scores. Stage 2 represents 41% of the weighted issue scores, and Stage 3 represents 51%. Both Stages 2 and 3 exceed 25% of the total, but Stage 1 does not. Thus, the global score in this case is Stage 2/3.

Step 17: Calculating the Weighted Average Score (WAS)
The same system of weights for chosen issues, nonchosen issues, and guess scores is used for calculating the WAS as was used for calculating global scores (see Step 16). To calculate the WAS:

1. Multiply each stage represented in the interview by the weighted points for that stage;
2. Sum the products for all the stages;
3. Divide the sum of the products by the total number of weighted points;
4. Multiply by 100.

Calculation of the WAS for the example used in Step 16 would be as follows:

Stage		Weighted points	Product of stage × weighted points
1	×	1	= 1
2	×	$5\frac{1}{3}$	= $10\frac{2}{3}$
3	×	$6\frac{2}{3}$	= 20
Total		13	$31\frac{2}{3}$

The sum of the products ($31\frac{2}{3}$) is divided by the total number of weighted points assigned (13) and then multiplied by 100 for the WAS.

$$31.67 \div 13 = 2.44$$
$$2.44 \times 100 = 244 = WAS$$

Reliability

Some issues regarding reliable scoring need to be noted. Using the MJI for research purposes requires scorers to obtain interrater agreement so that valid comparisons may be made across studies.

Agreement may be determined in one of two ways, depending upon individual research requirements. A subsample of the pool of data under investigation may be selected, scored, and the scores compared to those of an expert rater.[1] This would be the method used if the sample or the quality of data diverge from the usual data obtained using the MJI. The second way to obtain interrater reliability figures is to obtain a sample data set from the Harvard Center for Moral Education. A scorer's results are compared to the scores obtained by expert scorers at the Center. Recommended sample sizes for either type of reliability method is 20 cases for each form of the MJI. Recommended agreement figures are at least 75% exact stage agreement on the 9 point scale, and agreement of at least 90% for within $\frac{1}{2}$ stage. In addition to percentage agreement, a product moment correlation between the weighted average scores of two raters should be reported. The correlation should be above .90.

Skills Sections

Skills Section for Step 2: Chosen Issue

The first problem in scoring responses to each dilemma is to determine which of the two standard issues is the subject's chosen issue and to note the choice on the score sheet.

[1] An expert scorer is considered to have at least 75% exact global agreement on the 9 point scale, and at least 95% agreement within $\frac{1}{2}$ stage with another reliable scorer.

In order to identify the chosen issue, read over the subject's answers on the dilemma, with this question in mind: What choice does the subject make? The dilemma requires a choice between two courses of action that we have identified as corresponding to the two standard issues. For example, the issues placed in conflict by Dilemma III are life and law. In this case, the subject is asked to choose either life (i.e., Heinz should steal the drug) or law (Heinz should not steal the drug).

Determining chosen issue is an important step in the scoring procedure because it can make a substantial difference in the overall stage score of the interview. This is because the score for a chosen issue is given $1\frac{1}{2}$ times the weight of the score for the nonchosen issue. A chosen issue must be assigned for the responses to each dilemma, even if the subject's choice is ambiguous. That is, there is no option of designating the dilemma as having "no chosen issue."

Where chosen issue is clear, assign it first, before proceeding to separate all the material by issue. Where chosen issue is ambiguous, begin with separation of material into the two issues instead of assigning chosen issue first. Then score all material on both issues. After having assigned stage scores to each issue on the dilemma, go back and assign weights to the issue scores by determining chosen issue. The chosen issue can be omitted if both issue scores are guesses.

In assigning chosen issue, the scorer should follow the rules enumerated in the step-by-step scoring procedures outlined earlier in this chapter.

The following examples illustrate the determination of chosen issue in cases that demonstrate considerable ambiguity with regard to choice:

DILEMMA III

Should he have done that?
If he liked his wife he should.

Is it wrong to do it?
Sure, he could go to court.

Would a good husband have to?
He wouldn't have to, no. If he didn't want to, he didn't have to. But if he loved his wife, he should.

Should he steal it for a friend?
If the friend had a lot of money, I wouldn't. He could buy it himself, or maybe they would let the doctor buy it.

Would a good husband do it or not?
If he wanted to stay out of trouble, he wouldn't.

What is the right thing to do here?
Don't steal — buy it. Get a loan. I'd go and get a couple of loans.

Would it be wrong if he took it and left $1,000?
No one should steal.

Would he be going against the storekeeper's rights?

I don't think he should have stole it, because if he would have gone to about two banks he could get the loan, the $2,000. And that's all he needs.

If there was no law setting a limit to the price, was he wrong to set the price that high?

I think so. Because if it could cure certain kinds of cancer, it wouldn't be wrong to have that high price because it would cure that disease – if the druggist was sure he could do it.

In this case, life is the chosen issue because it represents the subject's first stated choice on the dilemma. This subject reverses his decision several times in the course of the interview in response to interview probes that go beyond a repetition of the original question. There are, then, two reasons for using the original life choice to indicate chosen issue: (1) The first reversal occurs in response to an interviewer probe other than repetition of the original question. (Note that ''Is it wrong?'' is not considered a repetition of the original question.) (2) Even if the first reversal had been spontaneous, the subject's first choice would determine chosen issue because the subject does not hold consistently to the opinion expressed in the second response.

This same kind of ''waffling'' occurs in response to Dilemma I for the same interview. In this case, too, the original choice (authority) determines chosen issue.

DILEMMA I *Should Joe refuse to give his father the money?*

I think he should give it to him. Fathers know better.

Is it his duty to his father?

Not exactly his duty, but he should.

Would it be wrong for him to refuse?

Yes, he could refuse, because he was the one that earned the money.

Would he be a bad son if he didn't give the money?

Not exactly, his father has no right to take the son's own money away.

If his father doesn't have the right, then why should he give it to him? You said his father knows best?

Yeah.

Does his father have the right to tell him to give him the money?

It's his son's own money. I don't see a law that says that the father can take the son's own money away. Unless it's for a good reason.

In the following example, life is the chosen issue because it seems to represent the central focus of the subject's thinking. Arguments against stealing or against imposing a moral obligation on Heinz serve to qualify the prostealing position rather than the reverse.

DILEMMA III *Should Heinz steal the drug?*

I don't know how many times I tapped this and how many times the questions were posed. I don't know how consistent I am, but it is always a struggle in

190

some ways if he should, because you look at it from the various points of view. If I interiorize myself as Heinz in this position and I see my wife in the position, I say yes, I am going to take the drug.

So do you think Heinz should steal the drug?

I don't know about Heinz, but if it was me, yes. I better do that because it is a life involved. It is close to me and that is more important to me than the other ramifications.

So you would steal the drug, but do you think Heinz should steal the drug?

If Heinz wants to, that is up to him. Each person has to make his own mind up about things like that. If you have to have some kind of should, I don't really care if he does or not.

Usually are you talking about another person more than yourself?

I think Heinz should do what he has to do, what he feels [is] important.

Say he stole the drug, do you think that would be right, that he stole the drug?

It's wrong to steal. It may have been an imperative for him to do so and there may be circumstances under which you can say yes, but if I do it, I acknowledge that it is wrong.

In the following interview, punishment has been designated as the chosen issue in spite of the ambiguity, because it seems that the basic focus is on the need for punishment with arguments for leniency serving as qualifiers.

DILEMMA III'

Should the judge give Heinz some sentence, or should he suspend the sentence and let Heinz go free? Why?

Sentence, but not jail, to show him he can't do it all the time, perhaps volunteer work with kids, etc. After all, he was saving a life.

Thinking in terms of society, why should people who break the law be punished?

To show them that it's wrong and they can't do it without sanctions. So they'll think twice in [the] future and to show others an example. Because [they're] affecting others and things are wrong if they are generally accepted to be wrong.

How does this relate to Heinz's case?

Would be showing Heinz that even though it's right, it's not accepted by everybody. So in the future, [he] will know the consequences if the situation arises again.

It should be noted here that in some dilemmas, e.g., Dilemma III, some of the probe questions in effect introduce new situational factors – Suppose Heinz doesn't love his wife or suppose the dying person is a stranger. Responses to these questions are not relevant in determining chosen issue. A subject who clearly states that Heinz should steal for his (presumably loved) wife and sticks by that decision, has chosen the life issue even if the subject judges that Heinz should not steal for an unloved wife or stranger.

Skills Section for Step 3: Classification by Issue

As described in the step-by-step scoring procedures, all responses to the Moral Judgment Interview must be classified as belonging to one of the two standard issues of the dilemma being scored. A critical factor in this classification is the question to which the material is a responses. Because the rules for issue classification differ somewhat according to the type of probe question under consideration, let us illustrate the process as it applies to each of the three types of questions.

Dilemma-related questions ask the respondent to make a judgment about what the dilemma protagonist should do under the original dilemma conditions or under altered conditions that are stated in the question. For example:

If Heinz doesn't love his wife, should he steal the drug for her?
Should Heinz steal the drug for a stranger?
Should Joe refuse to give his father the money?
Should Dr. Jefferson give her the drug that would make her die?
When a pet animal is badly wounded and will die, it is killed to put it out of its pain. Does the same thing apply here?

Responses to dilemma-related questions are classified according to the dilemma choice that they support. For example, the following Dilemma III material argues in support of stealing the drug and is therefore classified under the life issue:

If Heinz doesn't love his wife, should he steal the drug for her?

Any human being should have stolen the drug to save the woman's life. However, if he hated her and wished her to die, he obviously wouldn't have committed the crime. If a life is in danger, it is a duty to save it if possible, so he is obligated to steal the drug, not because she is his wife, but because she is a person.

It should be clear that the first and third sentences to this response uphold the prostealing choice and thus the life issue. The second sentence is not classified with regard to issue at all since it is clearly not prescriptive. Were it prescriptive, it would be designated ''law issue'' since it offers a reason not to steal.

In many cases, the response to a single question will include material corresponding to both standard issues:

Should the judge sentence Heinz?

The judge has been appointed to uphold a set of laws. To fulfill his duty he must sentence Heinz. But he shouldn't sentence Heinz because of the stake of human life involved.

In this example, the first two sentences argue for sentencing Heinz and are thus punishment issue material. The third sentence argues for leniency and is morality and conscience material.

In some cases, the content of the material in question may seem to correspond to one issue whereas the choice being supported corresponds to the opposite issue. For example, a response to the question "Should Joe refuse to give his father the money?" might be "Yes, because his father is abusing his authority. The authority of a father is limited and must be deserved." This response tells us about the subject's conception of authority, but it is giving a justification for refusing to give the money. The material is classified as contract issue because it is a response to a dilemma-related question and justifies the choice defined as contract – refuse to give the money. That the content of the material is authority is indicated by designating the material as representing the authority norm. Content focus (other than choice) of the material is irrelevant in issue classification but enters into norm classification.

Issue-centered questions probe the value of a particular issue in the context of the moral dilemma. For example:

It is against the law for Heinz to steal. Does that make it morally wrong?
Is the fact that Joe earned the money himself important in this situation?
It is against the law for the doctor to give the woman the drug. Does that make it morally wrong?

These questions are designed to elicit material that presents the best arguments for upholding the issue of the question. They often succeed in doing so and in such cases, the issue of the response corresponds to the issue of the question. Sometimes, however, the subject does not argue for the value of the issue being probed but instead denies the validity of upholding that value in the context of the dilemma. In some cases, both sides of the conflict will be presented. For example, in the following response, reasons are given both for upholding the law in general and for violating it in this case:

What's to be said for obeying the law in this situation or in general?

The law is meant to provide rules for society to live by. It is never meant to be inhumane. Heinz disobeyed a law that was keeping his wife from surviving. He knew he was disobeying it and should be prepared to take the consequences. The law cannot be flouted in general and must be enforced, but it was not wrong to break it in this case.

In this example, life and law material are intertwined in a way that is somewhat difficult to disentangle. The important thing to remember is that arguments for stealing the drug are life issue and arguments against stealing or for obeying the law are law issue. The first sentence of this example is law material. The second sentence, a qualification of the first, is life issue. The third and fourth sentences are somewhat ambiguous as to issue. In order to make the decision, it is helpful to review the CJs of the two issues to see whether a CJ for one of the issues resembles the interview material. In this case, we find nothing at all similar on the life issue, but law CJ#27 is very close to the interview material in question. This indicates that the material ought to be classified as law issue. The fifth and final sentence begins with law issue material, "The law . . . must be enforced, . . ." but ends with life issue material ". . . but it was not wrong to break it in this case." When both issues are intertwined in a single response in this complex way, it is generally helpful to use the transposition procedure to construct a coherent statement supporting each of the two issues.

General-issue questions ask for an explication of the value of an issue in a way that is generalized rather than embedded in the context of a particular moral dilemma. For example:

In general, should people try to do everything they can to obey the law? Why or why not?
Thinking in terms of society, should people who break the law be punished? Why or why not?
In general, why should a promise be kept?

Usually, responses to general-issue questions will not refer to the moral dilemma. These responses are classified under the issue of the question. For example, the following subject has argued consistently that Heinz should steal the drug, yet he is also able to appreciate the importance of upholding the law in general:

How do you feel about upholding the law in general?

I think it is important, because there have to be laws in order for civilization to survive.

Sometimes, however, the subject will refuse to answer the general question in the abstract and will relate it back to the dilemma. In such a case, the response is classified according to the decision it supports.

Skills Section for Step 5: Classification into Interview Judgment (Classification by Norm and Element)

The unit of moral judgment scoring is the interview judgment, which is defined as the intersection of dilemma, issue, norm, and element. That is, rather than being defined as a single sentence or the response to a single question, the scoring unit in Standard Issue Scoring is defined as what amounts to a complete and conceptually unitary moral idea. Material representing a particular idea or interview judgment is sometimes spread across the responses to many questions. Sometimes the response to a single question includes material representing two or more distinguishable interview judgments. The accurate identification of interview judgments is perhaps one of the most difficult steps in Standard Scoring, but it is a very important step on which valid comparison between criterion judgments and interview judgments depends.

The process of isolating interview judgments within material on a given issue is guided by an awareness of the moral norms and elements and by a familiarity with the available criterion judgments for the issue against which the interview judgments will eventually be compared. Sometimes norms and elements are clearly identifiable within the responses to a dilemma, and sometimes either the norm or the element (or both) is ambiguous and obscure. In the former case, the norms and elements can be used to guide the scorer to an appropriate identification of norms and elements and thus interview judgments. Often the process involves a working back and forth between the Table of Criterion Judgments for the issue and the interview material for the issue. This can perhaps be illustrated best by presenting the full set of responses given by a subject to a dilemma and pulling out of that set of responses all interview judgments on each of the two issues. Consider, for example, the following case:

DILEMMA III
(CASE 12-C)

1. *Should Heinz have done that?*

   The devotion for life, the companionship, the object of stealing is wrong, but when you're devoted to someone like this, irregardless of how social pressures are, man has set up laws, but man did not set up the standards for love, which makes a tremendous difference. I think he had the full right to do this.

2. *What gives him the right?*

   His devotion to his wife in the form of love. If I was in his state, I would probably do the exact same thing. And in my opinion I would be doing right. Of course, I know I would be punished for it, even though I thought I was doing the right thing.

3. *Well, is it actually right or wrong?*

   In his eyes he's right and many other people having the same situation be right, but in the eyes of the state and the laws of the nation he's wrong.

4. *I'm not quite sure I understand why you believe he's right in doing it.*

   He had no alternative in the matter. He thought it was going to save his wife's life. At a time of desperation of this type, like I say I'd do the same thing and I very seldom do anything that I think is wrong. If I knew it was wrong I wouldn't do it and this type, I for my own situation, my own self-needs I would know it's right, even though, on the same hand, I would know that it's wrong due to the fact of the state's law.

5. *Well, you said that you yourself know that it's right. How do you know it's right?*

   If it was going to, if you, if the love in this situation is strong enough to break in to steal, there is, I don't know exactly how to phrase this – the situation where he has this devotion to another person to steal, in this manner, to bring this, I would say this is where I get the basis for my right opinion, as far as what he did. He acted probably, acted rationally on this. Anyone who does steal without planning a robbery, the situation is done rationally.

6. *Rationally, you say?*

   Yeah, quickly, you know. But I think he could do better in – did it say the time on that, I wasn't sure.

7. *No.*

   No. Well, now with the forms of the nation that we have as far as government control there is organizations he could have went to.

8. *Well, is it a husband's duty to steal the drug for his wife if he can get it no other way?*

   No, I don't see where the combination of a husband would really make any difference whether it would be any individual for another individual who had such a compelling that if you really thought that this was going to help this individual, if you had the devotion towards this individual.

9. *What about if the husband does not feel very close or affectionate to his wife? Should he still steal the drug?*

   No, like I said I think it's entirely the object of devotion in this situation that has brought him to do this.

195

10. *So if he does it . . .*

    If you don't I've seen too much of it already in the fact that if you don't care for an individual, no matter what you do would be enough or to any extent in this situation where the woman is dying, she may die anyhow and in the eyes of someone who is doing it just to save her life not as actually for, more or less for their own regards, feel that I did this to prolong their life. This is probably would be the general conception of an individual who didn't have a love for this person.

11. *You mean they are doing it for selfish gratification?*

    Um-hum.

12. *So then it, would you say it would be wrong to steal the drug for somebody to whom you are not devoted?*

    Right.

13. *Why, because it's selfish?*

    More or less yes. I would say ninety percent of the people would do this for their own self-comfort more or less. Feel that I've neglected somebody along the line of life. Or in this situation I would say in my opinion, I would if I was this devoted to a person being a mother or sister, my wife, friend, etcetera.

14. *What do you mean by devoted?*

    There's just a, in my opinion there's a definite difference between love and devotion. I don't know what definition Webster gives for love. I don't even know what my definition for love would be. But the idea of devotion to a person would be something that you could not, no matter what you could do at a time of need you couldn't do enough. You'd surpass your own desires, your own right for this person, in this case of stealing, knowing you may be sent to jail for stealing this drug. You're surpassing that in your own opinion in going into the, stealing the object, not for yourself but for this other person.

15. *Does the devotion make you duty bound or? . . .*

    No, not at all. Devotion is something you would obtain on your own opinion. It would be taken from. This is not something in a code of ethics book, under devotion you would do such and such and such and such. This would be, in my opinion, you could not do enough. You would completely, as far as your own life goes, forget your own life to help someone.

16. *Suppose it wasn't Heinz's wife who was dying of cancer but it was his best friend. Should Heinz steal the drug for his friend in that case?*

    This again would be how close these friends are. In the world today, you don't really know who your friends are. There may be a few, there's tremendous difference between a friend and companion you may say. To go to this extent to steal it for a friend you'd have to be extremely close and have this devotion that I was referring to.

17. *You mean otherwise you wouldn't want to, or otherwise it wouldn't be right?*

    In my opinion it wouldn't be right.

18. *Why wouldn't it be right to steal for a stranger?*

You see him laying there on the street dying. She didn't know what he was dying from. I mean you found out some way that this drug was going to save his life. You don't know, you don't have any idea of what this person has done during their life, whether this person even wants to live. And after you have saved their life whether this may be the worst thing you could possibly do for this person. They may want to die.

19. *Did the druggist have the right to charge that much when there was no law actually setting a limit to the price?*

Yes and no. Under the situation the druggist had, it was his business, no law set on it. In the world as it is today, which is one of the problems, I think, everybody's out to get as much as they can off of whomever they can. Which is quite a normal situation. Everybody wants to better themselves. And about one of the only means you can in this world is by means of your wallet. If you have an opportunity to make money, and you have no conscience about this, in this form or of being life and death to someone, well, if you're this type of individual and you can live with yourself, well, fine.

20. *Then the druggist has the right?*

Definitely. He's just trying to better himself from this. But like I say, if you can live with yourself after bettering yourself in this manner that's another situation entirely.

21. *But whether or not the druggist has the right to do that depends on whether or not his conscience would bother him afterwards, and if it doesn't bother him then he has the right to do it? Is that what you're saying?*

Yes, it's his business, he's trying to get ahead, he had an opportunity to make money. We'd all do the same, I'm almost sure.

Before attempting to isolate the interview judgments, we must complete Step 3, classification by issue. Using the guidelines presented in Step 3, it should be clear that the responses to questions 1, 2, the first half of 3, 4, 5, 8, 13 (last sentence), 14, 15, and 16 are arguments *for* stealing the drug and are thus life issue material. The responses to Questions 3 (second half), 7, 9, 10, 11, 12, 13 (three sentences), 17, 18, 19, 20, and 21 present arguments against stealing and are thus law issue material. Let us begin with the life issue material.

The norms used on the life issue are listed at the beginning of the Table of Life Issue Criterion Judgments. They are life, property, affiliation, law, and conscience. In reading over the life issue material on this interview, the norm that stands out most clearly is the affiliation norm. This norm, referring to the relationship or feelings between Heinz and his wife, is evident in Responses 1, 2, 5, 8, 13 (last sentence), 14, 15, and 16. Whether this material represents a single Interview Judgment or several depends on whether one or more elements are used in conjunction with the life issue and the affiliation norm. For someone unfamiliar with Standard Scoring, it may be extremely difficult to determine by reading over the material just which element (or elements) is present. Therefore, it is useful to turn to the Table of Life Issue Criterion Judgments for guidance.

In a rough, initial stage assessment of the material, you will probably guess that the most likely stages to consider are Stages 3, 2/3, and 2. Let us begin by considering the CJs at Stage 3. There are four CJs at Stage 3 that use the affiliation norm. Combining the same norm with four different elements results in four quite distinctive moral ideas. In the first, CJ#12, the relationship of love is seen as the basis for approving of what Heinz had done or for exempting him from blame. In the second, CJ#13, the affiliative relationship is construed in terms of duty, Heinz's role or duty as a good husband. In the third, CJ#14, affiliation is seen from the point of view of the family and the consequences of acting or not acting for the family. In the fourth, CJ#15, affiliation is construed in terms of reciprocity, Heinz's gratitude or appreciation toward his wife. The first of these four ideas, CJ#12, is clearly the closest to the central idea expressed in the interview: [Heinz should steal the drug] out of love or concern for his wife; *or* because he would feel so close to her or the relationship would be so close.

After determining whether any other IJ can be identified on this issue, the scorer would proceed to evaluate the match between CJ #12 and the corresponding IJ expressed in Responses 1, 2, 5, 13, and 14–16. There is no evidence at all of the group consequences (CJ#14) or reciprocity (CJ#15) elements in the life issue, affiliation norm material for this interview so these CJs may be dropped from further consideration. The duty element in relation to the affiliation norm does, however, come up in the interviewer's Question 15: ''Does the devotion make you duty bound or? . . .'' When asked directly whether he is arguing for stealing on the basis of the affiliation norm and duty element, the subject says that he is not. That is, the duty element is represented in the interviewer's question but not in the subject's reasoning. It appears, then, that all of the life issue material represents a single interview judgment. Just to be sure, however, the scorer should review the other CJs at stages 3, 2/3, and 3 to determine whether any seem to correspond to material in the interview. The only Stage 3 CJ that is evocative of the interview material is CJ#16, in which the blaming (approving) element is combined with the conscience norm rather than the *affiliation* norm. In this CJ, the focus is on Heinz's intentions as being good rather than on love or devotion as a reason to justify stealing. A parallel idea is represented at Stage 2/3 in CJ#8. Evidence that this combination of norm and element is present in the interview can be seen in the response to Question 4. In evaluating this IJ–CJ match, it will become clear that the IJ is closer to CJ#8 than to CJ#16. However, CJ#8 is included with CJ#12, so if our first proposed match is verified, the conscience norm material is not scored. In summary, the life issue for this subject includes two interview judgments – affiliation norm, blaming (approving) element; and conscience norm, blaming (approving) element.

Turning to the Table of Law Issue Criterion Judgments, we see that the norms potentially usable for this issue are life, property, affiliation, law, and conscience. We will again guess that the material is most likely to be Stage 3, 2/3, or 2. In analyzing the law issue material, let us begin by grouping together material that seems to be expressing a single idea. The responses to Questions 9, 10, 11, 12, 13, 17, and 18 seem to be expressing an idea that is very similar to that identified as life issue, affiliation norm, namely, the blaming (approving) element. On the law issue, the ''flip side'' of the same idea is being expressed: ''Heinz shouldn't steal for a stranger or unloved wife because he wouldn't be doing it out of love or devotion.'' That is, the same norm, affiliation, is being used along with the same element but in the context of the law rather than life issue. A review of the Table of Law Issue Criterion Judgments reveals that this idea is expressed in Law Issue CJ#13, which does in fact resemble the interview material and is labeled as representing the proposed norm and element.

A second quite salient norm in the law issue responses is the property norm as expressed in responses to Questions 19–21. The element is also fairly clear in this material. It is "having a right." Since there is no CJ at Stage 3 on the law issue, with norm property and element having a right, let us review the CJs at the adjacent stages. Stage 2 CJ#6 provides a potential match and confirms our suggestion that the responses yield an IJ defined by the law issue, the property norm, and the having a right element.

The only remaining material for this issue is the responses to Questions 3 and 7, both of which appear to represent the law norm as well as the law issue. The response to Question 3 states that stealing is wrong in the eyes of the state and the laws of the nation but does not explain why. The fact that the law norm is expressed without any identifiable element makes this material unscorable. The response to Question 7 also appears to be unscorable since it is a statement of what Heinz *could do* rather than what he *should* do and *why*. However, a review of the CJs at Stage 3 reveals that the interview material bears at least some resemblance to CJ#14, law norm, obeying (consulting) element. The scorer should at least consider whether the interview material represents this CJ idea in an ambiguous and implicit way.

The law issue, then, yields two clear interview judgments – affiliation norm/blaming (approving) element and property norm/having a right element. It also yields a very ambiguous possible IJ representing the law norm/obeying element. As a further illustration of identifying interview judgments, let us consider the same individual's responses to Dilemma I.

1. *Should Joe refuse to give his father the money?*

Yes, it was his money. He wanted to go. He worked for, he saved for it. He's still under his father's protection as far as the age limit goes. But you do have to, even at the age of 14, do have to stand up for some rights.

2. *Would it be right or wrong to refuse?*

I think it would be right.

Why?

Because this money meant something to him. He worked for it. He had a definite goal for this. It's the basis for life, you know, if you don't start at that age and prove that your money is going to do something for you, this is really the time to start a child on, in his mind what he has to do in order to accomplish what he wants. So in turn by doing this, his father is going to take and distort any image as far as financial ideas this child may have.

3. *Does his father have the right to tell Joe to give him the money?*

No, I don't think so. As I say, he did work for it, and it is his entirely and it should be his.

4. *Does giving the money have anything to do with being a good son?*

No, basically not. No matter what it is between a good father and a good son, good mother or daughter, no matter what you, as far as financial terms or physical means will not accomplish being something good. You can buy anything to impress people or give them money to this extent or take their money. But this does not mean you're going to be a good person from this.

5. *Which is worse, a father breaking a promise to his son or a son breaking a promise to his father?*

Basically the father because most sons will imagine themselves after their father and distorting an image of the father at this early age, especially at this age, could be quite harmful.

6. *In what way could it be harmful?*

The object of, he's at 14. His basics and it's more than likely his father has around approximately this age explained the facts of life. The son is trying to set up a life's meaning from his father, this is the only male, probably the only male he has to follow. So in other words, everything is from something like this, his father, his father taking the money could just completely shatter any ideas that this son would have about him. And any beliefs, you know, like well, he told me this, he told me that . . . baloney with him. Forget it.

7. *Why should a promise be kept?*

If your word's no good, you're no good.

8. *What do you mean?*

If you can't unless it's physically impossible to go along with what you've done, or what you stated you were going to do. This would really ruin your own life as far as this goes. Because no matter what this was, the boy and the wolf or something like that, you know, he's always crying. And then at the time he really needed help when his word was desperate for the boy's safety, it was no good.

9. *You mean if you break promises people won't believe you anymore?*

Right. Somehow or other they just get fed up with listening to your problems or something like this, you know, and forget you.

Before attempting to isolate interview judgments, we must separate the responses into the two standard issues for this dilemma, contract and authority. Contract issue responses are given in answer to Questions 1 (all but the fourth sentence), 2, 3, 4, 7, 8, and 9. Authority issue responses are given in answer to Questions 1 (fourth sentence), 5, and 6.

Turning to the Table of Contract Issue Criterion Judgments, we see that the norms relevant to the contract issue are property, affiliation, authority, contract, and conscience. In a preliminary analysis of the contract issue material in the example, it appears that at least three separate ideas are expressed. In Response 1 and the beginning of Response 2, the idea is that it would be right for Joe to refuse because it is his money that he worked for and saved. This appears to be the property norm. In the remainder of the response to Question 2, the subject is talking about the lesson Joe could learn from this incident about life and money. The norm here is not immediately obvious, but may also be property since the idea concerns learning about how to handle money. In Questions 7 through 9 the idea expressed appears to be that if you don't keep your word you can ruin your life because people will no longer believe what you say. This discussion of the importance of keeping promises is the contract norm. Let us return to the latter two responses, after having completed the element classification of the first property norm material. In Response 1 and the first two sentences of Response 2, the subject refers to the son's right to keep the money based on the fact that he worked for and saved it. This suggests either the having a right element or the reciprocity (positive desert) element. As in Dilemma III, the material appears at first glance to be in the Stage 2, 2/3, 3 range. In reviewing the property norm CJs at these stages, two CJs can be identified as potential matches: Stage 2 CJ#4 (property norm/having a right element) and Stage 3 CJ#12 (property norm/reciprocity element). It may seem strange that these two seemingly parallel ideas are identified with different elements. The reason for this is that the reciprocity, positive desert element is taken to imply a notion of deservingness as a mediator between working for or owning something and having a right to it. This concept begins to be used only at Stage 3. At Stage 2 the judgment that if one owns or works for something, one can do what one likes with it is not mediated by an implication of deservingness. In a case such as this, one cannot make a final decision about which element is more appropriate until one has decided which of the two CJs is the appropriate match for the interview material. Based on an initial reading of the material, the Stage 2 *having a right* element CJ appears to be more appropriate. This must, of course, be verified by reference to the critical indicators, stage structure, and so on.

In the second idea expressed in response to Question 2, the norm again appears to be property and the element is also fairly clearly identifiable. The idea here appears to be that this incident is important in that it can teach the son about life and about handling money. Responses that refer to an individual's development are almost invariably classified as expressions of the *upholding character* element. Unfortunately, we cannot find a CJ with the property norm and upholding character element at any of the stages that seem most appropriate. If this happens, two things should be done. First, you ought to check against adjacent and even nonadjacent stages to see whether they yield a CJ of the norm and element you have identified in the interview. In this case there is a property, upholding character CJ at Stage 4 (CJ#23). The IJ should be evaluated against the critical indicators and stage structure of CJ#23 in spite of the fact that it does not correspond to our original stage estimate. In addition to checking for a particular norm and element combination at other stages, it is also important to check CJs with other norms and elements at the stages that appear most likely just in case the classification by norm or element was incorrect. In this case, none of the other CJs appears to be similar to the IJ material.

Finally, turning to the contract norm material in Questions 7–9, it is not easy to tell what element is being expressed in the material. In this case, the best approach is to check the contract norm CJs in the Table of Contract Issue Criterion Judgments to look for an idea that looks like the IJ. CJ#8 at Stage 2/3, contract norm, good (bad) reputation element, sounds very much like the IJ, and the element designation makes sense in relation to the idea expressed. Therefore the critical indicators and stage structure ought to be scrutinized in order to decide whether the CJ provides a match to the IJ. Note that CJ#16 expresses a parallel idea and is defined by the same norm and element. Stage 2 CJ#6 is also a parallel idea, but in this case the element is different, indicating that at Stage 2 the idea focuses on the instrumental consequences of promise keeping and breaking. At Stages 2/3 and 3 this concern for instrumental consequences is transformed into a concern for approval that is captured by the reputation element rather than the reward element. All of these parallel ideas should be checked carefully before deciding which, if any, provides the appropriate match score.

Turning to the Table of Authority Issue Criterion Judgments, we see authority and affiliation listed as the two norms used with this issue. In reading through the authority material in responses to Questions 1, 5, and 6, it appears that all of the material can be classified as authority norm since it treats the father–son relationship as one of the father's authority over the son rather than one of mutual affection or affiliation. The fourth sentence in the response to Question 1 refers to the son's obligation to respect or obey his father. The statement represents the authority issue, authority norm, and obeying (consulting) element. This combination occurs at Stages 3 (CJ#14), 3/4 (CJ#18), and 4 (CJ#21). All of these CJs should be evaluated as potential matches for the IJ, beginning with the CJ that appears to resemble the IJ most closely. The responses to Questions 5 and 6 deal with the father as a model for his son. This idea is captured by the upholding character element. The responses to these two questions represent a single interview judgment defined as authority issue, authority norm, and upholding character element. This combination occurs at Stage 3 (CJ#15), Stage 3/4 (CJ#19), and Stage 4 (CJ#23). All three CJs constitute potential matches for the IJ and should be scrutinized carefully to determine whether a match score can be assigned.

It should be clear from this case material that classification by norm and element requires a flexible approach with clues being taken from both the interview material and from the tables of CJs. Norm and element classification is not as straightforward as classification by issue. Occasionally, the designation may seem arbitrary. The important thing to remember is that this step is simply a way of identifying all potential IJ–CJ correspondences so that these correspondences can be evaluated in regard to whether they justify assignment of a match score. The aim is to uncover potential matches; classification by norm and element is simply a means to this end, not an end in itself.

Skills Section for Step 6: Scorability Criteria

To be used in match scoring an IJ must (1) provide a reason that (2) is considered valid by the subject and (3) is at least implicitly prescriptive. If an IJ is to be used for guess scoring, it need not meet the third criterion, prescriptivity. Examples pertaining to each of the three criteria are presented in this section.

1. An IJ must offer a reason or justification for the action or value being defended. Assertions not supported by specific reasons are often made in interviews (as they are in general conversation). As we have noted in the instructions, in the absence of a moral reason or supporting value, a statement is not considered scorable. Statements unsupported by reasons are often easily spotted. They include simple yes and no responses to questions (e.g., *Should Heinz steal the drug?* "Yes," "I don't know," "Perhaps," "I think he should," and so on) as well as unelaborated repetitions of the information from the question, for example,

If he was a judge would he think so?
No, because he was a judge.

Other "no reason" responses were discussed earlier in the step-by-step instructions:

Stealing is wrong.
He should pay the druggist for the drug.

Often, however, the presence or absence for a reason is less obvious. The reason may be implicit or may require disentanglement from other parts of the interview. An effort should be made to construe meaning if meaning exists. In the instructions we used the example "He should be made to pay for what he has done" and suggested that unlike the statement "He should pay the druggist for the drug," the first statement implies the value retribution and therefore is usable for a guess score. The following two responses to the question "Should Heinz steal the drug?" also contain implicit reasons:

Heinz should steal the drug because his wife is dying.
Heinz should steal the drug because without the drug his wife will die.

In both cases the action of stealing is justified by implicit reference to the value of the wife's life.

In other cases it is more difficult to decide whether a reason is being offered. The scorer must use the transposition process to restate the interview response. If the response can be restated as a reason for action (or in support of a value), it is considered to pass the first scorability criterion even though it is not stated by the subject in the form of a reason. Transposition was discussed under Instructions for Standard Issue Scoring. It involves restating the relevant interview material in a way that is more coherent than the subject's own expression of his or her thoughts. In restating the subject's response, the scorer is attempting to answer the following question: What does the subject really seem to be saying; what does he really mean by the response he has given? In answering this question, one must be very careful neither to read extraneous ideas into the subject's judgments nor to exclude relevant material from the restated version. The idea is to establish first of all a more concise or focused representation of the subject's idea. This entails making rearrangements, distillations, or other grammatical alterations – but no *substantive* modifications of the response. This means that the scorer should restate what the subject is saying in a way that is (a) relatively intelligible or syntactically coherent; (b) pithy or stripped of material not relevant to the IJ norm and element (be especially careful here); and (c) direct or explicit. Draw on the subject's own words as much as possible in the transposition and bracket any words not used by the subject that you have introduced. (If possible, avoid introducing any of your own words at all.)

Some of the criterion judgments themselves seem to offer only opinions about *what* should be done or *when* something should be done rather than reasons *why*. A transposition or restatement can be offered in each case to show the sense in which the criterion judgment can be interpreted as presenting a reason in support of a judgment. Consider the following examples:

CRITERION JUDGMENT #7, DILEMMA III, LIFE ISSUE

[Heinz should steal the drug] if he needs, likes, or loves his wife or wants her to live; **OR** because she might return the favor some day; **OR** if he thinks it would be worth the trouble, penalty, or risk.

This criterion judgment states the conditions under which Heinz should steal the drug. However, it is easy to discern an implied *reason* for stealing being right (in those cases where it is right). That is, we could restate the criterion judgment in the following way without significantly altering its meaning: "If (or when) stealing the drug is right for Heinz to do, it is right *because* he needs his wife, wants her to live, would think it's worth the risk, and so on." (The action of stealing the drug is justified by an implied reference to the value of the wife's life for Heinz.)

CRITERION JUDGMENT #9, DILEMMA IV, LIFE ISSUE

[The doctor should give the woman the drug] if he consulted all the relatives, and/or the law, and/or other doctors and they agreed that he should kill the woman.

Restated version:

It could be right for the doctor to give the woman the drug because if he has consulted all the relatives, law, and/or other doctors, and they agree to it, then that makes it all right. (The action of euthanasia is justified by reference to social consensus – element, consulting, obeying.)

If the interview response you are evaluating is as fully elaborated as the criterion judgments, you should have no trouble making comparable transpositions to determine whether a reason is offered. It is, of course, much more difficult in borderline cases, but the same principle applies.

The following are examples of statements that do not meet the criterion of offering a reason and thus are not usable even for a guess score. These examples are easily seen to offer no moral reason since they are essentially yes or no answers to a probe question.

DILEMMA III, LIFE ISSUE

What do you think you would do?

I think I would probably do the same thing.

DILEMMA I, AUTHORITY ISSUE

Which is worse, a father breaking a promise to a son or a son breaking a promise to a father?

I can't see where there'd be any difference.

DILEMMA III, MORALITY AND CONSCIENCE ISSUE

Should Heinz get full punishment?

No, in this case he should still be punished but yet it should not be as severe.

Another type of "no reason" response involves stating *what* action should be taken rather than *why* the action is recommended. (This kind of response occurs fairly frequently on the punishment issue of Dilemmas III' and IV' but can occur on any issue.)

DILEMMA III', PUNISHMENT ISSUE

What punishment should the judge give him?

He might give him some outrageous sentence . . . He could give him 5 or 10 years probably.

(Note that this example also fails to meet the prescriptivity criterion.)

DILEMMA III', PUNISHMENT ISSUE

Punishment?

He should be made to pay for the drug.

2. *An IJ must be accepted as valid by the subject.* Judgments that fail this criterion are those that are clearly disavowed or rejected by the speaker.

The italicized material in the following response might be considered for scoring under the law issue.

Did the druggist have the right to charge that much when there was no law saying he couldn't?

The druggist could charge anything he wanted, but he was just out to make money as far as I am concerned. **Everybody's out to make a buck and I think this was wrong** because he is dealing in human life. Human life comes very high to me, it is not something you play around with. I think he should have thought of that before he charged $2,000 for the drug. He was probably the only druggist in town so he could charge what he wanted.

The statements "The druggist could charge anything he wanted" and "Everybody's out to make a buck" sound similar to Dilemma III law issue CJ#6: ("Heinz should not steal the drug because the druggist discovered or made the drug and can do what he wants with it.") However, the subject goes on to reject that line of reasoning: ". . . and I think this was wrong." Therefore, the material is not usable even for a guess score.

A subject may also disavow a judgment by attributing it to the interviewer:

Does the father have the right to tell Joe to give him the money?

He's boss over him, if that's what you mean. I don't think he should have the right to take the money. Joe worked for it.

The judgment "He's boss over him" would be a match candidate for CJ#1 of the Dilemma I authority issue if it were not for a disavowal that follows, ". . . if that's what *you* mean. I don't think he should have the right."

In order for a judgment to be ruled out as unscorable, the validity of that judgment must be clearly rejected. The following response to Dilemma IV, for example, would be suitable for scoring because the subject suggests that although the position is not his own, it is "equally as good":

For the kind of reasons you are saying, your personal feeling?

That is my personal feeling. Now if you want to look at it from society's viewpoint, you can say these people are a drag on society and they are using up resources, they really are of no use to society anymore. I suppose they could make equally as good rationalization for legalizing it. (67-D)

In cases where the validity attributed to the judgment is ambiguous, the material should not be used to assign a match score but may be used as the basis for a guess score if no match scores have been assigned for the issue. In the following example, the italicized material presents an argument for the Dilemma III life issue that is not rejected as *completely* invalid but that is not considered by the subject to be a morally valid reason to steal the drug. Thus it can be used for a guess score but not for a match score.

What if there was no other way to get it?

Certainly he is in a difficult position if he loves his wife, but the point that I have to consider is the fact that we are all under some kind of duress, we all need things and if we all disobeyed the law to fulfill those needs, then there would be a breakdown in the structure of society. Maybe somebody would steal from him the $2,000 that he stole from somebody else. And he is taking it to the pharmacy to pay the bill. Because if it is all right for him to do it, then maybe somebody else has a reason to do it to him.

If Heinz does not love his wife, should he steal the drug?

It is not a matter of if you love your wife or not as far as I am concerned. It is just as wrong to steal it whether you love your wife or not. **The thought that you would want to get the money and help her because you love her is very good and even if you didn't love her, but you valued her as a human being, you still might want to have the money, but the fact is that I still say I don't think that you should steal.**

Suppose it was a stranger, should he steal the drug?

Well, obviously if I am not going to steal for my wife and I love her, the possibility of stealing for a stranger would be even more remote.

There are two possible CJ matches for the life issue material presented here, CJ#9 and CJ#12. However, because the arguments as presented in the interview are not accepted as valid by the subject, the material cannot be used to assign a match score. (Material on the law issue contained in the same passages can, of course, be used for match scoring on the law issue.) Let us look more closely at the material on the two possible life matches.

Life CJ#12 states, "Heinz should steal the drug out of love or concern for his wife." The subject appears to be expressing the same Stage 3 affiliation norm ideas as are presented in the CJ: "Certainly he is in a difficult position if he loves his wife . . . The thought that you would want to get the money and help her because you love her is very good." However, the validity of these Stage 3 ideas must be viewed in the context of the subject's assertion.

"It is not a matter of if you love your wife or not as far as I am concerned. It is just as wrong to steal it whether you love your wife or not. The thought that you would want to . . . help her because you love her is very good . . . but the fact is that I still say I don't think that you should steal." Although attributing some value to the ideas corresponding to CJ#12, the subject has denied the validity of these arguments as reasons for stealing. Therefore, the material is suitable only for a guess score.

The possible match with Life CJ#9 runs into the same difficulty. This criterion judgment holds that Heinz should steal the drug even if he doesn't love his wife because "we are all human beings" and "human life is always precious." The apparently matching statement by the subject (". . . even if you didn't love her, but you valued her as a human being, you still might want to have the money . . .") is again contradicted by "but the fact is that I still say I don't think that you should steal." Given the ambiguity of the subject's acceptance of the reason as valid, the match could be considered only for a guess score.

Arguments in both of the following examples are more clearly rejected as invalid and are, therefore, not usable even for guess scoring.

DILEMMA III, LAW ISSUE

What kind of criterion do you use?

I mentioned earlier, the sort of conflict here between social responsibility. "Thou shalt not steal" is one of the Ten Commandments, but at the same time, life is a pretty precious thing, too. It seems to me the conflict here is that it is right if it will save a life – I think. Because the loss the druggist will feel is hardly the loss Heinz would feel from the death of his wife. I would tend to put that on a higher priority. The consequences **of the theft are something you have to take into consideration, too. I guess you shouldn't judge right or wrong on the consequences in that sense.**

What consequences?

To him if he steals it and gets caught.

Are you saying that if he gets caught that makes it wrong?

What I'm trying to say is that you shouldn't do it on that basis, but it is a consideration that is unavoidable. Like you read so often the kids cheating in school – that sort of thing, it is all right if you don't get caught. I don't think that is a valid argument.

DILEMMA I, AUTHORITY ISSUE

What would be the most important reason for giving his father the money?

There isn't any. **No moral reason,** he might not want to get a beating.

    3. *To be used for match scoring, an IJ must be at least implicitly prescriptive.* In the following example, the nonprescriptivity of the statement is clear. Since this example also fails the criterion of offering a reason, it is not usable for either match or guess scoring.

DILEMMA III', PUNISHMENT ISSUE

What punishment should the judge give him?

He might give him some outrageous sentence . . . He could give him 5 or 10 years probably.

    In the following two examples, the prescriptivity of the judgment is not explicit. However, because these responses are implicitly prescriptive, they can be used for match scoring.

DILEMMA III, LIFE ISSUE

Suppose it wasn't Heinz's wife, but a stranger. Should he still steal the drug?

If you're in the spot of helping someone without hurting someone else emotionally or physically, it's an ideal value to save someone and jeopardize yourself for humanity.

    Although the subject in the preceding example does not say that Heinz *should* steal the drug for a stranger, the reference to saving that person as ''an ideal value'' implies prescriptivity.

    The following example is implicitly prescriptive because it seems to be an argument for stealing being *right* ''in this situation.''

DILEMMA III, LIFE ISSUE

Why is it right to steal?

Well, in the large picture, it may not be so, because it is only one life. But in this situation it's this man's wife, and he naturally would want to do anything he could to save her.

207

In the following three examples, the prescriptivity of the judgments is ambiguous. Thus, the material can be used to assign a guess score, but should not be used as the basis of a match score.

DILEMMA III, LAW ISSUE

Should Heinz steal the drug?

No, I don't think so, because if I were put in that position, I would never just go and steal it.

DILEMMA III, LIFE ISSUE

Should Heinz steal the drug?

Sure, I would do it. *Why?* Because people are very important to me. I enjoy helping people, and I would feel like a murderer if I didn't do all I could to save a human life. I would never destroy one.

DILEMMA IV, LIFE (QUALITY) ISSUE

Why should Dr. Jefferson give the woman the drug?

I just don't see how he could just sit there and watch this woman just waste away.

Skills Section for Steps 7–10: Evaluating a CJ–IJ Match

We shall seek to illustrate Steps 7 through 10 together (locating a match, making surface and structural evaluations of the proposed match, and accepting or rejecting the match). We shall illustrate the process with a series of examples beginning with those involving clear-cut matches and proceeding to those presenting difficulties of various kinds.

DILEMMA III, LIFE ISSUE

Should Heinz steal the drug?

In that case he might. His wife was dying and maybe they had children and he might need someone home to look after them. But maybe he shouldn't steal it because they might put him in prison for more years than he could stand.

The second sentence of this response offers a reason for stealing the drug and thus provides material on the life issue. The third sentence offers a reason against stealing and thus provides law issue material. In this example we shall attempt to score the life issue and thus shall consider the second sentence alone:

His wife was dying and maybe they had children and he might need someone home to look after them.

Assuming that this statement is the only one in the interview in which the subject expresses this thought, we would treat the material as a single interview judgment and attempt to use it as the basis for a match.

The statement clearly provides a reason for stealing that is not rejected by the subject as invalid (although counterarguments are presented). The judgment is not literally prescriptive as it stages what Heinz might do rather than what he should do. But given the preconventional failure to distinguish between *should* and *would*, this judgment would be considered functionally prescriptive if it were scored at the preconventional level. The IJ thus provisionally passes all three scorability criteria.

Phase 1 (Orientation):

The emphasis in the IJ on Heinz's needs is suggestive of the instrumental egoism characteristic of Stage 2. Therefore, the search for a CJ that resembles the

IJ begins with Stage 2. A review of the Stage 2 CJs in the Table of Life Issue Criterion Judgments produces a possible match with CJ#7:

[Heinz should steal the drug] if he needs, likes, or loves his wife or wants her to live; **OR** because she might return the favor some day; **OR** because he thinks it would be worth the trouble, penalty, or risk.

At first glance, there does not seem to be much question about the suitability of the match. The subject states that Heinz "might" steal the drug because "he might need" his wife to "look after" their children, if they had any. The suggestion, in other words, is that Heinz should steal the drug if he needs his wife – exactly the judgment expressed in the first part of the CJ.

However, a score for the proposed match must not be entered until after an evaluation of the correspondence has been made in terms of the CJ's critical indicators, stage structure, and distinctions. We turn for this evaluation to the explicated version of CJ#7 reproduced in Table 6.6.

Phase 2 (Surface Evaluation): In the example at hand, the consideration that Heinz "might need someone home to look after" the children straightforwardly satisfies Critical Indicator (a), which stipulates an appeal to "Heinz's needs or wishes." Because only one of the three critical indicators must be fulfilled, the interview judgment has passed the surface evaluation and therefore it receives a "clear pass" for Phase 2.

Phase 3 (Structural Evaluation): We must now proceed to double-check the structural level of the material being assessed. In doing so, we must keep in mind the conceptual differences between parallel ideas expressed at different stages. Our initial tentative evaluation of this response placed it at Stage 2. We have found a CJ that seems to match it and whose critical indicators it satisfies. It is still possible, however, that something in the response could lead us to question whether the statement in fact reflects a Stage 2 structure. To avoid scoring as Stage 2 a judgment that reflects a higher or lower stage structure, a comparison of the IJ is made with both the Stage Structure and Distinctions and Inclusions sections of the explicated CJ.

In terms of the stage structure of CJ#7, we see that an appeal to Heinz's needs is based on a "self-interested conception of the relationship between Heinz and others, and an appreciation of the instrumental value which stealing the drug may have for Heinz." Is the IJ consistent with this underlying structural idea? Indeed, the response does seem to embody the idea of the structure notion that Heinz should save his wife because he might need her to take care of their children certainly seems to reflect "a self-interested conception of the relationship between Heinz and others." Furthermore, there seems to be no basis for supposing that the ideas in the IJ are more representative of another stage. To be certain, each of the distinctions referred to in CJ#7 should be checked. Clearly, neither the Stage 3 CJ (#12) nor the Stage 4 CJ (#24) referred to in the Distinctions and Inclusions section of CJ#7 would provide an appropriate match for the IJ we are scoring. A pass is assigned for Phase 3.

The IJ has passed both the surface and structural evaluations and has satisfied the three scorability criteria. Therefore, a "clear match" is assigned for the IJ and CJ#7. (The score is a clear match, not a marginal match, because there is no doubt about the presence of the critical indicators.) The need for such an

Table 6.6. *Criterion judgment #7*

DILEMMA:	III
ISSUE:	Life
NORM:	Affiliation (conscience)
ELEMENT:	Seeking reward (avoiding punishment) (7)
STAGE:	2

Criterion judgment

1. [Heinz should steal the drug] if he needs, likes, or loves his wife, a stranger, or pet, or wants them to live; **OR** because they might return the favor some day; **OR** if he thinks it would be worth the trouble, penalty, or risk.

2. [Heinz should save his wife but not a pet] because you can always get another dog but you can't get another wife.

Stage structure

This justification is based on an individually self-interested conception of the relationship between Heinz and others, and an appreciation of the instrumental value which stealing the drug may have for Heinz. Heinz's "love" is contingent upon, the relative to, Heinz's wishes rather than being a shared normative value (Stage 3). The relative value of animal and human life (dog and wife) depends on the difficulty or ease of replacing them if they are lost.

Critical indicators

Required for a match is an appeal to any of the following: (a) Heinz's needs or wishes; (b) Heinz's judgment that saving his wife would be worth the risk or trouble; (c) past or anticipated benefits to Heinz, or possible exchanges between Heinz and another (wife, friend); or (d) the pragmatic difficulty of replacement.

Distinctions and inclusions

Within Stage 2
Do not confuse with the parallel point on the law issue (CJ#8) that Heinz should not steal the drug if he does not love his wife, nor for a stranger, because it would not be worth the trouble.

Between Other Stages
Do not confuse this self-interested conception with the Stage 3 conception of the relationship in terms of unique affectional ties or loving concern (CJ#12). The cited Stage 3 point includes the idea of this judgment *except when Indicator (c) is present.*

The idea of return benefit should not be scored Stage 2 when it is part of Stage 4 societal reasoning (see CJ#24, Match Example #1).

Distinguish carefully between the transitional "3 1/2" concern with weighing conflicting social values and Heinz's perspective (CJ#22), which includes this point.

Match examples

1. *You mean if the drug didn't work . . .*

Well, if this man was caught in the act, it sure wouldn't do him any good but if he was able to take the drug home and have it work, **I think it would be worth a few years in prison.** [65-0]

2. *Is it up to Heinz to decide?*

It's up to Heinz to decide **how badly he wants to save his wife.** [23-0]

3. *Does he have a duty to do it for a friend?*

Table 6.6. (*cont.*)

Match examples (*cont.*)	Yes, if his friend was very sick and **he knew that his friend would help him when he was sick himself.** If his friend was real close, he'd want to save his life and maybe his friend would sometimes save his life.
	4. *Should he have done that?* **If he liked his wife he should.** *Would a good husband have to?* He wouldn't have to, no. If he didn't want to, he didn't have to. **But if he loved his wife, he should.** [22-0]
	5. *Should Heinz steal the drug?* Yes. He wants it for his wife, because she is sick . . . He wants his wife to get better.
Marginal match example	6. *Why should he steal it for a friend?* Because they are going to die if they don't have any drugs. You wouldn't have any friends if everybody died.
Nonmatch example	*What should he do? Not would or might, but should.* It depends again, to me what the trade-off or risk will be, you know. What it will mean in terms of, if he is going to sacrifice his life in place of his wife, I don't know if that would help either of them really. I don't know if the sum total of their happiness is going to be increased if he is going to go to prison for the rest of his life. Again, it is the same thing for his friend. I would say you probably would feel that obligation to steal the drug for either your wife or your friend and hope to hell that you didn't suffer too much for it later. (Although this response fits Critical Indicator [b] of CJ#7, it is inconsistent with that judgment's stage structure because of its perspective of mutuality in the relationships [''the sum total of their happiness,'' etc.]. The unelaborated idea of obligation that Heinz might feel suggests that the structure of this response is Stage 3/4.)

intricate system of evaluative criteria as that described earlier will become more apparent as we proceed with examples that are less easily scored.

The following example of material on the life issue illustrates the idea of an essential rather than literal match to the critical indicators. It represents a marginal pass on the surface evaluation and a marginal match overall.

DILEMMA III, LIFE ISSUE

Is it a husband's duty to steal the drug for his wife if he can get it no other way?

In this case I would say yes, it is, based on the general duties of a husband to a wife or a wife to a husband, what a mate must do for either her husband or his wife.

How is it good for Heinz to steal?

Because he is fulfilling his duty as a husband and as a human being.

Phase 1
(Orientation):

The subject's concern with the "general duties" of a husband is suggestive of societally defined role responsibilities discussed in the general description of Stage 4. With this tentative stage assessment in mind, we scan the Table of Life Issue Criterion Judgments for a CJ that resembles our example. The closest similarity is provided by CJ#27:

[Heinz should steal the drug] because of the marital responsibility he accepted; **OR** because he is obligated by or must honor the covenant of marriage or the wedding vows.

We turn to the explicated CJ to evaluate the proposed match (Table 6.7).

Phase 2 (Surface Evaluation):

The IJ does not *clearly* satisfy the critical indicators since the evident concern in the judgment with Heinz's marital responsibility entails no explicit idea of Heinz's having "accepted or chosen" that responsibility as required in Indicator (a). Neither are the "general duties of a husband" explicitly defined in terms of "wedding vows or marriage contract" as required by Indicator (b). Therefore, we can not give the IJ a clear pass on Phase 2. On the other hand, the essence of what the subject seems to be saying comes very close to the idea in Critical Indicator (b). The reference to "the general duties of a husband or his wife" can be plausibly interpreted as a reference to the marriage contract, albeit indirect. At Stage 4, marriage defines a set of societal roles and obligations. As such, the referents for the IJ's "general duties" and the CJ's "marriage contract" seem to be the same. Thus, there is some evidence for an "essential match" between the IJ and the critical indicator. Because in this case the IJ neither fails nor passes the critical indicators in an unambiguous way, and because in essence the subject seems to be expressing an idea that does not differ significantly from that of the critical indicator, we give the IJ a marginal pass on Phase 2.

Phase 3 (Structural Evaluation):

When an IJ has been given only a marginal pass on Phase 2, particular care must be used in making the structural evaluation. The subject's failure to express the critical indicator ideas exactly may result from the fact that his thinking is not really Stage 4 rather than from a failure to elaborate the ideas fully or to express them using the language of the CJ. In such cases the scorer must look very carefully at the stage structure descriptions and the IJ for evidence that the IJ is inconsistent with the stage structure of the proposed CJ. In this case, we can find no such indication that the IJ is structurally inconsistent with Stage 4 nor does it clearly exhibit the structure of another stage. The role duties are not based on feelings of affection between a husband and wife as at Stage 3 or on an explicitly contractual agreement as at Stage 5. (We can also easily rule out the instrumental Stage 2 and physicalistic Stage 1 conceptions of the relationship.) In fact, as we noted in discussing the orientation phase (Phase 1), the IJ seems to give positive evidence for a Stage 4 conception of general, societally defined role obligations that each spouse must fulfill in relation to the other.

In order to be sure we have not made a mistake in this structural evaluation, we must check the distinctions provided by CJ#27. The reference to Stage 4/5 CJ#32 (Heinz's deep and mutual commitment with his wife) seems clearly inapplicable. The Stage 3 CJ#13, which involves concern with shared norma-

Table 6.7. *Criterion judgment #27*

DILEMMA:	III
ISSUE:	Life
NORM:	Affiliation
ELEMENT:	Having a duty (5)
STAGE:	4

Criterion judgment

[Heinz should steal the drug] because of the marital responsibility he accepted; **OR** because he is obligated by, or must honor, the covenant of marriage or the wedding vows.

Stage structure

This judgment expresses an institutionalized view of marriage in which obligation toward another person in marriage is based on defined rules for a role a person commits himself or herself to in taking on the role. These rules are defined in relation to religious or societal order. Sometimes the definitions are given a legal or "written contract" flavor.

Critical indicators

Required for a match is an appeal to either (a) Heinz's having *accepted* a marital *responsibility;* or (b) Heinz's *obligation* from the marriage *contract* (covenant, vows).

Distinctions and inclusions

Between Other Stages

Do not confuse this idea of a societal obligation with the Stage 3 concern with shared normative expectations for good role-behavior (CJ#3), where the role obligation is defined in terms of the dyadic relation. Distinguish from a transitional 3/4 idea of the responsibility as something Heinz would naturally feel (CJ#21).

Do not confuse with the Stage 4/5 appeal to Heinz's deep and mutual commitment with his wife (CJ#32). This judgment includes the cited Stage 3 and 3/4 points and is itself included within the Stage 4/5 point.

Match examples

1. *So you mean the wife really does have the right to expect him to steal the drug, because of this mutual thing?*

   Yes. I mean, if we were dating, my wife and I were just dating, and all of a sudden I found out that she was – I don't think I would have the actual obligation, even though there might be just as much love. *Why not?* I don't know, maybe just **because of the laws of marriage.** *Why does that make it more binding?* It is just the simple contract of marriage. I don't know if I am sounding too – *What is the contract?* Just service and a devotion to each other and just obligation. There is where obligation comes in. [9-D]

2. *Getting back to this story, suppose the husband doesn't feel very close or affectionate to his wife. Should he still steal the drug in that case?*

   Well, I don't know, I think he'd be **obligated anyway, just from a marriage contract alone,** I mean the idea that he should help her in any time or any kind of stress, that morally he still should have done it. [23-B]

3. *What makes it his duty?*

   In most marriages, **you accept the responsibility to look after one another's health** and after their life and you have the responsibility when you live with

Table 6.7. (cont.)

Match examples (cont.)	someone to try and make it a happy life. And it's not going to be a happy life if his wife is dead. [41-D]
Marginal match example	4. *Suppose that Heinz has tried everything and nobody is going to help him. Should he steal it or not?* I think I would feel more personal, emotional, and logical responsibility to my wife rather than this guy whose behavior is rather antisocial in the sense that he is trying to make a lot of money on it. I think I would steal it. [42-C] (Marginal because the reference is to responsibility, not accepted responsibility.)
Guess examples	1. *Is it a husband's duty to steal the drug for his wife if he can get it no other way?* In this case I would say yes, it is, based on the general duties of a husband to a wife or a wife to a husband, what a mate must do for either her husband or his wife. [44-B] (Note that the term *duties* is also in the question.)
	2. *If the husband does not love his wife, is he obligated to steal the drug for her?* He still is morally obligated to do so, although he may be less inclined to do so. The marriage vows still hold and so, as long as he is still her husband, he must do anything in his power to save her. [9-E] (Guess because acceptance of responsibility is implicit.)

tive expectations for good role behavior, is less easily ruled out. Table 6.8 presents the explicated version of CJ#13.

The fully explicated Stage 3 CJ#13 clearly does not provide as appropriate a match for our example as does the Stage 4 CJ#27. The IJ does not focus on affection or loving concern between Heinz and his wife as does CJ#13 (Heinz should love or care about her, should help her because he once loved her, etc.). In fact, the contrast between the IJ and the examples provided for the Stage CJ#13 increases our confidence that the Stage 4 CJ#27 is the correct match.

Since the proposed correspondence has been given a marginal pass on Phase 2 and a pass on Phase 3, it is assigned an overall score of marginal match (Stage 4). This means that we are sure enough of the correspondence to assign a full-weight (rather than guess) Stage 4 score, but there is enough ambiguity in the correspondence to require us to note that the match is only marginally rather than clearly appropriate.

Sometimes the appropriate stage is not immediately apparent in Phase 1, nor is it always clear which CJ provides the best approximation to the IJ being scored. In the following example, the relative merits of CJs at several stages must be considered. This case also illustrates the usefulness of the transposition procedure as a means of evaluating the IJ at each of the three phases.

DILEMMA I, AUTHORITY ISSUE	*Does his father have the right to tell Joe to give him the money?* How old is he again? *Fourteen.* Fourteen, he has a right to, yes, by law. He is under his home and under the rule of the father, but by all codes of ethics, no.

Table 6.8. *Criterion judgment #13*

DILEMMA:	III
ISSUE:	Life
NORM:	Affiliation
ELEMENT:	Having a duty (5)
STAGE:	3

Criterion judgment

1. [Heinz should steal the drug, or it is Heinz's duty to steal the drug] because he should care about her, or love her; **OR** because he is supposed to stick close to her; **OR** because he shouldn't just sit back and watch her die.

2. [Heinz should steal the drug even if he doesn't love his wife] because he must have loved her at one time or should still care about her; **OR** because he is still her husband.

Stage structure

As in Criterion Judgment #12, stealing is justified insofar as it conforms in this case to a norm of affiliation and concern between husband and wife or friends. There is a focus in this criterion judgment on obligation as based on shared expectations for prosocial role behavior.

Critical indicators

Required for a match is an appeal to either (a) how Heinz should feel (should care about her, love her, must have loved her once, should still care about her, etc.); or (b) proper empathic conduct (shouldn't just sit back and let her die).

Distinctions and inclusions

Within Stage 3
Do not confuse with alternative Stage 3 points that focus on Heinz's prosocial character motives in general (#16), or on the concern Heinz *would* feel (CJ#12).
Between Other Stages
Do not confuse this prescription for Heinz to care with the ambiguous Stage 3/4 idea of the responsibility Heinz would feel (CJ#21).

Distinguish from the Stage 4 understanding of role norms in terms of societal responsibilities or contractual obligations (CJ#27). This point should be included with the cited Stage 3/4 or Stage 4 judgments.

Match examples

1. *Is there a good reason to steal if Heinz does not love his wife?*

   Yes, just to try to save a life. **He, at some time, must have loved her and he is still her husband.**

2. *Is it a husband's duty to steal the drug for his wife if he can get it no other way? Would a good husband do it?*

   I don't think any husband should sit back and watch his wife die. It is his duty to save her life.

How do you mean that? Say more about the difference between under the law and by codes of ethics.

Well, his father has supported him for fourteen years, he lived at . . . It doesn't say whether he has a nice home or not; what kind of family background he has, but he's in your imagination, probably lives in an average-type home and eats three meals a day and just in general, is comfortable and where his father could

– his father still has the power over his son to say what to do and what not to do.

Why does he have this power?

Well, this is the father's job no matter what, until you're out on your own, to put down certain laws.

Phase 1 (Orientation): On inspection of the Dilemma I Table of Authority Issue Criterion Judgments, we encounter some difficulty in making our initial orienting stage guess. One possibility is the fixed societal responsibilities discussed in regard to Stage 4. A review of the Stage 4 CJs in the Table of Criterion Judgments suggests CJ#21 as a possible match:

[Joe should give his father the money] out of respect for his father's legitimate position of authority or right of guardianship; **OR** because his father is responsible for making decisions concerning his son; **OR** because legally Joe is still a minor.

This is not the only possible candidate, however. We might also consider a transitional CJ characterized by ambiguous conceptions of authority that are broader than interpersonal considerations yet not clearly societal in nature. Specifically, in the Table of Criterion Judgments at Stage 3/4 there is CJ#18:

1. [Joe should give his father the money] because he or a good son is supposed to respect, honor, or obey his father; **OR** because his father is head of the household and should be obeyed.
2. [The most important thing a son should consider is] that he or a good son should respect, honor, or obey his father.

Insofar as the IJ also appeals to the father's having "supported" the son, we may even consider the idea of interpersonal reciprocity represented at Stages 3 and 2/3. Transitional 2/3 CJ#9 could be considered a third possible CJ match:

1. [Joe should give his father the money] because his father brought him up or raised him; **OR** because Joe should think about how much his father has done for him; **OR** because Joe wouldn't be in this world without him.
2. [The most important thing a son should consider is] that his father brought him up or raised him; **OR** that Joe should think about how much his father has done for him; **OR** that Joe wouldn't be in this world without him.

How are we to decide which of these possible candidates for a match is the one that would be best to pursue? In order to answer this question, we must first answer another question: What does the subject *really* seem to be saying, what does he really *mean* by the response he has given? One must be very careful in answering this latter question. In making inferences about the meaning of a response, we do not want to read ideas into the subject's judgment that simply are not there; but on the other hand, we also do not want to relegate to a guess level judgments that essentially match a particular CJ but that happen to be expressed a bit incoherently or idiosyncratically.

Let us restate the subject's remarks in an attempt to clarify their meaning. A transposition of the example might read: "Joe's father has the right to tell Joe to give him the money, because Joe is only fourteen and still living at home and by law is under the rule of the father. The father has supported Joe, and until Joe is out on his own the father has the power over his son to say what he can't and can do. It is the father's job to put down certain laws for his son until he is out on his own.''

Once we have double-checked to make sure that our transposed version of the subject's interview judgment is faithful to the raw data, we can reapproach the Phase 1 orientation to stage. In the case at hand, the transposition makes the task of identifying the most likely CJ candidate a little easier. We can rule out the Stage 2/3 CJ#9 because the reference in the IJ to the father's ''support'' for Joe seems to be meant to explicate the father's ''job'' and authority, rather than to indicate the father's deservingness through exchange as in CJ#9. This distinction was not as clear in the raw version of the response. Of the remaining possibilities, it is less clear whether the Stage 3/4 CJ#18 or the Stage 4 CJ#21 is the better correspondence. An irrevocable decision about the best match is not necessary in Phase 1. The Phase 2 and Phase 3 evaluations will afford the opportunity to reconsider our preliminary decision. In this tentative spirit we can select the Stage 4 CJ#22 as a potential match, since this CJ specifically encompasses the consideration that ''legally Joe is still a minor,'' a consideration that is absent from the Stage 3/4 CJ#19 and that seems to be a dominant idea in the IJ. The reader should turn to the explication for CJ#21 in Volume II, Form A.

Phase 2 (Surface Evaluation):

A dominant feature of the IJ is the consideration that the father's power derives from the fact that Joe is only ''fourteen'' and hence ''by law'' subject to the father's ''rules.'' The subject seems to be saying, in effect, that Joe is still legally subordinate, still a minor. A second emphasis in the IJ is that the father's right to tell Joe what to do derives from the fact that Joe is living at home, is being supported by his father, and is subject to his father's authority until he is out on his own. The idea expressed here seems analogous to Critical Indicator (a), ''the father's right as a guardian.'' Although only one critical indicator is required, the IJ also seems to match Critical Indicator (c), which requires a legal definition of the son's role. In making these inferences, we can be reasonably sure that we are not giving any gratuitous conceptual ''credit'' to the subject; we are not merely penalizing him for having expressed this legally oriented thought somewhat indirectly. The subject seems to be saying that Joe is still a minor and that his father has the rights of a guardian. These considerations satisfy Critical Indicators (a) and (c). Because the evidence for the critical indicators within the IJ depended on a certain amount of inference and transposition, we rate the proposed correspondence a marginal pass on Phase 2. (Note that this is true in spite of the fact that we have inferred references to two of the three critical indicators whereas explicit reference to only one is required. As mentioned in Instructions for Standard Issue Scoring, a match cannot make up in quantity [reference to more than the minimum number of critical indicators] what it lacks in quality [directness, explicitness, lack of ambiguity] in the critical indicator references.)

Phase 3 (Structural Evaluation):

The stage structure of CJ#21 requires the presence of the idea that the son has a responsibility to show unilateral respect for the father's authority because it is a symbol of society or because the father has ''responsibility . . . in the system.'' The IJ being scored seems consistent with this underlying idea. At the very least, there is nothing in the IJ that seems to contradict the idea.

The distinctions do remind us of the possibility that the Stage 3/4 CJ#18 might be a better candidate, but in fact a quick inspection shows that this is not the case. The legal emphasis in the IJ is simply not to be found in the normative and stereotyped Stage 3/4 focus described as the basis for CJ#18. It is precisely the legal orientation of the IJ that renders plausible the possibility that the structure underlying it is Stage 4. Thus, the IJ passes the stage structure test of CJ#21.

With a marginal pass on the surface evaluation and a pass on the structural evaluation as well as a pass on the three scorability criteria, the IJ receives a marginal match on CJ#21.

In the next example, a transposition again has been used to clarify the IJ. In this case, the transposition helps us to see that all three phases are clearly passed and therefore, the IJ can be assigned a clear match.

DILEMMA III, LIFE ISSUE

Why is it important to care about a fellow human being? Why should it be important to care?

I think it's one of the responsibilities we all have.

Why? Should it be our responsibility to care about fellow human beings?

Yes. Because we're all here together.

Is it important for people to do everything they can to save another's life?

Yes, insofar as it doesn't injure someone else. *Why?* That goes back to the responsibility and the love. That one of the reasons we're here or, one of the things we must do when we are here is to help each other.

Why must we help each other?

We have to. It's only through that that any kind of advances will be made — progress. Or that people can live harmoniously.

Phase 1
(Orientation):

Focusing especially on the final response of this example, we orient to Stage 4 and choose Life Issue CJ#24 as a possible match:

[People should do everything they can to save another's life] because people must have some sense of responsibility for others for the sake of society or humanity; **OR** because people must be willing to save others if society is to survive, not decay, or advance.

Phase 2 (Surface Evaluation):

Let us transpose the example to read:

Caring about a fellow human being or helping each other is one of the responsibilities we all have, because it is only through that that any advances or progress will be made or that people can live harmoniously.

This statement seems to be a fairly straightforward reference to the ideas required by the critical indicators (see explicated CJ#24, Form A, Volume II): ''helping others . . . (b) for the sake of society or society's . . . advancement.'' Thus the IJ receives a clear pass for Phase 2.

218

Phase 3 (Structural Evaluation):	The response is not only consistent with the Stage 4 structure, it seems to positively embody the stage structure described in the explicated CJ: "helping others has to be a generalized practice if society or humanity is to survive and improve." The CJ referred to in the distinctions is not relevant as it concerns the druggist's responsibility. The response appears to be prescriptive and accepted as valid by the subject. As it passes Phases 2 and 3, it is rated a clear match.

The next example illustrates a marginal match for the same CJ. It should be contrasted with the previous clear match example.

DILEMMA III, LIFE ISSUE	*If Heinz does not love his wife, should he steal the drug for her?*
	Yes. I'm tempted to say no, but then survival of the species is more important than social rules – man should act to aid the survival of another.

Phase 1 (Orientation):	Although none of the life issue CJs sound just like this example, the closest seems to be again the Stage 4 CJ#24 (see earlier discussion).

Phase 2 (Surface Evaluation):	Let us transpose the example slightly to make it more grammatically parallel to the critical indicators:

Man should act to aid in the survival of another because [this is important for] the survival of the species [which] is more important than social rules.

As transposed, the IJ seems to fulfill the critical indicator requirements, although not as clearly as did the previous example. Thus the IJ receives a marginal pass on Phase 2.

Phase 3 (Structural Evaluation):	Again, the IJ seems positively to embody the stage structure of CJ#24 and to bear no particular resemblance to the CJ mentioned in the distinctions paragraph. It is rated a pass for Phase 3. As it received a marginal pass on Phase 2 and meets the three scorability criteria, it receives a marginal match overall.

In the following example, difficulties arise at both Phases 2 and 3 in spite of surface similarity between the IJ and the proposed CJ. Our conclusions will be that the example is not even a guess level representation of the CJ against which we compare it.

DILEMMA I, AUTHORITY ISSUE	*What is the most important thing a son should be concerned about in his relationship to his father?*
	He should be concerned about dealing with his father as a person.

Why is that the most important thing?

I mean, they should do things because it is a person-to-person relationship, not a father-and-son relationship. A son should be concerned with giving his father what he deserves.

What do you think is the most important thing a father should be concerned about in his relationship to his son?

He should be concerned with seeing his son as a person. He should try to give his son as much opportunity as he can.

Why is that the most important thing?

219

He owes it to his son as far as his son's development goes. He has a huge responsibility and he should try to do the best he can.

Phase 1 (Orientation):

Although the structural stage significance of this example is somewhat ambiguous (we can be sure it is at least conventional), we can locate in the Table of Authority Issue Criterion Judgments a CJ that seems to be a possible match candidate, Stage 5, CJ#28 (see explicated CJ, Volume II, Form A).

[The most important thing a father/son should consider is] that the other person should be respected as an individual human being; **OR** that the other person is a free and unique individual, a human being with rights or independence; **OR** a person of worth whose point of view should be respected.

Phase 2 (Surface Evaluation):

The IJ provides clear evidence of passing Critical Indicator (a). The subject states: "He should be concerned about dealing with his father as a person. . . . it is a person-to-person relationship, not a father-and-son relationship. . . . He should be concerned with seeing his son as a person." For this CJ, however, reference to *two* of the four critical indicators is required. We see no direct reference to (b) rights, (c) respect for freedom or independence, or (d) a unique point of view that must be respected. Thus, we cannot assign a clear pass for Phase 2. We must still ask whether the IJ *essentially* matches any of the three remaining critical indicators. The subject explicates the importance of the son seeing the father as a person by saying, "A son should be concerned with giving his father what he deserves." In light of earlier references within the responses to this dilemma, we interpret this statement to mean: "A son should not base his judgment about how to act toward the father (especially about whether to give him the money) on the fact that this *is* his father but should instead decide the case on its own merits – give the money if the father deserves it. Don't give it if he does not." This idea does not seem to be very closely analogous to any of the critical indicator ideas. In explicating the importance of the father seeing the son as a person, the subject says, "He should try to give his son as much opportunity as he can. He owes it to his son as far as his son's development goes." The idea here seems to be that the son should be seen as a developing person and should therefore be given as many opportunities as possible. This idea seems vaguely related to some conception of the importance of the son's freedom or independence. However, it would be reading in too much to say that the idea expressed by the IJ is essentially a reference to the intrinsic importance of individual autonomy, which is the essence of the critical indicator idea. We must conclude that our proposed correspondence fails Phase 2.

Phase 3 (Structural Evaluation):

Although the IJ is not clearly *inconsistent* with the Stage 5 structures, it does not seem positively to embody the structural features described in the explicated CJ of Stage 5 generally. There is no evidence of respect for individual rights of liberty and autonomy as ends in themselves. Because there are no glaring violations of stage structure, the IJ would have been considered a pass if Phase 2 had been a clear or marginal pass. However, Stage 5 does not provide our best possible guess for the IJ if a guess score is required. The emphasis on desert as the basis for property distribution and on the father's responsibility for the son's development suggests a conventional rather than postconventional structure, probably Stage 4. The IJ, therefore, is a nonmatch for the Stage 5 CJ and would receive a guess score of Stage 4 if a guess score were required.

The next example is similar in that it fails both Phases 2 and 3 in relation to the CJ it initially seems to resemble most closely.

DILEMMA III, LIFE ISSUE	*Should Heinz steal the drug?* If I loved my wife and was totally devoted to her in an ideal sense, I would put her above myself so that by stealing I might be ruining my life but I would be doing something that would prolong her life.
Phase 1 (Orientation):	Again it is difficult to make an initial structural stage guess, but Stage 4/5 CJ#32 suggests a possible correspondence: Heinz should steal the drug for his wife or a friend insofar as they have developed a deep or total commitment to one another in their relationship.
Phase 2 (Surface Evaluation):	The critical indicators (see explicated CJ, Form A, Volume II) require reference to mutual commitment. The IJ, however, does not refer to mutual commitment, but rather to unilateral devotion. Thus, Phase 2 is failed.
Phase 3 (Structural Evaluation):	The emphasis in the IJ seems to violate the Stage 4/5 structure in which obligations in relationships are based on mutual contract or commitment as distinguished from or in addition to emotional love. In the distinctions paragraph, we are told that CJ#32 is sometimes confused with a parallel idea at a lower stage, CJ#12: [Heinz should steal the drug] out of love or concern for his wife; **OR** because he would feel so close to her or the relationship would be so close.

The preceding example, in its reference to devotion "in an ideal sense," seems to go beyond the Stage 3 idea represented in CJ#12. It is difficult to make a confident assessment of the stage of this judgment, partly because it is only ambiguously prescriptive. However, because the idea does seem to be above Stage 3 and below Stage 4/5, it could be assigned a Stage 3/4 or Stage 4 as a guess score.

The next example illustrates the difficulties that may arise when several CJs seem to be equally appropriate match candidates for one IJ.

DILEMMA I, AUTHORITY ISSUE	*What do you think is the most important thing a son should be concerned about in his relationship to his father?* Respect. If a son can't respect his father, he has no reason to respect his other elders. Wait, I don't know if I can say that or not. A son should have a high standard for his father. He knows that his father knows more than he does. He knows he can help him if he's in trouble. He should respect, love, and trust his father.
Phase 1 (Orientation):	This authority issue example is difficult to relate to a single CJ. The subject's statement is somewhat unclear so we should begin by trying to restate it. Consider the following transposition:

A son should respect, love, and trust his father. He should have a high standard for his father. He knows that his father knows more than he does and can help him if he's in trouble.

As we will discuss later, the meaning of the second sentence is unclear. It may mean, given the context, that he should have high regard for his father.

Even after transposition, several CJs suggest possible matches: CJ#14 (Stage 3), CJ#18 (Stage 3/4), and CJ#21 (Stage 4). On an initial check, CJ#21 can be ruled out since the IJ being scored does not evidence the required legalistic orientation (father as guardian, legal definition of son's role). This leaves CJ#14 and CJ#18 to be evaluated in greater detail. Let us begin with CJ#14:

[Joe should give his father the money or it is important for a son to consider that] his father has his best interests at heart, is acting for his own good; **OR** is doing his best to bring up his son.

Phase 2 (Surface Evaluation): The subject's judgment that a son should respect his father because his father knows more than he does or can help if he's in trouble is very close to the critical indicator idea that a son should respect his father because the father knows what is best for the son, cares for his son, and so on. However, the assumption of parental benevolence as required by the CJ is only ambiguously present in the IJ. Therefore, the IJ receives only a marginal pass on Phase 2.

Phase 3 (Structural Evaluation): The IJ is consistent with the Stage 3 structure; e.g., the subject seems to assume that the father would help the son if he were in trouble. We must be cautious, however, because in the distinctions we see a reference to a "Stage 3/4 concern" that sons should respect and honor their parents without an assumption of the benevolent motives of a father. Because in our Phase 2 assessment we noted the ambiguity of the example with regard to the father's benevolent motives, we must go on to evaluate the relative adequacy of the Stage 3/4 CJ for our example rather than to simply enter a Stage 3 marginal match on the basis of CJ#14. Let us now consider the Stage 3/4 CJ#18:

[The most important thing a son should consider is] that he or a good son should respect, honor, or obey his father.

Phase 2 (Surface Evaluation): The IJ statement that a son should have a high standard for and respect his father because he knows more than he does could be seen to match Critical Indicator (a): "Reference to what is generally expected of a son in his role." The correspondence between the IJ and the critical indicator is ambiguous, however, since it is difficult to determine whether the subject intends his statement to mean something like "sons in general should respect and have high regard for their fathers because their fathers are more knowledgeable, experienced, and so on" (a Stage 3/4 idea), or "a son should respect his father because his father is benevolent, altruistic, wise, and so on" (a Stage 3 idea). Given the ambiguity, a marginal pass is assigned on Phase 2.

Phase 3 (Structural Evaluation): Given the Stage 3/4 interpretation of the IJ just posed, there is no clear contradiction of the Stage 3/4 structure by the material to be scored. Since our IJ has been assigned a Phase 2 marginal pass for both CJs #14 and #19 and seems to be *consistent* with either stage structure, we must now proceed to ask which

CJ seems to provide a better match for the IJ. A careful scrutiny of the critical indicators, stage structures, and examples of both CJs suggests that the IJ more clearly embodies the structure of the Stage 3 CJ#14. For example, the congruence of the IJ with the stage structure of CJ#14 is quite close (fathers are seen as benevolent or having superior wisdom). It does not clearly "go beyond the Stage 3 notion of the father as authoritative because of his stereotypical qualities," as specified in CJ#18. Because the IJ is very close to both CJs #14 and #18, however, either of these would be acceptable as the basis for a marginal match score.

Due to the hierarchical nature of the moral judgment stages, ideas are often expressed within a higher stage context that, when taken literally or out of context, would be scored at a much lower stage. The function of the Phase 3 structural evaluation is to weed out or "veto" those literal matches for which the stage of the CJ is not a true reflection of the structural significance of the interview material. The idea expressed in an IJ may resemble the CJ but may also differ in essential ways. In such cases, the significance of the IJ may differ from that of the CJ because the former is embedded in a broader perspective or a more complex structure. This rather difficult and subtle use of structural veto of Phase 3 should be applied only when there is clear evidence for the non-CJ stage. The following example illustrates the "experienced scorer's structural veto."

DILEMMA III, LIFE ISSUE

Suppose it is a pet animal that he loves. Should Heinz steal to save a pet animal?
No.

Why not?

Because I think that Heinz's life is a lot more important than an animal's life. I really believe that you should let animals die naturally. I don't think Heinz should give up his life for that of an animal.

Is it important for people to do everything they can to save another's life?

It depends on what the illness is. As long as the person can be cured then it is fine. I think if it is just a question of prolonging life then it might not be all right. I think that you should do everything you can within certain boundaries. But in this case it is beyond the boundaries and into the field of risk. That's like beyond his duty in this case. You can't just give yourself. There is a balance. You have to weigh out how much your life is worth to you and how much the other person's life is worth to you. You can give up and sacrifice just what that other person is worth to you. Even in the sense of the pet. If the pet was the whole world to some old lady then I would say it would be worth it for the lady to do whatever she had to do to save it.

Phase 1 (Orientation):

The interview material is suggestive of a Stage 2 self-interested pragmatic orientation. Stage 2 CJ#7 presents a possible match. Let us consider the correspondence:

[Heinz should steal the drug] if he needs, likes, or loves his wife or wants her to live; **OR** if he thinks it worth the trouble, penalty, or risk.

Phase 2 (Surface Evaluation):

The IJ provides clear evidence for Critical Indicator (b), which stipulates a judgment that "saving (a life) would be worth the risk." Thus the subject

223

states, "You have to weigh out how much your life is worth to you and how much the other person's life is worth to you. . . . I would say it would be worth it . . . to do whatever she had to do to save it." Since the CJ requires reference to only one of the three critical indicators, the correspondence is given a clear pass for Phase 2.

Phase 3 (Structural Evaluation):

In order to evaluate structurally the idea that seems to underlie the IJ response, let us transpose the IJ. The following transposition provides what seems to be the most plausible interpretation:

> Heinz must weigh and balance the sacrifices he is willing to make (his self-interest) against the welfare of the other person or the value of the other person's life for him. If it is just a question of helping another person, you should do everything you can. Beyond certain boundaries, though, you have entered the field of risk. For someone to go beyond the boundaries and into the field of risk is like going beyond his duty. [You can't be expected to] just give up yourself. When it comes to sacrificing something for someone else (taking a big risk), Heinz has to weigh it out in his own mind. He would have to decide if he was willing to give up a part of himself for another person.

The judgment seems to be based not on a self-interested conception of the husband–wife relationship, but on a relativistic conception of moral obligation or duty. The individual faced with the dilemma must decide how much of herself she is willing to sacrifice for another person and does not have a *duty* to give up herself for another. This kind of orientation has been described as the central feature of a relativistic type of transitional phase between Stage 3 and 4 and between Stage 4 and 5. A comparison of our interview material with Stage 3/4 CJ#22 and Stage 4/5 CJ#33 indicates a closer similarity to Stage 3/4 than to Stage 4/5. There is no evidence of a weighing of obligations to society versus one's own hierarchy of values, which is characteristic of the Stage 4/5 transition.

Let us consider, then, the Stage 3/4 CJ#22:

> [Heinz should steal the drug because] if he really loves her, then it would be right from his viewpoint, or then it would be important enough to him to risk going to jail; **OR** if he feels strongly enough that saving her life is more important than obeying the law.

Phase 2: (Surface Evaluation):

Although the IJ resembles CJ#22 fairly closely, it does not clearly exhibit the required critical indicators, particularly Indicator (b): "justifiable from Heinz's perspective." This idea may be implicit in the IJ, but it is not sufficiently clear to justify a match to CJ#22.

Phase 3 (Structural Evaluation):

A comparison of Stage Structure paragraphs for CJs #7 and #22 reveals that the IJ is in essence closer to CJ#22 than to CJ#7. The judgment exhibits subjectivity and relativity at the conventional level rather than a "self-interested conception of the relationship" and thus is more appropriately scored as a guess Stage 3/4 than as a match for Stage 2.

In a number of the scoring examples discussed in the preceding section, the proposed IJ–CJ match was scored as a "fail" but the IJ was deemed usable for assigning a guess score. We shall now consider some of the special techniques for guess scoring that were discussed in the instructions for step-by-step scoring.

We stated that if no interpretable guess material can be found for an issue, you may turn to the other issues for help by (1) using material on the opposing issue as context for interpreting material on the issue you are trying to score; (2) extracting reasons on the issue from material classified under the opposing issue; or (3) comparing an IJ from the issue being scored with a CJ from a different issue. We will present examples here of the latter two of these approaches (no examples are available of the first approach).

2. Sometimes an interview yields no responses that can be classified in their entirety under a particular issue (usually the nonchosen issue). In such cases, material classified under the opposing issue may be usable for a guess score on the empty issue *as long as the arguments for that issue are not rejected by the subject as invalid* (Scorability Criterion 2).

The following example is taken from a Dilemma III' interview in which all the responses focus on the punishment issue. The following excerpt is the only one containing possible material for the morality and conscience issue.

Should the policeman report Heinz?

Yes. Both men are acting on conviction. Heinz is acting on the conviction that he loves his wife and the law officer should already have decided within himself if he is convicted [*sic*] to the law. If he isn't, then he shouldn't be a police officer.

This response would normally be classified under the punishment issue (as it supports reporting Heinz). In the absence of any material for scoring the morality and conscience issue, however, we can try to extract morality and conscience material from this response. The morality and conscience issue question to which we would be seeking a response is, "Is there any reason that can be given on the side of leniency for Heinz?" In this case we can extract an answer to the morality and conscience question from the punishment issue response; i.e., "A reason for leniency would be that Heinz is acting on conviction. He is acting on the conviction that he loves his wife." Note that we have not substantially modified the reason given. We have simply used it as a presumably valid – though overridden – argument for an action that has not been chosen. Although the action choice has been rejected, the reason itself seems to have some validity for the subject. Thus we can use it for guess scoring.

Although the idea expressed here does not match any of our morality and conscience issue CJs, it most closely resembles Stage 3/4 CJ#20:

[The judge should be lenient] because breaking the law out of love for one's wife or to save someone's life could have been the right decision for Heinz or could have been right in Heinz's view.

The IJ cannot be used as a match to this CJ because the validity attributed to the idea expressed is ambiguous. CJ#20 does provide the basis for a fairly confident guess, however.

In contrast, another subject has said that Officer Brown should *not* report Heinz because "if he did that he would be placing the letter of the law above the moral truth, which says that human life is more valuable than excess profit, or for that matter, property." All material on Dilemma III' was classified as morality and conscience. We cannot salvage a punishment issue score from the subject's reference to the "letter of the law" because she is *rejecting* this notion as a basis for reporting Heinz.

Sometimes material salvaged from the chosen issue is very minimal, and some work is needed to determine whether it satisfies the first scorability criterion, i.e., whether it offers a moral reason or justification for the issue value or action. In the following example we have concluded that a position including a reason can be constructed and therefore a guess score must be assigned.

DILEMMA III', MORALITY AND CONSCIENCE ISSUE

There is and should be a punishment for each crime. **Even though he saved his wife,** he has to suffer consequences for stealing. Because he did commit a crime **although he was doing good.**

A position on the morality and conscience issue might be the following: "A reason for leniency would be that he saved his wife . . . he was doing good." This qualifies as guess material because the action choice of leniency is justified by reference to the value of Heinz's wife's life and to Heinz's good intentions. We would assign a "guess Stage 3" on the basis of this material.

In the next example, we can construct what appears to be a reason. The reason constructed does not refer to a moral value (norm or element) and thus cannot be used to assign a guess score.

DILEMMA III', PUNISHMENT ISSUE

Heinz broke in the store, stole the drug, got caught. Should the judge send Heinz to jail for stealing or should he let him go free?

If I were the judge I would put him out on probation probably. To begin with, any jury that would sentence a man for something like that, such circumstances in a situation like that, it would really be unfair I think and I don't know if a jury would sentence a case like this. **I mean his stealing is wrong, yes,** but then again that is why we have a jury to decide if this man took the right steps to save his wife or what.

A restatement might be: "[A reason for punishing Heinz is that] his stealing is wrong." No information is provided as to what value underlies the judgment that stealing is wrong. Thus, the response is not scorable.

3. Sometimes correspondence of an IJ on one issue with a CJ on another issue provides the basis for a guess score (but never for a match score). The following contract issue example illustrates the use of a CJ from the opposing issue as the basis for a guess.

DILEMMA I, CONTRACT ISSUE

Should Joe refuse to give his father the money?

Joe's father had the right to take the money from him, but that isn't teaching him very well. But as far as Joe thinking about refusing to give him the money, this was wrong. He should do what his father said and give him the money. Joe's father is not showing very good teaching to do this to his son. It is going to stick in Joe's mind and affect him for the rest of his life possibly. But Joe's father is completely within his rights to ask his son for the money.

Why should a promise be kept?

When you break a promise it leaves a mark on one's mind, especially in a 14-year-old boy. It'll leave a mark, a grudge, that maybe he will never be able to overcome. I don't think his father would want him to hate him for this, but it is not a good idea to break a promise, especially to a small child or a 14-year-old boy.

Although this idea resembles but does not match contract issue Stage 3/4 CJ#21, it perhaps more closely approximates transitional Stage 3/4 CJ#19 from the authority issue. Because it seems to embody the 3/4 stage structure of these two CJs and is not a better structural match to any other stage, the contract issue is assigned a guess Stage 3/4 on the basis of this material. (The reason for scoring the material under the contract issue is that it is in response to the question ''Why should a promise be kept?'' which is a general issue question for the contract issue.)

In using a CJ from another issue to assign a guess score, one must be careful not to overlook clues from other CJs just as in match scoring or use of ''same issue CJs'' for guessing. At first glance the following morality and conscience response seems to correspond to a transitional Stage 4/5 CJ on another issue (life issue CJ#31), but after close examination we conclude that the structural significance of the response is not likely to be Stage 4/5.

DILEMMA III', MORALITY AND CONSCIENCE ISSUE

Should the judge sentence Heinz to jail for stealing or let him go free?

In a court of law I think the whole case should be brought out, about the druggist treating him in an unjust manner and the drug to save his wife's life. I think that the druggist should be brought into court, too, and the drug should be examined and the cost in making it and then the amount of profit that the druggist could make should be set.

Assuming they go over the whole case, what should the judge do?

Under any of these circumstances I think that Heinz has justification to steal the drug. I don't think it would do any good to send the husband to jail and I think the druggist is the party at fault. I think when there is a drug like this the government should take it over and it should be available at little or no cost to those who need it. And those who can't afford it.

The statements ''the amount of profit that the druggist could make should be set'' and ''I think when there is a drug like this the government should take it over and it should be available at little or no cost to those who need it. And those who can't afford it'' are reminiscent of the life issue transitional Stage 4/5 judgment (CJ#31) that such drugs are a public resource that society should control or that ''products basic to life must be widely shared or distributed in society.'' However, the former statements do not seem to imply an appreciation of a ''rational hierarchy involving societal regulation and distribution,'' which is said to underlie the Stage 4/5 criterion judgment. They seem instead to imply a conventional perspective like that expressed by life issue CJ#20, a transitional Stage 3/4 criterion judgment (''disapproval of the druggist's conduct in relation to the value or usefulness of the drug for everyone in society who needs the drug''). Although the response to be scored is ambiguous, it is generally more appropriate, when in doubt, to assign the lower score. That is, the response could be consistent with the Stage 4/5 CJ but in the absence of evidence of postconventional perspectives, the more appropriate guess is Stage 3/4.

In some interviews, particularly those conducted by unskilled interviewers, a great deal of material may be available on an issue, but the material may yield no match scores for the issue at all. In such cases, the overall stage on the issue should be assessed by first assigning individual guess scores to each IJ unit and then making a judgment about the overall stage(s) of the issue. The following presents just such a case:

DILEMMA III, LAW ISSUE

Should Heinz steal the drug?

No he shouldn't. Because it is against the law.

So why shouldn't he?

It is illegal to steal and take something that doesn't belong to you.

Can you explain why he shouldn't do it even though it is a question of life and death?

I don't know if I can explain why he shouldn't. Other than the fact it is against the law. That is not saying I wouldn't.

Suppose the person is a stranger?

No. Again I just feel it is easy for someone else that you are not involved with to say that, because you don't know their feelings. But then again, you can say you don't want to get in trouble.

Say the stranger does not have a husband. A poor lonesome person is in the hospital dying and this drug could save her.

I still think not. For the same reasons, maybe because I would not be involved, I would hate to be involved with a stranger, in that respect. Not hate, but of course, again, you are looking at what my experiences are. It seems to me that a person has enough problems with his own family life, to get along by yourself, as opposed to going out looking for somebody else.

What is to be said for the law in general? Why should we obey laws?

To protect us from ourselves. If you have one person stealing, then it is legal for everybody else. Lawfully stealing. If someone steals there should be a law for it. If your neighbor had something you like and you could go over and take it, why couldn't he come over and take something of yours. This winds up in all kinds of arguments and the mighty would rule.

What would be so bad about a situation where the strongest would rule? A lot of people have suggested it over the years.

If you want a king and queen and a servant, I guess it is okay.

Put it more positively, you are in favor of a more democratic system?

Because of the freedom that most people, the general public would have. If you want to go back to the days of kings and queens and rulers – sometime in the middle of the night you might have a knock on your door, let the mighty rule, they could drag you out, and make laws of their own, all in favor of them.

We can group this material into three separate interview judgments: (a) He shouldn't steal ''because it is against the law. It is illegal to steal and take something that doesn't belong to you. I don't know if I can explain why he shouldn't, other than the fact it is against the law." (b) "I just feel it is easy for someone else that you are not involved with to say that, because you don't know their feelings. But then again, you can say you don't want to get in trouble." (c) "To protect us . . ." (last three responses).

The material in the first unit (a) is similar to the transitional Stage 1/2 CJ#4. However, when guess scoring, the level of material on the issue as a whole is taken into account. We would not give much weight to this first material as we have subsequent evidence of substantially higher stage thinking. The unit (b) material is also very ambiguous. That the judgments are not clearly prescriptive leads us to doubt that they really reflect reasoning as low as the Stage CJ#8 that they resemble. The concern for limiting one's obligations to members of one's own family could reflect anything from a Stage 2 to a transitional third unit (c). This concern for the law as essential to group welfare seems to fall between Stage 3 (CJ#16) and Stage 4 (CJ#25). It resembles but does not match transitional Stage 3/4 CJ#18. Because we can be fairly confident that our third unit represents a Stage 3/4 conception of law and because the earlier material is very ambiguous, we will consider unit (c) our only confident guess and will assign a guess Stage 3/4 for the issue.

The preceding example involved guessing on an issue with a substantial amount of material. Sometimes, however, the only material available on an issue is sparse and ambiguous with regard to stage. In such cases, a best estimate of the stage significance of the material on that issue must still be made and a guess score entered. These estimates can be based on specific criterion judgments or one's general understanding of the stages.

The responses in the following example are minimal and difficult to evaluate structurally.

DILEMMA I,
AUTHORITY ISSUE

Should Joe refuse to give his father the money?
I think he should give it to him. Fathers know better.

Is it his duty to his father?
Not exactly his duty, but he should.

The response bears some resemblance to authority CJ#1, Stage 1, and to authority CJ#14, Stage 3. In other words, the norm authority and the element obeying/consulting seem clear, but the stage significance cannot be determined with much confidence. We assign a guess score Stage 1/2 because the response does seem to go somewhat beyond the Stage 1 CJ but show no clear evidence of Stage 3 mutual role taking or assumption of the father's benevolence.

APPENDIX A: PROBE QUESTIONS CLASSIFIED BY TYPE

Moral Judgment Interview, Form A

*(Starred questions may be eliminated if time for interviewing is limited.)

Dilemma III

In Europe, a woman was near death from a special kind of cancer. There was one drug that the doctors thought might save her. It was a form of radium that

229

a druggist in the same town had recently discovered. The drug was expensive to make, but the druggist was charging ten times what the drug cost him to make. He paid $400 for the radium and charged $4,000 for a small dose of the drug. The sick woman's husband, Heinz, went to everyone he knew to borrow the money and tried every legal means, but he could only get together about $2,000, which is half of what it cost. He told the druggist that his wife was dying, and asked him to sell it cheaper or let him pay later. But the druggist said, "No, I discovered the drug and I'm going to make money from it." So having tried every legal means, Heinz gets desperate and considers breaking into the man's store to steal the drug for his wife.

1. *Should Heinz steal the drug? (Dilemma related)*
1a. *Why or why not?*

Questions 2 and 3 are designed to elicit the subject's moral type and should be considered optional.

*2. *Is it actually right or wrong for him to steal the drug?*
*2a. *Why is it right or wrong? (Dilemma related)*
*3. *Does Heinz have a duty or obligation to steal the drug?*
*3a. *Why or why not? (Dilemma related)*
4. *[If subject originally favors stealing, ask:]*
   If Heinz doesn't love his wife, should he steal the drug for her?
4. *[If subject originally favors not stealing, ask:]*
   Does it make a difference whether or not he loves his wife?
4a. *Why or why not?*
5. *Suppose the person dying is not his wife but a stranger.*
5a. *Should Heinz steal the drug for the stranger?*
   Why or why not? (Dilemma related)
*6. *[If subject favors stealing the drug for a stranger, ask:]*
   Suppose it's a pet animal he loves. Should Heinz steal to save the pet animal?
*6a. *Why or why not? (Dilemma related)*
7. *Is it important for people to do everything they can to save another's life?*
7a. *Why or why not? (General issue)*
*8. *It is against the law for Heinz to steal. Does that make it morally wrong?*
*8a. *Why or why not? (Issue centered)*
9. *In general, should people try to do everything they can to obey the law?*
9a. *Why or why not? (General issue)*
9b. *How does this apply to what Heinz should do? (Issue centered)*
*10. *In thinking over the dilemma, what would you say is the most responsible thing for Heinz to do?*
10a. *Why? (Dilemma related)*

*Dilemma III'
Heinz did break into the store. He stole the drug and gave it to his wife. In the newspapers the next day there was an account of the robbery. Mr. Brown, a police officer who knew Heinz, read the account. He remembered seeing Heinz running away from the store and realized that it was Heinz who stole the drug. Mr. Brown wonders whether he should report that Heinz was the robber.

*1. *Should Officer Brown report Heinz for stealing?*

*1a. *Why or why not? (Dilemma related)*

*2. *Suppose Officer Brown were a close friend of Heinz, should he then report him?*

*2a. *Why or why not? (Dilemma related)*

Dilemma III'

Officer Brown did report Heinz. Heinz was arrested and brought to court. A jury was selected. The jury's job is to find whether a person is innocent or guilty of committing a crime. The jury finds Heinz guilty. It is up to the judge to determine the sentence.

3. *Should the judge give Heinz some sentence, or should he suspend the sentence and let Heinz go free?*

3a. *Why is that best? (Dilemma related)*

4. *Thinking in terms of society, should people who break the law be punished? (General issue)*

4a. *Why or why not?*

4b. *How does this apply to how the judge should decide? (Issue centered)*

5. *Heinz was doing what his conscience told him when he stole the drug. Should a lawbreaker be punished if he is acting out of conscience? (General issue)*

5a. *Why or why not?*

*6. *Thinking back over the dilemma, what would you say is the most responsible thing for the judge to do? (Dilemma related)*

*6a. *Why?*

[Questions 7–12 are designed to elicit the subject's theory of ethics and should be considered optional. They should not be scored for moral stage.]

*7. *What does the word conscience mean to you, anyhow? If you were Heinz, how would your conscience enter into the decision?*

*8. *Heinz has to make a moral decision. Should a moral decision be based on one's feelings or on one's thinking and reasoning about right and wrong?*

*9. *Is Heinz's problem a moral problem? Why or why not?*

*9a. *In general, what makes something a moral problem or what does the word morality mean to you?*

*10. *If Heinz is going to decide what to do by thinking about what's really right, there must be some answer, some right solution. Is there really some correct solution to moral problems like Heinz's, or when people disagree is everybody's opinion equally right? Why?*

*11. *How do you know when you've come up with a good moral decision? Is there a way of thinking or a method by which one can reach a good or adequate decision?*

*12. *Most people believe that thinking and reasoning in science can lead to a correct answer. Is the same thing true in moral decisions or are they different?*

Dilemma I

Joe is a fourteen-year-old boy who wanted to go to camp very much. His father promised him he could go if he saved up the money for it himself. So Joe worked hard at his paper route and saved up the $100 it cost to go to camp and a little more besides. But just before camp was going to start, his father changed his mind. Some of his friends decided to go on a special fishing trip, and Joe's father was short of the money it would cost. So he told Joe to give him the money he had saved from the paper route. Joe didn't want to give up going to camp, so he thinks of refusing to give his father the money.

1. *Should Joe refuse to give his father the money?*
1a. *Why or why not? (Dilemma related)*
*2. *Does the father have the right to tell Joe to give him the money?*
*2a. *Why or why not? (Dilemma related)*
*3. *Does giving the money have anything to do with being a good son?*
*3a. *Why or why not? (Issue centered)*
*4. *Is the fact that Joe earned the money himself important in this situation?*
*4a. *Why or why not? (Issue centered)*
5. *The father promised Joe he could go to camp if he earned the money. Is the fact that the father promised the most important thing in the situation?*
5a. *Why or why not? (Issue centered)*
6. *In general, why should a promise be kept? (General issue)*
7. *Is it important to keep a promise to someone you don't know well and probably won't see again?*
7a. *Why or why not? (General issue)*
8. *What do you think is the most important thing a father should be concerned about in his relationship to his son?*
8a. *Why is that the most important thing? (General issue)*
9. *In general, what should be the authority of a father over his son? (General issue)*
9a. *Why?*
10. *What do you think is the most important thing a son should be concerned about in his relationship to his father?*
10a. *Why is that the most important thing? (General issue)*

[The following question is designed to elicit the subject's moral type and should be considered optional.]

*11. *In thinking back over the dilemma, what would you say is the most responsible thing for Joe to do in this situation?*
*11a. *Why?*

Moral Judgment Interview, Form B

*(Starred questions may be eliminated if time for interviewing is limited.)

Dilemma IV

There was a woman who had very bad cancer, and there was no treatment known to medicine that would save her. Her doctor, Dr. Jefferson, knew that she had only about six months to live. She was in terrible pain, but she was so weak that a good dose of a painkiller like ether or morphine would make her die sooner. She was delirious and almost crazy with pain, and in her calm periods she would ask Dr. Jefferson to give her enough ether to kill her. She said she couldn't stand the pain and she was going to die in a few months anyway. Although he knows that mercy killing is against the law, the doctor thinks about granting her request.

1. *Should Dr. Jefferson give her the drug that would make her die?*
1a. *Why or why not? (Dilemma related)*
*2. *Is it actually right or wrong for him to give the woman the drug that would make her die?*
*2a. *Why is it right or wrong? (Dilemma related)*
3. *Should the woman have the right to make the final decision?*
3a. *Why or why not? (Dilemma related)*
*4. *The woman is married. Should her husband have anything to do with the decision?*
*4a. *Why or why not? (Dilemma related)*
*5. *What should a good husband do in this situation? (Dilemma related)*
*5a. *Why?*
6. *Is there any way a person has a duty or obligation to live when he or she does not want to, when the person wants to commit suicide? (Issue centered)*
6a. *Why or why not?*

[The following question is designed to elicit the subject's moral type and should be considered optional.]

*7. *Does Dr. Jefferson have a duty or obligation to make the drug available to the woman?*
*7a. *Why or why not? (Dilemma related)*
8. *When a pet animal is badly wounded and will die, it is killed to put it out of its pain. Does the same thing apply here?*
8a. *Why or why not? (Issue centered)*
9. *It is against the law for the doctor to give the woman the drug. Does that make it morally wrong?*
9a. *Why or why not? (Issue centered)*
10. *In general, should people try to do everything they can to obey the law?*
10a. *Why or why not? (General issue)*
10b. *How does this apply to what Dr. Jefferson should do? (Issue centered)*
*11. *In thinking back over the dilemma, what would you say is the most responsible thing for Dr. Jefferson to do? (Dilemma related)*
*11a. *Why?*

*Dilemma IV'

Dr. Jefferson did perform the mercy killing by giving the woman the drug. Passing by at this time was another doctor, Dr. Rogers, who knew the situation Dr. Jefferson was in. Dr. Rogers thought of trying to stop Dr. Jefferson, but the drug was already administered. Dr. Rogers wonders whether he should report Dr. Jefferson.

*1. *Should Dr. Rogers report Dr. jefferson?*
*1a. *Why or why not? (Dilemma related)*

Dilemma IV'

Dr. Rogers did report Dr. Jefferson. Dr. Jefferson is brought to court and a jury is selected. The jury's job is to find whether a person is innocent or guilty of committing a crime. The jury finds Dr. Jefferson guilty. It is up to the judge to determine the sentence.

233

2. *Should the judge give Dr. Jefferson some sentence, or should he suspend the sentence and let Dr. Jefferson go free?*

2a. *Why is that best? (Dilemma related)*

3. *Thinking in terms of society, should people who break the law be punished?*

3a. *Why or why not? (General issue)*

3b. *How does this apply to how the judge should decide? (Issue centered)*

4. *The jury finds Dr. Jefferson legally guilty of murder. Would it be wrong or right for the judge to give him the death sentence (a legally possible punishment)?*

4a. *Why? (Dilemma related)*

5. *Is it ever right to give the death sentence? Why or why not? What are the conditions when the death sentence should be given in your opinion? Why are these conditions important? (Issue centered)*

6. *Dr. Jefferson was doing what his conscience told him when he gave the woman the drug. Should a lawbreaker be punished if he is acting out of conscience?*

6a. *Why or why not? (General issue)*

*7. *Thinking back over the dilemma, what would you say is the most responsible thing for the judge to do?*

*7a. *Why? (Dilemma related)*

[Questions 8–13 are designed to elicit the subject's theory of ethics and should be considered optional. They should not be scored for moral stage.]

*8. *What does the word conscience mean to you, anyhow? If you were Dr. Jefferson, how would your conscience enter into the decision?*

*9. *Dr. Jefferson has to make a moral decision. Should a moral decision be based on one's feelings or on one's thinking and reasoning about right and wrong?*

*10. *Is Dr. Jefferson's problem a moral problem? Why or why not?*

*10a. *In general, what makes something a moral problem or what does the word morality mean to you?*

*11. *If Dr. Jefferson is going to decide what to do by thinking about what's really right, there must be some answer, some right solution. Is there really some correct solution to moral problems like Dr. Jefferson's, or when people disagree is everybody's opinion equally right? Why?*

*12. *How do you know when you've come up with a good moral decision? Is there a way of thinking or a method by which one can reach a good or adequate decision?*

*13. *Most people believe that thinking and reasoning in science can lead to a correct answer. Is the same thing true in moral decisions or are they different?*

Dilemma II

Judy was a twelve-year-old girl. Her mother promised her that she could go to a special rock concert coming to their town if she saved up from baby-sitting and lunch money so she would have enough money to buy a ticket to the concert. She managed to save up the $15 it cost plus another $5. But then her mother changed her mind and told Judy that she had to spend the money on new clothes for school. Judy was disappointed and decided to go to the concert anyway. She bought a ticket and told her mother that she had only been able to save $5. That Saturday she went to the performance and told her mother that she was spending the day with a friend. A week passed without her mother finding out. Judy then told her older sister, Louise, that she had gone to the performance and had lied to her mother about it. Louise wonders whether to tell their mother what Judy did.

1. *Should Louise, the older sister, tell their mother that Judy had lied about the money or should she keep quiet?*
1a. *Why or why not? (Dilemma related)*
*2. *In wondering whether to tell, Louise thinks of the fact that Judy is her sister. Should that make a difference in Louise's decision?*
*2a. *Why or why not? (Issue centered)*
*3. *Does telling have anything to do with being a good daughter?*
*3a. *Why or why not? (Issue centered)*
*4. *Is the fact that Judy earned the money herself important in this situation?*
*4a. *Why or why not? (Issue centered)*
5. *The mother promised Judy she could go to the concert if she earned the money. Is the fact that the mother promised the most important thing in the situation?*
5a. *Why or why not? (Issue centered)*
6. *Why in general should a promise be kept? (General issue)*
7. *Is it important to keep a promise to someone you don't know well and probably won't see again?*
7a. *Why or why not? (General issue)*
8. *What do you think is the most important thing a mother should be concerned about in her relationship to her daughter?*
8a. *Why is that the most important thing? (General issue)*
9. *In general, what should be the authority of a mother over her daughter?*
9a. *Why? (General issue)*
10. *What do you think is the most important thing a daughter should be concerned about in her relationship to her mother?*
10a. *Why is that the most important thing? (General issue)*
*11. *In thinking back over the dilemma, what would you say is the most responsible thing for Louise to do in this situation?*
*11a. *Why? (Dilemma related)*

Moral Judgment Interview, Form C

*(Starred questions may be eliminated if time for interviewing is limited.)

Dilemma V

In Korea, a company of Marines was way outnumbered and was retreating before the enemy. The company had crossed a bridge over a river, but the enemy were mostly still on the other side. If someone went back to the bridge and blew it up, with the head start the rest of the men in the company would have, they could probably then escape. But the man who stayed back to blow up the bridge would not be able to escape alive. The captain himself is the man who knows best how to lead the retreat. He asks for volunteers, but no one will volunteer. If he goes himself, the men will probably not get back safely as he is the only one who knows how to lead the retreat.

1. *Should the captain order a man to go on the mission or should he go himself?*
1a. *Why? (Dilemma related)*

235

2. *Should the captain send a man (or even use a lottery) when it means sending him to his death?*

2a. *Why or why not? (Dilemma related)*

3. *Should the captain go himself when it means that the men will probably not make it back safely?*

3a. *Why or why not? (Dilemma related)*

[Questions 4 and 5 are designed to elicit the subject's moral type and should be considered optional.]

*4. *Does the captain have the right to order a man if he thinks it is best?*

*4a. *Why or why not? (Dilemma related)*

*5. *Does the man who is selected have a duty or obligation to go?*

*5a. *Why or why not? (Dilemma related)*

6. *What's so important about human life that makes it important to save or protect?*

6a. *Why is that important? (General issue)*

6b. *How does this apply to what the captain should do? (Issue centered)*

*7. *In thinking back over the dilemma, what would you say is the most responsible thing for the captain to do?*

*7a. *Why? (Dilemma related)*

Dilemma VIII

In a country in Europe, a poor man named Valjean could find no work, nor could his sister and brother. Without money, he stole food and medicine that they needed. He was captured and sentenced to prison for six years. After a couple of years, he escaped from the prison and went to live in another part of the country under a new name. He saved money and slowly built up a big factory. He gave his workers the highest wages and used most of his profits to build a hospital for people who couldn't afford good medical care. Twenty years had passed when a tailor recognized the factory owner as being Valjean, the escaped convict whom the police had been looking for back in his home town.

1. *Should the tailor report Valjean to the police?*

1a. *Why or why not? (Dilemma related)*

2. *Does a citizen have a duty or obligation to report an escaped convict?*

2a. *Why or why not? (Issue centered)*

3. *Suppose Valjean were a close friend of the tailor. Should he then report Valjean?*

3a. *Why or why not? (Dilemma related)*

4. *If Valjean were reported and brought before the judge, should the judge send him back to jail or let him go free?*

4a. *Why? (Dilemma related)*

5. *Thinking in terms of society, should people who break the law be punished?*

5a. *Why or why not? (General issue)*

*5b. *How does this apply to what the judge should do? (Issue centered)*

6. *Valjean was doing what his conscience told him to do when he stole the food and medicine. Should a lawbreaker be punished if he is acting out of conscience?*

6a. *Why or why not? (Issue centered)*

*7. In thinking back over the dilemma, what would you say is the most responsible thing for the tailor to do?

*7a. Why? (Dilemma related)

[Questions 8–13 are designed to elicit the subject's theory of ethics and should be considered optional. They should not be scored for moral stage.]

*8. What does the word conscience mean to you, anyhow? If you were Valjean, how would your conscience enter into the decision?

*9. Valjean has to make a moral decision. Should a moral decision be based on one's feelings or on one's thinking and reasoning about right and wrong?

*10. Is Valjean's problem a moral problem? Why or why not?

*10a. In general, what makes something a moral problem or what does the word morality mean to you?

*11. If Valjean is going to decide what to do by thinking about what's really right, there must be some answer, some right solution. Is there really some correct solution to moral problems like Valjean's, or when people disagree is everybody's opinion equally right? Why?

*12. How do you know when you've come up with a good moral decision? Is there a way of thinking or a method by which one can reach a good or adequate decision?

*13. Most people believe that thinking and reasoning in science can lead to a correct answer. Is the same thing true in moral decisions or are they different?

Dilemma VII

Two young men, brothers, had gotten into serious trouble. They were secretly leaving town in a hurry and needed money. Karl, the older one, broke into a store and stole $1,000. Bob, the younger one, went to a retired old man who was known to help people in town. He told the man that he was very sick and that he needed $1,000 to pay for an operation. Bob asked the old man to lend him the money and promised that he would pay him back when he recovered. Really Bob wasn't sick at all and he had no intention of paying the man back. Although the old man didn't know Bob very well, he lent him the money. So Bob and Karl skipped town, each with $1,000.

1. Which is worse, stealing like Karl or cheating like Bob?

1a. Why is that worse? (Dilemma related)

2. What do you think is the worst thing about cheating the old man?

2a. Why is that the worst thing? (Dilemma related)

3. In general, why should a promise be kept? (General issue)

4. Is it important to keep a promise to someone you don't know well or will never see again?

4a. Why or why not? (General issue)

5. Why shouldn't someone steal from a store? (General issue)

6. What is the value or importance of property rights? (General issue)

7. Should people do everything they can to obey the law?

7a. Why or why not? (General issue)

*8. Was the old man being irresponsible by lending Bob the money?

*8a. Why or why not? (Dilemma related)

APPENDIX B: SAMPLE CASE

Dilemma III:

1. *Should Heinz steal the drug?*

   Yes.

   Why?

   Because he is desperate for one he loves. Stealing is wrong, but sometimes you don't have any other choice, and that's what you have to do. And ask God to forgive you.

2. *If Heinz doesn't love his wife, should he steal the drug for her?*

   Yes. Because this is a human being, and he's married to this woman. And I'm sure one time he loved her. Love keeps coming to my mind.

3. *Suppose the person dying is not his wife but a stranger. Should Heinz steal the drug for the stranger?*

   Well, I don't . . . no . . . I don't know. *Why?* Because she is a stranger and other than feeling sorry for her as a human being, but not like a closeness that you have for one you love. I would have to have a strong feeling for someone before I could do it or dear friend.

4. *(Question not asked.)*

5. *Is it important for people to do everything they can to save another's life?*

   Yes, I think so. *Why?* Because people are human beings and would be if you're normal. It's a normal reaction to want to help someone in trouble.

6. *It is against the law for Heinz to steal. Does that make it morally wrong?*

   No. *Why Not?* It's helping another human being because he has feelings. It's instinct to reach out and help another human.

7. *Should People try to do everything they can to obey the law?*

   Yes. *Why?* If they didn't, God, I'd hate to see where we'd be today if they didn't have law. Nothing is always right or always all wrong, so [you] have to have laws [to] say what is right and wrong. We have people who are crazy and unstable, so we have to have the law.

8. *How does this apply to what Heinz should do?*

   That shouldn't apply to him at all in this situation. *Why?* The man can't raise the money to save his wife and has no other way. And he isn't killing anybody. The mere fact that he's stealing to help someone he loves. So [I] don't see how that applies to the law.

APPENDIX C: STANDARD SCORING SHEET

STANDARD SCORING SHEET

DATE:
INTERVIEW No./S name:
SCORED BY:

FORM A/FORM B/ FORM C (circle one)

(Circle Chosen Issue)

DILEMMA III (FORM A) OR IV (FORM B) OR
V (FORM C)

LIFE (FORM A) or LIFE-QUALITY
(Forms B & C) ISSUE

LAW (FORM A) or LAW/LIFE-PRESERV.
(Forms B & C) ISSUE

Q#	CJ#/Norm & Element	Stage (Notes)	Q#	CJ#/Norm & Element	Stage (Notes)

ISSUE SCORE: ISSUE SCORE:

(Circle Chosen Issue)

DILEMMA III' (FORM A) OR IV' (FORM B) OR
VIII (FORM C)

MORALITY & CONSCIENCE ISSUE   PUNISHMENT ISSUE

Q#	CJ#/Norm & Element	Stage (Notes)	Q#	CJ#/Norm & Element	Stage (Notes)

ISSUE SCORE: ISSUE SCORE:

(Circle Chosen Issue)

DILEMMA I (FORM A) OR II (FORM B) OR
VII (FORM C)

CONTRACT ISSUE   AUTHORITY ISSUE

Q#	CJ#/Norm & Element	Stage (Notes)	Q#	CJ#/Norm & Element	Stage (Notes)

ISSUE SCORE: ISSUE SCORE:

Summated   1 _____   OVERALL PROTOCOL SCORE
Weightings   2 _____   GLOBAL: _____
From Issues: 3 _____
               4 _____   WAS: _____
               5 _____

Seven

Annotated Practice Cases

with Anat Abrahami

This chapter presents an opportunity to practice the procedures described in chapter 6 for scoring moral judgment interviews. It offers a number of typical moral judgment interview protocols along with annotated scoring sheets that indicate what scores were assigned and why.

As noted in previous chapters, the Standard Issue Moral Judgment Interview includes three parallel forms: Forms A, B, and C. This chapter includes sample cases only from Forms A and B. Although the three forms vary in the specific content of their dilemmas, the scoring techniques, rules, and procedures are identical across the three forms. Thus, the cases presented here should yield a firm grasp of how to score moral judgment interviews regardless of which form is used.

In selecting these cases, an attempt was made to ensure a representative sample in terms of difficulty in scoring and an inclusive range of stages and transitions.

The chapter is divided into four sections. The first and third sections include 16 transcripts of moral judgment protocols of Form A ($n=9$) and Form B ($n=7$), respectively. The second and fourth sections present the same cases as the preceding sections, scored and annotated. This annotation provides a detailed explanation of scoring decisions that were made where difficulties arose.

In order to practice Standard Issue Scoring, you should attempt to score all of the protocols in a single form (A or B) *before* going to the next section. In this way, the annotated cases can be used as both a learning experience and as a way to assess your progress toward reliable scoring.

Moral Judgment Practice Cases, Form A

Case #410

Dilemma III

1. *Should Heinz steal the drug?*

   No, because it's a rule [that you're] not supposed to steal. It's not right. It's a crime.

2. *If Heinz doesn't love his wife, should he steal the drug for her? Does it make a difference if he loves his wife or not?*

   [If Heinz loves his wife] no, he should try to make the drug. [If he can't make it] he'll just have to suffer.

2a. *Why or why not?*

[If he doesn't love his wife] no, because he should be kind to everybody and his wife. *Why is that kind?* It's wrong.

3. *Suppose the person dying is not his wife but a stranger.*
   Should Heinz steal the drug for the stranger?

   No, it's not right.

4. *Suppose it's a pet animal he loves. Should Heinz steal to save the pet animal?*

   No, it's not right for him to steal drugs from the store.

5. *Is it important for people to do everything they can to save another's life?*

   Yes, like they can help you in other ways. And then you can help them in other ways.

6. *It is against the law for Heinz to steal. Does that make it morally wrong?*

   Yes, it's against the law.

7. *Should people try to do everything they can to obey the law?*

   Yes. They don't want to get hurt or have accidents and die. It could be safety. Like, you obey the stop signs and street lights and walk beside your bicycle across the street because you could run people's feet over and get them hurt.

7b. *How does this apply to what Heinz should do?*

   The man who owns the store might catch him and put him into jail.

Dilemma III'

1. *Should Officer Brown report Heinz for stealing?*

   Yes, he disobeyed the law. He's not supposed to disobey it. *Why else?* He saw him running away. And because it was in the newspaper.

2. *Officer Brown finds and arrests Heinz. Heinz is brought to court, and a jury is selected. The jury's job is to find whether a person is innocent or guilty of committing a crime. The jury finds Heinz guilty. It is up to the judge to determine the sentence. Should the judge give Heinz some sentence, or should he suspend the sentence and let Heinz go free?*

   [The judge should] give him a sentence for breaking the law of stealing. What sentence? A punishment – to be put in jail for two years. *Is that bad?* Yes.

3. *Thinking in terms of society, should people who break the law be punished?*

   Yes, if they didn't know about the law, they shouldn't be punished. Give them another chance. [If they did know] then they will be put in jail. *Should they?* Yes.

3b. *How does this apply to how the judge should decide?*

   To be put in jail because he broke the law twice. He tried to take the drug. [If he broke the law only once] let him go – because he only did one thing.

4. *Heinz was doing what his conscience told him when he stole the drug. Should a lawbreaker be punished if he is acting out of conscience?*

   Yes, he did wrong.

Dilemma I

1. *Should Joe refuse to give his father the money?*

   Yes, because he earned his money up. He tried all he could to go to camp because he never went there before.

2. *Is the fact that Joe earned the money himself the most important thing in the situation?*

   Yes, because Joe never went to camp before and he should go to camp before it's all over.

3. *The father promised Joe he could go to camp if he earned the money. Is the fact that the father promised the most important thing in the situation?*

   Yes, because he wanted to go so much to learn . . . reading, math, spelling.

3a. *Why or why not?*

   If the father went fishing, he should let the boy have his chance and not be selfish. [If the father doesn't go fishing] that's his fault – he had the money to let the son go to camp, but he said – earn it and you can go to camp. And then the father changed his mind and he said he needed the money. The son went and thought about it. He wanted to go to camp so much that he didn't want his father to go with his friends.

4. *Is it important to keep a promise?*

   Yes. You promised it. You promise stuff and you can keep it and that's what Joe should do – keep his promise because he wants to go to camp.

5. *Is it important to keep a promise to someone you don't know well and probably won't see again?*

   No. Because he's gone so long. And if you don't see him again, you can't keep it.

6. *What do you think is the most important thing a son should be concerned about in his relationship to his father?*

   Be nice to them, love each other, and care for them – everybody. So they can be kind to you and won't have to shout at you.

7. *What do you think is the most important thing a father should be concerned about in his relationship to his son?*

   That the children should go along with the mother and father – because the mother and father brought them up. Children should obey them even into their hundred years old because in their father's and mother's way – of growing up.

Case #506

Dilemma III

1. *Should Heinz steal the drug?*
   Yes.

1a. *Why or why not?*

Because Heinz is working from a hierarchy of values, in which life (at least the life of his wife) is higher than honesty (although he tried that route too – a lower but real value – until it proved incapable of serving a higher imperative). From my point of view, as distinct from Heinz's, human life and its presentation – at least as presented here – must take precedence over other values, like Heinz's desire to be honest and law-abiding, or the druggist's love of money and his "rights." All values stem from the ultimate value of life.

2. *What's to be said for obeying the law in this situation or in general?*

The law should be obeyed only insofar as it supports – or at least does not contradict, counteract, or weaken – the more fundamental moral imperatives.

3. *In this situation, law and life come into conflict. How can you resolve the conflict taking the best arguments for both into account?*

Law, its supporters will claim, is the way of preserving the value of life in society, and as such, it should not be violated. They focus on the end result – a better society for life to flourish in – and can dispense with more "minor" losses. But life cannot be so relegated. It must be the foremost concern in both means and ends.

4. *If the husband doesn't love his wife, is he obligated to steal the drug for her? Why or why not?*

Love should make no difference to moral *obligation* here, although it will certainly affect his *inclination*. We *must* distinguish here between common or romantic notions – individual notions – of *love,* and the kind of *love* that is the basis of all moral imperatives – love for fellow men. If the husband lacks this, he is outside the realm of moral action and influence.

5. *Why is it important to save the woman's life? Would it be as right to steal it for a stranger as his wife? Why?*

It would probably be more fully *satisfying* to the man to save his wife than a stranger – for all the intimate shared experience they have. But it is in no way less morally important to save the life of the stranger.

Dilemma III′

6. *Heinz steals the drug and is caught. Should the judge sentence him or should he let him go free? Why?*

The judge in our legal system would have to assign some guilt or punishment, or case being part of that system. But aside from such considerations, the judge *should* let him go free, for he has answered to the highest morality.

7. *Thinking in terms of society, what would be the best reasons for the judge to give him some sentence?*

A sentence, it would be held, would discourage the man from thinking honesty could be avoided in the future – perhaps for the less pressing reasons. And it would impress upon the man the demands and balances of his own society as structured – make obvious the gap between his ideal action and the mundane society.

8. *Thinking in terms of society, what would be the best reasons for the judge to not give him some sentence?*

To not sentence him would be to give greater authority to the impulses of high morality that are in conflict with existing legal structures. Carefully handled, this could lead to a general increase in moral consciousness – true and independent response by all to moral imperatives that originate in human nature and not in a particular code.

Dilemma I

1. *Should Joe refuse to give his father the money?*

Yes, though he can't back it up.

1a. *Why or why not?*

Joe's father is instilling a lack of trust and incoherence in him by vacillating on this issue of such great personal importance in Joe's growth. Joe can neither respond with compliance with the untrustworthy and incoherent or with just rebellion and assertion of his well-founded rights versus arbitrary authority.

2. *Is the fact that Joe earned the money himself the most important thing in the situation?*

Joe, in giving up the money, might learn some lesson of nonattachment and the fickleness of material benefits. But this would require a maturity of vision that he probably yet lacks. He might learn, too, how it feels to give up one's own desires for those of another – as, presumably, his father has done for him many times in the last 14 years.

3. *Is the fact that Joe earned the money himself an important consideration here? Why or why not?*

Not in the *most* important senses of trust, coherence, and just authority. That factor would, of course, be important as a supplementary and sentimental issue to Joe. It is *more* important that Joe's father set *conditions* to be met for a reward, and then did not fulfill the confidence instilled in Joe.

4. *Why should a promise be kept?*

A promise partakes in the sacred realm of relationships of trust. Trust is among the highest human values, and must not be abrogated except on the demand of a higher value.

5. *What makes a person feel bad when a promise is broken?*

He has a sense that he has weakened one of the essential links between all men, that if the thing that he has just weakened disappears, so does humanity.

6. *Why is it important to keep a promise to someone you don't know well or are not close to?*

Because, although the sentimental motivations are not present here, trust is a value that must exist between all men if it is to be a real seminal value. Claiming lack of close relationships is a rationalization and a guise to obscure the uneasiness of abrogated trust.

245

7. *Trust is one important thing in a good father–son relationship. What are some other important considerations that a good father should recognize in his relations with this son? Why is that important?*

He should communicate a sense of authority – but *just* authority, that can be at least in some sense assented to and understood by his son. He should encourage transmission of love and concern through and above the authority and trust. He should show his son that he is ultimately concerned with his full and true development. He should not bludgeon his son with the law, or with his whim, but help him to embrace what is right. Because these are values by which men should live.

8. *How is a good parent–child relationship similar to any good human relationship? Why is that?*

Though modified by the difference in age, the same vital aspects of relationship are at work among parent and child as among any people. The moral bases are identical, and in a way delicate with a child because his morality is being developed.

Case #247

Dilemma III

1. *Should Heinz steal the drug?*

He should talk to the man and see if he would let him pay for it on time.

2. *There is no other alternative.*

Well, depending on what he thinks of his wife, he should steal it, I suppose, if he really wants to save her.

3. *What would he think of his wife?*

If he really loves his wife, if he didn't want to see her die, he should steal it. It's wrong, but he has not other choice; the man is put in a corner, he has to fight his way out of there.

4. *Why is the amount of love he has for his wife, why is that the important thing?*

If he didn't care for his wife, if he didn't care what happens to her; but if he really loves his wife, and doesn't want to live without her, then there is no other choice. He has to steal it or she is going to die.

5. *If he does not love his wife should he steal the drug?*

Well, he should because it is not right to let the woman die, but if he doesn't want her around anymore, he would have to break the law to get it, so he could legally let the woman pass on, it would be up to him. Yeah, I suppose he should, if the person is going to die a senseless death, the cure is there, but he just can't get it, legally he can't just go in and buy it or charge it, so he steals it or she dies.

6. *Suppose the person dying is a stranger. Should he steal the drug for a stranger?*

Should he? He shouldn't, because I say it is not right to steal in the first place, he doesn't know the person, really what does he care, if it is a complete stranger, he just shouldn't. Why should he care what happens to a stranger?

7. *But you said he should steal for his wife?*

For a loved one.

8. *Even if he doesn't love his wife?*

If he doesn't love his wife, he should. He knows her, he has to have some feeling for her, it might not be love, but it might be friendship or just a knowing of a person, but a stranger, he can't have any emotional attachment, to a stranger.

9. *What is to be said for obeying the law in this situation or in general?*

Well, it's wrong to steal, he can be punished for it. Then again, what kind of law is protecting him from a guy who is jacking the price up to ten times the original amount? He is not breaking a law, he can just do what he wants, but it's wrong, the person would be dying because he was greedy for money and I guess the law is going to be on his side, but again, the guy is wrong, but he is still going to get punished for it if he gets caught. They might, in a situation, justice might be easy on it, but he is still breaking the law.

10. *But what is there about the law that you say in general it is bad to steal, it is against the law? Why is it bad to go against the law?*

Well, they are rules set down by the people over the years, if he has to do it that way, which is the legal way, everybody else has to do it that way and you know if you don't do it that way you are going to get punished for it, you are breaking the law and going against the majority of the people. They set the laws as standards of the country, so you are breaking something that people are living with. So if you can do it that means somebody else can do it, and if you get a slap on the wrist, that person is going to get a slap on the wrist, or shouldn't get a slap on the wrist, and you are just breaking something that people set up for rules to be followed.

11. *Heinz might think it is important to obey the law and save his wife, but can't do both. Is there a way to resolve the conflict between life and law taking the best arguments for both into account?*

Give me some idea of the way I can get started on this one.

12. *Why don't you just take a crack at it?*

I don't really understand how to get into that. Well, one way, I said it, he is forced if he really wants to save his wife, he is forced to steal, if there is no other way this man is going to get this medicine, but now, like I have been saying, the laws have been set up for everyone to be followed, and if they are not followed, the man is in trouble. Now how can you resolve both of them – the man could steal and the next day the law could be easy on him. Kind of give him his punishment but not to the point where the guy is really going to suffer for it. You don't want to see anybody dying senselessly, which would be if he couldn't get it. I don't know any other way to answer it, he's got to get it, but then he would break the law, and the law could be easy on him, that's about the best I can do for you on that one.

247

Dilemma III'

1. *Should Mr. Brown arrest Heinz or not?*

   He should, because the man's got a job to do, he saw Heinz steal, it is his job to arrest the man, he should. But then again, he could see the way this guy Heinz feels and kind of oversee it, but then again, he is actually breaking the law again, but – by not reporting what he had seen and he is not doing his job by arresting the man.

2. *So what do you think he should end up doing?*

   Arrest him.

3. *Brown finds and arrests Heinz. Should the judge sentence Heinz or let him go free?*

   Well, he should sentence him, he did break the law and he should be punished. I feel myself that the man should not be punished severely because the man did it saving a loved one, but he has to punish the man, he did do wrong, and then every other Tom, Dick, and Harry is going to be doing something that shouldn't be done, and they are going to be thinking, if this man can do it, why shouldn't I? So he should be given some kind of punishment, but not too severe.

4. *What about the fact that he is saving a life?*

   He is saving a life, but he did break the law. Some other person can come along and do the same thing and say I had to have this, or to have money for this to help my family out, and they will be breaking the law and some guy is always going to be losing. You rob anything, somebody else is suffering because you had to have this or that. It doesn't have to be a serious punishment, if the guy only robbed what he needed, he didn't rob for greed, he wanted to save somebody.

5. *The guy should give him probation?*

   Probation, something light, a slap on the wrist, something like that.

6. *The judge has to think about society. Thinking in terms of society, what is the best reason for the judge to give Heinz a sentence?*

   Just to show that he had done something wrong, and the man should have some sort of punishment for it. Which seems to be a joke nowadays anyway.

7. *Do you agree with that reason? If you were the judge would this be your decision?*

   Do I agree he should give him a sentence, yeah, I agree he should give him a sentence.

8. *You said that people would get the idea that here was somebody who was getting away with breaking the law, if he did not get sentenced. But if you are thinking in terms of the general interpretation that this case would have, why wouldn't you think in terms of the interpretation that someone is saving a life, and should be rewarded for it?*

   Because to save a life, he had to break a law, he can't do something wrong in order to do something right, but he did something wrong, so he should be punished. I know I say in everybody's eyes, the guy is going to look like a hero, because he had to do it, but still there are written laws that millions of people have to follow, or you end up in prison or getting punished and he did break a law, it says here, he did break in and stole it, so he is going to have some sort of reprimand, to let everybody know that the man did wrong and had to be punished for it some way or another.

9. *Why is it generally important to punish people who break the law?*

    I just answered that anyway.

10. *But is it important to punish the people?*

    It is to show the other people who might be thinking the same thing, that they do the same thing, they are going to know they would be punished for it.

11. *What is the purpose of showing everybody?*

    If one person sees or other people see that this man can do this and get away with it, then why can't they do it and get away with it, then you will have chaos, because you will have everybody breaking into stores and stealing the man's merchandise and money and whatever he had and then everybody can do it and what kind of society do we have. A man is walking down the street – you don't like his looks – you shoot him. If he can do it, I can do it. If he can get away with it, then I should be able to get away with it.

Dilemma I

1. *Should Joe refuse to give his father the money?*

    I can see two sides of this one too. Should Joe give his father the money? I would say if Joe is the son, he should give the money to his father, because it is his father, on that end of it, but then again I also feel that he shouldn't give it to his father, because his father did promise him, the kid did work for it, to go, and the kid did work, he saved, and he had his heart set on going to camp and then I could say he should refuse him. How I could answer anymore than that?

2. *Which side will you take?*

    I think his father is being selfish on the point there, the kid has worked and saved his money and like his father promised him, he did promise him he could go to camp, I think I would feel more towards the kid refusing his father, but then again, I couldn't do it to my father. I say it is just the way you are brought up with your father, but . . .

3. *You said the main reason of his thinking of not refusing was – is his father. What is there about a father that would make you not refuse to give the money?*

    When you are a boy, you always love your father. I respect my father, I would do anything for my dad. I feel now, still being a son, but being older, that I would like to see my dad do everything that he could possibly do. I still have a full life ahead of me and my dad could be coming to the end of his, of course I could too, the way things are going. I would do it to be able to see my dad do some-thing else, enjoy a little more or something. I could always go – if I was counting on a vacation, I could always go on a vacation to camp next year, but my father may not be able to go on a fishing trip next year and he has a chance to be able to get together with his buddies, and my dad doesn't really do, hang around with his buddies and if he had a chance to go fishing with his friends, I would really like to see him go. I would give him the money, no problem and then plan a vacation for the next year.

4. *Is the fact that Joe earned the money himself an important consideration here?*

   His dad is not giving him the money and he is not counting on his dad, he is using his own money over his dad's, he should be able to do with it what he wants to, but I say the kid is still young and it could mess the kid up and bother the kid, too, here his dad gives him a promise and the kid does everything he has to do to fulfill the promise and then his dad shuts him off. The kid could lose trust in his father. He promises him to do this and then he doesn't do it.

5. *Does the fact he earned the money himself, does that matter?*

   He earned the money himself and he should be able to do with the money what he wants to do with the money, but he is still living at home, his father is still paying all the other bills and he is living there, living off his father and his father is dressing him and schooling him, so really his – the kid does owe his father anyway, but a 14-year-old might not be able to understand that shit anyway.

6. *Why does he owe his father something if his father is providing material things?*

   It is not that he owed him, his father had him by his own choice, most fathers had them – but it is his dad, he is raising him, giving him loving care, and he is taking care of him, if something happens to you, you kind of owe your dad, you always do. I owe my dad, he is doing everything he can for you.

7. *The fact that he is doing everything he can for you, what does that have to do with it?*

   He is doing everything he can, you should do a little in return. The father is doing this for you, why can't you do a little for him? You give him a little for what he gives you. He gives you a lot. In a normal case, the father is showing you love. Dad wants to have a little fun, if you can help him, why not?

8. *Is it important for a father to respect his son's property?*

   Yeah, it is something that the kid had to go out and work for. He earned it himself, with no help from anybody else, it's his. It is his to do with what he wants to really, if he really wants to go to camp, then it should be up to him, because it's his money and it should be his to spend as he wants to. The father maybe should ask him say hey, can I have it, but not demand it from him, it's not his.

9. *Why should a father respect his son's property?*

   He should respect his son's property if he wants his son to respect his property. If he goes out and earns his money or his house, or whatever, he – his son should respect it to a point, the kid, now he has gone out and earned a little bit and his father should respect him, this is yours, to do with what you want, if he goes and demands his money, why shouldn't the kid say well listen, give me this or that, too.

10. *What is the basic value or importance of property rights in general?*

    I really couldn't tell you, it is something that belongs to somebody, it doesn't belong to you, what this person has, you shouldn't go and take it from him, it doesn't belong to you. A man has worked or earned it to be his. What gives anybody else the right to just come along and take it from that person? There is no right to that.

11. *Why should he be able to keep it? Because you worked for it?*

Because you went out and worked for it, you had to give up something in return for something else. Now it belongs to you, it should be yours to do with it what you want to do with it.

12. *Not only did Joe earn the money, but his father made a promise. Is that important?*

Yeah, I think so, when the father made the promise the boy had to feel well, if I do this I can do that, and if I earned the money, I am going to camp. If this happened, the kid should feel I am going to camp now, I got the money and I can go. All of a sudden if the father comes along and knocks the stops out of him, the kid has got to be hurt and confused. The father told him he can do it if he does this and he does it and now he can't do what the promise was.

13. *Why should a promise be kept in general?*

When you make a person a promise, the person expects you will do what you promised, and all of a sudden you tell him he can't do, probably the person won't trust you again, you can go up to him next time and say I promise this and he will say, hey you broke one promise to me, is he going to do it again, he is going to be a little not sure of the person making the promise, if he breaks one, he is going to break another one. How can you show respect to a person, or believe this person or trust him, anymore?

14. *What would be the consequence, or wrong with losing his trust?*

Well, the person who is breaking the promise, if he tells a person something, the person is just not going to believe him, how can you believe a person that keeps on lying to you, saying one thing to you to get you to do something else and then when you do this other thing, they say I am going to not do it anyway. I was kidding you, I am not going to keep my end of the bargain.

15. *Is it important to keep a promise to someone you don't know well or are not close to?*

It is important to keep a promise to anybody. To anybody you break a promise to is just going to feel the same way as anybody else. A person who is closer to you is going to maybe feel a little more hurt, but a person who does not know you, who comes in contact with you occasionally is not going to trust you.

16. *The issue you were talking about was that this particular person will not trust you anymore, somebody you don't know well or probably won't see again, so would the same thing hold true?*

For yourself it is. If you lie to people to benefit yourself, then you start doing that, you are going to do it to anybody, but who is going to care, you are not going to see that person again anyways, so you say I am not going to see him, what do I care, but to yourself, you are kind of cheating yourself in a way, too, you just go along trying to take advantage of everybody, I will tell this guy this to get what I wants and he can go fly a kite. To yourself, I think you are lowering yourself a little bit just trying to get everything you want for yourself and the heck with everybody else. The other person. You are not being fair with yourself, are you?

17. *Why wouldn't you consider it fair with yourself, no one is ever going to know about it. How is it really hurting you?*

You are kind of lowering yourself, you are not being an upstanding person, you are kind of cheating everybody, you don't care how you are going to get ahead, you are going to go around hurting everybody that comes in contact with you, you don't see the guy, so what, you are not going to care, but — I just don't feel like you are being fair with yourself, you are taking advantage of anything or anyone, just to help yourself out, I think you're lowering your standards.

18. *What is the most important thing for a son to consider in his relationship to his father?*

I think that the son trusts his father and by the father breaking promises to the boy, the boy is going to lose trust in his father, that the father is not telling the son really the truth, he is telling him something, he can do this, and then the next step he is telling him, I am only kidding you can't do it, why should the son trust him if he tells him again something and his father breaks his promise again, the boy can't trust his father, the boy doesn't know if the man is going to be telling the truth or not. He is not going to trust his father anymore.

19. *Why should trust be important?*

If he can't trust his father, I don't think when he grows up he is going to be trusting anybody else that tells him something. If he is growing up under a father who breaks his promises, why should he trust anybody else, why should he believe anything else. He would not believe anybody.

20. *What would be so bad about that?*

I don't see how they would get along, if somebody tells you something, you should believe the man, but you think back oh, my father told me something too and he didn't follow through, why should this man. Sometimes when guys tell me something at work, I don't know if they are putting me on or if I should believe them, like that. You just don't know. I don't think it is from my bringing up, I think it is just from my working where I work, but if you lose faith in anybody, you just don't believe anybody, and if you go through life like that, I think you are in trouble. Don't believe people.

21. *In what sense do you trust them?*

If a man tells you, you do this and this happens — you think, well, what's to say? If I do this, something else doesn't happen, or if you do something and you get in trouble. A guy at work tells you you have to do a job this way and you think maybe he is . . .

Case #138

Dilemma III

1. *Should Heinz steal the drug?*

Yes.

1a. *Why or why not?*

Because the druggist is an asshole. Because his wife deserves to live. It's more important than that man's money.

2. *If Heinz doesn't love his wife, should he steal the drug for her?*

Sure.

2a. *Why or why not?*

Because it's another life. You should always try to save another life. *Why?* Because humankind is important.

3. *Suppose the person dying is not his wife but a stranger. Should Heinz steal the drug for the stranger?*

If he wanted to risk it, sure. It's still another life.

4. *What's to be said for obeying the law in this situation or in general?*

I think life is more important than law. Because you don't want to end up in prison for one. *Any other reason?* Well, it's immoral to break the law. The druggist is breaking the law. *Why is it immoral?* Laws are there to protect the people. If you go breaking them, you harm someone else. If he killed the dude in stealing it, it would be hypocritical.

Dilemma III'

1. *Should Officer Brown report Heinz for stealing?*

No.

1a. *Why or why not?*

If he knows the situation, he should be sympathetic with Heinz and he should put that before law. He could always say he didn't see it or something.

2. *Officer Brown finds and arrests Heinz. Heinz is brought to court, and a jury is selected. The jury's job is to find whether a person is innocent or guilty of committing a crime. The jury finds Heinz guilty. It is up to the judge to determine the sentence. Should the judge give Heinz some sentence, or should he suspend the sentence and let Heinz go free?*

Let him go. The druggist shouldn't charge such a high price. The judge should be sympathetic. If he had a wife, he would know.

3. *The judge has to think about society. Thinking in terms of society, what is the best argument for the judge to give Heinz a sentence?*

The law is the law and Heinz broke it. It was obvious — anyone who broke the law must pay for it. He knew he was breaking the law, so he should pay for it. *Why should you pay for it if you break the law?* Because the law was written and Heinz knows the law. *Why should penalties be attached to laws?* The laws would be no good. People would go around breaking them. If you don't have punishment, you won't have laws.

3a. *If you disagree with this argument, why?*

The judge should sympathize with Heinz. He should be able to put human life before the law.

4. *Heinz might think it's important to obey the law and to save his wife, but he can't do both. Is there a way to resolve the conflict between law and life, taking the best arguments for both into account? How or why not?*

Not in this case. You either do one or the other. *In this case?* The law is going counter to saving a life. He should save a life in this case.

Dilemma I

1. *Should Joe refuse to give his father the money?*

   Sure.

1a. *Why or why not?*

   Because he worked hard for the money. Because it was something he wanted to do. The father didn't work for it. Besides, he promised him he'd let him go.

2. *Is the fact that Joe earned the money himself the most important thing in the situation?*

   Yes, because he had his heart set on it. If he worked hard for it, it meant he worked on it, and saved it, and didn't blow it.

3. *Joe might consider the money something he earned and that he has property rights in this case. Is it important for a father to respect his son's property? Why or why not?*

   Yes. Because he would expect his son to respect his property. It's do unto others as you would have them do unto you. The other part is don't do unto others if you don't want them to do it unto you. People who steal will get stolen from. It's not revenge. If things are happening to you, you have to think of who you are dumping on.

4. *What is the basic value or importance of property rights, in general?*

   Normally something that means something to one person, doesn't mean the same to another. People who steal have to think of how important the thing is to the person they are stealing from. Property don't have to be material, like embarrassing you in public.

5. *Not only did Joe earn the money, but his father made a promise. Is that an important consideration here? Why or why not?*

   Yes. *Why?* First of all, he shouldn't make a promise if he doesn't intend to keep it. O.K., he probably did intend to keep it, but something came up. So he should put his son before himself, because he did make the promise and his son was counting on it.

6. *Is it important to keep a promise?*

   If you promise somebody something, they assume you intend to keep it, and they are counting on it. They are making plans to do what they want with it. And then it fucks them up.

7. *Is it important to keep a promise to someone you don't know well and probably won't see again?*

   Sure. A promise is a promise. The above applies.

8. *What do you think is the most important thing a son should be concerned about in his relationship to his father?*

He should probably think "Would my father do this for me?" If he thinks he would, then he should give it to him. If not, no. It depends on the relationship, whether it's good or not. It's the same with my friends.

9. *What do you think is the most important thing a father should be concerned about in his relationship to his son?*

He should think along the same lines. If the situation were reversed, the father should think, "Would my son do this for me?" Again, it depends on the relationship.

Case #131

Dilemma III

1. *Should Heinz, the husband, have done that? Why?*

Yes. Well, the guy that was selling the drug, it cost him $200 and for $1,000 he'd still be making a profit and he'd still be saving someone's life, and the guy he wanted to save his wife and he might have got $1,000 for the druggist to keep. *But he didn't, but you say he was right to do this anyway?* No, it's not right to do it, but he should have, well, . . . *It's not right to do it?* Well, if you have a good reason, your wife is dying and you want to save her – that doesn't make it right – it's still against the law. *But you have to do it for something like that?* Well, he was desperate, he probably didn't know what he was doing. He just wanted to save his wife's life.

1a. *Is it a husband's duty to steal it?*

Yes, to save his wife's life, 'cause she was dying. If she died he wouldn't be near her anymore and he'd probably feel sorry for himself. *Why is it his duty?* I don't know. *He just wants to save his wife's life?* Yeah. He loves her a lot. *You say a husband should do that but it isn't right to do it.* It isn't right to do it, but he would probably do it to save his wife's life.

2. *If her husband didn't like her, should he steal the drug for her?*

[No answer.]

3. *Suppose it were for a friend?*

That's up to Heinz, what he wanted to do. If he wants to get caught or something – he probably would get caught if he started to steal the drug for his friend – maybe he could go to a loan company. *Say they tried that? Should he steal the drug to save his friend's life?* It all depends on how close his friend is. If it was a friend that was like a brother to him, maybe he wouldn't but maybe he'd still do it to save his friend's life. He might get about six months or a year. *Should he do it?* No, I don't think so.

4. *Did the druggist have the right to charge that much for the drug?*

He was making too much of a profit from the $200 he paid for it to $2,000. I think he asked too much. He should charge about $1,000, maybe cheaper than that, maybe $750. *Why is that?* Well, then more people could use the drug to save more people's lives. *Doesn't he have the right to charge that much?* Oh, he has the right to do it, if he discovered it. *But it isn't the best thing to do to charge that much. He has the right?* Yes. *Are you sure?* No, not positive. *Then?* He can try it

255

and see what he can do with it, and if it did save his friend's life he'd be happy about it and he'd probably have to serve six months or so. *So it wouldn't make much difference?* No, but if he didn't try nothing for it then this friend's family would feel kinda bad toward him.

Dilemma III'

1. *Heinz stole the drug, should the judge send Heinz to jail?*

   He shouldn't let him go free, he should give him a sentence. It all depends on how bad the crime was. As I said before, it might be only six months to a year. *Why should he give him a sentence?* Well, he broke in the store and that's robbery and that's against the law. *I see.*

2. *Would the judge think Heinz should have stolen the drug?*

   Well, the judge might have done it for his wife, but it was his duty to enforce the law, so he probably say no then, 'cause it hasn't happened to him. If it ever did then he just might steal it. *The judge would say that Heinz shouldn't have stolen the drug but actually if he himself got in this situation he probably would.* Yes. *So you say the judge wouldn't say that Heinz should have stolen the drug?* Yes. *He'd think Heinz shouldn't have stolen it?* Yes.

Dilemma I

1. *Should Joe refuse to give his father the money? Why?*

   I think he should refuse him, because he's the one who saved it up working, and his father could have saved some of his money instead of spending it. *Well, his father didn't know this fishing trip was coming up.* Still, Joe had plans to go on his camping trip and his father wouldn't be half as disappointed as Joe is because Joe has been planning on it since he started his paper route and he's been saving up the money for it. *His father wouldn't be as disappointed. Is that one of the reasons Joe should refuse?* Yes. *Are there any others?* Well, it's Joe's money and it's not his father's. If Joe could save money his father surely could.

2. *Does his father have the right to tell Joe to give him the money?*

   No, I don't think he does. *Why not?* it's Joe's money, he saved it up all by himself.

3a. *Which is worse, a father breaking a promise to his son or a son breaking a promise to his father?*

   Father breaking a promise to his son. *Why?* Well, the boy is still growing up yet and his father has learned how to take it, I guess, I don't know.

Case #332

Dilemma III

1. *Should Heinz steal the drug?*

   Yes. Human life is more important than social rules. A higher moral principle . . . Stealing is wrong, but not in this case because a human life is more important.

2. *Should he steal even if he does not love his wife?*

Yes. Human life as a whole is more important than social rules. It doesn't matter if he loves her – she's a human being. Any human being should be saved in this case.

3. *Should he steal for a stranger?*

Yes. Human life should be saved regardless of whether you know the person or not.

4. *Should he steal it for a pet that he loves?*

No. Animals must be distinguished from people. In saving the wife we are concerned with survival of the species. We save other people because they can think or feel – like us.

5. *Is it important to do everything to save a life?*

Yes. Life is the highest moral principle. Above social regulation naturally.

6. *If it is against the law, does that make it morally wrong?*

No. Because his moral standards extend beyond the regulations of his society.

7. *Should people do everything they can to obey the law?*

The law is a general set of rules and everyone should obey them except when they conflict with higher personal moral standards, which should take precedence.

7b. *So What should Heinz do?*

He should steal the drug.

Dilemma III'

1. *Should Officer Brown report Heinz?*

Yes. His obligation is to fulfill the law. He does not know the circumstances. He has no reason not to fulfill his legal obligation to the state. No conflict with a higher principle.

2. *What should the judge do?*

Heinz should have to pay for the drug gradually and should go free. The judge should realize his moral decision is right and take circumstances into consideration. He should recognize Heinz's conflict – that Heinz pay for the drug is a reasonable social demand.

3. *Why punish lawbreakers from society's view?*

We have to maintain order to control people – order is set up by the law and the vast majority of people and situations will fall within the law.

3a. *How does this apply to Heinz's case?*

The judge must make an exception here since he must recognize the need to act according to principles when they conflict with laws.

4. *Why punish someone who breaks the law if he is following his conscience?*

When acting out of conscience it is necessary to have a subjective decision made by an impartial judge who decides based on circumstances. The judge

257

is the representative of authority and must make a judgment in cases where law and principle conflict.

Dilemma I

1. *Should Joe refuse to give his father the money?*

   Yes. Because the money is his. He earned it. Joe is an individual with equal rights to things he's earned.

2. *Is the fact that he earned it important?*

   No. His father's honesty is more important. Respect is essential in forming a sense of justice and his father helps to instill it by serving as an example.

3. *Is the fact that his father promised important?*

   Yes. Joe has to be able to trust his father in order for him to be able to respect others. His father serves as a role model and his action will greatly affect Joe's development of a sense of justice.

4. *Is it important to keep promises?*

   Yes. One treats others in the ways he's treated. One should keep a promise because it is an obligation to another and the basis for social contract.

5. *Is it important to keep a promise to a stranger?*

   Yes. A promise transcends situation, it is a basic responsibility for another human.

6. *What should the son be concerned about in relation to his father?*

   Full and open communication and mutual respect for each other as people. Respect based on caring and not fear. [This is] important because father serves as model and son learns respect from him and learns a sense of justice. Respect for feeling and concern for others.

7. *What should the father be concerned about in relation to his son?*

   Treating son as a person, as an equal. Equal rights and deserving equal care and love. Important because the son must feel like a valuable human being and he will develop this feeling as a young child if his father always respects him. Also he will respect others.

Case #191

Dilemma III

1. *Should Heinz steal the drug?*

   Yes. There is no dilemma — life is more precious than anything else.

2. *If Heinz doesn't love his wife, should he steal the drug for her?*

   Any life I value. It is a human life. I can't take the responsibility of the supreme being.

3. *Suppose the person dying is not his wife but a stranger. Should Heinz steal the drug for the stranger?*

   Depends how the stranger asks for it.

4. *Suppose it's a pet animal he loves. Should Heinz steal to save the pet animal?*

Depends how he feels about the pet animal. It is life, too, and part of his humanity and what his attitude is towards human life.

5. *Is it important for people to do everything they can to save another's life?*

One, if the tables were turned. Two, I think life is precious — you only have it once. It should be preserved. Three, it depends how the other person feels about brotherhood, humanity, an expansion of his point of view, personality, principles, etc.

6. *It is against the law for Heinz to steal. Does that make it morally wrong?*

I don't think in society you can have things as right or wrong — or else life would be based on a light switch — off/on — light/darkness. There are different schools of thought pertaining to moral standards. This moral right to property is probably someone who is morally wrong. It would be morally wrong if the person really cared. It would show to me more insensitivity of the person.

7. *Why should people generally do everything they can to avoid breaking the law, anyhow?*

I don't think it should be "avoid" if you agree to it. It's unhealthy to be a servant of society, not its master. If it's possible to change things you should do it out front — actively try to change. You have a responsibility to accept the results of what you do. Just to know that if you challenge the law, why are you doing it and what you are going to do.

7a. *How does this apply to what Heinz should do?*

The law is the line, it provides. Reason may be example why and how. A person should be responsible. The laws are made like people — people like you. Everyone has more or less an equal chance.

Dilemma III'

1. *Should Officer Brown report Heinz for stealing?*

Some people who are principled because they do what is right . . . I wouldn't report in this hypothetical . . . If I was his good friend, I would know about his wife. I could understand Heinz. We would share the same outlook on life.

2. *Officer Brown finds and arrests Heinz. Heinz is brought to court, and a jury is selected. The jury's job is to find whether a person is innocent or guilty of committing a crime. The jury finds Heinz guilty. It is up to the judge to determine the sentence. Should the judge give Heinz some sentence, or should he suspend the sentence and let Heinz go free?*

Punish him. Explain to the court why. He should show everyone what he did that was wrong, what he did that was right. Any court ruling sets a precedent. *Why?* This isn't the only case like this — in morals you just can't measure. He is a servant of the law. He is not omnipotent. If I were Heinz, I'd explain why I did it. I don't think they would be so heartless so as not to understand.

3. *Thinking in terms of society, should people who break the law be punished?*

I wouldn't necessarily call it punished. It depends on the crime — how it was done and why it was done. A person who commits the crime should be put in a situation where he benefits and society benefits because he is part of society. Society is made up of individuals just like him.

Dilemma I

1. *Should Joe refuse to give his father the money?*

   At that age if he stands up for his rights, it shows the father is not right and fathers are not humans. The father is human, too. Right – justice – He fervently saved up that money. The father was inconsistent in the first place. If I were in his position . . .

2. *Is the fact that Joe earned the money himself the most important thing in the situation?*

   He made a special effort – it showed responsibility, determination, and maturity to do that.

3. *The father promised Joe he could go to camp if he earned the money. Is the fact that the father promised the most important thing in the situation?*

   He gave his word. It shows his worth in a moral sense. His moral value.

4. *Is it important to keep a promise?*

   It's not only the action of making it but the thought behind what's being said. He should be responsible for his actions.

5. *Is it important to keep a promise to someone you don't know well and probably won't see again?*

   If you have a conscience – if you like yourself, you should. You just cheated yourself of something. You have gone against yourself and it's on your conscience. The people who don't feel that aren't human. They are missing what makes human life feel so special.

6. *What do you think is the most important thing a son should be concerned about in his relationship to his father?*

   He is a person. He makes mistakes, too.

6a. *Why is that the most important thing?*

   A lot of kids forget this – to err is human, to forgive is . . .

7. *What do you think is the most important thing a father should be concerned about in his relationship to his son?*

   Kids are very impressionable. Things set precedents that are understood. To break a promise – he has made two errors: One, his word is bad, two, he is not a very consistent person.

7a. *Why is that the most important thing?*

   His honor, his authority – it's not honorable to do something like that. It's nonetheless human to do something so vain and gutless.

Case #168

Dilemma III

1. *Should he have done that?*

   If he liked his wife he should.

2. *Is it wrong to do it?*

   Sure, he could go to court.

3. *Would a good husband have to?*

   He wouldn't have to, no. If he didn't want to, he didn't have to. But if he loved his wife, he should.

4. *Should he steal it for a friend?*

   If the friend had a lot of money, I wouldn't. He could buy it himself, or maybe they would let the doctor buy it.

5. *Would a good husband do it or not?*

   If he wanted to stay out of trouble, he wouldn't.

6. *What is the right thing to do here?*

   Don't steal it – buy it. Get a loan. I'd go and get a couple of loans.

7. *Would it be wrong if he took it and left $1,000?*

   No one should steal.

8. *Would he be going against the storekeeper's rights?*

   I don't think he should have stole it, because if he would have gone to about two banks, he could get the loan, the $2,000 and that's all he needs.

9. *If there was no law setting a limit to the price, was he wrong to set the price that high?*

   I think so because if it could cure certain kinds of cancer it wouldn't be wrong to have that high prices because it could cure that disease – if the druggist was sure it could do it.

Dilemma III'

1. *What punishment should the judge give him?*

   Send him to jail for about 10 years.

2. *Should the judge drop the case if the druggist asks him to?*

   I think so, because the druggist has a right to say the case should be dropped because it's his own medicine. He could do what he wanted, the judge, but I think he should send him to jail or drop the case, he should do what the store-keeper wanted him to do.

Dilemma I

1. *Should Joe refuse to give his father the money?*

   I think he should give it to him. Fathers know better.

261

2. *Is it his duty to his father?*

Not exactly his duty, but he should.

3. *Would it be wrong for him to refuse?*

· Yes, he could refuse, because he was the one that earned that money.

4. *Would he be a bad son if he didn't give the money?*

Not exactly, his father has no right to take the son's own money away.

5. *If his father doesn't have the right, then why should he give it to him? You said his father knows best?*

Yeah.

6. *Does his father have the right to tell him to give him the money?*

It's his son's own money. I don't see a law that says that the father can take the son's money away. Unless it's for a good reason.

7. *If the law said the father has ownership of the son's money, would that be a bad law?*

I think it would be a bad law.

8. *Was it wrong for the father to break his promise to his son?*

I think it was wrong.

9. *Is it worse for the father to break a promise to a son or a son to his father?*

Father breaking his promise to his son, because maybe when the son grows up, he will break all his promises to his sons.

10. *Joe lied; what should the father do?*

Scold him. Because I don't think Joe should lie to his father. And if he wanted to go to camp next year, I wouldn't let him go.

11. *Would the punishment do the son any good when the father had broken his promise in the first place?*

No. Because Joe's father promised him he could go to camp. Then Joe's father wanted to go fishing and didn't have enough money and he took some of the money away from Joe. Joe just gave him $10. He should have given him $40.

Case #7

Dilemma III

1. *Should Heinz steal the drug?*

Yes.

1a. *Why or why not?*

This has to be one of the cleanest-cut dilemmas possible. It comes down to simply a question of two values: what's more important, respect for life or respect for property. As we know, Heinz will break the law but this isn't really all that important. Laws are designed to protect life and property, and are tools to this end, not sacred ends in themselves. So Heinz has a very simple problem and very simple solution: steal the drug, as life is more important than property.

2. *If Heinz doesn't love his wife, should he steal the drug for her?*

Yes.

2a. *Why or why not?*

It is not Heinz's love for his wife that is paramount, but the life itself. Heinz is possibly under a greater obligation than most as this is his wife, but it seems to me that anyone else who hears of the problem would be under an obligation to act similarly. To repeat, it is not the relation of someone to the life that's important, but rather the life.

3. *Suppose the person dying is not his wife but a stranger? Should Heinz steal the drug for the stranger?*

Yes.

3a. *Why or why not?*

As stated above, the feelings someone has for the person in question are irrelevant. The importance of life over property transcends the relationships or feelings involved.

4. *What's to be said for obeying the law in this situation or in general?*

The laws are tools for the protection of life and property. They have no meaning unless they serve this purpose. If in a situation, the ends are not served by the laws, then one is no longer under any obligation to obey the laws. To do so would be counterproductive. If though, one is not in a situation where the laws and the laws' ends are not at cross-purposes, then it could be argued that one should obey the laws. Whether or not it is a moral duty to obey the laws is highly questionable though, and personally, I doubt it.

5. *Heinz might think it's important to obey the law and to save his wife, but he can't do both. Is there a way to resolve the conflict between law and life, taking the best arguments for both into account? Why or why not?*

As stated above, you obey the laws if you feel the laws will help you to reach the proper goals. If they don't, you don't. I am not at all sure what you mean by resolving the conflict. He cannot serve both masters at once in some situations. In conflict situations, he should perform his moral obligations, not his legal ones.

It could be argued that he solves the situations by serving the law's ends rather than their specific means. This argument has some validity, but it does not take into account that generally speaking laws value property as much, if not more, than life. This is possibly necessarily so to promote a more harmonious society which benefits the individual and therefore is valid on a global level. On an individual level, one should choose life over property.

So, while one can resolve the conflict in terms of what one actually does on an individual level, because of global considerations, it seems impossible to resolve the conflict so that one serves both laws and life.

Dilemma III′

1. *Should Officer Brown report Heinz for stealing?*

No.

263

1a. *Why or why not?*

While on an institutional level this policy of turning the other cheek could not be rationalized as a good policy, on an individual level it seems the best policy to follow. Mr. Brown could say that it is up to the courts to decide but this would be a shirking of personal responsibility for his decision.

2. *Officer Brown finds and arrests Heinz. Heinz is brought to court, and a jury is selected. The jury's job is to find whether a person is innocent or guilty of committing a crime. The jury finds Heinz guilty. It is up to the judge to determine the sentence. Should the judge give Heinz some sentence, or should he suspend the sentence and let Heinz go free?*

I'm sure that through enough legal trickery it could be rationalized that Heinz can be let go free and the "holiness" of the laws upheld. This is the optimal result.

2a. *Why?*

While Heinz is "guilty," it would be a farce to punish him. It would serve no functional purpose and would not redress the moral balance of the universe.

3. *The judge has to think about society. Thinking in terms of society, what is the best reason for the judge to give Heinz a sentence?*

On the familiar deterrence argument. If the judge doesn't slap Heinz down, then all sorts of evildoers will run rampant causing horrendous suffering to lots and lots of people. As the judge would be a believer in deterrence, he would also almost have to be a believer in utilitarian theory. Therefore, he would say that more harm — more suffering for lots and lots — would be done than the harm to Heinz. Lesser of two evils and all of that.

3a. *Do you disagree with this reason? Why?*

Yes. On utilitarian reasons for one, i.e., more harm is done. If institutions treat one person as an object, they will tend to treat all persons as objects, and this will result in greater harm being done to both the individuals who stand before our noble courts, and for the average peasant who will view the law with fear and misgivings.

On deontological grounds, it is also objectionable. It is wrong to treat individuals as objects towards a greater end. Besides being self-defeating, it is horrendously cruel and dehumanizing.

4. *Why is it important, generally, to punish people who break the law?*

Deterrence is the big reason. Prevent the particular and the others from doing nasties. Get a nicer society and the peasants are better off. It doesn't work well, but if the deterrence aspect was removed altogether, it's possible that our society would be even shittier than it is.

4b. Another reason is that the person deserves, i.e., is entitled, to be punished. If he is an individual, he deserves to be responsible for his actions; if you don't punish him, you rob him of his responsibility and thus his personhood. Lovely theory. Again in practice, if you ever see the slugs in question who are punished by our courts, it would strongly shake your faith in the practicality of the theory.

Dilemma I

1. *Should Joe refuse to give his father the money? Why or why not?*

   Joe has no moral obligation to give dad the money. Therefore whether or not he should – in a nonmoral sense – depends on other variables such as how much he likes daddy, whether or not he really wants to go to camp, etc.

2. *Is the fact that Joe earned the money himself an important consideration here? Why or why not?*

   Yes and no. What's important is not whether he earned it or not, but the fact that it's his. If it wasn't his, then he wouldn't have much say, would he? As you can see I'm a strong believer in the rights of capitalistic ownership in certain situations. Income redistribution for the poorer peasants is one thing, but abandoning my $40 is something altogether different.

3. *Joe might consider the money something he earned and that he has property rights in this case. Is it important for a father to respect his son's property? Why or why not?*

   It's important for anyone to respect anyone else's property. That doesn't mean that the respect won't be overridden in cases such as Heinz's. *Why?* Well we're grubby creatures. We like to lay claim to the material we find around us. Taking away our material makes us feel hurt.

4. *What is the basic value or importance of property rights in general?*

   The basic importance is the right to the property, not the property itself. If someone can establish some reasonable rationale as to why the property is his, then if we take it we are violating his personhood.

5. *Not only did Joe earn the money, but his father made a promise. Is that an important consideration here? Why or why not?*

   All of us moralists believe in promises. We hate breaking contracts. But, be that as it may, it's not of overwhelming importance in this case. Joe already has his rights, the fact that a promise exists just makes the case stronger.

6. *Why should a promise be kept?*

   The real reason is because we hurt others if we break the promise. Why this is so, I don't know. Just another one of those "intuitively obvious" things. Rationally, one talks of the self-defeating aspects of promise making and then breaking, etc.

7. *Is it important to keep a promise to someone you don't know well or are not close to? Why or why not?*

   No. A promise is a promise. Your relation to the promised part of the situation is irrelevant.

8. *Can you say what is the most important thing for a son to consider about his relationship to his father in this or other situations?*

   That he can hurt his father very deeply because of his relation to him. But, so I won't be inconsistent, the relation itself is not important. It's the effect, the deep hurt, etc., that's really the biggie here.

265

8a. *Why is that important?*

Intuitively obvious that we shouldn't hurt others if possible.

9. *What is the most important thing for a father to consider about his relationship to his son in this or other situations?*

Parents are very exploitative their children. (I know, I am one.) Children are people. They have rights. Your rights as a parent are not necessarily "more right" than theirs. Consider whether you are exploiting him/her, abusing his/her rights because of your relation. Would you do what you're doing to him/her to someone else?

9a. *Why is that important?*

Because children are people. People have rights. Abuse the rights and you hurt them. Hurting is bad.

Annotated Scoring Sheets for Form A – Practice Cases

This section and the fourth section of this chapter present detailed illustrations of how the experienced scorer approaches typical difficulties that may arise in scoring the MJI. For each interview protocol, a completed Standard Scoring Sheet is provided. When a scoring procedure is straightforward (e.g., a clear match between IJ and CJ), no explanation is given. When a difficult or unusual scoring rule is applied, or when a scoring procedure is not self-evident (e.g., guess score), an explanation is provided. A superscript alphanumeric following a score corresponds to the explanation of that score. Parentheses ( ) indicate matches that might seem appropriate to the new scorer but that, for the reason explained in the annotation, do *not*, in fact, constitute matches.

Case #410

Explanation of Scoring

a- Unscorable material – nonprescriptive.

b- This is a straightforward match – see the CJ's "Note."

c- Again, this is a clear match; the special requirements elaborated in the CJ's "Note" are all met.

d- Since no match score can be assigned to this issue, we give it a guess. The guess is based on the material (Q#3b) from the M&C issue plus the material from the opposing issue (punishment), in accordance with Rule 4a of the Rules for Guess Scoring.

e- Both these CJs are matched. They have the same norm (property) and different elements. Since, however, the two CJs express the same idea, at different stages, the inclusion rule is applied. Therefore, only the higher stage score (2/3) is assigned.

f- This material can only be guess scored. However, since a match score has already been assigned, we do not enter any guess score.

g- This match score is based on Critical Indicator (b) of CJ#14.

h- In assigning the overall global score to the protocol, only pure and transitional stage scores are used. No distinction is made between major and minor stage scores. (See chap. 6, Step-by-step Scoring, Steps 16 and 17 [calculating the global stage and the weighted average scores, respectively].)

STANDARD SCORING SHEET

DATE:
INTERVIEW No./S name: # 410
SCORED BY:

FORM A / FORM B/ FORM C (circle one)   *(FORM A circled)*

DILEMMA III (FORM A) OR IV (FORM B) OR
V (FORM C)   *(III circled)*

(Circle Chosen Issue)

LIFE (FORM A) or LIFE-QUALITY (Forms B & C) ISSUE

Q#	CJ#/Norm & Element	Stage (Notes)
5	7 aff (7)	2
ISSUE SCORE:		2

LAW (FORM A) or LAW/LIFE-PRESERV. (Forms B & C) ISSUE   *(LAW circled)*

Q#	CJ#/Norm & Element	Stage (Notes)
1,3,4,6, 7ᵃ	2 law (2)	1
7b	3 law (9)	1ᵇ
ISSUE SCORE:		⓪

(Circle Chosen Issue)

DILEMMA III' (FORM A) OR IV' (FORM B) OR VIII (FORM C)   *(III' circled)*

MORALITY & CONSCIENCE ISSUE

Q#	CJ#/Norm & Element	Stage (Notes)
3b		
ISSUE SCORE:		G ½ᵈ

PUNISHMENT ISSUE   *(circled)*

Q#	CJ#/Norm & Element	Stage (Notes)
1, 2, 3b	2 law (2)	1ᶜ
ISSUE SCORE:		①

(Circle Chosen Issue)

DILEMMA I (FORM A) OR II (FORM B) OR VII (FORM C)   *(I circled)*

CONTRACT ISSUE   *(circled)*

Q#	CJ#/Norm & Element	Stage (Notes)
1	4 prop (4)	2
3, 3a	7 prop (8)	2/3ᵉ
4, 5ᶠ		
ISSUE SCORE:		②/③

AUTHORITY ISSUE

Q#	CJ#/Norm & Element	Stage (Notes)
6	4 aff (7)	2ᵍ
7	9 auth (15)	2/3
ISSUE SCORE:		2(3)

Summated Weightings From Issues:

1 3+3+.5=6.5×1 = 6.5
2 2+.5+1.5+1=5×2 = 10
3 1.5+1=2.5×3 = 7.5
4
5

6.5+10+7.5 = 24 ÷ 14

OVERALL PROTOCOL SCORE

GLOBAL: 1/2ʰ

WAS: 171

Case #506

Explanation of Scoring

a- Although this is clearly a Stage 5 protocol, the particular way in which the subject responds to this dilemma makes it difficult to score; the subject distinguishes the legal system from the sociomoral one (Q#6 and 8). This distinction by itself is indicative of a Stage 5, prior-to-society perspective. However, what makes scoring somewhat confusing is that the subject often addresses the questions from the "society as presently structured" perspective (Q#6 "in our legal system"; Q#7, "a sentence, *it would be held*," etc.), and not from the prior-to-society perspective, which he holds. For example, regarding the question of punishing Heinz, the subject believes that Heinz *should* be free from punishment since "he has answered to the highest morality" (Q#6). However, given "our legal system . . . some guilt or punishment

STANDARD SCORING SHEET

DATE:
INTERVIEW No./S name: 506
SCORED BY:

(FORM A)/FORM B/ FORM C (circle one)

DILEMMA (III) (FORM A) OR IV (FORM B) OR
V (FORM C)

(Circle Chosen Issue)

(LIFE) (FORM A) or LIFE-QUALITY (Forms B & C) ISSUE

LAW (FORM A) or LAW/LIFE-PRESERV. (Forms B & C) ISSUE

Q#	CJ#/Norm & Element	Stage (Notes)	Q#	CJ#/Norm & Element	Stage (Notes)
1a,5	36 life (13)	5	2,3	32 law (13)	5
ISSUE SCORE:		⑤	ISSUE SCORE:		5

DILEMMA (III)ᵃ (FORM A) OR IV' (FORM B) OR
VIII (FORM C)

(Circle Chosen Issue)

(MORALITY & CONSCIENCE ISSUE)

PUNISHMENT ISSUE

Q#	CJ#/Norm & Element	Stage (Notes)	Q#	CJ#/Norm & Element	Stage (Notes)
6,8	[34 law (12)]	G5ᵇ			
ISSUE SCORE:		(G5)	ISSUE SCORE:		G5ᶜ

DILEMMA (I) (FORM A) OR II (FORM B) OR
VII (FORM C)

(Circle Chosen Issue)

(CONTRACT ISSUE)

AUTHORITY ISSUE

Q#	CJ#/Norm & Element	Stage (Notes)	Q#	CJ#/Norm & Element	Stage (Notes)
4-6	42 cont (17)	5	2ᵈ		
			7	30 auth (17)	5ᵉ
			7b	27 auth (10)	5ᶠ
ISSUE SCORE:		⑤	ISSUE SCORE:		5

Summated   1 _____
Weightings   2 _____
From Issues: 3 _____
                  4 _____
                  5 3+2+1+1+3+2 = 12 x 5 = 60
                     60 ÷ 12

OVERALL PROTOCOL SCORE
GLOBAL: 5
WAS: 500

would have to be assigned." If "carefully handled" (Q#8), this punishment "could lead to a general increase in moral consciousness" (Q#8), so that people would start to respond to "moral imperatives that originate in human nature" and not in the law (Q#8). Given these unique responses, we assign a Stage 5 guess score to both (M&C & punishment) issues.

b- The material in Q#6 and 8 is similar to CJ#34, which is a law (serving social ideal and harmony) point. Although the material meets Critical Indicators (a) and (b), it fails (c). Therefore, we can not use it as a match score; instead, we give it a guess 5 score.

c- See a.

d- This material is *not* a match for CJ#16, which is a Stage 3 *authority* (reciprocity or positive desert) point. Although the subject uses what might be considered a similar argument ("He might learn, too, how it feels to give up one's own desires for those of another – as presumably, *his father has done*

STANDARD SCORING SHEET

DATE:
INTERVIEW No./S name: #247
SCORED BY:

FORM A / FORM B / FORM C (circle one)

DILEMMA III (FORM A) OR IV (FORM B) OR
V (FORM C)

(Circle Chosen Issue)

LIFE (FORM A) or LIFE-QUALITY
(Forms B & C) ISSUE

Q#	CJ#/Norm & Element	Stage (Notes)
2,3,4	8 life (2)	2/3
8,5	13 aff (5)	3
9	10 prop (2)	3

ISSUE SCORE: ③ᵃ

LAW (FORM A) or LAW/LIFE-PRESERV.
(Forms B & C) ISSUE

Q#	CJ#/Norm & Element	Stage (Notes)
6,8	13 aff (2)	3
10,12	18 law (9)	3/4
10	20 law (14)	3/4

ISSUE SCORE: 3 (4)

(Circle Chosen Issue)

MORALITY & CONSCIENCE ISSUE

Q#	CJ#/Norm & Element	Stage (Notes)
3,4	14 M+C (2)	3 marginalᵈ

ISSUE SCORE: 3

DILEMMA III (FORM A) OR IV' (FORM B) OR
VIII (FORM C)

PUNISHMENT ISSUE

Q#	CJ#/Norm & Element	Stage (Notes)
1	16 pun (3)	3
3,6,8,10	18 law (9)	3/4
3	[12 pun (16)	2/3ᶠ
11	[14 law (9)	3ᶜ]

ISSUE SCORE: ③ (4)

(Circle Chosen Issue)

CONTRACT ISSUE ᵉ

Q#	CJ#/Norm & Element	Stage (Notes)
2,5,11	12 prop (15)	3
4	13 aff (12)	3
12	17 cont (8)	3
13,14,18	18 cont (18)	3
16,17	22 cont (6)	3/4 marginal

ISSUE SCORE: ③

DILEMMA I (FORM A) OR II (FORM B) OR
VII (FORM C)

AUTHORITY ISSUE

Q#	CJ#/Norm & Element	Stage (Notes)
3,5,7	16 auth (15)	3
18-21	19 auth (10)	3/4

ISSUE SCORE: 3 (4)

Summated Weightings From Issues:

1 _____
2 _____
3 3+1+2+3+1 = 12×3 = 36
4 1+1+1 = 3×4 = 12
5 _____

36 + 12 = 48 ÷ 15

OVERALL PROTOCOL SCORE

GLOBAL: 3

WAS: 320

---

*for him many times in the last fourteen years''), we give it a structural veto.
What the subject is in fact saying is that if Joe were to give up his own desires
(i.e., the money with which he can go to camp), it would be for moral virtue
rather than gratitude. This is clearly higher than Stage 3.

e- See Match Example 1, CJ#30.

f- Since Q#7 has two major ideas, we separate it into two IJs. Q#7b includes
''he should show his son,'' etc., and is matched to CJ#27, Critical Indicator
(b).

Case #247

Explanation of Scoring

a- In the total calculation of the issue score, the Stage 2 is dropped because the
Stage 3 points comprise more than 75% of the issue score.

b- Do not confuse CJ#12, a 2/3 point, with CJ#18, a 3/4 point. In CJ#13, the reason for punishment is to prevent people from thinking that they are actually given permission to break the law. In CJ#18, the reason originates in people losing sight of right and wrong.

c- Although Q#11 is a match to CJ#14, it is dropped from the total issue score based on the inclusion rule (CJ#14 and CJ#18 have the same norm and element), and they express the same basic idea but at different stages.

d- Although none of the CIs are explicitly met, Critical Indicator (a) seems to be quite clearly implied. In addition, the Stage Structure is also implicitly inferred from the response; thus we give it a marginal match score.

e- Review the rules for designating chosen issue (chap. 6); remember that designating no chosen issue is *not* an option. Although the subject spontaneously answers the question with arguments for both sides of the dilemma, he appears to be leaning more toward the contract issue than toward the authority issue. In addition, the subject appears to be making a distinction between his own father (Q#3) and fathers in general. Justifying "giving the money" is grounded in the subject's actual, personal life and not in a prescriptive argument. This supports our decision to designate contract as the chosen issue.

Case #138

Explanation of Scoring

a- Q#4 is a law question and is scored under the law issue. However, the first sentence under 4, "I think life is more important than law," is a clear expression of the same Stage 3/4 point under life, and thus should be included under the life issue.

Q#1a, "Because the druggist is an asshole," *fails* CJ#11: Critical Indicator (c) is not met (see also Distinctions section). In addition, reference to the druggist's bad character as a reason for stealing (Stage 3) is a lower stage idea than the 3/4 hierarchy ("life is *more important than* . . . money") point, which is expressed repeatedly in Q#1a and #4. The higher and, in this case, more salient idea is scored.

b- Although CJ#9 is a match score it is not included in the total issue score because of the inclusion rule. CJ#9 and CJ#19 involve the same norm and element but different stages. That is, parallel, yet developmentally distinct, concepts are being expressed by the subject. According to the inclusion rule, only the higher stage concept is counted in issue scoring.

c- The idea that laws are there to *protect* people ("If you go breaking them, you *harm* someone else") by itself is nondiscriminatory as to which stage it presents (3 or 5). Therefore, there is no appropriate CJ for it. It can only be guess scored. We give it a G3/4 because of the conventional concept of hypocrisy. "Is's immoral to break the law. The druggist is breaking the law . . . if he killed the dude in stealing it, it would be hypocritical" (Q#4). Implicit in this response is the conventional notion of moral character that should be upheld. To kill while stealing would be hypocritical from the perspective of that moral character. It implies going against one's own moral standards. What is still missing here is a constructivist view of the law and less stereotypical terminology, which would make it Stage 4.

d- In Q#1a, the only part that is scored under this CJ is the idea of sympathy: Officer Brown "should be sympathetic with Heinz." The idea of leniency is supported here on the basis of sympathetic role taking with Heinz, Officer Brown, and the judge.

STANDARD SCORING SHEET

DATE:
INTERVIEW No./S name: #138
SCORED BY:

(FORM A) FORM B/ FORM C (circle one)

DILEMMA (III) (FORM A) OR IV (FORM B) OR
V (FORM C)

(Circle Chosen Issue)

(LIFE) (FORM A) or LIFE-QUALITY (Forms B & C) ISSUE			LAW (FORM A) or LAW/LIFE-PRESERV. (Forms B & C) ISSUE		
Q#	CJ#/Norm & Element	Stage (Notes)	Q#	CJ#/Norm & Element	Stage (Notes)
1,4,5	19 life (13)	3/4 ^{a}	4		G 3/4 ^{c}
2a, 3	[9 life (13)	[3] ^{b}			
ISSUE SCORE:		(3/4)	ISSUE SCORE:		G 3/4

(Circle Chosen Issue)

DILEMMA (III') (FORM A) OR IV' (FORM B) OR
VIII (FORM C)

(MORALITY & CONSCIENCE ISSUE)			PUNISHMENT ISSUE		
Q#	CJ#/Norm & Element	Stage (Notes)	Q#	CJ#/Norm & Element	Stage (Notes)
1,2,3a	18 M+C (14)	3 ^{d}	3	22 pun (14)	3/4
3a	20 life (13)	3/4	3	18 life (12)	3/4 ^{e}
ISSUE SCORE:		3(4)	ISSUE SCORE:		3/4

(Circle Chosen Issue)

DILEMMA (I) (FORM A) OR II (FORM B) OR
VII (FORM C)

(CONTRACT ISSUE)			AUTHORITY ISSUE		
Q#	CJ#/Norm & Element	Stage (Notes)	Q#	CJ#/Norm & Element	Stage (Notes)
6,2,3^f	12 prop (15)	3	8,9		G 2/3 ^{i}
6	9 cont (8)	2/3			
4,5	17 cont (8)	3 marginal ^{g}			
ISSUE SCORE:		(3) ^{h}	ISSUE SCORE:		G 2/3

Summated Weightings From Issues:	1 _____
	2 .5 X 2 = 1
	3 1.5+.5+2+1+3+.5 = 8.5 X 3 = 25.5
	4 1.5+.5+1+1 = 4 x 4 = 16
	5 _____
	1 + 25.5 + 16 = 42.5 ÷ 13

OVERALL PROTOCOL SCORE

GLOBAL: 3/4

WAS: 326

e- What is scored under the CJ is the second part of Q#3, which attaches penalties to laws because without them, "The law would be no good. People would go around breaking them. If you don't have punishment, you won't have laws." This fits Critical Indicator (b) of CJ#18 and thus gets a match score.

f- This response manifests the common Golden Rule concept, which by itself is considered nondiscriminatory among stages above 2/3. Therefore, it is not scored. If we had no other scorable points under this issue, a Guess 3 Score would have been given to this material.

g- The scorable material in Q#4 is the notion that "people who steal have to think of how important the thing is to the person they are stealing from. Property don't have to be material, like *embarrassing* you in public." This implies a concern for the other person's feelings as a manifestation of the value of keeping and upholding property rights. In Q#5, a similar idea is expressed in relation to the importance of keeping the promise to Joe because "he [father] should *put his son before himself* [and] because . . . his son was *counting on it*." We give it only a marginal score because there is an *ambiguous* fit with a Critical Indicator of CJ#17 ([a]: demonstrating *care or concern* for the other person).

h- CJ#9 and CJ#17 have the same norm and element. Based on the inclusion rule (see note b), only CJ#17 is scored. CJ#12 is also a Stage 3 point. Therefore, the total score under the contract issue is Stage 3.

i- Similar to Q#4 on the law issue, the major concept advocated is that of the Golden Rule. Here it is being applied to the father–son relationship. Since the Golden Rule by itself is nondiscriminatory, we give it only a guess score. It is a guess 2/3 point because of the concrete and relationship-dependent interpretation of the Golden Rule: "It *depends on the relationship*, whether it's good or not." In other words, one should treat another person as one would like to be treated *only* when the relationship is good (i.e., the Golden Rule should be applied only when a favorable outcome is *certain*).

Case #131

Explanation of Scoring

a- The prescriptive material supports life, and therefore that is the chosen issue.

b- CJ#12, which is a Stage 3 point, sounds like the argument in Q#1 and Q#1a yet it is not quite Stage 3. (See both Stage Structure and Critical Indicators.) Therefore, we match it to CJ#8, Stage 2/3.

c- This material resembles CJ#25; however, it fails Critical Indicator (b).

d- We match Q#4, "Oh, he has a right to do it, if he discovered it," to CJ#6, which is a Stage 2, property (having a right) point.

e- See chapter 6, Rules for Designating Chosen Issue.

f- We give this CJ a structural veto, since there is *no* reference to the idea of the *role* (of a judge, a police officer, etc.) as governing behavior and defining obligation. The fact that the subject spontaneously mentions the word *duty* does not by itself warrant a Stage 3 score. The whole issue, therefore, is assigned a guess 2/3 score.

g- The material in Q#2 resembles CJ#9, which supports punishment based on balancing perspectives or role taking. However, none of the Critical Indicators are met. Therefore, we give it, and the total issue, only a guess Stage 2 score.

h- See note on Critical Indicator of CJ#7: "References to Joe's disappointment in his father because of the breakdown of expectations in the relationship are scored at Stage 3." CJ#4, which is a clear Stage 2 point, is therefore not a match for this IJ.

i- The total issue is a guess 2/3 score, based on the material in Q#3a ("the boy is still growing up," etc.), which is an authority (upholding character) point. There is also an authority (upholding character) point at Stage 3 (CJ#15). Since, the material is clearly not Stage 3 (neither Critical Indicator nor Stage Structure of CJ#15 is met), we give it a guess 2/3 score.

Case #332

Explanation of Scoring

a- See Match Example 3, CJ#34.

b- There is very little material on the law issue, and no match CJ. According to

STANDARD SCORING SHEET

DATE:
INTERVIEW No./S name: # 131
SCORED BY:

FORM A / FORM B/ FORM C (circle one)

DILEMMA III (FORM A) OR IV (FORM B) OR
V (FORM C)

(Circle Chosen Issue)

LIFE (FORM A) or LIFE-QUALITY (Forms B & C) ISSUE

LAW (FORM A) or LAW/LIFE-PRESERV. (Forms B & C) ISSUE

Q#	CJ#/Norm & Element	Stage (Notes)	Q#	CJ#/Norm & Element	Stage (Notes)
1, 1a	8 aff (8)	2/3 b	4	6 prop (4)	2 d
1	[25 life (13)	4] c			

ISSUE SCORE: 2/3

ISSUE SCORE: 2c

(Circle Chosen Issue)

DILEMMA III (FORM A) OR IV' (FORM B) OR
VIII (FORM C)

MORALITY & CONSCIENCE ISSUE

PUNISHMENT ISSUE

Q#	CJ#/Norm & Element	Stage (Notes)	Q#	CJ#/Norm & Element	Stage (Notes)
2	[9 pun (14)]	G2 g	1,2	[16 pun (15)	3] f

ISSUE SCORE: G2

ISSUE SCORE: G 2/3

(Circle Chosen Issue)

DILEMMA I (FORM A) OR II (FORM B) OR
VII (FORM C)

CONTRACT ISSUE

AUTHORITY ISSUE

Q#	CJ#/Norm & Element	Stage (Notes)	Q#	CJ#/Norm & Element	Stage (Notes)
1,2	7 prop (8)	2/3	3a	[15 auth (10)	3] i
2	[4 prop (4)	2] h			

ISSUE SCORE: 2/3

ISSUE SCORE: G 2/3

Summated
Weightings
From Issues:

1 _____
2 1.5 + 2 + 1 + .5 + 1.5 + .5 = 7 x 2 = 14
3 1.5 + .5 + 1.5 + .5 = 4 x 3 = 12
4 _____
5 _____

14 + 12 = 26 ÷ 11

OVERALL PROTOCOL SCORE

GLOBAL: 2/3

WAS: 236

Rules for Guess Scoring (chap. 6), if a response does not resemble a CJ from its "own" issue, but resembles that of another issue, then this correspondence may be used for a guess score. CJ#7 resembles CJ#33 on the life issue and, therefore, we use it to guess score the whole issue. The issue receives a 4/5 guess score.

c- Q#2 cannot be matched. CJ#24, which is a Stage 4 point, *is not* a match.

d- The material in Q#3 sounds like a Stage 4 "maintaining law and order" point. CJ#25 is very close, yet none of the Critical Indicators can be matched. Therefore, it is not a match but a guess. However, because we already have a match Stage 4 point on this issue, the guess score is dropped.

e- Since there is very little probing in this protocol and responses are short, it is often difficult to identify the correct element used in the argument. Bearing this in mind, we match Q#1 to CJ#38 (property, serving human dignity and autonomy) and *not* to CJ#39 (property, maintaining equity), based on the au-

STANDARD SCORING SHEET

DATE:
INTERVIEW No./S name: # 332
SCORED BY:

(FORM A)/ FORM B/ FORM C (circle one)

DILEMMA II (FORM A) OR IV (FORM B) OR V (FORM C)

(Circle Chosen Issue)

LIFE (FORM A) or LIFE-QUALITY (Forms B & C) ISSUE / **LAW (FORM A) or LAW/LIFE-PRESERV. (Forms B & C) ISSUE**

Q#	CJ#/Norm & Element	Stage (Notes)	Q#	CJ#/Norm & Element	Stage (Notes)
1,2,3,5,6	34 M+C (12)	4/5ᵃ	7		G 4/5ᵇ
ISSUE SCORE:		(4/5)	ISSUE SCORE:		G 4/5

DILEMMA III (FORM A) OR IV' (FORM B) OR VIII (FORM C)

(Circle Chosen Issue)

MORALITY & CONSCIENCE ISSUE / **PUNISHMENT ISSUE**

Q#	CJ#/Norm & Element	Stage (Notes)	Q#	CJ#/Norm & Element	Stage (Notes)
3a,4,2c	31 law (14)	4/5	1	2 pun (5)	4
			3	[25 law (1)	G 4ᵈ
ISSUE SCORE:		(4/5)	ISSUE SCORE:		4

DILEMMA I (FORM A) OR II (FORM B) OR VII (FORM C)

(Circle Chosen Issue)

CONTRACT ISSUE / **AUTHORITY ISSUE**

Q#	CJ#/Norm & Element	Stage (Notes)	Q#	CJ#/Norm & Element	Stage (Notes)
1	38 prop (13)	5ᵉ	6	28 auth (13)	5
2,3	31 cont (10)	4	7	29 auth (16)	5
4,5	23 cont (17)	5			
ISSUE SCORE:		5 (4)	ISSUE SCORE:		5

Summated Weightings From Issues:

1 _____
2 _____
3 _____
4 1.5+.5+1.5+2+1 = 6.5 = 26
5 1.5+.5+1.5+2+2 = 7.5 = 37.5

26 + 37.5 = 63.5 ÷ 14

OVERALL PROTOCOL SCORE
GLOBAL: 4/5
WAS: 453

tonomy element: "Joe is an individual with equal rights to things he's earned." Also, there is *no* reference to *equity* between father and son, which is needed for CJ#39.

Case #191

Explanation of Scoring

a- The idea that "life is *more important than* anything else" doesn't imply a hierarchy of values, which is a clear 3/4 point (see Critical Indicator [c] of CJ#19). Since the IJ passes the Critical Indicator of CJ#9 we give it a match Stage 3 score. In Q#5, the same idea of the preciousness of life is expressed. It is scored together with Q#1.

b- This is a straightforward match for CJ#18. Both (a) and (b) of the Critical Indicators are passed.

STANDARD SCORING SHEET

DATE:
INTERVIEW No./S name: #191
SCORED BY:

FORM A/ FORM B/ FORM C (circle one)

DILEMMA III (FORM A) OR IV (FORM B) OR V (FORM C)

(Circle Chosen Issue)

LIFE (FORM A) or LIFE-QUALITY (Forms B & C) ISSUE

Q#	CJ#/Norm & Element	Stage (Notes)
1,5	9 life (13)	3ᵃ
2	18 life (4)	3/4ᵇ
5,6		[G3]ᶜ

ISSUE SCORE: 3(4)

LAW (FORM A) or LAW/LIFE-PRESERV. (Forms B & C) ISSUE

Q#	CJ#/Norm & Element	Stage (Notes)
7, 7a	27 law (14)	4

ISSUE SCORE: 4

DILEMMA III' (FORM A) OR IV' (FORM B) OR VIII (FORM C)

(Circle Chosen Issue)

MORALITY & CONSCIENCE ISSUE

Q#	CJ#/Norm & Element	Stage (Notes)
2F		

ISSUE SCORE: G 3/4ᵍ

PUNISHMENT ISSUE

Q#	CJ#/Norm & Element	Stage (Notes)
2	29 pun (5)	4ᵈ
3	31 pun (10)	4ᵉ

ISSUE SCORE: (4)

DILEMMA I (FORM A) OR II (FORM B) OR VII (FORM C)

(Circle Chosen Issue)

CONTRACT ISSUE

Q#	CJ#/Norm & Element	Stage (Notes)
2	24 prop (8)	4ʰ
3	29 cont (6)	4ⁱ Either one
11	33 cont (17)	4
5	32 cont (11)	4

ISSUE SCORE: (4)

AUTHORITY ISSUE

Q#	CJ#/Norm & Element	Stage (Notes)
6,6a	13 aff (14)	3
7, 7a	19 auth (10)	3/4

ISSUE SCORE: 3(4)

Summated Weightings From Issues:

1 _____
2 _____
3 .2+.5+2 = 4.5 × 3 = 13.5
4 1+2+.5+3+1 = 10.5 × 4 = 42
5 _____

13.5 + 42 = 55.5 ÷ 15

OVERALL PROTOCOL SCORE
GLOBAL: 3/4
WAS: 370

c- Part 3 of Q#5 sounds like CJ#22, which is a 3/4 relativistic point. Since, however, it does not meet the Critical Indicator, we give it only a Guess 3. In the total calculation of the life issue, this guess score, like any other guess score that appears together with a match score, is dropped.

d- Punishment is the chosen issue (Q#2: "Punish him"). Justification for punishment is based on the ideas that (a) the judge "is the servant of the law," and (b) "he is not omnipotent." CJ#29 is a clear match, on both Critical Indicators (a) and (b).

e- The idea of rehabilitation as a punishment within a *societal* perspective is a Stage 4 (CJ#31) idea. Although the subject does not use the word *rehabilitation*, the concept is implicit in the response: "*I wouldn't necessarily call it punishment . . . A person who commits the crime should be put in a situation where he benefits and society benefits because he is part of society.*" Critical Indicators (a) and (b) are both passed. Thus, we assign a Match 4.

f- In Q#2, the idea that "any court ruling *sets a precedent* . . . [because] in morals you just can't measure," though it may resemble CJ#25 on M&C, fails the Critical Indicator and the Stage Structure. Similarly, the statement, "If I were Heinz, I'd explain why I did it. I don't think they would be *heartless* so as not to understand," sounds like CJ#17 on M&C, which is based on a role-taking argument. Here again, the judgment fails both the Critical Indicator and the Stage Structure because it lacks prescriptivity.

g- The total issue score is a guess Stage 3/4. Although the closeness of part of the response to a particular CJ (as shown earlier) should not constitute a guess for the *whole* issue (i.e., an issue guess score is based on *all* the material on the issue), it nevertheless can help the scorer's general orientation. Thus, we give it a G3/4.

h- The idea in Q#2 that by earning the money himself, Joe showed "responsibility, determination, and maturity" is implicit in the Critical Indicator of CJ#24. Therefore, we give it a match score 4.

i- Both CJ#29 and CJ#33 are Stage 4 contract CJs. The former is based on a reputation element, the latter on a maintaining social contract element. Since Q#3 can be validly interpreted as either one of these elements, it is up to the scorer to choose. In either choice, the score is a Match Stage 4.

Case #168

Explanation of Scoring

a- See chosen issue discussion, chapter 6, section entitled Identification of Chosen Issue.

b- The scorable material concerns the following ideas: (Q#2) "Sure, because he could go to court"; (Q#3) "He wouldn't have to, no. If he didn't want to, he didn't have to"; (Q#5) "If he wanted to stay out of trouble, he wouldn't." They match CJ#7, Critical Indicator (b).

c- In general, we distinguish between predictive statements (e.g., Q#4) that are considered nonmoral judgment material and prescriptive ones (e.g., Q#1). (For further discussion of prescriptivity, see chap. 6, section on Scorability Criteria.) In a low-stage case, the identification of prescriptive material is not as self-evident as it is in higher stage cases. Keeping in mind that a scorable response must (a) assert that some action or value is morally preferable; (b) offer a reason or justification for the recommended action; and (c) be accepted as valid by the subject helps to differentiate between scorable and nonscorable material.

d- "No material" is designated under the punishment issue because the material under this issue does not count as an IJ. The reason for supporting punishment is absent.

e- Guess 2 is based on the idea that "fathers *know* better." Had it been a physicalistic consideration, we would give it a guess 1.

f- Q#9, "Is it worse for the father. . ." is an authority probe question that is not used in the current MJI. It is scored under the authority issue. The notion that it is worse for the father to break his promise to the son "because . . . when the son grows up, he will break all his promises to his sons," is an authority norm and upholding character (10) element. This combination of norm and element first appears at Stage 3 (see CJ#15 under the authority issue). Since, however, the material under consideration fails even the Stage Structure description of CJ#15, we give it a guess 2/3.

STANDARD SCORING SHEET

DATE:
INTERVIEW No./S name: #168'
SCORED BY:

FORM A/FORM B/ FORM C (circle one)

DILEMMA III (FORM A) OR IV (FORM B) OR V (FORM C)

(Circle Chosen Issue)

LIFE (FORM A) or LIFE-QUALITY (Forms B & C) ISSUE			LAW (FORM A) or LAW/LIFE-PRESERV. (Forms B & C) ISSUE		
Q#	CJ#/Norm & Element	Stage (Notes)	Q#	CJ#/Norm & Element	Stage (Notes)
1,3	7 aff (7)	2	2,3,5,4ᶜ	8 law (7)	2ᵇ
ISSUE SCORE:		②ᵃ	ISSUE SCORE:		2

(Circle Chosen Issue)

DILEMMA III (FORM A) OR IV' (FORM B) OR VIII (FORM C)

MORALITY & CONSCIENCE ISSUE			PUNISHMENT ISSUE		
Q#	CJ#/Norm & Element	Stage (Notes)	Q#	CJ#/Norm & Element	Stage (Notes)
2	7 M+C (4)	2		no material	
ISSUE SCORE:		2	ISSUE SCORE:		Nmᵈ

(Circle Chosen Issue)

DILEMMA I (FORM A) OR II (FORM B) OR VII (FORM C)

CONTRACT ISSUE			AUTHORITY ISSUE		
Q#	CJ#/Norm & Element	Stage (Notes)	Q#	CJ#/Norm & Element	Stage (Notes)
3,4,6	4 prop (4)	2	1,2	[auth (10)]	G 2ᶜ
			9		G 2/3ᶠ
ISSUE SCORE:		2	ISSUE SCORE:		G 2/3ᵍ

Summated Weightings From Issues:	1 _____
	2 $3+2+2+2+.5=9.5\times2=19$
	3 $.5\times3=1.5$
	4 _____
	5 _____
	$19+1.5=20.5\div10$

OVERALL PROTOCOL SCORE

GLOBAL: 2

WAS: 205

g- Review Rules for Guess Scoring (chap. 6). Because a guess score is given the lowest weight (1 point) even if it is on the chosen issue, a major–minor guess score 2(3) and a transitional guess score 2/3 are treated the same; 1/2 point is assigned to each stage. Therefore, in the present case the total guess score under the authority issue can be designated as either 2(3) or 2/3 and receives 1/2 point for each stage.

Case #7

Explanation of Scoring

a- This is only a marginal match point because (a) there is lack of explicit reference to an individual's right to life (see Stage Structure) though it is strongly implied in the response, and (b) the element (13) – serving human dignity and autonomy – is ambiguous (see Distinctions section in CJ).

STANDARD SCORING SHEET

DATE:
INTERVIEW No./_S_ name: M
SCORED BY:

(FORM A) FORM B/ FORM C (circle one)

DILEMMA II (FORM A) OR IV (FORM B) OR
V (FORM C)

(Circle Chosen Issue)

LIFE (FORM A) or LIFE-QUALITY
(Forms B & C) ISSUE

LAW (FORM A) or LAW/LIFE-PRESERV.
(Forms B & C) ISSUE

Q#	CJ#/Norm & Element	Stage (Notes)	Q#	CJ#/Norm & Element	Stage (Notes)
1,2,3	36 life (13)	5	4,5	32 law (23)	5 marginal [a]
			5	28 law (12)	4/5 [b]

ISSUE SCORE: (5)   ISSUE SCORE: 5 (4)

DILEMMA III (FORM A) OR IV' (FORM B) OR
VIII (FORM C)

(Circle Chosen Issue)

MORALITY & CONSCIENCE ISSUE

PUNISHMENT ISSUE

Q#	CJ#/Norm & Element	Stage (Notes)	Q#	CJ#/Norm & Element	Stage (Notes)
1a,5	32 cont (10)	4/5 [c]	3,9		
2	[31 law (14)	G 4/5] [d]	4	[26 law (9)	4] [h]
3a		[G 5] [e]	4a	[32 pun (14)	4] [i]

ISSUE SCORE: (4/5) [f]   ISSUE SCORE: G 5 [j]

DILEMMA I (FORM A) OR II (FORM B) OR
VII (FORM C)

(Circle Chosen Issue)

CONTRACT ISSUE

AUTHORITY ISSUE

Q#	CJ#/Norm & Element	Stage (Notes)	Q#	CJ#/Norm & Element	Stage (Notes)
3,4,6 [L]	38 prop (13)	5 [k]	8,8a [m]		
			9	29 auth (16)	5
			9a	28 auth (13)	5 [h]

ISSUE SCORE: (5)   ISSUE SCORE: 5

Summated 1 _____
Weightings 2 _____
From Issues: 3 _____

OVERALL PROTOCOL SCORE
GLOBAL: 5
WAS: 480

4 $1 + 1.5 = 2.5 \times 4 = 10$
5 $3 + 2 + 1.5 + 1 + 3 + 2 = 10.5 \times 5 = 52.5$
$10 + 52.5 = 62.5 \div 13$

b- The second part of Q#5, "to promote a more harmonious society," etc., is match scored to CJ#28 based on both the norm (law) and the element (serving social ideal and harmony).

c- This is a matched point because both Critical Indicators (a) and (b) of CJ#32 are present in the IJ.

d- Since Critical Indicator (a) of CJ#31 is missing, this response warrants only a guess score.

e- Usually Q#3 is scored under the punishment issue (Should a lawbreaker be punished?). However, when, as in the present case, the probe question addresses disagreement with the subject's prior argument (Q#3), a reassessment of the scored issue is in order. Since the subject rejects his "punishment as deterrence" argument, the scored issue for Question 3a is M&C. The argument the subject presents is based on a combination of a punishment norm with a serving human dignity and autonomy element. This is a rare and idiosyncratic argument and, therefore, it has not been represented in the manual as a CJ. However, it warrants a guess Stage 5 score. For the scorer, such in-depth analysis is necessary *only* when there are *no* other scorable points. Otherwise, it can be ignored.

f- The two guess scores are dropped based on the guess scoring rules, which state that if one or more match scores have been assigned to an issue, no guess scores are entered.

g- No score is assigned because the subject *rejects* (in Q#3a) the utilitarian argument for punishment as deterrence, which he projected onto the judge.

h- Although the argument in Q#4 *sounds* like CJ#26, which is a Stage 4 law (good group consequences) point, it *lacks* emphasis on deterrence as protecting social functioning and social maintenance (see both critical indicators and matched examples of CJ#26, Form A, Volume II).

i- Here again, as in Q#4, the response might be mistakenly identified as a Stage 4 punishment point based on balancing perspectives or role taking (CJ#32): A lawbreaker has to pay the consequences of his/her actions or be held *responsible*. However, the subject claims that an individual "*deserves* to be responsible for his actions [because] if you don't punish him, you rob him of his responsibility and *thus* his *personhood*." In other words, punishment is needed, not in order to maintain social order (as in Stage 4), but to maintain personal integrity or personhood, which is a Stage 5 idea.

j- The guess score is needed here because of the idiosyncratic expression of ideas in this protocol such that though structurally scorable as Stage 5, this particular manifestation of the structure expressed by the subject has not been represented among CJs in Form A, Volume II. It is structurally a Stage 5 idea because (a) the subject clearly stands outside of society; (b) he advocates a constructivist view of the law – i.e., law comes from within and not from without; (c) punishment is necessary in order to maintain personal integrity and not for maintaining social order and smooth social functioning (as at Stage 4).

k- Both Critical Indicator (a) and (b) of CJ#32 are present: (a) "the basic importance is the *right* to the property, *not the property* itself"; and (b) "if we take [someone's property], we are violating his *personhood*."

l- The notion that a promise should be kept because "*we hurt others* if we break the promise" by *itself* is unscorable; concern with hurting other's *feelings*, for example, is a Stage 3 response, while concern with hurting others' sense of autonomy and personhood is a Stage 5 idea.

m- Although this question is usually scored under the authority issue, here it includes contract material. See (l) as to why it is not scored.

n- This is a clear Stage 5 response. Two CJs are assigned because of the two different elements presented: CJ#28 is matched on the basis of the serving human dignity and autonomy (13) element: "children are people . . . people have rights." CJ#29 is matched on the basis of the maintaining equity (13) element: "Your rights as a parent are not necessarily '*more right*' than theirs."

General Note: Case #7 is a particularly difficult case to score. This is largely due to the idiosyncratic expression of the subject's ideas. Since most of the material is Stage 5 or 4/5, it makes scoring even harder. In addition, the probe questions are fairly uncommon. This complicates even the relatively easy process of assigning material to the correct issue.

Moral Judgment Practice Cases, Form B

Case # 116

Dilemma IV

1. *Should Dr. Jefferson give her the drug that would make her die?*

   Yes. To get her out of her pain so she doesn't have to live for the next six months in pain – to get her out of her pain. If she wants to die anyway, and she is going to die anyway. She is just taking up a bed in the hospital and there are other people who might be helped who would need the treatment.

2. *Should the woman have the right to make the final decision?*

   Yes. Because it is her own life and especially her, because she is in so much pain. *Why is it important that it is her life? What do you mean?* She is the one in pain. She knows she won't live long. She's in pain, not the doctor.

3. *The woman is married. Should her husband have anything to do with the decision?*

   No. He would probably say no anyway. He wouldn't want her to die. He would want to keep her as long as he could.

4. *Is there any way a person has a duty or obligation to live when he or she does not want to, when the person wants to commit suicide?*

   It depends on the circumstances. A person in pain who is going to die anyway should be able to [commit suicide]. A person who just wants to get out of trouble – it's pretty stupid. *Why is this stupid?* Because he/she has hope for something. He/she can probably work whatever is wrong out.

5. *It is against the law for the doctor to give the woman the drug. Does that make it morally wrong?*

   No.

5a. *Why or why not?*

   Because if he feels that he should give the woman the drug because she feels that she should die, then he should [give her the drug]. Sometimes the law has to be bent too – you can't keep going by the law. *Why should the law be bent in this case?* The lady is in too much pain for the law to butt in on her life.

6. *Should people try to do everything they can to obey the law?*

   So they won't get in trouble and go to jail. There is no reason to break the law on purpose just to go to jail.

6a. *How does this apply to what Dr. Jefferson should do?*

   He can make it so that he didn't break the law, if he just gave her a little too much ether.

Dilemma IV'

1. *Should Dr. Rogers report Dr. Jefferson?*

   It depends on how good a friend he is with him, and all that. If he was a good friend, I don't think he would want to send him to jail.

2. *Should the judge give Dr. Jefferson some sentence, or should he suspend the sentence and let Dr. Jefferson go free?*

He should suspend the sentence.

2a. *Why?*

Because he didn't hurt anyone in doing it. He helped her – he got her out of the pain.

3. *Thinking in terms of society, should people who break the law be punished?*

I don't think that everyone who breaks the law should be punished. It depends on why they did it. Say they rob a store or shoplift because they don't have enough food, that would be a good reason [to break the law] I think.

3a. *How does this relate to Dr. Jefferson's case?*

Like before, I said, he shouldn't be punished because he didn't hurt anyone and it was needed that she be killed.

4. *The jury finds Dr. Jefferson legally guilty of murder. Would it be wrong or right for the judge to give him the death sentence (a legally possible punishment)? Why?*

No. Because the lady asked him to kill her. Anyone else wouldn't want to be in pain like that without dying.

5. *Is it ever right to give the death sentence? Why or why not? What are the conditions when the death sentence should be given in your opinion? Why are these conditions important?*

Yes, if someone kills people for no reason at all, that doesn't make any sense. They should be put to death.

6. *Dr. Jefferson was doing what his conscience told him when he gave the woman the drug. Should a lawbreaker be punished if he is acting out of conscience?*

It depends on what the case is, first of all. If someone's conscience was telling him that he didn't like someone, and he didn't want him around, and he just killed him for that – there would be no reason for it. That would be selfish. If it was like Dr. Jefferson, he was trying to help someone in doing this. He wouldn't feel right seeing the lady in pain every day.

Dilemma II

1. *Should Louise, the older sister, tell their mother that Judy had lied about the money or should she keep quiet?*

She should keep quiet and mind her own business.

1a. *Why?*

I don't know how she thinks, but I feel that the mother was wrong changing her mind after she had saved up the money. Since Judy worked to save up the money, the mother let her down. That just doesn't make any sense.

2. *In wondering whether to tell, Louise thinks of the fact that Judy is her sister. Should that make a difference in Louise's decision?*

No. Because it was wrong for the mother to change her mind. Judy shouldn't tell her mother that she went to the concert. She saved the money for it and she had to go to it.

3. *Is the fact that Judy earned the money herself the most important thing in this situation?*

She had to sacrifice some of her lunch and give up a lot of her time to get the money. She proved that she could earn the money. If the mother wants her to buy clothes, she should give her the money.

4. *The mother promised Judy she could go to the concert if she earned the money. Is the fact that the mother promised the most important thing in the situation?*

The promise is important for the mother. She shouldn't promise something and then change her mind and let the kid down.

5. *Why in general should a promise be kept?*

I'm not saying that all promises should be kept, because a person plans for what the promise was and expects it and it shouldn't be changed for a dumb reason.

6. *Is it important to keep a promise to someone you don't know well and probably won't see again?*

No.

6a. *Why or why not?*

Not really, because if you will never see them again and you don't know them well, it's probably not an important promise. If it really meant something to the stranger, then you should keep it.

7. *What do you think is the most important thing a daughter should be concerned about in her relationship to her mother?*

That she is going to do something that is against what her mother said. Then she shouldn't tell her just to keep her mother happy.

7a. *Why is that the most important thing?*

So they will stay on friendly terms. *Why?* If she doesn't stay on friendly terms, her mother can do a lot of things that wouldn't be nice.

8. *What do you think is the most important thing a mother should be concerned about in her relationship to her daughter?*

When she makes a decision she should make sure it isn't selfish.

8a. *Why is that the most important thing?*

The daughter or whomever wouldn't respect her mother or any decision that she makes. She wouldn't be as friendly with her.

Case #239

Dilemma IV

1. *Should Dr. Jefferson give her the drug?*

   Yes. Because everyone has the right to decide if they have lived long enough or want to end their life. She isn't strong enough to end it herself.

2. *Why does she have that right?*

   I think it's part of your basic freedom to live your life the way you choose within certain limits, and the right to choose to die is just a continuation of this basic right.

3. *Can you say a bit more about self-determination and why that is a right?*

   It's bound up with being allowed to make certain choices about how one wants to live, how one wants to raise children. There are many societies where one isn't given those choices, but I think that is the best way for human beings to live. I don't think that is a God-given right, I just have the feeling that that is the way things should be. It can be justified in terms of the alternatives being forms of tyranny and these can be argued against in terms of being cruel and immoral. They may be more efficient but they are unkind.

4. *Suppose the woman is married? Should her husband be involved in the decision?*

   I would think it would be a good thing for two people who are married to discuss it. He's obviously involved in it being closer to her than anyone. If they are close and have a very good relationship I think yes he should have a lot to do with it. But ultimately the decision is hers because especially this is a time in her life (dying) when she should make the decision herself.

5. *Is there any way one has an obligation to live if you don't want to?*

   Depends on the circumstances. If you're a healthy young mother but depressed, and have responsibilities to husband and children, then I think it could be incredibly selfish. In this situation, though, the woman is going to die anyway, she is in tremendous pain and is really not a functioning human being and not the person she was to her husband and children and friends. She's more a breathing machine than a human with human qualities. So it's a different situation. I still believe people have a right to do with their lives what they want but it's important to recognize a certain point when you have to think about other people. Trouble is, in a suicide case the person is usually too involved with themselves to think like this, or are doing it to scare someone – so it's hard to generalize.

6. *Mercy killing is against the law. Does that make it morally wrong?*

   Well, moral right and legal right often overlap but not necessarily. I think generally, in a free society, laws are made to protect the rights I talked about before and function in a moral framework. But the process by which laws are made by men and women account (through inculcation) for the overlap with morality, even though there is nothing inherent in the legal system to make this happen. It is rather a system that builds upon itself – at this point anyway; it's self-refer-

283

ential. Also views of what is right and wrong often change and the machinery of the law takes time to catch up. Also the law reflects old ideas and the law's view of mercy killing and suicide are based on the Christian ethic as being a sin against God. Probably in the end though, things even out. I guess I think the law and morality should be as much alike as possible, the more alike the better. Its just that the law system is very self-contained. But actually in the last couple of years we have seen the legalization of abortion: People changed their view of what was right and wrong and the laws did change to reflect this. But that is another example of morality being so subjective so now some people feel that the law is out of step with morality whereas it was in line before. I have a strong opinion that the law now on abortion is right. But I can understand others having another opinion and respect that. So the law is always more tangible than people's views of morality and it has to be because society functions on the basis of its legal laws.

7. *Do you think your position is more valid than others'?*

It's hard to say. Every issue has its nuances. I feel strongly about the abortion issue. I feel people have a right to abortion but also feel strongly against people telling other people whether they can or not. It's hard to criticize people when they take a stand through a strong concern with the issue of life. But if they were antiabortion because of reasons of illegality then I would definitely say they were wrong.

8. *What are the criteria by which you reason these responses?*

It's based on certain premises: fundamental convictions about what is just and unjust. My opinion and feelings stem from that, and also a lot of it is just gut reactions.

9. *Insofar as you feel people should obey the law, why do you think they should?*

Insofar as the law protects those freedoms we talked about and enables people to have those rights in society.

10. *How does this apply to this dilemma?*

What this doctor is doing is just helping this woman who couldn't do her chosen act herself because she was physically weak. Crimes that are directed against oneself fall into another category: prostitution and drug abuse (victimless crimes) where society or the law decides we have to protect people from themselves – it's paternalistic. I think the law should be more to protect people from each other, from rape and pillage, where their rights are infringed. Whereas the decision made between this woman, her husband, and the doctor doesn't really affect society, it is just between themselves. I don't think the law should tell people how to live their lives except when this affects other people. Laws based on moral precepts about how to live with other people are good, but it shouldn't tell people how to live their own lives.

Dilemma IV'

1. *Do you think Rogers should report him?*

I think not. But it depends on the doctor. If he feels that mercy killing is wrong then I can understand he would feel compelled to report him. But I don't feel that way. If I were in that situation I would probably discuss it with Dr. Jefferson, I wouldn't just go and report him. It's a hard thing because you probably do have an obligation to the hospital. A lot of loyalties come into conflict. I don't think I would end up reporting him but that is based on the premise that I agree with what he is doing here, and because I feel that he might lose his job. That's why you have to discuss it with Dr. Jefferson. I'm remembering the case of a doctor in Canada a couple of years ago who was well respected and performed a lot of abortions. He wanted to show how wrong the abortion law was and used himself as a test case. He was very courageous but he did succeed in drawing attention to the issue. Though I can understand another doctor not wanting to crusade like that. I don't think Dr. Jefferson has an obligation to do that.

2. *What sentence if reported?*

I think leaving aside whether you think what he did was justified, I think nothing would be served by having the judge give some sentence because the purpose of jail is to deter crime and from repetition of crime. This is a man who is valuable to society and you will make it impossible for him to help if he is imprisoned. Then also I don't think what he did was wrong. I accept the verdict that there was a legal crime committed but that leaves out other concerns. I see you have to respect the decision of the jury but the judge may not consider what he did was wrong.

3. *Why does the judge have to respect the decision of the jury?*

You have a complicated structure in which people who are guilty do get punished usually. To ensure justice is served you do have to use the system and it does have safeguards in it, like safeguards. So there is no point going through all these procedures if then at the end you just ignore it.

4. *Anything more about why lawbreakers should be punished?*

Not really. In this case, no matter how right he thought he was, he's not going to do it again, so in terms of the state trying to deter him punishment is irrelevant. The whole business of having to go through the trial would, I imagine, put the doctor off ever doing this again. And the publicity from the trial would be adequate deterrent to other doctors. Not that I think that is right, but I'm thinking from the judge's point of view and his concern to deter crime. Generally I'm against capital punishment but lately I've come to see there are certain situations where it might be the best solution: like terrorism. However, in general I do think it is wrong. There is the possibility of mistakes happening. And I don't think the state should be put in the role of murderer, which is what happens. But as I say, there are exceptions: In the terrorism case, if the state does not execute then it may be the indirect cause of many more murders. Capturing terrorists and putting them in jail does not deter them, in fact it only inflames them.

5. *What is wrong with the state being a murderer in other cases than terrorism punishment?*

I think the state has to have less of a personal vindictive attitude. In this country we avoid feudal eye-for-an-eye stuff by our legal system which is more detached and I think ultimately that safeguards against rash behavior. I think to maintain respect for the law it is important that the law remain detached and not assume the role of murderer. But I really haven't thought it out too well.

Dilemma II

1. *Should Louise tell the mother?*

    No. She'd be violating her sister's trust. It would be after the fact and therefore no purpose would be served. It's important not to violate the trust because that would damage the relationship with the sister. Very soon Judy wouldn't tell Louise anything.

2. *Is it important that Judy earned the money herself?*

    Yeah, sure. The fact that she earned it gave her a right to do with it what she wanted. She worked for it with something in mind – she probably baby-sat twice as much as she would have otherwise because she wanted to go to the rock concert.

3. *Why should one have that right in general?*

    If you are in a society where you know that you have no choice about what you do with your property it's different but here you have the freedom if you work for something to do that thing. There is an implicit promise which is then broken. And this is what happened in this case – the mother promised and then broke her word.

4. *Was the promise important?*

    Oh yes, crucial because if she had told her mother in the beginning and her mother had said she thought it was wrong to go, then they could have argued about it there and probably Judy would have stuck by and accepted the decision. But as it is Judy sacrificed and worked hard and then at the last minute her mother tells her to buy school clothes. It is not fair. It is central because Judy expected to be able to do something and then couldn't. Judy's disobedience would have been more severe if she had known in advance.

5. *Why in general is it important to keep promises?*

    It's back to the thing about the relationship with the sisters. It's a foundation for trust. If you break promises it affects the basis of what human relationships are founded on.

6. *How about a stranger?*

    Yes. Maybe less important because you don't have a relationship to endanger with them. But it is still important because one should have a society in which you take what people say at face value and know that they will follow through. Such a society is good because you have human relationships and know where you stand. If I were the stranger I'd rather someone say no they can't do this for me than promise and then break their word. It's a question of honesty and knowing where you stand.

7. *Most important thing in daughter's relationship with mother?*

    To love that person, trust them, and have mutual respect.

8. *Mother's relationship to daughter?*

    Same thing. Well love may not be the foundation for all human relations. But it is for all close human relations and family relations. Mutual respect is important for people to relate to each other and accept certain things or it will get screwed up. In mother–daughter relations there are other factors because parents raise children and you are responsible for instilling those very things in them. There is also a question of obedience, which I think is important for safety – like not riding your bicycle in the street, or eating a boxful of cookies.

In the Judy situation it would be different if Louise told before the fact realizing what Judy proposed to do might be dangerous. Like everything in life there is a trade-off: Would it be worth breaking the trust to look after sister's safety (i.e., something higher)? But this situation is different because there is no question about safety.

9. *What do you mean by "instilling"? What justifies it?*

I don't know if it is justified. Some people do it more consciously especially if they are religious. On the other hand I think parents do it whether they want to or not by example – it's unavoidable. It's not a question of right or wrong; if you have children that live with you they see how you act as they grow up. I think it's justifiable to consciously instill your values on your children – that's one of the reasons people have children, they want to perpetuate something of themselves and their ideals and that is all right within reason. I don't think it's really a question of right or wrong though. Parents just have a responsibility to raise their children to an awareness of morality. But children naturally react against it – it's a pendulum thing. So it's not right or wrong.

Case #114

Dilemma IV

1. *Should Dr. Jefferson give her the drug that would make her die?*

If she signed a written contract that she requested it and said that she was sane, then I don't know why she couldn't do it. It isn't like Karen Quinlan because she couldn't decide. The cancer didn't affect her mind. It would keep the doctor from getting in trouble. If the doctor let her make a decision where there's a question of whether she is stable, then it is his fault whether she signed a contract.

2. *Should the woman have the right to make the final decision?*

Yes. [It is] any person's right to decide to live or die. I don't believe in a religion that says it is against some law to take your life. It is your life to decide what to do with it. Speaking in terms of being sane, if she is insane, she should be treated for that.

3. *The woman is married. Should her husband have anything to do with the decision?*

No.

3a. *Why or why not?*

The laws of marriage have nothing to do with the law of living. Obviously, it would hurt him, but I would be hurt more to see her live in pain. [It's the] same as abortion.

4. *Is there any way a person has a duty or obligation to live when he or she does not want to, when the person wants to commit suicide?*

To other people or to themselves. Themselves – to find out if there is a way they could live. Only duty to others if the disease isn't fatal. If it is, then they will die anyway. It puts them out of misery sooner. If the disease is not fatal, then killing themselves would be wrong to themselves and would put pain to loved ones that could be saved.

5. *It is against the law for the doctor to give the woman the drug. Does that make it morally wrong?*

No.

5a. *Why or why not?*

Because the law applies to specific cases and every case is different. It might have been morally right when the law was made, but it might not apply to this person.

6. *Should people try to do everything they can to obey the law?*

Because if everyone thought nothing of breaking the law, there would be no point in having that law. It can't be a fling to break the law. It has to be a well-thought-out decision.

6b. *How does this apply to what Dr. Jefferson should do?*

Dr. Jefferson should break the law. And he has thought about it; he is not doing it *just* to break the law. That is not his reason.

Dilemma IV'

1. *Should Dr. Rogers report on Dr. Jefferson?*

It depends on whether Dr. Rogers agrees with Dr. Jefferson. If he does report Dr. Jefferson, it won't help the woman. But if he feels that Dr. Jefferson was irrational and would hurt others, he should. But he should discuss with Dr. Jefferson and find out that he is not just an irrational man that likes to kill many.

2. *Should the judge give Dr. Jefferson some sentence, or should he suspend the sentence and let Dr. Jefferson go free?*

Former case – sentenced to go to small town. That is fair. He would still go on helping people but would be forced to do without some former luxuries. I don't think he should be put in jail for something as delicate as a moral decision. And, though I agree with his decision, if he was found guilty it is not right for the judge to let him go free. So it is a. . . .

3. *Thinking in terms of society, should people who break the law be punished?*

Because if people could break laws without any penalty, then there would be no point to the law. Though I don't agree with the choice of penalty, in general, jails. They are not helpful to people who break laws. It breaks the man and they end up back in the same place.

3a. *How does this apply to how the judge should decide?*

In Dr. Jefferson's case, it is a question of the law, which is why we have the ability to change law. We should have a chance to discuss whether that law is applicable.

4. *The jury finds Dr. Jefferson legally guilty of murder. Would it be wrong or right for the judge to give him the death sentence (a legally possible punishment)? Why?*

Why should we kill people who kill people just to show that killing people is wrong? It won't do any good. And I don't believe it was murder. If he had a contract, it couldn't be murder. They'd probably say. . . .

5. *Is it ever right to give the death sentence? Why or why not? What are the conditions when the death sentence should be given in your opinion? Why are these conditions important?*

If it is requested by the accused. When a man requests a death sentence after committing a crime, how can that be right and not a mercy killing case? What gives judges the right to kill and not a doctor?

6. *Dr. Jefferson was doing what his conscience told him when he gave the woman the drug. Should a lawbreaker be punished if he is acting out of conscience?*

Because he's not breaking the law just to break it. He must feel that breaking the law is the only way to perform the job he has sworn to do.

Dilemma II

1. *Should Louise, the older sister, tell their mother that Judy had lied about the money or should she keep quiet?*

Keep quiet.

1a. *Why?*

I would. It's nice for my brother and I to keep secrets. Especially when her mother promised her and then changed her mind. If her mom wants her to learn to respect a promise and not lie, then she has to be a good model. Judy could take her broken promise as a lie.

2. *In wondering whether to tell, Louise thinks of the fact that Judy is her sister. Should that make a difference in Louise's decision?*

Yes. Because she is her sister, she shouldn't tell. [See first question.]

3. *Is the fact that Judy earned the money herself the most important thing in this situation?*

[The] money won't buy many clothes. It seems like a feeble reason for a mother to keep her from going to the concert.

4. *The mother promised Judy she could go to the concert if she earned the money. Is the fact that the mother promised the most important thing in this situation?*

Yes.

4a. *Why or why not?*

Her mother made her a promise on the condition and she met the condition. And then her mom broke the promise. Her mother should set a model or next time Judy could break her promise to the mother. Her mother would then punish her.

5. *Why in general should a promise be kept?*

For the principle of the promise. If you make a promise, it is a bond that says, "I won't change my mind" and if you change your mind, then there is no point to having made the promise.

6. *Is it important to keep a promise to someone you don't know well and probably won't see again?*

You have to be consistent in your beliefs for yourself. You are lying to yourself if you keep promises to someone you know and not to someone else.

7. *What do you think is the most important thing a daughter should be concerned about in her relationship to her mother?*

Have an honest relationship.

7a. *Why is that the most important thing?*

Honest not just without lies and promises, but also talking to one another, about experiences. A daughter has traits like her mom and if she can learn from her mom's experience, she will be helped.

8. *What do you think is the most important thing a mother should be concerned about in her relationship to her daughter?*

Not to be overprotective, but not too unprotective, and try and understand. It can make the girl unable to be an individual; it can make her irresponsible and [she] needs that to live alone.

8a. *Why is that the most important thing?*

If she can't understand then it will make for fights. Things are said that aren't meant. Doesn't accomplish anything but bad feelings.

Case #867

Dilemma IV

1. *Should Dr. Jefferson give the drug?*

Yes. *O.K., why should he give her the drug?* She was in a lot of pain and . . . and . . . it's her life, and I guess, the people who love her, they have to feel her pain, and especially if they really care about her, and it's painful for them to feel her pain.

2. *Should the woman have the right to the final decision?*

Yes. *Why? Her word over everyone else's? In other words, should it be her decision whether she lives or dies?* No. *Why not?* Well, yes. *You changed your mind? Why would you say she should?* Because she lives her life, and she feels she's in so much pain, it hurts her to live, she has nothing to live for. She has nothing to look forward to . . . She just isn't a person. *You mean being in such pain?* Yeah. It's costing the people she loves a lot of money to just keep her alive, when she feels she really doesn't . . . she's lived her life, and she's going to spend six more months being, well, in agony. *That's an interesting answer.* I think she would rather die a quiet death, than a violent death, painless. If I die, I'd like to die in calm.

3. *Should her husband have anything to say about the decision?*

Yeah . . . and her close friends. *Why? Why?* Because they're like a part of her, they care about her . . . and they're the ones who should help her.

4. *Does she have an obligation to live?*

Depending on the reason. *O.K., what kind of reasons do you think would be good reasons to live, even though you wanted to commit suicide?* You've lived your live, you've lived it to the full extent, you feel fulfilled with your life. *Suppose you were in terrible pain, like the woman in the example, and you wanted to commit suicide, for whatever reason. Would you have any reason to stay alive, even though you didn't want to?* No, unless someone else's life depends on you . . . let's say there's some ridiculous situation, unless her being able to say something about something else to clear something up. *Can you give an example of something that someone would have to live for?* Maybe that small chance that there might be some miracle drug or something. Or maybe to wait for a certain event that she's been waiting for, a special event. *Like Christmas?* Whatever . . . the last Christmas or something.

5. *It is against the law; does that make it morally wrong?*

Yeah . . . well, I think it should go through the court process to see if there is a good reason to just cut the wires. *What do you mean, a court process?* To really see if this person has not much to live for. *But now it's against the law. Going back to the original story, the doctor is thinging about giving her the drug, even though it's against the law. Does that make it morally wrong?* I don't think it would be his decision . . . Oh. He's the one who's going to be giving it to her. *Right.* So that doctor would be liable for her death, even if he placed the drugs next to her bed, and she took it herself. *That's right, there have been times when that has happened to doctors.* No, it's not right for him to give her the drug. *Why not?* You know, discussing it with her husband and friends and staff. *Suppose her husband disagreed? Suppose he didn't want her to be given the drug?* Depending on the reason. Just because he can't face her with the fact that she's dying, you know, he just might not be able to face the fact that she's dead. He wants to think it over. She's actually going to be gone in awhile. And he's just holding on to her for his selfish reasons. And she really feels . . . well, how much it's hurting.

6. *In general, should laws be obeyed?*

Yeah. *Why?* Because usually the laws are reasonable, they're made for the best, because people made the laws. *How does this apply to what Dr. Jefferson should do?* Well, maybe in that case the law is not the best. *On one hand you're saying that you should obey the law, and the law is reasonable, but on the other hand* . . . Well, not all of it is for the best. *When should people break the law, and when should people follow the law?* I don't think the doctor should really give this woman the drug. I think it should go through legally, because this guy would be liable, and he'd be put down for murder, and they'd take his doctorate license, you know, his future would be at stake. *But you said in Question 5* . . . But if that could not be done . . . I think what I'd do if I were the doctor, I'd have a big mix-up, as to who gives it where and how . . . maybe a mix-up as to who put it there, you know? So they couldn't really pin it on one person. If it couldn't go through a court process.

Dilemma IV'

1. *Should Rogers report Dr. Jefferson?*

   No, unless there was . . . no. *Why not?* Because this doctor felt that he did the humane thing . . . and the right thing to do, and I wouldn't feel that . . . I was going to say killing, but it really isn't – because actually, she was dead. *What do you mean dead? She's still alive.* You know in such pain and everything, except for a few rare moments of sanity. She felt herself that she was dead, you know, that she was not contributing anything to society. She's just out of it.

2. *Should the judge give a sentence or set him free?*

   The judge should let him go free . . . *You mean Dr. Jefferson did?* Yeah, he felt obligated to this woman as a fellow human being. *And so?* He just shortened the time she had to live. *What do you think it means to be obligated to another human being?* To do . . . I don't know. If the word obligated means . . . like he felt . . . *Do you feel obligated to another human being?* Sometimes. *When?* I wouldn't say obligated in the same sense . . . but I borrowed things, you know, someone did something for me, you know, and I feel obligated to do something for them.

3. *In general, should people who break the law be punished?*

   If the laws that they break were reasonable laws, you know, laws in the best interest of the people. But you know, some laws aren't right. *Why aren't they right?* Some people might just say to the doctor, they're in pain but it's going to blow over, or they might say, "Doctor, doctor, pull the plug . . . take the machine away from me, I just want to go up to heaven" . . . you know . . . I think that's why the law is bad. *Which law?* The law . . . I don't know how the law states . . . for a doctor to indirectly kill a patient, because they just say so. You know, just give me this drug . . . it will make me feel better that I die in a shorter time, I don't mind." *What about if people break a law that's reasonable?* No . . . well, and it's not reasonable for that person to go against the law? Well, then I think that person should be punished. *How does this apply to what the judge should decide, in the case of Dr. Jefferson?* If I was that doctor, and I was taking care of this patient, and she was going through a great deal of pain, and I would feel a great deal of relief, and I guess everyone else would, you know, to give the drug. *But how does this apply to the judge?* What should the judge do? Yes. I guess just put himself in the doctor's shoes. I said to myself, what would I do if I were the doctor.

4. *What about giving the death penalty?*

   It would be wrong, because he did not commit brutal murder, out of insanity or hate. He didn't feel any hate.

5. *What about the death penalty in general?*

   In some cases, the death sentence should be given, people who just kill people out of total insanity, or hate, and mass murderers. You know this guy, Son of Sam? He's saying things like "Sam made me do it." I don't watch the news too much, but if he's saying this, and psychiatrists find this true, that he's getting vibes, that just totally take over him, it would be kinda hard to kill this guy. *If Sam could prove this was true should he get the death sentence?* No. *Why not?* It was not him who did it. It might have been his fault for accepting those vibes, but he might not have wanted, or known what he was doing. You don't really say, "I won't really accept these spirits," or whatever.

6. *Should a lawbreaker be punished if he is acting out of conscience?*

I don't understand. *Do you know what the word conscience means?* Like your inner self. *Suppose your conscience told you that you should do something that was against the law?* If I did it to achieve something good, it would be O.K. *What would be something good?* I don't know, something like the story. *The doctor?* Yes. *Should a lawbreaker be punished then, if he is acting out of his conscience?* It was his decision to give it to her, but it was her decision to take it.

Dilemma II

1. *Should Louise tell her Mother?*

She should keep quiet. *Why?* I want to know one thing. Is this a middle-income family? *Why does that make a difference?* To me, eight dollars won't go far, for someone who doesn't get eight dollars so often, it goes a long way. *Suppose it was someone like us?* She shouldn't tell, because in the beginning the mother said yes, she could go. She was probably disappointed. *That's why Judy went. But what about Louise?* Because it's important to Judy to go to the concert. Because she told her sister in secret. I'd get very mad if I told someone in secret, and thought they weren't going to say anything, and they went and told.

2. *Does it make a difference that it's her sister?*

No. Maybe she doesn't like her sister. Judy might know something about her, so it would make a difference. It could put more pressure on her to tell her mother, because it's in the family. If I told a friend something, I'd even be more upset if he told my mother on me.

3. *Does it make a difference that Judy made the money herself?*

Yes. Because the money she gets is hers to do with. I personally think that her mother should supply her clothes. When you're 12, you don't get much money, and what money you get you want to spend on extras . . . fun things to do. That's money she doesn't have to ask her mother for.

4. *Which is more important, the fact that she earned the money or that her mother promised?*

I think both of them are about equal, the money and the promise. Judy earned the money herself, and her mother said she could go before. Of course, if her mother found something about the kind of concerts these people give, and what goes on at them, you know, that she was concerned about her young daughter. *So what if the mother was concerned?* I think then the mother should have said, "I really don't think it would be wise for you to go." *Even though she had promised?* Yeah, because before the mother didn't know what kind of concert it was going to be, she had no knowledge.

5. *Why is it important to keep a promise?*

Because you get your hopes up, you plan for this, you really get up hopes, and when someone doesn't live up to that promise, it's really not right. *What about your promises, the promises you make?* Because I said yes all right to that

293

person, they're expecting me to do it. I can't say, "Well, I don't really have to do that." If I later found out that it was going to hurt me to do that promise, I might not want to do it.

6. *Should you keep a promise to a stranger?*

I don't think it's as important. *Why not?* If you break a promise to someone else, you can't get promises back. With a stranger, you're not going to get promises back, but you . . . do let that person you don't know down. They expect you to do it. You might say to someone in your class, "O.K., you take these notes, and I'll take these notes." If that person doesn't take those notes, I'm going to be very upset, because I lost out a lot. I might not know the person very well, but that person had an obligation. I could have done it myself, but that person said, "All right, I'll do it."

7. *What's the most important thing for a daughter to be concerned about in a daughter–mother relationship?*

Trust. *Why?* If you've got trust with someone, you call, tell him why, I don't know. If . . . now that girl can't trust her mother. When something awful happens or something, it's important to tell a mother. *Why is that important?* Because your mother might be able to help you with it. If the girl got older, and had a past record of not being able to trust her mother, to talk to her, and have her mother not blow up at her if she did something wrong, and be really made at her, and punish her, and take away privileges, so that the girl can come to her for help, without really worrying about it.

8. *What's the most important thing for a mother to be concerned about in a mother–daughter relationship?*

Trust, the same thing. *Because?* So that she always knows what's going on in her daughter's personal life, everything. Because that's what a parent wants, they want trust between two people, they can tell each other what's happening . . . how they feel about things . . . you know.

Case #275

Dilemma IV

1. *Should Dr. Jefferson give her the drug that would make her die?*

No.

1a. *Why or why not?*

Because he might not be sure that she might die.

2. *Should the woman have the right to make the final decision?*

Yes.

2a. *Why or why not?*

Because it's her life.

3. *The woman is married. Should her husband have anything to do with the decision?*

Yes.

3a. *Why or why not?*

Because he's her husband.

4. *Is there any way a person has a duty or obligation to live when he or she does not want to, when the person wants to commit suicide?*

Yes.

4a. *Why or why not?*

I don't know.

5. *It is against the law for the doctor to give the woman the drug. Does that make it morally wrong?*

Yes. He could get arrested for it.

6. *Should people try to do everything they can to obey the law?*

Yes. Because if everyone obeyed the law there wouldn't be crime and stuff.

6b. *How does this apply to what Dr. Jefferson should do?*

[Long pause] I don't know.

Dilemma IV

1. *Should Dr. Rogers report Dr. Jefferson?*

Yes. Because if Dr. Jefferson gets punished, he won't do it again.

2. *Should the judge give Dr. Jefferson some sentence, or should he suspend the sentence and let Dr. Jefferson go free?*

Well, maybe just about a little sentence. So he'd learn his lesson for doing it.

3. *Thinking in terms of society, should people who break the law be punished?*

Yes. Because they committed a crime and killed somebody.

4. *The judge finds Dr. Jefferson legally guilty of murder. Would it be wrong or right for the judge to give him the death sentence (a legally possible punishment)? Why?*

For a life sentence? Could you repeat that again, please? [Interviewer repeats the question.] Wrong. Because the lady kept begging him to give her the drug.

5. *Is it ever right to give the death sentence? Why or why not? What are the conditions when the death sentence should be given in your opinion? Why are these conditions important?*

It matters what crime is. The death sentence should be given when somebody kills somebody, something. *Always? Or are there special cases when you wouldn't give it?* Special cases. *Why are these special cases important?* Because somebody might kill somebody for no reason.

6. *Dr. Jefferson was doing what his conscience told him when he gave the woman the drug. Should a lawbreaker be punished if he is acting out of conscience?*

Sort of in the middle of that one. Because he might want to do it and his conscience — he might not want to do it and his conscience will keep saying, "Do it" and stuff.

295

Dilemma II

1. *Should Louise, the older sister, tell their mother that Judy had lied about the money or should she keep quiet?*

   She should tell her mother. Because the girl disobeyed her mother.

2. *In wondering whether to tell, Louise thinks of the fact that Judy is her sister. Should that make a difference in Louise's decision?*

   No. Because she was not still doing wrong and it doesn't matter if she's her sister or not.

3. *Is the fact that Judy earned the money herself the most important thing in this situation?*

   I don't know.

4. *What do you think is the most important thing in the story?*

   The mother telling her that she could go. *The mother promised Judy she could go to the concert if she earned the money. Is the fact that the mother promised the most important thing in the situation?* Yes. Because the girl was saving up all her money to go and stuff. And she probably told all her friends that she was going.

5. *Why in general should a promise be kept?*

   Yes. Because they could go tell on their friends and it would spread and stuff and she probably asked her friend if she could go with her. And her friend probably asked their mother if she could go with her.

6. *Is it important to keep a promise to someone you don't know well and probably won't see again?*

   No. Because you wouldn't be able to do that promise or play with them or something if you never saw them again.

7. *What do you think is the most important thing a daughter should be concerned about in her relationship to her mother?*

   The love that she has for her mother.

7a. *Why is that the most important thing?*

   Because if there wasn't love, they wouldn't get along that good.

8. *What do you think is the most important thing a mother should be concerned about in her relationship to her daughter?*

   The same thing.

8a. *Why is that the most important thing?*

   I don't know.

Case #980

Dilemma IV

1. *Should Dr. Jefferson give the drug that will make her die?*

I've thought about this since the last time and I'm still not sure on what basis to make the decision. I can certainly think of a justification in the sense of putting her out of pain and her right to decide being respected. But I can also see the argument for not doing it out of respect for life. I don't know how to decide.

2. *Say more about her right to decide.*

It's her decision as a free agent. An individual should be allowed to do that unless it goes beyond some limit where it affects society or other people. There is a question as to whether it transgresses some higher value. In this case it's hard to weigh. I would say the sanctity of life is a basic value, but I also think there are circumstances under which I'd choose to die. *The New York Times* ran a series on suicide pacts among people who were faced with slavery: They were acting on a higher principle, saying their beliefs were more important than life. I don't think self-preservation is the highest value; I don't think I could live under any circumstances. There are religious passages which say you have to die in order not to be a murderer, or not to be incestuous. I do think there are higher principles than self-preservation; and I don't mean you accept that because you have faith in a particular religion that tells you that, but because it's a matter of rationality and then of spirituality as well.

To say life is the highest value is not to say self-preservation is the highest value. *What do you mean life is the highest value?* The problem with euthanasia is that sometimes I feel life is sacred – and I can't explain why. It doesn't necessarily raise the question of God; you can just argue that you can't have other values like love unless there is life first. But if by living you have to deny those values you hold then that is perhaps a reason to end life. To deny one's values just for the sake of living does not seem to make sense either. Another problem with euthanasia is someone deciding for someone else about their life. In this case it's O.K. because the woman asks to die. It's hard to weigh the value of holding on to life, though painful, as long as you can against pointless suffering. I'm not sure how the individual or society can decide. I can see myself administering a lethal dose, or anyway seriously considering it. But unless you are really faced with it, it is so complex and difficult it's hard to decide.

3. *Is there any way a person has an obligation to live if they don't want to?*

I've been leaning towards saying there are obligations to live. With the exception of when that entails giving up all your beliefs and values, or if you're senile. But then I don't know you can say that a person who *doesn't* martyr themselves is immoral. I've implied that suicide cases have an obligation to live because they're bummed out and feeling sorry for themselves – they're not treating life with respect and that is wrong. The obligation to live is based on the idea that life is sacred and meaningful. But if life has meaning then the prerequisite is that you hold life to be meaningful.

4. *Does the fact that mercy killing is against the law make it morally wrong?*

The concept of law and that of society restraining itself and finding a way to live together is important. So it is important to respect the law as a contract for living together: The laws themselves don't have inherent value but the concept does. There should be a way of creating stability and a relationship between people in society that works. If everyone were a law unto themselves you'd have an anarchic chaotic situation. The problem with that general statement "you should obey the law" is the implication that each law in itself has intrinsic value, and I'm suggesting that is false: I'm saying you should have respect for the law except when it contradicts one's higher and better ideas. But still at that point you have to take responsibility for the law because of the value of maintaining the social fabric. Why society is important is that it is a way of furthering and bettering life and art. *What are these values?* I don't want to give you a list: Respect for life is a pretty inclusive one but it's hard to extract one. I could say "liberty" but there are so many definitions of it and ways of applying it to society.

Also it doesn't always hold that you must be responsible for the law even if you break it because if you were in Nazi Germany and there was a law that you had to turn in Jews you obviously wouldn't go along with even the spirit of it. The difference is that in Nazi society there is repression and it is immoral in its way of treating people. In the U.S.A. at least the idea behind antieuthanasia laws is to protect people. Also in this society laws are changed through principled challenges, but in a society that supports money over life principled challenges would be impotent. In this society, knowing that there is a controversial law, I think people should stand up and argue. But if it were the case the society punished mercy killing with immediate death without a trial then it would be silly for the doctor to make a public stand. The time before when I answered this question my answer was in the context of a society that tries to deliberate on these questions. A good mechanism for discussion is public trial.

Dilemma IV'

1. *Should Rogers report Jefferson:*

   Yes. [See preceding answer, last paragraph.] There's probably a hospital ethics committee that he should go to. *Why is that a better way than a public trial?* I don't know that it is – I'm not sure a society should allow each profession to police itself. I don't think doctors should make decisions on life and death. On the other hand I don't want to make it sound as though the law is the only way to deal with questions – maybe you could turn the whole question over to a bunch of clergymen or psychiatrists.

2. *What kind of a sentence?*

   I would say the jury's verdict acknowledges that the act is against the law as it stands which is to say Jefferson is accountable for his actions and is not a law unto himself. But I would think in these circumstances and since the law is controversial that he should get a suspended sentence. He certainly shouldn't be put in jail for five years. It's not equitable with homicide: The reason for leniency is that it is a difficult moral dilemma and society is still in the process of considering. It's a harder question if it is a society which takes a very definite negative stance towards mercy killing so that Jefferson is more of a law unto himself: You can't really have the judge and Jefferson defying the whole of society and its values. I would admire a judge in Nazi Germany who said he didn't want to be any part of their system. But to get back to the present day and the U.S.A., the reason for leniency would be marking that this is an important law issue that can be dealt with from many different perspectives, it is not settled, it is obvious yours was not a malicious act. But the guy has to be held accountable until through a process the law is changed. And you could consider this the first move in the process that will get that law changed. But I wouldn't consider it O.K. for the judge to say that he would single-handedly subvert the legal system and nullify the jury decision, because law as a value must be respected as a way to have people live together and be protected from others. Our society needs a morality that will allow a pluralism of views while safeguarding individual freedoms. Without that minimum standard of morality you would lose that freedom.

3. *In general should people who break the law be punished?*

   I want to distinguish between different societies and different laws. I am not saying that because the law is the law you should be punished. What I am saying is that if you are going to have equality before the law, people being treated as equal by a system of rules, then if you transgress a rule you have still to apply the sanctions of the rule, otherwise it is meaningless and equality before the law is meaningless. That says nothing about substance.

4. *What about the death penalty?*

   Not for this crime. I think it's justifiable in the case of terrorism and murder of a prison guard or in the case of someone who has murdered before. I would base it on the rationale that you are attempting to preserve other life. I remember I said before that retribution was a value but is not by itself sufficient to warrant capital punishment. I think if you ask someone to guard dangerous criminals you should offer some safeguards and the death penalty for murdering prison guards is a deterrent in this vein. If you decided it was not a deterrent to other people, then the death sentence would only serve as retribution which is wrong as a basis for killing someone because life is a higher value. Of course it gets difficult if you consider that with the money it costs to keep someone in jail you could keep 20 people on kidney machines, for you could argue for killing one person to save 20 others. I think retribution is an illegitimate principle up to a point. I have nothing against punishing someone on the basis of deterrence or rehabilitation, nor with a concept of retribution which helps the criminal get over the crime. It seems to me that the victims are relying on the system too. But I don't think it should be taken as far as to torture the criminal.

Dilemma II

1. *Should Louise tell the mother?*

   Not after the fact. Sibling trust and loyalty are values and shouldn't be betrayed for no good reason. Was there a problem about the younger sister's safety?

   I think there's a value of sibling trust and loyalty and for her to betray that relationship for some other reason would not be right. If, on the other hand, she left and she found out that she was gone off by herself . . . Did she go by herself? *No, I think she went with somebody, it doesn't really say, but I think we can assume she went with somebody.* If she thought she were in danger, it would be a reasonable thing, a 12-year-old unescorted girl going to some rock concert, her sister should tell on her in that case, because she had a higher idea of her in danger, that's important. *She should tell on her after?* No, before. Once she's gotten back and she's okay, you say, that was stupid, you're lucky you're back here, I'm not going to tell this time, but think about what you're doing before you do it. But the before case, if she thought she was in danger, if she snuck off and went to the zoo, or something like that. But I think it is significant it was a rock concert. It seems to be they could have said the ice cream parlor down the street.

With parental responsibility, an individual is a free agent and being independent is an important value, but not at every age. We assume that children under a certain age need guidance and they don't have the experience and knowledge. It isn't being responsible for a parent to say, "Well, I want my kid to be independent, to go out with this motorcycle gang if that's what she wants to do." It is a parental responsibility to have certain guidelines for the child. Now, obviously, if you can't cross the street when you're twelve years old, that would be ridiculous. *What would be the focus of the guidelines? What kind of guidelines are legitimate?* I think I've said this before, but not in the same context, with the idea that to raise a child to make these decisions for herself, and grant more independence as the child accepts more responsibility. But the child has to be willing to assume the responsibility. As far as certain guidelines, it's difficult to say, well you do this or do that, but generally the two come together. But you teach the child what is smart to do, what is moral to do, not just "You do this because I said so," and that this is right, this is wrong. Maybe at an earlier age when they can't understand, you have to explain to them why they can't go to the rock concert.

3. *Why do you think that it's so important that you not just teach them what is right and what is wrong?*

Because some day you're going to be gone. You want a person to be independent and part of being free is self-restraint and being responsible for one's actions. You can't be responsible for your actions unless you are able to understand the consequences of them, what's going to happen to you, otherwise they aren't really free, and that's an important value. *In what sense are they not really free?* If you have to run to your mother and ask her if it's right or wrong to do it, you're not going to be an adult, independent, free-thinking, and all that stuff.

4. *Do you think that the fact that the mother promised is an important factor in the situation?*

That's difficult because if the mother found out about the rock concert at a later date – first of all she should explain it. She should say, well when I first promised (promises are important) but I shouldn't have made it because I didn't have all the information about this group has live sex on stage, and it really isn't appropriate, so therefore, I feel that I can break my promise. In general, it is important to keep one's promises. The whole idea of establishing trust and responsibility for one's actions, and if you're going to say something, you should do it.

5. *Could you elaborate on the importance of establishing trust? What do you mean by that and why is that important?*

First of all, on a personal level, for the parent and child, or for anyone to have a relationship, if it means anything, you need to have trust. It is the basis for any relationship to depend on a person and on what they say and it's going to coincide with their actions. On another level, on the perspective of rearing the child, the idea that you want the child to be independent and responsible. Part of the thing is that you're having to act, speak, say what you're going to do, etc., like what I was saying before, is being responsible for one's actions. You can't teach it unless you exemplify it. If the child sees that what you say doesn't correspond, you're not teaching the child what is a very important value. On a societal level, trust and acting responsible as contracts in law and living together and that value. *Why is it important to keep a promise, perhaps you could tie that in?*

6. *Why is it important, in general to keep a promise?*

The personal, the individual, interpersonal issue and the idea of the person in society and the idea of society as a whole having trust. You do have to enforce contracts and all because there's a difficulty in interpreting them, but sometimes people just want to break them. They don't mean what they say. To have things like . . . if you don't want to have an authoritarian society with police enforcing everything on you, then you have to have a consensus, you have to have a trust, liberty, freedom and equality, you have to have a standard of morality then you can have policemen walking down the street, that certain common beliefs are shared by people, and one of those is people meaning what they say and acting on it, doesn't mean a thing. If you have causality in the world, no correspondence about what people say and do, then there's nothing. . . . When you speak of everyday actions, you don't think in these terms. When you don't pay a parking ticket, or you get one, you say well, – I'm happy that they're acknowledging that I broke the law.

7. *What do you think is the most important thing a daughter should be concerned about (or a son, a child) in relationship to their parent?*

From a child's point of view, or the parent? *I want both.* I would like the child establishing, to be able to trust, to be able to display affection to the parent, to have a loving relationship with the parent. I want to learn from the parent, to look to the parent for guidance, and to respect the parent and hope their parents respect them. *Why?* Those are important things to learn when growing up, to learn how to – I think that a lot of new relationships are based on relationships with parents as models. Now, the idea of what you can do, your abilities, encouragement from parents, their guidance and how to think about the world comes from the parents, to an extent. If we are going to get to all these other values that we like, it's important to have this kind of environment for the child. He can feel that there are limits to what he can do, that there are, have a sense of morality, a sense of right and wrong so that he will have that when he's an adult. But I just want to stress that it's a matter of the parents being an authority figure, nothing else is going to teach him, there obviously has to be a lot of affection and love so that the person can also express that, because I think that's an important part of humanity. *Now, from the parents' perspective?* It's just the converse. He should love the child, give the child affection and part of that is being able to discipline the child and to explain to them why they're doing it, so that they'll understand. Try to teach them to think for themselves, to have an idea of right and wrong and value judgment. To encourage the child in improving and learning, etc. As I think I've said before, I would bring the child up, I certainly wouldn't say, "Well, you don't have to follow my values at all." I think one of the values is being able to think for yourself so you can be critical of them. In the beginning, when they aren't able to, I would try to express my values which I am thinking. I think that's important.

Case #947

Dilemma IV

1. *Should Dr. Jefferson give her the drug that would make her die?*

   Yes.

1a. *Why or why not?*

   Because she's in great pain – it's correct and right. *Why?* Because it's her life and her own personal decision.

2. *Should the woman have the right to make the final decision?*

   Yes.

2a. *Why or why not?*

   It's her life – I believe in self-determination – it's her life.

3. *The woman is married. Should her husband have anything to do with the decision?*

   Yes. Well, if you believe in the traditional, conventional views of marriage, the bond between husband and wife – he should have a say in it. But since just now I talked about self-determination, I guess it's still her decision.

4. *Is there any way a person has a duty or obligation to live when he or she does not want to, when the person wants to commit suicide?*

   Yes.

4a. *Why or why not?*

   Perhaps she has an obligation to her husband or maybe kids – maybe they are hoping for a miracle cure. *There isn't one.* Well she's going to die in six months and her husband and/or family should be able to accept her decision because she's in such pain. They would not want her to suffer any longer.

5. *It is against the law for the doctor to give the woman the drug. Does that make it morally wrong?*

   No.

5a. *Why or why not?*

   Well I see a difference between legal and moral judgments in our society. Most legal judgments are based on or reflect moral judgments – but I see a gap between those kind of laws and crimes which are trivial or victimless, like this case – there's no correlation between legal and moral judgments.

6. *Should people try to do everything they can to obey the law?*

   Generally, yes.

6a. *Why or why not?*

   Well, without law there would be chaos. The general philosophy of laws is to preserve order for civilized people.

6b. *How does this apply to what Dr. Jefferson should do?*

Well, obviously he broke the law, but he didn't do anything immoral – he fulfilled the wishes of the dying patient – it was a noble step. This is one of what I called before a trivial or victimless crime – it doesn't specifically threaten the order of society.

Dilemma IV'

1. *Should Dr. Rogers report Dr. Jefferson?*

   This is a dumb question, uh, hospital regulations . . . well . . . for example, all complications aside, like my safety, I would report a bank robbery or something, but if I was Dr. Rogers, I wouldn't report him.

1a. *Why or why not?*

   Well, I believe in mercy killing. *Why?* If the person is in great pain, there is no hope for a cure, I think they should have the choice of dying.

2. *Should the judge give Dr. Jefferson some sentence, or should he suspend the sentence and let Dr. Jefferson go free?*

   I'm not sure what the word *should* means here – if you're talking about the smooth functioning of the legislative system, the criminal justice system, then yes he should be sentenced, as a deterrent, but this is an isolated case about Dr. Jefferson.

2a. *Why?*

   If *should* refers to this particular case, no, he should not get a sentence be-cause of the specific type of crime here; what I said before about victimless crimes applies here.

3. *Thinking in terms of society, should people who break the law be punished?*
   Yes.

3a. *Why or why not?*

   To preserve order – set up a system or set of expectations of what right and wrong is and punishment resulting from behavior of certain types.

3b. *How does this apply to how the judge should decide?*

   Once again, the law should act as a deterrent, but this is a special case like I said before in the last question [2a].

4. *The jury finds Dr. Jefferson legally guilty of murder. Would it be wrong or right for the judge to give him the death sentence (a legally possible punishment)? Why?*

   Definitely wrong – this situation was vastly different from premeditated first-de-gree murder or voluntary manslaughter – this was the noble, worthwhile termi-nation of a life due to a personal, dignified decision. There's a big difference.

5. *Is it ever right to give the death sentence? Why or why not? What are the con-ditions when the death sentence should be given in your opinion? Why are these conditions important?*

   I don't know. I'm torn between the liberal sixties tradition of not taking lives for any reason and the cold, practical reasoning of the seventies – a great deal of crime and the death penalty as a deterrent. But I don't think so — life is sacred, but if I said yes, it would have to be for the most heinous of crimes. . .

6. *Dr. Jefferson was doing what his conscience told him when he gave the woman the drug. Should a lawbreaker be punished if he is acting out of conscience?*

    Yes — conscience is a very nebulous term — it could be an easy rationalization for crimes — like Raskolnikov justified his crime by saying his conscience felt he had to rid the earth of certain people.

Dilemma II

1. *Should Louise, the older sister, tell their mother that Judy had lied about the money or should she keep quiet?*

    No.

1a. *Why?*

    She'd be a tattletale — it could be a learning experience for Judy, maybe she can come forward herself — it sounds like a first-time thing. *And if not?* Well if it's happened a lot, perhaps Louise should intervene. *Why?* Obviously there is something wrong or lacking in communication between Judy and Mom.

2. *In wondering whether to tell, Louise thinks of the fact that Judy is her sister. Should that make a difference in Louise's decision?*

    No. I don't think that that gives her the right to tell — well maybe more than if it was just a friend. *Why?* Well, the family is the basic unit of society and they have many shared experiences particularly if she is only 12.

3. *Is the fact that Judy earned the money herself the most important thing in this situation?*

    No bearing at all.

3a. *Why or why not?*

    The money could have come out of a piggy bank — the thing here is the raised expectations about going to the concert.

4. *The mother promised Judy she could go to the concert if she earned the money. Is the fact that the mother promised the most important thing in the situation?*

    Yes.

4a. *Why or why not?*

    Raised expectations — an important part of interpersonal relationships is to be able to rely on others, have faith and trust in others.

5. *Why in general should a promise be kept?*

    Because of what I just said.

6. *Is it important to keep a promise to someone you don't know well and probably won't see again?*

    Yes — again the importance of relying on others and that one has an obligation to others.

7. *What do you think is the most important thing a daughter should be concerned about in her relationship to her mother?*

Love.

7a. *Why is that the most important thing?*

Love encompasses a lot of things – like fostering trust, respect, and honesty – these things are the important qualities for people and their relationships and dealings with others.

8. *What do you think is the most important thing a mother should be concerned about in her relationship to her daughter?*

Same things.

8a. *Why is that the most important thing?*

A mother should be especially concerned with instilling these qualities in her young child.

Annotated Scoring Sheets for Form B – Practice Cases

Case #116

Explanation of Scoring

a- This is neither a match nor a marginal match point to CJ#5; see Note, CJ#5, Volume II, Form B.

b- *Do not* match this IJ (Q#6) to CJ#7; see Note, CJ#7, Form B, Volume II.

c- Since there are no match points under this issue, we can only assign a guess score. The general structure is Stage 2; thus, a guess 2 score is assigned.

d- *Do not* match this IJ (Q#4) to CJ#5; see Note on CJ#5, Form B, Volume II.

e- Do not match this IJ (Q#1) to CJ#7; see Critical Indicator (a).

f- Although there is some reference in this response to the importance of "good personhood" of the parent as acting unselfishly (Critical Indicator [b]), it is only implicit. It *does not,* therefore, warrant a match score. Since we already have a match score on this issue, this IJ is not used for a guess score either.

Case #239

Explanation of Scoring

a- What is matched here is the following (Q#10): "I think the law should be more to protect people from each other . . . where their *rights are infringed* . . . I don't think the law should tell people how to live their lives *except* when this affects other people," etc.

b- The main argument for this point is presented in Q#5, where the subject states his opinion *against a personal* vindictive attitude, and for a detached attitude of the state or the law toward criminals. The Stage Structure is passed, although there is *some* ambiguity in regard to the Critical Indicators. Therefore, we give it a marginal Stage 4/5 score.

c- Here again, the Stage Structure of the CJ is passed, yet there is *some* ambiguity as to whether the Critical Indicators are perfectly met. Therefore, we give it a marginal score.

STANDARD SCORING SHEET

DATE:
INTERVIEW No./S name: 116
SCORED BY:

FORM A/FORM B) FORM C (circle one)

(Circle Chosen Issue)

DILEMMA III (FORM A) OR (IV) (FORM B) OR
V (FORM C)

(LIFE) (FORM A) or LIFE-QUALITY
(Forms B & C) ISSUE

LAW (FORM A) or LAW/LIFE-PRESERV.
(Forms B & C) ISSUE

Q#	CJ#/Norm & Element	Stage (Notes)	Q#	CJ#/Norm & Element	Stage (Notes)
1,5	8 life (8)	2/3	3	[5 aff (7)	2]ᵃ
4,2	5 aff (4)	2	6	[7 law (7)	2]ᵇ

ISSUE SCORE: 2 (3)   ISSUE SCORE: G 2ᶜ

(Circle Chosen Issue)

DILEMMA III' (FORM A) OR (IV) (FORM B) OR
VIII (FORM C)

(MORALITY & CONSCIENCE ISSUE)

PUNISHMENT ISSUE

Q#	CJ#/Norm & Element	Stage (Notes)	Q#	CJ#/Norm & Element	Stage (Notes)
1	11 m+c (8)	2/3	5	9 pun (2)	2
2,3,6	9 life (8)	2/3			
4	[5 m+c (2)	2]ᵈ			

ISSUE SCORE: 2/3   ISSUE SCORE: 2

(Circle Chosen Issue)

DILEMMA I (FORM A) OR (II) (FORM B) OR
VII (FORM C)

(CONTRACT ISSUE)

AUTHORITY ISSUE

Q#	CJ#/Norm & Element	Stage (Notes)	Q#	CJ#/Norm & Element	Stage (Notes)
1	[7 aff (4)	2]ᶜ	7a,8a	6 aff (7)	2
2,3	16 prop (15)	3	8	[18 auth (10)	G 3]ᶠ
1a,4,5,6	13 cont (18)	2/3			

ISSUE SCORE: 3 (2)   ISSUE SCORE: 2

Summated   1 _____
Weightings   2 2+1+1.5+2+1+2 = 9.5 X2 = 19
From Issues: 3 1+1.5+2 = 4.5 X 3 = 13.5
                4 _____
                5 _____

OVERALL PROTOCOL SCORE
GLOBAL: 2/3
WAS: 232

19 + 13.5 = 32.5 ÷ 14

d- The novice scorer may try to match Q#2 material to CJ#16, which is a Stage 3 point that emphasizes Judy's right to the money as positive desert (she worked hard, earned it, etc.). However, in Q#3, the subject suggests what he believes to be the important issue: "There is an *implicit* promise which is then broken." Therefore, CJ#16 is structurally vetoed and Q#2, #3, and #4 are scored together. Either CJ#40 or CJ#44 can be used to guess score this material to Stage 4/5. The IJ does not exhibit the Critical Indicators of either CJ.

e- CJ#32 is a possible match to Q#9. Yet, because Critical Indicator (b) is not present, we give it a Stage 4/5 guess score.

Case #114

Explanation of Scoring

a- The argument that "it is any person's right to decide to live or die" (Q#2) *does not* match CJ#2, Stage 2 life (having a right) point. First, it fails Critical

STANDARD SCORING SHEET

DATE:
INTERVIEW No./S name: #239
SCORED BY:

FORM A (FORM B) FORM C (circle one)

DILEMMA III (FORM A) OR (IV) (FORM B) OR
V (FORM C)

(Circle Chosen Issue)

(LIFE) (FORM A) or LIFE-QUALITY (Forms B & C) ISSUE			LAW (FORM A) or LAW/LIFE-PRESERV. (Forms B & C) ISSUE		
Q#	CJ#/Norm & Element	Stage (Notes)	Q#	CJ#/Norm & Element	Stage (Notes)
1,2,4	29 life (13)	5	6,9	38 law (13)	5
			10	39 law (16)	5ᵃ
ISSUE SCORE:		(5)	ISSUE SCORE:		5

DILEMMA III' (FORM A) OR (IV) (FORM B) OR
VIII (FORM C)

(Circle Chosen Issue)

(MORALITY & CONSCIENCE ISSUE)			PUNISHMENT ISSUE		
Q#	CJ#/Norm & Element	Stage (Notes)	Q#	CJ#/Norm & Element	Stage (Notes)
2	33 pun (9)	4	3	53 law (18)	5 marginalᶜ
4,5	38 life (16)	4/5 marginalᵇ			
ISSUE SCORE:		(4 (5))	ISSUE SCORE:		5

DILEMMA I (FORM A) OR (II) (FORM B) OR
VII (FORM C)

(Circle Chosen Issue)

(CONTRACT ISSUE)			AUTHORITY ISSUE		
Q#	CJ#/Norm & Element	Stage (Notes)	Q#	CJ#/Norm & Element	Stage (Notes)
1,5,6	48 cont (17)	5	7		[G 4/5]
2,3,4	[40 prop (9)	G 4/5]ᵈ	8,9	28 auth (10)	4
			9	[32 auth (17)	G 4/5]ᶜ
ISSUE SCORE:		(5)	ISSUE SCORE:		4

Summated Weightings From Issues:	1		OVERALL PROTOCOL SCORE
	2		GLOBAL: 4/5
	3		WAS: 473
	4 2+2 = 4 × 4 = 16		
	5 3+2+1+2+3 = 11 × 5 = 55		
	16 + 55 = 71 ÷ 15		

Indicator (b). Second, even the closeness of the Stage Structure is somewhat ambiguous; the subject *does not* advocate an *unlimited, concrete* control over one's life (as in Stage 2). Therefore, we give it a guess Stage 2. Also, see Distinctions Section in CJ#2: Do not confuse this material with CJ#29, a Stage 5, life (autonomy) point.

b- It is ambiguous as to whether we can interpret the statement "but I would be hurt *more* to see her live in pain" (Q#3a) as referring to the woman's *husband*. Had the subject *explicitly* stated the husband's concern or empathic suffering with the wife, we would match it to CJ#14, a Stage 3 point. As the argument appears in Q#3a, we can only guess score it.

c- Q#6b cannot be scored since the subject only makes a content choice with no structure or reason given to support the choice.

d- Based on the argument given in a and b above, we guess score the whole issue as Stage 2/3.

307

STANDARD SCORING SHEET

DATE:
INTERVIEW No./S name: #114
SCORED BY: _____   FORM A (FORM B) FORM C (circle one)

DILEMMA III (FORM A) OR (IV)(FORM B) OR
V (FORM C)

(Circle Chosen Issue)

(LIFE)(FORM A) or LIFE-QUALITY (Forms B & C) ISSUE

Q#	CJ#/Norm & Element	Stage (Notes)
1,2	[2 life (4)]	G 2 [a]
3a	[14 aff. (8)]	G 3 [b]
6 b [c]		
ISSUE SCORE:		(G 2/3) [d]

LAW (FORM A) or LAW/LIFE-PRESERV. (Forms B & C) ISSUE

Q#	CJ#/Norm & Element	Stage (Notes)
4	12 aff (8)	3
6	14 law (9)	3 (See match ex.#1)
ISSUE SCORE:		3

(Circle Chosen Issue)[e]

(MORALITY & CONSCIENCE ISSUE)

Q#	CJ#/Norm & Element	Stage (Notes)
6, 3b [f]	21 m+c (5)	3/4 (see match ex#1)
4,5	[20 life (4) G 3/4] [g]	
ISSUE SCORE:		(3/4)

DILEMMA III' (FORM A) OR (IV) (FORM B) OR VIII (FORM C)

PUNISHMENT ISSUE

Q#	CJ#/Norm & Element	Stage (Notes)
3	16 law (9)	3
ISSUE SCORE:		3

(Circle Chosen Issue)

(CONTRACT ISSUE)

Q#	CJ#/Norm & Element	Stage (Notes)
1a	20 auth (10)	3
4	16 prop (15)	
5	39 cont (17)	4 marginal [h]
6	38 cont (11)	4 (see match ex.#2)
ISSUE SCORE:		(3/4)

DILEMMA I (FORM A) OR (II) (FORM B) OR VII (FORM C)

AUTHORITY ISSUE

Q#	CJ#/Norm & Element	Stage (Notes)
7,8	24 auth (10)	3/4 marginal
ISSUE SCORE:		3/4

Summated
Weightings
From Issues:

1 _____
2 .5 X 2 = 1
3 .5+2+1.5+2+1.5+1 = 8.5 X 3 = 25.5
4 1.5 +1.5+1 = 4 X 4 = 16
5 _____
    1 +25.5 +16 = 42.5 ÷ 13

OVERALL PROTOCOL SCORE
GLOBAL: 3/4
WAS: 326

e- Determination of the subject's chosen issue here is somewhat difficult. In general, M&C is the chosen issue if the subject feels that the judge should *not* punish the individual *or* should *impose only token punishment.* Alternatively, punishment is the chosen issue if the subject *advocates more than a token punishment.* The ambiguity here centers around the question of the "token punishment," that is, whether the subject considers sentencing the doctor "to go to a small town" a token punishment. Supporting the doctor's decision all along, the subject views the necessity of the punishment as simply derived from the jury's verdict: "Though I agree with his [the doctor's] decision, if he was found guilty [by the jury], *it is not right for the judge* to let him go free" (Q#2). In addition, the statement "I don't think he should be put in jail for something as delicate as a moral decision," supports the subject's apparent objection to punishing the doctor. Therefore, we interpret the punishment as a token one and conclude that M&C is the chosen issue.

STANDARD SCORING SHEET

DATE:
INTERVIEW No./S name: # 867
SCORED BY:

FORM A (FORM B) FORM C (circle one)

DILEMMA III (FORM A) OR (IV) (FORM B) OR
V (FORM C)

(Circle Chosen Issue)

(LIFE) (FORM A) or LIFE-QUALITY
(Forms B & C) ISSUE

Q#	CJ#/Norm & Element	Stage (Notes)
1	14 aff (8)	3
2,5	11 life (8)	3
1,2	[12 life (14)	G 3]a
ISSUE SCORE:		(3)

LAW (FORM A) or LAW/LIFE-PRESERV.
(Forms B & C) ISSUE

Q#	CJ#/Norm & Element	Stage (Notes)
3	[12 aff (8)]	G 3b
6	[7 law (9)	3]c
4	[28 aff (5)]	G 4d
4,5,6		G 4e
ISSUE SCORE:		G 3/4 f

(Circle Chosen Issue)

DILEMMA III' (FORM A) OR (IV) (FORM B) OR
VIII (FORM C)

(MORALITY & CONSCIENCE) ISSUE

Q#	CJ#/Norm & Element	Stage (Notes)
1,2	14 m+c (12)	3
3	19 pun (14)	3
ISSUE SCORE:		(3)

PUNISHMENT ISSUE

Q#	CJ#/Norm & Element	Stage (Notes)
4,5	17 m+c (2)	3
ISSUE SCORE:		3

(Circle Chosen Issue)

DILEMMA I (FORM A) OR (II) (FORM B) OR
VII (FORM C)

(CONTRACT ISSUE)

Q#	CJ#/Norm & Element	Stage (Notes)
5,6	13 cont (8)	2/3
ISSUE SCORE:		(2/3)

AUTHORITY ISSUE

Q#	CJ#/Norm & Element	Stage (Notes)
7-8	[11 aff (9)]	G 3
	[12 aff (6)]	G 2/3 g
ISSUE SCORE:		G 2/3

Summated   1 _____
Weightings   2 1.5 + .5 = 2x2 = 4
From Issues: 3 3 + .5 + 3 + 2 + 1.5 + .5 = 10.5 X 3 = 31.5
                 4 .5 x 4 = 2
                 5 _____

4 + 31.5 + 2 = 37.5 ÷ 13

OVERALL PROTOCOL SCORE
GLOBAL: _____3_____
WAS: _____288_____

---

f- Structurally this material (Q#3a) is Stage 3/4 – a constructivist approach to
law. Since there is no CJ, we can only guess score this material.

g- Q#4 and #5 are a close match to CJ#20. However, there is *no explicit* statement of either Critical Indicator (a) or (b). Therefore, it can only be a guess
Stage 3/4.

h- It is ambiguous whether we can interpret the statement *"For the principle
of the promise . . . it is a bond that says . . . ,"* etc. (Q#5) as an *explicit*
reference to the promise as a serious *contract, pact, formal agreement,* etc.
(See Critical Indicators of CJ#39.) Therefore, we give it a marginal match
score.

Case #867

Explanation of Scoring

a. It is ambiguous whether the statement (Q#1) "They *have* to feel her pain, and
especially if they really care about her," etc., is a prescriptive statement or a

descriptive one. Therefore, we only guess score this material to CJ#12 (see both Stage Structure and Critical Indicator), a Stage 3 point.

b- Q#3 fits the SS of CJ#12 but fails the CI. Therefore, it can only be guessed to Stage 3.

c- Q#6 should not be *mistakenly* match scored to CJ#7, a Stage 2 point. Since Q#6 is in response to the *general* question of why obey the law (see CJ Note), we do not give it a match score.

d- Q#4, "No, unless someone else's life *depends* on you," resembles CJ#28, a Stage 4 affiliation (having a duty) point. Because there is not enough material that *explicitly* supports this argument we can only guess score it.

e- In Q#4, #5, and #6, there is the beginning Stage 4 idea of objective process ("court process") in decision making about fundamental issues such as life and death. There is also the beginning realization of the nature and inherent limitations of the law as *man-made:* "Usually the laws are reasonable, they're made for the best; because people made the laws . . . Maybe in that *case* the law is not the best" (Q#6). Although there is no CJ that matches it, this argument falls conceptually under Stage 4 law (maintaining social ideal). Therefore, we give it a guess score.

f- We guess score the whole issue as Stage 3/4, based on the material already discussed (a, b, c). Evidence for both Stage 3 and Stage 4 structures is present.

g- The total issue can only be guess scored 2/3. This is based on two alternative CJs: #11, an affiliation (good group consequences) point, or #12, an authority (good reputation) point. In CJ#11 Critical Indicator (b), the reciprocal aspect is missing; in CJ#12, both Critical Indicators (a) and (b) are absent. Since the IJ is consistent with the Stage Structures of both of these CJs, we give it a Stage 2/3 guess score.

Case #275

Explanation of Scoring

a- This is a nondiscriminatory statement that can appear in Stages 1, 2, or 3 protocols; therefore, it is not scored.

b- Q#2, though extremely short, has nevertheless the same norm (life) and element (having a right) as CJ#2. Since there is not enough material for a match score, we give it a guess 1/2.

c- Q#3 should *not* be matched to CJ#2, a Stage 1 law (blaming) point, because it is a response to a general question regarding a lawbreaker.

d- Q#1 and 2 cannot be scored since they are nondiscriminatory among various (1, 2, 2/3) stages.

e- Q#7a resembles CJ#6, though it fails both the Critical Indicator and the Stage Structure. Therefore, we give it a guess Stage 2.

f- See CJ#6, Critical Indicator (c): "a simple reference to the fact that Judy worked for, earned, or saved the money," *if unprobed* should be *used only as a guess.* We use the similarity between the CJ and the material to guess score the total issue as G2.

Case #980

Explanation of Scoring

a. Scorable material is in the first part of Q#2: "an individual should be allowed to do that *unless it goes beyond some limit where it affects society or other people.*" It is matched to CJ#30, the second stem.

STANDARD SCORING SHEET

DATE:
INTERVIEW No./S name: _275_
SCORED BY:

FORM A (FORM B) FORM C (circle one)

DILEMMA III (FORM A) OR (IV) (FORM B) OR
V (FORM C)

(Circle Chosen Issue)

LIFE (FORM A) or LIFE-QUALITY   (LAW)(FORM A) or LAW/LIFE-PRESERV.
(Forms B & C) ISSUE   (Forms B & C) ISSUE

Q#	CJ#/Norm & Element	Stage (Notes)	Q#	CJ#/Norm & Element	Stage (Notes)
2	[2 life (4)	2]^b	5	4 law (7)	1/2
			6^a		
ISSUE SCORE:		G 1/2	ISSUE SCORE:		(1/2)

(Circle Chosen Issue)

DILEMMA III' (FORM A) OR (IV) (FORM B) OR
VIII (FORM C)

MORALITY & CONSCIENCE ISSUE   (PUNISHMENT ISSUE)

Q#	CJ#/Norm & Element	Stage (Notes)	Q#	CJ#/Norm & Element	Stage (Notes)
4	5 M+C (2)	2	1,2	8 pun (8)	1/2
			5	9 pun (2)	2
			3	[2 law (2)	1]^c
ISSUE SCORE:		2	ISSUE SCORE:		(2 (1))

(Circle Chosen Issue)

DILEMMA I (FORM A) OR (II) (FORM B) OR
VII (FORM C)

CONTRACT ISSUE   (AUTHORITY ISSUE)

Q#	CJ#/Norm & Element	Stage (Notes)	Q#	CJ#/Norm & Element	Stage (Notes)
4	[6 prop(5)	G 2]^f	1,2^d		
6		G 2	7, 7a	[6 aff (7)]	G 2^e
ISSUE SCORE:		G 2	ISSUE SCORE:		(G 2)

Summated	1	1.5 + .5 + 1 = 3 × 1 = 3	OVERALL PROTOCOL SCORE
Weightings	2	1.5 + .5 + 2 + 2 + 1 + 1 = 8 × 2 = 16	GLOBAL: _1/2_
From Issues:	3		WAS: _172_
	4		
	5		

3 + 16 = 19 ÷ 11

b- In Q#4, the statement "you should have respect for the law *except* when it contradicts one's higher and better ideas. But *still . . . take responsibility for the law because of the value of maintaining the social fabric,*" sounds very much like CJ#37, second stem. Although the Stage Structure is definitely passed, it is questionable whether the Critical Indicators are met, (a, yes; c, no; b, debatable), we give it a guess 4/5. In the total calculation of this issue, this score is dropped, since we already have a clear Stage 5 match on the first part of Q#4.

c- Review the rules for the chosen issue. Justification for leniency (M&C) as the designated chosen issue is found in the following statements: (Q#2) ". . . in these circumstances and since the law is controversial . . . he should get a suspended sentence. The reason for leniency is . . . ," etc.

d- In Q#4, the statement, "if you decided it *was not* a deterrent . . . then the death sentence would only serve as a retribution which is wrong . . . ," re-

STANDARD SCORING SHEET

DATE:
INTERVIEW No./S name: **980**
SCORED BY:

FORM A/(FORM B) FORM C (circle one)

DILEMMA III (FORM A) OR (IV)(FORM B) OR
V (FORM C)

(Circle Chosen Issue)

(LIFE)(FORM A) or LIFE-QUALITY
(Forms B & C) ISSUE

LAW (FORM A) or LAW/LIFE-PRESERV.
(Forms B & C) ISSUE

Q#	CJ#/Norm & Element	Stage (Notes)	Q#	CJ#/Norm & Element	Stage (Notes)
2,3	26 life (13)	4/5	4	40 law (17)	5
2	30 life (6)	5ᵃ	4	[37 law (12)	G 4/5]ᵇ

ISSUE SCORE: **5 (4)**

ISSUE SCORE: **5**

DILEMMA III' (FORM A) OR (IV) (FORM B) OR
VIII (FORM C)

(Circle Chosen Issue)

(MORALITY & CONSCIENCE ISSUE)ᶜ

PUNISHMENT ISSUE

Q#	CJ#/Norm & Element	Stage (Notes)	Q#	CJ#/Norm & Element	Stage (Notes)
4	[43 pun (12)] G	4/5ᵈ	2	43 law (12)	4/5ᵉ
			3	49 pun (16)	4/5ᶠ

ISSUE SCORE: **G 4/5**

ISSUE SCORE: **4/5**

DILEMMA I (FORM A) OR (II) (FORM B) OR
VII (FORM C)

(Circle Chosen Issue)

(CONTRACT ISSUE)

AUTHORITY ISSUE

Q#	CJ#/Norm & Element	Stage (Notes)	Q#	CJ#/Norm & Element	Stage (Note)
4,5,6	48 cont (17)	5	1,3,7	33 auth (10)	5
5	[42 cont (10)	G 4/5]³			

ISSUE SCORE: **5**

ISSUE SCORE: **5**

Summated Weightings From Issues:

1 _____
2 _____
3 _____
4 1+.5+1=2.5×4=10
5 2+2+.5+1+3+2 =10.5×5= 52.5
10+52.5= 625 ÷13

OVERALL PROTOCOL SCORE
GLOBAL: **5**
WAS: **480**

sembles CJ#43, which is a Stage 4/5 (punishment and serving ideal) point. Yet, Critical Indicators are failed since the subject *does not deny* the legitimacy of either deterrence or retribution. Therefore, we only give it a guess 4/5 score.

e- Scorable material is in the following argument (Q#2): "But the guy has to be held accountable *until, through a process,* the law is changed. And you could *consider this the first move in the process that will get that law changed.*"

f- In Q#3, the argument "*if* you are going to have *equality before the law*, people being treated as equal . . . then *if you* transgress . . . ," etc., is matched to CJ#49, Stage 4/5. This point supports punishment on the basis of maintaining *equity* before the law.

g- Q#5 *does not* match CJ#42, since the Critical Indicator is failed. Since, however, the Stage Structure is passed, we give it a guess score.

STANDARD SCORING SHEET

DATE:
INTERVIEW No./S name: 947
SCORED BY:

FORM A / (FORM B) FORM C (circle one)

DILEMMA III (FORM A) OR IV (FORM B) OR
V (FORM C)

(Circle Chosen Issue)

LIFE (FORM A) or (LIFE-QUALITY)
  (Forms B & C) ISSUE

LAW (FORM A) or LAW/LIFE-PRESERV.
  (Forms B & C) ISSUE

Q#	CJ#/Norm & Element	Stage (Notes)	Q#	CJ#/Norm & Element	Stage (Notes)
1,3,5,6	[21 life (8)]	G4ᵃ	6a	30 law (9)	4
4a	[14 aff (8)	3]ᵇ			
ISSUE SCORE:		(G4)	ISSUE SCORE:		4

DILEMMA III' (FORM A) OR (IV) (FORM B) OR
VIII (FORM C)

(Circle Chosen Issue)

MORALITY & CONSCIENCE ISSUE

(PUNISHMENT ISSUE)

Q#	CJ#/Norm & Element	Stage (Notes)	Q#	CJ#/Norm & Element	Stage (Notes)
1,2a,4	[37 life (13)	4/5]ᶜ	2,3,3a	35 law (9)	4
			6	25 m+c (2)	3/4 marginalᵈ
ISSUE SCORE:		G4	ISSUE SCORE:		(4 (3))

DILEMMA I (FORM A) OR (II) (FORM B) OR
VII (FORM C)

(Circle Chosen Issue)

(CONTRACT ISSUE)

AUTHORITY ISSUE

Q#	CJ#/Norm & Element	Stage (Notes)	Q#	CJ#/Norm & Element	Stage (Notes)
1-3		[G 3/4]	2	24 auth (9)	4ᶜ
4-6	26 aff (12)	3/4	7,8	22 aff (12)	4
ISSUE SCORE:		(3/4)	ISSUE SCORE:		4

Summated   1 _____
Weightings 2 _____
From Issues: 3 |+1.5 = 2.5 X 3 = 7.5 _____
           4 |+2+2+1+1.5+| = 8.5 X 4 = 34
           5 _____
           7.5 + 34 = 41.5 ÷ 11

OVERALL PROTOCOL SCORE
GLOBAL: _____ 4
WAS: _____ 377

Case #947

Explanation of Scoring

a- We used CJ#21 to guess score the total issue as Stage 4. The Critical Indicators are failed, and the Stage Structure is passed.

b- *Do not* match the material in the last sentence of Q#4a to CJ#14. It is not prescriptive material and thus should not be scored.

c- We guess score the whole issue as Stage 4. CJ#37, a life quality (serving human dignity) point, fits the material superficially (see Q#5a), but not the structure. We are using this Stage 4/5 CJ as our reference point, to guess the total issue as Stage 4.

d- Q#6 fits the Stage Structure of CJ#25 and Critical Indicators (a). Critical Indicator (b), ''not necessarily eliminate the *wrongness* or harmfulness of the

313

conduct," is implicit in the material. Therefore, we give it a marginal score.

e- This question is usually scored under the contract issue. However, since the material clearly refers to the role of the family in the society, we score it under the authority issue, and match it to CJ#24.

Heteronomy and Autonomy in Moral Development:
Two Types of Moral Judgments

Mark Tappan, Lawrence Kohlberg, Dawn Schrader, Ann Higgins,
Cheryl Armon, and Ting Lei

> By mere analysis of the concepts of morality we can quite well show that the principle of autonomy is the sole principle of ethics. For analysis finds that the principle of morality must be a categorical imperative, and that this in turn commands nothing more nor less than precisely this autonomy.
>
> Immanuel Kant

What is moral autonomy? How does it develop? How do autonomous judgments differ from other types of judgments, both moral and nonmoral? These are all questions that were central to the work of Immanuel Kant, and they remain important today in research on the development of moral judgment. The purpose of this chapter is to present one approach to the study of moral autonomy, and one set of possible answers to these questions.

The natural ontogenesis of *autonomy* in moral judgment – where autonomy is defined as an independent and self-legislative stance taken in making moral judgments in the domain of justice – has been of particular interest to Kohlberg from the start of his work in the field of moral development. Initially, his dissertation research (Kohlberg, 1958) was designed to explore what was hypothesized to be a progressive increase in moral autonomy in early adolescence. In fact, the original title of the thesis was to have been "The Development of Moral Autonomy in the Years 10 to 16." In formulating this hypothesis Kohlberg relied heavily on Piaget's (1932/1965) distinction between heteronomous and autonomous types of morality. The findings of Kohlberg's dissertation research, however, suggested that a six-stage developmental typology was more useful in describing the observed differences in moral reasoning than was Piaget's heteronomy–autonomy distinction. Nevertheless, Kohlberg (1958) retained a focus on moral autonomy as one of the central aspects of his analysis of moral development in adolescence. As such, the six-stage sequence was designed, in part, to chart the progressive development of moral autonomy from Stage 1 (defined in 1958 as "Type 0") to Stage 6 ("Type 5"). In addition to Piaget's work, Kohlberg used the work of Baldwin (1897, 1906–1911) and Kant (1785/1948) to define the central features of the autonomous form of moral judgment toward which the developmental sequence led.

Kohlberg and his colleagues continued to work on the elaboration and clarification of the six-stage sequence and its associated scoring methodology through the 1960s and early 1970s (see chap. 1; see also Colby, 1978; Kohlberg, 1978). Throughout this process the development of autonomy in moral reasoning re-

315

mained an important, although at times less salient, research interest. The stage sequence did retain a certain focus on the progressive development of autonomy. With the gradual separation of content from structure in the stage definitions, however, many of the autonomous characteristics that Kohlberg (1958) had originally used to describe the postconventional stages were redefined as stylistic features of moral judgments that did not hold up as strictly developmental under close structural scrutiny. Thus defined to a large degree as nonstructural, moral autonomy lost its central place in Kohlberg's structural-developmental theory of the development of moral reasoning.

At the same time that these changes in his theory were taking place, however, Kohlberg and his colleagues began to explore whether an autonomous type or form of moral judgment could be identified *within* each of the stages of moral reasoning. This ''micro''-examination of the development of autonomy within each stage, as opposed to the ''macro''-examination of the development of autonomy across the stages, led Kohlberg (1976) to suggest that each stage might include two separate ''substages'': a heteronomous ''Type A'' substage and an autonomous ''Type B'' substage. The substage hypothesis allowed Kohlberg and his colleagues to retain a focus on moral autonomy, while at the same time separating it from the strict structural-developmental definition of the stages themselves. In addition, it provided the opportunity to explore the development of autonomy on a level that had not been addressed previously – the micro- or within-stage level.

Ultimately, however, the quasi-developmental assumptions of the substage hypothesis were not supported by the data obtained using that approach. At that point the research team whose work this chapter reports was formed, and we[1] began once again to explore the issue of moral autonomy and to develop a methodology for the assessment of the development of autonomous moral judgments on the micro- or within-stage level. We have used Weber's (1949) ideal-typological approach to identify characteristics of an ideal autonomous ''type'' of moral judgment. We have contrasted this autonomous type with an ideal heteronomous type (following Piaget and Kant), and have labeled them Types B and A, respectively. We have developed a coding scheme to assess the heteronomy–autonomy ideal-type distinction in moral judgment, and have used this scheme in several studies, the results of which will be reported later in this chapter.

The aim of this chapter, then, is to present our current theoretical and empirical work on the heteronomy–autonomy typology in some detail. The chapter begins with a historical review of the two major approaches that Kohlberg and his colleagues have used in studying moral autonomy. The second section presents our current theoretical formulation of the heteronomy–autonomy typology, based on nine criteria that we have taken to define the autonomous and heteronomous types of moral judgment. This section includes a review of the work of Piaget, Baldwin, and Kant on moral autonomy, since they have provided the major theoretical inspiration for our current work. It also contains several general hypotheses regarding the typology, taken from our theoretical sources. The third section describes the coding scheme we have developed to assess autonomous and heteronomous moral types. The actual coding manual itself can be found in Volume II. The fourth section describes six empirical

---

1 Throughout the rest of this chapter the use of the pronoun *we* refers to the authors of this chapter and the members of the research team whose work this chapter reports.

studies that have used our coding scheme and presents data on the reliability and validity of the scheme. Finally, the chapter concludes with a brief summary and discussion section, which includes additional theoretical speculations and suggestions for further research.

Historical Review

The purpose of this section is to set the context for our current approach to the identification of autonomous and heteronomous types of moral judgment. It will discuss the two major efforts that Kohlberg and his colleagues have made to operationalize and measure the development of moral autonomy: the 1958 developmental typological approach and the 1976 substage approach.

The Developmental Typological Approach

The aim of Kohlberg's (1958) original study of moral reasoning was to study the development of autonomy in the moral judgments of children between the ages of 10 and 16 using Piaget's (1932/1965) distinction between heteronomy and autonomy. This research was designed to explore the viability of extending the search for moral autonomy into adolescence, an age range that Piaget's initial research did not cover. Kohlberg hypothesized that certain social and environmental antecedents would have an effect on the development of moral autonomy. Three antecedent variables of interest were chosen for investigation: (1) participation in secondary social institutions as measured by socioeconomic status (following G. H. Mead, 1934); (2) idealization of and identification with significant adult role models, as measured using a Q-Sort ranking of adult roles and occupations (following J. M. Baldwin, 1906); and (3) peer group participation as measured by sociometric status (following Piaget, 1932/1965).

To test these hypotheses, Kohlberg (1958) developed a series of hypothetical moral dilemmas that he presented to a sample of boys between the ages of 10 and 16. This method was initially designed to differentiate Piaget's heteronomous and autonomous types, and thereby to measure the development of moral autonomy. Each dilemma pitted conformity to authority and/or rules against fairness as equality, reciprocity, or human rights. The choice made on a dilemma was thought to be one criterion that would distinguish an autonomous from a heteronomous response. Other criteria taken from Piaget's work that were designed to identify an autonomous type included references to mutual respect, reciprocity, equality, and contract or free agreement as a basis for moral obligation.

In terms of the three dilemmas that now make up Form A of the Standard Moral Judgment Interview (MJI), Kohlberg (1958) hypothesized that on the Heinz dilemma (Dilemma III), the autonomous type would choose to steal as opposed to obeying the law because he would support the wife's right to life, would focus on the mutual relationship between Heinz and his dying wife, and would perceive the druggist's demands to be unfair. In considering Heinz's punishment (Dilemma III'), the autonomous type would take a nonretributive stance because he would favor restitution rather than retribution, and he would consider Heinz's motives and intentions instead of the simple commission of the act. Finally, in considering the father's broken promise to his son Joe (Dilemma I), the autonomous type would think that Joe should refuse to give his father the money because he would emphasize the importance of the contract, the promise, and the right to reciprocal maintenance of what Joe worked to earn; he would also discuss the father–son relationship in terms of mutual respect.

In the analysis of interview responses to these dilemmas, however, a very important finding emerged: It became clear that Piaget's two ideal types were not sufficient to classify and categorize all of the types of moral reasoning that had appeared in response to the hypothetical dilemmas. This led Kohlberg to formulate a developmental sequence of *six* ideal types or "stages" and to abandon Piaget's (1932/1965) simple twofold typology.[2]

In short, Kohlberg's (1958) findings raised some important questions regarding the applicability of Piaget's moral typology for use in assessing the development of moral autonomy in adolescence. This was particularly striking when Kohlberg's first two types (Type 0 and Type 1) were compared with Piaget's two types (heteronomy and autonomy). Kohlberg's initial assumption had been that his Type 0 would correspond to Piaget's heteronomous type, and that his Type 1 would correspond to Piaget's autonomous type. When responses that Kohlberg scored as Type 0 and Type 1 were analyzed in detail, however, they did not appear to reflect the influence of two different types of social relationships, or the presence of two different types of respect, as Piaget had suggested is the case for heteronomy and autonomy. Type 0 did not appear to be tied to a sense of heteronomous respect for adults and rules that was grounded in a sense of reverence and awe. Instead it appeared to be tied more to a deference to superior power, and to a concern with obedience and punishment. These concerns were reflected not only in relations with adults, but also in relations with peers. Similarly, Type 1 did not appear to be oriented to an intrinsic feeling of mutual respect and solidarity among peers. Rather it seemed to reflect an instrumental understanding of relationships with both adults and peers.

For example, consider the responses of Tommy, one of Kohlberg's (1958) original subjects. At age 10 he responded to the dilemma of whether a child should tell on his brother to his parents (Dilemma II) using reasoning that was scored as Type 0, by saying:

In one way it was right to tell, because his father might beat him up. In another way it's wrong because his brother will beat him up if he tells.

Whether in relation to an adult or a peer, Tommy responds to the avoidance of punishment and retribution. At age 13 Tommy responded to the same dilemma using reasoning that was scored as Type 1, by saying:

The brother should not tell or he'll get his brother in trouble. If he wants his brother to keep quiet for him sometime, he'd better not squeal now.

It is clear that Tommy at Type 1 (age 13) is more oriented to reciprocity than he was at Type 0. However, his responses do not suggest his awareness of a

---

2 These six types provided the foundation for the current structural stage sequence that charts the development of moral reasoning (see chap. 1). In Kohlberg's 1958 dissertation they were numbered "Type 0" to "Type 5," which corresponds to the later Stage 1 to Stage 6 designations. For purposes of historical accuracy we will use the 1958 type designations while discussing the six types as used in the dissertation. The reader should remain cognizant of how the labels of the 1958 types relate to the labels of the later six stages.

peer system of autonomy, social solidarity, and mutual respect distinct from a child–adult system of heteronomy and intrinsic unilateral respect. In other words, Kohlberg's Type 1 was not oriented to the ideal *intrinsic* mutual respect of peers and equals that stands at the core of Piaget's description of the autonomous type. Type 1 did seem to use some form of mutual respect, but it took the form of instrumental and calculated reciprocity. Kohlberg (1958) concluded that whereas for Piaget (1932/1965) mutual respect can include instrumental reciprocal negotiations and considerations among peers and equals, *true* autonomous intrinsic mutual respect, following Kant (1785/1948), involves treating persons as ends, and not simply as means.

Similarly, Kohlberg's (1958) analysis raised some questions about the correspondence between Piaget's heteronomous type description and what Kohlberg called Type 0 reasoning. As Tommy's first response indicates, Kohlberg's Type 0 was marked by heteronomous respect for his father's authority. But was it a sui generis mixture of love, fear, and awe that prompted Tommy's feeling of obligation toward the father, as Piaget suggests is the case in the heteronomous stage? Or was it more a direct and absolutistic fear of physical punishment? The latter interpretation was ultimately adopted, and Kohlberg's descriptions of both Type 0 and Type 1 were based much more heavily on Baldwin's (1897, 1906–1911) view of the early stages of moral development than they were on Piaget's. Table A.1 presents a comparison of Piaget's heteronomous and autonomous types and Kohlberg's (1958) Types 0 and 1, following Baldwin.

This analysis led Kohlberg (1958) to conclude that although Piaget's heteronomy–autonomy typology suggested some aspects or dimensions of moral judgment related to age and cognitive development, it did not define stages or even developmental types as "structured wholes" or interlocked, consistent patterns of moral judgment (see Kohlberg & Helkama [in press] for a recent statement of this view). In order to define such a sequence, and to trace the full development of moral autonomy in adolescence, Kohlberg ultimately abandoned Piaget's dichotomous typology, in favor of a more finely differentiated developmental typology. Kohlberg also drew heavily on Baldwin's (1897, 1906–1911) work to define the characteristics of moral autonomy toward which this developmental sequence led: the Type 5 (now Stage 6) "conscience or principle" form of moral reasoning.

Kohlberg's dissertation research failed to validate Piaget's heteronomy–autonomy distinction as a useful way to measure the development of moral reasoning in adolescence. Nevertheless, Kohlberg's (1958) developmental-typological system did ultimately include some components derived from Piaget's 1932 monograph, such as the focus on consequences rather than intentions in judging moral responsibility in the first three types (stages). Moreover, Kohlberg maintained Piaget's focus on moral autonomy as a central feature of mature moral reasoning.

In sum, then, Kohlberg's (1958) dissertation research ultimately represented an effort to trace the development of moral autonomy in adolescence through a sequence of six developmental typological "stages." His original plan to use Piaget's typology to measure moral autonomy was abandoned, for the reasons already outlined here. Instead, Kohlberg developed a new typology, and he defined a different view of moral autonomy – a view that was much closer to Baldwin's and Kant's views of moral autonomy than it was to Piaget's. The six-stage sequence traced the development of various formal components of

Table A.1. *Piaget's stages of moral development compared with the first two Kohlberg stages*

Stage 1 (heteronomous stage)

1. Value and conformity are "egocentric" or "syntelic" (Baldwin). (Manifested in absolutism of value or unawareness or moral perspectives.) Our interpretation similar to Piaget's.

2. Conformity is "realistic" or "projective" (Baldwin). Judgments of bad are made in terms of physical properties and consequences of action rather than in terms of the act's psychological intentions or functional appropriateness to some norm. Manifested in objective responsibility, in physicalistic definitions of lies, and in belief that punishment is a physically automatic response to deviance (immanent justice and expiative, rather than restitutive or reforming, punishment).

   Piaget: There is a confusion of rules and things. Rules are oriented to as fixed sacred things. Deviance is always wrong. Acts are evaluated in terms of the "letter of law," and in terms of consequences instead of intentions.

   Our interpretation: "Objective responsibility" is merely an expression of "projective" modes of value and a failure to differentiate moral good from other kinds of good. It does not imply an orientation to rules in the usual sense of a concept of a rule orientation. We find Type 1 not oriented to rules as entities, but oriented to projectively bad acts and to obedience to persons, not rules.

3. Conformity is "heteronomous" or based on unilateral respect or "objective necessity" (Baldwin), i.e., might makes right. Manifested in beliefs that obedience to adults or other power figures is right when it conflicts with other rules or welfare considerations, and in belief that punishment makes an act wrong necessarily.

   Piaget: "Duty" is based on a sense of heteronomous respect for adults transferred to their commands and rules. This respect, compounded of love and fear, leads to an overevaluation and sense of sacredness of authority and rules.

   Our interpretation: Adults must be seen representing something beyond themselves before they are "respected." While we find children of Type 1 oriented to obedience, we find little evidence that they respect authorities in any sense beyond recognizing that they are more powerful. Various kinds of response used by Piaget as indicating a sense of the "sacredness" of adults are interpreted as indicating cognitive naïvete, independent of emotional overevaluation. Often they indicate a lack of awareness of moral rule, against which the adult is to be measured rather than an idealization of the adult.

Stage 2 (autonomous stage)

1. Value and conformity are relativistic.

2. Conformity and punitive justice are flexible and oriented to intentions and functional needs.

   Piaget: Rules are seen as the expression of human understandable purposes and as means to those purposes. Deviance may be justifiable in terms of an intent to conform to the "spirit" or purpose of the rule or in terms of a particular unusual situation. Acts are evaluated in terms of their intent.

   Our interpretation: Rules may be seen as merely instrumental acts, as commands based on the individual needs of authority. Deviance may be justified on the basis of an act being a means to a natural end. The end is not itself evaluated in terms of its worthiness for a moral self. Rules are seen as a basis for shared action but not as a basis of shared evaluation or judgment.

3. Conformity is autonomous or based on mutual respect. Manifested in sense of the need to conform to peer expectations, in concern about distributive equality, in the importance of exchange or reciprocity, in the notion that peer vengeance is similar to authority's punishment, and in the notion that adult punishment is not the ulti-

Table A.1. *(cont.)*

Stage 2 (autonomous stage) (cont.)

mate criterion of wrong but is only a painful consequence to be considered in decision making.

Piaget: Conformity is based on empathic identification with the needs of others, shared goals, maintenance of agreement and a concern for approval by those approved of by the self. Conformity as to the attitude of other equals.

Our interpretation: These attitudes may be invoked as a basis of conformity without any really internalized conformity, shared goals, or concern for others. There may be no differentiation between "legitimate" and other needs of self and all may be hedonistically oriented. Needs of others empathized with is based on the degree to which the other comes within the boundaries of the self. Equality is not a norm but a fact. "I and my needs are as good as anyone else's." A seeking to maximize quantity of approval by direct instrumental techniques.

Source: Kohlberg (1958), pp. 345–346.

moral reasoning in addition to autonomy, however. Thus Kohlberg's view of moral development as it took shape in 1958 was ultimately not restricted to a focus on moral autonomy.

As the moral judgment stage definitions were later reformulated and refined, the structural features of the stages were gradually separated from content focus and stylistic features. This meant that many of the characteristics of moral autonomy that had informed Kohlberg's early research were identified as content or stylistic orientation, and thus removed from the structural definitions of the stages. As a result, charting the gradual development from heteronomy to autonomy in moral reasoning lost its place as the central focus of Kohlberg's theoretical and methodological enterprise.

Kohlberg's "Continuities in Childhood and Adult Moral Development Revisited" (1973) presented his first statement of the theoretical and methodological changes that resulted from the more complete separation of structure and content. The fundamental impetus for this presentation was a reconsideration of the data reported by Kohlberg and Kramer (1969), which seemed to indicate that some of Kohlberg's longitudinal subjects who were scored as morally autonomous and postconventional in high school "regressed" to a relativistic, skeptical, and egoistic phase during the college years. (See chap. 1, this volume, for a discussion of the Kohlberg and Kramer [1969] findings and Kohlberg's [1973] reinterpretation.)

Kohlberg's (1973) revised interpretation, based on a more strictly structural analysis of the interviews in question, and in light of a new round of longitudinal interviews, suggested instead that the college relativists had not truly shown structurally postconventional reasoning in high school, but had been misscored using the 1958 scoring system. This misscoring was due to a confusion between content and structure. Primarily this confusion centered around content characteristics of *autonomous* moral reasoning that these high-school-aged subjects had shown in their responses to moral dilemmas. Hence Kohlberg and Kramer's (1969) autonomous subjects were scored as Stages 5 and 6 based on the *content* of their reasoning, not on the *structure* of their reasoning. This interpretation provided the final impetus for the separation of content from structure in Kohlberg's theory and method. The Standard Issue Scoring System, described in detail in chapter 2 of this volume, represents the final product of that effort.

This interpretation also refocused theoretical and empirical attention on the issue of autonomy in moral judgment. How was the autonomous content or character of the college relativist's "pseudo" postconventional reasoning during high school to be captured? Kohlberg's (1973) tentative solution to this problem was to postulate the existence of a Type B *substage* at the conventional stages. This Type B substage was understood to exhibit the content characteristics of autonomous moral reasoning that Kohlberg (1958) had originally designated as postconventional *within* the structure of the conventional Stages 3 and 4. It also introduced the possibility of analyzing the development of moral autonomy on a more micro- or within-stage level, as opposed to the macro- or across-stage level.

The Substage Approach

The first fully elaborated statement of the substage construct appeared in Kohlberg's (1976) presentation of his revised structural approach to moral development theory and research. In this article Kohlberg tied the development of moral autonomy to a strict structural-developmental notion of substages. In doing so he followed Piaget's work on stages of cognitive development, which suggested that within each logical stage there are a number of substages through which development proceeds in a specific order (see Inhelder & Piaget, 1958). Consequently, Kohlberg (1976) defined two substages in the moral domain: Substage A and Substage B.

The definition of these two substages was based on four moral orientations that were used to distinguish features of different types of moral judgments made at the same stage of moral reasoning. Taking categories from moral philosophy used to classify different types of moral theory, Kohlberg (1976, p. 40) identified and described the four moral orientations as follows:

1. *Normative order:* Orientation to prescribed rules and roles of the social or moral order. The basic considerations in decision making center on the element of rules.
2. *Utility consequences:* Orientation to the good or bad welfare consequences of action in the situation for others and/or the self.
3. *Justice or fairness:* Orientation to relations of liberty, equality, reciprocity, and contract between persons.
4. *Ideal self or perfectionistic:* Orientation to an image of the actor as a good self, or as someone with conscience, and to his or her motives or virtue (relatively independent of approval from others).

The first two orientations, normative order and utility consequences, were grouped together to define Substage A at each stage, and the last two orientations, justice and ideal self, were grouped together to define Substage B at each stage.

Kohlberg (1976) hypothesized that these two groupings would form relatively clear substages at each stage, with the B substage being more developmentally advanced than its A counterpart. Kohlberg (1976) described the differences between the two substages this way:

> Type A makes judgments more descriptively and predictively, in terms of the given "out there." Type B makes judgments more prescriptively, in terms of what ought to be, of what is internally accepted by the self. The Type B orientation presupposes both awareness of rules and a judgment of their fairness. (pp. 40–41)

As such, it was assumed that Substage B represents a more highly equilibrated version of the sociomoral perspective of its particular stage, a sociomoral perspective that is first constructed at Substage A. (See chap. 1, this volume, for a discussion of the sociomoral perspective that underlies each stage of moral judgment.) In this view the perspective of Substage B is more balanced than that of Substage A, which allows judgments made from it to be more prescriptive, universalistic, and internally generated. In other words, Substage B represents the *morally autonomous* version of the judgment structure characteristic of a particular stage.

In addition, Kohlberg (1976) suggested that although the full development and consolidation of the sociomoral perspective at each stage are defined by the justice and fairness orientation (and hence the B substage), stage development can and does occur through all four moral orientations. He also claimed that in ontogenetic moral development, individuals will move through a particular stage from the A to the B substage, but never vice versa (for example, 3A to 3B, but never 3B to 3A). That is, it was expected that any substage change within a stage would be from A to B. When stage transition is involved, Kohlberg predicted, movement would be from the B substage of the earlier stage to the A substage of the later stage. It was hypothesized that individuals might skip the B substage entirely, however, and move directly to the A substage of the next highest stage (for example, 3A to 4A).

The next statement that referred to the substage approach to moral autonomy appeared in 1977, as a part of a preliminary edition of the Standard Issue Scoring Manual (Kohlberg, et al., 1977). This statement clarified several components of the substage approach. For one, it served to flesh out the formal developmental criteria for Substage B more completely than the 1976 statement. It claimed that Substage B judgments more closely approximate the formal philosophical criteria of an adequate moral judgment because judgments made at Substage B are more equilibrated and reversible than judgments made at Substage A of the same stage. This argument proceeded as follows:

> While philosophers disagree on the details of an adequate moral judgment, nearly all accept certain minimum characteristics, including universalizability, generalizability, pre-emptiveness, internal consistency, impartiality, and the quality of having been made by an autonomous, rational moral agent. However, it is exactly those judgments that are reversible, i.e., can apply equally to any character in a moral situation, which are best able (within their social perspective) to meet these formal criteria. (Kohlberg et al., 1977, p. 71)

The authors also discussed the methods available for coding moral substages. They suggested that the researcher "determine the degree to which the moral judgment [in question] approximates the dimensions of formal ethical adequacy" (p. 72), by identifying which of the four moral "orientations" best describes that judgment. This was accomplished through the identification of 17 moral "elements," each of which fell under one of the moral orientations. These elements represent the ways in which an individual expresses his or her orientation toward a particular moral norm, by indicating what value that norm holds in his or her moral judgment. (See chap. 1, this volume, for a discussion of elements and norms and their role in Standard Issue Scoring.) To use the element scoring system to determine substage, according to Kohlberg et al. (1977), the element that an individual is using in making each moral judgment must be identified. That element will indicate what orientation and, hence, what substage that judgment represents.

The substage approach, as operationalized through the element scoring system, continued to be elaborated and refined for several years. A simple scoring algorithm was developed to be used in conjunction with the element system: First, the number of B element Criterion Judgment (CJ) scores an interview received was tallied. (See chaps. 1 and 7, this volume, for a discussion of the Standard Issue Scoring System and the use of Criterion Judgments in determining moral stage score.) Then, if the B scores represented more than 50% of the total CJ scores, the interview was given a B substage score (and if not, it was given an A substage score). Although this procedure was somewhat tentative, it did provide a way to test empirically the hypotheses associated with the substage approach.

Theoretical refinements in the formulation of the substage construct also continued during this time period. Colby's (1978) discussion of moral judgment substages abandoned the strong theoretical reliance on the four moral orientations as the sole basis for making the A–B substage distinction. Instead, a more formal psychological and philosophical view of moral autonomy was adopted. It served as the foundation for understanding the developmental distinction between the substages. As Colby put it:

These general A–B differences are differences in moral orientation. Judgments at substage A tend to stress external considerations or literal interpretations of role, duties, or rules, and to be unilateral and particularistic rather than generalized or universal in orientation. Judgments at substage B, while remaining within the same sociomoral perspective, have developed within that perspective toward greater reversibility, universality, and generalizability, and toward a deeper comprehension of the "spirit rather than the letter" of the roles and rules. In a sense, the B substage is a consolidation or equilibration of the social perspective first elaborated at the A substage. It is as if a new social contract (involving a new level of perspective) were negotiated at each A substage. At the B substage this new social contract is made more general, reciprocal, and reversible. It reaches a more stable equilibrium. (1978, p. 94)

Although Colby's statement still presented the substages as moral "orientations" in a certain sense, the description of the autonomous character of the B substage relied much more heavily on the formal characteristics of moral autonomy first elaborated by Kohlberg in 1958 than it did on the two philosophical orientations used to define Substage B by Kohlberg in 1976. As such, this statement represented an attempt to combine a renewed focus on the formal characteristics of moral autonomy with a continued interest in a strict structural notion of substages.

In spite of these empirical and theoretical refinements, the substage approach to the study of moral autonomy was ultimately abandoned because the hypotheses associated with the approach were disconfirmed by the empirical results obtained using the element scoring system. The most important results in this regard were obtained when the element system was used to score Kohlberg's American longitudinal sample for moral judgment substage. These results have not been previously published; we present them in the context of this discussion of the history of the substage approach to illustrate the problems associated with this method.

The results of the American longitudinal substage analysis were as follows:

1. With regard to substage as a developmental characteristic, there was a clear age-developmental trend toward increased usage of the B substage as subjects increased in age.

2. Within any given time-testing interval, there was a somewhat greater tendency for individual subjects to stay within the same substage than to change substage. However, when substage change did occur, it was twice as likely to be changed from A to B as it was from B to A.

3. Although the substages did exhibit some developmental characteristics, they did not define a strict structural-developmental sequence like the one defined by the stages of moral reasoning for several reasons. First, subjects were often found to move from the B substage to the A substage while their moral judgment stage remained the same (for example, movement from 3B to 3A). This disconfirmed Kohlberg's (1976) most important hypothesis concerning the substage construct; namely, that developmental movement would always be from Substage A to Substage B within the same stage. In addition, the longitudinal data did not support the other pattern to be expected if the substages were truly structural; namely, that entrance to a stage be via its A substage and that developmental movement always be from the A substage to the B substage, and then to the A substage of the next stage (for example, 3A to 3B to 4A to 4B).

4. Finally, if substages were not a strictly structural aspect of moral development, they might exhibit a weaker developmental characteristic; namely, that the B substage would be more equilibrated than the A substage. If this were true, it would be expected that whenever an individual terminated stage development, he or she would stabilize or consolidate at the B substage. These data seemed to support this hypothesis: 80% of the subjects who were stabilized in their stage development were scored as Substage B, whereas only 20% of the stabilized subjects were scored as Substage A.

These results suggested that even though there was a shift to increased usage of the B substage with age, substage change in general did not appear to represent structural-sequential development, since many subjects violated the invariant sequence pattern that must hold if structural development is present (that is, they moved from the B substage to the A substage within the same stage). Subjects *were* more likely to move from A to B than from B to A from one testing time to the next, however, and there was a clear association between Substage B and stabilization of stage in adulthood. This suggested that the orientation to justice, and the universalizability and reversibility of the autonomous Substage B, did represent a better equilibrium than that of Substage A.

Nevertheless, this analysis marked the end of the substage approach to the study of moral autonomy.[3] The assumptions underlying the substage construct

---

3 In spite of the abandonment of the substage approach and the element scoring system, two recently completed cross-cultural studies already underway at that time did use the element scoring system to score for substage. Nisan and Kohlberg's (1982) study of moral judgment in a Turkish population found that there was a significantly greater number of late adolescent and young adult subjects living in an urban setting who were scored as Substage B than there were subjects of the same age living in a rural village setting. Snarey's (1982) (see also Snarey, Kohlberg, & Reimer, 1984) cross-sectional and longitudinal study of subjects living on an Israeli kibbutz found that a vast majority of these subjects were scored as Substage B relatively early in their lives. Both of these

that Kohlberg adopted in 1976, following Piaget's formulation of substages in the development of logicomathematical thought, were not supported by the element scoring system. The existence of an autonomous form or type of judgment within each of the stages of moral reasoning, particularly the conventional Stages 3 and 4, continued to be a very robust phenomenon in need of explanation, however. But the substage construct did not provide an adequate one.

Thus, because the A–B differences seemed very real, but because they did not appear to represent *substages,* we moved to an ideal-typical approach that defines two moral types: the heteronomous type and the autonomous type. This approach retains some developmental features associated with the substage approach, but it is fundamentally different in a number of ways. It is to the current theoretical formulation of this approach that we now turn.

Theory

Our current formulation of the heteronomy–autonomy distinction represents, as we have suggested, an ideal-typical approach to the study of moral autonomy. The purpose of this section is to present our current conceptualization of these two types of moral judgment in some detail. In order to formulate this typology we have returned to the sources that guided Kohlberg's (1958) initial research on the development of moral autonomy: Jean Piaget, J. M. Baldwin, and Immanuel Kant. Consequently, a major portion of this section is devoted to a review of Piaget's, Baldwin's, and Kant's theories of moral autonomy as they relate to our current work. This review is preceded by a general overview of our current formulation of the heteronomy–autonomy typology.

It is important to stress at the outset what our adoption of the "ideal-typical" approach implies. A particular typology may be purely conceptual, purely empirical, or a mixture of the two, the latter termed ideal by Weber (1949). A purely conceptual typology, such as the one developed by Parsons (see Parsons & Shils, 1951) for the study of values, represents the various permutations and combinations that seem important to the typologist. A purely empirical typology would be represented by a simple-structure multiple factor analysis of between-person correlations. The ideal-typical method, however, involves observing a great mass of more or less qualitative material and seeking the joint presence of various elements that have some "understandable" relationship to each other. In other words, in the ideal-typical approach, a cluster of chosen content themes is assumed to hold together because of an underlying postulated, but not observable, "structure" that makes one element of content compatible with the others. Thus it involves simultaneous willingness to select and stress empirical consistencies that can be coherently interpreted, and willingness to revise and reform principles of observation and interpretation as new empirical patterns seem to emerge (see chap. 1 for further discussion of the ideal-typical approach; see also Kohlberg, 1958).

studies are reprinted in this volume, minus the report of the substage analyses (see chap. 4 and 5, respectively). In addition, Kohlberg, Levine, and Hewer's (1983) monograph contains a rather lengthy discussion of A and B *substages.* As will become clear in the next section, however, that discussion much more closely follows the heteronomy–autonomy ideal-typical distinction that we have adopted subsequent to the substage approach than it does the strict assumptions of the original substage construct. In other words, the Kohlberg et al. discussion, although very recent, represents the use of an old term to describe a new construct, and not a continuation of an approach that has, for all intents and purposes, been abandoned.

It is also important to stress that the notion of "structure" assumed by the ideal-typical approach is very different from Piaget's (1960, 1970) cognitive-developmental structuralism that has been adopted by Kohlberg to define structural stages of moral judgment. In the ideal-typical approach a structure is an organization of interrelated elements or content themes that define a particular ideal type (like Weber's "rational bureaucracy"), but do not bear any logical relationship to each other, as Piagetian structures do. Ideal-typical assessment, therefore, resembles Loevinger's (1976) "sign" approach (see Kohlberg, 1981b), whereby the existence of an underlying group of interrelated elements is hypothesized or abstracted from the presence of various surface signs and content indicators. In other words, assessment of moral types using an ideal-typical approach is very different from *structural* stage scoring using the Standard Issue Scoring System, because structural assessment demands that the underlying logical structure be explicitly observed in a way that ideal-typical assessment does not.

Weber (1949) has considered the nature, function, and limitations of this approach most fully in his methodological writings. He stresses that the ideal-typical method implies the accentuation of a certain point of view toward a trait or traits. This accentuation serves the purpose of synthesizing individual objects or persons into a unified analytical construct. It also serves the related purpose of stressing those traits and the interpretation of those traits that bring out the genetic implications of the object – implications as to what the object will develop into or become. Thus Weber (1930), taking as an object "Protestantism," in comparison with other religions, stresses those elements in it and an interpretation of them that were conducive to the development of capitalism.

Although the ideal type is "ideal," it is not simply a theoretical construction. An ideal type refers to and develops out of the study and interpretation of concrete historical objects. It must describe concrete traits observed or defined in relatively nontheoretical terms, and the type must show some empirical fit to each object as a whole.

We have altered Weber's approach slightly, in that our formulation of the ideal autonomous type has used a "bootstrapping" or "abductive" process (see chap. 1 of this volume; also Kohlberg, 1981b) that has involved an ongoing conversation between empirical data and theoretical constructs. Thus, the nine criteria we have developed to define the ideal autonomous type reflect at once both empirical responses to the dilemmas we use, and theoretical aspects of various theories of moral autonomy. We claim that these nine criteria form a coherent empirical cluster of aspects of moral judgment that ideally define the autonomous type of moral judgment. Every individual will make moral judgments that can be categorized as corresponding to one of our two types to some degree, but no one's moral judgment can be completely characterized by either the autonomous type or the heteronomous type. Nevertheless, we can and do characterize an individual according to which type of judgment (autonomy or heteronomy) seems to predominate over the other. (See Coding Scheme, later in this chapter, for a complete outline of our empirical methodology.) When we study individuals or groups, analysis using such a hermeneutic provides a useful designation for descriptive and comparative purposes. In sum, we claim that the nine criteria form a construction that is necessary for our analysis of moral autonomy, but that it is an *ideal* construction to which the moral judgment of individuals corresponds to a greater or lesser degree.

We also want to stress that the typology as we have defined it is much more strongly oriented to the identification of the ideal *autonomous* type of moral judgment in the justice domain than it is to the identification of the ideal heteronomous type. We have focused primarily on autonomy in the initial stages of this work, instead of developing a full definition of both ideal types. Thus both our current theoretical formulation of the autonomy–heteronomy typology and our empirical coding methodology more fully define and measure autonomy, leaving heteronomy to be defined primarily as a "not-autonomy" category. We are presently working to correct this imbalance.

Our current ideal-typical formulation of the autonomy–heteronomy distinction is defined by nine general criteria, taken from the work of Piaget, Baldwin, and Kant on moral autonomy. These nine criteria are *freedom, mutual respect, reversibility, constructivism, hierarchy, intrinsicalness, prescriptivity, universality,* and *choice.* Each represents an important aspect or characteristic of moral autonomy that serves to distinguish the autonomous type from the ideal heteronomous type. In our brief review of Piaget's, Baldwin's, and Kant's theories of moral autonomy we will describe these criteria in more detail, and indicate their sources.

Piaget

Jean Piaget's work on moral autonomy is central to our own conception of autonomy, and to our distinction between the autonomous type of moral judgment and the heteronomous type. We follow Piaget in making the basic distinction between heteronomy and autonomy, but although we have adopted his terminology we have not completely adopted either his theoretical or his methodological assumptions. We also look to his work to help us define four of our nine criteria: freedom, mutual respect, reversibility, and constructivism. Finally, Piaget's work has suggested the three major hypotheses that we have adopted regarding the heteronomy–autonomy typology (these will be presented later in this section).

Piaget's (1932/1965) monograph, *The Moral Judgment of the Child,* defines two general "stages" or "types" that trace developmental advance in the natural ontogenesis of moral judgment in children: a heteronomous stage followed by an autonomous stage. Piaget uses the term *stage* to characterize heteronomy and autonomy, but he does not define these two stages according to the strict stage criteria he applies to stages of logicomathematical thought (see Piaget, 1960). Instead he employs an ideal-typical approach following Weber (1949); hence the use of the ideal-typical approach in our current work also represents the adoption of Piaget's initial approach to the same issues.

Following Kant and in part Durkheim, Piaget sees morality as respect for rules and ultimately respect for the persons originating the rules. Piaget identifies two basic types of social relations in which this respect is grounded, corresponding to the two basic moral types or orientations. The first type of social relation is that of *unilateral respect* for parents or other authorities and the rules and laws they prescribe. This corresponds to the heteronomous type of morality and is marked by a "sui generis mixture of affection and fear or awe" directed toward authority figures. The second type of social relation is that of *mutual respect* among peers and equals; it includes respect for the rules that guide the interaction of equals. Mutual respect corresponds to the autonomous types of morality; its underlying structure is that of fairness in the sense of reciprocity and equality (as opposed to conformity and obedience to authority and to authority-made rules that mark the underlying structure of the heteronomous type). As Piaget (1932/1965) argues, "Autonomy therefore appears only with reciprocity, when mutual respect is strong enough to make the individual feel from within the desire to treat others as he himself would wish to be treated" (p. 196).

The following passage provides a helpful overview of Piaget's (1932/1965) views on the two types of social relations that lead to the two types of morality:

Our earlier studies led us to the conclusion that the norms of reason, and in particular the important norm of reciprocity, the source of the logic of relations, can only develop in and through cooperation. Whether cooperation is an effect or a cause of reason, or both, reason requires cooperation in so far as being rational consists in "situating oneself" so as to submit the individual to the universal. *Mutual respect* therefore appears to us as the necessary condition of *autonomy* under its double aspect, intellectual and moral. From the intellectual point of view, it frees the child from the opinions that have been imposed upon him while it favors inner consistency and reciprocal control. From the moral point of view, it replaces the norms of authority by that norm imanent in action and in consciousness themselves, the norm of reciprocity in sympathy.

In short, whether one takes up the point of view of Durkheim or of M. Bovet, it is necessary, in order to grasp the situation, to take account of two groups of social and moral facts – *constraint* and *unilateral respect* on the one hand, *cooperation* and *mutual respect* on the other. Such is the guiding hypothesis which will serve us in the sequel and which will lead us in examining the moral judgments of children to dissociate from one another two systems of totally different origin. Whether we describe the facts in the terms of social morphology or from the point of view of consciousness (and the two languages are, we repeat, parallel and not contradictory) it is impossible to reduce the effects of cooperation to those of constraint and unilateral respect. (pp. 107–108, emphasis added)

Piaget (1932/1965) considers the domain of morality as justice to be the focus of his typology. He claims that the most fundamental form of justice is distributive justice. In the autonomous orientation, distributive justice is reducible to equality and equity (equal distribution according to need) – both forms of reciprocity. (See chap. 1, this volume, for a discussion of equality, equity, and reciprocity as "justice operations.") In addition, Piaget examines corrective or retributive justice, which in the autonomous orientation is also directed to equality and reciprocity. Piaget characterizes the autonomous type of these two forms of justice as follows:

Towards 11–12 we see a new attitude emerge, which may be said to be characterized by the feeling of equity, and which is nothing but a development of equalitarianism in the direction of relativity. Instead of looking for equality in identity, the child no longer thinks of the equal rights of individuals except in relation to the particular situation of each. In the domain of retributive justice this comes to the same thing as not applying the same punishment to all, but taking into account the attenuating circumstances of some. In the domain of distributive justice it means no longer thinking of a law as identical for all but taking account of the personal circumstances of each (favouring the younger ones, etc.). Far from leading to privileges, such an attitude tends to make equality more effectual than it was before. (p. 317)

Piaget (1932/1965) then goes on to ask how constraint is to be distinguished from cooperation in considering the development of these ideas of justice? He also asks whether it is unilateral respect, the source of constraint, or mutual respect, the source of cooperation, that is the precipitating factor in the evolution of equalitarian and autonomous justice. His answers to his own questions are quite clear: Authority as such cannot be the source of justice, because the development of justice presupposes *autonomy* (p. 319). He acknowledges that the influence of adult authority probably does play an important role in the moral evolution of the child, but he is clear that it does not by itself create a sense of autonomous justice. This, he says, requires cooperation and mutual respect – "cooperation between children to begin with, and then between child and adult as the child approaches adolescence and comes, secretly at least, to consider himself as the adult's equal" (pp. 319–320).

Piaget's (1932/1965) concluding remarks with respect to his discussion of justice provide a very useful summary of his theory of heteronomous and autonomous morality. We quote him in full:

In conclusion, then, we find in the domain of justice, as in the other [domains] already dealt with, that opposition of two moralities to which we have so often drawn the reader's attention. The ethics of authority, which is that of duty and obedience, leads, in the domain of justice, to the confusion of what is just with the content of established law and to the acceptance of expiatory punishment. The ethics of mutual respect, which is that of good (as opposed to duty), and of autonomy, leads, in the domain of justice, to the development of equality, which is the idea at the bottom of distributive justice and of reciprocity. Solidarity between equals appears once more as the source of a whole set of complementary and coherent moral ideas which characterize the rational mentality. The question may, of course, be raised whether such realities could ever develop without a preliminary stage, during which the child's conscience is moulded by his unilateral respect for the adult. As this cannot be put to the test by experiment, it is idle to argue the point. But what is certain is that the moral equilibrium achieved by the complementary conceptions of heteronomous duty and of punishment properly so called, is an unstable equilibrium, owing to the fact that it does not allow the personality to grow and expand to its full extent. As the child grows up, the subjection of his conscience to the mind of the adult seems to him less legitimate, and except in cases of arrested moral development, caused either by decisive inner submission (those adults who remain children all their lives), or by sustained revolt, unilateral respect tends of itself to grow into mutual respect and to the state of cooperation which constitutes the normal equilibrium. It is obvious that since in our modern societies the common morality which regulates the relations of adults to each other is that of cooperation, the development of child morality will be accelerated by the examples that surround it. Actually, however, this is more probably a phenomenon of convergence than one simply of social pressure. For if human societies have evolved from heteronomy to autonomy, and from gerontocratic theocracy in all forms to equalitarian democracy, it may very well be that the phenomena of social condensation so well described by Durkheim have been favourable primarily to the emancipation of one generation from another, and have thus rendered possible in children and adolescents the development we have outlined above. (pp. 324–325)

In terms of the criteria we have taken from Piaget's work to define our conception of the autonomous type, freedom and mutual respect are the two that emerge most clearly from the foregoing discussion. Autonomous moral judgments are made under conditions of freedom, according to Piaget, because they are made without reference to external parameters, such as authority, tradition, or law, for justification or validation. This sense of freedom leads to a view of justice as equity and reciprocity, where equalitarianism is tempered with an appreciation for individual circumstances and particular situations. Autonomous freedom, for Piaget, is contrasted with heteronomous constraint. Heteronomous judgments fall under the constraint of external parameters for justification and validation. Piaget calls heteronomy the "ethics of authority and constraint," where what is just or right is confused with what the laws or rules say to do.

The following judgment represents the autonomous form of the freedom criterion in response to Dilemma III', the Officer Brown dilemma (the examples in this section are taken from the Moral Type Coding Manual, Appendix, Volume II):

How does this apply to how the judge should decide?

It takes the judge's own moral conscience to determine whether he should punish Heinz. (SAS 259.1)

The following heteronomous judgment reflects a lack of *freedom,* and the presence of constraint, in response to the same dilemma:

How does this apply to what the judge should decide?

The judge should do what he committed to do. He should follow the rules hard out. (SAS 220)

Mutual respect points to the fact that the autonomous type of moral judgment reflects an awareness of the importance of cooperation among equals in coming to just moral decisions. As Piaget says, mutual respect also entails reciprocity and involves treating others as one would like to be treated. The heteronomous type of moral judgment, on the other hand, exhibits unilateral respect for authority, tradition, or law, and clearly reflects the constraints imposed by those entities. Unilateral respect means that only certain powerful people or institutions deserve respect – respect that determines the outcome of moral decisions.

The following judgment represents the autonomous form of the mutual respect criterion in response to Dilemma I, the Joe dilemma:

What is the most important thing a father should be concerned about in his relationship to his son?

I guess one should honor those persons, parents, as you would want to be treated.

Why is that important?

Basically honoring rights, you know, the basic Golden Rule. (TR 302)

The following heteronomous judgment reflects a lack of mutual respect, and the presence of unilateral respect, in response to the same dilemma:

Which is worse, a father breaking a promise to his son, or vice versa?

For a son to break a promise to his father. Because a son should honor the father much more than the father should honor the son . . . after all, the father tells him what he can and what he can't do. (265–72)

Two other criteria, reversibility and constructivism, are also taken from Piaget's discussion of the autonomous and heteronomous types. Piaget suggests that mutual respect leads to autonomy because the true cooperation among peers that mutual respect entails also leads to a new conception of moral rules and laws (which he examined in the context of children's games). Rules become something that can be changed and altered if it is agreed upon by the group, for the truth of a rule no longer rests on tradition, but on mutual respect, agreement, and reciprocity (p. 95). Any change is possible or worthy of consideration, as long as new decisions are respected. As Piaget puts it; ". . . democracy follows on theocracy and gerontocracy" (p. 65). The child no longer relies on an all-wise tradition to determine each and every rule, and he no longer believes that everything has been done for the best in the past, nor that the only way to avoid trouble is by religiously respecting the established order (heteronomy). The child at the autonomous stage believes in the power and value of experiment as long as it is sanctioned by collective, cooperative opinion.

In this context Piaget (1932/1965) raises the concept of equilibrium and suggests that

this analysis will have shown how new in quality are the results of mutual respect as compared with those that arose out of unilateral respect. And yet the former is the outcome of the latter. Mutual respect is, in a sense, the state of equilibrium towards which unilateral respect is tending when differences between child and adult, younger and older, are becoming effaced; just as cooperation is the form of equilibrium to which constraint is tending in the same circumstances. In spite of this continuity in the facts it is necessary, nevertheless, to distinguish between the two kinds of respect, for their products differ as greatly as do autonomy and egocentrism. (p. 96)

From this discussion we have taken the criterion of reversibility to characterize the autonomous type of moral judgment, and we have tied it to Piaget's notion that the autonomous type achieves a degree of *equilibrium* that is not achieved in the heteronomous type of judgment. For Piaget (1967), a system or structure is reversible when it is in equilibrium (see also Kohlberg, 1981a). Autonomous moral judgments are more reversible or equilibrated than heteronomous judgments because they explicitly involve some form of mutual and reciprocal role taking. Thus all the actors in a particular situation are understood to consider each other's interests, claims, and points of view, before a just or fair solution to the problem at hand can be reached. The heteronomous type of judgment does not engage in role taking to this degree and tends to focus on a particular moral problem from only one perspective. Hence the solutions to a moral dilemma proposed by heteronomous judgments are not as reversible as those proposed by autonomous judgments.

The following judgment represents the autonomous form of the reversibility criterion in response to Dilemma III, the Heinz dilemma:

Is it important for people to do everything they can to save another's life?
I would think so. If the roles were switched, and I was the cancer victim I would appreciate help from others. (SAS 256.1)

The following heteronomous judgment reflects a lack of reversibility in response to Dilemma III':

Doesn't the judge have to consider Heinz's reasons for stealing?

It depends on the judge and the situation. The judge considers some things, but he can't consider everything. He has to give him a punishment . . .

So you think he is obligated to punish him?

Yes. Either him or the druggist. But I think Heinz deserves more in spite of wanting to save her. (288–73)

The constructivism criterion also finds clear expression in the preceding discussion. Constructivism implies that the autonomous type of judgment is aware that the rules, laws, and principles used to guide and frame moral decisions are actively constructed by the human mind, in the context of a social group based on cooperation among autonomous equals. This means that these rules and laws are not sacred entities, but that they are flexible and able to adapt to special situations and circumstances. The heteronomous type of judgment, by comparison, has a much more rigid view of rules and laws. Consequently the heteronomous type is much less likely to advocate flexibility in interpretation and/or enforcement of the standards than is the autonomous type.

The following judgment represents the autonomous form of the constructivism criterion in response to Dilemma III':

How does this apply to how the judge should decide?

It [the law] doesn't apply because sometimes there are extenuating circumstances requiring the law to be relaxed. (SHS 408–1)

The following heteronomous judgment reflects a lack of constructivism in response to the same dilemma:

Thinking in terms of society, should people who break the law be punished?

Judges are expected to punish criminals. Exceptions to [certain] cases can't be allowed, otherwise the whole system could become ambiguous in enforcements . . . Laws cannot be based on individual consciences because they are so diverse. (SAS 219)

Just as we have taken the four criteria described earlier from Piaget's work to help us to define our current conception of the heteronomy–autonomy typology, we have also used his work to guide our formulation of three general hypotheses regarding our typology. First, we assume that our heteronomy–autonomy moral typology, as defined by the nine criteria we have listed, is a developmental typology. Piaget assumes that his typology is a developmental typology in the sense that it is related to age. As a child grows older, she is more able to enter into peer relationships of mutual respect and solidarity, leading to the development of autonomous morality and the abandonment of heteronomous morality. And because heteronomous morality is less equilibrated than autonomous morality, there is a natural push toward the stable equilibrium of autonomy with increase in age, according to Piaget.

Whereas Piaget's (1932/1965) research on moral judgment focused primarily on children, it is important for our work to consider, given this age developmental hypothesis, whether it is possible for *adults* to remain within the heteronomous orientation. Piaget does assume that many adolescents and adults can and do remain heteronomous. At one point, in discussing how justice is viewed from the heteronomous orientation, and how from this standpoint what is just is confused with what is law, he claims that "justice is identified with formulated rules – as indeed it is in the opinion of a great many adults, of all, namely, who have not succeeded in setting autonomy of conscience above social prejudice and the written law" (p. 319).

Early in his monograph, Piaget asks, "How is it that democratic practice is so developed in the game of marbles played by boys of 11–13, whereas it is still so unfamiliar to the adult in many spheres of life?" (p. 76). His answer, in part, is that children of 11–13 have no superiors in the game of marbles – no one to impose pressure by virtue of their greater status, power, or prestige. Consequently, children of 11–13 are able to become *"conscious of their autonomy"* much sooner than if the game of marbles lasted until the age of 18, and 13-year-olds had to play with 18-year-olds. Piaget suggests that this *absence* of social pressure due to prestige and status, especially with regard to the pressure of one generation on another, is not as common in the adult world (p. 76). This suggests again that although Piaget's typology is fundamentally age related, it is possible for adults to make heteronomous judgments in a number of different moral spheres. We agree with this formulation.

According to Piaget (1932/1965), however, a developmental predominance of autonomous morality is dependent, at least in part, on the kind of social relations or society in which the child lives. Piaget expects that in traditional or "gerontocratic" societies based on what Durkheim calls "mechanical solidarity," heteronomous morality will extend into adulthood. It is only in societies based on "organic solidarity," cooperation, and "equalitarian democracy" that support the emancipation of one generation from another that the development from heteronomy to autonomy will proceed as he has outlined it (p. 325).

We adopt this argument as the basis for our second general hypothesis. We suggest, following Piaget, that the type of sociocultural environment and social relationships an individual is exposed to will have an effect on the development of autonomy in moral judgment. Environments that stress cooperation, mutual respect, organic solidarity, and equalitarian democracy will foster the development of autonomy. On the other hand, environments that stress constraint, unilateral respect, authority of the elders, and traditional laws and rules will inhibit the development of autonomy and support stabilization in heteronomy.

This view of the effect of social relations on the development of moral judgment is supported by current work of Damon (1983) and Youniss (1980). Both propose, following Piaget, a "two-worlds" hypothesis. They suggest that the two worlds that the child shares with parents and adult authorities, on the one hand, and peers and friends, on the other, contribute equally but differently to the child's development (Youniss, 1980). Our extension of this view is simply to suggest that different types of social relations influence the development of moral autonomy across the life span, not just in childhood.

Our third general hypothesis is based on Piaget's (1932/1965) observation that there is a marked difference between the heteronomous type and the autonomous type regarding the relationship between moral consciousness (or moral judgment) and moral action. Children at the heteronomous stage have a very profound and powerful respect for the rules, to the extent that they believe that rules cannot be changed, even by group agreement. When it comes to children's own individual application or practice of the rules, however, they are very idiosyncratic and egocentric, and exhibit only a slight awareness of the rules when they actually play the game. Children of this stage play more or less as they choose; they know the rough outlines of the rules or the pattern of the game, but they do not bother to obey the rules they know, and they are not troubled by even the most serious infraction in practice (p. 61). Yet when asked about the rules per se, they are adamant in their overriding respect for them. "With regard to [these] moral rules," Piaget claims,

> the child submits more or less completely in intention to the rules laid down for him, but these, remaining, as it were, external to the subject's conscience, do not really transform his conduct. This is why the child looks upon rules as sacred though he does not really put them into practice. (p. 62).

Piaget concludes that this striking difference between the egocentric ignoring of the rules in practice, and the unilateral, heteronomous respect exhibited for the rules in consciousness can be easily explained. He claims that this powerful respect is a function of a moral consciousness fashioned not by free cooperation among equals, but by adult constraint. True cooperation can only arise among *equals,* Piaget argues. He sets as his task in discussing moral autonomy to show how true cooperation among equals brings about not only a gradual shift in the child's *practical* attitude toward the rules of the game, but also an abandonment of the mystical feeling about authority (p. 62).

Piaget claims that at the autonomous stage the child, in losing this mystical feeling of respect for a law or rule, gains a practical respect for rules and laws in action – rules and laws understood to be constructed in an autonomous fashion through cooperation and mutual respect among equals. As Piaget describes this new view of rules; "Autonomy follows upon heteronomy: the rule of a game appears to the child no longer as an external law, sacred in so far as it has been laid down by adults; but as the outcome of a free decision and worthy of respect in the measure that it has enlisted mutual consent" (p. 65).

This autonomous view of rules and laws leads, Piaget argues, to a very strong relationship between autonomous moral judgment and moral action. This suggests our third hypothesis: Persons who make autonomous moral judgments will be more likely to engage in what might be called "moral action" than persons who make heteronomous moral judgments. This hypothesis is illuminated by Piaget's discussion of autonomous judgment and autonomous action in the simple context of the game of marbles. As he puts it:

> It is from the moment that it replaces the rule of constraint that the rule of cooperation becomes an effective moral law. . . . [That is,] when a rule ceases to be external to children and depends only on their free collective will, it becomes incorporated in the mind of each, and individual obedience is henceforth purely spontaneous. True, the difficulty reappears each time that the child, while still remaining faithful to a rule that favors him, is tempted to slur over some article of the law or some point of procedure that favors his opponent. But the peculiar function of cooperation is to lead the child to the practice of reciprocity, hence of moral universality and generosity in his relations with his playmates. (pp. 70–71)

We would argue that this relation between moral autonomy and moral action holds across the life span, and in many contexts other than the game of marbles. In doing so we follow Derek Wright (1982, 1983), who claims that Piaget's moral typology is primarily directed to the child's sense of practical obligation and to the social sentiment of respect from which it derives. On this view the heteronomy–autonomy distinction is very useful in examining situations of real-life choice and action. It also leads Wright to argue that Piaget's typology contributes to the understanding of the relation of moral judgment to moral action.

Baldwin

James Mark Baldwin's work, although not as central to our current formulation of the heteronomy–autonomy distinction as is Piaget's, nevertheless represents a very important theoretical source for the typology described in this chapter. Baldwin's general view of moral autonomy has influenced our thinking greatly. His work (and Kant's) also has enabled us to flesh out four additional criteria that we use to define our ideal typology: hierarchy, intrinsicalness, prescriptivity, and universality. Finally, like Piaget, Baldwin makes the very strong claim that the attainment of autonomy in moral judgment is a developmental achievement. His rationale for this lends support to our first general hypothesis – that the heteronomous–autonomous ideal-type distinction is developmental.

The core of Baldwin's (1897, 1906–1911) theory of moral autonomy in his description of three stages or levels of moral judgment. These ethical stages arise from Baldwin's theory of the development of genetic logic (1906–1911), which involves a successive set of differentiations between what he calls the "subjective" and "objective" poles of experience (Kohlberg, 1982; also Broughton & Freeman-Moir, 1982). Baldwin's stages or levels of moral judgment are parallel steps in the gradual differentiation of the subjective and the objective in the area of ends, values, and duties, rather than in the area of facts or objects. These three stages are summarized in Table A.2.

Baldwin calls his first ethical stage the objective or adualistic stage. He claims that the thought of very young children is adualistic in that values are assumed to be "syntelic"; that is, it is uncritically assumed by the child that his or her value attitudes are shared by everyone, or that what is a value for one is a value for all. Baldwin also claims that the thought of a young child is adualistic because it is "projective": There is no differentiation between the objective and physical properties of an object and the subjective and psychological value of that object. The adult ordinarily views the values of objects not as intrinsically located in the perceptual-physical attributes of the object, but as based on some relation of the object to the satisfaction of some subjective state, desire, or ideal held by some persons. The adualistic child does not make this differentiation; projective valuing leads to a confusion of the perceptual or physical qualities of an act or an object with its value, whether this value is instrumental or moral. In short, the adualistic stage is marked by a confusion between physical and moral values, resulting in the endowment of physical properties with quasi-moral value and moral values with quasi-physical properties.[4]

Baldwin calls his second ethical stage the dualistic, prudential, or intellectual stage. It is dualistic, according to Baldwin, for two reasons. The first concerns the fact that values are seen as "relative"; that is, judgments of value (for example, right and good) are based on self-interest, and relative to those interests. Judgments of value are understood to conflict where interests conflict. The

---

4 The current definition of moral Stage 1, the stage of morality defined in terms of obedience and avoidance of physical punishment, is based heavily on Baldwin's description of the adualistic stage.

Table A.2. *J. M. Baldwin's ethical stages*

I. Objective or adualistic stage

1. Value is *syntelic*. Failure to localize or distinguish for whom a bad event is bad. The value of an event to another person is shared by the self without basis; or the evaluation of the event by the self is believed to be held by others without basis.

2. Value is *projective*. Failure to see the value of an event as a means to an end, on which its value is strictly contingent, or as an expression of a purpose which defines its value. Value of an act is dependent on its consequences and on irrelevant perceptual similarities to other valued acts. There is a general failure to differentiate good and right from other meanings of good and right.

3. Duty is perceived as based on *objective* or external necessity. "Duty" or right action is identified with that which the self "has to do" or is compelled to do by external forces, authority, and sanctions.

II. Dualistic, prudential or intellectual stage

1. Value is *relativistic*. Judgments of right and good are relative to self-interest and judgments may be seen as conflicting where interests conflict.

2. Value is *instrumental* and based on need. The value of an object or act is based on its relation to an actual need or end involved in the particular situation.

3. "Duty" is perceived as a *hypothetical* imperative. Direction of action is not by compelling prescription or external pressure but is advisory and contingent on needs or motives of the actor.

III. Ethical or ideal stage

1. Value is public or *synomic*. The moral value accorded by the self to the event is that which it is believed could be accorded to it by anyone. At the same time this value which the public could hold is a value based on the self's own legitimate perspective in the situation. The value is not the opinion poll value but the value which the self perceives when taking the role of "any rational man" in the society, or which we think society ought to take.

2. Value is ideal or objective. Events are valued not in terms of ideal desires which the self *does* have, but in terms of ideal desires which the self *should* have. It is felt that objects or events *should* be valued in certain ways, that value requires an effort of judgment and appreciation.

3. Duty is perceived as based on inner compulsion, or moral necessity, on conscience. Action takes the form of a moral categorical imperative derived from the right in general, e.g., "I ought to or must do this because it is right, because I know or feel it to be right."

Source: Kohlberg (1958), pp. 344–345.

second concerns the fact that values are seen as "instrumental"; that is, judgments of value are based on need. The value of an object, act, or person is based on its relation to an actual need or end of interest to the individual in the particular situation.[5]

Baldwin's third and final ethical stage is the ethical or ideal stage. The term *ethical* is appropriate for this level, because it defines the content of the true moral realm itself. As such, values are understood to be "public" or "synomic"; that is, "the primary subject of ethical investigation is all that is included under the notion of what is good and desirable for man; all that is rea-

---

5 The present definition of moral Stage 2, the stage of individualistic, instrumental morality, is based heavily on Baldwin's description of the dualistic stage.

sonably chosen or sought by him, not as a means to some ulterior end, but for itself'' (Sidgwick, 1887). In Baldwin's second stage, the dualistic stage, the fact of desire or need is the end point of value. In the ethical stage *intrinsic* values are defined: values or purposes that are *desirable* rather than simply being *desired*. In addition, values at this stage are understood to be ''ideal''; that is, there is a differentiation between the desires people *do* have and the desires they *should* have. At the dualistic stage one has an ''ideal self'' only in the sense of wishing to possess objects or traits that are seen as means to satisfy given or nonideal needs or ends (for example, wealth, strength, power, beauty, etc.). At the ethical stage, though, one has an ''ideal self'' in the sense of wishing to possess ethical, good, or desirable motives or ends.

Expressed as the development of the means–ends dichotomy, an ''ideal self'' at the ethical stage means having the ability to view desires simply as means, and not as ends. There is a search for some further end to which various desires are means, and in terms of which they may be evaluated. Put in terms of objects, there is the conception that various acts or objects *should* be desired, regardless of whether in fact they *are* desired; ''ethical'' values are thus more objective than ''dualistic'' or ''instrumental'' values. This is not a return, however, to the adualistic or projective stage, where objects have a quasi-perceptual intrinsic value. At the ethical stage the intrinsic worth of the object is still the product of an act of value judgment by an observer; it is intrinsically ''there'' only in the sense that an *ideal observer* would judge it to be truly there. Some effort toward ''appreciation'' of the object is required, some process of judgment and experience by which the value of the object comes to be genuinely recognized – some further perspective on it to be gained. The actual value resides in this standard, and it is the subsuming of the experience or object *under* this standard that gives it value.

Ethical values are also more universal than instrumental values, according to Baldwin. In this sense the ethical stage resembles the adualistic stage, which holds that the valued is shared and that the shared is valuable. However, at the ethical stage, values are said to be shared in the sense of being public or synomic rather than syntelic. Ethical values are values that the individual believes everyone *should* hold, whether they do so or not. Efforts to state ethical *principles* are efforts to state rules and values that every human being *ought* to accept, whether or not they do accept them. The shared character of synomic valuing or moral principles is similar to that involved in scientific judgment. The standard of truth of scientific observation and inference is the standard that anyone else, in a similar situation, could make the same observation and inference. In fact, the scientist in her experiment observes something that no one else has observed, and often draws conclusions at variance with general or group belief. She asserts the validity of her own personal interpretation on the grounds that anyone else would come to the same conclusions if he or she followed the same methods of observation and inference (Kohlberg, 1982).

We have thus far discussed Baldwin's moral stages as stages in the understanding of the desired or the good, but they have corresponding meaning in the sphere of the required or the ought. Corresponding to the definition of ethics as the field of the intrinsic or the ideal good is the definition of ethics given by Kant (1785/1948) and others, as the field of intrinsic or unconditional duty – of the categorical as opposed to the hypothetical prescription of action. According to Baldwin, the categorical imperative or internal compulsion view of duty of the ethical stage must be distinguished not only from the hypothetical imperative of the dualistic stage but also from the earliest sense of external compulsion or necessity characteristic of the adualistic stage:

> First, there is the case in which the sanction is objective and unconditional, which we may call "objective necessity." "I am compelled to do this," or, "I must do this for you compel me," is its form. Second, the case of personal selection and decision within a whole of objective or possible social sanctioning, giving the "hypothetical imperative," "I should do this under certain conditions," or, "I should do this if I want this to happen," or, "I am impelled by prudence, by my interests, to do this." This in turn passes over, third, into the "moral necessity" of ideal conformity: "I must do this because it is right," or, "I ought to do this" [the categorical imperative]. (1906–1911, vol. 3, pp. 139–140)

At the stage of objective necessity, the child would say, "I have to go inside because it is raining." At the stage of the hypothetical imperative, he would say, "If I don't want to get wet, I'd better go inside." In the first case the child merely presents some unusually compelling external event. In the second case he simply states a means–end relationship and makes action dependent on the existence of a natural motive in the self on the particular occasion in question.

At the third stage, however, a person makes an assertion that an act should be done regardless of whether there is at the moment a corresponding need or external press. This necessity is based on a line of reasoning, thought, and feeling – not on physical pressure. The "value" that directs the reasoning does not defer to another self or aspect of the self to make the choice. There is, then, a certain necessity and impersonality associated with obligation at both the first and the third stages. At the third stage, though, this impersonality and disregard of the self's needs are those of the conscientious self oriented "only to duty." Although the definition of duty may be highly personal and strongly focused on providing for the needs and feelings of others, the acting subject who follows such a definition of duty feels that as a duty, it is distinct from his or her own feelings toward those needs. In contrast, at the first stage, it is not the action and conformity of the subject that is impersonal, it is the pattern or object *conformed to* that is impersonal and indifferent to needs. Outer authority or law may be seen as completely indifferent to the intention, needs, or welfare of anyone, but the self's reasons for obeying authority are based completely on personal need, or fear of punishment. This is not the case at the third stage.

Baldwin's theory of moral autonomy, as we have suggested, provides the source for four additional criteria that we use to distinguish the ideal autonomous type of moral judgment from the ideal heteronomous type. The first of these is the hierarchy criterion. We take this criterion primarily from Baldwin's notion that moral value at the ethical or autonomous stage is ideal and objective. That is, ideal, ethical, or moral value is understood to stand above all other values in a hierarchy of values. It implies that a person making autonomous judgment frames a clear hierarchy of values in response to a moral dilemma – a hierarchy that places the value of the moral consideration in the dilemma above all other values or considerations. Thus moral values and prescriptive duties are placed above pragmatic, descriptive, consequentialist, or aesthetic considerations. The heteronomous type, on the other hand, does not impute such value to these moral considerations and gives much more weight to the nonmoral consideration, as Baldwin describes in the context of the adualistic and dualistic stages.

The following judgment represents the autonomous form of the hierarchy criterion in response to Dilemma III:

Should Heinz have done that?
Yeah. He was justified, I feel.

Why?
Well, human life is infinitely more precious than money, which can be replaced. (45-C)

The following heteronomous judgment reflects a lack of a clear moral *hierarchy* in response to the same dilemma:

Should Heinz steal the drug?
No, if he's caught he will never get to see his wife and will spend a lot of time in jail. (SHS 319)

The intrinsicalness criterion is the second one taken from Baldwin's work. Intrinsicalness reflects Baldwin's notion that at the ethical or autonomous stage *intrinsic* values that are desirable rather than simply desired are defined. Intrinsicalness also refers to the autonomy of the moral personality as the primary object of moral respect, following Kant's (1785/1948) dictum: "Treat each person as an end, and never simply as a means." The autonomous type justifies moral decisions with reference to the value of persons in themselves, tied to a fundamental respect for moral personality, personal autonomy, and human dignity. The heteronomous type, in comparison, has a much more instrumental and pragmatic view of persons. Consequently, the heteronomous type is much more likely to advocate treating persons as a means to another end to which he or she imputes ultimate value than is the autonomous type. This is similar to the instrumental view of value that Baldwin defines in the context of the dualistic stage.

The following judgment represents the autonomous form of the intrinsicalness criterion in response to Dilemma III:

What is it about a person's life that makes it right to steal the drug?
You cannot compare anything to a human. Even the most expensive medicine in the world to a human life.

What about compared to law?
Ever since the beginning of the world, human life . . . is still different. (SAS)

The following heteronomous judgment reflects a lack of intrinsicalness in response to the same dilemma:

Is it important for people to do everything they can to save another's life?
Yes, in a way, but not always. If a person loves another then he should steal the drug, but if he does not have feelings which are deep, he should not risk his own consequences. (SHS 402)

The third criterion, prescriptivity, is taken from the instrinsic, unconditional, and categorical view of duty, which defines the nature and form of autonomous moral duty at the ethical stage for Baldwin. The autonomous type has a strong view of moral duty that prescribes a certain set of moral actions regardless of the inclinations of the actor, or various pragmatic considerations. That is, duty is perceived as based on inner compulsion, moral necessity, or conscience. The heteronomous type, on the other hand, is much more likely to have either an *objective* or a *hypothetical* view of moral duty, to use Baldwin's terminology.

The following judgment represents the autonomous form of the prescriptivity criterion in response to Dilemma III:

Why is it important to do everything you can to save another's life?

Because if you have a chance to save somebody, if you have a chance to let someone live longer, then I think you should do it . . . because people have a duty to help each other.

A duty?

Yes. Responsibility. I think they should feel responsible for other people's lives, whether or not they know them. (TR 232)

The following heteronomous judgment reflects a lack of unconditional prescriptivity, and a much more hypothetical view of moral duty, in response to the same dilemma:

If he doesn't love his wife, should he still steal the drug for her?

If he doesn't love his wife, why is he considering stealing for her?

What do you mean?

I don't think there's a should or shouldn't to it. It's his own initiative stealing the drug. Again, I don't think he has to put his life, his own freedom in jeopardy for her if he doesn't want to, and if he doesn't love her, he has no reason to want to, then, well, he shouldn't. (TR 984)

The fourth and final criterion taken from Baldwin's work, universality, is a crucial one with respect to our formulation of the autonomous type. It reflects Baldwin's understanding of the synomic, public, or universal character of moral values held at the ethical or autonomous stage. For Baldwin, moral autonomy involves the ability to generalize and universalize one's moral judgments, to apply them to anyone and everyone in the same or relevantly similar circumstances. The autonomous type generalizes and universalizes moral judgments made in response to a specific situation, in order that they apply to *anyone* in that situation. The heteronomous type, on the other hand, does not universalize or generalize his or her judgments. Instead heteronomous moral values are either syntelic – uncritically assumed to be held by everyone – or relative to instrumental self-interest.

The following judgment represents the autonomous form of the *universality* criterion in response to Dilemma III:

Suppose the dying person is a stranger, should he steal the drug?

Yes, he should steal because a life will be saved. Everybody carries a life no matter who they are . . . But let me spend five to six months in jail for the sake of humanity since I am a human being. (M.Y.-1976)

The following heteronomous judgment reflects a lack of *universality* in response to the same dilemma:

Do you think it is right to steal for a stranger?
No, I would never do it for a stranger.

Why?
Well, I'd say another guy with his wife, if he won't do it for his wife, why should I do it for his wife, or if he won't do it for his friend, why should I . . . It's not really a responsibility, I know it sounds like a responsibility, but it's really not, for him to steal for his best friend or for his wife . . . I guess it would be [if you] respect [or] like your best friend or your wife, depending on the case and your feelings for them naturally. (59-D)

To recapitulate, then, for Baldwin, when an individual attains the third stage of moral development, the ethical or ideal stage, the individual has attained true moral *autonomy*. Baldwin's view of the ethical stage is very similar, in many respects, to Piaget's description of the autonomous stage or type (see Broughton & Freeman-Moir [1982] for a discussion of the influence that Baldwin's work had on Piaget). The most important similarity is that Baldwin, like Piaget, claims that the attainment of the ethical, ideal, or autonomous stage is a developmental achievement. As such we use Baldwin's work, in addition to Piaget's, to support our first general hypothesis regarding the heteronomy–autonomy typology; namely, that the typology is a developmental one.

However, whereas Piaget claims that autonomy arises through cooperation and mutual respect in the context of interaction between peers and equals, Baldwin suggests that equality and reciprocity in what he calls the "bipolar" self–other relationship arise out of imitation, due to the subordination of both self and other to the ideal self or conscience. The "premoral" bipolar self becomes the ideal or moral self with the recognition that there are rules and norms that the model or authority (for example, the father) obeys or accommodates to even though he is the dominant partner in the bipolar self–other relationship. At this point the child begins to understand that there are rules and norms to which everyone in the family group (or everyone in general) has to conform. The self that is to conform to such moral norms is the ideal self: an imaginative self that the child is to become, and one that the parents only imperfectly represent or model. (See Kohlberg [1958, 1969, 1982] and Hart and Kohlberg [in press] for a fuller discussion of Baldwin's theory of the origins of the social and moral self.)

Baldwin's theoretical account of the genesis of autonomy differs, then, in significant ways from Piaget's. Although we have primarily adopted Piaget's view in our current formulation of the heteronomy–autonomy typology, we have no interest in joining this debate at the present time.

Immanuel Kant's work on moral autonomy has not only profoundly influenced our current work, but his "Groundwork of the Metaphysics of Morals" (1785/1948), and his views on the distinction between autonomy and heteronomy, inspired both Piaget's and Baldwin's work in the same area. In fact, it is not inappropriate to see both Piaget's and Baldwin's efforts (and our own) as attempts to operationalize Kant's seminal philosophical insights in psychological terms. We have used Kant's work to help us define our general view of moral autonomy and to distinguish it from heteronomy, as well as to justify the centrality of autonomy to our conception of mature moral judgment. We also have drawn on his work to define the following criteria: freedom, reversibility, constructivism, hierarchy, intrinsicalness, prescriptivity, and universality.

The central feature of Kant's moral theory, as it is presented in the "Groundwork," is his theory of moral autonomy. Kant claims that the fundamental characteristic of human beings is their ability to act *autonomously:* to act according to moral laws that they set for themselves, not according to external laws or determinations of nature; or to act so as to choose a particular end in itself, and not simply to choose the best means to a given end. Kant bases his view of autonomy on the human capacity for reason and freedom. He claims that when human beings act in pursuit of their desires they are actually slaves to something outside themselves, and hence they are not being truly rational or truly free. This state of nonautonomy Kant calls *heteronomy.* Acting on account of one's desires is heteronomous because it means acting because of external forces presented by nature. Similarly, acting heteronomously means acting for the sake of some particular goal, and thus acting becomes a *means* to a given end instead of being seen as an end that is intrinsically valuable in itself.

Kant's primary aim in the "Groundwork" is to discover how it is that human beings come to feel a sense of unconditional or autonomous moral obligation (or duty) to perform certain acts that they may in fact not be inclined to perform by reason of their own self-interest. Kant takes as his starting point ordinary human reason, and the fact that human beings experience feelings of moral obligation. His interest, therefore, is to investigate the source of these feelings of moral obligation, and to understand how it is that true moral obligation arises. Kant assumes that ordinary moral judgments concerning duties and obligations legitimately may claim to be true. The task he sets for himself, then, is to determine the *conditions* that must hold if these claims are to be justified (Paton, 1948, p. 15). Kant hopes that by following this course it will lead him to the ultimate condition of all valid moral judgments – the "supreme principle of morality."

For Kant, the search for the supreme principle of morality is the search for what he calls "the moral law." The moral law is not, however, a specific law that prescribes particular actions. Rather, it is a *formal* law, a law that designates the pure *form* of all genuinely moral duties, and genuine moral judgments, regardless of their content. Paton (1948), in his analysis of Kant's argument in the "Groundwork," acknowledges that some may find Kant's conception of the moral law empty, if not revolting. Nevertheless, he goes on to make the following argument in favor of Kant's view:

Yet is not Kant merely saying the minimum that can and must be said about morality? A man is morally good, not as seeking to satisfy his own desires or to attain his own happiness (though he may do both these things), but as seeking to obey a law valid for *all* men and to follow an objective standard not determined by his own desires. (p. 22)

Moral autonomy, according to Kant, is the key to the supreme principle of morality. Kant's primary thesis is that human beings as moral agents are subject only to those laws that they have made as reasonable and rational beings that are at the same time *universal*. In addition, they are bound only to act in conformity with a will that is their own, and which has, as nature's purpose, the making of universal law (p. 94, 432). Kant uses this thesis to suggest why all other previous attempts have failed to discover the supreme principle of morality. He claims that previous efforts have thought of persons merely as being subject to a law (whatever it might be) that had to carry with it some interest in order to attract or to compel. Since such a law did not spring as a law from human will, in order to conform to the law the will had to be necessitated by something else to act in a certain way. Such a conclusion meant that the supreme principle of absolute duty was never found, only the necessity of acting from a certain interest. This interest, says Kant, might be one's own or another's; but on such a view the imperative was bound to be always a conditioned one and could not possibly serve as a moral law (pp. 94–95, 432–433). Rawls (1982) suggests that Kant here is giving voice to an idea found in Rousseau (1762/1964) that greatly influenced him: namely, that liberty is acting in accordance with a law that we give to ourselves (see *The Social Contract*, book I, chap. viii).

The distinction that Kant draws between his view of morality and all other efforts to discover the supreme principle of morality in conditioned principles is essentially his distinction between autonomy of the will and heteronomy of the will. Autonomy of the will, argues Kant, *is* the supreme principle of morality. It is the property the will has of being or legislating a law unto itself (independently of every property belonging to external objects of volition). Hence the principle of autonomy, Kant says, is "never to choose except in such a way that in the same volition the maxims of your choice are also present as universal law" (p. 101, 440). He goes on to claim that an analysis of the concepts of morality clearly shows that the principle of autonomy is the sole principle of ethics. Analysis finds, he argues, that the supreme principle of morality (the moral law) must be a "categorical imperative" that commands nothing more nor less than precisely this autonomy.

Kant calls the moral law the *categorical imperative*, because it appears as a law that one *ought* to obey for its own sake. The categorical imperative, however, does not yield the content of any particular moral action. Rather, it provides a way of *evaluating* particular maxims of action, to see if they pass the test implicit in the form of the moral law. Maxims are accepted our rejected as being morally acceptable in terms of a law that is valid for all persons to follow, not in terms of the individual benefits they may bring to the actor.

In the "Groundwork," Kant presents three different formulations of the categorical imperative. The first is the Formula of the Universal Law:

Act only on that maxim through which you can at the same time will that it should become a universal law. (p. 84, 421)

Rawls (1982) suggests that the first formula outlines a procedure (the "CI Procedure") that describes the way a reasonable and rational (autonomous) human being goes about determining whether the action he or she is about to undertake conforms to the moral law, and hence is morally good and in accordance with moral duty. In other words, it defines the strict method that is to be used to specify the content of the moral law. As Rawls (1982) says, "It sets up the guiding framework that an agent is to use in moral deliberation in order to ascertain the requirements of pure practical reason" (Lecture VIII, p. 1). If a maxim does not pass the test entailed by the CI Procedure, that maxim cannot be considered to prescribe an action that is morally obligatory.

The second formula of the categorical imperative is the Formula of the End in Itself:

> Act in such a way that you always treat humanity, whether in your own person or in the person of any other, never simply as a means, but always at the same time as an end. (p. 91, 429)

Rawls (1982) suggests that this formula is designed by Kant to look at the categorical imperative from the standpoint of other persons, and not from the standpoint of the deliberating moral actor. It does not alter the content of the moral law, or affect the outcome of the CI Procedure entailed by the first formula. But it does, says Rawls (1982), represent a further perspective from which to regard and to understand the force of the consistent and intelligent application of the categorical imperative (Lecture VIII, p. 1).

The third and final formula of the categorical imperative is perhaps the most important for our purposes here. It is the so-called Formula of Autonomy:

> So act that your will can regard itself at the same time as making universal law through its maxim. (p. 93, 430–431)

Rawls (1982) claims that the significance of the third formula is that it focuses on the perspective of the deliberating autonomous moral agent, but this time as someone who *makes* the moral law, not as someone subject to the moral law (cf. the first formula). As such, "The CI Procedure is viewed as that procedure the adherence to which, with a full grasp of its meaning, enables us to regard ourselves as making universal law for a possible moral community (realm of ends)" (Rawls, 1982, Lecture VIII, p. 1).

In contrast to autonomy as described by the three forms of the categorical imperative is heteronomy of the will, which is the source of all spurious principles of morality, according to Kant. Because of its crucial role in our understanding of the distinction between autonomy and heteronomy, we quote Kant's discussion of heteronomy in full:

> If the will seeks the law that is to determine it *anywhere else* than in the fitness of its maxims for its own making of universal law – if therefore in going beyond itself it seeks this law in the character of any of its objects – the result is always *heteronomy*. In that case the will does not give itself the law, but the object does so in virtue of its relation to the will. This relation, whether based on inclination or on rational ideas, can give rise to only hypothetical imperatives: "I ought to do something *because I will something else.*" As against this, the moral, and therefore categorical, imperative, says: "I ought to will thus or thus, although I have not willed something else." For example, the first

says: "I ought not to lie if I want to maintain my reputation"; while the second says: "I ought not to lie even if so doing were to bring me not the slightest disgrace." The second imperative must therefore abstract from all objects to this extent – they should be without any *influence* at all on the will so that practical reason (the will) may not merely administer an alien interest but may simply manifest its own sovereign authority as the supreme maker of law. Thus, for example, the reason why I ought to promote the happiness of others is not because the realization of their happiness is of consequence to myself (whether on account of immediate inclination or on account of some satisfaction gained indirectly through reason), but solely because a maxim which excludes this cannot also be present in one and the same volition as a universal law. (p. 102, 441)

In short, Kant is convinced that no command or imperative issuing from an *external* source could be unconditionally binding on the human will (Schrader, 1963). He wants to distinguish clearly the heteronomous duty that results from such hypothetical imperatives from the autonomous duty that results from the categorical imperative. The unconditional nature of the moral laws constructed by the autonomous will is due to the fact that although the moral actor is bound by the laws that she makes, those laws are truly moral laws because they pass the universalizability test inherent in the first formula of the categorical imperative.

Hawes (1983) in his analysis of personal autonomy, provides a very helpful interpretation and summary of Kant's views on moral autonomy. He stresses the fact that, for Kant, unconditional and autonomous moral obligation must be *intrinsic*. Kant believes that unconditional moral obligation cannot be based on some nonmoral motive, inclination, or interest, because then the nature of the nonmoral consideration would constitute a condition for the application of moral obligation and the performance of moral action. Thus Kant rejects theories of morality that explain moral obligation and moral action by reference to nonmoral motives and considerations, and instead bases his view on instrinsically moral motives. "When Kant first mentions 'autonomy,'" says Hawes, "all we can clearly understand about it is that it is supposed to include or to provide for a motive for moral action that is intrinsically moral. He expresses this by saying that the moral motive is part of the person's own will" (1983, pp. 13–14).

In addition, Hawes (1983) also discusses Kant's view of the relationship between freedom and autonomy. He suggests that there are three separate senses in which Kant's concept of autonomy, defined as the condition of a reasonable and rational person obligated by an unconditional moral law, is related to the concept of freedom:

1. The autonomous person is free in that he is not determined by physical causes to act contrary to his moral obligation.
2. The autonomous person is the originator, as a rational being, of his moral action: he is the agent who makes the moral law for his action.
3. The autonomous person is the agent of judgment, the moral authority who judges what the correct application of moral principles is in his own situation. That he is the authority does not mean that he is always correct, but it does mean that he has the capacity to be correct and that he is the one whose responsibility it is to judge. (p. 30)

Finally, Hawes summarizes Kant's explanation of what unconditional moral obligation is and how it is possible by pointing to three central elements of Kant's view of moral autonomy. First, an actor must have an intrinsically moral motive to act according to his or her obligation. This motive must be intrinsic to the nature of the actor. Autonomous moral action cannot be done for the sake of some extrinsic, nonmoral motive, if moral obligation is to be unconditional (otherwise it is conditional and heteronomous). Second, moral action must be done on the basis of knowledge, both of the fact that the actor is obligated in general, and of what the actor's particular obligation is in any particular circumstance. Third, the actor must be seen as having the power to act on the basis of his moral obligations. If the actor did not have the power to act he could not be obligated to act. Nor could he be seen as responsible for his actions, if the power to act were not his to employ according to his own choice. These three elements form the core of Kant's theory of moral autonomy (Hawes, 1983, p. 33).

As a way of summarizing Kant's work and its relevance for our present conception of the heteronomy–autonomy ideal typology, let us briefly point to the specific criteria that his work helps to illuminate. In terms of the *freedom* criterion we follow Hawes's (1983) interpretation of Kant's work in assuming that the autonomous type will stress the autonomy of the moral domain over the nonmoral domain. Also, an autonomous judgment will be made under conditions of personal freedom. A heteronomous judgment, on the other hand, will stress personal or nonmoral considerations and will not be made under conditions of freedom.

With respect to the *reversibility* criterion, there is a close connection between Kant's conception of universality and Piaget's notion that a structure or system that is in *equilibrium* is also *reversible*. This relationship between universality and reversibility in justice reasoning is clearly brought out in the writings of Frankena (1973), Hare (1963, 1981), Rawls (1971, 1980), and other "Kantian" and "Neo-Kantian" moral philosophers. It is also elaborated in Kohlberg's (1981a) essay, "Justice as Reversibility." Here we need simply to note that to universalize a norm or obligation is to make it reversible. It is giving oneself an obligation one wishes all others to adhere to as well. In so doing it implies reversibility or interchangeability between one's own point of view and the point of view of others – reconciling what one expects of oneself, what one expects of others, and what expectation of others one will accept for oneself.

Kant's work has also influenced our thinking regarding the *constructivism* criterion. Kant's constructivist view of the way in which autonomous agents act on laws that they construct and give themselves is a crucial aspect of his moral theory. For Kant the essence of autonomy is to be self-legislating with respect to rules and laws. And the essence of heteronomy is to hold a nonconstructivist view of moral laws, and to act only according to externally imposed parameters.

In terms of the *hierarchy* criterion, Kant's work suggests that autonomous moral judgments will involve the rational construction of a moral hierarchy in which the intrinsically moral considerations will be placed above the nonmoral considerations. Thus hierarchy is very closely tied to the *intrinsicalness* criterion. As Hawes (1983) emphasizes, according to Kant unconditional and autonomous moral action or moral judgment is based on intrinsically valuable moral considerations, and not on nonmoral motives, inclinations, or interests. Heteronomous actions and judgments *are* based on these nonintrinsic considerations, however, and thus a hierarchy is often constructed that is the inverse of the autonomous hierarchy.

The *prescriptivity* criterion finds its strongest expression in Kant's notion of unconditional and autonomous moral duty. The categorical imperative expresses the obligation inherent in the moral law. Thus autonomous moral judgments based on intrinsic moral considerations necessarily involve unconditional or categorical moral obligation, according to Kant. Heteronomous judgments, on the other hand, do not entail such categorical obligations. Instead they are based on hypothetical imperatives.

Finally, the *universality* criterion is directly tied to the universalizability test implied in the first formula of the categorical imperative. For Kant, moral autonomy involves the ability to generalize and universalize one's moral maxims so that they apply to anyone and everyone in the same or relevantly similar circumstances as if by a law of nature. If the maxim can be universalized and still be logically held, then the maxim prescribes a truly autonomous moral duty. Heteronomous judgments are not universalizable in the same way, and thus do not pass the test inherent in the CI Procedure.

In conclusion, Kant's work clearly plays a very important role in our current formulation of the heteronomy–autonomy typology. It is not necessary, however, to accept all of Kant's moral philosophy in order to find his distinction between heteronomy and autonomy useful. We do not subscribe to all of Kant's system, especially his strict application of the categorical imperative to define the only true moral duty. We *do* look to his work on moral autonomy for general inspiration, though, especially as it influenced both Piaget and Baldwin.

Summary of Current Theoretical Formulation and Hypotheses

The preceding presentation of our current theoretical formulation of the heteronomy–autonomy ideal typology has been organized around nine criteria that distinguish heteronomous from autonomous moral judgments. In our presentation of the theoretical sources for those criteria, however, we have discussed only eight of them. The ninth criterion, *choice,* has not yet been addressed. This is because the choice criterion is in a somewhat different class than the first eight. It emphasizes content in a different way than do the other criteria, and consequently it is less formal, and more probabilistic. In short, this criterion reflects the action choice advocated as the solution to a particular hypothetical moral dilemma. Each dilemma on the MJI has an action choice that represents the solution to the dilemma that is generally seen as fair and just from the standpoint of the postconventional stages of moral judgment. An individual who makes autonomous moral judgments is much more likely to choose and justify this solution than is a person who makes heteronomous judgments. For example, on Form A, the autonomous choice on Dilemma III is for Heinz to steal the drug, on Dilemma III' it is for the judge to set Heinz free, and on Dilemma I it is for Joe to refuse to give his father the money.

Table A.3 presents the nine criteria we use to define the heteronomy–autonomy typology in summary form. These criteria represent an empirical cluster of characteristics that serve to define the ideal forms of our two types. We have looked to the work of Piaget, Baldwin, and Kant on moral autonomy to provide theoretical support and rationale for the criteria we have identified. And we have developed a coding scheme based on these criteria that will be described in the next section.

One final word about Piaget and Baldwin before turning to a review of our three general hypotheses: It is important to distinguish between the contribution

Table A.3. *Criteria upon which heteronomy–autonomy distinction is based*

1. *Freedom:* Autonomous judgments are made without reference to external parameters, such as authority, tradition, or law, for justification or validation. Heteronomous judgments fall under the constraint of external parameters for justification and validation.

2. *Mutual respect:* Autonomous judgments reflect an awareness of the importance of cooperation among equals in coming to just and fair moral decisions. Mutual respect also entails treating others as one would like to be treated. Heteronomous judgments exhibit unilateral respect toward authority, law, tradition, or power – whether in the form of persons or institutions.

3. *Reversibility:* Autonomous judgments are reversible or equilibrated because they explicitly involve some form of (at least rudimentary) mutual and reciprocal role taking. Thus all the actors in a particular situation are understood to consider each other's interests, claims, and points of view before a just or fair solution to the problem can be reached. Heteronomous judgments do not involve explicit role taking to this degree, and tend to focus on a particular moral problem from only one perspective.

4. *Constructivism:* Autonomous judgments reflect an awareness that rules and laws used to guide and frame moral decisions are actively formulated by the human mind, in the context of a social group ideally based in cooperation among equals. Thus rules and laws are understood to be flexible and able to adapt to special situations and circumstances. Heteronomous judgments reflect a sacred, rigid, and inflexible view of rules and laws.

5. *Hierarchy:* Autonomous judgments reflect a clear hierarchy of values that places moral values and prescriptive duties above pragmatic, descriptive, consequentialist, or aesthetic considerations in the resolution of a moral dilemma. Heteronomous judgments do not reflect a clear moral hierarchy. Instead nonmoral and pragmatic considerations are weighed heavily in the resolution of a moral dilemma.

6. *Intrinsicalness:* Autonomous judgments are based on a fundamental valuing of persons as ends in themselves, tied to a basic respect for moral personality, personal autonomy, and human dignity. Heteronomous judgments are based on a much more pragmatic and instrumental view of persons. Consequently, heteronomous judgments are much more likely to advocate treating persons as means to another end than are autonomous judgments.

7. *Prescriptivity:* Autonomous judgments reflect a view of moral duty that prescribes a certain set of moral obligations and actions regardless of the inclination of the actor, or various pragmatic considerations. Moral duty is based on inner compulsion, moral necessity, or conscience. Heteronomous judgments reflect an instrumental or hypothetical view of moral duty.

8. *Universality:* Autonomous judgments reflect the willingness to generalize and universalize moral judgments in order that they apply to anyone and everyone in the same or relevantly similar circumstances. Heteronomous judgments are not explicitly universalized or generalized. Instead heteronomous moral judgments or values are either uncritically assumed to be held by everyone, or understood to be relative to instrumental self-interest.

9. *Choice:* In response to a particular moral dilemma, the individual who makes autonomous moral judgments is much more likely to choose and justify the solution to the dilemma that is generally seen as *just* and *fair* from the standpoint of the postconventional stages of moral judgment than is the individual who makes heteronomous judgments.

that both Piaget's and Baldwin's work has made to Kohlberg's definitions of the *stages* of moral judgment and the contribution that their work has made to our new definition of the heteronomous and autonomous moral *types*. There are clear parallels between Kohlberg's stages and Piaget's and Baldwin's types, stages, and levels, because to a certain extent Kohlberg relied on Piaget's and Baldwin's work to define his structural stages. However, we have also used the same types, stages, and levels in Piaget's and Baldwin's work to define our two ideal moral types. This has been possible to achieve without contradiction because from our point of view both Piaget and Baldwin confounded stage and type in their descriptions of moral development. Thus we view our current work as a refinement of Piaget's and Baldwin's theories of moral development. As such we have attempted to separate the aspects of their descriptions that are characteristic of structural moral judgment stages from the aspects that are characteristic of heteronomous and autonomous ideal types.

The three general hypotheses regarding the heteronomy–autonomy typology that we have adopted, following Piaget, are as follows: The first general hypothesis reflects our assumption that the heteronomy–autonomy distinction defines a developmental typology. Under this general hypothesis we posit two specific hypotheses: The first is that there is a relationship between moral type and chronological age such that as age increases subjects will be more likely to be scored as making autonomous moral judgments on the MJI. Here we follow Piaget and Baldwin, both of whom postulate a strong relationship between increase in age and the attainment of the autonomous or ideal moral stage. We understand this to be our weak developmental hypothesis, in that any construct that is deemed to be developmental must bear a necessary relationship to age. Increase in age provides a precondition for development that does not *explain* developmental advance, per se, but does provide a ''floor'' with respect to the attainment of a developmental attribute. As such age is a predictive indicator of, or *proxy* for, life experience and/or education that has a positive effect on the development of moral autonomy in the domain of justice.

The second specific developmental hypothesis we hold concerns the developmental pattern shown by the heteronomy–autonomy typology over the course of the natural ontogenesis of moral judgment. Again following Piaget and Baldwin, we assume that the attainment of moral autonomy is a developmental achievement, and that it naturally occurs at one particular point in an individual's life. Consequently, we expect that in an individual set of longitudinal interviews the moral type pattern will be as follows: an initial series of heteronomous type scores, then at some point *a one-time shift to moral autonomy,* followed by stabilization at the autonomous type. Ideally we expect this one-time shift to be irreversible; hence individuals who have attained moral autonomy will not return to a heteronomous type of moral judgment. However, in reality we can only predict that there will be a *tendency* for this one-time shift to occur and to stabilize. We expect to find some ''reversals'' in these patterns, due both to measurement error associated with our ideal-typical coding method and to the fact that moral type, as we have defined it, is very responsive to specific social environments. That is, we expect that a change in social environment from one that is supportive of moral autonomy to one that is not may cause an individual to change from making autonomous to making heteronomous moral judgments. We also claim, however, following Piaget, that not all individuals will make the developmental shift to autonomy. As such, we expect to find some adults in our longitudinal studies who have never made the shift to autonomy, and who are living stable and fully functioning lives.

Our second general hypothesis, following Piaget, is that the type of sociocultural environment and social relations that an individual is exposed to will have a direct effect on the development of autonomy in moral judgment. As such, we expect sociocultural environments and social relations that stress democracy, equality, cooperation, and mutuality of relationships to be likely to exert a positive influence on the development of autonomous moral judgment. In contrast, we expect environments that are authoritarian, where a strict traditional social hierarchy is followed, and where obedience and generational respect are stressed, to be less likely to facilitate the development of autonomy, and to be more likely to perpetuate heteronomy. In short, following Piaget, we expect that social environments that stress cooperation and mutual respect lead to autonomy, whereas those that stress constraint and unilateral respect lead to heteronomy. This includes both the environments encountered by children and those encountered by adults.

Our third general hypothesis concerns the relationship between moral type and moral action. Following Piaget, again, we expect that the individuals scored as making autonomous judgments will be more likely to engage in moral action than will subjects scored as making heteronomous judgments. This assumption is based on Piaget's extensive examination of the difference between children at the heteronomous stage and those at the autonomous stage concerning the actual respect shown the rules of the game in practice. We have extrapolated from this finding to suggest that the heteronomous and autonomous types found across the life span also bear a similar relationship to action performed in accordance with "moral" rules. The autonomous type, because of his or her intrinsic respect for moral rules and principles that indicate what is the right, just, or fair thing to do in a particular situation, is much more likely to act on those rules and principles than is the heteronomous type. This is due to the fact that the autonomous type accepts the obligations inherent in moral rules and principles that are autonomously constructed under conditions of mutual respect and cooperation. The heteronomous type, on the other hand, is constrained by rules and laws that he does not experience as intrinsically obligating. Hence the autonomous type will be more likely to act justly and fairly than the heteronomous type in a situation that calls for a deliberate moral action.

Before we conclude this section it is important to review another current typological approach in the moral domain – an approach that resembles ours in several ways. We have in mind the typology based on the work of Erich Fromm (1947), as operationalized by Martin Hoffman (1970a, b). Fromm's psychology of ethics centers on a neopsychoanalytic-typological approach to social character. In one form his typology represents a series of developmental types: the Receptive, the Exploitative, the Hoarding, the Marketing, and the Productive orientations.[6] Although in one form Fromm's (1947) typology represents a developmental series, it also reduces to a productive–nonproductive dichotomy with the first four developmental types being classified as nonproductive.

---

6 In this form, the typology is close to the psychological typology of character development of Peck and Havighurst (1960): the Amoral, the Expedient, the Conforming, the Irrational-Conscientious, and the Rational-Altruistic. Peck and Havighurst assessed their types through clinical case ratings of motives and conduct, including interviews, projective tests, and parent, teacher, and peer ratings.

The productive–nonproductive dichotomy derives from Fromm's (1941) analysis of the authoritarian personality embodied in the German and Italian fascist movements.

Fromm's (1947) central contrast is between an *authoritarian* and a *humanistic* ethic. According to Fromm a humanistic ethic is rooted in the Enlightenment, with its belief in reason as a basis for knowledge and goodness, and its optimism concerning progress toward solving the problems of want, disease, war, and other human evils. In addition to its optimistic belief in reason, the post-Enlightenment humanistic ethic is rooted in respect for human personality and the dignity of humankind. Opposing this ethic are modern authoritarian ethics, sometimes relativistic and cynical like the Nazi ideology, sometimes absolutistic and transcendental like the pre-Enlightenment medieval Christian ethic.

According to Fromm (1947):

Authoritarian ethics can be distinguished from humanistic ethics by two criteria, one formal, the other material. *Formally,* authoritarian ethics denies man's capacity to know what is good or bad; the norm giver is always an authority transcending the individual. Such a system is not based on reason and knowledge but on awe of the authority and on the subject's feelings of weakness and dependence; the surrender of decision-making to the authority . . . ; its decisions cannot and must not be questioned. *Materially,* or according to content, authoritarian ethics answers the question of what is good or bad primarily in terms of the interests of the authority, not the interests of the subjects; it is exploitative, although the subjects may derive considerable benefits, psychic or material, from it. . . . For the developing person "Good" is that for which one is praised; "Bad," that for which one is frowned upon or punished by social authorities or by the majority of one's fellow men. Indeed, the fear of disapproval and the need for approval seem to be the most powerful and almost exclusive motivations for ethical judgment. This intense emotional pressure prevents the child, and later the adult, from asking critically whether "good" in a judgment means good for him or good for the authority. . . . The unforgivable sin in authoritarian ethics is disobedience or rebellion, the questioning of the authority's right to establish norms and of its axiom that the norms established by the authority are in the best interests of the subjects. Even if a person sins, his acceptance of punishment and his feeling of guilt restores him to "goodness" because he then experiences his acceptance of the authority's superiority. . . . *Humanistic* ethics, in contrast to authoritarian ethics, may likewise be distinguished by formal and material criteria. *Formally,* it is based on the principle that only man himself can determine the criteria for virtue and sin, and not an authority transcending him. *Materially,* it is based on the principle that "good" is what is good for man and "evil" what is detrimental to man; *the sole criterion of ethical value being man's welfare.* (pp. 147–176; emphasis added)

Fromm stresses that each of these types of ethics has a distinctive *conscience*. An authoritarian conscience "takes disobedience and criticism of authority as the basis for guilt," whereas a humanistic conscience "takes actions violating [one's] own integrity, [one's] own care for the self, or care for others, as the basis for guilt" (Fromm, 1947, pp. 147–76).

Hoffman (1970a, b) attempted to operationalize Fromm's neopsychoanalytic typology by selecting two groups of seventh-grade middle-class children, groups similar in showing an equal level of "internalization" or guilt both on a story completion test and in acceptance of blame for a misdeed based on parent and teacher ratings. Two types of indicators were used to define humanistic as opposed to conventional or authoritarian moralities. The first was the use of appeals to harm to others, as opposed to rule or institution violation per se. The second was consideration of extenuating circumstances in judging an act right or wrong. Two of the Kohlberg (1958) dilemmas were used to pull for these indicators. Dilemma III (the Heinz dilemma) was used to pull for concern for extenuating circumstances, and Dilemma VII (which is worse, stealing or breaking a trust?) was used to select indicators of concern for defining wrong in terms of institutional rules versus intrinsic harm to others. The major differences found by Hoffman (1970a, b) were that "humanistic" subjects were more tolerant of antimoral impulses, more apt to experience guilt as a result of awareness of the consequences of their behavior to others, and more identified with the personal rather than the power aspects of their parents' role. The conventional or authoritarian subjects appeared to be more repressed, to experience guilt as a result of impulse expression rather than harm to others, and to be more identified with the power aspect of their parents' role. Their parents reported more reliance on love withdrawal and induction of guilt about harm to themselves than did the parents of the humanistic subjects.

In summary, Fromm's neopsychoanalytic theory of socialization and of social character was used by Hoffman to define types somewhat similar to our moral types on two of our moral dilemmas. Some confirmation of the hypothesized relationship of the two types to types of guilt on the one hand, and to types of parental discipline and socialization on the other, were found. From the point of view of our more cognitive-developmental and structural approach to the heteronomous and autonomous moral types, the Fromm-Hoffman types do not appear to define ideal types with clear developmental implications to the extent that our current types do. Their work does, however, point to a certain important consistency between our types and types derived from a neopsychoanalytic socialization approach.

Coding Scheme

The aim of this section is to present an overview of the coding scheme we have devised to assess heteronomous and autonomous moral types. It is designed to code moral judgments that are elicited using the Moral Judgment Interview (MJI). This coding scheme represents our effort to operationalize the construct presented in the previous section: the ideal-typical distinction between moral heteronomy and moral autonomy.

Our coding scheme represents a relatively simple clinical approach to the assessment of moral types. Following Weber's (1930) ideal-typical approach, as discussed earlier, it is designed to yield a single dichotomous score for the moral judgments that an individual subject makes in response to the MJI: heteronomous Type "A" or autonomous Type "B." Our coding scheme is also designed to be used in conjunction with Standard Issue Scoring (see chap. 1, 2, and 7 of this volume), so that from the same MJI a subject's structural stage and moral type can be assessed. It is important to note, however, that these two assessment procedures are independent.

The nine criteria outlined in the previous section form the core of our moral type coding scheme. The coding manual itself consists of a specific translation of these theoretical criteria into coding criteria for each of the three standard hypothetical dilemmas on Forms A, B, and C of the MJI.

In line with our ideal-typical approach to this construct, we have developed idealized forms of each of the nine criteria for each dilemma: a "B" form that represents the idealized autonomous judgment, and an "A" form that represents the idealized heteronomous judgment. The scorer's task is to determine which of the two forms of the criterion in question a given subject's moral judgment most closely resembles. The scorer has only a dichotomous choice in this regard – a response must be given either an A or a B on the appropriate criterion.

The "unit of analysis" for this coding scheme, therefore, is the individual dilemma as a whole. This is similar to the approach adopted by Kohlberg (1958) in his original ideal-typical study of moral judgment development. In this approach an individual's responses to a particular dilemma on the MJI are assessed using the nine criteria described earlier. The underlying "structure" of either the ideal heteronomous or autonomous type of judgment is then inferred based on the nine scoring criteria for the dilemma as a whole. We have found that using the dilemma as a unit of analysis yields much greater consistency than was obtained by the old element scoring system associated with the substage construct, which used individual interview judgments as the unit of analysis. As stated earlier, the element scoring system was abandoned, partially because of the lack of consistency within an interview obtained by scoring each individual IJ–CJ match for substage as well as for stage. No internal consistency or structured wholeness could be inferred using this method because the most common pattern was to have an even split between Substage A and Substage B element scores within any given interview. The larger unit of analysis associated with the current coding scheme, and ideal-typical approach, has yielded a much greater degree of consistency within dilemmas than was ever obtained using the element system.

Table A.4 presents information taken from the appendix to Volume II (Coding Moral Types) and provides examples of the way in which the nine theoretical criteria have been translated into specific coding criteria for this dilemma. The manual also presents the idealized A and B forms (called Pass and Fail) for each criterion, and provides examples taken from cases to illustrate the two forms of the nine criteria.[7]

One of the most difficult aspects of translating the nine general criteria from the theoretical level to the coding level was applying the general criteria to the specifics of each dilemma. Table A.4 shows that for Dilemma III, as for all the dilemmas, some of the criteria become tied to specific questions and issues in the dilemma, whereas others refer to a more general approach to the dilemma as a whole. For example, in Dilemma III, the universality criterion is tied to the specific question of whether or not Heinz should steal for a stranger, whereas the freedom criterion refers to the subject's overall approach to the dilemma. In other words, because the structure of each of the dilemmas is not identical, not all of the nine criteria play an equally strong role in distinguishing autonomy from heteronomy in every dilemma.

In order to address this phenomenon we have identified "critical" criteria for each dilemma. These four or five criteria are the ones that empirically have been found to be the most robust and consistent for the dilemma in question, that is, the ones that are most useful in distinguishing autonomous judgments

---

7 Note that the criteria are presented in a different order here than they are presented in Table A.3. This is because the order followed in Table A.4 is the natural order in which the nine criteria appear in the dilemma, due to the structure of the dilemma.

Table A.4. *Coding criteria for Dilemma III*

Choice:
B: Heinz should steal the drug.

Should Heinz steal the drug?
Yeah, he should. Because life is more important than anything else, it's more important than money or anything in this world. (67-E)

Choice:
A: Heinz should not steal the drug.

Should Heinz steal the drug?
No, because people can't go around stealing from others no matter what the situation is. (SAS 271)

Hierarchy:
B: The wife's life, the (moral) value of her life, or her right to life takes precedence over, or is more important than, the law, the druggist's property rights, the fact that Heinz may be punished for his actions, or Heinz's own needs.

Should Heinz have done that?
Yes. Because life is more important than any amount of money. (SHS 115)

Hierarchy:
A: The law, the druggist's property rights, the fact that Heinz may be punished for his actions, or his intrapersonal or instrumental need takes precedence over, or are more important than the (moral) value of saving the wife's life.

Should Heinz steal the drug?
No, because people can't go around stealing things from others no matter what the situation is. (SAS 271)

Intrinsicalness:
B: The wife's, friend's, or stranger's lives in particular, or human life in general, has (moral) value in itself. The life in question is valuable, and thus should be saved, regardless of social status, potential productivity, or personal benefit to Heinz.

What do you see that is important about life?
Just the being, the person. Each one is unique, every person is unique and I think every person is important, has his own or her own worth. (67-E).

Intrinsicalness:
A: The life of the wife, friend, or stranger is not seen as having (moral) value in itself. The life in question may be seen as having instrumental or personal significance to Heinz, or instrumental value to society.

Should Heinz steal the drug for a stranger?
I think from nature, from man's nature, that to those who are near him, he relates as if they are more equal. If all are equal then there are those who are more equal and those who are less equal (or could be translated as "worth more/less"). (211-78)

355

Table A.4. (*cont.*)

Prescriptivity:
B: Heinz has a duty, obligation, or responsibility to steal the drug to save his wife's life, whether he loves her or not.

If he doesn't love his wife should he steal?

He should steal. It's his duty to her, his human duty. *What is human duty?* People should help each other, people are living beings above all. (B., 1976)

Prescriptivity:
A: Heinz has no duty, obligation, or responsibility to steal the drug to save his wife's life. [In addition, taking such an action may be seen as solely dependent on Heinz's own feelings or inclinations.]

It is against the law for Heinz to steal. Does that make it morally wrong?

Yeah. *Why?* Because if he likes prison he should steal it, if he don't then he shouldn't steal it. (TR 196)

Universality:
B: Given the same or similar circumstances, it is morally right (justified) for Heinz to steal the drug to save the life of a friend or stranger.

Suppose the dying person is a stranger, should he steal the drug?

Yes, he should steal because a life will be saved. Everybody carries a life no matter who they are . . . But let me spend five to six months in jail for the sake of humanity since I'm a human being. (M., 1976)

Universality:
A: Given the same or similar circumstances, it is not morally right (justified) for Heinz to steal the drug to save the life of a friend or stranger.

Do you think it is right to steal for a stranger?

No, I would never do it for a stranger. *Why?* Well, I'd say another guy with his wife, if he won't do it for his wife, why should I do it for his wife, or if he won't do it for his friend, why should I . . . It's not really a responsibility, I know it sounds like a responsibility, but it's really not, for him to steal for his best friend or for his wife . . . I guess it would be respect like your best friend or your wife, depending on the case and your feelings for them naturally. (59-D)

Freedom
B: Heinz must act according to his conscience or his self-chosen moral values or principles that advocate saving a life regardless of the external constraints imposed by the law, or other external considerations.

Can you say what you mean by moral law?

I would say that the moral law would be something that each person possesses; it would be distinct from the universal or national laws, and the moral laws could apply to virtually every interaction a person takes. And there are certain judgments which he has to decide upon. He's going to make a decision: is it right; is it wrong? The basis of that is that he should be governed by this judgment of right or wrong on a separate basis as opposed to these general laws that have been written. (TR 227)

Table A.4. *(cont.)*

Freedom:
A: Heinz is bound by the constraints of the law, the social system, or some other external influence.

Should people try to do everything they can to obey the law?

Yes . . . *How does this apply to Heinz?* The law rules and is supreme! He can get around the law, but why not let others take their chances instead? (SHS 402)

Mutual respect:
B: Heinz should respect his wife as he would want her to respect him. Mutual respect involves treating persons as ends, not merely as means.

Is it important to save another person's life?

Yes. People must respect other's lives and wills to live as they value their own. (SAS 236)

Mutual respect:
A: The actors in the dilemma do not treat each other as equals, and there is a lack of respect between them. [For example, Heinz should unilaterally respect the law in spite of the wife's right to life.]

Reversibility:
B: Heinz and/or the druggist should take into account the interests, concerns, and claims of the dying person. He must view the dilemma from the perspective of the dying person, as well as from his own.

How does this (breaking the law or not) apply to what Heinz should do?

He should do, all things considered, what is best for everyone involved. (SAS 273)

Reversibility:
A: Heinz and/or the druggist is understood to view the dilemma *only* from his particular point of view.

How does this apply to what Heinz should do?

Well if he stole the drug, it would involve the druggist who invented the drug and it would be wrong. (SAS 271)

Constructivism:
B: Rules, laws, and norms are humanly constructed, and must remain flexible and open to interpretation in order to respond to special situations and circumstances.

Should people do everything they can to obey the law?

Yes and no. *Why?* Yes, because the laws were made for the benefit of the majority. No, because the laws weren't made for everybody, and some of the laws may be inapplicable in some cases. (SAS 258-1)

Constructivism:
A: Rules, laws, and norms are not, and should not be, flexible and open to interpretation. They must be applied consistently in *all* cases and circumstances.

Table A.4. (*cont.*)

It is against the law for Heinz to steal the drug. Does that make it morally wrong?

Yes it is. Stealing is a crime. A crime is a crime no matter if it was for a good cause or a bad cause. (SHS 419)

---

from heteronomous judgments for that dilemma. These critical criteria are the ones most likely to be elicited by the structure of the dilemma in most subjects; some subjects may spontaneously raise other, noncritical criteria, but that is rare. Thus more weight is given to the critical criteria for each dilemma than to the noncritical criteria. As such, the dilemma-scoring algorithm demands that to be given a Type B score on the dilemma as a whole, a subject must be given a B score on a majority of the critical criteria that appear in the dilemma, and not be given an A score on *any* critical ones. Because the noncritical criteria for each dilemma are often simply not represented in the course of a subject's response to the dilemma, even though they are theoretically expected to be a part of the cluster of criteria that define the ideal type, the algorithm makes no specific demands vis-à-vis these criteria. If noncritical criteria are present they are scored, and they provide additional information about the character of a subject's moral judgment. Their absence, however, has no effect on the outcome of the coding process.

A brief word about the *choice* criterion, which is critical on *all* of the dilemmas: The initial dilemma choice is an important indicator of moral type, as we have defined it, and thus a subject who clearly chooses the autonomous choice, and sticks with it, is given a B score on the *choice* criterion. Most subjects who make the autonomous choice go on to justify that choice using the autonomous forms of the other criteria, and their overall dilemma score is a clear Type B. On the other hand, a subject who clearly chooses the heteronomous choice, and sticks with it, is given an A score on the *choice* criterion. Most subjects who make the heteronomous choice go on to justify that choice using the heteronomous forms of the other criteria, and their overall dilemma score is a clear Type A. There are a number of cases, however, where subjects are unclear, ambiguous, or simply undecided about the initial dilemma choice, and offer arguments supporting both possible action choices, or equivocate about the choice and never really make up their minds. These subjects are given an "ambiguous" or "unscorable" score on the *choice* criterion, and that criterion is not used in determining the overall dilemma score (see the Appendix in Volume II, for a further discussion of this issue).

Finally, even though theoretically we understand that the autonomous type is strictly defined in terms of all nine criteria of moral autonomy, in practice many subjects who receive heteronomous dilemma scores actually receive Type B scores on some of the criteria, while receiving Type A scores on a majority of the critical criteria. Thus although the autonomous criteria do seem to cluster in subjects who are scored as making Type B judgments, subjects who are scored as making Type A judgments often also exhibit one or more characteristics of moral autonomy, as defined by a B score on a particular criterion. We think this phenomenon is related to the ideal-typical definition of these criteria. Both the autonomous and heteronomous types of moral judgment are *ideal* types – they do not necessarily reflect all of the possible responses to these dilemmas. Ultimately we are interested in finding the closest fit between an individual subject's moral judgments and the ideal-typical criteria of either autonomy or heteronomy. Necessarily there is a certain degree of uncertainty in this assessment procedure, leading to a certain level of measurement error. Our scoring algorithms are designed to compensate, to a certain extent, for this uncertainty.

We have developed two primary scoring algorithms to determine a subject's overall moral type score from her or his responses to an MJI. We have already introduced *dilemma* algorithm: B scores on a majority of the critical criteria and no A scores on any of the critical criteria result in a Type B score for the dilemma; one A score on a critical criterion, no matter how many B scores on critical or noncritical criteria, yields a Type A score for the dilemma. And if any criterion is scored as ambiguous or unscorable it is not considered in determining the dilemma score.

The *form* algorithm is designed to determine the overall moral type score for a complete MJI (Form A, B, or C). It is based on a simple rule of two out of three: The form score is the moral type represented by at least two out of the three dilemmas on a form. At this point no distinction is made between *pure* type scores on a form (that is, all three dilemmas scored as Type A, or all three scored as Type B), and *mixed* type scores (that is, two out of three dilemmas scored as Type A, or two out of three scored as Type B). The only problem that can arise in determining the form score occurs when one or more dilemmas are designated as unscorable; that is, the dilemma was not presented to the subject, or the subject's answers are so brief or unclear as to make scoring for moral type impossible. If one dilemma is unscorable and the other two are in agreement (for example, both are Type B), the form score is the score of the two dilemmas that agree. But if one dilemma is unscorable and the other two dilemmas are in disagreement (for example, one is Type A and the other is Type B) then the overall form is designated as unscorable. And if two dilemmas are unscorable the overall form is also designated as unscorable, because individual dilemma scores are not robust enough to determine a subject's overall moral type.

Again, we want to stress that the somewhat arbitrary nature of both the dilemma and form algorithms is due to our ideal-typical conceptualization of moral autonomy. The ideal-typical approach means that assessment involves determining whether the moral judgment of the subject in question does, or does not, conform to the idealized form. This means that the score yielded by our coding scheme is necessarily a dichotomous one. We have not attempted to develop a continuous score to reflect, for example, the percentage of Type A and Type B scores for a particular subject. This is because at the present time that kind of quantification does not fit our understanding of moral autonomy. We are interested in identifying when a subject attains the fully consolidated characteristics of autonomy in moral reasoning (i.e., Type B), as we have defined them here. A subject who does not fully exhibit these ideal-typical characteristics is scored as a heteronomous Type A.

This, then, represents a brief overview of the coding scheme we have developed to assess heteronomous and autonomous moral types. The complete Moral Type Coding Manual is contained in Volume II. It was developed using a "bootstrapping or "abductive" method (see Kohlberg, 1981b; and chap. 1 of this volume) involving several longitudinal construction cases, taken from

Kohlberg's American longitudinal sample. It has been validated on the rest of that sample, as well as on several other samples. These studies will be described in some detail in the next section. As a clinical ideal-typical coding methodology it has several important limitations, to be discussed in the conclusion to this chapter. However, it also represents a significant advance over earlier methods used to investigate the development of moral autonomy and to assess the distinction between heteronomous and autonomous moral types. As such it has provided a relatively simple method for coding the construct in question. We will report specific data concerning the reliability and validity of the scheme in the next section.

Empirical Studies

The purpose of this section is to present the results of six studies that have used the moral type coding scheme for the identification of heteronomous and autonomous moral types. These studies have involved the analysis of data collected from various longitudinal, cross-sectional, and cross-cultural samples using the Standard Moral Judgment Interview. The six studies we will be reporting here are (1) a reliability study, which examined the reliability of the moral type coding scheme; (2) the American longitudinal study, which used Kohlberg's 20-year longitudinal sample of 58 males; (3) the Israeli kibbutz study, which reports Snarey and Schrader's (1984) reanalysis of Snarey, Reimer, and Kohlberg's (chap. 5, this volume) longitudinal sample of adolescent and young adult kibbutzniks; (4) the Turkish study, which used Nisan and Kohlberg's (chap. 4, this volume) longitudinal sample of 22 adolescent and young adult males; (5) the Taiwanese study, which reports Lei's (1983) cross-sectional and longitudinal study of subjects ranging in age from 7 to 25; and (6) a judgment–action study, which reports two analyses from Kohlberg and Candee's (in Kohlberg, 1984) review of research on the relationship between moral judgment and moral action. In these analyses the coding scheme described in the preceding section was used to investigate the relationship between moral type and moral behavior.

The Reliability Study

The reliability study was designed primarily to examine the interrater and test–retest reliabilities of the moral type coding scheme. The sample for this study was selected from the test–retest sample used to assess the reliability of the Standard Issue Scoring System (see chap. 2, this volume). This sample was chosen from among volunteers in several New England elementary schools, high schools, colleges, and graduate schools. Our sample, a subset of the Standard Issue Scoring test–retest sample, consisted of 40 subjects: 20 with test–retest interviews on Form A and 20 with test–retest interviews on Form B. Of the 20 Form A subjects, 11 were female and 9 were male. Of the 20 Form B subjects, 9 were female and 11 were male. Subjects ranged in age from approximately 8 to 28 years on both forms.

Two raters independently scored 10 Form A test–retest interview pairs and 10 Form B test–retest interview pairs (40 interviews in all, 20 per form) to assess *interrater* reliability for Forms A and B. The remaining interviews were divided equally between the two raters. The total sample was used to assess *test–retest* reliability. All interviews were scored blind with respect to structural moral stage, age, sex, and responses to the other interview in the test–retest pair.

The interrater reliability figures obtained from this sample were as follows: Rater 1 and Rater 2 (the first and third authors of this chapter, respectively) achieved a 90% agreement rate for the 20 Form A interviews scored in common, and an 80% rate for the 20 Form B interviews scored in common; the total percent agreement across both forms was thus 85%. Using Cohen's κ to correct for chance agreement, given the fact that our measure yields only two dichotomous categories (plus an "unscorable" designation), the corrected interrater reliability figures were 79% for Form A, 62% for Form B, and 71% across forms.

We also determined interrater reliability for Form C of the MJI, based on scores obtained from the American longitudinal sample. Across 10 interviews coded in common, four trained scorers achieved a 100% agreement rate.

Test–retest reliability figures were as follows: Form A showed test–retest agreement of 95%, and Form B showed 94% agreement. In other words, only 5% of the Form A test–retest subjects and 6% of the Form B test–retest subjects were assigned discrepant scores across the two testing times. Exactly half of these discrepant scores reflected a Type A to B change (2.5% on Form A), and half represented a Type B to A change (3% on Form A). This is a higher test–retest reliability figure than that reported for Standard Issue Stage Scoring, which yields between 70% and 80% complete agreement between Time 1 and Time 2 for both Forms A and B.

To determine *alternate form* reliability, we used data collected from the American longitudinal sample. Each of the subjects in the longitudinal sample was given both Forms A, B, and C at each time he was interviewed. Thus, this sample provided the basis for comparing the moral type score yielded by each form for the same subject at the same testing time.

Since all 58 American longitudinal subjects were given both Forms A and B at each time of testing, we had approximately 215 alternate form comparison points (eliminating any comparisons that included an "unscorable" score for either of the two forms). Of these 215 observations, 75% showed consistency across forms (that is, they were scored either Type A on both forms or Type B on both forms). Of the 25% that were inconsistent, 5% were scored as Type A on Form A and Type B on Form B, and 20% were scored as Type B on Form A and Type A on Form B. This suggests that a subject is slightly more likely to be given a Type B score on Form A than he is on Form B.

When the moral type scores for Form C were compared to the scores from Forms A and B a somewhat different pattern emerged. Out of 150 alternate form comparison points between Form A and Form C, 66% showed consistency across forms. Of the 34% that were inconsistent, 8% were scored as Type A on Form C and Type B on Form A, and 26% were scored as Type B on Form C and Type A on Form A. Out of 156 alternate form comparison points between Form B and Form C, 58% showed consistency across forms. Of the 42% that were inconsistent, 4% were scored as Type A on Form C and Type B on Form B, whereas 38% were scored as Type B on Form C and Type A on Form B. This analysis suggests that a subject is more likely to be given a Type B score on Form C than on either Form A or Form B.

Similar figures have been reported for the alternate form reliability of Standard Issue Scoring. Chapter 2 of this volume reports 85% agreement within 1/2

Table A.5. *American longitudinal sample, percentage of interviews on each MJI form scored as Type A, Type B, and Form C*

	Form A	Form B	Form C
Type A	65%	80%	51%
	(149)	(175)	(83)
Type B	35%	20%	49%
	(79)	(43)	(80)
N	228	218	163

stage between forms on the American longitudinal sample, with Rater 1 scoring Form A and Rater 2 scoring Form B. On the test–retest sample, with the same rater scoring both forms, Chapter 2 reports 75% exact agreement using 9 categories, 67% exact agreement using 13 categories, and 100% agreement within 1/3 stage.

Examination of the simple frequency of Type A and Type B scores given by form across all the testing times of the American longitudinal study further indicated the higher frequency of Type B scores assigned to Form C interviews, and the lower frequency of Type B scores assigned to Form B interviews. These frequencies are presented in Table A.5.

It is important to note that these are not independent observations, but rather repeated measures on 58 subjects. Also, any interview that received an "unscorable" designation was removed prior to these analyses. Nevertheless, this table provides another indication that a subject is most likely to be given a Type B score on Form C, and least likely to be given a Type B score on Form B; the likelihood of being given a Type B score on Form A lies somewhere in between.

Finally, the test–retest sample also provided information regarding possible sex differences in moral type. On Form A 66% of the males and 55% of the females received a Type B score; on Form B the percentages were exactly reversed (66% of the females and 55% of the males received a Type B score). These differences are not statistically significant on either form (Form A: $\chi^2 = 2.10, p > .10$; Form B: $\chi^2 = .94, p > .30$).

The American Longitudinal Study

In the American longitudinal study 58 males were followed longitudinally over a 20-year period, with subjects interviewed approximately every 4 years, beginning in early adolescence (ages 10–16) and concluding in young adulthood (ages 30–36). These interviews were conducted using the hypothetical moral dilemmas that are at present designated as Forms A, B, and C of the MJI. The complete description of this sample and of the study is presented in chapter 3 of this volume.

This sample was used primarily to examine our first general hypothesis regarding moral types – the developmental hypothesis. As such it enabled us to investigate the relationship between moral type and age, since each subject was followed throughout virtually the entire course of adolescence and young adult-

Table A.6. *American longitudinal sample, Form A: percentage of interviews scored at each age by type*

	10	13–14	16–18	19–22	23–26	27–30	31–33	36
Type A	95%	81%	78%	74%	55%	56%	41%	30%
	(18)	(25)	(32)	(28)	(17)	(23)	(11)	(3)
Type B	5%	19%	22%	26%	45%	44%	59%	70%
	(1)	(6)	(9)	(10)	(14)	(18)	(16)	(7)

Table A.7. *American longitudinal sample, Form B: percentage of interviews scored at each age by type*

	10	13–14	16–18	19–22	23–26	27–30	31–33	36
Type A	100%	86%	86%	84%	75%	75%	64%	50%
	(18)	(30)	(37)	(31)	(21)	(27)	(16)	(4)
Type B		14%	14%	16%	25%	25%	36%	50%
	(0)	(5)	(6)	(6)	(7)	(9)	(9)	(4)

hood. It also allowed us to identify the developmental pattern that the heteronomy–autonomy distinction followed over the course of a 20-year time period. Finally, although we made no assumptions about it a priori, this sample allowed us to investigate the relationship between moral type and moral stage, since each subject also had a moral stage score for each form at each testing time.

The interviews from this sample were scored using three different strategies. All the Form A interviews were scored by two raters, and discrepancies in scoring were discussed and resolved. Then, upon the attainment of an acceptable level of interrater reliability, the Form B interviews were divided equally among the two raters, and scored separately. Finally, four additional raters were trained, attained a very high level of interrater reliability, and then scored equal numbers of the Form C interviews. All interviews were scored blind with respect to moral judgment stage.

We turn first to an examination of the relationship between moral type and age. Specifically, we will report the percentage of subjects scored as making Type B judgments in eight age categories, ranging from age 10 to 36. All of the longitudinal interviews for each subject on Forms A, B, and C were available for this analysis – 238 Form A interviews, 230 Form B interviews, and 163 Form C interviews (all of which represent nonindependent observations – minus "unscorable" interviews). These percentages are presented in Table A.6 (Form A), Table A.7 (Form B), and Table A.8 (Form C).

On all three forms there is a monotonic relationship between age and the likelihood of making morally autonomous judgments. That is, as age increases, subjects are more likely to be scored as making Type B judgments.

We turn next to an examination of the longitudinal developmental patterns found in the American sample. On Form A the patterns were as follows:

Table A.8. *American longitudinal sample, Form C: percentage of interviews scored at each age by type*

	10	13–14	16–18	19–22	23–26	27–30	31–33	36
Type A	79%	64%	53%	46%	46%	32%	20%	
	(15)	(18)	(18)	(6)	(17)	(7)	(2)	(0)
Type B	21%	36%	47%	54%	54%	68%	80%	
	(4)	(10)	(16)	(7)	(20)	(15)	(8)	(0)

1. Thirty-three percent of the 58 subjects exhibited a one-time shift in their moral type score from Type A to Type B. That is, they began as making Type A judgments, were consistently Type A up to some point, then switched to making Type B judgments, and then remained consistently Type B throughout the remaining testing times.
2. Five percent of the subjects started as making Type B judgments, and remained Type B throughout all the testing times.
3. Thirty-eight percent of the subjects started as making Type A judgments, and remained Type A throughout the 20 years of the study.
4. Twenty-four percent of the subjects showed an irregular pattern that included both A to B movement and B to A movement across the testing times. That is, they showed at least one movement from making Type B judgments to making Type A judgments – a movement not predicted by the theory – from one testing time to the next.

A further analysis examined the change in individual subjects' moral type scores at adjacent testing times (that is, from T_n to T_{n+1} *within* each subject). This analysis yielded 174 adjacent longitudinal comparisons (after the removal of "unscorable" interviews) and the following patterns:

1. Eighteen percent of the comparisons showed an A to B developmental shift.
2. Twenty-one percent of the comparisons showed a stable B to B pattern.
3. Fifty-three percent of the comparisons showed a stable A to A pattern.
4. Eight percent of the comparisons showed a change from B to A (compare to the 2.5% test–retest B to A shift representing measurement error on Form A).

On Form B, the individual subjects' longitudinal patterns were similar:

1. Twenty-nine percent of the 58 subjects showed a one-time shift from making Type A judgments to making Type B judgments at some point in their development. Once the shift to Type B was made, it was maintained throughout the remainder of the study.
2. None of the subjects started out as making Type B judgments and remained Type B throughout the course of the study.
3. Fifty-two of the subjects started out as making Type A judgments and remained Type A throughout the study, across all interview times.
4. Nineteen percent of the subjects showed an irregular pattern that included both A to B movement and B to A movement.

The following are the patterns of within-subject longitudinal comparisons of adjacent testing times, given 165 observations on Form B:

1. Fifteen percent of the comparisons showed an A to B developmental shift.
2. Nine percent of the comparisons showed a stable B to B pattern.
3. Sixty-nine percent of the comparisons showed a stable A to A pattern.
4. Seven percent of the comparisons showed a change from B to A (compare to the 3% test–retest B to A shift representing measurement error on Form B).

Finally, on Form C, the individual subjects' longitudinal patterns were as follows:

1. Twenty-one percent of the 52 subjects showed a one-time shift from making Type A judgments to making Type B judgments at some point in their development. Once the shift to Type B was made, it was maintained throughout the remainder of the study.
2. Twenty-nine percent of the subjects started out as making Type B judgments and remained Type B throughout the course of the study.
3. Twenty-five percent of the subjects started out as making Type A judgments and remained Type A throughout the study, across all interview times.
4. Twenty-five percent of the subjects showed an irregular pattern that included both A to B movement and B to A movement.

The following are the patterns of within-subject longitudinal comparisons of adjacent testing times, given 98 observations on Form C:

1. Twenty-four percent of the comparisons showed an A to B developmental shift.
2. Thirty percent of the comparisons showed a stable B to B pattern.
3. Thirty-six percent of the comparisons showed a stable A to A pattern.
4. Ten percent of the comparisons showed a change from B to A.

Given these patterns, our next area of interest concerned the relationship between moral type and moral stage. To assess this relationship we began by examining the simple relationship between moral stage and the percentage of each moral type found at each stage. The results of the stage assessment of this sample using the Standard Issue Scoring System are reported in chapter 3 of this volume. We used the stage scores reported in that chapter for each of the 58 subjects at each testing time, and compared them with the moral type scores we obtained for each subject at each testing time. These data are reported in Tables A.9, A.10, and A.11. These tables report both the percentages, and the absolute number, of the interviews at each stage that were given Type A and Type B scores for each form (the interviews that were given "unscorable" type scores have been removed from these analyses). These tables indicate a moderate monotonic relationship between stage and type, on all three forms. That is, as moral judgment stage increases, subjects are more likely to be scored as making Type B judgments.

Finally, as discussed in the historical review introducing this chapter, Kohlberg's (1958) initial dissertation research on the American longitudinal sample was designed to examine the effects of peer-group integration and social class on moral development viewed in Piagetian terms. And, in chapter 3 of this volume, significant sociometric and social class differences in moral stage development were reported. Because, however, the original intent of Kohlberg's dissertation research was to use sociometric differences to help explain the development of moral autonomy as defined by Piaget (1932/1965), and, in light

Table A.9. *American longitudinal sample, Form A: percentage of interviews scored at each stage by type*

	1	1/2	2	2/3	3	3/4	4	4/5
Type A	100%	100%	100%	84%	62%	66%	42%	7%
	(1)	(9)	(12)	(27)	(28)	(63)	(8)	(1)
Type B				16%	38%	34%	58%	93%
	(0)	(0)	(0)	(5)	(17)	(33)	(11)	(13)

Table A.10. *American longitudinal sample, Form B: percentage of interviews scored at each stage by type*

	1	1/2	2	2/3	3	3/4	4	4/5
Type A	100%	100%	88%	79%	80%	87%	71%	10%
	(1)	(14)	(22)	(23)	(43)	(56)	(15)	(1)
Type B			12%	21%	20%	13%	29%	90%
	(0)	(0)	(3)	(6)	(11)	(8)	(6)	(9)

Table A.11. *American longitudinal sample, Form C: percentage of interviews scored at each stage by type*

	1	1/2	2	2/3	3	3/4	4	4/5
Type A	100%	87%	67%	59%	45%	44%	25%	
	(1)	(13)	(8)	(17)	(17)	(24)	(2)	(0)
Type B		13%	23%	41%	55%	56%	75%	100%
	(0)	(2)	(4)	(12)	(21)	(30)	(6)	(1)

of the roots of our moral type conception in Piaget's work, it seemed especially important to examine the relation of sociometric integration to moral type, in addition to its relation to moral stage. We did this at two age points for this sample, age 16–17 and age 24–26. Moral type for each subject in this analysis was obtained by using a two-out-of-three rule across Forms A, B, and C. That is, a subject was scored as Type B if he received a Type B score on all three forms, or on two out of the three forms – otherwise he was scored as Type A.

The relation of sociometric status (scored as either isolate or integrate) to moral type in adolescence (age 16–17) is reported in Table A.12. This table indicates some general tendency of the sociometric integrates to be Type B more frequently than the isolates, but this difference is not statistically significant (Fisher's exact test: $p < .37$). The relation of sociometric status to moral type in young adulthood (age 24–26) is presented in Table A. 13.

Here there is a somewhat stronger tendency for the sociometric integrates to be Type B more frequently than the isolates, but again this difference fails to

Table A.12. *American longitudinal sample, age 16–17: Tabulation of sociometric status (rows) by moral type (columns)*

	A	B	
Isolates	15 (83.33%)	3 (16.67%)	18 (43.90%)
Integrates	17 (73.91%)	6 (26.09%)	23 (56.10%)
	32 (78.05%)	9 (21.95%)	

Table A.13. *American longitudinal sample, age 24–26: Tabulation of sociometric status (rows) by moral type (columns)*

	A	B	
Isolates	8 (72.73%)	3 (27.27%)	11 (42.31%)
Integrates	7 (46.67%)	8 (53.33%)	15 (57.59%)
	15 (57.69%)	11 (42.31%)	

achieve significance (Fisher's exact test: $p < .18$). It is interesting to note that although sociometric status as a factor affecting moral stage development drops out by young adulthood (see chap. 3 of this volume), there is still a suggestive trend indicating sociometric influence on moral type in young adulthood. The relative weakness of this trend, however, fails to give much support to Piaget's (1932/1965) hypothesis that an autonomous moral orientation is developed primarily through strong peer relations.

As noted earlier, Kohlberg (1958) also postulated the development of a more autonomous moral orientation in the higher socioeconomic group. An elaboration of this rationale has been given by Kohn (1977), who relates the administrative complexity of work and the autonomy of the work decision making of fathers to their valuing of "traits" of autonomy as opposed to "traits" of conformity and obedience in their children in consistently replicated large studies. Thus both through the child's sense of greater perceived power participation and autonomy in the society on the part of his family, and through the parent's own autonomy-oriented behavior toward his children, it would be expected that the middle-class subjects would be more likely to be Type B than the working-class subjects.

The relation of socioeconomic status (scored as either high or low) to moral type in adolescence (age 16–17) is reported in Table A.14. While indicating a trend in the predicted direction, these social class differences fail to attain statistical significance (Fisher's exact test: $p < .37$). The relation of social class

Table A.14. *American longitudinal sample, age 16–17:*
Tabulation of sociometric status (rows) by moral type
(columns)

	A	B	
High	1	17	6
	(73.91%)	(26.09%)	(56.10%)
Low	15	3	18
	(83.33%)	(16.67%)	(43.90%)
	32	9	41
	(78.05%)	(21.95%)	

Table A.15. *American longitudinal sample, age 24–26:*
Tabulation of sociometric status (rows) by moral type
(columns)

	A	B	
High	8	7	15
	(53.33%)	(46.67%)	(57.69%)
Low	7	4	11
	(63.64%)	(36.36%)	(42.31%)
	15	11	26
	(57.69%)	(42.31%)	

of origin and moral type in young adulthood (age 24–26) is presented in Table A.15. This trend, although suggestive, also fails to achieve significance (Fisher's exact test: $p < .45$). As was the case for sociometric status, the weakness of these social class differences and trends fails to provide strong support for the Kohlberg and Kohn view of the influence of social class on moral autonomy.

The Israeli Kibbutz Study

The third study entailed Logan, Snarey, and Schrader's (1984) reanalysis of the longitudinal data from Israel previously reported by Snarey (1982) and Snarey et al. (chap. 5, this volume). This study, as well as the two studies that follow, allowed us to investigate the cross-cultural validity of the heteronomy–autonomy distinction. These studies also provided an opportunity for a very preliminary exploration of potential sociocultural effects on moral type and the development of moral autonomy – our second general hypothesis.

A description of the sample and the original analyses of the Israeli kibbutz study are reported by Snarey et al. (this volume). From the original group of 92 adolescents in the study, Logan, Snarey, and Schrader (1984) limited their analyses to the 64 subjects who were kibbutz residents and who had been followed longitudinally. However, of those 64 subjects, 12 were omitted because

Table A.16. *Israeli longitudinal sample, Form A: percentage of interviews scored at each age by type*

	12–13	14–15	16–17	18–19	20–21	22–23	24–25	26+
Type A	77%	61%	42%	24%	10%		17%	
	(10)	(11)	(8)	(5)	(1)	(0)	(1)	(0)
Type B	23%	39%	58%	76%	90%	100%	83%	100%
	(3)	(7)	(11)	(16)	(9)	(6)	(5)	(4)

their interviews had not been translated into English. Thus the final sample for this study consisted of 42 subjects, 17 females and 25 males. These subjects were between the ages of 12 and 17 at their first interview, and between the ages of 18 and 26 at their final interview. Half the subjects were interviewed three times; the other half were interviewed twice.

All of the interviews from this sample were conducted using Form A of the MJI. Each interview was scored for both moral stage and moral type. The results of the moral stage analyses are reported in chapter 5 of this volume.

We report the results of Logan, Snarey, and Schrader's (1984) analyses of the Israeli data following the same form of presentation as the results of the American longitudinal study. This is to permit clear comparison across the two cultures vis-à-vis our second general hypothesis. That is, the analyses reported here focus on the relationship between age and moral type, the developmental patterns exhibited by the two types, and the relationship between moral type and stage.

Logan, Snarey, and Schrader's (1984) examination of the relationship between moral type and age in the Israeli sample entailed the calculation of the percentage of subjects who were scored as making Type B moral judgments at eight separate age categories, ranging from age 12 to 27. All of the scorable Form A interviews for the 42 subjects in this sample were available for this analysis: that is, 97 interviews (nonindependent observations). The percentage of subjects receiving Type A and B scores in each age category is presented in Table A.16. In the Israeli sample, as in the American, there is a moderate monotonic relationship between age and the morally autonomous type of moral judgment. As age increases, subjects are more likely to be scored as making autonomous moral judgments.

In terms of the longitudinal developmental patterns evidenced by the moral type data obtained from the Israeli sample, the following patterns emerged:

1. Forty percent of the 42 subjects exhibited a one-time shift from Type A to Type B.
2. Forty-two percent of the subjects started as making Type B judgments, and remained Type B throughout all the testing times.
3. Nine percent of the subjects started as making Type A judgments, and remained Type A throughout the longitudinal study.
4. Nine percent of the subjects showed an irregular pattern that included both A to B movement and B to A movement.

Logan, Snarey, and Schrader (1984) also examined the changes between adjacent testing times (from T_n to T_{n+1}) *within* subjects. This analysis yielded

Table A.17. *Israeli longitudinal sample, Form A: percentage of interviews scored at each stage by type*

	2	2/3	3	3/4	4	4/5
Type A	100%	57%	46%	21%		33%
	(1)	(8)	(13)	(9)	(0)	(1)
Type B		43%	54%	79%	100%	67%
	(0)	(6)	(15)	(33)	(8)	(2)

53 adjacent comparisons (after the removal of "unscorable" interviews) and the following patterns:

1. Thirty-eight percent of the comparisons showed an A to B developmental shift.
2. Forty percent of the comparisons showed a stable B to B pattern.
3. Fifteen percent of the comparisons showed a stable A to A pattern.
4. Seven percent of the comparisons showed a change from B to A (compare to the 2.5% test–retest B to A measurement error on Form A).

Using the stage scores obtained for each subject at each testing time, Logan, Snarey, and Schrader (1984) examined the percentage of Israeli subjects scored at each moral stage who were also scored as Type A, versus the percentage of subjects who were scored as Type B. Table A.17 reports both the absolute number and the percentage of the scorable interviews at each stage that were given Type A and Type B scores for this sample. As in the American sample, there appears to be a moderate monotonic relationship between stage and Type B moral judgments for the Israeli sample. As stage increases, subjects are more likely to make Type B judgments.

Finally, Logan, Snarey, and Schrader (1984) looked for sex differences in moral type score in the Israeli sample. When the total number of interviews was compared across males and females, 59% of the female interviews and 65% of the male interviews were scored as exhibiting Type B judgments. These differences are not statistically significant ($\chi^2 = .37, p > .50$).

The Turkish Study

The fourth study, the Turkish study, entailed the reanalysis of the data reported by Nisan and Kohlberg (see chap. 4, this volume). Specifically, we reanalyzed the data from 22 of Nisan and Kohlberg's longitudinal subjects. Eighteen were from a rural Turkish village and 4 were from an urban setting. All were male. They ranged in age from 10 to 25 at the first time they were interviewed, and from 12 to 35 at the last time they were interviewed; each subject was interviewed from two to four times over a 12-year period. The moral type scores reported there are based on Form A Moral Judgment Interviews scored by the author of this chapter.

We turn first to an examination of the relationship between moral type and age in the Turkish sample. We examined the percentage of subjects who were scored as making Type B moral judgments in each of nine age categories, ranging from age 10 to 26 and older. All of the scorable Form A interviews for the 22 subjects in this sample were available for this analysis, that is, 56 inter-

Table A.18. *Turkish longitudinal study, Form A: percentage of interviews scored at each age by type*

	10–11	12–13	14–15	16–17	18–19	20–21	22–23	24–25	26+
Type A	100%	100%	60%	67%	80%	75%	60%	100%	50%
	(8)	(13)	(3)	(6)	(4)	(3)	(3)	(1)	(3)
Type B			40%	33%	20%	25%	40%		50%
	(0)	(0)	(2)	(3)	(1)	(1)	(2)	(0)	(2)

views (nonindependent observations). The percentage of subjects scored as making Type A and Type B judgments in each age category is presented in Table A.18. Unlike in the American and Israeli samples, there does not appear to be any clear relationship between age and the morally autonomous type of moral judgment in this sample. Certainly it appears that at the younger ages subjects are much less likely to be scored as Type B than they are at the older ages.

Second, we examined the longitudinal developmental patterns evidenced by the moral type data obtained from the Turkish sample and the following patterns emerged:

1. Thirty-two percent of the 22 subjects exhibited a one-time shift from making Type A judgments to making Type B judgments.
2. None of the subjects started as making Type B judgments and remained Type B throughout all the testing times.
3. Fifty-nine percent of the subjects started as making Type A judgments, and remained Type A throughout the longitudinal study.
4. Nine percent showed an irregular pattern that included both A to B movement and B to A movement.

As in our analysis of both the American and the Israeli longitudinal data, we also examined the developmental patterns based on a comparison of individual adjacent longitudinal observations from T_n to T_{n+1} *within* subjects. This analysis yielded 33 adjacent comparisons (after the removal of "unscorable" interviews) and the following patterns:

1. Twenty-seven percent of the comparisons showed an A to B development shift.
2. Three percent of the comparisons showed a stable B to B pattern.
3. Sixty-four percent of the comparisons showed a stable A to A pattern.
4. Six percent of the comparisons showed a change from B to A (compare to the 2.5% test–retest B to A measurement error on Form A).

We did not perform an analysis of the relationship of stage and type in this study.

The Taiwanese Study

The fifth study, the Taiwanese study, reports results from Lei's (1983) ongoing research. Lei's sample consisted of 217 native Taiwanese subjects drawn from seven age groups ranging from age 7 to 25. There were approximately 30 subjects in each age group, and each group included roughly equal numbers of

Table A.19. *Percentage of moral Type B at each age by cultural setting*

	Age	N	Moral Type B %
Taiwan	7	30	3
Taiwan	9	30	7
U.S.A.	10	25	6
Taiwan	12	30	13
U.S.A.	13	25	19
Taiwan	14	38	8
U.S.A.	16	41	22
Taiwan	18	29	10
U.S.A.	19	31	32
Taiwan	23	43	23
U.S.A.	22	30	43
Taiwan	25	17	59
U.S.A.	25	39	41

Source: Lei (1983), p. 25.

males and females. Although the bulk of the study was cross-sectional, Lei did include a small longitudinal sample: 17 of the age 25 subjects were drawn from the original age 23 group and were reinterviewed 2 1/2 years later.

All of the subjects were given Form A of the MJI. Each interview was scored for moral stage using the Standard Issue Scoring System, translated into Chinese by Lei. Lei also scored each of the interviews for moral type, using the coding scheme described earlier.

Lei's (1983) analysis of moral type scores included a comparison of the Taiwanese data with the American longitudinal data. To perform these comparisons, Lei selected two subsamples from the American Form A data – one matched for age to his cross-sectional sample, the other matched for stage. He then compared the percentage of moral type score by age, and by stage, of the Taiwanese sample with the American "cross-sectional" samples matched for age and for stage. We will consider each of these comparisons briefly in turn.

Lei's (1983) cross-cultural comparison of moral type matched for age is presented in Table A.19. This table gives the percentage of subjects receiving Type B scores at each age in the Taiwanese sample and in the matched American sample. The percentage of subjects scored as making Type B judgments is smaller in the Taiwanese sample than in the American sample at most age groups. However, the difference between the two samples is significant only for the 18-year-old group (Lei, 1983, p. 22). Lei also suggests that the age trends with respect to the number of subjects making Type B judgments indicate clear cultural differences. The age trend for the American sample shows a roughly linear increase, whereas the Taiwanese curve is quite flat before the age of 18, after which it rises rapidly.

Lei's (1983) cross-cultural comparison of moral stage and moral type (Table A.20) indicates clearer differences between the Taiwanese and American samples. The difference between the percentage of subjects scored as making Type

Table A.20. *Percentage of moral Type B at each stage by cultural setting*

	Stage	N	Moral Type B (%)
Taiwan	1	2	0
U.S.A.		1	0
Taiwan	1/2	12	0
U.S.A.		8	0
Taiwan	2	15	0
U.S.A.		8	12
Taiwan	2/3	37	8
U.S.A.		19	16
Taiwan	3	59	12
U.S.A.		6	50
Taiwan	3/4	61	13
U.S.A.		25	56
Taiwan	4	22	32
U.S.A.		3	67
Taiwan	4/5	9	89
U.S.A.		2	100

Source: Lei (1983), p. 25.

B judgments in the American sample compared with the Taiwanese sample is significant at both Stage 3 ($\chi^2 = 6.08$, $p < .05$) and Stage 4 ($\chi^2 = 17.11$, $p < .01$) (Lei, 1983, p. 22). Lei also examined the strength of the relationship between stage and moral type within the Taiwanese sample alone. He found that this relationship was also significant (Cramer's V = 0.40, $\chi^2 = 33.72$, $p < .0001$) (Lei, 1983, p. 28).

Finally, as in the American test–retest and the Israeli samples, Lei found no significant sex difference in moral type score in the Taiwanese sample.

The Judgment–Action Study

For the sixth and final study, the judgment–action study, we review the results of several earlier analyses by Kohlberg and Candee (in Kohlberg, 1984). These analyses entailed an examination of the heteronomy–autonomy distinction that used the old "substage" labels, instead of the more recent moral type labels. When these analyses were conducted the substage *construct* had already been replaced by the ideal-type construct, but the terminology had not yet been changed. In addition, the assessment of the A–B distinction carried out in the Kohlberg and Candee analyses did not use the fully elaborated coding scheme described earlier, but rather an early prototype that clinically yielded the same scores as the one described here (the prototype was not, however, as complete). We review the results of these analyses in spite of these small discrepancies, because the differences are minor in the face of the similarities between the Kohlberg and Candee methodology and the methodology used in the other studies reported in this section.

Kohlberg and Candee report the reanalyses of data from two different stud-

Table A.21. *Percentage of subjects sitting in by stage and substage of moral reasoning*

	Stage			
	3	3/4	4	4/5
Substage A				
% Sitting in	0%	21%	21%	60%
(*N* at Stage)	(30)	(85)	(57)	(5)
Ambiguous B				
% Sitting in	44%	44%	53%	58%
(*N* at Stage)	(9)	(41)	(40)	(12)
Substage B				
% Sitting in		57%	67%	83%
(*N* at Stage)	(0)	(7)	(18)	(18)

Source: Kohlberg and Candee (1984).

ies. The first is an examination of the relationship of moral stage to participation in the illegal occupation of an administration building during the Berkeley Free Speech Movement (FSM) in the mid-1960s (see Haan, Smith, & Block [1968] for the original report of this study). Written forms of the MJI were given to 339 students, 129 of whom had been arrested for sitting in, and 210 chosen at random from a cross-section of the Berkeley campus. All the interviews were rescored for moral stage, and for moral type (''substage'') by Candee and Kohlberg. The relationship between moral stage, moral type, and moral action (sitting in or not sitting in) was then examined.

The data from the FSM study are reported in Table A.21. It presents the relationship of moral stage and moral type (substage) to sitting in, and gives the percentage of subjects scored at each stage and type who actually sat in during the FSM demonstration. It includes moral Type A, moral Type B, and an intermediate group that Kohlberg and Candee scored as ambiguously or marginally morally autonomous (ambiguous Type B). These data suggest that the effect of moral stage and moral type on sitting in is additive. At each higher stage, and at each moral type closer to the unambiguous Type B, more subjects sat in. This effect held even when controlling for deontic moral choice, i.e., within the group of subjects who judged the sit-in to be the right course of action. In other words, among all the subjects who said it was right to sit in, subjects scored as moral Type B (and as ambiguous Type B) were still much more likely to perform the action that they define as moral than were those subjects scored as Type A.

The second study reported by Kohlberg and Candee is an early version of Milgram's well-known experiments on obedience to authority. In those experiments naive subjects were recruited to ''shock'' an innocent victim under the guise of studying the effects of punishment on memory. Some of these subjects refused to continue the experiment once they felt the ''victim'' was being hurt, but others continued all the way to the end of the experiment, following the orders of the experimenter. All 26 subjects in this sample were given the MJI, and it was scored for stage and type by Kohlberg and Candee. These data

Table A.22. *Percentage of subjects quitting Milgram situation by stage and substage of moral reasoning*

	Stage			
	3	3/4	4	Substage totals
Substage A				
% Quit	0%	0%	0%	0%
(*N* at Stage)	(2)	(6)	(1)	(9)
Ambiguous				
% Quit	100%	0%	100%	18%
(*N* at Stage)	(1)	(9)	(1)	(11)
Substage B				
% Quit	100%	50%	100%	86%
(*N* at Stage)	(1)	(2)	(4)	(7)
Stage totals	50%	6%	87%	
	(4)	(17)	(6)	(27)

Note: Method of Scoring: 1980 Standard Issue Scoring.
Source: Kohlberg and Candee (1984).

provided a second opportunity to examine the relationship between stage, type, and moral action. The data from this study are reported in Table A.22. This table suggests that there is a monotonic increase in the percentage of subjects who performed the moral action (quit the experiment) when moral Type ("substage") B is compared to ambiguous Type B and Type A. No moral type A subjects quit, 18% of the ambiguous Type B subjects quit, and 86% of the Type B subjects quit. Again, moral type, especially autonomous Type B, appears to be one predictor of moral action.

Summary, Discussion, and Conclusion

This section summarizes the various components of this chapter and draws some general conclusions from the data and theory presented here. As part of this section we will also discuss the significance of the moral type distinction in terms of current work in the field, and offer some suggestions regarding directions for further research.

Our current understanding of the heteronomy–autonomy distinction focuses on nine ideal-typical criteria that define the nature of the autonomous type. In order to distinguish between autonomy and heteronomy, we developed a clinical coding scheme. This system codes the moral type of an individual's responses to the hypothetical moral dilemmas found on the Standard Moral Judgment Interview (MJI).

The *interrater* reliability figures for the moral type coding scheme are adequate. The percentage of exact agreement between two trained raters is 90% for Form A and 80% for Form B. When adjusted for chance agreement, these percentages are in the high 70s for Form A and in the low 60s for Form B. Although these figures are somewhat lower than the interrater reliability figures reported for the Standard Issue Scoring System (high 80s to mid-70s complete agreement using nine categories), they show that our coding scheme *can* be used by a trained rater to reliably score interview protocols for moral type.

The *test–retest* reliability figures are crucial for our analysis of the empirical studies. This information provides a way to interpret the significance of longitudinal patterns, since a longitudinal design is a form of test–retest, or repeated measures design. The test–retest reliability figures are high. When the MJI was given twice separated by a 1-month interval, the level of type inconsistency for Form A was 5% (2.5% Type A to B shift and 2.5% Type B to A shift) and for Form B it was 6% (3% Type A to B shift and 3% Type B to A shift). These levels are used as a standard for distinguishing meaningful change in type from apparent change due to measurement error in the three longitudinal studies.

The *alternate form* reliability of the moral type coding scheme is somewhat more problematic. Consistent and significant differences exist between the frequency of moral Type B scores yielded by Form A as compared to those yielded by form B in all of the Form A–Form B comparisons (based on data from the American longitudinal study). The percentage of discrepant scores between the two forms is quite high (25%). In addition, the fact that on Form A the total percentage of Type B scores for the American longitudinal sample was 35%, whereas on Form B it was only 20%, suggests that it is more difficult to attain a Type B score on form B than on Form A.

Because moral types include considerations of content, we would not expect as high a degree of consistency across dilemmas as is found for moral stage, a more purely structural construct. Although the decision choice for any dilemma is the most obvious content criterion in the moral type coding scheme, the other criteria, such as mutual respect, intrinsicalness, and constructivism, also reveal specific views or attitudes about the social relations and norms presented in each dilemma. Unlike the system for scoring stages that holds content constant (norms and elements) and abstracts structure from that content, the scheme for coding moral types represents a use of Weber's ideal-type methodology that clusters a set of theoretically connected concerns. An individual's responses, then, indicate the particular set of concerns that he or she brings to the dilemma in trying to solve it. Some of these concerns are captured by moral types.

It is important to say a word about our findings regarding sex differences in moral type. In those studies reported here that include both male and female subjects (the test–retest sample, the Israeli sample, and the Taiwanese sample), *no* sex differences in moral type scores were found. This is a very important finding, because it serves to answer in advance a potential criticism of our work, namely, that our identification of the autonomous type of moral judgment represents characteristics that are stereotypically thought of as male (see Gilligan, 1982). In this stereotype, autonomy is confused with independence in the sense of isolated individualism. In contrast, in the theories of Piaget and Baldwin, autonomy arises out of and supports social relationships of sharing and cooperation. Our findings suggest that autonomy, as we have defined it, is just as likely to characterize moral judgments made by women as those made by men. In addition, autonomy appears most frequently in the least "individualistic" cultural setting – the Israeli kibbutz.

With respect to the three general hypotheses we proposed regarding the heteronomy–autonomy distinction, the six studies reported in this chapter appear to support them all. Our first major hypothesis is that moral type is a developmental variable. One indication of this is that across all four longitudinal and cross-sectional samples we found a significant relationship between age and moral type. As subjects get older, they are more likely to make autonomous moral judgments. This supports our first specific subhypothesis under the developmental category – that there is a relationship between age and moral type.

A stronger developmental claim than age relatedness is that developmental movement should always be from moral Type A to Type B, and not the reverse. Piaget (1932/1965) did not claim that his heteronomous and autonomous types defined true stages representing a hierarchical, invariant sequence. However, he did claim that autonomous morality is not only more age-developmentally advanced, but also better equilibrated. From this theoretical assumption we formulated our second subhypothesis under the developmental category: that movement from Type B to Type A in our system is an unlikely occurrence.

The three longitudinal samples (American, Israeli, and Turkish) lend partial support to this hypothesis. Although the majority of subjects in each sample shifted once from A to B, or remained stable at either A or B, a number of subjects in each sample showed a "regressive" B to A pattern. When individual longitudinal observations at adjacent testing times were analyzed, however, it was discovered that in each sample the percentage of longitudinal comparisons that showed a B to A pattern represented only 6%–8% of the total number of comparisons. In evaluating the invariant upward structural stage sequence hypothesis in chapter 3, the regressive shifts in the American longitudinal data were compared with the regressive shifts in the test–retest data. This comparison suggested that the downward shifts in the longitudinal data were fewer than those found in the test–retest data. Thus, longitudinal "regression" was attributed to measurement error.

In making the same comparison between longitudinal "regression" and test–retest measurement error for the moral type data, we must compare the 6%–8% figure for the B to A reversals found in the three longitudinal samples with the percentage of B to A reversals in the test–retest sample. The test–retest inconsistency was reported to be 5% for Form A and 6% for Form B; however, only about half of that inconsistency (2.5% and 3%) is attributable to the B to A reversal pattern. Within the limits of our data, then, there are somewhat more B to A "reversal" shifts than can be attributed to measurement error.

A claim for the absence of "regression" or reversal from Type B to Type A is not a necessary theoretical claim, since we distinguish our moral types from invariant sequential hierarchical moral stages. The actual findings do show that the developmental shift from Type A to Type B is two to four times as likely in our samples than is the Type B to Type A reversal. This supports the general hypothesis that the types are developmental without claiming that they fit a strict invariant stage model.

Another developmental aspect of the nature of the moral types that was not part of our original hypothesis but that emerged from our analysis of the data concerns the relationship between moral type and structural moral stage. The data from the American, Israeli, and Taiwanese studies suggests that there is a relationship between moral type and moral stage. Specifically, the relationship seems to be a monotonic one, in which the higher a subject's moral stage score, the more likely he is to be scored as making autonomous moral judgments. (Conversely, the lower a subject's stage score, the more likely he is to be scored as making Type A judgments.) With age partialed out, there is still a significant relationship between stage and moral type for the American and Israeli samples, the only two for which we had the data necessary to do the partial correlation analyses.

From a logical point of view, the moral realism and the heteronomous respect for authority partially characterizing the first moral stage preclude a subject at Stage 1 from making Type B moral judgments. On the other hand, at the upper end of the stage sequence it is logically possible but highly unlikely that a subject at moral Stage 5 would make heteronomous moral judgments. The more formal criteria of the autonomous type – hierarchy, intrinsicalness, and universality – are also part of the formal features of moral Stage 5. A large majority of Stage 5 subjects choose the Type B action choice in many of the dilemmas, including all three on Form A (Kohlberg, 1984, chap. 7). Combining all of our samples, 36 subjects scored at Stage 4/5 and none at Stage 5. Of the 36 at 4/5, 32 (89%) were scored as making Type B moral judgments.

What, then, is the theoretical relationship between moral stages and moral types? Both are empirically age developmental, and development along both dimensions increases the likelihood that there will be consistency between moral reasoning or judgment and moral action. Although the stages are defined more by structure of reasoning, formal considerations also enter into our conception of the moral types. Judgments of Type B are more prescriptive and universalizable than judgments of Type A, dimensions earlier stressed as aspects of the stage sequence (Kohlberg, 1981a). In this volume we have stressed two additional formal characteristics of the moral stage sequence: greater inclusiveness in sociomoral perspective, and integration and reversibility of justice operations (see chap. 1). These, we believe, represent dimensions of greater adequacy in moral reasoning about justice problems. Moral autonomy, in contrast, refers to a mode of interpretation and application of the particular sociomoral perspective and set of justice operations that a subject brings to bear on a moral decision. Type B judgments reflect more freedom from fixed norms, external authority figures, and pragmatic considerations than do Type A judgments, even from within the same sociomoral perspective.

A rather impressive finding that serves as a bridge between our first and second general hypotheses is that moral type appears to be a developmental variable in *four* very different Western and non-Western cultures. The Israeli and American cultures are usually thought to be fundamentally democratic, and the Turkish and Taiwanese cultures lay more emphasis on gerontocratic respect for elders and authority. For instance, in Taiwan the norm of filial piety is still functionally strong. However, in all four cultures we find both the heteronomous and autonomous types, and in all four we find development or movement from Type A to Type B more frequently than movement from B to A. Thus, autonomous moral judgments are not limited to Western cultures that value various forms of individualism.

Our second general hypothesis, then, is that social relations and sociocultural environment would have an effect on the development of moral type. Following Piaget (1932/1965) we expected that in traditional or gerontocratic societies a large proportion of adults would continue to make heteronomous moral judgments because they would still be embedded in a hierarchical system of social relationships. Somewhat to our surprise, almost the same percentage of the American male subjects below the age of 26 were scored as making type A judgments as were the male Turkish subjects and the male and female Taiwanese subjects of the same age. Thus our second general hypothesis was only partially supported by our data.

The cultural group that most clearly supports the Piagetian hypothesis that an autonomous type of judgment would be most likely found in a social system stressing cooperation, sharing, and equality is the Israeli kibbutz sample. In that sample, by age 16 a majority of the men and women were making Type B judgments, and by age 20 essentially all the subjects were making Type B judgments. In contrast, a majority of the American males were not making Type B judgments until their early 30s. A majority of the 25-year-old Taiwanese male and female sample made Type B judgments, as did half of the small sample of 26-year-old Turkish males.

In summary, the Israeli kibbutz sample stands out as showing the relationship between sociocultural setting and moral type predicted by our theoretical assumptions. There are two possible explanations for this finding. The first is that we capture cultural content in the scoring criteria for Type B on Form A. The sanctity of life is a strong cultural value in all of Israel, and individual property rights are not a strong value on the kibbutz. From this point of view the hierarchical valuing of life over property on the Heinz dilemmas (Dilemmas III and III′) may represent the transmission of the content of cultural values as an explanation for the high frequency of subjects scored as making autonomous type B judgments on the Israeli kibbutz.

On the other hand, an explanation closer to Piaget's (1932/1965) and our own would be that the underlying structure of social relations on the kibbutz is more truly characterized by equality, cooperation, and mutual respect than is true of the structure of social relations in the other cultural groups studied. We would add that the structure of social relations in the other three cultures seems to be a more complex mixture of both the gerontocratic and democratic forms, as described by Piaget.

Our third general hypothesis concerns the relationships between moral type and moral action. Following Piaget (1932/1965), we suggested that individuals who make autonomous moral judgments would be more likely to engage in "moral action" than individuals who make heteronomous moral judgments. We presented data analyzed by Kohlberg and Candee (in Kohlberg, 1984) that tend to support this hypothesis. Their analysis of both the Berkeley FSM subjects and subjects engaged in a version of the Milgram experiment showed that subjects who were scored as making either Type B judgments or ambiguous Type B judgments were more likely to sit in or quit the experiment, respectively, than those who were scored as making Type A judgments. In both of these studies the kind of moral action predicted for subjects scored as making Type B judgments was one that involved resisting the expectations of authorities in order to recognize individual rights. Further research is needed to show that just action that does not involve resistance to authority can also be predicted using the moral type distinction. It should be added that the current data suggest that moral Type B is more consistent in relating action to moral judgment choice. That is, persons making Type B judgments appear to make moral judgments of responsibility for their own moral actions in a way that those making Type A judgments do not (Kohlberg, 1984, chap. 7). Much further research is needed to verify this interpretation.

This concludes our summary and discussion of the empirical results presented in this chapter. We now turn to a discussion of three additional issues regarding the heteronomy–autonomy distinction that require further research. The first of these issues concerns the limitations of our present coding scheme for the assessment of moral type. At present, our methodology is designed to identify clearly only the ideal Type B moral judgment. Consequently, the Type A score is not an ideal type score so much as it represents a large category into which everything that is "not ideally B" is placed. Upon clinical examination of Type A interview protocols, we recognize that Type A can be called a "wastebasket" category including within it individuals who exhibit some Type B criteria as well as individuals who exhibit none. This suggests the need for further analysis of Type A interviews. True to the dichotomous and typological theories of Piaget and Baldwin, it seemed wise to begin as we did with an ideal-typical method emphasizing the ideal characteristics of moral autonomy. We recognize the need at this point to refine our methodology.

A second issue requiring further research concerns the relationship of the heteronomous and autonomous types to variables of personality or character. In our theoretical introduction we discussed the possible relevance of Fromm's and Hoffman's typology of social character – the authoritarian and the human-istic – to our own typology. Social character types cover a broader range of values than do our moral types, and are less clearly linked to development. More generally, it is possible that correlations between our types and socio-moral attitudes, on the one hand, and personality traits, on the other, may be found that broaden our understanding of the relationship between moral devel-opment and social character, attitudes, and actions.

A third area that demands further research is the study, both naturalistically and through intervention efforts, of the effects of social institutions *within* cul-tures on the development of moral autonomy. Of particular interest is the in-corporation of the moral type variable into evaluations of moral education in-terventions. Moral autonomy, in its underlying nature, should not be susceptible to direct didactic or indoctrination approaches. Since our ideal-typological as-sessment is a mixture of content and structure, however, moral educators who use moral type as a part of their evaluation procedures should take special care to avoid teaching to the surface aspects of the measure. The "just community approach" to moral education is an example of an intervention that should enhance the development of autonomous moral judgment, since it attempts to create a democratic system of social relations based on equality, mutual re-spect, and cooperation within the high school (Kohlberg, 1980).

In conclusion, let us point to several key concepts and findings that suggest that the heteronomy–autonomy moral type distinction is a useful and important research tool. First, it captures the theoretical ideas of Piaget, Baldwin, and Kant about what constitutes adequate and mature moral judgments that are not captured by the moral stages themselves. Second, it relates moral judgment to moral action in ways not derivable from the moral stages. Finally, it is an indicator of differences in sociocultural environments and social relations that have an effect on the development of moral judgment – differences that are not adequately assessed using the structural stage variable.

References

Arbuthnot, J., Sparling, Y., Faust, D., & Kee, W. (1983). Logical and moral development in preadolescent children. *Psychological Reports, 52*, 209–210.

Aristotle. (1962). *Nicomachean ethics* (M. Ostwald, Trans.). Indianapolis: Bobbs-Merrill.

Baldwin, J. M. (1897). *Social and ethical interpretations in mental development.* New York: Macmillan.

——(1906–1911). *Thoughts and things or genetic logic* (3 Vols.). London: Swan Sonnenschein.

Berry, J. (1971). Ecological and cultural factors in spatial perceptual development. *Canadian Journal of Behavioral Science, 3*, 324–336.

Blasi, A. (1980). Bridging moral cognition and moral action: A critical review of the literature. *Psychological Bulletin, 88*, 1–45.

——(1983). Bridging moral cognition and action: A theoretical view. *Developmental Review, 3*, 178–210.

Blatt, M. (1969). *The effects of classroom discussion programs upon children's level of moral judgment.* Unpublished doctoral dissertation, University of Chicago.

Blatt, M., & Kohlberg, L. (1975). The effects of classroom moral discussion upon children's level of moral judgment. *Journal of Moral Education, 4*, 129–163.

Bloom, A. H. (1977). Two dimensions of moral reasoning: Social principledness and social humanism in cross-cultural perspective. *Journal of Social Psychology, 101*, 29–44.

Bloom, B. (1964). Stability and change in human characteristics. New York: Wiley.

Boyd, D. (1977). The moralberry pie: Some basic concepts. *Theory into Practice, 16*, 67–72.

Broughton, J. M. (1978a). The cognitive-developmental approach to morality: A reply to Kurtines and Grief. *Journal of Moral Education, 1*, 81–96.

——(1978b). The development of concepts of self, mind, reality, and knowledge. In W. Damon (Ed.), *New directions for child development: Vol. 1. Social cognition.* San Francisco: Jossey-Bass.

Broughton, J. M., & Freeman-Moir, D. S. (Eds.) (1982). *The cognitive developmental psychology of James Mark Baldwin.* Norwood, NJ: ABLEX.

Colby, A. (1978). Evolution of a moral-developmental theory. In W. Damon (Ed.), *New directions for child development: Vol. 2. Moral development.* San Francisco: Jossey-Bass.

——(1975.) The relationship between cognitive and moral stages. Unpublished manuscript, Harvard University, 1975.

Colby, A., Kohlberg, L., Fenton, E., Speicher-Dubin, B., & Lieberman, M. (1977). Secondary school moral discussion programmes led by social studies teachers. *Journal of Moral Education, 6*(2), 90–111.

Colby, A., Kohlberg, L., Gibbs, J., & Lieberman, M. (1983). A longitudinal study of moral judgment. *Monographs of the Society for Research in Child Development, 48*, 1–124.

Cole, M., Gay, J., Glick, J., & Sharp, D. 1971. *The cultural context of learning and thinking.* New York: Basic Books.

Damon, W. (1977). *The social world of the child.* San Francisco: Jossey-Bass.

——(1983). *Social development from childhood through adolescence.* New York: Norton.

Edwards, C. P. (1975). Society complexity and moral development: A Kenyan study. *Ethos, 3*, 505–527.

——(1981). The comparative study of the development of moral judgment and reasoning. In R. H. Munroe,

R. L. Munroe, & B. B. Whiting (Eds.), *Handbook of cross-cultural human development*. New York: Garland Press.

——(1982). Moral development in comparative cross-cultural perspective. In D. Wagner & W. Stevenson (Eds.), *Cultural perspectives on child development*. San Francisco: Freeman.

Erickson, V. Lois. (1980). The case study method in the evaluation of developmental programs. In L. Kuhmerker, M. Mentkowski, & V. Lois Erickson (Eds.), *Evaluating moral development*. New York: Character Research Press.

Erikson, E. H. (1963). *Childhood and society*. New York: Norton. (Originally published 1950)

Faust, D., & Arbuthnot, J. (1978). The relation between moral and Piagetian reasoning and the effectiveness of moral education. *Developmental Psychology, 14*, 435–436.

Flavell, J. J. (1971). Stage related properties of cognitive development. *Cognitive Psychology, 2*, 89–112.

Fowler, J. W. (1981). *Stages of faith: The psychology of human development and the quest for meaning*. San Francisco: Harper & Row.

Frankena, W. K. (1973). *Ethics*. Englewood Cliffs, NJ: Prentice-Hall.

Fromm, E. (1941). *Escape from freedom*. New York: Holt, Rinehart & Winston.

——(1947). *Man for himself: An inquiry into the psychology of ethics*. Greenwich, CT: Fawcett.

Gibbs, J. C. (1977). Kohlberg's stages of moral judgment: A constructive critique. *Harvard Educational Review, 47*, 43–61.

Gibbs, J. C. (1979). Kohlberg's moral state theory: A Piagetian revision. *Human Development, 22*, 89–112.

Gibbs, J., Arnold, K., & Burkhart, J. (1983). Sex differences in the expression of moral judgment. *Child Development, 55*, 1040–43.

Gibbs, J., Schnell, S., Berkowitz, M., & Goldstein, D. (1983, April). *Relations between formal operations and logical conflict resolution*. Paper presented at the biennial meeting of the Society for Research in Child Development, Detroit.

Gilligan, C. (1977). In a different voice: Women's conceptions of the self and of morality. *Harvard Educational Review, 47*, 481–517.

——(1982). *In a different voice: Psychological theory and women's development*. Cambridge, MA: Harvard University Press.

Gilligan, C., & Belenky, M. (1980). A naturalistic study of abortion decisions. In R. Selman & R. Yando (Eds.), *New directions for child development: Vol. 7. Clinical developmental psychology*. San Francisco: Jossey-Bass.

Gilligan, C., Kohlberg, L., Lerner, J., & Belenky, M. (1971). *Report to the U.S. Commission on Obscenity and Pornography*, Vol. 1 (No. 52560010). Washington, DC: U.S. Government Printing Office.

Gilligan, C., & Murphy, J. M. (1979). Development from adolescence to adulthood: The philosopher and the dilemma of the fact. In D. Kuhn (Ed.), *New directions for child development: Vol. 5. Intellectual development beyond childhood*. San Francisco: Jossey-Bass.

Gorsuch, R. L., & Barnes, M. L. (1973). Stages of ethical reasoning and moral norms of Carib youths. *Journal of Cross-cultural Psychology, 4*, 283–301.

Grimley, L. (1973). *A cross cultural study of moral judgment development in India, Japan, and Zambia*. Unpublished doctoral dissertation, Kent State University, Ohio.

Haan, N., Smith, B., & Block, J. (1968). Political, family, and personality correlates of adolescent moral judgment. *Journal of Personality and Social Psychology, 10*, 183–201.

Habermas, J. (1984). Interpretive social science vs. hermeneutics. In N. Haan, R. B. Bellah, P. Rabinow, & W. Sullivan (Eds.), *Social science as moral inquiry*. New York: Columbia University Press.

Hanes, K. (1983). *Personal autonomy*. Unpublished doctoral dissertation, Harvard Graduate School of Education, Cambridge, MA.

Hare, R. M. (1963). *Freedom and reason*. New York: Oxford University Press.

——(1981). *Moral thinking*. Oxford: Clarendon Press.

Harsanyi, J. C. (1982). Morality and the theory of rational behavior. In A. Sen & B. Williams (Eds.), *Utilitarianism and beyond*. Cambridge: Cambridge University Press.

Hart, D., & Kohlberg, L. (In prep.). Theories of the social self of J. M. Baldwin and G. H. Mead. In L. Kohlberg (Ed.), *Child psychology and childhood education*.

Hawes, K. (1983). *A conception of moral autonomy.* Unpublished doctoral dissertation, Harvard University, Cambridge, MA.

Hickey, J., & Scharf, P. (1980). *Toward a just correctional system.* San Francisco: Jossey-Bass.

Hoffman, M. L. (1970a). Conscience, personality, and socialization techniques. *Human Development, 13,* 90–126.

——(1970b). Moral development. In P. H. Mussen (Ed.), *Manual of child psychology* (3rd ed., vol. 2). New York: Wiley.

Holstein, C. (1976). Irreversible, stepwise sequence in the development of moral judgment: A longitudinal study of males and females. *Child Development, 47,* 51–61.

Horton, R. (1967). African traditional thought and Western science. *Africa, 37,* 50–71, 155–187.

Inhelder, B., & Piaget, J. (1958). *The growth of logical thinking from childhood to adolescence.* New York: Basic Books.

James, W. (1978). *The meaning of truth.* Cambridge, MA: Harvard University Press. (Original work published 1909)

Kant, I. (1948). Groundwork of the metaphysics of morals. In H. Paton (Ed. and Trans.), *The moral law.* London: Hutchinson. (Original work published 1785)

Kegan, R. (1982). *The evolving self.* Cambridge, MA: Harvard University Press.

Kohlberg, L. (1958). *The development of modes of moral thinking and choice in the years ten to sixteen.* Unpublished doctoral dissertation, University of Chicago.

——(1963). The development of children's orientations toward a moral order. 1. Sequence in the development of moral thought. *Vita Humana, 6,* 11–33.

——(1968). Early education: A cognitive-developmental approach. *Child Development, 39,* 1013–1062.

——(1969). Stage and sequence: The cognitive-developmental approach to socialization. In D. Goslin (Ed.), *Handbook of socialization theory and research.* Chicago: Rand-McNally.

——(1970). The moral atmosphere of the school. In N. Overley (Ed.), *The unstudied curriculum: Its impact on children.* Washington, DC: Association for Supervision and Curriculum Development.

——(1971a). *Structural issue scoring manual.* Unpublished manuscript, Harvard University, Center for Moral Development and Education, Cambridge, MA.

——(1971b). Cognitive-developmental theory and the practice of collective moral education. In M. Wolins & M. Gottesman (Eds.), *Group care: An Israeli approach.* New York: Gordon & Breach.

——(1971c). From is to ought: How to commit the naturalistic fallacy and get away with it in the study of moral development. In T. Mischel (Ed.), *Cognitive development and epistemology.* New York: Academic Press.

——(1973). Continuities in childhood and adult moral development revisited. In P. B. Baltes & K. W. Schaie (Eds.), *Lifespan developmental psychology: Personality and socialization.* New York and London: Academic Press.

——(1976). Moral stages and moralization: The cognitive-developmental approach. In T. Lickona (Ed.), *Moral development and behavior: Theory, research, and social issues.* New York: Holt, Rinehart & Winston.

——(1978). Revisions in the theory and practice of moral development. In W. Damon (Ed.), *New directions for child development: Vol. 2. Moral development,* San Francisco: Jossey-Bass.

——(1980). High school democracy and educating for a just society. In R. Mosher (Ed.), *Moral education: A first generation of research.* New York: Praeger.

——(1981a). *Essays in moral development: Vol. I. The philosophy of moral development.* New York: Harper & Row.

——(1981b). *The meaning and measurement of moral development.* The Heinz Werner Lecture Series, vol. XIII. Worcester, MA: Clark University Press.

——(1982). Moral development. In J. M. Broughton & D. J. Freeman-Moir (Eds.), *The cognitive developmental psychology of James Mark Baldwin.* Norwood, NJ: ABLEX.

——(1984). *Essays in moral development: Vol. II. The psychology of moral development: Moral stages, their nature and validity.* San Francisco: Harper & Row.

Kohlberg, L., & Armon, C. (1983). Three types of stage models for the study of adult development. In

M. Commons, R. Richards, & C. Armon (Eds.), *Beyond formal operations: Late adolescent and adult cognitive development*. New York: Praeger.

Kohlberg, L., & Bar-Yam, M. (1971). Cognitive-developmental theory and the practice of collective moral education. In M. Wolins & M. Gottesman (Ed.), *Group care: An Israeli approach*. New York: Gordon & Breach.

Kohlberg, L., & Candee, D. (1983). *The relation of moral judgment to moral action*. Paper presented at Florida University International Conference on Morality and Moral Education, Miami Beach, Florida, December 1981. To appear in W. Kurtines & J. L. Gewirtz (Eds.), *Morality, moral behavior, and moral development: Basic issues in theory and research*. New York: Wiley Interscience.

——(1984). The relation between moral judgment and moral action. In L. Kohlberg (Ed.), *Essays on moral development: Vol. II. The psychology of moral development*. San Francisco: Harper & Row.

——(Eds.). (In press). *Research in moral development*. Cambridge, MA: Harvard University Press.

Kohlberg, L., & Gilligan, C. (1971). The adolescent as philosopher. The discovery of the self in a postconventional world. *Daedalus, 100*, 1051–1086.

Kohlberg, L., & Helkama, K. (In press). Research on Piaget's theory of moral judgment. In L. Kohlberg & D. Candee (Eds.), *Research in moral development*. Cambridge, MA: Harvard University Press.

Kohlberg, L., & Kramer, R. (1969). Continuities and discontinuities in childhood and adult moral development. *Human Development, 12*, 93–120.

Kohlberg, L., Levine, C., & Hewer, A. (1983). Moral stages: A current formulation and a response to critics. In J. A. Meacham (Ed.), *Contributions to Human Development* (Vol. 10). Basel: S. Karger.

Kohlberg, L., Colby, A., Gibbs, J., Speicher-Dubin, B., & Power, C. (1977). *Standard Issue Scoring Manual* (preliminary edition). Unpublished manuscript, Harvard University, Center for Moral Development and Education, Cambridge, MA.

Kohlberg, L., Selman, R., & Schultz, L. (In press). The relationship between social perspective-taking and moral judgment development. In L. Kohlberg & D. Candee (Eds.), *Research in moral development*. Cambridge, MA: Harvard University Press.

Kohn, M. (1977). *Class and conformity. A study in values* (2nd ed.). Chicago: University of Chicago Press.

Kohn, N. (1969). *Performance of Negro children of varying social class background on Piagetian tasks*. Unpublished doctoral dissertation, University of Chicago.

Kramer, R. (1968). *Moral development in young adulthood*. Unpublished doctoral dissertation, University of Chicago.

Kuhn, D. (1976). Short-term longitudinal evidence for the sequentiality of Kohlberg's early stages of moral judgment. *Developmental Psychology, 12*, 162–166.

Kuhn, D., Langer, J., Kohlberg, L., & Haan, N. (1977). The development of formal operations in logical and moral judgment. *Genetic Psychology Monographs, 95*, 97–188.

Kurtines, W., & Greif, E. B. (1974). The development of moral thought: Review and evaluation of Kohlberg's approach. *Psychological Bulletin, 81*, 453–470.

Kusatsu, O. (1973). Ego development and socio-cultural process in Japan. *Journal of Economics, Tokyo, 3*, 41–128.

Lakatos, I. (1976). Falsification and methodology of scientific research programmes. In I. Lakatos & A. Musgrave (Eds.), *Criticism and the growth of knowledge*. Cambridge: Cambridge University Press.

Lapsley, D., & Serlin, R. (1983, April). *On the alleged degeneration of the Kohlbergian research program*. Paper presented at the biennial meeting of the Society for Research in Child Development, Detroit.

Lasker, H. M. (1974a). Stage specific reactions to ego development training. In *Formative research in ego stage change*, Study No. 3. Willemstad: Humanas Foundation.

——(1974b). Self-reported change manual. In *Formative research in ego stage change*, Study No. 4. Willemstad: Humanas Foundation.

——(1977). *Interim summative evaluation report. An initial assessment of the Shell/Humanas OD program*. Cambridge, MA: Harvard University Press.

Lei, T. (1983). *Toward a little but special light on the universality of moral judgment development: A study of moral stage and moral type in a Taiwanese sample.* Unpublished qualifying paper, Harvard Graduate School of Education.

Lei, T., & Cheng, S. W. (1982). *An empirical study of Kohlberg's theory and moral judgment in Chinese society.* Unpublished manuscript, Harvard University, Cambridge, MA.

Lerner, D. (1958). *The passing of traditional society.* Glencoe, IL: Free Press.

Limoges, J. (1978). *French translation of the sentence completion test.* Unpublished manuscript, University of Sherbrooke, Canada.

Lockwood, A. L. (1975). Stages of moral development and students' reasoning on public policy issues. *Journal of Moral Education, 5,* 51–63.

——(1977). *The effects of values clarification and moral development curriculum on school-age subjects: A critical view of recent research.* Unpublished manuscript, University of Wisconsin, Madison.

Loevinger, J. (1976). *Ego development: Concepts and theories.* San Francisco: Jossey-Bass.

Loevinger, J., & Wessler, R. (1970). *Measuring ego development: Vol. I. Construction and use of a sentence completion test.* San Francisco: Jossey-Bass.

Loevinger, J., Wessler, R., & Redmore, C. (1970). *Measuring ego development: Vol. II. Scoring manual for women and girls.* San Francisco: Jossey-Bass.

Logan, R., Snarey, J., & Schrader, D. (1984). *Heteronomous and autonomous moral types among Israeli kibbutz adolescents: A cross-cultural, longitudinal study.* Unpublished manuscript, Harvard University, Center for Moral Development and Education, Cambridge, MA.

Mead, G. H. (1934). *Mind, self, and society.* Chicago: University of Chicago Press.

Moir, J. (1974). Egocentrism and the emergence of conventional morality in preadolescent girls. *Child Development, 45,* 299–304.

Nicolayev, J., & Phillips, D. C. (1979). On assessing Kohlberg's stage theory of moral development. In D. Cochrane, C. Hamm, & A. Kazepides (Eds.), *The domain of moral education.* New York: Paulist.

Nisan, M., & Kohlberg, L. (1982). Universality and cross-cultural variation in moral development: A longitudinal and cross-sectional study in Turkey. *Child Development, 53,* 865–876.

Nunnally, J. C. (1978). *Psychometric theory* (2nd ed.). New York: McGraw-Hill.

Oser, F. (1980). Stages of religious judgment. In J. Fowler & A. Vergote (Eds.), *Toward moral and religious maturity.* Morristown, NJ: Silver-Burdett.

Parikh, B. (1980). Moral judgment development and its relation to family environmental factors in Indian and American families. *Child Development, 51,* 1030–1039.

Parsons, T., & Shils, E. (Eds.). (1951). *Toward a general theory of action.* Cambridge, MA: Harvard University Press.

Paton, H. J. (1948). *The moral law.* London: Hutchinson.

Peck, R. F., & Havighurst, R. J. (1960). *The psychology of character development.* New York: Wiley.

Perry, W. G., Jr. (1970). *Forms of intellectual and ethical development in the college years.* New York: Holt, Rinehart & Winston.

Piaget, J. (1929). *The child's conception of the world.* London: Routledge & Kegan Paul.

——(1960). The general problems of the psychobiological development of the child. In J. M. Tanner & B. Inhelder (Eds.), *Discussions on child development: Proceedings of the World Health Organization study group on the psychobiological development of the child* (Vol. IV). New York: International Universities Press.

——(1965). *The moral judgment of the child.* Glencoe, IL: Free Press. (Originally published in 1932)

——(1967). *Six psychological studies.* New York: Random House.

——(1970). *Structuralism.* New York: Basic Books.

——(1971). *Biology and knowledge.* Chicago: University of Chicago Press. (Originally published in 1965)

Piaget, J., & Inhelder, B. (1969). *The early growth of logic.* New York: Norton.

Price-Williams, D. R. (1975). *Explorations in cross-cultural psychology.* San Francisco: Chandler & Sharp.

Puka, B. (1979). A Kohlbergian reply. In D. Cochrane, C. Hamm, & A. Kazepides (Eds.), *The domain of moral education.* New York: Paulist.

Rawls, J. (1971). *A theory of justice.* Cambridge: MA: Harvard University Press.

——(1980). Kantian constructivism in moral theory. *Journal of Philosophy, 87,* 515–572.

——(1982). *Lectures on Kant.* Unpublished lecture notes, Harvard University.

Reimer, J. (1977). *A study in the moral development of kibbutz adolescents.* Unpublished doctoral dissertation, Harvard University, Cambridge, MA.

Rest, G. (1977). *Voting preference in the 1976 presidential election and the influences of moral reasoning.* Unpublished manuscript, University of Michigan, Ann Arbor.

Rest, J. (1973). The hierarchical nature of moral judgment. *Journal of Personality, 41,* 86–109.

——(1979). *Development in judging moral issues.* Minneapolis, MN: University of Minnesota Press.

——(1983). Morality. In J. H. Flavell & E. Markman (Eds.), *Manual of child psychology* (4th ed.). *Vol. 3: Cognitive development.* New York: Wiley.

Rest, J., Davison, M. L., & Robbins, S. (1978). Age trends in judging moral issues: A review of cross-sectional, longitudinal, and sequential studies of the Defining Issues Test. *Child Development, 49,* 263–279.

Rest, J., Turiel, E., & Kohlberg, L. (1969). Level of moral development as a determinant of preference and comprehension of moral judgments made by others. *Journal of Personality, 37,* 225–252.

Rousseau, J. (1964). *The social contract* (C. Frankel, Ed. and Trans.). New York: Hafner. (Originally published in 1762)

Schrader, G. (1963). Autonomy, heteronomy, and moral imperatives. *Journal of Philosophy, 60,* 65–77.

Schweder, R. (1982). Review of Lawrence Kohlberg's *Essays on moral development, Vol. I: The philosophy of moral development. Contemporary Psychology,* June. 421–24.

Selman, R. L. (1971). The relation of role-taking to the development of moral judgment in children. *Child Development, 42,* 79–91.

Selman, R. (1976). Social-cognitive understanding. In T. Lickona (Ed.), *Moral development and behavior.* New York: Holt, Rinehart & Winston.

——(1980). *The growth of interpersonal understanding.* New York: Academic Press.

Selman, R., and Damon, W. (1975). The necessity (but insufficiency) of social perspective taking for conceptions of justice at three early levels. In D. DePalma & J. Foley (Eds.), *Contemporary issues in moral development.* Hillsdale, NJ: Erlbaum.

Selman, R., & Jaquette, D. (1977). Stability and oscillation in interpersonal awareness. In C. Keasey (Ed.), *Nebraska symposium on motivation* (Vol. 25). Lincoln: University of Nebraska Press.

Sidgwick, H. (1887). *Methods of ethics.* London: Macmillan.

Siegel, S. (1956). *Nonparametric statistics.* New York: McGraw-Hill.

Simpson, E. L. (1974). Moral development research: A case study of scientific cultural bias. *Human Development, 17,* 81–106.

Snarey, J. (1982). *The social and moral development of kibbutz founders and sabras: A cross-sectional and longitudinal study.* Unpublished doctoral dissertation, Harvard University, Cambridge, MA.

——(1983). *The cross-cultural universality of social-moral development: A critical review of Kohlbergian research.* Paper presented at the meeting of the Association for Moral Education, Boston, MA.

——(In press). A review of cross-cultural studies in moral judgment development. In L. Kohlberg & D. Candee (Eds.), *Research on moral development.* Cambridge, MA: Harvard University Press.

——(1985). Cross-cultural universality of social-moral development: A critical review of Kohlbergian research. *Psychological Bulletin, 97,* 202–32.

Snarey, J., & Blasi, A. (1980). Ego development among adult kibbutzniks: A cross-cultural application of Loevinger's theory. *Genetic Psychology Monographs, 102,* 117–157.

Snarey, J., Reimer, J., & Kohlberg, L. (1984). The socio-moral development of kibbutz adolescents: A longitudinal, cross-cultural study. *Developmental Psychology, 21,* 3–17.

Turiel, E. (1966). An experimental test of the sequentiality of developmental stages in the child's moral judgment. *Journal of Personality and Social Psychology, 3,* 611–618.

——(1969). Developmental processes in the child's moral thinking. In P. Mussen, J. Langer, and M. Covington (Eds.), *New directions in developmental psychology.* New York: Holt, Rinehart & Winston.

——(1977). Distinct conceptual and developmental domains: Social convention and morality. In H. E. Howe and C. P. Keasey (Eds.), *Nebraska symposium on motivation* (Vol. 25). Lincoln: University of Nebraska Press.

——(1979). *Social-cognitive development: Domains and categories.* Paper presented at the 9th Annual Symposium of the Jean Piaget Society, Philadelphia.

——(1983). Domains and categories in social-cognitive development. In W. Overton (Ed.), *The relationship between social and cognitive development.* Hillsdale, NJ: Erlbaum.

Turiel, E., Edwards, C. P., & Kohlberg, L. (1978). Moral development in Turkish children, adolescents, and young adults. *Journal of Cross-cultural Psychology, 9,* 75–85.

Vetter, M. (1978). *Dimensionen des Selbstkonzeptes und Ich-Entwicklung.* Unpublished thesis, University of Mainz, Federal Republic of Germany.

Walker, L. J. (1980). Cognitive and perspective taking prerequisites for moral development. *Child Development, 51,* 131–139.

——(1982a). The sequentiality of Kohlberg's stages of moral development. *Child Development, 53,* 1330–1336.

——(1982b, June). *Sex differences in the development of moral reasoning: A critical review of the literature.* Paper presented at the Canadian Psychological Association, Montreal.

——(1983). Sex differences in the development of moral reasoning: A critical review. *Child Development, 54,* 1103–1141.

Walker, L. J., DeVries, B., & Bichard, S. L. (1984). The hierarchical nature of stages of moral development. *Developmental Psychology, 20,* 960–966.

Walker, L. J., & Richards, B. S. (1979). Stimulating transitions in moral reasoning as a function of stage of cognitive development. *Developmental Psychology, 15,* 95–103.

Weber, M. (1930). *The Protestant ethic and the spirit of capitalism* (Talcott Parsons, Trans.). London: Allen & Unwin.

——(1949). *The methodology of the social sciences.* New York: Free Press.

White, C. B. (1975). Moral development in Bahamian school children: A cultural examination of Kohlberg's stages of moral reasoning. *Developmental Psychology, 11,* 535–536.

White, C. B., Bushnell, N., & Regnemer, J. L. (1978). Moral development in Bahamian school children: A three-year examination of Kohlberg's stages of moral development. *Developmental Psychology, 14,* 58–65.

Wright, D. (1982). Piaget's theory of moral development. In S. Modgil & C. Modgil (Eds.), *Jean Piaget: Consensus and controversy.* New York: Praeger.

Wright, D. (1983). "The Moral Judgment of the Child," revisited. In H. Weinreich-Haste & D. Locke (Eds.), *Morality in the making.* New York: Wiley.

Youniss, J. (1980). *Parent and peers in social development: A Sullivan-Piaget perspective.* Chicago: University of Chicago Press.

Name Index

Subject Index

action: moral value of, 52; *see also* moral action

action choice, 46, 47; autonomous moral judgment in, 348; justification of, 51; in scoring, 160, 162

additive model (stage development), 7–8

adolescence, 315, 317, 318, 319; heteronomous stage in, 333–4; *see also* kibbutz adolescents study

adults remaining in heteronomous orientation, 333–4, 351

affectional relations, 16

affiliation, 42, 43, 49, 54–5

agape, 31

age: and moral development, kibbutz adolescents study, 130, 140–2, 148; and moral development, U.S. males study, 79, 81, 100–3, 107, 110–12; and moral judgment, Turkish males study, 119, 120, 122, 124–5; and moral maturity scores, U.S. males study, 107; and moral type, 362–5, 369, 370–3, 377

alternate form reliability: assessment of moral type, 361–2, 376; Standard Issue Scoring, 65–6, 69, 70, 71, 72; U.S. males study, 115

anthropological method applied to Kohlberg theory, 129, 130

aretaic judgments, 23

authoritarianism, 351, 352–3

authority, 8, 49, 115, 330, 334; external, 339, 346, 378; respect for, 378; in Stage 1 reasoning, 25; in Stage 4 reasoning, 28

authority issue (dilemmas), 47, 57

authority relations, 328–9, 330, 335

autonomous moral judgment, 315, 328; criteria for defining, 327, 328, 330, 333, 336, 339–42, 343, 347–8, 349, 353, 354–9, 375, 376, 378; justification and validation of, 330–1; ontogenesis of, 315; reversibility of, 332–3; *see also* moral judgment(s)

autonomous moral type (Type B), 316, 350, 375–80; coding scheme

for assessment of, 353–62, 380; historical review of, 317–26; kibbutz adolescents study, 368–70; in Piaget, 328–36; Taiwanese study, 371–3; Turkish study, 370–1; U.S. males study, 362–8; *see also* moral type

autonomy in moral development, *see* moral autonomy

autonomy of the will (Kant), 344, 345

Bahamas (the), 119

Berkeley Free Speech Movement (FSM), 374, 379

bias, 120, 126; in cross-cultural studies, 149; in interviews, 156, 157; scorer, 75

blame, 352

"bootstrapping" ("abductive") method, 36, 327, 359–60

care and response orientation, 24

caring, 31, 35

categorical imperative, 10, 25, 338–9, 344–5, 346, 348; first formulation, 344–5, 348; second formulation, 345; third formulation, 345

choice: culturally defined, 130; issues, norms, elements in, 58–9

choice (criterion, autonomy/heteronomy distinction), 328, 348, 358, 376

chosen issue, 185; identification of, 161–2, 188–91; scoring, 161–2, 186, 187t

circularity, 40, 74–5

civil rights, 50

clear pass (match) (IJ–CJ match), 175, 179, 209–11, 218, 224

coding, substages, 323

coding manual, 316

coding method, ideal-typical, 350

coding schemes: autonomous/heteronomous moral types, 316–17, 348, 353–60, 373; autonomous moral judgment, 327; reliability study, 360–2, 375–6, 380

cognition and role taking, 13

cognitive development, domains in, 8–9; and moral development stages, 77–8, 113–14; stages in, 6–7, 13, 117

cognitive development theory, 4–5; stage concept in, 6–7, 83–4, 117; universality of stage and sequence in, 119–20; U.S. males study consistent with, 117

cognitive domain, 1, 12–15

cohort effect, U.S. males study, 103–4

college-age relativism (regression), 38, 78; U.S. males study, 114, 321, 322

common good, 28

community, 32

commutative justice, 24, 26, 27, 28, 29, 30, 61

compensation, 24

competence, distinct from performance, 5, 8, 15

comprehension of moral judgments made by others, 7, 78, 116, 117

concrete individual perspective, 16, 17, 22

concrete operations, 12, 13

conflict between issues (dilemmas), 46–7

conflict resolution, 26, 28, 49

conformity, 317, 328

conscience, 20, 28, 322, 330, 342; authoritarian/humanitarian, 352; autonomy of, 334

conscience issue (dilemmas), 47, 48

conscience or principled form of moral reasoning (Stage 6), 319

consciousness and action, 334–6

consistency, 28, 29, 40; stage descriptions, 43; *see also* internal consistency

constraint and moral autonomy, 329–30, 331, 332, 334, 335, 351

construct validity, 69, 70, 75, 130, 134

construction cases, 40, 75

constructivism, 1, 4–5

constructivism (criterion, auton-

LaVergne, TN USA
10 February 2011
215948LV00003B/47-78/P

9 780521 169103